AGE OF
THE FRENCH REVOLUTION
by Claude Manceron

AGE OF
THE FRENCH REVOLUTION

I

Twilight of the Old Order 1774-1778

CLAUDE MANCERON

Translated from the French by Patricia Wolf

A TOUCHSTONE BOOK
Published by Simon & Schuster Inc.
NEW YORK · LONDON · TORONTO · SYDNEY · TOKYO

Touchstone
Simon & Schuster Building
Rockefeller Center
1230 Avenue of the Americas
New York, New York 10020

10   9   8   7   6   5   4   3   2   1   Pbk.

Library of Congress Cataloging-in-Publication Data
Manceron, Claude.
  [Hommes de la liberté. English (Simon and Schuster, Inc.)]
  Age of French revolution/Claude Manceron.
    p.   cm.—(A Touchstone book)
  Translation of: Hommes de la liberté.
  Reprint. Originally published: 1st American ed. New York: Knopf, 1977–
(French revolution)
  Includes bibliographies and index.
  Contents: v. 1. Twilight of the old order.
  1. France—History—Revolution, 1789–1799—Biography.
2. Revolutionists—France—Biography.   I. Title.
[DC145.M3513   1989]   89-31196
944.04'092'2—dc19   CIP

ISBN 0-671-68018-8

ILLUSTRATION CREDITS

Bibliothèque nationale: pages 12, 15 (Marie Antoinette), 23, 33, 41, 48, 58, 64, 68
(Mirabeau père), 72, 88, 103, 114, 149, 157, 162, 185, 209, 217, 230, 249, 255,
320, 356, 363, 377, 382, 412, 428, 482 (Marie Antoinette), 494, 504, 528, 534,
541, 550, 555, and 572; *The Granger Collection:* page 189 (Danton); *Musée du Louvre:*
pages 5 and 482 (Louis XVI); *Photo Bulloz:* pages 68 (Mirabeau fils), 223, 332, 423,
and 456; *Photo Giraudon:* pages 15 (Fersen), 18, 26, 79, 108, 137, 187, 189 (Talleyrand), 200, 261, 391, and 520; *Photo H. Roger-Viollet:* pages 29, 37, 114, 119, 132,
267, and 297; *photo Marburg:* page 313; *U.S.I.S:* page 244

*Most of the illustrations were provided through the courtesy of the Service iconographique of
Editions Robert Laffont.*

To Anne
Through Anne

Personally, I am stubbornly resolved to turn the impossible into something possible; otherwise one is forced to accept "irremediable reality," as the poet Vinaver calls it, "the world's incurable despair," in the popular poetry, and still attempt the *impossible* if society is to be made fit for human habitation . . .

At a certain moment in the history of the Revolution, a reversal of perspectives occurs in which the accents, as well as the scale of values and the personalities lately "in play," change, fracture, and are rearranged—so differently that one no longer knows who really was "bad," who "important," and what precisely someone did to upset the world's balance. The Revolution has its own secrets, which are not so readily accessible.

—DUSAN MATIC, letter to Alain Jouffroy
in *Les Lettres françaises,* June 9, 1971

Personal approach: simplify, trace the biography of history, as if it were a man's, as if it were my own.

—MICHELET, *Journal,* October 1834

Biographical and anecdotal history is the least explanatory but the richest in information, for it considers individuals in their particularity, detailing subtle distinctions of character for each, tracing their motives and the phases of their deliberations . . . The historian's relative choice, with respect to each domain of history he gives up, is always between history which teaches more and explains less and history which explains more and teaches less.

—CLAUDE LÉVI-STRAUSS, *La Pensée sauvage*

Contents

Acknowledgments

In 1954, thanks to Robert Laffont, I was able to attain the position of author. The confidence and friendship he has always shown has permitted me to conceive, prepare, and now to write The *Age of the French Revolution*. May he be thanked forever for it. My gratitude extends to the whole group at Editions Robert Laffont, where I have so often found support in getting through the rough spots.

I have indicated in the reference notes the names of those who contributed to the elaboration of this or that part of my text, particularly with bibliographical information or by the loan of materials. Many other names will be found in the notes of the volumes yet to appear. I would like here simply to say again to all those who have helped me morally or materially for so many years that this book is also theirs.

I must mention the valuable help that Marguerite Puhl-Demange and Henri Amouroux have given in permitting me to pursue the career of columnist alongside my work as historian. Thanks to them, I did not feel myself relegated to the dust of the past, and I was able, each week, to engage the present.

The friendships of Louis Aragon, of Henri Guillemin, of François Mitterand have illuminated my way. Professor Marcel Reinhard, who holds the Chair of the French Revolution at the Sorbonne, has given me invaluable advice and helped me overcome the complexes of an autodidact whom polio had turned away from the academic path.

Introduced to the National Archives by George Bordonove, my wife and I found in M. Mahieu an indispensable guide. Earlier, the helpfulness of M. Rieunier, general secretary of the Bibliothèque nationale, had permitted me to compensate for the handicap of my invalidism by giving me double access to the department. M. Suirey of Saint-Rémy has done the same at the Library of the City of Paris. The lamented Paul Fleuriot de Lange had accorded us a work-haven at the Library Marmottan; we thank M. Foucart for continuing this favor.

Morvan Lebesque came to Saint-Privat on May 20, 1970. He was the first to hold the beginning of this manuscript in his hands. He encouraged me to persevere, in terms that barred the path of doubt, and this was at the worst moment. I see again his last gesture of farewell, in the evening, in front of the Palais des Congrès at Béziers: there he was, large, solid, happy to be going to Brazil several days later. Our car pulled away. His lips moved. We could no longer hear him. He made a signal to us that said: "Write! Write! To work!"

I try, Morvan.

Chronology of Principal Events
1774-1778

1774

FEBRUARY	26	Beaumarchais is censured by the Parliament of Paris.
APRIL	5	Returning from Russia, Diderot stops in The Hague.
	11	Marriage of Gilbert de La Fayette and Adrienne de Noailles.
	15	The English Parliament passes the "Five Intolerable Acts" against the American colonies.
	19	The Paris première of Gluck's *Iphigénie*.
LATE APRIL		Marat publishes *The Chains of Slavery* in London.
MAY	10	Death of Louis XV. Accession of Louis XVI.
	20	Louis XVI chooses Maurepas as a minister.
JUNE	2	Resignation of the Duc d'Aiguillon.
AUGUST	22	Beaumarchais is arrested in Vienna (he will be released on September 22).
	24	"The Ministers' St. Bartholomew" at Versailles. Dismissal of Maupeou and the Abbé Terray. Turgot becomes comptroller general of finance.
SEPTEMBER	13	Turgot decrees the free circulation of grain.
	15	Arrest of Pugachev in Iaïtsk (he will be executed on January 10, 1775).
	20	Mirabeau confined to the Château d'If.
	22	Death of Pope Clement XIV (Ganganelli).
NOVEMBER	12	Louis XVI recalls the old parliaments.

1775

FEBRUARY	15	Election of Pope Pius VI (Braschi).
	23	Première of Beaumarchais's *The Barber of Seville* in Paris.
APRIL	18	The first battle of the American Revolution: Lexington.
APRIL 18 to MAY 10		Series of riots in France, known as the Grain War.
JUNE	11	Coronation of Louis XVI in Rheims.
	15	Washington named commander-in-chief of the revolutionary forces.
JULY	21	Malesherbes becomes a minister.
NOVEMBER	1	Publication of *Le Paysan perverti* by Restif de La Bretonne.
	4	The Chevalier d'Eon commits himself to dressing as a woman.

1776

MARCH	12	Turgot imposes edicts of reform.
	28	The British evacuate Boston.
MAY	12	Dismissal of Turgot and Malesherbes.
JUNE	11	Goethe is named counselor to the Weimar court.
JULY	4	Philadelphia: Congress proclaims the independence of the United Colonies.
AUGUST	24	Pontarlier: Mirabeau helps Sophie de Monnier to escape.
	27	Battle of Long Island. The British retake New York.
OCTOBER	18	Necker named deputy comptroller general of finance.
	24	Jean-Jacques Rousseau's accident in Mesnil-Montant.
DECEMBER	7	Franklin arrives in Nantes.
	25	Washington's victory at Trenton after a long retreat in New Jersey.

1777

FEBRUARY	13	Sade imprisoned in Vincennes.
MARCH	15	La Fayette leaves Paris for America.
APRIL	18	Arrival of Joseph II in Paris.
	20	La Fayette and his companions leave Los Pasajes to cross the Atlantic.

MAY	14	Mirabeau and Sophie de Monnier are arrested in Amsterdam. Mirabeau will be imprisoned in Vincennes.
JUNE	13	La Fayette arrives in Georgetown.
SEPTEMBER	11	La Fayette is wounded in the Battle of the Brandywine. The Americans abandon Philadelphia.
OCTOBER	17	Victory of the Americans at Saratoga.

1778

FEBRUARY	10	Voltaire's arrival in Paris.
MARCH	2	Ailing Voltaire signs a Catholic "profession of faith."
	20	Franklin is officially presented at Versailles.
	30	Voltaire's "triumph" in Paris.
APRIL	19	Announcement of Marie Antoinette's first pregnancy.
MAY	30	Death of Voltaire.
JUNE	17	Battle of *La Belle Poule* against the *Arethusa* (beginning of the Franco-British war).
JULY	2	Death of Jean-Jacques Rousseau.

Twilight of the Old Order

I

DECEMBER 1773

We Are Disgusted with the Universal Scene

Saint-Denis, where the kings of France have lain buried since Dagobert's time. Late on the night of December 24, 1773, two young men appear at the Arbalète, a cheap little tavern huddled, with others, against the great Gothic abbey, welcoming travelers to the first coach stop on the road north from Paris. Two dragoons, cavalrymen, without horses or luggage, one in green, the other in blue with white facings. No one seems to notice them in the bustle of Christmas Eve. From every inn rise fragrant aromas of the regional specialty, the best matelote in the Ile-de-France—stewed in red wine with onions, without eel but with plenty of fish from the Seine provided by bargemen from the island below Saint-Denis.

The two men boarded the mail coach on the Rue Notre-Dame-des-Victoires in Paris. Beyond the gate of Saint-Denis the broad, well-paved road bordered by handsome trees cuts straight across vast vegetable fields. They have passed the village of La Chapelle on the left; on the right, the monastery of Notre-Dame-du-Bon-Secours, where barren Parisian wives come to pray to the Virgin and St. Geneviève. How odd to get off the coach after just two leagues, with the journey barely begun. But for them it was the end of all journeying.

They dine heartily, take a room, do not attend midnight mass. The next morning, after walking around town, they return to the inn at noon and ask to have brioches and a bottle of wine sent up to their room. Shortly afterward they order a second bottle and some writing paper, bolt the door, and fire two shots. Unable to enter the room, the innkeeper runs to the soldiery next door for help; the soldiers break down the door. The two dragoons are discovered dead, across the table from each other, "of a pistol shot fired into the mouth."[1] In plain view are a letter and a "will" written by the younger of the pair, who signs himself "Bourdeaux, former pupil of the schoolmasters, then

assistant pettifogger,* monk, dragoon, and finally nothing . . .," the contents
of which obligingly provide investigators with this information:

> Humain is the taller of us and I, Bourdeaux, am the shorter. He is regimental
> drum major in the first company and I am simply a Belzunce dragoon . . .
> Humain is only twenty-four; as for me, I am not yet twenty . . . No pressing
> urgency compels us to cut short our careers . . . a disgust for life is our sole reason
> for ending it . . . We are disgusted with the universal scene; the curtain has fallen
> for us, and we leave our roles to those weak enough to wish to play them out
> awhile longer. A few grains of gunpowder have just burst the springs of that mass
> of moving flesh which our haughty brethren like to call king of creatures.
>
> Gentlemen of the law, our bodies await your disposal; we scorn them too
> much to fret about their fate . . .
>
> The maidservant of the inn shall take my handkerchiefs and neckbands as
> well as the stockings I wear and all other linen. Our remaining possessions will
> pay for the futile investigation and proceedings that will be conducted on our
> account. The three-livre piece on the table covers the wine we have drunk.
>
> Saint-Denis, this Christmas Day, 1773
> Bourdeaux — Humain

Despite his seniority, poor Humain had done no more than meekly
endorse his own death warrant in signing a lengthy, resolute defense of suicide
set forth by Bourdeaux, who apparently called the tune to the very last for this
manifestly equivocal pair. Gazetteers later reported that "both had been cited
less than honorably in the police records with respect to conduct as well as
morals." Perhaps Humain might have wanted another plate of fish stew,
another mug of wine, might have wished to join others on the road to Epernay
bound for a visit to the latest attraction, a new laundry—"the biggest in the
world," its sign assured, "ready to wash for the whole of Paris." But Bourdeaux had decided for them both, and Humain followed him in death as in
life. Bourdeaux left a second letter, addressed to the only human being for
whom he seemed to hold any affection, his lieutenant in the Belzunce regiment, M. de Clérac:

> . . . I think I told you several times how discontent I am with my present situa-
> tion . . . After examining my thoughts more seriously, I realized that this disgust
> embraced everything, and that I was also fed up with every existing situation, of
> mankind, of the whole world, of myself; I was bound to act upon this discovery.
>
> When one is tired of everything, it is time to give up everything. The
> calculation was simple; there was no call for using geometry; now I am about to
> rid myself of the certificate of existence I have possessed for almost twenty years,
> and which has burdened me for fifteen . . . I owe no one an apology. I am
> deserting, which is a crime; but as I am going to punish myself, the law will be
> satisfied . . . Farewell, my dear Lieutenant . . . Keep flitting from flower to
> flower and extracting the nectar from all knowledge and all pleasures . . . When

*Undoubtedly a law clerk.

you receive this letter, it will already have been more than 24 hours since I ceased to be, with sincere esteem, your most affectionate servant.

The schoolmasters who raised Bourdeaux had at least taught him to die with stylish elegance even if they never managed to imbue him with a zest for life. But Humain's silence echoes starkly against the bloodied walls of that room from which the bodies were dragged, soon to be publicly exhibited naked upon the hurdle, each with a stake driven through its heart, for the horrified distraction of Saint-Denis's inhabitants, then burned with the town refuse. Suicide was a crime "which had to be punished more severely than another," according to prevailing canons enforced by the police and courts of Paris: "the soul is damned to Hell, and, in this world, the flesh to the gibbet, and confiscated property passes to the seigneur." In this case the seigneur of these two dragoons was the king of France himself, who gained precisely nothing. Their pockets were empty, and the sale of their personal effects did not even pay court costs, in which the Arbalète's owner was obliged to share. At least they were not instrumental in inflicting on anyone the disgrace and persecution reserved for families of suicides; they were alone in the world. No one would mourn them.

LOUIS XVI AND HIS
GRANDFATHER, LOUIS XV

2

JANUARY 1774

France and the World in 1774

That happened just steps away from the tomb in which Louis XIV had reposed for fifty-eight years. His successor, Louis XV, apparently was not the only victim of deadly boredom in fossilized France, where ten thousand gentlemen of leisure ruled twenty-three million souls.[1] Troops had not seen battle for ten years; the army, sole justifiers for the nobility's supremacy, grew fat and lazy in garrison. And because military rank, down to that of second lieutenant, had to be bought, for what future would Humain have been fighting had he chosen to defy Bourdeaux? Average life expectancy: twenty-eight years and nine months.[2] If Bourdeaux had known this, he could have claimed to have deprived his comrade of only four years. To these desperate young men, France at Christmastide of 1773 must have seemed as ancient as her sixty-four-year-old king. An ancient land of little patriarchs proud of having reached old age in defiance of the prevailing mortality. The whole country is private property;

you may not enter, you may not even budge: religion, landholding, social status, trade or profession, all are prescribed and immutable. Obedience is the rule from cradle to grave; to the priest above all, who ordains each gesture of daily life; to the fief-owning seigneur or his intendant; to the regiment's proprietary colonel; to the hereditary officeholding magistrate; to the shop master; and, on entering the domestic prison, obedience to the father, who may be a hundred but still has the right to scrutinize his children's affairs.

Obedience to the king? Certainly, he being both pinnacle and symbol of this human pyramid. But he remains an abstraction for most of his subjects, so remote from them at Versailles, which he rarely leaves now except to make the ritual tour of neighboring palaces at Fontainebleau, Marly, Saint-Germain, and Choisy. Well-informed persons know about his official mistress; the less informed know about the feud—of elders, to be sure—which magistrates of the old and new Parliament have been waging for three years in an effort to shift ever so slightly the balance of power among men of privilege. This stirring performance fascinates a few thousand "enlightened" souls all over Europe, whereas nine out of ten Frenchmen are totally indifferent, being in no way involved. The distinction between a Lamoignon and a Maupeou escapes the man in the street.

Bourdeaux's misfortune is to have devoured, but not digested, stacks of pamphlets and clandestine books printed in Neuchâtel, London, or Amsterdam, which circulate under the very noses of the royal dragoons. Voltaire's *Dictionnaire philosophique* was burned publicly seven years before along with the Chevalier de La Barre's headless body—on Maupeou's orders. These readings simply confirmed for Bourdeaux the evidence of an immobile France; impasse. Budding awareness turning into nausea; the vision of evil and stupidity without the weapons to combat them. "Disgust with the universal scene." Lucidity plus impotence. Vertigo.

But exactly what "universal scene" was in his mind? What image of the world had the schoolmasters given him if he looked outside France for reasons to go on living? What did someone like Bourdeaux know about the universe in this third quarter of the eighteenth century?

The solar system is still firmly planted in the center, and it was not so very long since the world had become round. Less than a century before, the proliferation of travelers bringing back honest accounts, long overdue, had opened a fissure in Christianity's padlocked edifice,[3] gravely threatening her self-image as the navel of the universe. For those able to obtain proscribed books—a minority once again—curiosity, or amused tolerance at any rate, had replaced infatuation. Persians, Chinese, even Moslems, not to mention the Noble Savage, no longer passed for Satan's henchmen or inferior creatures. Confrontation replaced domination and proselytism. But all this was still fluid: a state of mind rather than a pattern of behavior. Those willing to go one step further and compare France realistically to other countries were confined to the approximations of the *Encyclopédie.* [4]

This pictured the world in four parts. Oceania does not exist. Beyond the only ocean of significance, "ours," bathing western shores, lies the New World, quickly encompassed: it includes western America, in which "New Spain" (Mexico) belongs to the Spanish and "Canada" to the English. In "Southern Canada" are to be found colonies such as Maryland, Virginia, "New York," or "New England," all of them just beginning to be heard of. South America, divided into the Spanish Main (Guiana and Venezuela), Peru, the Land of the Amazons, Brazil, Chile, Paraguay, and "Magellanic Land," is the preserve of Spain and Portugal. Finally, "in the sea," a spray of islands, at times enormous, Windwards or Leewards, stretches from Newfoundland to Tierra del Fuego via the Antilles, several of which belong to France.

Africa? A "Land of Whites," meaning Arabs: Barbary (present-day Maghreb), Egypt, Numidia, up and down the Nile. A "Land of Blacks" vaguely bounded by great mysterious rivers like the Niger, virtually uncharted beyond their deltas; Nigritia, Guinea, Nubia. Eastward lies Ethiopia, known to contain a strange sect of Christians. "In the sea," whole islands, except Madagascar, confiscated for European ports of call.

Asia? Five roughly equal empires in this summary vision, each as fabulous as the next, infinite source of dreams: Tartary, China, India (where vastly overrated authority is ascribed to the Great Mogul), Persia, and Turkey. "In the sea," another cluster of islands, the Japanese string assessed on a par with the Philippines, the Moluccas, the Sundas, or the Maldives.

As for Europe: a magma of powers entangled with a Germany viewed as a basketful of hopelessly contentious Catholic or "presumably Protestant" princes, chief rivals among whom, for the moment, are the Hapsburgs of Vienna held in check by the Hohenzollerns of Berlin. In the north, a declining Sweden and Denmark; a Muscovy, or Russia, persistently seen as a Western power and whose expansion is feared. To the east, Poland's decay encouraged. Bordering France: the United Provinces, or Holland, contained by England, and the Austrian Netherlands, where Belgians have traded Spanish for German occupation; this same situation exists beyond the Alps in northern Italy, where whatever does not belong to the pope or Austria is a prize for pirate dynasties. The thirteen Swiss cantons huddle in their valleys. Spain and Portugal, still wearing proud faces, are eroded by the Inquisition. Far to the southeast, the Balkans, nearly as mysterious as China, and Greece are merely "Turkey in Europe." And right next door, just across the Channel, lies the enemy, the obsession: England.

This vague interest in the rest of the globe does not dissuade an enlightened Frenchman from the conviction that his is the richest continent, the most civilized, and the most populous. In fact Europe, including Russia, numbers

150 million inhabitants as compared to 440 million Asians, nearly 15 million in North and South America combined, and about 100 million in Africa.* Less than 800 million people on earth in 1774.[5]

Wherever organized societies exist, the only societies which interrelate, the social structure is identical to that of France even if it wears a modestly liberal veneer, or an exotic tinge as in Asia. Humanity continues to tolerate the universal trademarks of tribalism or feudalism. A privileged few own the earth and the sources of life; the rest pray or die—like Bourdeaux and Humain.

Still, if they had only known, the fools!

3

JANUARY 1774

The Men of Liberty

Bourdeaux is nineteen, the same age as the dauphin, destined to become Louis XVI in five months. The same age as a young man from Strasbourg whose own obstructed future will force him to seek his fortune in the Austrian army: Jean-Baptiste Kléber. The age of Miranda, pining for action in Venezuela, South America's first *libertador* after helping to win the Battle of Valmy. The age of Brissot, coming Girondist leader, and of a pert little Parisian named Manon Phlipon, the future Madame Roland. Of Hébert, known as "Père Duchesne," founder of popular journalism. Of Fabre d'Eglantine, author of the revolutionary calendar. Of Cloots, "the Orator of Mankind." And, if Bourdeaux had chosen to view the world solely in terms of riches, of Barras and Talleyrand.

At twenty-four, Humain is the age of Mirabeau and the Abbé Grégoire, an obscure parish priest from Lorraine who will proclaim the French Republic. Of Jeanbon Saint-André, savior of the revolutionary fleet. Of Romme and Soubrany, "Martyrs of Prairial," two of the century's most heroic figures. And this year Goethe turns twenty-four.

A host of other men and women in France and all over the world are approaching the age of twenty innocent of the fact that for each of them Louis

*Approximate rounded figures. What later came to be called Oceania then had 2 million inhabitants.

XV's death will mark the start of one of the most prodigious human adventures ever, for no adventure can match man's search for man, you roamers of the seven seas, blessed egoists, dear devourers of women and diamonds! How pale it will seem, your eternal conflict with yourselves pursued down to the sands or to the depths of a lagoon, compared to these glowing lives that will alter Life.

They don't know each other. Unawares, they will approach one another during the fifteen-year reign which rejected the Revolution, thereby endowing it with its messianic character: a cleavage in time to serve all time. Once under way, the Revolution will set the stage for their meeting: they will love, unite, defy, tear to shreds, destroy each other—or survive now and then owing to luck, betrayal, or patience. From 1789 to 1797 they will enact a *chanson de geste* each episode of which is part of our existence, destined to become the very tissue of it: the Peters, Johns, and Magdalens, the Pontius Pilates and Judases bearing the glad tidings of liberty. If Bourdeaux and Humain had not taken their own lives, they would have been thirty-nine and forty-four at the Battle of Fleurus. Something worth waiting for. Now some of you may insist it was better to die instantly than risk being beheaded. At any rate, so it seems from today's perspective . . . The difference is that these two poor lads died without having lived. Fifteen years hence, where will our own battles be fought?

I shall deal with all the famous personalities of the French Revolution and a number of its most significant observers or interpreters around the globe, at the age they were in 1774. I shall follow them to their deaths, or at least to Babeuf's death on May 27, 1797, marking the Revolution's temporary burial. A sampling: Robespierre is 16; those who become his lifelong—and deathlong —friends: Couthon, age 19, Lebas 9, Saint-Just 7.

Danton is 15 and Camille Desmoulins 14. If we stay on the Mountain,* Marat is already 31 (Charlotte Corday 6), Carnot 21, Barère 19, Cambon and Billaud-Varenne 18, Fouché 15.

The Girondists? Vergniaud is 21, Roland 40, Guadet 16, Pétion 18, Louvet and Buzot 14, Barbaroux 7. Rabaut-Saint-Etienne, the Protestant, 31; Condorcet, the atheist, 30.

What about the moderate royalists, known as *monarchiens*? Bailly is 38, Clermont-Tonnerre 27, Malouet 34, the Lameth brothers 24, 21, and 18, La Fayette 17, Mounier 16, Dupont 15, Barnave 13.

The "Fanatics"? Jacques Roux is 22, Chaumette 11, Carrier 18.

Fouquier-Tinville is 28.

The great soldiers? Bernadotte is 11; Davout, Desaix, Hoche, Joubert, Marceau, Murat, Ney, and Lannes all are under 10 years old; Brune, Cham-

*The extremist party, occupying the highest rows in the Chamber. [*Trans.*]

pionnet, and Jourdan under 15. Masséna 16. Berthier 21. Kellermann 39 and
Dumouriez 35.*

The literary personalities? Voltaire is 80, Rousseau 62, Diderot 61 like
Raynal, Buffon 67, Mably 65, Holbach 51—all but Raynal would die *before*,
having made the first assaults. Among those who will live the Revolution and,
in some cases, die of it: Beaumarchais is 42, Restif de La Bretonne 40, Bernardin de Saint-Pierre 37, Chamfort and Laclos 33, Mercier 34, Sylvain Maréchal
24, and Volney 17. Still children under 12: Germaine Necker, the future
Madame de Staël; André Chénier; Chateaubriand; Benjamin Constant; Paul-
Louis Courier. Two future masters of polemics are 19 and 12: royalist Rivarol
and republican Loustalot.

Goldoni is 67, Kant 50, Alfieri 25, Schiller 15, Hegel and Hölderlin 4.
Sade is 34.

Fragonard is 42; David 26.

Among the scientists, Guyton de Morveau is 37, Lavoisier 31, Monge 28,
Volta 29, Humboldt 7.

The bankers? Necker is 42, Perrégaux 24, Laffitte 7, Ouvrard 4.

Philippe d'Orléans, later Philippe Egalité, is 37. His son Louis-Philippe
has just been born, destined to be the last King of the French after the nation
puts up with Louis XVIII (the Comte de Provence, 19 years old in 1774) and
Charles X (the Comte d'Artois, 17).

Mozart is 18, Beethoven 4, Goya 28.

Toussaint L'Ouverture is 31.

Bonaparte is 5; Babeuf 14.

We will meet some born after Louis XV's death: for example, Bolívar, La
Mennais, Stendhal, and Byron. A host of so-called secondary figures will step
from the shadows along the way: peasants out of the *cahiers*,**sans-culottes* from
the faubourgs, workers from the first "coalitions," volunteers of the Year I,
all those who *were* the Revolution (along with *Chouans*† and émigrés who *were*
the Reaction), whereas the figureheads symbolized it. Whenever possible I
shall try to bring them out of obscurity, to personify them, to capture the
reality of their daily lives.

Over a thousand people, then, a hundred of whom we shall stalk. Their
biographies are woven into the main thread of chronological events. Running
heads give the reader his bearings at every stage of the way: at the right, a

*Of those destined to lead, against some of their own ranks, the Vendéan uprising, d'Elbée is 22,
Stofflet 23, Cathelineau 15, Bonchamp 14, Charette 11, Cadoudal 3, Henri de La Roche-Jacquelin
2.

**Documents drawn up by the parishes at the king's invitation, which set forth their grievances
and were presented to the States-General in 1789. [*Trans.*]

†Anti-revolutionary peasant insurgents in the Normandy region who waged intermittent guerrilla
warfare. [*Trans.*]

summary of the episode in progress; at the left, the date.* The alphabetical index at the back of the volume will aid readers who prefer to take in the career of a given person all at once, be it La Fayette, Collot d'Herbois, or even Joséphine de Beauharnais. Numbered notes refer to bibliographical indications or details for researchers which are grouped together at the back of the volume. On the other hand, asterisks, daggers, et cetera, refer to footnotes, the few that are absolutely essential for immediate comprehension of the narrative.

Instead of chapters, sequences. A guiding rule: objective truth as to dates, facts, acts, spoken and written words. A bias: the desire to enter into the psychology of each person, whatever his role in the Revolution—hence respect for Charette as well as Marceau—in an attempt to reconstitute his inner movement. A technique: combining anecdotal material with events to provide the background for a portrait and to make a figure live again in his own times through simultaneous sensations and impressions. The Revolution was *also* David, Talma, Gossec, Ledoux, balloons, visual telegraphy, and Fulton's experiments, just as the Liberation of France was *also* Aragon, Eluard, Camus, Giacometti, Gérard Philipe, and Le Corbusier. An ambition: to steer a course midway between the analysis of economic and social spheres that shape mankind and the study of a particular person's unpredictable influence on those spheres, thereby exploding the framework of determinism. Napoleon and revolutionary Europe; Lenin and the Russia of 1917; De Gaulle and the French Resistance. In other words, the passionate interference of individual destinies in the collective destiny. If that is indeed the meaning of dialectics, well and good; if it is roughly equivalent to a position halfway between Marx and Freud, why not? But in no case does it point to a syncretistic mediation between two systems, ultimately producing a peculiar intellectual molasses; this "between" implies a constant shuttling back and forth, which can only be a sign of humility, for it describes the journey of the ant. Back and forth.

Finally, an explanation: my sifting through thousands of episodes resulted in retaining (trifling as they may seem—an operatic aria, an epigram, an academic reception, a love letter) only those things which enhance the understanding of a quarter-century containing all centuries. A conceivable, if insufferable, subtitle comes to mind: "Poetic and historic manual for bringing about instant total change in myself and others."

---

*In running heads the spelling of names is that of the revolutionary period; in the narrative, however, it is that of the period to which the episode belongs. Thus the title "Dumouriez, a Privileged Prisoner" refers to the adventures in 1774 of Colonel du Mouriez, and "Biron Courts the Queen" deals with the person known as the Duc de Lauzun in 1775.

Except where indicated, spelling and punctuation have been modernized in citations.

Let's begin. May the reader forgive this preamble; I shall be silent, or pretend to be, for five thousand pages, which is the best way to write. Let the others speak and act. On my desk sit ten thousand silent file cards, twenty years of my life: "Son of man, dost thou think these bones shall live?" Flesh, heart, and blood appeared. Are we not told that history is the field of a battle forever lost, a Waterloo abandoned to the vultures? I was not alone in thinking differently during all those years when each day I could feel the lives of the Men of Liberty flowing into my own, giving it meaning. There were many others, men and women, who helped me—mostly through their faith in this insane undertaking. Their names appear one after another in the notes, but now as I set out from base camp, my thoughts turn to them. They have done credit not to me but to a certain positive conception of history.

BENJAMIN FRANKLIN

4

JANUARY 1774

We Have Not Kept Him

Inside him, everything is falling to pieces. Can one start a new life at sixty-eight? Yet Benjamin Franklin betrays no anxiety this morning, January 29, 1774; more than a half-century of wily dealings with powerful interests on both sides of the Atlantic—in Boston, Philadephia, and London—has instilled self-discipline.

The thirty-five men before whom he stands arraigned are indeed among the most powerful of the power elite, being the King of England's Privy Council. In full, generally somber regalia, they stare at Franklin out of hostile faces, buried under long flaxen wigs oddly perpetuating among officials of the British crown a custom of Louis XIV's court which the French have abandoned. What a peculiar country in which His Majesty's council sits in a tavern!

Of course, the Cockpit Tavern is no ordinary public house; more like a club than a luxury inn, with its high oak-paneled ceilings blackened with pipe smoke, its narrow, thick-paned casements admitting only the faintest light already bleached out by the fog along the Thames. Outside is London in winter, the world's largest city, a million inhabitants, grayness. Here, one of England's most distinguished meeting rooms, far more comfortable than West-minster for deliberations behind tankards of that beer Franklin will never get used to, "as black as bull's blood and as thick as mustard."[1] Where is his American beer, blond and pale as the fair maids of his youth? And where the cocky youngster, the bantam who once busied himself about the shop of his father, Josiah, the candlemaker of Milk Street, Boston?

Benjamin Franklin holds himself erect despite the pains in his knees and thighs—oh, this London climate! Standing with his back to the flaming logs in the fireplace, he looks squarely at his accusers with solemn eyes peering out of a face slightly too large for his body, slit by a pair of thin lips. Until now he "has had them." He has built a reputation in Boston, New England, the thirteen colonies, and finally in the mother country, has risen from nowhere, from a job as foreman in his brother James's printing house. A man so "low-born" may never have set foot in this tavern before and in America is, for a while longer, postmaster general and in London agent for the Pennsylvania, New Jersey, Georgia, and Massachusetts assemblies. Scientific circles on both sides of the ocean esteem him as highly as Newton; he has tamed the thunderbolt.

But he has yet to discover the secret of taming human folly. These men are resolved to make him pay for his insolence, to bring him down. As for a state execution, he too has put on his largest wig, his fine gentian-blue suit of figured Manchester velvet, and has taken the hollow walking stick he uses to perform magic tricks for the amusement of friends. Unflinching, he is about to endure two solid hours of torrential insults delivered by Wedderburn, the solicitor general, whose fists pound the polished oak table. Franklin is charged with having abused his position as postmaster general to intercept and publish some letters written by Thomas Hutchinson, crown-appointed Governor of Massachusetts. There is truth in the charge. He is not innocent. His customary prudence failed to avert this blunder.

Hutchinson, persistent advocate of colonial exploitation for the sole benefit of English merchants, has been one of the principals responsible over long months for squeezing American exasperation to the bursting point. Vexations pile up one upon another, unilateral, always from London. Import levies grow oppressive; English troops must occupy ports in order to collect them. Four years ago they fired on the crowd in Boston. Yet Franklin has pledged his life to the lofty ideal of a single, united Anglo-American empire, with the Atlantic serving the same function as the Mediterranean for Rome, an immense federation of English-speaking peoples ruled by a tolerant Caesar in London. Not an impossible dream in the light of France's defeat in 1763; the Treaty of Paris has sanctioned English sovereignty over all North America, India, and the African coast.

But these petty men cannot shoulder their victory. Facing Franklin at the far end of the table is Lord North, England's prime minister, the epitome of self-satisfied mediocrity, corpulent, inflexible—and bearing a singular resemblance to George III, whose bastard brother he is said to be. He has refused Franklin a private hearing. Against the latter's plea for a community of peoples working together as equals in joyful competition, they oppose—every last one of them—the supremacy of the United Kingdom squeezing its colonies like so many lemons, and are in the process of fomenting civil war after they have won the foreign one.

Now if discreet circulation of those cynical, provocative, and fatuous letters of Hutchinson had succeeded in alerting the English public to the policies its government was pursuing . . . The public was aroused, yes, but against Cassandra. Embarrassed by his "professional slip," Franklin found himself isolated, alienated, forced to resort to half-truths and personal excuses. A botched affair: what he had tried to do was not "seemly."

Toward midday the solicitor general concludes his charge, having declared Franklin a spy, traitor, thief, would-be assassin—rebel. The elegant audience clustered about the table applauds the censure as Franklin leaves the room in silence—to respond would not have been "seemly"—limping slightly, shoulders drooping, shaking hands with the last of his friends. A letter to his son the next day discloses that, deep beneath his impassive countenance, a private upheaval has shattered the illusions of a brilliant mind. He has lost faith in England. Until just this morning he had still believed in her king, George III, whose accession he had eagerly greeted fourteen years before: a young, temperate, and pious monarch, the "bourgeois king" come at last, the anti-Louis XIV, an idealistic projection shared by Franklins all over the globe. In November 1760 he had noted in his diary, *Poor Richard*: "His virtue and the consciousness of his intentions to make his people happy will give him firmness and resolve in his decisions and in supporting the honest friends he will choose to serve him. When this firmness is generally perceived, factionalism will dissolve and be dissipated like the morning mists before the rising sun, leaving the rest of the day serene and cloudless . . . "

His Privy Council having declared itself, George III, also unwilling ever to grant Franklin an audience, signs a letter on January 31, 1774, withdrawing his appointment as postmaster general. The philosopher Hume wrote to Franklin in 1762: "America has sent us many good things: gold, silver, sugar, tobacco, indigo, etc.; but you are the first philosopher, and indeed the first great man of letters for whom we are beholden to her. It is our own fault that we have not kept him."[2]

MARIE ANTOINETTE

5

COUNT HANS AXEL FERSEN

JANUARY 1774

The Dauphine Spoke to Me at Length

The first private conversation between Marie Antoinette and Count Hans Axel Fersen* takes place at a masked ball at the Paris Opera on January 30, 1774. She is the wife of the dauphin; he is the eldest son of an eminent Swedish official, leader of Parliament. They are nineteen and eighteen.

That year Axel began keeping a regular diary of his travels and pleasures in the rough, ungainly, precise French adopted for everyday use by the family at his father's insistence. " 'Writing French is not enough,' he told his children; 'you must learn to think in French, otherwise you will never really learn the language.' "[1] This was not eccentric because most scions of European nobility, from Saint Petersburg to Lisbon, were reared in the same tradition. Francophilia, however, proved to be a distinctive trait of the Fersens. Axel's father, virtual ruler of Sweden until a few years earlier, had led the pro-French Hat party for three decades, in opposition to the pro-Russian Cap party. Swedish aristocrats gravely referred to those halcyon days as the "Era of Freedom" inasmuch as a noble oligarchy controlled a puppet monarch. The "revolution" all Europe has been talking about for a year was Gustavus III's coup d'état. Old Senator Fersen sulks in his palace on the isle of Saint Blaise, a residence nearly as lavish as Stockholm's royal castle, which it faces and withstands comparison with. His son has influence with the young monarch, who treats him as a friend. Axel can expect to become a royal adviser or minister on his return to Sweden.

Right now, as part of his so-called education, Fersen is winding up that eighteenth-century "grand tour" that enabled sons of the rich to cultivate a knowledge of foreign languages, society, the military profession, and the salons. In three years, flanked by his tutor, he has "done" Denmark, Germany, Switzerland, Italy, and since November 15, 1773, has been savoring the expedition's supreme reward: Paris. There he leads the life of a dandy, caught up in the social whirl and dismayed by its relentless pace. He is entertained

*Who organized the French royal family's flight in June 1791 and drove the coach himself on the disastrous journey that ended at Varennes. [*Trans.*]

to the verge of exhaustion. What a life! How did he manage in a single day to attend Madame du Deffand's and Madame Geoffrin's salons (two-word entry in his diary for December 3: *"vieilles savantes"*); the Théâtre des Italiens; concerts at the Vauxhall, the Opera, and the Théâtre Français; to pay his respects to the royal favorite at Versailles and to the Orléans family at the Palais Royal; then to sit in on a physics lecture at the Sorbonne with Diderot's daughter? And those wretched Parisian tailors who can't produce overnight the suit he fancies! "I had ordered my carriage for eight o'clock, but was kept waiting, fuming with rage, until quarter to nine for the tailor to deliver the fur suit I had ordered the previous morning." Somehow he finds time to linger with the ladies, for whom he already shows a lively taste. It is reciprocated: Marie-Angélique Diderot* "approached me first, to make my acquaintance. I took her about in my carriage every morning; she was very gay and witty, but not very pretty."[2]

On Sunday, January 30, he noted: "Creutz** took me to Princess de Beauveau's and to a concert at Count Stroganov's; at nine o'clock we went to supper together at M. d'Arville's; I left at one to go on to the Opera ball. It was a great social event: Madame la Dauphine, Monsieur le Dauphin, and the Comte de Provence† came and were at the ball half an hour before anyone recognized them. The dauphine spoke to me at length without my knowing who she was; when at last she identified herself, everyone rushed to her side and she withdrew to her box. At three o'clock I left the ball."

That's all. They have met recently at Versailles when Fersen was presented at court; they will meet again, infrequently and always publicly, two or three times during the Mardi Gras festivities. He will leave for London on May 29, go on to Sweden, and not see Marie Antoinette for four years, but their adventure begins tonight: she has noticed and will not forget him. From a sense of "professional duty," to begin with: the son of the Hat party's leader and friend of Gustavus III is someone a dauphine is brought up to respect. From an affinity to foreigners, whom she prefers to Frenchmen. But also because he is a remarkably handsome fellow: "tall and slender, with an easy manner, long and exquisitely shaped legs, graceful movements, elegant gestures, an impeccable wardrobe, he possessed every conceivable attraction at the mere age of eighteen: regular features, velvety skin, indescribably blue and sparkling eyes that converged slightly when he looked at you [a squint-eyed glance—the ultimate gallantry], a soft mouth, and an even softer voice, which his Scandinavian accent modulated with timidity . . ."[3] Mental indolence and

---

*Who was actually Madame Caroillon de Vandeul. After two years of marriage she had just given birth to a daughter.
**Swedish ambassador to France.
†History remembers them as Marie Antoinette, Louis XVI, and Louis XVIII.

self-satisfaction simply enhanced his plumage in the tiny colony of strutting peacocks attending the dauphine.

His interest is strictly in the dauphine, not the budding woman barely emerged from prolonged childhood. She will not grow anymore, fortunately. Her shoulders are still rather narrow, but her bosom is shapely, her neck superb, and she has discovered her greatest physical asset: a carriage at once stately and graceful, the result of good posture. Her face is disappointingly plain beneath the reddish-brown hair and thick brows: long and oval, with the pouting Hapsburg lip and a perpetually disdainful expression relieved only by flashes of composure or anger. Just who is this woman, this child on whom the fairest kingdom on earth may soon depend? Nobody knows. Her personality, if she has one, does not project. Now there is open talk of her husband being dull-witted, even if he surprises his public tonight by cheerfully parading from one group to the next, waddling and tongue-tied like a shy, oafish schoolboy. If Louis XV dies, Europe will have a third reigning princess, Marie Antoinette, in addition to Maria Theresa and Catherine II. But will she ever rule? No sign of pregnancy after three years of marriage. Dynastic hopes waver between her brothers-in-law: Provence, who may be impotent, and Artois, the young rake who took a wife just three months ago in a swirl of celebrations—or there is the option currently in favor that the king remarry (a Spanish princess, for example). Certain factions at court would relish this chance to pick off two birds with one stone: banish the favorite and remove the barren dauphine, who, for the moment, is simply a little Dresden doll, a winning card in the Austrian hand, carefully screened from affairs of state—tomorrow's mistress of France or nothing at all.

Fersen was among the few who did not recognize her instantly. Despite her masquerade (gray velvet mask under the hood of a loose-fitting silk domino, not unlike a monk's cowl), Marie Antoinette's arrival sends a stir through the hall—if only because the princely battalion is escorted by security agents of dubious anonymity—the minute she appears in the doorway leading to the Opera loges from a passageway connected with the Duc de Chartres's apartments in the Palais Royal. The conversation is watched and commented on by dozens of curious persons feigning total absorption in the minuet. Fersen, like every other partner, extends his fist, on which she places the palm of her hand for one step, three steps, a *"demi-coupé échappé,"* three more steps. This on a platform set level with the first-balcony loges, like perfumed sweat baths where dancers may go for refreshment or a chat. A sea of people under immense chandeliers lit by a hundred wax candles (a recently invented improvement over the foul-smelling tallow variety). "The bigger the crowd, the more reason to be pleased with oneself next day for having attended . . . Kept women, duchesses, bourgeoises, all hide beneath the same domino."[4] Three "firemen" stand duty, one on the stage, another in the audience, the third at the main entrance in case of the ultimate disaster, for the opera house is a

gigantic wad of gas, pasteboard, timber, and wax that goes up in flames every
five years. A panic would leave hundreds of dancers asphyxiated or trampled
to death.

Smiling, the dauphine at last retires to her box. For the length of a minuet
she has outwitted boredom. "She kept imagining that no one ever recognized
her, and everyone always did. Masked balls were organized on some pretext
or other to allow her the pleasure of appearing incognito. She was especially
eager to intrigue foreigners; this only gave rise to endless gossip. I did not
want her to attend this ball," laments the Prince von Ligne, one of her inti-
mates, "not only for that reason but also because of the aftermath . . . Her
endless chatter about masquerades, what she had said and what others had told
her, was insufferable." [5]

BEAUMARCHAIS

6

FEBRUARY 1774

Don't Deprive Me of My Bitterness

On February 26, 1774, Madame du Deffand sends news of Paris to an old
English friend, Horace Walpole, a few hasty lines in the outsize, awkward
scrawl common to sightless persons, guided onto paper with the aid of a
perforated metal plate:

"Today we await a great event: the judgment of Beaumarchais . . . M.
de Monaco has invited him to give a reading this evening, one of his comedies
called *Le Barbier de Séville* . . . The public has gone wild over its author; his
case is being decided as I write to you. A harsh verdict is expected, and it may
turn out that instead of supping with us he will be banished or even pilloried."

She was right. The guest of honor sent his excuses shortly after midday:
"Beaumarchais, infinitely grateful for the honor extended by M. le Prince de
Monaco, replies from the law courts where he has been closeted since six this
morning, where he has been brought before the bar, and where he awaits
judgment that is indeed slow in arriving . . . He begs M. le Prince de Monaco
therefore to defer his kind invitation to another day." [1]

Who is this Beaumarchais? Today, the most celebrated man in France;
yesterday, virtually unknown to the general public and unpopular among the
literati. In February of this year Grimm notes in his *Correspondance littéraire* that
he was "the horror of Paris a year ago, and everyone, based on neighborhood

gossip, believed him capable of the foulest crimes." And yet "the public raves about him today and defends him for what he has written . . . What a darling child is the French nation! When vexed, how spiteful it turns; when made to laugh, how good-natured and well behaved . . . *Le Barbier de Séville* was to be given on Saturday, February 12; the play was announced and posted; loges were sold out for the first five performances;* then, on Friday the 11th, it was announced that the authorities had banned the play. The public . . . lamented its loss in whispers, and loved the author all the more."[2] But the dramatist is not the topic of conversation. The *Barber* is known only by hearsay, and his two previous plays have rarely been staged. At this moment he is both plaintiff and defendant in the Goëzman trial.** A polemist.

The rest is simply a patchwork of rumors involving an elusive individual defying all descriptions and interpretations, one Pierre-Augustin Caron de Beaumarchais, son of a clockmaker. The "de Beaumarchais" part is something of a joke, referring to a tiny plot of ground at Vert-le-Grand in the district of Arpajon, the estate of Beau Marché, which he stole from his first wife. He put up with that rich widow, six years his senior, for only ten months before poisoning her—oh yes, it was common knowledge—so as to inherit her property sooner. Ah, but he inherited nothing because her will had not been *recorded,* meaning legally validated. All the same, his second wife also died, obligingly, after just a year of wedlock, in time to leave him a nice little pile. Twice a widower and not even forty; odd, wouldn't you say? Of course, the second wife died in childbirth with five doctors looking on. Unlikely scenario for a poisoning. On top of that his son died, three-year-old Augustin, his adored child: "I laugh to think that I am working for him." Would you accuse him of poisoning the boy, too?

In any event, he is headed for a fall climaxing a series of leaps, tumbles, and gyrations in every direction. Music master to Louis XV's daughters—not bad for a commoner! But now they slam the door in his face. While Jack-of-all-trades in the service of Paris-Duverney, one of the richest bankers in France and founder of her military academy, how did he manage to extract fifty thousand écus—a fortune—from his benefactor six months before he died? . . . Oh yes, it was a blank piece of paper signed by the banker, which Beaumarchais filled out in the appropriate amount—this according to the dead man's heir, the Comte de La Blache, who won't give up a sou. Lawsuit. And from that suit another sprouts, the Goëzman case, like the multiplying brood of the Old Woman Who Lived in a Shoe. Meanwhile, what was he doing in Spain if not spying, perhaps for the monarchy? But would a spy have acted so incongruously, triggering an obscure quarrel to defend the honor of one of his sisters, and raising such a row that this Clavijo affair incensed the Spanish

---

*Performed by the Comédiens Français. Molière had died a hundred years earlier.
**Pronounced according to the spelling: Go-ëz-man. Often called "Guzman" when mistaken for the transparent name of the Judge in *Le Mariage de Figaro,* Don Guzman Brid'oison.

court? And the worst was that verbal brawl over an actress last year, under his own roof, with the Duc de Chaulnes, which brought the police and a prison sentence for Beaumarchais at For-l'Evêque. He is headed for trouble. No intriguer can afford to act on impulse. To make things worse, he sold off timber illegally from the forest of Chinon.* He purchased a minor appointment as "lieutenant general of the hunt" from the royal game warden's office, "guardians of the king's pleasures." They are out to divest him of that along with everything else.

Will those judges ever finish deliberating? The "assembled Chambers" have dragged out the agonizing wait for more than twelve hours. Beaumarchais has been "on the hook," as it were, since morning in this city of the law in the heart of Paris: the Palace of Justice, its maze of courts, passageways, and buildings occupying nearly half the Ile-de-la-Cité. He has elbowed his way through crowds gathered to witness the event, a mixture of gowns and swords, lawyers and prostitutes, curious spectators, litigants, and shopkeepers lined up by the dozen in their stalls below the Altar of the Red Mass in the Salle des Pas Perdus.

> In approaching the courtroom, I was impressed but unmoved by the distant din of voices; yet I confess that on entering, a single Latin word cried out repeatedly by the clerk who went before me and the profound silence greeting the word, affected me intensely. *Adest! Adest!* He is present, the defendant is here, lock up your feelings for him! *Adest!* This word will ring in my ears for a long time. Then I was taken before the court. At the sight of a room resembling a temple, somber and imposing in the dim light, the majestic assembly of sixty magistrates all dressed alike and staring at me . . . suddenly my heart shriveled, as if a drop of congealed blood had fallen on it, arresting its beat. [But] one of the things I have studied most earnestly is the mastery of my emotions in time of crisis; thus the courage to discipline oneself has always struck me as being among the noblest efforts upon which an intelligent man could pride himself.[3]

Pierre-Augustin holds fast. Is this the end? Or does it mean a fresh start? Here he is, dangling from a thread at the age of forty-two. His real life still lies ahead, he knows, despite the succession of false starts behind him. The art of living has coarsened his features ever so slightly. His handsome head of graying hair, upswept above a high forehead, falls in neat rolls; round, merry eyes flicker restlessly on either side of his long, aquiline nose.

Can these officers of the law possibly grasp what is at stake in the Goëzman trial? Is there to be a new Molière or not? For twelve solid hours the case they are discussing, which has already been heard and dismissed, must be rehashed. Did Beaumarchais really intend to bribe the judge investigating his dispute with La Blache over the Paris-Duverney legacy? Of course he did, for the

*Crown property. [*Trans.*]

practice of buying justice has not changed since *Les Plaideurs.** That's where
the trouble starts: the "crime" was practically essential to winning the case, but
subject to severe penalties if exposed. The judge was Goëzman, a sour, ludicrous fellow with a twisted grin clamped onto his face. Apparently it was best
to approach him through his wife, a young actress "who looked eighteen when
trying to look thirty." Beaumarchais had advanced her a hundred louis of the
two hundred she had asked for, plus a jeweled watch, plus fifteen louis for the
secretary. In exchange for which he obtained an exceedingly brief, hostile
audience with the judge, who obviously had received a bigger bribe from La
Blache, and lost the case. Never would he see those fifty thousand écus.** He
faced imminent bankruptcy, having staked everything he owned on winning
the suit. Goëzman's wife—a "decent" sort, it seems—returned his hundred
louis and the watch. But not the fifteen louis for the secretary—who never got
them, as Beaumarchais discovered.

Rather than keep silent, he had exploded. What else was there to lose?
Did he set out to rock the columns of the Temple, and did he suspect that
"those fifteen louis would shake the very foundations of Louis XV's parliament"? At first he could not see that far; he fought for himself instinctively,
like a hunted man, regardless of who else stood to benefit. He demanded his
fifteen louis in an open letter to Madame Goëzman. When it was published,
the couple, instead of returning the money (the wife undoubtedly pocketed
it without her husband's consent), counterattacked with a subpoena ordering
Beaumarchais to appear in court on charges of attempting to bribe a magistrate. The Goëzmans and La Blache had mustered support from some twenty-
five disreputable publishers and second-rate journalists—while the court was
investigating the case, Beaumarchais has torn them to shreds in four *Mémoires* † which Europe's intelligentsia has read avidly. In the end, what remains
of Pierre-Augustin's adversaries? A mound of mud. His pen alone has ground
them to dust: Bertrand, Arnauld Baculard, and especially Marin the gazetteer,
informer, and censor: "When walking, he crawls like a snake; when rising to
his feet, he sprawls like a toad. In short, creeping and clambering, by leaps and
bounds, forever rushing along, he has busied himself so diligently that in our
own time we have seen the corsair headed for Versailles in a coach-and-four,
his arms emblazoned on the sides . . . a despised figure, representing Europe,
wrapped in a short cassock lined with gazettes and surmounted by a doctor's
cap bearing this legend on the tassel: *Ques-a-co* Marin?"

"*Ques-a-co*"? Apparently, this was the fellow's theme song whenever he

---

*Racine's satire on the law courts (1668). [*Trans.*]
**In modern figures, Beaumarchais lost approximately 600,000 current francs [about $120,000],
an écu then being worth three livres. He paid the equivalent of 16,000 modern francs [$3200]
for the audience with Goëzman (200 louis). And the fifteen louis on which the dispute hinged
amounted roughly to 1000 current francs [$200].
†Exposés in pamphlet form of the issues being litigated. [*Trans.*]

poked around for information in La Ciotat,* "a little town in Provence, where little Marin hummed his tune, for little people, on a little organ, in a little parish . . . "⁴ Not just Marin was involved here; Beaumarchais's readers understood that rich, powerful men, judges in the Maupeou Parliament, subject to the king's pleasure, were the real targets. "The outraged public protests. And if at any time judges pass sentence on each citizen, at all times the mass of citizens passes sentence on each judge . . . Every citizen unquestionably is subject to the magistrates; but what magistrate can forgo the citizens' respect? . . . "⁵

Two hundred seventy-three pages have set the judicial system afire . . . The dauphine orders caps à la ques-a-co** for winter wear; a young German author, Goethe, frames a drama around the Clavijo affair; Madame du Barry has the Mémoires staged and played before the king; and Voltaire writes about Beaumarchais to D'Alembert: "What a man! He combines everything, wit, seriousness, reason, gaiety, force, compassion . . . he confounds his adversaries while teaching his judges a lesson . . ."⁶ And an obscure writer vegetating in poverty sends a message to Pierre-Augustin: "I salute a man of letters destined to attain Molière's reputation . . . Signed: Bernardin de Saint-Pierre."⁷

Can that make him feel any better? By nine in the evening he is exhausted, registers his address with the court clerk, leaves the palace and crosses the Seine to spend the night with his sister, the wife of Lépine the clockmaker, only a stone's throw from his judges. They know where to find him if prison is to be his lot. He is worn out and resentful: the dauphine, Du Barry, the throngs cheering him along the quays of the Seine, Voltaire, and all the rest, what have they done to help? He is certain to be convicted; do judges ever reverse a colleague's ruling? Nothing beats esprit de corps. His house has been attached, his father and his other sisters have retired to a convent. He has no carriage or servants. His latest play is banned. "And my friends advise me to reply with moderation, to argue my case without humor, and above all without gaiety! . . . Gaiety, my friends! Ah, don't deprive me of my bitterness and leave me nothing but disgust."⁸ Somehow he manages to fall sound asleep. "Much as I may weep, laughter never fails to seep through."⁹ "I had lost everything, except my courage. I brushed away everyone's tears, saying: Hide your grief from me, friends; don't ease my burdened soul while it still bears the strain of indignation."¹⁰

A distant uproar sweeps through the gates of the Palace of Justice onto the Pont Neuf and out along the Tuileries promenade. Cheers, bursts of applause. Impromptu fireworks at the Place Dauphine, with firecrackers popping. Gudin, his devoted friend, wakes Beaumarchais:

*Marseilles region. [Trans.]
**A Provençal locution roughly equivalent to "What's up?" It became a fashionable idiom largely owing to Beaumarchais's usage. [Trans.]

"Hear them cheering for you!"

"Am I acquitted?"

"No, convicted. But the crowd nearly gave it to the judges, who scurried out the back way. They decided against having you appear before them for censure. People are lining up at the concierge's to leave their names and pay you compliments. The Prince de Conti has invited you tomorrow and the Duc de Chartres the day after . . . "

He got out of bed calmly, master of his own acts and thoughts. "Let's see now what else I must do," he said . . . [11]

Madame Goëzman was also officially disgraced and the judge's career virtually ruined. In effect, both parties lost. Beaumarchais is aware, however, that long after applause has faded, the conviction will stand ordering him "to be brought before the chamber for censure, on his knees, and to pay a fine of three livres to the king," his *Mémoires* to be "torn to shreds and burned at the foot of the great stairway in the Palace by the high executioner, as containing expressions and imputations which are ill-advised, scandalous, and injurious to the magistracy in general . . . " It "prohibits said Caron de Beaumarchais from publishing any more statements of this kind on pain of corporal punishment, and for having done so, orders him to give alms, providing bread for prisoners in the Conciergerie of the Palace, in the amount of twelve livres, for which his possessions are attachable." The jargon amounted to civil disfranchisement: denial of the right to engage in any public activity or to publish a word. He would never set eyes on Paris-Duverney's fifty thousand écus. Let the public heap praise on him—flowers for his own funeral. La Blache and a host of others rub their hands gleefully: "The law itself will punish Beaumarchais and his kind for their insolence . . . The justice he is owed will suffice to purge society of this venomous breed."[12]

GENERAL DU MOURIEZ

7

MARCH 1774

The Bastille Is a Sickness

N'adresse point au ciel une plainte importune,
Et, quel que soit le cours de ton sort incertain,
Apprends de moi que l'infortune
Est le creuset du genre humain.

[Address not to heaven thy tiresome complaint,
Unsurely though thy path may wind;
Learn from me that adversity
Is the crucible of mankind.]

Proud of this poetic effort engraved with a belt buckle on the wall of his cell
in the Bastille, another recalcitrant had carefully signed his initials to the
quatrain, C.-F.D.P.D.M., Charles-François du Périer du Mouriez (or du
Mourier), thus adding his own speculations to those of previous tenants such
as La Bourdonnaye, La Chalotais, and de Lally-Tollendal, the last having gone
from there to the scaffold eight years earlier.[1]

From the moment he arrived on September 13, this devilish du Mouriez
has infuriated everyone, including the warden, the guards, and his interroga-
tors. They are scared to death of him—you can see why at a glance. He looks
like a thug, older than his thirty-five years, cool-headed as a veteran cam-
paigner. Prussian grapeshot riddled him at Klosterkamp; two hundred grains
of it had to be removed one by one from his face. And when he makes a motion
to his judges with his right hand, from which the middle finger is missing, he
is threatening to strip and show them his three other battle scars. Impossible
to reason with the man, safe in the knowledge that he enjoys royal protection
in a royal prison—what a situation! They don't know what to make of it, except
that they must keep an eye on him, treat him politely, interrogate him, ignore
his replies, and await his ascent—to power or to the scaffold, depending on
which way the wind shifts.

The day he entered prison he had asked for chicken. Out of the question:
it was Friday, a fast day.

"What of it? I'm sick. The Bastille is a sickness. Besides, you're supposed
to guard *me,* not my conscience."[2]

Receiving permission to have books, he promptly procured the complete
works of Cicero and Horace, two German grammars, six large maps of the
European states, and some twenty treatises on travel and philosophy. With
supreme relish, he devoured Beaumarchais's *Mémoires* the moment they were
printed, and read excerpts to his jailers. A double kinship links the two men:
their adventurous spirit and their skepticism. At sixteen, du Mouriez longed
to become a priest. To cure him of the notion, his father made him read all
of Montaigne, Bayle, and Voltaire in eight months. "I'll be anything you name
except a monk!" His appetite for reading never left him. One night "he forgot
to snuff the candle always burning on his bedside table, where his trousers and
stockings lay, as well as two towels, which caught fire. Flames woke the
prisoner, who grabbed his water pitcher and doused them, thus putting out
the fire."[3] Another time, roused to exasperation over his narrow cell, he
began ripping up the floorboards and discovered directly below him "a man
of about fifty years, naked as the palm of your hand, with a long gray beard

and shaggy hair, bellowing wildly as he flung the broken plaster [*sic*] back up through the hole. He wanted to talk to the poor mad creature. Later he found out that the man's name was Eustache Farcy, a captain in the Piedmont regiment imprisoned for writing a song about La Pompadour."[4] Du Mouriez was moved to much better quarters, twenty-six feet by eighteen, with an excellent bed once tenanted by a young lady named Tiercelin, a mistress of Louis XV's, "who had spent a month upon it for excessive ambition." Old Jumilhac, warden of the prison, has tried his best to butter up the mystery prisoner, on orders from the highest echelon, but has only managed to indulge his gluttony. Du Mouriez is perpetually hungry because he never got enough to eat in his adventurous youth. At midday dinner they stuff five courses into him, three more at supper, and every day the warden personally delivers a supply of lemons, sugar, coffee, port, and Malaga wine. In February the captive begins to warm up to the daily visits, but remains doggedly insolent during interrogations:

"Do you know why you are in the Bastille?"

"I have my suspicions, but the question smacks of a grilling. I'm defending the site; it's up to you to fire first . . ."

"Be careful! Whatever you say against the Duc d'Aiguillon reflects on the king."

"The king himself has taught me to distinguish his sacred person from his ministers; during the seventeen years I have served him His Majesty has disgraced or dismissed twenty-six ministers . . ."

The tale is out: du Mouriez was arrested by order of the Duc d'Aiguillon, minister of war, whose rise is aided by La Du Barry. The duke is eager to know what this colonel-diplomat-spy was doing in Hamburg without official sanction. Or, rather, he knew, but wanted to hear from du Mouriez's own lips that the latter was working with the Comte de Broglie, director of the "King's Secret," a diplomatic nursery game devised by Louis XV for keeping tabs on, and occasionally countermanding, his own ambassadors. Du Mouriez thus was serving the king, who preferred not to know about it, and who enjoyed watching Aiguillon and Broglie play cat-and-mouse at the expense of this too independent and too political-minded agent. In 1773 did he *have* to write: "I give the great Revolution of this kingdom until 1780 to arrive. It is time this lethargy ceased if the awakening is not to be fatal"?[5] Six months in the Bastille will do him no harm. He is simply being asked to keep his mouth shut and conform to a system in which no one speaks to anyone, least of all officials to their sovereign, or vice versa. The comedy reaches its climax in February when, in order to satisfy Aiguillon, Louis XV banishes Broglie to his country estates—and instructs him to continue directing the secret sevice from under his own roof, unbeknownst to officialdom. And because du Mouriez kept quiet, he deserves a reward; the king sends word discreetly to Aiguillon: "He has suffered for a long time and is not really guilty . . ."

Aiguillon reels. To save face, he will not release du Mouriez all at once. The prisoner is transferred to the fortress of Caen, a pet boarder with a fine suite of rooms, a vegetable garden, visiting and visitors' privileges.

On March 8, 1774, a comfortable carriage rolled over the Bastille's drawbridge taking Colonel du Mouriez to Caen with five hundred louis in his pocket, a "loan" from the warden. He has no complaints. Shrugging his shoulders, he daydreams about the next chapter of a saga that has already landed him in Poland, Stockholm, Hamburg . . . Just after asking insolently if it wasn't true that as a child Louis XV had had a page for a whipping boy.[6]

THE MARQUIS AND
MARQUISE DE LA FAYETTE

8

APRIL 1774

My Grandfather Had Arranged My Marriage

At noon on April 11, 1774, the Abbé Paul de Murat,* vicar general of the archbishopric of Sens and chaplain to the Comtesse de Provence, performed the marriage ceremony for his cousin Marie-Paul-Yves-Roch-Gilbert du Motier, the Marquis de La Fayette, and Marie-Adrienne-Françoise de Noailles, "minor daughter of Jean-Paul-François de Noailles, the Duc d'Ayen, lord of the principality of Tingry, and of Henriette-Anne-Louise d'Aguesseau de Fresne, the Duchesse d'Ayen." The scene is the private chapel of the Noailles mansion in Paris, on the Rue Saint-Honoré near the Tuileries, and it is one of the greatest matches of the century. It takes a squad of notaries three days to collect signatures on the marriage contract "of relatives and friends in their domiciles," authenticating a union between members of the highest aristocracy: the Noailles, great landowners, with the La Fayettes and La Rivières, and the *noblesse de robe,* the nobility of the legal profession, with the D'Aguesseaus. An entire page of the contract is set aside for the signatures of Louis XV and the royal family.[1] Even the setting—the Noailles mansion with its two main wings each 138 feet long, situated on the Right Bank of the Seine between the cloisters of the Feuillants and the Jacobins, a district rich in gardens reserved for the aristocracy and contented priests—is "a Versailles scaled for a great family."[2] The main courtyard accommodates forty coaches. Guests attending the evening reception (only relatives were invited to the chapel) will

*No relation to Joachim Murat, imperial marshal and King of Naples under Napoleon.

find themselves in a museum, surrounded by Boulle furniture, Chinese porcelains, paintings by masters of the Renaissance and of current times, Raphael to Fragonard.

What pageantry for the wedding of two children! Gilbert is going on seventeen; Adrienne, fifteen. It is stipulated that she will continue living with her mother, who promises to take in the intruder whenever he is on leave from his military unit or the court. Adrienne receives the marriage sacrament before the Eucharist; she will make her first communion next year on the first Sunday after Easter, 1775.

Two well-behaved children decked out in the new finery of their new life: silk, brocade, and gold braid; how expertly they do and say what is required of them. A wheeling parade of feathers smothers them with compliments: this spring, aigrettes and plumes are all the rage. Madame de Boufflers says that it resembles moving day. The powder gilding the faces of fashionable ladies is now reddish or blond. Women look more like well-tanned Hindu idols than the blanched, flour-and-starch scarecrows of ten years before. On her wedding day Adrienne de La Fayette is not obliged to "cover her fifteen-year-old head with all the hoarfrost of age and winter."[3] Flushed, smiling, self-conscious, she accepts this overgrown boy of a husband for what he is: her first experience of a man. She has only sisters, "the Noailles nestlings," and her father, the Duc d'Ayen, lives as far as he can from her mother.

La Fayette is barely full-grown and still on the gawky side. Slender and totally vertical, even to his tapered, delicate face with its mild expression at once cold or vacant, depending on how you see it. Arched brows lend him a perpetually quizzical air. Attractive aquiline nose; well-etched lips that women envy. Red hair neatly rolled, falling behind the neck in a massive knot that accents his girlish appearance. His obsessive desire to "look right" carries him a bit too far, making him look ill at ease. There is something provincial about the lad despite excellent schooling at the Collège du Plessis and the two years he has just spent with the Black Musketeers,* in the same regiment his grandfather had commanded. A lieutenant's uniform was awaiting him at the age of fourteen. He has already had "the honor of passing in review before the king, of escorting the royal coach to Versailles and having the king tell me on the way that maintaining order was an easy matter, and reporting this news to the musketeers' commander, who had it drummed into his ears 365 times a year." But the greatest influence was his feudal boyhood in Auvergne: "I had not the slightest curiosity to see the capital. I recall my amazement in finding that every passer-by on the highway did not doff his hat to me as they did in Chavaniac, where I was the young lord of the village."[4] As long as he could remember, he had always dressed like a gentleman in a silk suit and knee breeches, with a toy sword at his side, the same sword he vowed to take into

*Various regiments of the king's musketeers were distinguished by the color of their horses. [*Trans.*]

the mountains, at the age of seven, to slay a wild beast terrorizing the Gévau-
dan region. "I am lord of this village and it is my duty to defend it." Rightly
so, for an English shell had killed his father in the Battle of Hastenbeck when
he was two. His mother was a remote lady in Paris, bored by Auvergne,
whom he had seen only during vacations; in 1770, at the age of thirty-three,
she too died. So an orphan is marrying a Noailles—but an orphan who came
into 120,000 livres*a year at age thirteen from the vast La Rivière landholdings in Auvergne and Touraine, in addition to the La Fayette** estates in
Auvergne, extending to Brioude, Vissac, and La Chaise-Dieu. He always liked
Chavaniac best, the massive château with its sturdy towers astride the crest of
a hill high enough to dominate the entire plain of Chaliergues; the froth of
rye fields in summer, but four months or more of snow in winter, the wind,
the pine trees, the crows, and wolves still roaming the forests; better than the
edge of the world—a forgotten world.[5] There, fatherless, he grew up adored
by three women in black, his grandmother and two aunts, who raised him in
a cult of modest self-worship. A female cousin also formed part of the
household, another child for him to play with and grow attached to, Charlotte,
"a year older than I. No brother and sister ever loved each other more
tenderly than we." But the court at Versailles was in a great rush to marry off
this fairytale heir. "I was turning fourteen when we received news that my
grandfather had arranged for me to marry Mlle de Noailles, who was then
twelve." Two children became engaged. He was not sorry; pride compensated
for his bewilderment. "I can say that I was very well liked at school; I had even
gained sufficient ascendancy over my schoolmates to find myself surrounded
by friends, mostly older than I and eager to look like disciples, whenever I
entered the schoolyard."[6] At the Hôtel de Noailles tonight there are many
such disciples readily accessible to a schoolboy on a yearly allowance of
120,000 livres. And La Fayette welcomes another adjunct, the young girl he
acquired in the lottery of appanages, and who decided instantly that hers was
a lucky number in the gamble. If he proves attentive, she may turn out to be
an annoyance, something slightly ridiculous in this society: a wife who loves
her husband. But he will adapt; after all, she *is* a Noailles . . . .[7]

*Equivalent to an income of 500,000 francs in 1970 [$100,000].
**Derived from *fage* or *faye, fagette, fayette* [kidney bean—*Trans.*], a name originating in that region
dotted with herds of black cattle, traversed by the col of the Fageolle.

9

APRIL 1774

Well Then, We Shall Encyclopedize!

Denis Diderot left Saint Petersburg "on the 5th of March [1774] in the evening."[1] He arrives in The Hague "on the 5th of April, in the morning" and settles down in the house of his friend Prince Galitzin, the Russian ambassador to Holland. The return has broken something inside him; he will never be the same. Not that the journey was particularly disagreeable, especially at the outset, in the spacious "English coach" expressly ordered for him by Catherine II and roomy enough for him to lie down in, which "he had adopted for his assigned residence between Petersburg and The Hague . . . It was a thankless task to transport a human being unwilling to stop either to sleep or eat." And there were those fateful accidents: the ice on the Dvina cracking under the coach wheels, sending sprays of water in every direction, and the escort armed with spiked staves floundering about and eventually fishing the travelers out. Then the imperial berlin broke down crossing the Aa. They had to change coaches three times, sending the heavy baggage on ahead in wagons, and were obliged to stay over a few days in Hamburg, where Diderot bought manuscripts of several keyboard sonatas from the composer Carl Philipp Emmanuel Bach, Johann Sebastian's son, apologizing for not calling on him in person: "I come from Petersburg, traveling by post, in a dressing gown under my greatcoat, without a change of clothes; but for that, I should not have failed to call upon such an eminent man."

He is back at last from a journey of well over four hundred miles in midwinter. Rather than complain, he makes an effort to be cheerful. On April 8 and 9 he writes several long letters to friends after the initial one to his Russian benefactress: "Madam, I trust that Your Imperial Majesty is as successful in everything as in her unstinting concern for the comfort of my journey . . . Piercing cold and snow in abundance as far as Riga. Between Riga and here, serene nights and summery, rather than springlike, days . . . Here and there the kind of perilous footing that induces self-knowledge and exposes courage and fortitude in those so endowed by nature . . . Remembering this is a constant source of pleasure; we talk of it endlessly and with such satisfaction that, on closer examination, life's perilous moments are rarely the ones we would choose to erase. Surely this is the record of Your Majesty's own soul."

But the fact remains that philosopher Denis Diderot is broken: "The damage was not done by the waters of the Neva; instead, double attacks of intestinal inflammation on the trip out, bouts of colic and terrible chest pains caused by the severe cold in Petersburg while I was there, and a fall on the ferry at Mitau coming back have almost done me in . . . My disjointed limbs need time to rejoin; rest will take care of this, and since my return I have been sleeping eight or nine hours at a stretch," he writes to Sophie Volland.[2]

He is only sixty-one. Yet so many things have left their mark on him before this Russian expedition, so much work, so much suffering, and the implacable thickening of his solid frame, "built like that of a sedan-chair bearer," ill-served by a sedentary existence. Wistfully he had observed the generous schedule of gymnastic training given to select orphans attending the imperial Academy for Young Ladies at Smolny. No French grammar school would have been prepared to instill the habit of physical exercise in him, and no occupation could have caused his body to deteriorate faster than those twenty years of solitary "apprenticeship" hunched over the plates and proofs of the *Encyclopédie* in a badly lit room on the Rue Tarranne in Paris. Petersburg society called him "the old man."

His returning trunks contain the final pages of the *Neveu de Rameau* and the beginning of *Jacques le Fataliste,* that glimpse of Rabelais in the age of Voltaire. Thus, Diderot is at once broken and at the peak of his literary form. He is stopping in The Hague to have a book printed in French, *Les Plans et statuts des différents établissements ordonnés par Sa Majesté Impériale Catherine II pour l'éducation de la jeunesse et l'utilité générale de son empire,* a monumental labor of Catherine's much-favored courtier Betzki. Diderot cherishes a burning hope, the only flame that can revive his flagging energies: to launch a new edition of the *Encyclopédie* with Catherine's financial sponsorship, all thirty-five volumes recast, reworked, produced from cover to cover under his sole direction. The desertions of Rousseau, D'Alembert, and others at last would be offset; the four inferior supplementary volumes printed without his approval by that rascal Panckouke, counteracted. Good-by to the unending succession of insipid columns aligned by Jaucourt, the Abbé Chappe, and Marmontel. History's most gigantic literary endeavor snatched from certain failure in the confusion, the heterogeneity which devours Diderot, which haunts and destroys him, and which will kill him sooner than Poland's frost or punishing roads if he is prevented from doing what God has never done: going back over his work to mold and perfect it. The complete *Encyclopédie* of Denis Diderot . . . "Before dying I shall take suitable revenge for the malice of my enemies . . . Before dying I shall imprint some marks upon the earth which time will not erase. I shall devote my last fifteen years to it, for have I anything

better to do?" He writes to Betzki: "Well then, General, we shall encyclope-
dize!"[3]

Added to this hope is a parvenu's naïveté. This son of a cutler from
Langres has just had sixty private talks with the Great Catherine. "The sovereign's private study is open to me daily from three in the afternoon until five
and sometimes six . . . Ah, my dears, what a sovereign! what an extraordinary
woman! . . . You will have to believe me when I describe her with her
own words; you will all agree that hers is the soul of Brutus in the body of
Cleopatra . . ."[4] "He entered and sat down opposite her at a small table that
she placed between them to shield her thighs from his too cordial gesticula-
tions. He managed nevertheless to seize her hand, to pump her arm, and had
no compunctions about pounding the table, as if it were Holbach's house or
the Régence."*[5] What tête-à-têtes they must have been between this artless,
agitated spirit, with neither polish nor elegance, whose face lit up when "enthusiasm became his state,"[6] and the attractive, buxom German coquette,
fluent in French and able to appraise a man at first glance. They got along
famously, no question about it. She must have liked being pushed around a
bit. He was aware that she had engineered her husband's murder ten years
earlier and managed to let her know that he respected her for it.

"What do they think of me in Paris?"

"Madam, some people believe you are innocent of Peter III's death and
think that he was a half-witted tyrant; others believe you are not innocent . . ."

"And those people?"

"Those people think like the others."

He had bombarded her with notes, lists of questions, of suggestions, of
diplomatic, pedagogic, political, and technical projects for Russia. But whose
Russia? The empire ruled over by Catherine, whom he took to be engaged
in creating a model of enlightened government. He had not heard the roar
of a rebel army led by Pugachev (a self-appointed Peter III returned from the
dead) echoing from the far reaches of the Caspian, sweeping Cossacks, Bashkirs, Kalmuks into its ranks, besieging city after city, alarming Muscovites into
staging a mass exodus . . . Between two cheerful interviews with Diderot,
Catherine had written to one of her generals: "In our misfortune, we may
consider ourselves fortunate that this rabble was checked for two solid months
at the gates of Orenburg."[7]

The insurgent hordes solidified the rebellious stirrings of "impoverished
peasants," miners, and factory workers, promising everyone "the land, the
seas, the forests, heaven and earth and all liberties."[8] When the cutler's son
announced his departure in a trembling voice to this latter-day Cleopatra,
Pugachev still had fifty cannon trained on Orenburg. Perhaps some trace of

*Coffee house on the Place du Palais-Royal, the setting of Diderot's *Le Neveu de Rameau.*
[*Trans.*]

the Russian reality may have rubbed off on Diderot, filtering through the polite hostility of Petersburg society, reflected in certain teasing remarks of the Empress, who would listen indulgently to "his sheer prattle," commenting that Diderot "was a hundred years old in certain respects and not ten in others."[9] Wasn't this one reason for his premature departure, in the snow, despite Catherine's efforts to restrain him? Did he feel adrift in an alien world, the world of illusion? He returned without having once strayed off the beaten path of enlightened northern Europe, where, from London to Saint Petersburg, society strove for conformity—in French. Same fashions, same manners, same juggling of ideas no weightier than soap bubbles. Diderot never saw Russia; he merely consorted with her rulers.

If he is really so proud of himself, then why the deep sigh of relief on settling down in the Galitzin household? Why is he in no hurry to return to France? He talks of weeks, but thinks of months and months in Holland, to rest, to wait, never quite sure for what. He hesitates, understandably, to rejoin his dragon of a wife: "The most obliging questions induce such harsh responses on her part that I address her only when absolutely necessary."[10] But what about those "dear Volland ladies," the mother and the two sisters, especially Sophie, even if tenderness and complicity are now the sole ties between them? Or the Holbachs? Or his beloved daughter Marie-Angélique, still recovering from childbirth? And her infant daughter, whom he has never seen? He says that he has much to talk about: "I am saving a host of interesting details for the fireside. Gradually I am losing the marks of age brought on by fatigue."[11] No, he will never lose them. His cheerfulness rings flat. "I am old indeed. You don't know how long it takes to age, and I do."[12] Did Denis Diderot's solid frame have to become bent before he could write this to Catherine: "I prostrate myself northward; once again I offer Your Imperial Majesty my solemn thanks for all her bounties, and once again my tears moisten her hand"[13] (from The Hague, April 8, 1774)? Diderot, "who, in all things, is different from other men," the empress later observed, musing, to Grimm.[14]

GLUCK

10

APRIL 1774

Nature's Plaintive Cry

During this month of April, Paris seethes with revolution—verbal, at any rate. Not since the Querelle des Bouffons* twenty years before, between partisans of Italian and French music, have its likes been seen. "The turmoil wrought by this revolution in the minds of Parisians is incredible"—writes Mannlich, a German observer. "*Iphigénie* is on everyone's lips. Beaumarchais's famous *Mémoires* attacking M. Goëzman and pleading the nation's cause in the gayest and wittiest fashion . . . all that was shoved aside, forgotten, replaced by such topics as recitatives, overtures, triad roots, major and minor thirds, dissonance and consonance. Yet the busiest tongues can hardly define a chord."[1]

A great musical event is in store, promised as long ago as October 1, 1772, when the *Mercure de France* announced that "the famous M. Glouck,** known throughout Europe, has written a French opera which he would like to see performed on the French stage." So it is to be an original work, the world première of an opera in *French* (libretto by Leblanc de Roullet, based on Racine's *Iphigénie en Aulide*) presented to a *Parisian* audience in a *cosmopolitan* musical style launched by the first Viennese composer to achieve renown. This last fact alone sows panic in the ranks of tradition: what can Austria possibly offer—or any country besides Italy, for that matter? Others argue the point fiercely. Revolution or civil war? "For two weeks now, all of Paris is thinking

---

*"In 1752 the curious strife broke out . . . known as the 'Guerre des bouffons,' which was occasioned by the advent [in Paris] of an Italian troupe with their own repertory of works and with singers trained in the fine art of vocalization. Their side was championed by the critics Grimm, Diderot, and Rousseau, and the court, the press, and the public for two years or more were sharply divided into two parties, between which the literary and social antagonism was intense (expressed, for instance, in some sixty pamphlets). The Italians ranked themselves under the name of the queen, the French under that of the king, and each sought by every means to discredit the other. The French party ultimately triumphed and the historic opéra comique followed"—Waldo Selden Pratt, *History of Music* (New York: Schirmer, 1930), p.287. [*Trans.*]
**Contemporary writers spelled the name any number of whimsical ways: Kluck, Clouc, Cluck, even Cloch. It should be spelled "Gluck" and pronounced "Glouck." Occasionally one finds it incorrectly written with a dieresis over the "u."

and dreaming music. It is the core of every dispute and every conversation, the soul of our dinner parties; to express interest in any other subject would appear utterly absurd . . . Need it be said that M. le Chevalier Gluck's *Iphigénie* is inciting the turmoil? And it is all the more heated because opinions are sharply divided and loyalties equally passionate. There seem to be three main factions: partisans of traditional French opera, the sworn apostles of Lully and Rameau; disciples of such composers as Jommelli, Piccinni, and Sacchini; and finally devotees of the Chevalier Gluck, who claims to have pioneered music best suited to the demands of dramatic action, music relying on the inexhaustible resources of harmony and the intimate ties between human emotions and sensations; music native to no country, whose brilliant composer has managed to adapt it to the peculiar locutions of our language."[2]

Every war has its decisive battle, and this one opened on April 19 at the première of *Iphigénie.* The immense, circular Opera, rebuilt in 1770 at an angle with the Palais Royal on the site of the hall which had burned in 1763, can accommodate nearly three thousand. They are all there now, having waited since early morning, jostling each other in a line reaching to the Tuileries, along with many others who will never get in. Sharpers comb the crowd, hawking tickets at double or triple their original cost. Earlier the city magistrate was forced to limit attendance to five hundred at the final rehearsals and summon a military guard. Wrangling in the audience reached such a pitch that the singers could hardly rehearse.[3]

At half past five a great commotion greets the arrival of the dauphin and his wife, and the Comtes and Comtesses de Provence and d'Artois, climaxing a procession of state coaches announcing the presence of princes and ministers of the crown. Only the king and Madame du Barry have yet to appear. The hall, under blazing chandeliers, is stifling. Standees pack the pit, ringed by gilt loges filled with notables. Opposite the dauphin's box sits the Gluck family: a pretty, anxious-looking young woman, a pale girl* of fifteen, and the strapping, powerfully muscled old man with his red, round, "horribly pockmarked" face. Gluck's cold, deep-set eyes probe the hall with rapid glances, but, facing the three most crucial hours of his life, he retains an unwonted Olympian serenity.

The curtain rises. On one side, the Greek camp; on the other, Agamemnon's palace—setting of a pasteboard war reflecting the struggle going on in the minds of a bewildered audience. No conventional allegorical prologue. No flights of vocal virtuosity, artfully engineered to show off individual voices. No more warbling. Besides, what style would you call this—Italian, German, or what? And who ever heard of music that compels you to listen to the words instead of dozing or gossiping? These lively airs, these rustic-sounding trios and quartets, don't they suggest a village fair instead of a tragedy? Anyway,

*Marianne, their adopted daughter, suffering from consumption.

it's always safe to complain about the acting. Sophie Arnould (Iphigenia) has aged a bit; her eyes no longer hold the "adventure and romance" once admired by La Pompadour. She is still impressive, though, and, miraculously, manages for once to sing on key. On the other hand, Agamemnon (Larrivée) lacks dignity, and Achilles (Le Gros) flails the air, declaiming at the top of his lungs. The chorus is weak; Gluck winces in distress, indicating that the fault is not his. The audience remains unreceptive, disconcerted, puzzled, anxious to see what neighbors will say when the curtain falls. Those frequent bursts of applause are on behalf of Marie Antoinette: everyone knows that Gluck was her music master in Vienna. "One may even venture to attribute most of the generous applause to a desire to please the dauphine. This princess seemed to be pressing a cause with her constant clapping, which obliged Madame la Comtesse de Provence, the princes, and all the loges to do likewise."[4] Rather than sheer caprice, it is the first test of her influence. Having been barred from politics, society, and the court, she resolves to conquer the musical world.

Gluck had waged an intense, merciless campaign for four months, advancing through the sinuous channels of operatic tradition with the dauphine as his shield, trampling iron rules, prejudice, and ill-will. He had hustled the chorus out of its conventional, trellis-like formation based not on height but on seniority; had raised havoc with prosody in the name of lyricism; had humiliated the actors and musicians. "He wanted movement, expression; it was too much to ask for." Every rehearsal turned into a psychodrama. Gluck would fling his wig on the floor, singing, miming, cursing: "How do you get these automatons moving? If only I could dispense with my chorus, but I need it, dammit, I need it!" He was drenched in sweat. Madame Gluck would mop his brow with a moist towel and change his shirt, to which he submitted in docile silence. Then, suddenly, his listlessness vanished and once again he began rushing around to various sections of the orchestra. Not only the chorus but the violins, basses, strings, and altos were betraying him. "He cut them short, sang the passage to bring out the desired accents, then stopped them again, bellowing: 'That's not worth a damn!' His theme song. Several times he just missed being hit over the head with an instrument. He offended everyone." In the evening, strollers in the Tuileries Gardens would step aside for this fellow in a gray topcoat and cropped wig gesticulating like a drunken coachman. Many who attended those rehearsals are hoping that he will wind up with a failure tonight. In any event, one man who stood in the pit two days ago, only to be forced to take a seat, does not share their view. Gluck proved himself a first-rate diplomat indeed by courting Jean-Jacques Rousseau like a royal patron. He had climbed upstairs to the master's sanctum on the Rue Plâtrière to show him parts of *Iphigénie.* In return for which the fifth evangelist descended from his lair and set out on foot for the Opera, wearing his flat collar, cropped wig, and buckled shoes, head drooping slightly to one side, hat tucked under his arm, looking "like a neatly dressed peasant," as his musician friend Grétry observed. Opera-goers waited breathlessly for his reactions. In defending the Bouffons at one time, had he not declared the French language unsuited to musical expression? And Rousseau had gone off without a word, leaving Gluck in despair, when one small urchin from the host of errand boys roaming the streets presented him with a note. Upon reading the sender's name, he grew excited and handed the message to his wife:

"Ah, my efforts were not in vain. Here, read this! Read it aloud."

> Monsieur le Chevalier Gluck,
>
> I have just come from your opera *Iphigénie.* I find it delightful. You have achieved what I believed was impossible until now. *Iphigénie* changes all my ideas. It proves that the French language is as adaptable as any other to a musical style at once strong, touching, and sensitive.
>
> Kindly accept my sincere compliments and my very humble greetings.
>
> Paris, April 17, 1774
> Jean-Jacques Rousseau

But neither Marie Antoinette nor Jean-Jacques Rousseau could save Gluck tonight if something were not passing away. Event. Advent. And there it goes. Even before the first-act curtain falls, a few men, a few women are reduced to utter silence, in the pit as well as the loges, carried away by the bold invention of Agamemnon's long recitative decrying the conflict between paternal love and the divine command to sacrifice his daughter. "Echoing in my breast, I hear nature's plaintive cry." Oboes take up the theme, sustaining and accenting the wail of man protesting his fate: "I shall not obey this inhuman command," the "I" ringing out like a manifesto. "Upon those twenty-four measures, interspersed with pauses, one could found a religion," someone wrote the next day. Lieder, tranquil melodies accompany man's painful conquest of himself, actually of the immortals, up to the final chorus, *"Partons! Volons à la victoire!"* A burst of voices sweeps across the stage as the orchestra surges to a crescendo over the ominous beat, heard for the first time at the Paris Opera, of kettledrums thundering like cannon. No need for further applause from the dauphine. Utter stillness greets the reprieve, as tears well up beneath the rind of powder, paste, and beauty patches. No one so much as glances at his neighbor, yet all have looked in the same mirror. In march tempo with bassoon accompaniment, the high priest, Calchas, exhorts his listeners: "At the pinnacle of glory, imperious mortals, behold your own frailty . . ." Over the incessant drum roll like a storm approaching from the depths of time . . .

"The audience filed out as if from church." In the front of the pit stood a youngish-looking man, conductor of the Prince de Conti's orchestra, who had wept despite himself: François-Joseph Gossec,* son of a Belgian plowman.

---

*One of the founders of the Paris Conservatory and a major influence in the development of French orchestral music. [*Trans.*]

II

APRIL 1774

What Won't It Take to Make the People Act?

Jean-Paul Marat is not going to follow Diderot's example and visit Catherine II. True, he wavered momentarily, in the dead of London's winter and in want, at the age of thirty-two, between a political and a literary career. An influential benefactor, Lord Lyttelton, had told him that the Russian court was engaging tutors for children of noble Petersburg families, advising him to call on Count Pushkin, the Russian ambassador, "who will inform you of something that may be highly advantageous to you."[1] Jean-Paul considered the proposal and rejected it. He had just finished writing *Les Aventures du Comte Potowski,* an unmarketable saga featuring Rousseauism spiced with eroticism, and characters engaged in political debates and acts in the tormented Poland left prostrate by the First Partition of 1772. Anxious concern for the world situation had prompted him to set his novel in that mutilated country. No, never would he seek his fortune at the court of a woman who "today forces the Poles to their knees with fire and sword" and smiles benignly at those horrid Encyclopedists, whom he cannot forgive for having scorned him in the past. "She hires mercenary pens to celebrate her."[2] Well, she won't buy the signature of Jean-Paul Maxa, Massa, Marsa, Mara—Marat, finally, the definitive spelling, with its Frenchified final "t," that he settled on fifteen years ago while a teacher in Bordeaux.

But has he really ended his search for a name and a country? Born in the Prussian province of Boudry, near Neuchâtel, of a Sardinian father and Languedocian mother, he admits to no other cradle than the human race. Right now, in 1774, he is tinkering with the notion of putting down temporary roots in England. Marat is thinking of becoming a British citizen and charges head first into the electoral fray. The contest for lord mayor of London is so heated this April that people speak of a revolution in England, a real one.

By all standards Wilkes is ugly, Wilkes has no breeding, Wilkes is a reveler, Wilkes worships money, Wilkes is cynical, vicious, fickle, a second-rate writer and orator. Yet he cannot fail to win the mayoralty. He is the idol of the London mob, the symbol of universal suffering under the tyranny of the crown, the government, the aristocracy—all one and the same since England's famed liberties began eroding. Just eleven years ago the whole city turned out to celebrate Wilkes's release by the Court of Common Pleas, following charges of seditious libel for attacking the speech from the throne in No. 45 of his periodical *The North Briton*. Overnight he became Mr. 45; "45" fashions sprang up, "45" shop signboards, "45" snuff. Now he is again under siege, after the crowded events following his triumph: a duel, a critical injury, exile and a momentous return, the pillory, bankruptcy, public contributions in his behalf, election, expulsion, re-election, re-expulsion . . . Who will finally win? Londoners, who want Wilkes, or the king, who doesn't?

Elections provide the English with a spectacle you are not likely to see in Paris. A ferocious festival; the nation takes to the streets. Everywhere shouts, debates, people drunk on stout, or ale, or just noise. Partisans of each candidate canvass the town, drumming up votes one by one. "You would think the Saturnalia were with us again: working women rush about like bacchantes, while ladies of the *beau monde** electioneer in the salons. A duchess did not hesitate to solicit her butcher's vote, which he refused to pledge. He held to his own opinion and insisted on supporting Wilkes."[3] In Covent Garden, where trees are putting forth their first timid shoots, impromptu orators mount the hustings and harangue the crowd. The mood can turn ugly at night, however, in the slums of St. Giles or on the docks along the Thames, wherever mobs gather, the antithesis of the *beau monde*, those "animals diseased with poverty" whom Hogarth had recently drawn. Permanent gibbets have been raised here and workmen hanged for marching on the shops and destroying machinery, the bodies left dangling for a week as an example. It seems that some of them prefer the scaffold to slow death from cold and starvation, or deportation to some strange city decreed by the machine, a new and fiendish despot they abhor. Children are sold to the workrooms in lots of fifty, more likely eighty, starting at the age of five. A thousand or so have just been shipped off to Lancashire. "Little ones are put to work almost as soon as they can walk, and their parents are the harshest masters." Clergymen, serving the district adjoining a factory in which apprentices are imprisoned until the age of sixteen, recommend "that no aid be given to children above the age of six who have not learned to weave, or to children over nine who cannot spin flax or wool."[4] Preachers of the gospel ended up recruiting the first victims of England's industrial expansion. The work day for "parish apprentices" in the infant textile industry varied from fourteen to eighteen hours.

The beasts of burden do not vote. Whom would they vote for anyway? Even Wilkes avoids mentioning them. Nor are there votes for the boxers whom office-seekers hire from entrepreneurs operating much like stud farmers

---

*"*Le beau monde*" as a current French expression which the English adopted intact to denote "smart society." It returned to favor in nineteenth-century France in the phrase "*Ça, c'est du beau monde!*"

"to fatten and fortify them on choice, succulent meats." These days you see them sparring with bare fists in the open air, sporting Whig or Tory colors, going at it until "the claret spurts" —a popular term for drawing blood, much in favor with the screaming crowd, which is not averse to seeing boxers fight to the death in the shade of a pub usually reserved for cockfighting.

The central issue in this election is crucial enough, though the neediest may not know it. The election, which is not required until March 1775, has been called prematurely by George III in order to take the opposition by surprise and to secure a new Parliament that can consider the urgent affairs of America undistracted by the prospect of an early dissolution. Lord North's government, solidly anti-American, labors assiduously to keep its big majority of country gentlemen. The only resistance comes from a solid core of liberal Whigs warning against the folly of colonial warfare: Fox, Burke, Sheridan, and Wilkes—always Wilkes.*

To aid their cause, Marat has just published *The Chains of Slavery,* English version of a tract he has been mulling over for ten years, his own *Spirit of the Laws* and *Social Contract*: *Les Chaines de l'esclavage,* "the first attempt in the eighteenth century to evolve a genuine theory of the Revolution."**

He has shut himself up in his Soho room, no longer visited by the pretty Swiss artist Angelica Kauffmann. This handsome, swarthy, high-strung man grated on her nerves, kept her from painting her subdued landscapes and ruins. Their affair had lasted just a year; he was not sorry to see it ended. For the first time he felt a tremor not unlike an electric current deep inside him: a nation awakening and beginning to stir. But "what won't it take to make the people act?"[5] Quickly now, hurl the firebrand, alert voters before they can be bought off in "rotten boroughs" by corrupt sheriffs. If only he can finish it in time. This book, which he wrote to serve the French, or Poles, or Swiss, or Americans, shall first serve the English. He labored twenty-one hours a day for three months to translate it into English and adapt it to the realities of British politics. He managed to hold out through the use of "diluted coffee, which he drank so excessively that it came nearer to killing him than lack of sleep." He had fallen "into a kind of prostration verging on stupor. He had lost his memory and for thirteen days remained in that lethargic state," from which he emerged around the 15th of April "with the aid of music and rest."[6]

At last the volume "is ready to come off the press": a hundred or so short chapters, each one to three pages long, the mere titles of which would have clapped him behind bars in France: "Hypocrisy of Rulers," "Ill-advised Moderation of the People," "On Superstition," "Connivance of Rulers and Priests," "Usurpation of Absolute Authority," "The People Are Forging Their Fetters" . . . A tedious but orderly approach: each chapter opens with

---

*But Wilkes was in a category all his own, at odds with the Whigs and their century-old craving for power.
**According to Gérard Walter.

an ideological assertion which is subsequently borne out in a series of illustrations from ancient or modern history, repeated tours of Greece, Rome, feudal Europe, Spain under the Inquisition, France under Louis XIV (viewed as a tyrant of the first order), in addition to contemporary despots: Frederick II, Catherine of Russia, Louis XV. Marat has turned out a methodical treatise based upon his systematic compilation "of thirty mortal volumes."

An obsession: venality. The corruption of tyrants eats away the fiber of free nations. A dominant theme: dismantling the process of building absolutism. "To keep people enslaved, rulers have found it safest to reduce them gradually to slavery, by lulling them to sleep, by corrupting them, by stripping them of all they possess—love, memory, even the very concept of liberty."

This sets off a flurry of admonitions. The book is indeed a manual of distrust. "Rulers deal liberty the opening blow not by boldly violating the law but by promoting ignorance of it. To enslave the public you must begin by rocking it to sleep . . . " "At first administration is so mild that it appears bent on augmenting freedom, a far cry from destroying it . . . " "The approach to despotism is frequently smooth and pleasant, all games, festivities, dancing, and singing. But the people do not see the evil lurking in these games; abandoning themselves to pleasure, they set the air ringing with joyous songs . . . " "To the power of time and festivals is added the distraction of activity: undertaking some national monument; constructing public buildings, highways, marketplaces, houses of worship. The people, who judge only by appearances, believe their ruler is totally preoccupied with the welfare of the state, whereas he is simply furthering his own devices . . . " "Any gift to the populace from its ruler should be suspect, unless made in the wake of a sudden disaster. The only honest way for a ruler not intent on becoming a tyrant to ease the lot of his subjects is by reducing their taxes . . . " "Who would believe it? Rulers have been known to approach despotism along paths that ordinarily lead away from it."

These rulers have their tools; their favorites, their "creatures," their army, their priesthood. "All religions lend tyranny a helping hand; yet I know none that indulges it more than Christianity." And speculators. In the first third of the book Marat denounces "the system of monopolies"—"Soon the nation falls prey to extortionists, financiers, publicans, swindling officials . . . " "In the trading nations, capitalists and investors generally make common cause with merchants, bankers, and speculators; the large cities contain but two classes of citizens, one of which vegetates in misery while the other wallows in superfluities . . . In republics, then, the extreme disparity in wealth leaves the mass of people subservient to a handful of individuals. That is what happened in Venice, in Genoa, in Florence, when commerce brought the riches of Asia pouring in. And that is what we find in the United Provinces [Holland], where affluent citizens, true masters of the republic, possess princely riches while the multitude cries for bread."

It is that view of the world which world citizen Jean-Paul Marat seeks to implant in England's citizenry in April 1774. Without much hope, for his mounting pessimism culminates in these final lines: "Liberty shares the fate of all human affairs: it yields to time, which destroys all; to ignorance, which confuses all; to vice, which corrupts all; and to force, which crushes all." Still, he makes every effort to promote the book, sending it to "the most advanced patriotic societies" and journeying all the way to Scotland to publicize it. Wasted time: *The Chains of Slavery* receives no notice. It is merely a ripple in the tide of election victories returning the Tories, with the sole compensation of carrying Wilkes into the lord mayor's office, where he makes himself at home in record time, out of weariness if not corruption. Marat is not the least surprised, considering that the great Wilkes did not even bother to thank him for the copy of his book.

```
ANECDOTES
       SUR
M. LA COMTESSE
DU BARRI.

Hec ubi suppofuit dextro corpus mihi lævum,
Ilia & Egeria eft; do nomen quodlibet illi,
Horat. L. I. Sat. II. vr. 125, 126.

A LONDRES.
MDCCLXXV.
```

12

APRIL 1774

Another Man Would Hang Himself for Less

Beaumarchais, too, is spending most of April in England, though paying scant attention to the elections. Still, some people are beginning to call him "the French Wilkes"—as if he didn't have troubles enough with his own government—a comparison advanced in social circles where No. 45 of *The North Briton* is mentioned in the same breath as the Goëzman pamphlets. In reality, the people's tribune and the man of letters have nothing in common except the brief outcries raised by their antagonists in London and Paris.

Pierre-Augustin is no fool. The last thing he needs is to dog Marat's footsteps and start poking his nose into British politics! He is there incognito, beyond the reach of the law. Even the name Caron has vanished, having been reversed, a passport issued to "M. de Ronac, French gentleman." The man all France was talking about just two months ago now travels unnoticed along the shortest route between Paris and London, the classic choice of hurried voyagers.

Chantilly, the Versailles of the Condés. Amiens, city of a hundred thousand, devoted to silk and to wool soft as silk. Abbeville, still scarred by the explosion of a powder magazine six months before, where one can see "the hole it made, and the heavy rocks hurled far and wide"; [1] the finest sheets in the world are woven there. Boulogne, with its fishermen and fish auctions along the Roman docks. The windswept coastal road skirting the Channel. Calais, pretty chalk-white city, no more than an innkeeper to travelers between France and England. The crossing aboard a slow, sturdy little vessel, anywhere from four hours to two days, depending on the winds. Dover, the cliffs, the boat overrun with "young rascals making a frightful racket, some trying to carry the luggage, others to conduct travelers to the inn, each one shouting in his own fashion." [2] The exorbitant rate of exchanging louis into guineas. Prices are double. White-and-green roads; "totally different manners, food, attitudes, way of life, even the method of constructing a house—in short, everything." [3] "The host of men, women and children sitting on the doorstep in the early morning sun, relaxing from their labors, offering beer, punch, and cakes to passers-by and acquaintances, while a boisterous circle of sailors laughs and disports with a half-dozen coachfuls of travelers . . . A rustic background richly decorated with poplars, fruit trees, country houses . . . Great numbers of cabriolets, as elegant as they are light, horses unrivaled for speed, impeccably dressed young men and ladies in riding habits, whose tightly veiled heads disclose only the whiteness of their skin and a distinctive modesty." [4] This is the road between Dover and London, a delight to newly arrived travelers from the continent. Seventy-two miles. Three changes of horses.

In London he plunges straight into the *beau monde,* making his way unobtrusively through the whirl of social events, whose harmony leaves the English aristocracy deaf to the rumbling in the streets. "The salons are superb. Soirées began at ten, the gentlemen not arriving before 11:30, after spending the evening at their club. During that interval the ladies waited patiently, elegantly gowned and bejeweled. At midnight a magnificent supper would be served." [5] Over the staircase at Lord Stanley's, bathed in colored lights, musicians play the hunting horn and clarinet; "vestals in white tend the sacred flame destined to produce tea . . . " At the French embassy, where the Comte de Guines presides and Beaumarchais is visible yet invisible, one whole side of the ballroom has been torn down to provide more space for the musicians "dressed in scarlet robes. Huge mirrors all around the room reflect the guests and the lights. The visual impact is dazzling . . . In the ballet of the seasons, dancers are dressed as shepherds and shepherdesses." [6]

Has Beaumarchais come there to dance? Not according to those who recognize him. He is testing the breeze, exploring, poking through the "nest of Frenchmen," that swarm of adventurers outlawed by Louis XV who have set up headquarters "in the land of Milord Sterling and Milady Guinea."* He did not come alone from France. With him is a florid-cheeked, imposing,

*Expression coined by the Chevalier d'Eon.

captivating gentleman, full of malice and abrasion, who acts as both his sponsor and his "cover" in this exclusive society: Louis-Léon de Brancas, the Comte de Lauraguais. This brash nobleman has already had his fill of the army, which bored him. He has haunted the corridors of the Comédie Française, has loved and left Sophie Arnould. The epigrams he fires at doctors, judges, and crown officials eventually send him from (gilded) prison into exile. He adjusts easily; temperamentally, he is Beaumarchais's clansman and has just published a *Mémoire pour moi, par moi* aimed at settling a few accounts. Lauraguais is like a fish out of water in London, "that immense pit hollowed out first by the Danes, then the Normans, and steadily deepened by the French, in which gold and universal folly are forever being swallowed up. When an Italian or a Frenchman has earned the noose in his own country, they both come rushing here. One proclaims on arrival that he has fled the Inquisition, the other, the Bastille . . . If they succeed in arousing pity and scorn in the rather uncouth crowd, they are offered a tankard in the corner alehouse. They remark politely that in England one toasts liberty whereas elsewhere one merely longs for it."[7] But Lauraguais is not here to philosophize about Great Britain; he is accompanying Beaumarchais on a secret mission, and, despite their offhand manner, they have no time to lose. Without Lauraguais, Beaumarchais could get in touch on his own with Théveneau de Morande, but not secure the "contact."

Now Pierre-Augustin's mission consists in arranging an immediate meeting with Théveneau de Morande and buying him off for the King of France. For some time now Lauraguais has carried on a singular relationship with that "rogue [Théveneau], who fancies himself something of a social lion because a few strumpets call him the Chevalier de La Morande instead of simply De Morande, and because he publishes a scandal sheet that sounds as if a coachman had adapted it from the diary of a bawd's kitchen slut."[8] Lauraguais himself provides that sketch of Théveneau de Morande, in whose arms he collapses with protestations of undying friendship when introducing Beaumarchais—after checking to make sure the meeting is indeed secret. Lauraguais had threatened once to have Morande beaten up; they used to curse each other publicly and privately; in fact they were the best of friends. Lauraguais furnished Théveneau with titillating details about the goings-on at Versailles. And as the count himself frequently ran short of funds, he in turn was not averse to dropping a scurrilous remark here and there, finding that an excellent way to relieve the pinch.

Charles Théveneau is no ordinary outlaw. Thirty-three, with a high forehead, pinched lips, and caressing eyes. Rotten to the core; relatives of his in Arnay-le-Duc insist that he was born that way. Having done everything, tried everything, known everything—extortion, women, prison, persecution—all he has left are a vigorous pen, undying hatred of mankind, and a voracious appetite for money. Three years ago in London he published *le Gazetier cuirassé,* *ou anecdotes scandaleuses de la Cour de France,* * "printed a hundred leagues from the Bastille, at the sign of Liberty,"[9] containing a curious frontispiece of Masonic inspiration depicting the god Vishnu consorting with Jupiter. In it, and with considerable wit, he demolishes La Du Barry and the king's ministers, sparing Louis XV only to diminish him by implication. The sheet sells like hotcakes all over "enlightened" Europe, indulging at times in something more than spicy anecdote: "There is one way to pocket three millions with no outlay: set up a scaffold on the Place des Sablons, hang Maupeou upon it, and collect an écu from every spectator."[10] Shades of Marat. Or this: "It is reckoned in France that out of about 200 colonels, equally divided among the infantry, cavalry, and dragoons, 180 can dance and sing little tunes, nearly the same number wear lace and red heels, and at least half know how to write and sign their name. Add to this calculation the fact that not four of them know the rudiments of their profession."[11] Morande sends galley proofs of his diatribes to the victims, offering to withdraw them from publication in return for money. He has just announced the appearance of a four-volume opus, *Les Mémoires secrets d'une femme publique,* with engravings, about the life of "La Comtesse du Tonneau," the very mention of which is enough to terrorize Du Barry and her circle.** It seems that Louis XV is depicted brewing coffee for "Chonchon," who asks him, laughing hysterically, "Can anyone believe that you rule twenty million subjects and that I am one of them?" . . . She calls in the Archbishop of Rheims to change her slippers, she removes Chancellor Maupeou's wig and covers his bald pate with her handkerchief—it's all simply beyond endurance! Someone has to put a stop to this! Panic at Versailles. Not that any popular rumblings threaten them because of these "revelations." The populace doesn't care a straw about Du Barry—and what workman reads Morande? No, the loss of privacy is what they dread, being confronted in print with their own intimate nocturnal whisperings, the slow torture of this cruel sport. They tried everything: first the French ambassador, then an agent, the Chevalier d'Eon, hired in case of emergency, despite his shady reputation. How much did Morande want?

Five thousand louis in cash and an annual allowance for life of four thousand livres, payable after his death to his wife and son.† Too much. So they tried to silence him some other way. A small expedition, armed with England's pledge of impunity, sailed for London: four civil police under the command of an army officer were to seize Morande and toss him on board a cutter moored at the mouth of the Thames. Amen. He would have been lucky to end up in the Bastille or Vincennes. Over the past ten years some twenty European pamphleteers kidnaped in that fashion had vanished from France, Spain, and Austria.

*The Armor-Plated Gazetteer, Or Scandalous Tales from the French Court. [*Trans.*]
***Tonneau* and *baril* (pronounced "barry") both mean "keg" or "barrel" in French. [*Trans.*]
†Roughly 400,000 current francs cash [$80,000] and 16,000 francs [$3200] allowance.

But word from Paris had alerted Théveneau de Morande. When the myrmidons of the law introduced themselves as "friends," he greeted them politely, borrowed thirty louis from each—among friends, right?—and instead of appearing at the appointed rendezvous, promptly and vehemently denounced this violation of English hospitality in all the gazettes. Crowds gathered at their hotel; they were assaulted and chased. The tardiest runner was caught, tarred, and thrown into the Thames. Fished out in a state of shock, he has been in Bedlam, the insane asylum, since February. The others simply took to their heels and fled. This Théveneau de Morande was certainly not the accommodating sort.

After twelve thousand copies of his book had been printed—half of them in Amsterdam, as a precaution—he issued his ultimatum to Versailles advising them that one word from him to the printer would put the volumes in circulation . . . At that moment Beaumarchais offered his services to Louis XV.

It was virtually the only course open to him. After the ephemeral triumph of his censure, everyone had clapped him on the back, then dropped him, as he expected. His Goëzman pamphlets had gone up in smoke at the foot of the grand staircase in the Palace of Justice. Subjected to civil disgrace, he stood deprived of resources, of his livelihood, of all means of expression. *Le Barbier de Séville* continued to be banned. In appealing the ruling, he had made it clear that either his judges must weigh the facts objectively and mete out harsher terms to an insolent offender from their own ranks, or else he, Beaumarchais, would attack them in a fresh series of pamphlets . . . But this threatened blackmail so disturbed the king that he ordered him silenced. Sartines, minister of police and presumably his friend, summoned Beaumarchais like a principal calling in a lazy student for a dressing down: "Sir, I advise you to make yourself scarce. Present goings-on irritate a great many people. It is not enough to be censured; one must also be humble. If the king should give an order, I would be compelled to carry it out, no matter how I felt. Above all, write nothing, for the king does not wish you to publish a word about this matter."[12]

Perhaps at that moment he was given to understand that things might go easier for him if he volunteered for certain small chores demanding versatility and cunning, plus the tact and prestige needed to intimidate Morande. But he must step forward; the King of France was not about to admit that he needed a Beaumarchais.

Pierre-Augustin then wrote to La Borde, another of those ubiquitous double-dealing agents, first gentleman of the king's bedchamber, which simply meant that he possessed one or two quarterings of nobility and frequently was alone in Louis XV's presence, his "service" not requiring him to lift a single finger. La Borde was actually a tax farmer—in other words, a millionaire—with literary and musical pretensions. A seat in the Academy was his cherished hope. Beaumarchais, whose kindred spirit he fancied himself to be, might help him obtain it one day. La Borde decided to invest a small amount of courage.

The bargain was sealed—verbally—during the month of March, through La Borde and Sartines, between the king and Du Barry on the one hand and Beaumarchais on the other. The latter agrees to try to cajole Morande and buy him off once and for all at the lowest price; the former pledge that if Beaumarchais succeeds, he will receive royal *lettres de relief* automatically reopening the Goëzman case.

M. de Ronac is in London, then, to restore M. Caron's civil rights.

Now D'Eon looked down his nose at Morande in their Burgundian homeland, the one a native of Tonnerre, the other of Arnay-le-Duc. He disdained him as a gentleman disdains a bourgeois, as a veteran bearer of state secrets scoffs at a common intriguer spying at bedroom keyholes. "M. Morande is from my district," the chevalier reported to his minister;* "he prides himself on being related to a branch of my family in Burgundy . . . For two months I refused to see him, and for good reasons. Since then he has hung about my door so persistently that from time to time I have allowed him entrance to avoid being saddled with a most excitable and impetuous young man, who knows no bounds and no moderation, who respects neither the sacred nor the profane . . . He married his landlady's daughter, who was in the habit of making and unmaking his bed with him . . . I know he needs money . . . but I would be delighted if he were to receive that money from some hand other than mine, lest . . . it be imagined that I acquired a single guinea from such an arrangement."[13] The cheerfully archaic tone is typical of D'Eon. The first thing to consider about this man is that in 1774 he has become a writer, even fancies himself a philosopher, and that all other aspects of his personality recede into the background, including the sexual ambiguity about which public whispers can now be heard. This year he is bringing out a gigantic tome, a mountain, the summary of his life, thirteen volumes entitled *Les Loisirs du Chevalier d'Eon de Beaumont, sur divers sujets importants d'administration*, dedicated by this everlasting Don Quixote to the great Choiseul, now in disgrace, for protection that no longer protects. As a writer, not to say moralist, he is about to act as witness—rather peeved at not being the principal agent—to the dealings between Morande and Beaumarchais. He will end up playing a substantial role as counselor. Bright and early one morning Morande appears on D'Eon's doorstep to announce that "two French gentlemen have come with a fortune in their pockets to persuade him to suppress his *Mémoires* against the Comtesse du Barry, but he will do nothing without first seeking advice:

" 'Where are they now?'

" 'In their carriage, on the street corner. They wish to talk to you.'

" 'What are their names? Where are their letters of introduction?'

" 'They insist on strict anonymity.'

*The Duc d'Aiguillon, interim minister of foreign affairs.

" 'Open my door to strangers? How do you know they are not police, spies, or adventurers? Let them go about their own business. Arrange whatever you like with them privately.'

" 'But what do you advise me to do?'

" 'My friend, I know the risks of your trade, the same as those of a highway robber. You have a wife, children, servants, and debts. Life in London is dear. Attack the fanciest coach that comes your way.' "[14]

D'Eon goes on to describe the transaction that took place, speaking of himself in the third person: "A few days later M. d'Eon learned that the two unknown gentlemen were the totally unknown M. Caron de Beaumarchais and the very prominent and well-known Louis François Brancas, the Comte de Lauraguais, and that on behalf of Louis XV they had concluded a compact with M. Charles Théveneau de Morande providing for suppression of his lampoon in return for the sum of fifteen hundred louis in cash, an annual allowance of four thousand francs during Morande's lifetime and, after his death, two thousand to his wife for life.* M. d'Eon thanked heaven and M. de Morande for such good fortune and told him jokingly that he was foolish not to have demanded a life pension for his children, legitimate and bastard, his dog, and his cat."

By the end of April, Beaumarchais is done in. He has been back and forth twice between Paris and London to obtain powers of attorney, and to Holland to see that all six thousand copies of the pamphlet were destroyed in Amsterdam. On his return to London, he will use D'Eon as a "technical consultant" in arranging to liquidate the remaining half of the edition. It is too bulky for the ordinary fireplace; last year Morande nearly incinerated the whole Lincoln's Inn district with another of his printings—a diatribe against Lauraguais, as a matter of fact—which roared up the chimney of a private citizen. This time Lauraguais is cooperating, along with Beaumarchais, to make "a magnificent bonfire" of the last six thousand copies in a brick oven a mile outside London, hired on the chevalier's advice.

Success is theirs and they are exhilarated. Morande has become an agent and pensioner of the king he lately vilified. Beaumarchais's return to favor and fortune is assured at last. Quickly now, head for home: the white road, the boat, Calais. Boulogne. A brief stopover, on May 3, to change horses. But why does everyone rush so for the news sheets?

"My dear sir, the king is dying!"

From Beaumarchais to Morande six days after Louis XV's death: "How different are our destinies! I work day and night for six weeks. I cover nearly seven hundred leagues . . . You acquire something from this operation . . . your peace of mind, whereas I cannot even be sure of having my travel

---

*Evidently Beaumarchais had managed to whittle down the cash figure by 70,000 current francs [$14,000] and to cut the survivor's pension in half.

expenses reimbursed . . . All I have left are my swollen legs and flat purse. Another man would hang himself for less, but since that choice will always be mine, I save it for the finale . . . and am presently waiting to see which of us, the devil or myself, will prove more obstinate, he in pitching me down, or I in picking myself up."[15]

LOUIS XVI HEARING OF
THE DEATH OF LOUIS XV

13

MAY 1774

My Dear Abbé, the Worst Is Yet to Come

The great sculptor Pigalle has just completed his four bronze Cardinal Virtues which support the pedestal of an equestrian figure of Louis XV standing in a square of still fluid contours, at the western entrance to Paris, before the Tuileries.* They are "four miserable creatures, flat, clumsy, and depressing, who will constantly inform passers-by on the Place Louis XV that by casting them, their creator showed a lack of genius and of taste . . . This equestrian statue of Louis XV cost the city of Paris more than two million."[1]**

Louis XV resembles the virtues which Pigalle heaped on him. He has the head of an old goose, mercilessly depicted by Van Loo in one of the last portraits of the monarch.[2] "His timid manner stems in large part from his stupidity," observed Choiseul, who knew him well, having been around him for twelve years.[3] A long, narrow face; large, vacant eyes; a nose curved like a beak, with a ruddy tip. Flabby flesh. Detached, but always majestic. And they expect him to remarry? Where would he find the courage? Anyone—including his daughter Louise, a Carmelite nun—who nags him about it is brushed aside like a fly. "I am aware that if people keep talking to me of marriage, it is to remind me of my age; that if they urge me to take a wife, they mean that I should give up my mistress."[4] He is content with things as they are, pleasant little supper parties of six or eight, including Du Barry. An erotic flush or two now and then—honor demands it—but generally slippers and coffee. A glimpse of the domestic bliss he never knew with Marie Leczinska or La Pompadour. Is this what he is supposed to surrender at the age of sixty-four, only to act like an ass for the benefit of some young Spanish or Austrian

*Now the Place de la Concorde. The equestrian statue itself was done by Bouchardon.
**Between eight and nine million current francs [$1,600,000 and $1,800,000].

princess? And fall back into the exhausting pattern of balls, military parades, and crowds which he gave up years ago?

In fact he has been decaying delicately for quite some time. "Death inhabits Versailles."[5] Sorba, the Genoese ambassador, often seen in the royal circle, gave the alarm by departing this earth in two minutes flat. Then the Abbé de La Ville, another obliging doormat, died during the king's levee. Next Chauvelin, his friend for twenty years and accomplice in the Parc aux Cerfs affair, one evening as they were playing piquet in Madame du Barry's apartments . . . Looking up, she sees him leaning on the king's armchair: "Monsieur de Chauvelin, what a face you're making!" By the time Louis XV had turned around, the Marquis de Chauvelin lay dead at his feet.

A desert is opening up. People hesitate to choose between Versailles and Chanteloup, near Amboise, where Choiseul has been holding court since his dismissal. "It is a completely new spectacle for France to watch . . . a king becoming unpopular, or, synonymously, unfashionable,"[6] observes the Englishman Walpole, who in fact was unacquainted with Louis XIV's last, desolate years. And just to make matters worse, that zealous young Abbé de Beauvais, Bishop of Senez, began fulminating from his pulpit on Maundy Thursday in the king's presence—not so much against Du Barry as against rising taxes, the misery of the poor, and the useless existence of his stunned listeners there in the chapel of Versailles: "Another forty days and Nineveh shall be destroyed!" Delectable shiver: the kind Louis XV relishes between dainty suppers, peppering passion with the notion of death.

Another type of shiver invaded him at Trianon on Tuesday, April 26, 1774. Not at the rose- and flesh-tinted Grand Trianon, deserted now for several years, but at the Petit Trianon, all sparkling white and new, a square "pavilion" most unlike a palace, with its Greek outlines adapted to French taste, planted by the architect Gabriel in the center of a botanical garden boasting every variety of strawberry Europe has to offer,[7] the scene of Bernard de Jussieu's experiments "on what causes grain to rot and how to prevent it." Louis XV has come here since 1768 for his diversions with La Du Barry.* Beauty, refinement, isolation, boredom. Perfect for intimate suppers, though not for sleeping—those small, low-ceilinged, and generally uncomfortable upstairs rooms.

So the king feels chilled and unwell on the evening of the 26th shortly after arriving for a rendezvous with Madame du Barry, surrounded by a small coterie schooled to the fact that they must never talk to him about anything: four men and three women.** "He finds everything tedious and has no appetite." Louis XV is no better the next morning. He attempts to "shake off

---

*Total cost of the Petit Trianon, financed from the ministry of foreign affairs's budget, 736,056 livres, 16 sols, 6 deniers, or approximately three million current francs [$600,000].[8]

**The Prince de Soubise, the Ducs d'Aiguillon, d'Ayen, and de Duras; Mesdames de Mirepoix, de Forcalquier, and de Flammarens.

his humors" by setting out for a bit of hunting in the woods between Versailles and Marly, directly accessible from the Trianons, but is compelled to dismount and sit huddled in the back of a coach. Splitting headache on his return. He goes to bed without eating, feels flushed and chilled by turns, cannot tolerate his mistress in the bed, lies on a sofa and shakes all night.[9]

On the morning of the 28th his chief physician is summoned, Lemonnier, Du Barry's trusted friend. "No alarming symptoms." If the court half a league away at the palace learns that His Majesty is ill, the whole barnyard will go wild. But can Versailles and Trianon keep secrets from each other much beyond five hours? Tales filter down through the servants. Some member of the royal family, probably one of the king's daughters, decides to dispatch the royal surgeon, La Martinière, a plain-spoken man:

"Sire, Versailles is the place to be ill."

That evening, as if echoing events to come, a mournful procession of coaches escorts the king back to neighboring Versailles. He is bundled up in his dressing gown, but still wholly lucid and unwilling to change his entourage: Du Barry and her friends continue to attend him.

A bad night on the 28th. His fever is mounting. The king becomes panicky; fear of death, or rather "dread of the devil," a constant obsession whenever he is ill, invades him. La Martinière and Lemonnier call for reinforcements. Bordeu joins them, another member of the Du Barry clan. Consultation. The medical profession has hardly budged since Molière's day. Serious debate as to whether the illness is "hyperacute," like apoplexy or "the English sweat"; "very acute," like burning fever; "inflammatory, legitimate, exquisite diseases" of "declining acuteness" (twenty to forty days); or "chronic." This is "the age of crudeness" when "nature and disease are at grips, when victory crowns neither side and there is extensive disordering of the machine."[10] Not knowing what else to do, they elect to bleed the patient, withdrawing the standard* three basins of blood. No effect, except to excite further commotion in the palace. Throngs of courtiers fill the antechamber. Second bleeding in the afternoon. The headache persists. When the doctors announce that they wish to bleed him a third time, Louis XV is terrified:

"A third bleeding? It will make me even worse. So I am really ill? I would prefer not to be bled a third time . . . You tell me that I shall recover soon, but you don't believe a word of it."

"The king held out his tongue for the doctors," relates La Rochefoucauld-Liancourt, grand master of the royal wardrobe. "Each in his own manner expressed satisfaction at the beauty and hue of this royal morsel . . . The same ceremony was repeated moments later for his stomach, which had to be thumped, while he suffered each physician, each surgeon, each apothecary to file past him, submitting cheerfully to the visit and summoning them one by one in order of rank."[11]

*About 400 grams. The two bleedings remove nearly a liter of blood.

Agitation gives way to turmoil at Versailles. The third bleeding means that the patient may suffer a stroke and die at any minute; it brings the indispensable priest to the bedside, confession, dismissal of the mistress and of the Duc d'Aiguillon, his liegeman. It warns that Choiseul may return to favor. Aiguillon rushes in, takes Bordeu aside. There will be no third bleeding. But the king is very weak. Eight physicians ring his bedside, allowing no one to approach—not even Du Barry, the first sign of a palace revolution.

Night of April 29. When the king soils his bed, they move him to a fresh one. The approaching candlelight reveals on his forehead and cheeks "red blotches encircling telltale pustules." Mercy-Argenteau, Austria's ambassador, who also acts as the dauphine's adviser and a listening post, reports to Vienna: "Smallpox has erupted. It is confluent and appears highly virulent, although no one will admit it."[12] Bordeu is anguished: "Smallpox, at the age of sixty-four and in the king's physical condition, is a dread disease." He knows that, bodily, Louis XV is frayed at the seams, as much from wear and tear on his nervous system as from the inferior fabric of his heredity, sporadic attacks of syphilis, and the ravages of sensual overindulgence. He cannot survive.

Smallpox was the scourge of these times, just as the plague had been in the seventeenth century, or leprosy toward the close of the Middle Ages. A medical treatise published in 1774 calls it "the most universal disease." In France ninety-five out of every hundred persons contracted it; one out of seven perished as a result.[13] The king is afflicted with the most virulent form: in "distinct" smallpox "the pustules are separate and individual"; in the "confluent" form "the pustules overlap and crowd together under a single scab . . . It is ordinarily complicated with crimson flushes and carbuncles;* patients frequently succumb on the eleventh day." They care for him as best they can; bleedings stop once the eruptions appear, replaced by "mild purgatives, infusions of black salsify, lentils, vincetoxicum, or boiled wart-cress."[14] In other words, expect the worst if the body's natural resistance fails.

The king is dying. By Sunday, the 1st of May, everyone knows it in Versailles, Paris, and France. Europe hears the news as it travels out in concentric circles to the rhythm of the swiftest post horses: England will learn about it on the 2nd, Austria and Rome on the 4th, Berlin the 5th, Saint Petersburg the 7th. A surge of emotion at first, though certainly not out of tender concern for the late Beloved—for whom no one has the slightest affection, except perhaps his daughters—but because most people identify the universe with Louis XV. Sixty years upon the throne! The world revolving around him like a stage. Now, however, will only the set change? What will the effect be? What will be different? A hundred thousand voices asking the same questions. Europe is likely to remain pretty much as it is, with closer ties between Paris and Vienna now that France has an Austrian queen. What about France? Two

*That is, heightened by severe attacks of fever and symptoms of anthrax.

raw and inexperienced youngsters of twenty on the throne. Who will guide them? Who will help them shake down the golden apples of prosperity, and in which direction will they roll? How to get rid of the ministerial triumvirate ruling France since Choiseul's disgrace, partisans of Du Barry? Aiguillon first and foremost, of course, with his "jaundiced countenance, his fondness for spying, and his bluntness—not to mention his unchallenged control of foreign affairs, war, diplomatic personnel, and military promotions: the hand of power abroad and in the armed forces. Chancellor Maupeou, "that swarthy, bushy-browed little man," another sallow, overworked face (overflowing bile was a trademark of the closing years of Louis XV's reign), "the most repugnant face upon which one could spit"—but also the power behind the magistracy and the attempts to reorganize it, power to make and enforce the law. And finally the Abbé Terray, a crook-backed giant with red blotches dappling his dismal face, haggard and sinister according to those who covet his high position: "Look, the abbé is laughing; has something awful happened to someone?"[15] —taxes, the budget, the economy are in his hands, the purse strings of power. Once and for all, is grain to be traded freely or not?

Who will replace these ministers? Parasites cluttering the sumptuous caravansary of Versailles whisper a single name: Choiseul. Louis XV's death equals Choiseul's return. They imagine the future purely as a recapitulation of the past.

But things have not yet reached that point. First question: should the patient be told of his condition? The knowledge that he is dying and must repent will activate the process of change. Like his doctors, Louis XV has seen and fingered his eruptions; he is convinced that he had smallpox as a child and is immune. Then how does he explain the headaches, the intense salivation, and the pustules? He does exactly what he has done all his life when faced with a problem: he wriggles. He retreats from the thing that frightens him most: decision-making. In this case, a few plain questions to the doctors would have constituted a choice on his part, for court etiquette forbade their initiating conversation with the monarch. He alone could broach the matter. As long as he drowses, or pretends to, the situation is locked in.

But he no longer dictates the daily routine at Versailles. Protocol brings his daughters to his bedside, thus resolving a second question: who will surround the king and claim his final moments? The dauphin and his wife and the king's two other grandsons have been removed to the farthest wing of the palace; smallpox is highly contagious. Sixty-five years ago, inside of a week it wiped out the Duchesse de Bourgogne, then her husband and their eldest son. An infant became heir to the throne. The memory of that hecatomb still haunts the court. None of the Mesdames* has ever had the disease, yet they all revel

*The king's daughters, "Daughters of France," were officially addressed as Madame even if spinsters.

in this display of daughterly heroism. They are resolved to possess their father at his death, having failed to exert any influence on his life. Three sour, neurotic spinsters, once beautiful perhaps, but never appealing, take revenge for having wasted their lives in virtuous incest. "Graille," "Coche," and "Loque"* he called them in the spring of their youth, husky-voiced Adelaide, pudgy Victoire, and timorous Sophie plant the standard of remorse in the bedchamber. Adelaide issues the orders—she is raw determination in the guise of bigotry.

Yet she acts cautiously, letting her father think at first that he has a simple erysipeloid infection. She does this because she heads, or claims to head, the *dévot* party—which, for the moment, happens to coincide with the Du Barry faction. A desperate struggle opens. The king's daughters abhor their father's mistresses, especially this one; but through generous outlays of favors and charity Du Barry and Aiguillon have managed to win over most of the court clergy and chaplains. Aided by Maupeou, they have tightened censorship, harassed the Encyclopedist movement, and censured Beaumarchais. The "freethinking" faction dares not attack the virtuous adultery of a king who champions established religion. Not a good idea to disturb the delicate balance of forces by recalling someone like Choiseul, Voltaire's and Madame de Pompadour's friend, who reads Aretino during the mass.

Monday, May 2. The plot, worthy of an operetta, is gradually emerging: "The *dévot* and Jesuit** party resisted the king's taking communion because it would inform him of his condition, Madame du Barry would have to be sent away, and power is harder to regain than to keep. The Choiseul party, including *philosophes* and skeptics, clamored for communion for exactly opposite reasons." Count Xavier of Saxony writes to his sister: "You wouldn't believe how many indecent, petty, and horrid cabals and intrigues go on here."[16] He has just watched the skeptics propel or, rather, carry the Archbishop of Paris, Christophe de Beaumont, an old bag of bones, into the sickchamber. Hard to tell whether he or the king may die first. The archbishop has gallstones and passes blood in his urine; a surgeon attends him in his coach. Most of his own priests detest his merciless attacks on Jansenism. But at least he is honest, they say; he will speak his mind. After all, a soul is in mortal peril. And in fact Louis XV trembles at the old man's approach, burying himself under the bedclothes as if Death had entered the room.

But the Duc de Richelieu is there, purveyor of the king's pleasures; it was he who procured Du Barry. Richelieu has just lectured Monseigneur de Beaumont in the antechamber: "You're not going to kill him with a theological argument, are you? . . . And, by the way, did you know that just last week

*Roughly equivalent to "Grackle," "Piggy," and "Limp Rag." [*Trans.*]
**The Jesuits were driven out of France in 1762, largely through Choiseul's efforts; their order, dissolved by papal decree, still has many nostalgic sympathizers.

the countess was again reminding His Majesty about applying to Rome for your cardinal's zucchetto?"

They confer privately for fifteen minutes. The archbishop is carried off. Adelaide approaches; even she cannot question her father to find out what was said. He is silent for a while, drowsing or dreaming, then heaves a sigh of relief, murmuring:

"He told me how beautiful the weather in Paris has been these past few days."

While his three daughters are at supper that evening, he summons Madame du Barry and kisses her hands.[17] The churchmen have won twenty-four hours "in the gambling and barter for the king's conscience."[18] Christophe de Beaumont's reputation for integrity will never be the same.

May 3. Truce. "While the Eucharist is roaming the corridors," the king turns completely black, covered with a kind of leprosy.[19] But these same corridors are crammed, according to Xavier of Saxony, "with an incredible priestly rabble." A few believe in God, the Abbé Maudoux for one, His Majesty's confessor, barred from the sickchamber all along and now threatening to force the door. Collectively, persistently, they are pressing for their own particular truth, which happens to be holy sacraments.

Wednesday, May 4. The patient is becoming delirious. Public prayers are ordered in Paris, then throughout France. The Abbey of Sainte-Geneviève exposes the saint's shrine for forty-eight hours. Processions of Parisian clergy will file past it after deliberating for an hour whether to wear black or purple. But the churches remain empty. Indifference, wholesale among the poor, also penetrates the bourgeoisie. Hardy, the bookseller and diarist, encounters a gloomy canon of Notre Dame: "When the king took ill at Metz in 1744, we sold six thousand special masses. In 1757, after Damiens's attempted assassination, six hundred masses. And do you know how many requests we have this time? Three."[20]

"One of the persons charged with his funeral oration has said that the people have no right to disobey, but they do have the right to remain silent when ill-governed. Never was this silence greater than in the churches. The Forty Hours' Devotion was ordained everywhere during the course of his illness, and everywhere the churches were deserted."[21]

. . . In any event, people are listening. They don't pray, they simply wait, hoping it won't last too long. The king's fate arouses self-pity. A twenty-year-old Parisian named Marie-Jeanne Phlipon (the future Madame Roland), daughter of an engraver employed in the Place Dauphine in Paris, writes to a school friend, Sophie Canet: "The news of his illness made an impression on me; I'd tell you why if I could write it.* Though my low birth, rank, and condition would seem to rule out my taking any interest in government, I can't help being affected by the general welfare. My country means something to me; my attachment to her is rooted deep inside me. How could I be indifferent to her? I care about everything. I think my soul is a trifle cosmopolitan; humanity and feeling unite me with every living thing: a Carib interests me, the fate of a Kaffir touches my heart . . . Is such extreme sensitivity an advantage? Doesn't one magnify the power of grief by being so vulnerable?" [22]

May 5. The infection has spread over his entire body, producing a sickening odor reaching all the way from the king's apartment to the Salon de l'Oeil-de-boeuf, thus named because of the shape of its bull's-eye windows. It becomes apparent that another graybeard is paid to tell His Majesty the truth: Cardinal de La Roche-Aymon, Grand Almoner of France. He performs his duty with great reluctance, having also a vested interest in maintaining Du Barry. She advances boldly into the royal bedchamber, smiling, eyes shining with pent-up tears. Bordeu has advised her that the time has come to make a proper end. Rarely has a royal mistress achieved such a decorous exit. She alone may defy the rules and address him first:

"Sire, what do you think of these *dévots* insisting that you receive the sacrament just as you are beginning to get better? I say you would do well to oblige them. I shall go away while you do this and come back to see you in a few days."

The love, or at least tenderness, between them is probably stronger now than ever before. Jeanne Bécu, raised as a courtesan, renamed Vaubernier, who caught the king's eye before she was twenty-five, has kept her side of the bargain. She barely managed to save Louis XV from a sordid old age by exposing him to six years of dignified living. She fought tooth and nail, but always in self-defense, never striking first at either Choiseul or Marie Antoinette. Now she bestows on this pathetic man the last of her favors: death without too many wrangles. He is spared the remorse of having to send her away, which he would have done in another five minutes.

Aiguillon, too, shows his pith.

Dismissing everyone else, the king addresses him privately: "That poor woman has spoken to you. I must take the sacraments." Raising his nightshirt, he displays his arms and chest. "And what will become of that poor woman?"

Aiguillon shrugs his shoulders. Even with his own world collapsing, he

*All mail was subject to postal censorship aimed at keeping tabs on public opinion and searching out dissenters.

will not desert his colors. "It doesn't matter where she goes as long as she leaves Versailles. I will invite her to stay with me at Ruel."*

"Do you think it will satisfy the priests?"

At three o'clock Du Barry steps into the duke's carriage. "Madame Lisp," fair-haired, with skin so white and soft, this pretty little nobody who has cost France the price of ten men-o'-war or a whole new city, rides off covered with gold and jewels, but without legal warranty, after subjecting European history to six years of her peacockery. Of course, Ruel is only an hour from Versailles, and the horses are saddled and waiting in case the king should make a miraculous recovery . . .

This is why, on the 6th of May—the eleventh, and normally fatal, day— confusion still reigns at the royal bedside, where His Majesty, all black and very weak, alternately calls for Du Barry and holy communion between expressions of alarm at the aphthous ulcerations mushrooming in his throat. Isn't the pus likely to contaminate the host? He can recite in detail the tortures reserved for high treason: is he doomed to share a corner of hell with Damiens, an eternity of fiery tongs and boiling pitch for having offended the viaticum on its way down? He listens patiently to the final negotiations preceding "his sacraments"; now there are as many priests as physicians in attendance. At three in the morning Aiguillon is called once more to His Majesty's bedside:

"THEY are not pleased. THEY want her farther away than Ruel and ask me to send her to her husband in Toulouse."

"But, Sire, that is impossible. She is legally separated from him."

"Then how about Chinon, at Richelieu's place?"

"That won't do either. THEY promised me something else. I will talk to THEM again."

Aiguillon, after all, is still virtual master of the kingdom, having the army at his beck and call. Entering the adjoining room, he vents his spleen on Cardinal de La Roche-Aymon, who, "as usual, splutters something in response to the duke." In the same breath he attacks the king's blind confessor, the Abbé Maudoux: haven't all his demands been satisfied? Confession, dismissal of the favorite? But to Ruel she must go, and not a step beyond. At length the duke manages to intimidate the Archbishop of Paris, now back at Versailles, transported here and there according to events. "The final arrangement was that Madame du Barry's retirement to Ruel would be acceptable."[23]

May 7, seven o'clock in the morning. Formal procession through the galleries and along the palace stairways. God is visiting the king. Courtiers in full regalia, decked out with swords and decorations, attend the ceremony marking the end of a world. They stand aside for the grand almoner bearing the holy

*Now Rueil-Malmaison. The Duc d'Aiguillon owned a small château there, submerged in greenery, near Louveciennes (then called Luciennes), where Du Barry had her *folie* and received friends.

to perform this task.* The casket was first enclosed in an aromatized packing case, which in turn was deposited in a second lead box, but all this could not prevent the odor from seeping through."¹ A troop of bodyguards, a coach-and-six, flickering torches and lanterns piercing the night: thus did Louis XV make his final journey along the carriage road built fifteen years earlier to link Versailles directly with Compiègne and spare him the sight and sound of complaining Parisians along the "Route de la Révolte." What were those churls up to anyway, trooping along the roadside, shouting: " 'Tallyho! Tallyho!' in that scornful tone of theirs as if they had just spotted a stag"?²

They were stablehands, it seems, but not the authors of a popular ditty written while the king was still alive and repeated all over Paris on May 11:

<table>
<tr><td>Louis a rempli sa carrière</td><td>[Louis has ended his career</td></tr>
<tr><td>Et fini ses tristes destins;</td><td>And met his sad fate;</td></tr>
<tr><td>Tremblez, voleurs; fuyez, putains!</td><td>Tremble, thieves; flee, harlots!</td></tr>
<tr><td>Vous avez perdu votre père.</td><td>Your father has forsaken you.]</td></tr>
</table>

Priests have resealed the crypt. "Here lies the one who gave us the system** at birth, war as he matured, famine in old age, pestilence on his deathbed."³

Indeed Versailles was acting as if the plague had hit. Absolute chaos. A flock of courtiers had rushed off to a remote wing of the palace where the dauphin and Marie Antoinette, now king and queen, were quarantined. At a distance, without kissing hands, they paid their respects to the painfully young and awkward couple standing there, eyes brimming with tears, looking scared to death. Officials who had lingered too long in the death chamber were not permitted to attend this audience. The master of the king's household, La Vrillière, in charge of the daily routine at Versailles, fretted anxiously: Mesdames had been bundled off in a coach like a colony of lepers, while the steady clatter of departing carriages bespoke everyone's impatience to escape the palace's befouled air. The age of Louis XV did not elect to share his pyre. And if there was to be any age of Louis XVI, better get the dauphin out of here as soon as possible. Marie Antoinette writes to her mother the next day: "It had been decided that we must depart the moment the king breathed his last, and so about four o'clock we left to come here."⁴ Here—Choisy—is a tiny hamlet of fishermen and bargemasters on the banks of the Seine, equidistant from Paris, Versailles, and Sceaux. During Louis XIV's reign La Grande Mademoiselle† built herself a château here, later acquired by Louis XV, who collected "small country houses" within an hour's journey of Versailles. He

---

*Actually, they were ditch-cleaners employed in the town of Versailles. But the term "laborer," lowest rung of the social ladder under the Ancien Régime, indicated that even without exercising any skill they "lived somewhere and did not beg."

**John Law's "system."   †The Duchesse de Montpensier. [*Trans.*]

sank a fortune into Choisy-Mademoiselle, renamed Choisy-le-Roi, demolish-
ing the old château because he found it depressing and constructing two new
ones in the park, the "grand," to lodge his household, and the "petit," where
he could enjoy privacy with his mistresses.* That arrangement may finally
prove useful. In the same letter Marie Antoinette informs her mother: "As it
is assumed that he [Louis XV] must have communicated his disease to my
aunts, they have been installed in the small château next to us; if they should
come down with it, their age** gives us cause to fear for them."

So here we have the new king and queen with their entourage (restricted
to those who had stayed out of the sickchamber) locked up in a charming rustic
prison for the first days of their reign, a few steps away from three aging
spinsters hovering between life and the hereafter. France forgets them temporarily, long enough to don mourning from north to south, tip to toe. A
fascinating diversion: the whole kingdom wears black, "from the mortuary
chapel at Versailles, the catafalque at Saint-Denis, and the funereal elegance
of the great houses, down to the suburban market stalls. Artisans, porters,
persons to whom the death of a king really means nothing, wear signs of deep
mourning. You would think each had lost his own father; indeed, long-stand-
ing custom equated grief for the two. Yet for some time now the epithet 'Louis
the Beloved' had fallen into disuse, and beyond . . . But in all the sanctuaries
'pride was harvested from beneath the king's ashes.' "[5]

Louis XVI begins at Choisy. Marie Antoinette's letters to her relatives on May
11 and 12 depict the young couple plagued by a sense of inferiority verging
on anguish: "Good heavens, what will become of us, M. le dauphin and I are
appalled at having to reign so young. My dear mother, pour out advice to your
unhappy children . . . " "I rely on your tender affection, dear brother, in the
dire situation facing me; I shall always do my duty, but I must know what it
is, the king [her husband] being too concerned with his own to go into details,
and I am afraid he will be induced to leave me to myself . . . These past four
years have been happy ones, but a new life is opening up, full of dangers; pray
for me and help me . . . " "The king's death presents us with a task even more
terrifying inasmuch as M. le dauphin remains totally ignorant of state matters,
which the king never discussed with him. Try as we did to prepare ourselves
for an event conceded to be inevitable two days before it happened, the first
impact was ghastly and left us both speechless. I felt something choking me
like a vise. I cannot tell you how shocked we were. The king has recovered
completely and dutifully wears a cheerful face, but such determination cannot
last, and after dictating his letters and issuing his orders, he feels compelled
now and then to come weep on my shoulder. Sometimes I shiver, I feel afraid,
and just this moment he was comparing himself to a man fallen out of a belfry."

*Both buildings are gone now.
**They were forty-two, forty-one, and thirty-nine.

Indeed this young German prince has tumbled quite by accident onto the throne of the fairest kingdom on earth and has not a tenth part of French blood in his veins. His mother was Saxon (and christened him Louis-Auguste after his grandfather, the Elector of Saxony), his grandmother Polish, his paternal forebears Piedmontese, Bavarian, Austrian, more Austrians, all the way back to Marie de Médicis, offspring of that tainted bloodline, who married Henri IV. In terms of genealogical ties to one of the reigning houses, he is far more Hapsburg than Bourbon. He is the walking image of degeneracy: a shapeless, limp, already corpulent body, "soapy eyes," an excessively high forehead, poor coordination, an "air of seeing and hearing nothing" largely the result of myopia,* protruding buttocks partly responsible for his waddle, and the prognathous jaw which, though buried beneath unwholesome mounds of flesh, marks the decline of several bloodlines.[6]

After such an inventory, one more fundamental quality of his remains to be noted: the will to survive. Silent determination.

His childhood was a nightmare. Born the Duc de Berry, he nearly died in infancy due to an incompetent nurse, mistress to La Vrillière, whom the latter foisted upon him. The wholesome air of Meudon miraculously saved the life of this neglected prince, whom no one cared about because the future of the monarchy resided with his older brother, the new Duc de Bourgogne, a sturdy, robust, gifted little fellow who pummeled his brother with his fists and humiliated him at every turn. Taking the short view, most courtiers resolved to curry favor with Bourgogne, which only heaped added scorn upon the puny Berry. He grew up in the general expectation of his death. Then, in 1760, both brothers fell ill, probably from tuberculosis. To everyone's astonishment, Bourgogne succumbed, while Berry simply grew punier than ever. The court, including his grandfather, Louis XV, and his father, the dauphin, went on expecting him to die in the interests of his infinitely more "presentable" younger brothers, Provence and Artois.

Yet Berry adored and idolized his father, from whom he learned to detest anything even remotely associated with Louis XV, mainly officials and women. He endured cheerfully the tortures of that peculiarly unbalanced education which his father, neurotically obsessed with sex and religion, inflicted on him, drowning the boy in Latin and theology. His father's death in 1765 made him the most unwelcome dauphin in French history, but at last forced Louis XV to stop ignoring him—and start brushing him aside. In the meantime he had acquired a preceptor, the pompous, inflexible, and rancorous La Vauguyon. Then, at twelve, he became engaged to an Austrian archduchess, and made a pretense of consummating the marriage in 1770. At twenty, he has a trifling appetite for sex, a gluttonous craving for sleep and food, an interest in scientific engineering, and a fondness for hunting and manual work, which, had he

*Kings of France and their royal offspring were denied the right to wear glasses until Louis-Philippe did so after 1830.

not been so lethargic, might have made him a more rounded personality.

He is spiteful—to a moderate degree, for excessive spite stirs the blood. He seems to delight in shooting down the cats that roam the palace rooftops at Versailles; in taking a stick to lame dogs and beating them senseless; in teasing his brothers and cousins mercilessly. He cannot conceive of rulership without fear: the day Artois said that he intended to have Marmontel thrashed for presuming to educate royalty in *Bélisaire*, Louis told him: "If I were king, I would have him hanged."[7]

Since becoming one a few days ago, he is utterly defiant. He has no friends and no desire for them. He may listen to his aunts on occasion because they are as bigoted as he and because his father loved them. Adelaide is his godmother and confides in him—but he doesn't encourage that either. His wife? She is Austrian. Overnight she learned not to discuss politics openly. Writing to Maria Theresa, she says: "The king, who never speaks, has not said a word about choosing a minister. I have proposed M. de Choiseul, who is well thought of here, but there has been no response . . . "[8]

She despises him and he knows it; his brothers envy him; the court spies on him; Europe ignores him. And he knows nothing, absolutely nothing, about running a government—less than the chief secretary in any ministry. He was not allowed to sit in Council. His grandfather never discussed the business of state with him. No official ever reported to him about anything—and now he is quarantined, compelled to communicate with all of them by letter. "The court waited, in fear and trembling, to see which way Louis XVI would go; and in this situation the young monarch was perhaps the most perplexed soul in the kingdom."[9]

He does have one conviction, however: never, never will he recall Choiseul to power. This should have been apparent from his first public statement before leaving Versailles, a few stammered phrases which the gazettes reported the next day: "I see that God so wills it. The decision was His. My only task now is to protect religion, which is sorely in need of protection, to eschew corrupt and wicked men, and to comfort my people."

Did Catholicism really need a shield in France? It was the state religion. Priests controlled the nation's civil and religious life. Dissenters were hounded by the police, stripped of their rights and their livelihood. Protestants—referred to as members of the "so-called reformist cult"—Jews, and Jansenists could choose starvation, exile, or apostasy. Declared atheists were hanged or broken on the wheel. At the same time, it is true that Louis XV's reign had been marked somewhere at the midpoint by the influence of an intelligent, liberal-minded woman. Louis XVI's father referred to her only as "La Pompon" or "Mama Whore"—the much maligned Madame de Pompadour, who grew so tired of being harassed by the *dévots* that she banished all officials linked to the dauphin—including Maurepas, Machault, and Argenson—in favor of her friend Choiseul, the man responsible for outlawing the Jesuits and protecting Voltaire. The man who never fasted on Friday. The man openly accused by Berry's clique of having poisoned the dauphin (whose widow used to have the dogs taste every dish brought before the young prince).

That was the only lesson Louis XVI's parents taught him: never trust Choiseul. The devil incarnate. A devil who found him a wife? Another reason for despising him. Secret, pleasurable guile begins to motivate some of his acts. He listens as others, including his wife, promote Choiseul, but he will never recall him. It is his first delight as king, and his first attempt to punish his wife. Let those who swore Marie Antoinette would rule France choke on their words.

Still, Louis XVI needs someone immediately to rely on, if only to write his speeches, advise him on official appointments, and tell him "what is proper and improper." A prime minister? Out of the question. The Bourbons would never stand for ministers of the caliber of Richelieu, Mazarin, or Fleury. One of the current ministers? Apart from the problem of quarantine, he execrates any tool of Du Barry's. They must find him someone "new." A young man? No such item at court. The middle generation, men between thirty and fifty, is Choiseul's clique and more or less pledged to him. For lack of new faces, they will seek out old ones. As Edgar Faure tells us, "It was impossible to eliminate the ghosts of Choiseulism except with superghosts of even longer-standing disgrace."[10]

Did Adelaide actually come from the *"petit palais"* next door to visit her nephew, thus threatening his life? Surely she must have been seething with impatience, knowing that this chance of a lifetime stared her in the face, something her father never had been willing to give her: a hand in ruling the kingdom. In any event, she presents the young monarch with a list of reliable (meaning anti-Pompadour) officials compiled by her dead brother the dauphin. The two top names are Maurepas and Machault, both seventy-four years old. Both good men forty years ago. Both banished to their estates for so long that Louis XVI had forgotten their existence.

His Majesty composes an "appeal" (without help, having a distinct flair for elegant prose):

> Sir,
>   Despite the overwhelming grief I share with the entire kingdom, there are duties I must perform. I am king; the word itself connotes many obligations, but I am only twenty years old. I do not presume to have learned everything I have to learn. Moreover, I cannot receive my ministers, all of whom were at the king's bedside during his illness. Much has been said in praise of your integrity and the high reputation which your profound knowledge of affairs has justly earned you. Therefore I beg you to aid me with your counsel and wisdom. Kindly come to Choisy at your earliest pleasure and I shall be happy to see you.
>   Louis-Auguste

Fine, but now whom to send it to, Maurepas or Machault? The former is impulsive, fond of epigrams, neither pious nor contentious, flexible, tactful, and pragmatic. The latter is taken for a Jansenist, has courage and ideals: they call him "burnished steel" and say he advocates tapping church resources to relieve the public debt.

A reformer or a politician? Louis XVI addresses the letter to Maurepas, though he may have preferred Machault and changed his mind in the wake of a last-ditch assault from his aunt. Whatever the circumstances, his first decision is an abdication. He has chosen the man of least resistance.

BRISSOT

15

MAY 1774

Something Real Lies Ahead

On May 20, 1774, Jacques-Pierre Brissot makes his first trip to Paris in the Chartres stagecoach. The lumbering vehicle drawn by four horses carries eight passengers and their baggage piled on the roof, and has been traveling the whole day. It is dark, but the slender, eager-eyed young man is so dazzled by the myriad lights at the southwestern approach to the city, the Conference Gate, flanked by statues of Brittany and Normandy, that he takes it for the gateway to paradise. Twenty years later he could still recall the thrill of that evening: "The Conference Gate is the most glittering entrance to Paris. The river, the bridges, the Champs-Elysées, the Tuileries Gardens all offered splendid views. Aglow with light, the embankment made an enchanting spectacle. As it was the period of mourning for Louis XV, I wore black and carried a sword, having heard that without this badge one could not expect to be received anywhere. But in spite of my mourning and my sword, I must have looked very provincial and ill at ease."[1]

Surely so, never having strayed beyond a radius of four leagues from Chartres. Dressed in black from head to toe, with the new rapier flapping against his shins and getting in the way when he sits down, he looks for all the world like a lost soul. He is alone. He has always felt alone. He is reticent, timid, and proud. Still written on his face is the strain of his first heartbreak, the girl of seventeen he honestly intended to marry, so perfectly did she fit the image "of his ideal heroine," and "who had blossomed into such a vigorous personality." He had never even declared his love, fearing it might change something between them. Now she has taken her own life, "weary of the world, of the stupidity of some, the corruption of others, the tyranny that prevails." Time for him to move on, too. The tedium was more than he could bear. "As the sphere of my ideas expanded, Chartres became intolerably confining. Rampant bigotry harassed me; ignorance was virtually universal. The listlessness, the torpor affecting everyone there contrasted so sharply with my own intellectual activity that it made life depressing." When a young man who considers himself something of a *philosophe* reaches that point, he needs "an immense city or the countryside," "solitude or stimulating company."[2] A sense of bewilderment coupled with the conviction that at last life is about to begin has welled up in him each time they changed horses, at Maintenon, Epernon, Rambouillet, and Versailles. Arriving at night is ideal, for everything looks like fairyland and fewer people will notice him. But how the devil does the driver avoid trampling people in the street? The lumbering coach rattles along the rough paving stones, coming to a halt in front of Sieur Angot's house at the corner of the Quai des Grands-Augustins and the Rue Saint-André-des-Arts. There the dream begins to fade: Jacques-Pierre can do without the effusive welcome tendered by his father's correspondent, Legrain, under whose roof he is to live. Legrain is a "poultry purveyor" or, if you will, "food broker for the Vale," meaning a wholesaler of poultry and game here in the district to which Brissot has come, a pier on the Seine popularly known as the "Vale of Misery" because of its high prices. Our young notary's clerk would have preferred a more distinguished host who would not make him so conscious of the fact that his father, Guillaume Brissot, "master chef and tavernkeeper," does business in Chartres on the Rue du Cul-Salé. For the past two or three years he has been operating under the name of Brissot de Warville—since he learned English, that is. Not out of sheer snobbery either; it is customary among the rural petty bourgeoisie for a father to name each son after one of his landholdings, regardless of how insignificant it may be. Ouarville, where Jacques-Pierre was put to nurse, is a hamlet boasting six houses, lost in a sea of grain fields, between Chartres and Pithiviers. "I took a fancy to giving my name an English tinge and substituted the English W for the French dipthong OU . . . If this is a crime, then I am guilty along with men of letters who, in recent centuries, saw fit to Hellenize or Latinize their names . . . Anglomania, if you choose to call it that, made me change mine, not the desire to reject my father's."[3]

At any rate, he has no love for his father; neither did others, it seems. A gruff man, Guillaume Brissot, tremendously energetic, blessed "with common sense, wits, and ambition." His hostelry business flourished; his fellow tradesmen chose him for their syndic, and the parish made him its churchwarden. But that was as far as he could go. Wedded for the rest of his life to his stove

and work table, "he was conscious of his ignorance" and could not forgive his
sons for the education he had given them—reluctantly. "He would tell my
mother: They despise me . . . " "The jealousy he often showed me stifled
fatherly affection in him and filial love and gratitude in me; he always treated
me harshly; never did I see a father's gentle smile on his face: despite my fine
record at school, when I used to come home laden with honors, my father's
curt embrace wounded me to the quick. He rejoiced in my success less than
he longed to have enjoyed it once himself . . . How often, in bitter secrecy,
did I regret not having a friend for a father."

His mother? A good woman who deserved credit for pressing her sons
to study hard. That was about it. "How often I wished that my parents and
I could speak the same language."[4] Brothers and sisters? A nestful: seventeen
in the brood. Jacques-Pierre is the thirteenth; only seven survived infancy. The
boys had to look after themselves, with little help from any brother. The sisters
were more loving and mothered Jacques-Pierre from time to time, especially
the eldest, Marie Louise, who would come to his room every morning on her
way to four-o'clock mass and leave the stub of her candle for him to read by.
Yet he could never understand why the huge nearby cathedral claimed more
of her attention than he; it swallowed her up like a forest of stone. "The priests
set up a barrier between her and me."[5] Their elder brother "was cast into the
clerical profession."

The heavy hand of the church dominated his entire childhood. As soon
as he could read, they sent him for instruction to the curate of Ecubley, a town
north of Chartres near Châteauneuf, in the Thimerais district. "I can still savor
the wonderful feasts I had, under a currant bush or a plum tree, devouring a
morsel of bread. It was there that I learned to appreciate the countryside."[6]
But all too soon he was back in town again, a network of fetid alleys where
it begins to dawn on him that ten thousand souls are slumbering their lives
away in the foul air of the tanneries lining the Eure.[7]

A tutor comes to board: the torment of force-fed Latin. Secondary school
at the age of eight. Discovering the delights of reading for pleasure, thanks
to the kindly Abbé Comuscle, who lets the boy explore his library. The seeds
of rebellion as well, on account of headmaster François Berthinot, "a hopeless
bigot, melancholy, even superstitious, and coldly cruel, who, for the slightest
fault, would beat the children mercilessly . . . Subjected to such barbarous
treatment, for seven years I remained a mere puppet being infused with ideas
and words."[8] Brissot quit school at fifteen, his fierce resolve "to be myself"
tempered by the ever present urge to escape into the pages of literary voyages,
"which changed my whole way of thinking." "I was forever injecting my
studies with romantic notions; they enchanted my solitude." But "you can well
imagine my reluctance ever to mention the daydreams that filled my somewhat
extravagant imagination. I felt instinctively that something real lay ahead, but
that life all around was too remote from that reality to hear me."[9]

Next he turned his back forever on the church, settling accounts in one lump sum with all the priests who ever lived. "I was a skeptic by conviction. My hatred of the priesthood thus led me to renounce God, yet my conscience brought me back to Him."[10] Reading Rousseau resolved the dilemma by turning him into an undogmatic deist. He found this blend of exoticism and "philosophism" useful in getting back at the townsfolk of Chartres when faced with the need to find work at a tender age. Untrained for any profession, what could he do? "Become a merchant? No such occupation in Chartres, where there were only shopkeepers. Enter the seminary? My sister urged me to do so, but I could not see myself as an outright fraud. That left only the bar, which I preferred. To get there entailed threading one's way through a maze of chicanery . . . I went to work for the best-known lawyer in Chartres."[11] Five years as a legal clerk were not entirely wasted, for he learned English and Italian.

Luck brought him in contact with Nolleau, a prosecutor in the Paris Parliament "reputed to be more cultivated than most members of his profession." And indeed he deserves the reputation for his warm reaction to Brissot's first creative effort, submitted as "a sample of his talent, personality, and style," a short essay modestly entitled *Du vol et de la propriété* [Of theft and property] of which the author is very proud. "It was a virtual tour de force . . . a paradox such as any young man might advance if he engages in intellectual gymnastics and shuns the beaten track. I set out to prove that social property did not derive from nature, and that theft did not exist in primitive times nor was cannibalism a crime."[12]

Nolleau promptly hired cannibalism's apologist for his staff: six months' apprenticeship with board and keep as prelude to the position of head clerk at four hundred francs a month.* A fortune for the present; the assurance of a legal career ahead. "No man's reputation could satisfy me then. People told me that I would be lucky to become as good a lawyer as Janvier, one of the finest orators of the Chartres bar." Do they think that could satisfy him? No one guesses the immense ambition lodged in this slender, black-clad young man stepping off the coach: "I felt humiliated by the comparison; my secret genius promised me far greater destinies."[13] "I had a prodigious yearning for fame; from the age of nine, it was my passion for fame that kept me studying at night in bed." "I hated kings right from the start; as a child, I was fascinated by the story of Cromwell; I would imagine myself the same age as the king and, in my innocent fancies, saw no reason why he should sit upon the throne when I was born an innkeeper's son."[14]

"My thoughts often strayed to this idea of revolution, which I never dared express; I fancied myself playing a major role in it."[15]

*About 1600 current francs [$320].

MIRABEAU PÈRE

MIRABEAU FILS

16

MAY 1774

A Wretched Creature Grovels at My Feet

Before choosing inept La Vauguyon, the future Louis XVI's parents had considered Mirabeau for the post of royal tutor. The Marquis de Mirabeau, dubbed the "Friend of Man" after the title of one of his best-known pamphlets, fancied himself a second Montesquieu. The heir to the throne would have been raised on doctrines of "economism" and physiocracy—a farmer king in the making. In the end, however, they rejected Mirabeau as too rugged an individualist. He remained in the wings during the closing years of Louis XV's reign, respected, but relegated to his estate at Bignon in the Gâtinais district, where, on March 9, 1749, one of his sons was born.

May 28, 1774. This "Mirabeau fils,"* as yet unknown to the nation, heaves a deep sigh of relief. He stands erect and calm in the small whitewashed room, like a self-service torture chamber, in which he has just extracted a confession from his own victim. The pale light serves only to accent his pitted, dissolute features. Smallpox at the age of three, "treated" with useless home remedies, permanently scarred his face—excessively broad to begin with. He has trouble controlling his voice: "I never shout when angry. I might demolish a wall, I might grab at a live cannonball, but I do not shout."[1] That made him even more terrifying to the woman whom he has just forced to sign a confession of adultery.

    The accused, the guilty woman, the victim, is his wife, Emilie de Marignane. He is twenty-five; she, twenty-two. Married two years, and now this mess.

    She, too, appears calm through the tears bathing her obstinate little face. You hold your head high when your family claims to possess the noblest blood in Provence. In firm, bold strokes, without a single alteration, she has penned the letter dictated by her husband[2] to her lover: "I see the error of my ways, sir, and my first act upon returning to virtue is to advise you that all relations between us are severed . . . "

*His official signature, and the only name his father authorized him to use.

The bright alpine sunshine of spring is already baking Manosque, where the young pair are more isolated than on some desert island at the end of the earth. It is indeed the end of the earth: sudden squalls, driving rains, icy blasts, echoes of their own sad tale. From a distance, the town is beautiful with its square ocher and carmine houses terraced above the Durance. But at close range, it is squalid poverty: narrow, badly paved streets littered with straw and dung. Manosque is simply a giant sheepfold, the home of shepherds, cheese-mongers, and a handful of petty nobles. Among the latter is the Gassaud family, friends who had taken in Mirabeau and his wife two months earlier when a *lettre de cachet* banished the young couple to this Godforsaken place. Not so accidentally, Emilie was already having an affair with the son of the household. [3]

Had the Mirabeaus ever been in love? For three months perhaps, cul-minating in the lucrative match he had pursued relentlessly and finally brought off by boldly seducing Emilie and compromising her in the eyes of Aix nobil-ity. It was his last desperate effort to escape a childhood choked with hatred for his father, the torment known as "training" at the Chotard boarding school, the military career denied him at Saintes, twenty years of being tossed back and forth by his parents, who used him as a pawn in their wrangles. [4] Deprived of a career in the army, of self-respect, of money, all he had was a string of debts and women. Marrying an heiress was the way out, the light at the end of the tunnel.

Somehow he had managed to turn his ugliness to great advantage. Emilie had loved him enough to accept it: "He requires strong odors, bad stews, monkeyshines." [5] In the beginning he had tried converting her to eroticism, but she quickly tired of it. Maybe if the satin sheets and champagne suppers had been permanent fixtures . . . She could not live without luxuries. For a week or two he had bluffed, pretending to smother her with them, giving costly parties and exploring the Château de Mirabeau, cradle of the Riqueti clan. (How they bragged about their Florentine ancestors, rivaled only by the the Medici, when in fact they descended from a Sieur Riquet, a successful dealer in scarlet stuffs in Marseilles under the Valois. [6]) But this ramshackle château, with cracks in every seam and timber, offered a standing invitation to the mistral, the mosquitoes, and creditors. And the young couple's credit was merely of the "hopeful" variety—dependent on Emilie's inheritance. Banking on his mother-in-law's failing health, Gabriel-Honoré* had borrowed recklessly to put up a front mainly for his wife's sake. All that collapsed in a single season. If the semblance of love was there, the patience to cultivate it was not, especially on Emilie's part. As domestic life grew stale, she visited her parents more and more frequently at Marignane. It was there she gave birth to a son, Victor, whose arrival left his parents hopelessly in debt and still living far beyond their means.

*Mirabeau generally went by the second of these names, Honoré.

The *lettre de cachet* hastily solicited from His Majesty by Mirabeau senior had temporarily relieved his son's plight: "under the king's protection" he was safe from the law, just as highwaymen used to take refuge in churches. Manosque was like an asylum without bars. Honoré arrived there with debts totaling 188,624 livres, "of which 136,275 were owed to the Jews."* In response to creditors' complaints, he declared that he was just another victim of an era addicted to speculation, in which anyone with a title and a "warranty" could borrow money . . . sometimes at three hundred percent. "I can honestly say, with respect to the value received for the sale of the jewels [which he had given to his wife a few months before] or actual cash, that I collected less than fifty thousand livres."[7]

Money had corroded love. Sharing close quarters at Manosque for the past two months had generated constant bickering because of Honoré's jealousy of young Gassaud, a Gray Musketeer distantly related to his wife, whose slender shape and graceful gestures were the antitheses of his own. Laurent-Marie de Gassaud had occupied a room adjoining Emilie's at Marignane the previous winter. She is pregnant again. By whom? Mirabeau really has no business asking such a question since one of his mistresses, his own cousin Madame de Limaye, has just given birth to a singularly large-headed daughter ("our left-handed niece," says the Friend of Man). Why start aping Georges Dandin in an age when marital fidelity was a virtual farce among the upper classes? Why torment Emilie? Laurent-Marie is stationed in Paris; his parents are the very soul of hospitality. Why does Honoré open his wife's letters? Because he is struggling desperately to escape from his own trap, a marriage that curtails his freedom and loans that have cost a fortune. Who else could manage to mess up his life so thoroughly by the age of twenty-five? He feels compelled to prove to the world that he can do even worse. On May 21, in the course of opening Emilie's correspondence, he came across a message from the marquis—for she had begun exchanging letters privately with this father-in-law she had never met, who reviles Honoré and righteously urges her to console herself as best she can: "I know you belong to a raving lunatic, to whom any show of affection on your part causes offense." [8] In similar fashion Honoré has just learned that his father submitted a petition of lunacy to the Châtelet court in Paris, a standard procedure for parents of feeble-minded or insane children. The law will declare him a perpetual minor. He may be rationed for the rest of his life, as in Manosque, where a daily allotment of seven pounds of meat, six of coarse bread, and three of white is provided for himself, his wife, and their four servants. When he protested, his father-in-law merely shrugged it off: "I must agree with you that they are cutting it a bit thin . . . " Gabriel-Honoré de Mirabeau a permanent ward of the state? He

---

*Nearly 800,000 current francs [$160,000]. Against this, the families of the young couple were giving them an annual allowance of only 20,000 [$4000] on the current scale.

would sooner be dead. "I cannot say whether all these humiliations have wounded or provoked me more."⁹

His chance came (the one he was secretly hoping for) when a billet-doux from Gassaud arrived for Emilie, ruling out any doubt that they are lovers. Laurent-Marie refers to Honoré as his "cruelest enemy." Honoré snatches at the only kind of satisfaction he can imagine: revenge. Adultery is winked at, of course, among the upper classes, but if a husband should press charges, his wife is liable to feudal chastisements ranging from confinement in a nunnery to public disgrace and life imprisonment. Honoré now possesses incontrovertible documentary evidence in case the matter ever comes to trial. The Marignane fortune is within his grasp if he can blackmail the family after first bringing their daughter to her knees.

In a series of brutal, carefully staged scenes witnessed by the astounded Gassauds—the musketeer's father, uncle, mother, and three sisters—Emilie is dragged through an elaborate comedy of self-recrimination and repentance in keeping with the social code. Besides, she really is rather frightened by the glint in those glaring eyes. How she will hate him later, after the storm abates . . . For the moment, she holds her tongue and, in a letter from Manosque dated May 28, 1774, obediently informs her lover that their affair is over, asking him to return the letter. The dismayed musketeer complies all the more readily under family pressure to repair "his fault" and in the face of a melodramatic eight-page dispatch from the offended husband: "Good Lord, what a scoundrel you are! You to whom hospitality, trust, and gratitude mean nothing, you who lacked the courage to try to kill me . . . Vile seducer! A woman I adored, and you knew it, who loved me, and you knew it, who was virtuous prior to your horrid advances, and you knew it . . . What made you so sure I wouldn't plunge a dagger into her breast, or fling her into some dark dungeon? . . . Preposterous indiscretion places a letter in my hands, the opening line of which has cast me into a hopeless state verging on madness . . . A wretched creature, whom I cannot bring myself to exterminate, grovels at my feet and kisses them; I see her remorse; her repentance disarms me . . . Villain, if your conscience were not such a sink of iniquity, it would torment you mercilessly . . . Your father and family are saving your life; but never again let me set eyes on you, for I swear to wipe you from the face of the earth . . ."

Laurent-Marie de Gassaud returns Emilie's letter; she hands it to Mirabeau, who signs it in the margin opposite the first and last lines: "Mirabeau fils *ne varietur,*" then locks it away permanently in a portfolio. It is his passport to fortune, the lottery ticket that may pay off one day. From that point of view, the flare-up at Manosque is not just another crisis in his life; it marks his savage determination to get back at *them.* To control *them.* "Mirabeau fils *ne varietur.*"

17

JUNE 1774

Maurepas Returns in Triumph

Mesdames* were taken ill shortly after arriving at Choisy. There they are, cooped up with their physicians in the *petit château* while the whole country waits for them to die. If they do, it will mean that Louis XV has truly departed. Ah, but their smallpox proves not to be "confluent" and their resistance to have gained from years of airtight existence. By the end of May they are out of danger. Madame du Deffand is inconsolable: "The avenging angel has sheathed his sword. Once again we shall find those three spinsters installed at the new court, weaving their petty intrigues."[1] Fresh panic on the king's account. It is sheer insanity to have lodged his aunts so close by when they could have gone to Trianon, but they insisted on supervising the new sovereign's first official acts at the risk of infecting him. Cardinal imprudence: Madame Adelaide's private chamber at Choisy became the setting for Louis XVI's introduction to Maurepas. It was only proper, of course, for someone acquainted with Maurepas to present him to the king, yet the poor woman was bright red, complaining that "her head was about to split open," and retired immediately afterward. Louis XVI managed to turn this situation into his second secret triumph by using the (very real) danger of infection as an excuse for leaving his aunts at Choisy and transferring his wife, brother, and household to the Château de La Muette on the fringe of the Bois de Boulogne. He is resolved never again to consult Mesdames—or Marie Antoinette, for that matter—about important affairs. They have saddled him with Maurepas, but that's as far as he means them to go. The man who will rule France is not so easily ruled.

What about Maurepas? The nineteen-year-old novice and the seventy-four-year-old ghost have opened a decorous war of wits. Each protests his satisfaction with the new association. The honeymoon is on. For a while, however, they will try to size each other up. Louis XVI wanted an adviser, not a prime minister; Maurepas wanted a free hand in running things. His title is to be simply "minister of state." Under those conditions they could work

*The late king's daughters. [*Trans.*]

together. Maurepas's ambition is not likely to get out of hand: having already
made his fortune,* he can afford to be honest. Besides, fate has dealt him an
undreamed-of windfall. His disgrace dated from 1740. Revenge, after thirty-
five years.

The king's summons had reached Philemon and Baucis (as the Maurepas
couple were playfully known) at Pontchartrain, their lavish estate thirty miles
outside Paris, whose park nearly rivaled that of Versailles. While appearing
to drag their feet, they rejoiced privately. Life flowed back into them. In no
time Maurepas was packed and ready to go, his wife to follow when an official
residence could be assigned them after the court's return to Versailles. Louis
XVI had decided to lodge them in no less a place than Du Barry's old suite
of rooms just above his own, connected by a secret staircase. The logistics of
this arrangement, which had once facilitated quite different assignations, set
people chuckling because the two men were notoriously unmanly:

Maurepas revient triomphant. [Maurepas returns in triumph.
V'là c'que c'est que d'être   There's the reward for
   impuissant.   impotence.
Le Roi lui dit, en l'embrassant: The king embraces him, saying:
Quand on se ressemble   Birds of a feather
Il faut vivre ensemble . . . ² Should nest together.]

Philemon and Baucis were childless—for an excellent reason. "If all the stories
are true, there never was, and indeed never could have been, any relationship
between them based other than on habit and intimacy."³ This simply made
it easier for Madame de Maurepas, daughter of the Duc de La Vrillière, to rule
her little spouse. "If a single individual somehow could combine husbandly
intelligence with wifely determination, he would make an ideal minister."⁴
She had done Maurepas a favor by cultivating his sarcasm and gloomy spirits.
"A size less than average," he compensated for his stature, as many small
persons do, by a certain starchiness and "gravity of demeanor."⁵ "He was not
exactly nasty"; it was just that "sarcasm and jibes are what one came to expect
from him."⁶ Louis XVI instantly welcomed that trait as assurance that no
conversation with the gray eminence would prove tedious. Besides, Maurepas
was a capable man whose only mistake was to have succeeded too early in life.
All of fourteen when he became minister of the navy, he had stepped into the
shoes of his father, Jérôme de Pontchartrain, whom the regent wanted to ease
out of office. At twenty-two, he had taken charge of the French fleet, as Louis
XV did not care to bother with it. To promote scientific research, he had sent
ships all over the world to test Newton's theories by measuring two remote
meridians, one south of the Equator, the other close to the North Pole,
thereby confirming the earth's oblateness. He had supported expeditions by
the botanist Jussieu to collect rare species on all the continents, and was

*An annual income of 120,000 livres (about 500,000 francs [$100,000]).

instrumental in establishing coffee plantations "in the French islands of America."[7] Bedchamber connivances put an end to all such constructive impulses. Maurepas's refusal to play the game with Madame de Pompadour cut short forty years of service to the crown, teaching him that the only way to survive at court was to register absolute zero. Self-preservation accounted in good part for his pessimism.

Nobody waited for Maurepas to settle accounts with Du Barry. So intensely did Marie Antoinette detest* the late sovereign's mistress that she insisted on her immediate removal.

After fawning for so long at Du Barry's feet, the Duc de La Vrillière wrote to her on May 12: "I trust, Madam, that you will understand how painful it is for me to inform you that you are forbidden to appear at court; yet I am obliged to execute the king's commands . . . At the same time His Majesty grants you permission to visit your aunt at the convent of Pont-aux-Dames,[8] and I shall write forthwith to the abbess to facilitate your arrival."

She expected far worse. They are letting her keep her estates and her jewels. It is easier to escape from a convent than from a prison, even though she is forbidden temporarily to correspond or receive visitors—except her jeweler, who for the moment serves as banker. The Ruel townsfolk watch this living image of an already historic past ride off "in her coach-and-six with a single chambermaid, escorted by a second carriage containing two private citizens, one of whom was a police agent."[9] Harsher measures will be taken against several of her clansmen, especially her "brother-in-law" (more accurately, her pimp) Du-Barry-le Roué, who had sold her first to the Duc de Richelieu, then to the king, and finally married her off to his obscure brother to try to clothe her in some semblance of social decency. Now the brother is in trouble. For months the capital has been gossiping about the four women he keeps: La Thévenet, La Morancé, La Dubois, and La Breba, while he boasts of having plowed through eighteen millions** since his mistress's "accession." He flees to Switzerland. "The coopers will have their work cut out for them; every last barrel has sprung† . . . "[10]

Growing concern in some quarters: it is a bad sign when a reign begins with acts of vengeance. The second of these is about to occur, for too many people, including the queen, want the Duc d'Aiguillon dismissed. Even if Louis XVI and Maurepas choose to take their time and feel around before replacing other

---

*Not because Jeanne Bécu had been Louis XV's mistress, but because she was a commoner. The Austrian archduchess could not tolerate his mingling with the rabble. Had he slept with the Duchesse de Grammont, favored by the Choiseul party, the whole story would have been different.
**Eighty million current francs [$16 million].
†Another play on the words *tonneau* and *baril*, as noted on p. 44. [*Trans.*]

officials, the duke knows which way the wind is blowing: he was too close to Louis XV and Du Barry, his abrasive manner too offensive at court. His family relationship to the Maurepas couple merely helps him to save face: on June 2, electing to resign rather than be ousted, he retires with a pension and a royal gift of 500,000 francs.* On this occasion Louis XVI announces that he is breaking with a tradition instituted by Louis XIV, who, when tired of his ministers, sent them into exile like common criminals.

Aiguillon held two portfolios: war and foreign affairs. Who would take his place? For the first post Louis XVI picked a name off the famous list he inherited from his father: no one objected when he appointed the Comte de Muy, a venerable gentleman of soldierly bearing but declining wits who, so late in life, is about to reap his reward for serving the former dauphin as page or games companion. Thirty years ago the count had distinguished himself at the Battle of Fontenoy. Those credentials appear to suffice.

Foreign affairs is another matter. Factions mobilize. The issue is charged with emotion because of so many conflicting interests at court, where there are pro-Austrians, pro-Prussians, pro-Russians, pro-Swedes, pro-Spaniards, not to mention a phenomenal pro-English contingent led by Lauzun. At the moment, the Austrian party seems in command, but should not let this fact go to its head. Marie Antoinette recognizes her husband's marked perversity. She has had her way about Du Barry and Aiguillon. Openly, she does not dare propose the Baron de Breteuil, an Austrian agent, for the post. Many people expect it will go to the Duc de Nivernais, descended from the Mancinis, an urbane, charming peacock, but a tool of the Prussians. Louis XVI picks another name from his father's list of recommendations: "M. de Vergennes is a professional diplomat; he is methodical, judicious, and capable of conducting lengthy negotiations according to accepted principles."[11] This certainly proves that Vergennes had the dauphin's approval and must have opposed Choiseul, who in fact dismissed him in 1768; but aside from this one good point, no one knows much about him. Fifty-five years old. A host of jobs in faraway places: ambassador to several petty German courts, then to Constantinople, where the length of his dispatches (thirty-two pages on occasion) annoyed Choiseul. Now he is in Sweden, having won favor with Gustavus III when the latter seized power. Ah, but his Burgundian pedigree is so very undistinguished. A wife he picked up in Turkey, lord knows where—maybe a slave market? His friends hasten to correct the error: the lady Testa was the widow of a surgeon in Pera, Constantinople's European quarter, where she was born of French parents. Still, neither her background nor the fact that he married without Louis XV's sanction brought him any credit. It was one of the reasons for the rupture with Choiseul. Now someone like Breteuil, flower of the French nobility, is quite a different story . . .

Louis XVI wavers between Breteuil and Vergennes. He allows Maurepas

*About two million current francs [$400,000].

to make the choice, and Maurepas in turn wavers for a whole day. Then along comes the Abbé de Véri, charter member of the thriving colony of urbane, opulent clerics. A good head on his shoulders, but too fond of scheming and meddling in everyone else's business; piercing eyes, a mouth without lips. His church income has always enabled him to live in high style, with a coach and six horses, twelve servants including a meat-roaster, a pastry-maker, and a household steward.[12] Véri had become acquainted with the Maurepas couple during the early years of their exile in Bourges, where he was vicar general. Actually, Madame de Maurepas had taken a shine to this priest twenty-five years her husband's junior. He became her confessor and constant dinner guest. Maurepas's return to power will make Véri one of the guiding forces behind the throne. "Maurepas controlled the king, Madame de Maurepas controlled her husband, and the Abbé de Véri controlled Madame de Maurepas." Tonight he is dining with them and protests at the mention of Breteuil's name: "In 1757 I happened to be at the Court of Vienna when he was there . . . Either rivalry or an arrogant and superior air on his part, which he artfully transforms into deference when it serves his interests, gave me a totally disgusting impression of him . . . "[13] Véri warns that Maurepas will never have a moment's peace if he appoints Breteuil, who will gradually take over. What of it if Vergennes is a nonentity? He will be easier to manipulate.

The next morning a messenger gallops off to Stockholm in quest of Vergennes. Meanwhile, life at La Muette is a blend of ritual and pastorale. "Returning through the park, the king found the queen and other princesses on a bench eating strawberries and cream; she had declined a chair, with or without arms; everyone was gathered round in informal fashion."[14] They are cheered for allowing townsfolk to enter the park at certain hours. The royal family attends Pentecost devotions in the town of Chaillot's smallest monastery (Franciscan). The interlude seems to drone on, all part of the irrepressible slackening that follows an aged king's demise. Summer bursts in. Marie Antoinette is less cautious now than when she was dauphine. Mercy-Argenteau, Austria's ambassador and chief spy, reports to Maria Theresa on June 7: "In her private chambers Her Majesty sees a good deal of the Princesse de Lamballe, née the Princesse de Carignan;* besides her sweetness and charm, she is extremely honest and in no way inclined to intrigue or impropriety. The queen has been a close friend of this young princess for some time, and the choice is excellent because Madame de Lamballe, though Piedmontese, has no ties either to Madame** or to Madame d'Artois."[15]

A shadow flits across the lawns of La Muette: the first public discord

---

*She is twenty-five; her husband, the Prince de Bourbon-Penthièvre de Lamballe, left her a widow at nineteen when he died of syphilis.

**Since Louis XVI's accession the Comtesse de Provence, wife of Monsieur, the king's eldest brother, had the honor of being addressed simply as Madame. She and her sister, the Comtesse d'Artois, were daughters of the King of Sardinia, whose court was in Turin.

between the royal pair. Again on Choiseul's account. Marie Antoinette had resigned herself to his temporary absence from the government, but was it right to let him go on moping forever at Chanteloup, on the banks of the Loire, banished like a common criminal? She makes her first scene, a stunning performance of pouts and sulks. Grudgingly, Louis XVI relents and allows Choiseul to come "pay him court." Whereupon the ugly, carrot-haired petty nobleman "with a pugdog's face" dons his gold braid and leaps into his coach on June 10, arriving in the capital on the evening of the 12th. Too hasty, too noisy an entrance. The public falsely assumes that Choiseul is really returning to power. Mobs gather at the Croix de Berny. Fishwives from the markets flock to see him. "M. de Choiseul was welcomed to Paris like Our Lord to Jerusalem; people clambered over rooftops to watch him pass."[16] Was "Europe's coachman," a stubbornly independent driver, about to climb back into his seat?

Nine o'clock the next morning at La Muette: icy silence. A wedge between the royal couple. Who will prevail? Betting is lively and tends to divide the court between husband and wife. Those who still shift with the wind perk up their ears to hear the queen complimenting Choiseul: "I am delighted to see you here and pleased to repay a debt to you. I owe you my happiness. It is only fitting that you should witness it."[17]

But they also observe His Majesty deigning to address the man of the hour only after conversing with two other persons, and then having this to say: "My, but you have put on weight and lost your hair, Monsieur de Choiseul . . . You are getting bald. Your forelock is thinning."

On Tuesday morning Choiseul declared that the sowing (or was it the mowing?) season required his presence at Chanteloup, though his wife and twenty stewards were managing the estate. He set off for home that very evening. His "return" had lasted forty-eight hours.

Marie Antoinette is shaken worse than he. At once delighted and remorseful at having offended her, Louis XVI sought to make amends with a handsome gift. But as he found it painful to give anything spontaneously, he preferred to wait until she asked for something. Mercy-Argenteau reports to Maria Theresa on June 7: "For a long time, while the archduchess was still dauphine, she yearned for a house of her own in the country . . . After the king died, the Comte and Comtesse de Noailles* sought to take charge of negotiations and to sound out the king on this matter. I found the whole officious procedure unseemly and undignified in regard to the queen . . . and I implored her to make the request herself, without advance preparations or intermediaries. Her Majesty accepted my idea, and when first she mentioned the Petit Trianon to the king, he replied instantly that this pleasure house was hers and he delighted in presenting it to her."[18]

*Cousins of La Fayette's in-laws.

Ask and ye shall receive. But having had to ask for Trianon, her gratitude is hardly overflowing. In the same week her husband doles out charity and hands her a serious rebuff through his efforts to humiliate Choiseul. Just a month has passed since Louis XV's death.

All that is partly forgotten in the uproar surrounding the inoculation of the king and his brothers. For the past thirty years most progressive physicians in England, Holland, and Germany have utilized this discovery, which revolutionized medicine: a drop of pus removed from a victim of benign smallpox was implanted in tiny incisions in the arm of a person seeking protection. This produced a low fever and brief rash, leaving the recipient immunized. Marie Antoinette and all Maria Theresa's other children had been inoculated in Vienna and thus were safe from smallpox. Catholic France, Spain, and Italy remained silent about this diabolic practice. Many priests banned its use: "Smallpox, a visitation of divine will, is a scourge to which we must submit, having no right to shirk the decrees of Providence by giving the disease to ourselves."[19] But the worldly clerics at Louis XVI's court valued their good fortune in having a ruler bound to "protect religion," and they intended to hang on to him. Yet the "avenging angel" still hovered over the royal nest. Yesterday Louis XV, today his daughters . . . Several hundred cases of smallpox were reported by the central hospital of Paris. Most of the royal physicians are pro-inoculation. They urge making the most of this interval before the court returns to Versailles, where the teeming palace population will only increase the risk of contagion. On June 15 word leaks out that the king and his brothers are at Marly, a roomier palace than La Muette and farther from the capital, and that "all three are undergoing preparations for the operation": eight or nine days of dieting, nightly dosages of calomel mixed with ground crayfish claws and "one-eighth grain of tartar emetic."[20] "Royal properties"* take a drubbing at the Exchange on the Rue Vivienne; if the avenging angel exterminates all three males of the main branch, the throne will pass to the Orléans side, with unpredictable repercussions. From afar, Voltaire adds his approval: "History will not forget that the king, the Comte de Provence, and the Comte d'Artois, all three of tender years, taught the French people, by undergoing inoculation, that one must risk danger in order to escape death."[21] It is "Sieur Richard, known ever after as Fearless Richard in honor of the occasion, who makes the insertion"—and everything turns out for the best, with Louis XVI complaining, at the week's end, of nothing more serious than "a bad taste in the mouth; his breath had the odor of smallpox." Marie Antoinette reassures her worried mother: "The king had a rather high fever for three days; the rash appeared two evenings ago and the fever gradually abated to the point where it has now disappeared. He will not have many pocks; a few noticeable ones are on his nose, wrist, and chest; they are already

*Negotiable shares of certain agricultural domains of the crown.

fading. He had had four small incisions, and these sores are now coming to a head, assuring his doctors that the inoculation was entirely successful."[22] Louis XVI's reign thus began with the triumph of immunization, which becomes standard practice thereafter. Smallpox will virtually disappear within two generations. Rarely will the laminated faces of zombies haunt the daily scene, whereas in 1774 they account for one out of every three or four. That liberation will proclaim itself, like other events of the day, in towering coiffures for women that soar to delirious heights, as if Louis XV's passing had blown out the ceiling. Bouffantes *à la mort du roi* came into fashion, displaying "at the left a tall cypress representing black worry, at the foot of which stretches a mourning band of the same color . . . But at the right is a fat sheaf of wheat resting on a cornucopia heaped with figs, grapes and melons."[23] The *coiffure à l'inoculation* depicts a snake, a club, a rising sun, and an olive branch. The snake symbolizes medicine; the club is the inoculation smiting the monstrous disease; the rising sun represents the young king; and the olive branch stands for universal optimism. Countless other fantasies will unfurl atop thousands of frivolous heads turned out by a dozen fashionable hairdressers, to be stared at in passing coaches (whose roofs need raising) by poor working women who go on wearing the same kerchiefs they have worn since feudal times.

MARIA THERESA
AND FAMILY

18

AUGUST 1774

The Slain Gentleman Who Laughs

Beaumarchais did not hang himself. He went instead to his "friend" Sartines, the minister of police. These two are bound not only by the delicate ties between employer and employee in the secret service, but also by a class conspiracy: the common denominator shared by Messieurs Caron and Sardines. For that was indeed the name of the minister's father, a Lyons grocer. Money and women had helped his son win favor first with La Pompadour, then Du Barry, and miraculously had preserved him from offending Marie Antoinette. For the past fifteen years he had presided over the French scene with the "meager talents of mediocrity,"* making expert use of an army of spies. He must have had a sense of humor to have included sardines in his coat of

*The phrase is Marmontel's.

arms and then changed one letter of his name when they ennobled him. Paris was his jurisdiction, where he improved street lighting and built the grain exchange. He had acquired a reputation for liberalism by making the Encyclopedists believe he was protecting them. His great weakness was a passion for wigs, of which he owned the finest collection in Europe, designed to minimize his jaundiced complexion and bony features.

Through Sartines, Beaumarchais passes a letter to Louis XVI early in June: "Last March the late king your grandfather alone knew my whereabouts; he had honored me with a very special and very delicate mission in England . . . Though he worried constantly about my delayed return before falling ill [*sic*], I was deprived even of the consolation of informing him that his secret commands had been executed fully . . . The account I settled for him is now Your Majesty's concern and contains some items for Your Majesty's ears alone."[1]

Sartines is instructed to look into this, and a week later hands the king a second profession of faith from Beaumarchais: "For whatever the king wishes to know, privately and promptly, for whatever he wishes done quickly and secretly—I stand ready. I pledge him my head, my heart, my right arm, and no tongue. Heretofore I would serve no employer; yet this one pleases me, for, being young, he is uncorrupted; Europe honors him, and the French adore him."[2]

That heady dose of flattery earned Beaumarchais another London assignment closely resembling the last one. This time, however, it was he who dug it up. He explained that the "nest of Frenchmen" had suffered a temporary setback owing to Du Barry's fall and was now "back-pedaling," aiming its venom, for lack of a royal mistress, at the next best target: Marie Antoinette. Through information probably supplied by Théveneau de Morande (who at last is beginning to earn his keep), Beaumarchais tells of a second libelous pamphlet bearing this formidable title: *Avis important à la branche espagnole sur ses droits à la couronne de France à défaut d'héritiers et qui peut mesme être très utile à toute la famille de Bourbon, surtout au roi Louis XVI.* *[3] It casts a glaring light upon the Achilles's heel of France's new sovereign, suggesting that all three of Louis XV's grandsons may be sterile. The sly allusion to Charles III of Spain is cruel, the latter having sired eleven children in seventeen years of marriage. "Intoxicated" by Beaumarchais, Sartines proceeds in turn to "intoxicate" Louis XVI, and "M. de Ronac" is dispatched anew to ferret out the pamphlet's author and buy his silence. Neither the king nor Sartines has read a word of it.

By this time Beaumarchais is altogether at home in London. He bombards Sartines with frenzied letters declaring that he has discovered the guilty party

*Important notice to the Spanish branch concerning its right to succession to the French throne in the absence of heirs, and which may also prove very useful to the entire Bourbon line, especially His Majesty Louis XVI. [*Trans.*]

and is in hot pursuit, but that his hands are tied until he receives a blanket power of attorney in the king's own hand: "If this piece ever appears, the queen will be justly outraged, knowing it could have been suppressed and that you and I are involved . . . She will be furious at us, not the least effect of which will be for her to hint to the king that you are an incompetent minister."[4]

Sartines instantly "hints" to His Majesty that he has no business permitting the rest of Europe to take him for an incompetent husband, and Beaumarchais receives signed orders by return post, the text of which he finds familiar enough, being his own, copied word for word by the king at Sartines's behest:

> Monsieur de Beaumarchais, entrusted with my secret orders, will leave as soon as possible for his destination. His discretion and promptness in executing them will be the best proof of his zeal in serving me.
>
> Marly, July 10, 1774   Louis[5]

Again by return post, Beaumarchais thanks His Majesty for a blanket license unique in the annals of the monarchy: "A lover hangs the portrait of his mistress about his neck, a miser hangs his keys, a pious man his cross; but I have made me an oval gold locket, long and flat, shaped like a lentil, in which I have placed Your Majesty's commission and hung it on a gold chain about my neck. . . ."[6] Engraved on the cover of this locket is the motto: "Emulation in my work"; in those days it was customary for lovers to wear a miniature of their loved one as a talisman.[7]

Louis XVI really has no cause for complaint. Shortly afterward Beaumarchais sends Sartines the text of an "agreement" signed with the slanderer on July 23, 1774.[8] The fellow is both an Englishman who goes by the name of William Hatkinson and a Venetian Jew who calls himself Guillaume Angelucci*—Beaumarchais makes sure that both appellations appear on the contract. Signing himself "Ronac," he promptly hands fourteen hundred pounds sterling** to the Anglo-Venetian-Semite in return for a pledge to destroy all printed copies of the pamphlet, half in London, half in Amsterdam. A curious repetition of the Morande scenario. Beaumarchais seems to be a regular commuter on the France-England-Holland circuit. The beginning of August finds him in Amsterdam supervising the destruction of all remaining copies. Feeling pleased with himself, he takes time out to tour the canals of this port city. Success at last . . .

But the plan backfires. Sartines receives alarming news that the beastly Semite has slipped through Beaumarchais's fingers and fled to Nuremberg with one last copy of the pamphlet, which he intends to reprint. How does Beaumarchais know where the man is headed? A mystery. He takes off in hot pursuit: "I am like a lion. I have no money left, but I have diamonds

---

*The name "Guillaume," specifically Christian in origin, was not used in any Semitic community.

**Approximately 100,000 current francs [$20,000].

and jewels which I will sell, and with rage in my heart I will take to the roads again . . . I'll travel day and night if I don't drop from exhaustion along the way . . . Woe to the cursed fellow who sends me three or four hundred leagues farther just when I thought I could rest. I'll strip him of all his papers, I'll kill him."[9]

Sartines rubs his eyes: an insane situation, but there's worse to come. Meanwhile Beaumarchais has hired "an English servant who speaks German," as he himself cannot understand a word of it. The two of them are off on the post road through Prussia—he finds the duchy of Cleves depressing, its inhabitants crushed by taxes—then on through the electorates of Treves and Cologne and the imperial dominions bordering the Danube.

About three o'clock on the afternoon of August 14, at the Langenfeld posting house ten miles outside Nuremberg, M. de Ronac and his servant climb into a two-wheeled chaise in charge of a postilion named Johann Georg Dratz, who assumes they are English. From this point on, two versions of the truth unfold: the postilion's—set forth in a police affidavit (executed at six o'clock before the district officer of Neustadt an der Aysch)—and Beaumarchais's account, or series of accounts, to the Nuremberg authorities at nine the next morning, to his correspondents in France, and finally, a week later, to Empress Maria Theresa at Schönbrunn.

The postilion: On the outskirts of Neustadt he turns around to find the "gentleman" standing in the carriage, removing a mirror and razor from his baggage. Does he plan to shave en route? Probably. What else would you expect from an Englishman? . . . But while crossing the Leichtenholtz, a scrubby band of pine woods, the passenger orders him to stop and darts in among the trees; the servant tells the driver to proceed at a walk. Nature's pressing call, no doubt. At the far side of the woods he halts the chaise and the two of them wait for "over half an hour," encountering only "three journeymen carpenters with axes slung over their shoulders and packs on their backs." At last the "gentleman" reappears "with his hand bandaged in a white handkerchief"; he tells his servant "that he had seen robbers but was not robbed." "The Englishman" appears so calm that Dratz assumes he must have mistaken the carpenters for robbers and whips up the horses. Shortly past Neustadt he notices that his passenger has a bloody neck and bloodstained clothes. Does he care to register a complaint here in the district? Absolutely not. After taking on fresh horses and a new postilion at the next relay station, they head straight for Nuremberg. To be on the safe side, Dratz makes his own report to the police. He heard no shouts or pistol fire. "It appeared to him that the passenger must have inflicted his own wounds with the razor he had taken with him." The affidavit goes into the files.[10]

Beaumarchais: Suddenly, in front of their post chaise, he sees "trotting along on a little bay a short man in a blond wig with a few black curls peeking out from under." There he is, the needle in the German haystack, the very fellow he has sworn to find! Turning, Angelucci recognizes him and gallops off into the woods. Without a word to the postilion, and like a good secret agent, Beaumarchais rushes off in pursuit and catches up with the wretch. They have a scuffle and he snatches the fellow's game pouch, in which he discovers the last copy of the famous pamphlet. Noble soul, he releases Angelucci, then finds himself face to face with two fierce brigands with daggers who step out from a clump of trees. Beaumarchais defends himself as best he can, first with his pistol, then his walking stick; the two men wrestle him to the ground and prepare to finish him off. Miracle: a knife aimed straight at his heart strikes the little gold locket instead, his amulet, and Louis XVI's message ends up saving his life. He escapes with only a neck wound. "I ought to change my name and instead of Censured Beaumarchais call myself Battered Beaumarchais. A battering, friends, that is bound to scar my success with the ladies. But what can you do? There's an end to everything."

In a last desperate effort he manages to knock out one of his assailants and put the other to flight. "My first concern, upon finding myself safe and sound . . . was to relieve myself in a hurry . . . I soaked my handkerchief in urine and wiped my wounds." So he is spared and has recovered the pamphlet. "As I am on my feet, it can't be the end for me . . . From now on I will rejoice to think that I am still alive." "But I must be insatiable . . . for who else has a life so cluttered with luck and misfortune? . . . I have lived two hundred years . . . You cannot imagine all the things I sensed, anticipated, stirred up, and performed in a quarter of a minute . . . But when my confounded shots missed the first robber, ah, how my heart shriveled."[11]

Late that night—and these are facts—he lodges in the Red Rooster inn at the gates of Nuremberg. He calls for no doctor and no assistance in this bustling "free city" of seventy-five thousand under Austrian dominion; no one examines his wounds. Konrad Gruber, the innkeeper, declares merely that his guest is extremely agitated, paces the room in all directions, and keeps opening the window "as if suffering from some mental derangement." Beaumarchais files a complaint early the next morning, hurriedly, declining to wait for a formal hearing, then boards a boat heading down the Danube for Vienna.

Why Vienna? What prevents him from returning to France now that he has what he came for? A theatrical stunt, a gamble, a fit of madness: turning his back on Paris, on Sartines and Louis XVI, he is off to obtain an audience with Empress Maria Theresa and show her the scurrilous pamphlet vilifying her daughter, the Queen of France.

Still a poet despite the touch of madness, he savors the journey in a six-oared boat and enjoys having peasants, who have heard his tale from Nuremberg postilions, gather around him at the water's edge. "My valet translates what they are saying: Come see the Frenchman who was killed in the Neustadt woods . . . I laugh, and they stare in wide-eyed wonder at the slain gentleman who laughs . . . It is plain to see that I am traveling in a civilized country; wherever I go, people are sympathetic and beg me for money . . . The rain has stopped. All up and down the mountains from ridge to valley floor, the varied hues of dusky pines, paler elms, and soft green meadows, this splendid canal carrying me along between two high slopes, cultivation of which has pushed back the forest to the very peak, are a delightful sight." On the 16th of August he vomits blood, or claims to, yet his spirits soar higher than ever: "How pleasant it is to vomit big thick clots of blood into the Danube! How clear is everything around me. The most rugged slopes are covered with vineyards on both sides of the river. Everywhere I see a miracle of agriculture. People here put forth their best efforts."*

In Ratisbon he lodges at the White Rooster (instead of the Red one), then enters the archduchy of Austria. "The high mountains pinch the river and make it run faster . . . I can sense our approach to a great capital: the farms, the shipping, the churches and forts all signal our arrival." At noon on August 20 he reaches Vienna.[12]

Acting more and more like a spy, he neglects to call on the French ambassador (the Prince de Rohan, who happens to be in France anyway). That same afternoon he goes straight to Maria Theresa's private secretary, the Baron de Neny, and hands him a letter signed by Ronac "for Her Imperial Majesty the Queen, exclusive of all other persons, and which Her Majesty is entreated to read in private": "Madam, from the farthest corner of western Europe I have traveled day and night to come here and inform Your Majesty of matters touching upon your happiness, your peace of mind, and, if I may be permitted to say so, the very depths of your heart." After alluding obscurely to an "assault" by some robbers in Nuremberg, he requests "a private and confidential audience secret from both your ministers and our ambassador."[13]

The tale might well have ended right there. This outrageously unconventional approach so horrified the secretary that he nearly sent Beaumarchais packing: "Because of my refusal to state my business and my battered face, he seemed to take me for an Irish officer or scarred adventurer bent on snatching a few ducats by soliciting Her Majesty's sympathy. He would have thrown me out had I not assumed an arrogant air to match his own."[14] This strategy had often worked for Beaumarchais and did so again, for an imperial secretary is

---

*A suspiciously optimistic picture of Austria. Knowing that letters he wrote during his trip down the Danube would be subject to imperial censorship, Beaumarchais included them in his plan.

not accustomed to dealing with insolent visitors. Dolefully, Neny transmits the message* to his sovereign: "I cannot fathom this business, Sacred Majesty;** but this Raunac [*sic*] seemed presentable and insisted so firmly on my delivering his message to Your Majesty that finally I dared not deny his request."[15]

Maria Theresa hesitates: "I doubt that the purported revelations amount to much . . . " But then, this "presentable" man comes from France, where her daughter now rules. She decides to let Count Seilern, Lower Austria's governor and her family adviser, handle the matter.

Summoned by Seilern on August 21, Beaumarchais finds himself face to face with one of those starchy, interchangeable, assembly-line products peculiar to the Viennese court, the typical Hapsburg servant. Taking the stage from M. de Ronac, Beaumarchais proceeds to melt Seilern's starch with a flourish of Louis XVI's handwritten note, warning that Marie Antoinette's honor is at stake. The count promptly orders his carriage and both leave at once for the imperial residence at Schönbrunn, just outside Vienna, one of many miniature Versailles that have sprouted all over Europe during the eighteenth century. By now Beaumarchais is under such tension that he neglects to admire the handsome white palace, its stately, tree-lined garden walks, and the tranquil countryside surrounding the hilltop on which workmen are laying the foundations of a small Roman temple, the Glorietta. He is brought directly before the empress in her private chambers.

She turns out to be a plump little woman encased in widow's weeds, mistress of central Europe, and Charles VI's heir. She rules nearly twenty million souls, a task shared for the past nine years (since the death of her husband, François I, Duke of Lorraine) with her eldest son, Joseph II. Having this ill-matched pair in harness produces such confusion and contradiction that few ministers can tell which of the two is attending to what. Officially, Maria Theresa remains in charge, but Joseph is forever kicking out against his complaining, bigoted mother, who fears, yet grudgingly yields to him. "Affairs of state are handed from one level to another without our even seeing each other . . . It is more painful than death to think how long I have lived uniquely for this son of mine, how I have idolized him . . . It is terrible to tell oneself that we love each other even when we quarrel, that we torment each other without either of us deriving the slightest satisfaction from it."[16] Maria Theresa, who recites the litany for the dead every afternoon, has no creed except remorseful yearning for the lost husband she venerated, and sullen resentment for the wretched deity who snatched him prematurely from her. She had borne him but sixteen children.

As a result, she is hostile to all men. Beaumarchais was wrong to think he could charm her as he had charmed countless other women. She intimidates

---

*Written in French, a second language to Maria Theresa.

**Obligatory form of address to Austria's emperors, otherwise known as "most apostolic kings."

him with her high forehead, the benign dimples riveted into plump cheeks, the pursed lips, and those blank, introverted eyes. He might have fared better man to man with Joseph II, but as the latter is away on a journey, Beaumarchais attempts to stir the heartstrings of maternal solicitude.

In he plunges, dragging up whatever he can think of: the threat of slander to the new queen, the connivance of Hatkinson-Angelucci, the incident in the Neustadt woods . . . On the strength of this preface, he then hands the pamphlet to Maria Theresa, who glances through it, blushes, and asks to keep it overnight. Beaumarchais throws caution to the wind and proposes to have one more copy printed in Vienna, shorn this time of any allusion to Marie Antoinette's frivolity, so that when he is back at Versailles he can show the king a pamphlet that does not compromise his queen.

Maria Theresa remains composed, though her "blood is boiling." Having managed thus far to shield herself successfully from the Enlightenment, she has no idea who Beaumarchais is. But she recognized her son-in-law's handwriting on the note and, being concerned for the childless royal couple, grows unduly alarmed at the reported antics of her daughter, which Mercy-Argenteau's dispatches have vastly exaggerated. A pamphlet now sits on her desk subjecting Marie Antoinette to the same treatment Du Barry received. She writes to Mercy on August 28: "Never has anything so atrocious appeared in print. I must say I did not believe that an inveterate hatred of Austrians, of my person, and of the poor innocent queen was still so deeply imbedded in the hearts of Frenchmen. So this is what the flood of adulation comes to! This is the love they bear my daughter! I am filled with the vilest scorn for this nation without religion, manners, or feelings."[17]

And he is thoroughly French, "that scoundrel" she would like "to treat like an abominable impostor, to send packing on short notice, if not banish from my realm to make it plain that we are not hoodwinked and are acting merely out of charity."[18] Hasn't this self-styled royal messenger just tried to pull a stunt that would make a fool of Louis XVI? She cuts short his muddled arguments. Rising, with an icy smile, she promises to send him news shortly. In the meantime: "Put yourself to bed and see that you are bled promptly."[19] A common remedy for ailing minds. The next morning, like a caged bear, Beaumarchais paces the room he has rented from a French landlady, Madame de Bert. Deflated and discouraged, he now realizes that he went too far. At any rate, he should never have suggested reprinting the pamphlet. That part was foolish. And the promised response still is not forthcoming; mortal silence stretches through the whole day . . . He sends a note to Seilern. No answer. Feverishly, he dashes off twelve pages to the empress, hoping to rectify his blunder but only enlarging it: "No, Madam, in retrospect I will not take that infamous pamphlet to the king . . . Not so much to an empress as to a concerned and justly alarmed mother I now address myself . . ."[20] At nine that evening he is still writing when into the room burst "eight grenadiers with fixed bayonets, two officers with drawn swords, and a secretary bearing Count Seilern's written advice that he submit to arrest."[21] Simple house arrest, as a favor, with a servant, a doctor, and meals provided by his landlady. Armed guards, however, will be posted around the clock.

Immediately after dismissing Beaumarchais, Maria Theresa had elevated this family matter to an affair of state. She summoned Kaunitz, her own Choiseul, "Europe's coachman" if ever there was one, responsible for upsetting alliances as well as arranging Marie Antoinette's marriage. In some remote corner of her grieving heart perhaps there was still a place for him. She relied on his counsel and closed her eyes to his foibles. For one whole week she had forbidden any reference at court to the disease afflicting Louis XV simply because the very mention of smallpox terrified her minister. Now, as she explains the situation to him, Kaunitz arches one brow in that elongated, cold-eyed Slavic face of his. Beaumarchais? Oh, yes, Beaumarchais. Maria Theresa writes to Mercy: "The name of this rascal aroused Prince Kaunitz's curiosity and interest, as he connected it with the man involved in that famous Goëzman suit that was in all the papers here last winter. I never read about it, for it distresses rather than amuses me to see how unwisely people employ their time and talents while worthier objects are derided."[22]

Kaunitz is the anti-Beaumarchais, the arch-conservative. He would leap for joy if he were capable of any emotion. Instantly assuming the worst, he concludes that Beaumarchais must have written and published the pamphlet himself and is only pretending to have rushed all over Europe during the past two months. Let that blasphemer and mischief-maker go now that he is in their hands? Never. Kaunitz has him arrested. They will write to Louis XVI and clear up the matter, but until the reply comes—in about a month—the fellow must remain under close guard. Only the note from his sovereign saves Beaumarchais from landing in a dungeon.

As always, he faces adversity with dignity and pride:

"Do not resist, Monsieur."

"I have been known to resist robbers, Monsieur, but never emperors."

His papers are placed under seal and he is forbidden to communicate with the empress. They take away his personal effects, "knife, scissors, even my shoe buckles."[23] A gleam of hope on August 23, when he obtains Seilern's permission to write to Sartines: "Upon my honor, they must think I have adopted the names Ronac and Beaumarchais for some evil purpose. At any rate, advise His Majesty at once of this strange misadventure and make haste to rescue your devoted friend from prison."[24]

Lack of news spares him further torment. If he had known the momentous events in store for the French court, on August 24, he might have lost heart. His letter will not find Sartines at the ministry of police.

TURGOT

19

AUGUST 1774

The Anticipated Revolutions

On the afternoon of August 24, 1774, Chancellor Maupeou and the Abbé Terray, ministers of justice and finance respectively, are dismissed. Turgot replaces Terray. Because this occurs precisely 202 years after an otherwise painful massacre, the day comes to be known as the "Ministers' St. Bartholomew." The Abbé de Véri, architect of this event (if it had one), reports in his diary: "The anticipated revolutions took place this morning."[1]

Everyone, including Maurepas, was on the verge of despair. The young king had needed so much prodding. The Duc d'Aiguillon's dismissal (June 2) plainly hinted that the ruling triumvirate had not long to rule; surely Maupeou and Terray would fall next.

But the reprieve continued, surprising no one more than they. Maupeou was especially unpopular, symbol of Louis XV's reign: "For some time now Chancellor Maupeou has been looking radiant; his complexion has even turned a shade lighter . . . Unfortunately, several visitors arriving unannounced in his private chamber while he was still dressing have found him unchanged; it can only be concluded that he paints his face, not as a woman . . . but as a veteran politician . . . He regularly applies a thick layer of white, followed by a layer of red, producing a lily-and-roses effect in stark contrast to the yellowish-olive, leaden flesh that once earned him the epithet 'Bitter Orange' . . . "[2]

His political cunning reaches back far into the past: forty years of skulduggery, which he could have avoided considering what life had handed him on a silver salver. From birth he enjoyed every advantage of the *noblesse de robe*,* rich bourgeois families prominent for the last two hundred years, clustered like a fungus deep beneath the moldering crust of the feudal aristocracy: the Lamoignons, the Pontchartrains, the D'Aguesseaus, "over fifty relatives or in-laws in the Paris Parliament alone."[3] His father had been a local potentate in the Paris law courts, where he had ruled almost as long as Louis XV. The

*The privileged legal caste. [*Trans.*]

son's sole misfortune was to have eclipsed him ever so little. When the elder
Maupeou died they buried him savagely:

> Ci-gît un vieux coquin qui mourut de colère
> D'avoir fait un coquin plus coquin que son père.

> [Here lies an old knave who died of ire,
> Having begat a knave more knavish than his sire.]

René de Maupeou had already married, and nearly destroyed the life of a
young and beautiful daughter of the high nobility. Like his father, by sheer
hard work he had gradually taken over the Palace of Justice in Paris. Nothing
else amused him: "Our Chancellor will breathe his last sooner than yawn; he
is not a man but a demon."* Toil, devotion, and cruelty: he was one of the
principals responsible for legally murdering the Chevalier de La Barre and
the Baron de Lally-Tollendal in 1766. For his steadfast service to Louis XV
he was made chancellor, a lifetime sinecure like an episcopate, making him the
foremost magistrate in France, and later was awarded the office of keeper of
the seals. In this last function he officiated solemnly each week with wax and
parchment; his role was to legalize the king's every whim, and indeed he
served His Majesty exclusively and well—to the detriment of his own brothers, cousins, and friends. The five-year struggle of the parliaments—the Aiguillon–La Chalotais episode, the royal musketeers invading the law courts—
stemmed from a statement made by Maupeou in 1770: "His Majesty is beholden to God alone for his crown; he alone is empowered to administer the
forces of public safety and is accountable only to God for his administration.
He alone invests magistrates with their authority; they are and of necessity
must be officers of His Majesty licensed to execute his will."[4] To this assertion
his peers retorted that money gave them rights and privileges which they were
not prepared to renounce. The informed minority sided with the nobles if only
because those nobles were banished to the four corners of the kingdom and
in constant contact with it.

In this atmosphere of chill hostility, the chancellor set about reforming
and reorganizing the French judicial system, exclusively for the benefit of
court circles, with aid from a few hundred "yellow" judges: the Maupeou
Parliament.[5]

To provoke Choiseul, he had recruited a competent but conniving comptroller general,** the Abbé Terray, whose highwayman's jaw inspired fear
and derision. Parental pressure had driven him into the priesthood through
no fault of his own. He avenged the injury ever afterward—rather successfully,
it seems, judging from the fortune and the women he collected. Like Aiguillon

---

*Madame du Deffand writing to Horace Walpole.
**Office combining the current jurisdictions of the French ministers of finance, the budget, and
economics. Only if the appointee were of ministerial rank did it also entail a seat on the "high
council," the most influential royal advisory body.

and Maupeou, he worked hard. Opposing the advocates of a free economy, he favored strict controls, especially over the grain trade, which was the burning issue of those times.

All during June their heads were expected to fall. Had the inoculation perhaps delayed it? But they were still there in July, more confident than ever while anxiety preyed all around. Who would govern in Louis XVI's name, Maurepas or Maupeou? Versailles was too small for the two of them. Maurepas knew this, but sought to avoid open conflict since both Maupeou and Aiguillon were distant relatives of his. People began whispering that he was decidedly uncordial.

Prudently, Maurepas had advanced a pawn: Louis XVI enjoyed torment-ing his naval minister, Bourgeois de Boynes, a corpulent, beer-swollen magis-trate whom Maupeou had appointed more or less accidentally. Though an authority on Roman law, Boynes couldn't tell a foresail from a mizzen. Now, the young king prided himself on his navigational expertise and would ply his minister with any number of treacherous questions. But the "king's tendency to indecision began to manifest itself. He wanted to dismiss M. de Boynes and could not bring himself to do it. M. de Maurepas was compelled to press him on Tuesday, July 19: Matters of state require decisions, he told him. You do not wish to keep M. de Boynes, and the last Council disgusted you more than usual because of the report he gave. Get it over with one way or another."[6]

Who would replace Boynes? Once again the Abbé de Véri came forth with an old schoolmate of his, whose name, as a matter of fact, was on the tip of many tongues (a new man at last), the intendant* of Limousin, which he had governed wisely for thirteen years: Turgot. It was rumored that he might replace Terray, but Louis XVI distrusted this friend of the Encyclopedists.

Take him for the naval ministry if you are still undecided what to do about Terray, counseled Maurepas.

This was done on July 19. At last things were getting off to a start, thought Turgot's good friend, a thirty-year-old scientist already known throughout Europe for his mathematical studies, Marie-Jean-Antoine-Nicolas de Caritat, Marquis de Condorcet. While some people scoffed at the notion of putting an economist in the naval post,** Condorcet wrote to Turgot: "Your appointment to the government is astonishing news . . . I think of our colonies and their wretched inhabitants, oppressed by Europe's outcasts who are sent off to make their fortune in the Indies; of those Negroes whom Louis XIII consigned to the mercy of barbarous masters in the pious hope of Christianizing them with the lash. I can picture the good you will do those unfortunate souls. It cheers

*District officials of the crown who enjoyed both administrative and judicial powers. [Trans.]
**The only ministerial post at the time which involved the handling of long-range investments, in connection with the naval shipyards.'

me to think that no heavenly angel is likelier to redeem our earthly sins than a vessel reaching the colonies laden with your consoling orders."[8]

Coincidence? Another newcomer arrived at Marly and pledged his oath to the king on July 21: Charles Gravier de Vergennes, whose journey from Stockholm had taken three weeks. Young courtiers in the queen's circle, instantly distrustful of any opposition to Choiseul, began whispering: so this was to be the new minister of foreign affairs, this stocky fellow of fifty-four who looked at least sixty? A small-minded diplomat. Polite but hollow. No conversation. They swore he wouldn't last; they would do him in; after all, his wife, "the Turkish slave," could never be presented at court, an intolerable affront . . . A week after his arrival the newcomer was busy reorganizing his office, setting up interdepartmental committees, and instructing embassies to word their dispatches in language "that does not resemble newspaper reports."[9]

On July 27 Louis XV was finally buried officially. A solemn ceremony took place in the cathedral of Saint-Denis, decked in funereal splendor, honoring an empty coffin—nobody would approach the real one for fear of contamination. Five hours of *Libera me* and *Miserere*. The royal armor, banded with crepe (helmet, coat of mail, shield, gauntlets, and spurs), had already been tossed into a yawning pit. "The king is dead. Let us pray for his soul's repose"; a pause, after which the grand master of ceremonies cries: "Long live the king! Let all join in shouting: Long live the king!" Drum rolls . . . The real news that day was made by a conspicuously absent duo: the Duc d'Orléans and his son the Duc de Chartres.* The princes of the younger branch refused to recognize "the Maupeou Parliament." Yielding to precedent (a decided ancestral trait of his) rather than anger, Louis XVI exiled his cousins to their estates at Villers-Cotterêts. The public grumbled: if Louis XV was to go on reigning forever, why bother burying him? Did the removal of two obnoxious ministers signal the arrival of two others equally obnoxious? When would the real decisions be made? The real changes? Louis XVI's days of grace were running out. Except for the necessary replacement of one entrenched group with another, the whole machine had been spinning idly for three months. Famine and sporadic risings were reported in and around the Pyrenees, the Dauphiné, Limousin, and Cévennes. The grain issue demanded attention. The rich urban bourgeoisie echoed the complaining poor: when will the real parliaments (sovereign territories of that same bourgeoisie) be summoned and permitted to act? More pressing still was the problem of a nearly bankrupt royal treasury, in debt to the tune of 150 millions,** despite the fact that Terray had managed to reduce the annual deficit from 63 millions to 19 millions inside of four years.

*The future Philippe Egalité.
**600 million current francs [$120 million].

When the deficit theme recurred too often, Louis XVI would simply hie himself to Compiègne for a hunting holiday.

Compiègne had long been his favorite country residence. North of Paris, its fresh, cool woods, alive with game, kept him from sweating too much. Eight years before, he had written a *Guide to the Forest of Compiègne* and printed it on a toy printing press. It was the last stop on the return to Versailles, which still intimidated him because there he had always been treated as a child. What an endless merry-go-round since his accession: Choisy, La Muette, Marly, and Compiègne, symbol of his retreat from decision-making. But there was no retreat from Maurepas, whose composure had finally given out.

On August 9 the king's mentor had nearly exploded over the issue of dismissing the two ministers: "Delays cause matters to pile up, disrupting but not settling them. You must not think this is the only business in need of attention. The moment you solve one problem, another will arise. This ever turning mill will be your lot for as long as you live."[10]

Right now Maurepas concentrated on getting rid of Maupeou, who, prompted either by pride or despair, was "snubbing" the king:

"Have you spoken to him of the parliaments and magistracy, Sire?"

"Not a word; he scarcely does me the honor of coming to see me. But the problem of a successor . . ."[11]

That reply indicated that Maupeou's fate was sealed, without specifying when. Each time Maurepas tried to pin him down, Louis XVI would revert to the same lame excuse of the fifty-year gap separating them: "I am indeed rather young to be reigning." Instead of an admission of inferiority, this became his sole acknowledged failing. Even now he was beginning to feel quite pleased with himself.[12]

Like Maurepas, Véri was losing patience: "If at first I commended his moderation, I no longer feel that way. The time has come for him to leave the government if he cannot lead it. Having no department, he would look ridiculous."[13]

The exchange grew heated. Proverbial Bourbon indecisiveness led to spite on the part of this immature monarch determined to have his own way. Maurepas pressed him: who will succeed Maupeou?

" 'If you would have the man with widest public acceptance, take Monsieur de Malesherbes. His talents and impeccable honesty go unchallenged.'

" 'I know well enough that he has public support, but he does not suit me, as I already told you . . . Let us speak of him no more; he is a highly dangerous Encyclopedist.' "[14]

Maurepas did not insist. He simply came up with another relative of his wife's, a parasite named Huon de Miromesnil, former president of Rouen's Parliament, whose mediocrity posed no problem.

A tentative decision was reached, but not formalized, as to the keeper of the seals. Maupeou continued to hold this office. And Terray? "The ministry of finance is the heart of the administration. Its influence reaches out in all directions: domestic policy depends on it; foreign policy is subordinate to it; no department can go against it; trade, agriculture, and the arts* all fall within its jurisdiction."[15] A trend had been building during the past month, a modest wave of support for Turgot. Despite Condorcet's touching vision of the colonies, not a single friend of Limousin's former intendant felt happy about his appointment to the naval ministry. All of them were campaigning for him, often without his knowledge: Encyclopedists, physiocrats, the salons, Voltaire from afar, Rousseau in Paris, Diderot in The Hague, the Duchesse d'Anville, the La Rochefoucaulds, Véri arm-in-arm with Maurepas, and the Abbé de Vermond, another politically inclined priest in the queen's circle. Julie de Lespinasse, confidante and counselor to many of them, was prompted to revise her prophecy of May 10, declaring that if her friend Turgot, "philosophy in action," was brought to power by Louis XVI, then "we may see better days." But she was torn apart at the time. In the throes of a passionate love affair, having been bedded six months earlier at the belated age of forty-one by Guibert, she was still mourning the loss, just three months before, of the other man she loved, the Marquis de Mora. Her one link with reality was the hope she set in Turgot.

The issue must be settled. Maurepas prods the king on the morning of August 24:

> "Your honor is at stake, not to mention the honor of your government and the interest of the state. If you wish to retain your ministers, declare it, and correct the public's impression that they are about to fall. Similarly, if you do not wish to keep them, say so and appoint successors."
>
> "Yes, I am resolved to change them. This will be on Saturday, after the dispatch council."
>
> "No, Sire, no. This is not the way to govern. Time, I repeat, is not a resource to be squandered at will. You have already lost too much of it, and affairs suffer. You must reach a decision before I leave this room."
>
> "But look here, I am only twenty and saddled with problems. All this makes me uneasy."
>
> "Only a decision will dispel the uneasiness."[16]

Maurepas had been summoned a hundred days earlier. The king must really have exhausted the older man's patience, raised his hackles. At noon everything is settled; the Duc de La Vrillière, astonished to find himself still in charge of His Majesty's household, performs his assignment to serve Maupeou with a *lettre de cachet* banishing him to Normandy. Apparently Louis XVI had renounced that practice only for two months. Maupeou hands over the

---

*In the "Encyclopedic" sense of the word, embracing science and technology as well as artistic expression.

seals, adding: "As for the office of chancellor, I will die in it; it is essential to my existence and my honor."

The privilege was his. Worse luck for Miromesnil, whose venality would compensate him for the loss of dignity: "A chancellor deprived of the seals is like an apothecary deprived of sugar."[17]

Rising from his chair, Maupeou opens the door to his audience chamber and announces to the waiting petitioners: "I can help you no longer. My ministry has just come to an end."[18]

As for Terray, instead of being exiled, he retires voluntarily to the country, barely escaping angry peasants beyond the city gates who recognize him. He had filled his purse.

But who will replace Turgot in the naval post? Sartines is available. Forget him; he knows no more about the job than Bourgeois de Boynes.

What about Turgot? The final question mark. His appointment as director of finance does not become official until he and the king have talked for an hour. Louis XVI long had maintained: "He is extremely systematic, and he is in contact with the Encyclopedists . . . "[19]

The king seems to have dropped his reservations, at least temporarily. Turgot's working habits appeal to him, the unhurried, unruffled manner that almost suggests a dawdler. He is urbanely cultured, and his immense yet inconspicuous learning ripples the surface of his discourse without drowning the response. And you can be sure that Turgot knows a topsail from a mizzen. Besides, if so many people insist on innovation (the king wonders why; his father never spoke about it), then it had best wear Turgot's features. Features that might be the king's own, for Louis XVI and Turgot look alike: barrel-headed, myopic, awkward, they both have difficulty expressing themselves and are ill at ease with women. Turgot turns purple at a ribald story. He has never married.

Facing each other in this decisive hour-long dialogue are two timid souls—court gossips call them two virgins—forty-seven and twenty years old. Anne-Jacques-Robert de Turgot has somehow managed to duplicate the king's corpulence and mildly lopsided stance. Pale-blue eyes, a round, serene face, thick black hair and brows, fleshy lips framed by ridges of disillusionment. The court discovers him and Louis XVI simultaneously. He had never frequented Versailles in all the years he struggled to improve conditions in impoverished Limousin, out there in his desert, where he drew praise first from Mirabeau (the elder), then from other physiocrat exponents of planned agriculture, a number of whose doctrines he shared. Actually, he is compelled to restrain this band of "advanced" friends who regard him as uniquely qualified to fulfill their dreams. They have already made him countless enemies, whom he knows of only by hearsay. Exactly what does this Turgot plan to do? What is he after?

He will wait and see. He has no program. He wants to think and act step by step, just as he did in Limoges.

One major difference between him and the king is that Turgot is not a Catholic. Still, he does not despair "of ultimate causes. I hold that these feeling, reasoning, purposeful beings who set goals and choose means for themselves constitute a system which is just as real and certain as that of purely material beings, as it were, responding to purely mechanical causes."* Unless militant, the piety of others does not antagonize him. Let the king court virtue, but always with the understanding that "Virtue, however you may construe the word, gives no dispensation from justice."[20] That is his creed—and he realizes that no newcomer at court had better flaunt it. He will do what he can: "Morally, I am the sworn enemy of indifference and the true friend of tolerance, which I as much anyone else need from time to time."[21]

"Sire, you must permit me to set forth my general ideas in writing and, if I may be so bold, my conditions as to the manner in which I would have you support me in this administration; for I confess that my superficial acquaintance with it makes me tremble."

Louis XVI clasps Turgot's hands: "Of course, just as you like. I pledge my word of honor to explore all your views and uphold whatever courageous decisions you may take. But really now, don't you want to be comptroller general?"

"I confess to Your Majesty that I would prefer to remain with the navy because the post is more secure and I am certain to fill it better; at the moment, however, I am dedicating myself not to the king but to the citizenry."

"You will not be disappointed."

Excellent beginning. The wind rises, spirits lift, and everyone rejoices. When the door to Louis XVI's inner sanctum at Compiègne opens and two seemingly fast friends emerge, the court gazes on the man of the hour, if not the era. For the first time since Colbert, a minister assumes office intent upon achievement as well as power.

Louis XVI celebrated his birthday the day before, the golden age of twenty. This feast day of St. Louis on August 25 is a long-remembered holiday, with dancing and merry-making throughout the land. "The anticipated revolutions" promise to be calm and peaceful. No great tragedy if, here and there, especially in the heart of Paris, the people burn straw-and-rag effigies of Maupeou in his magistrate's robes and Terray in his cassock. Officers of the watch look the other way when mobs at the Place Sainte-Geneviève tear life-size figures limb from limb, as if breaking them on the wheel:

Sur la route de Chatou	[On the ro-ad to Chatou
Le peuple s'achemine	People hurry along
Pour voir la fichue mine	To see the sour face

---

*To Condorcet, May 18, 1774.

Du Chancelier Maupeou,	Of Chancellor Maupeou,
Sur la roue . . . Sur la roue . . .	On the ro- (wheel). On the ro- (wheel).
Sur la route de Chatou. [22]	On the ro-ad to Chatou.]

Alleluia! In the Louvre's chapel the Académie Française joins in the traditional "musical mass" celebrating the feast of St. Louis. Each year's panegyric to the paragon of Capetian saintliness brings a different orator to this prestigious pulpit. Two years ago it was the Abbé Maury;* now, the Abbé Fauchet,** a bony little priest. And each year *philosophes* in the audience wait for mention of the Crusades to clear their throats and emit indignant grunts. Fauchet won't have to put up with such minor embarrassments, having chosen to extol a new saint, Louis XVI by the grace of God, seated beneath his ancestral oak. "Applause attended him, meaning that in the chapel of the Louvre people clapped just as in the theater."[23]

Carried away by the general euphoria, Louis XVI announces an important measure. Because Terray, lately, and now Turgot have both advised retrenching the budget for the king's household, he decides to "curtail expenses for the royal lap dogs," a savings of two hundred thousand francs.†[24]

20

SEPTEMBER 1774

Times of Grief

Beaumarchais has been under house arrest for thirty-one days. Like a good watchmaker, he divides them into "forty-four thousand six hundred and forty minutes; for whereas the hours rush by so speedily for happy persons that their passing is scarcely noticed, unhappy souls chop up times of grief into minutes and seconds, finding each very long, taken individually."[1] His sole impressions of Vienna are the sounds of a city sweltering in the summer heat of central Europe, and the rattle of carriages traveling more swiftly than Parisian ones, along broader avenues. "They prohibited me from leaving my room; I did not set foot outside the door. They forbade my looking into the street; I

*Future spokesman of the monarchist cause during the Constituent Assembly, then Archbishop of Paris under Napoleon.
**Later known as the "Girondists' Bishop."
†800,000 current francs [$160,000].

had not the slightest impulse to open the shutters."[2] Evening brought some relief, the cool fragrance of chestnut trees along the Prater, Vienna's imperial promenade which Joseph II had opened to the public purely to antagonize his mother.

After letting the prisoner simmer for a few days, Kaunitz dispatches an unusual investigator to interrogate him, thoroughly but courteously, Chief of Police Sonnenfels, who turns out to be an educated law officer with a flair for writing and serious literary ambitions. The two become fast friends, and Beaumarchais later dedicates his memoirs to the chief. But despite generally favorable reports from Sonnenfels, Chancellor Kaunitz's private catechism is merely reinforced by information from Nuremberg and Neustadt, the postilion's deposition and the remarks of the innkeeper and the authorities . . . Kaunitz gradually becomes convinced that the scurrilous pamphlet is the work of his prisoner, and less charitably inclined upon discovering that it hints at an intimate relationship between himself and the empress. Spitefully, he retards his dispatches—a habit of his that Maria Theresa deplores: "On this last point, you must be extremely patient; now that he is growing older, Kaunitz is in less of a hurry than ever, and, in this respect, implacable."[3]

Back at Versailles, finding the whole business appalling, Mercy, Austria's ambassador, resolves to act discreetly and clear it up. Rather than alerting Lenoir, the new police commissioner, he shields Beaumarchais by approaching Sartines, who continues to serve the king clandestinely. Though furious at Beaumarchais's carelessness, Sartines is instantly prepared to "cover" for him since his own career hangs in the balance. The blame would be his if this "special agent" were proved guilty.

Embarrassed, he explains the situation as best he can to Louis XVI, who dispatches a courier to Maria Theresa at once to thank her for having locked up Beaumarchais and to solicit his release. He also asks to have the pamphlet delivered to him personally along with any confiscated documents.

On September 22 Sonnenfels appears on Beaumarchais's doorstep to offer him a thousand ducats.

"You are free to remain or depart, sir, according to your desire or your health."

A flash of wounded but consenting vanity: "Even if it meant dying on the way, I would not stay a quarter of an hour in Vienna."

He rejects the money—halfheartedly, until it is thrust into his hands—finally accepting it for "traveling expenses" and for the purchase of a harp—a thank-you present for his landlady, Madame de Bert—then sets off at once for Paris, arriving there nine days later.

Kaunitz cannot conceal his disapproval and contempt for a regime that employs such representatives. Ever afterward he laments the lost opportunity to hang Beaumarchais: "Added to his remarkably loose morality, M. de Sar-

tines selfishly appears unwilling to take the blame for what is clearly his doing
. . . In France, as I see it, all signs point to a pitiful government."[4]

The *Chanson de Robin,* which Beaumarchais composed on the way back to
Paris from Vienna, throbs with the joy of his release; it is a hymn to rediscov-
ered freedom.

Toujours, toujours, il est	[Ever, forever the same:
toujours le même:	Never was Robby
Jamais Robin	Acquainted with grief;
Ne connut le chagrin;	On drear days or fair,
Le temps sombre ou serein,	In lean times or fat,
Les jours gras, le carême,	Morning or night,
Le matin ou le soir,	Black or white,
Dites blanc, dites noir,	Ever, forever the same.]
Toujours, toujours, il est	
toujours le même.	

It had been a close shave. THEY almost got him, when all along he thought
he had THEM! No, of course he didn't write the pamphlet. Yes, of course
Angelucci does not exist.* Beaumarchais was always in league with its author,
either Morande or Lauraguais. He simply bit off more than he could chew,
seeking power to act in the king's name in order to impress Maria Theresa.
He grabbed with both fists hoping to curry favor with two sovereigns. The
pamphlet never left his luggage. He cut himself with his own razor in the
Leichtenholtz. He invented the ambush. If they had put him on the wheel or
hanged him, he would have been his own executioner. Not the least contrite,
he sings:

Robin, dansons ce branle que	[Robby, let's strike up the jig
tant j'aime;	I love to dance
Sans le presser,	And not hurry it.
Robin vient le passer.	Robby skips through it once.
Robin, j'en veux danser	Robby, let me dance it
Un second, un troisième;	A second and third time,
Je veux recommencer,	Let me do it over and over
Je ne veux plus cesser:	And never stop.
Toujours, toujours, il est	Ever, forever the same.]
toujours le même.[5]	

Gallop, coachman! Another Maria Theresa is waiting, and this time she won't
disappoint him: Marie-Thérèse de Willer-Mawlaz, a pretty Swiss miss of
twenty, with hair piled high on her head *à la ques-a-co,* who had come to borrow
a harp from him in March. She is naïve and maternal, the very qualities he
seeks. Sartines is not about to abandon him; neither is Louis XVI, who has

*Beaumarchais, who rarely buries a grudge, never again mentions this person.

every right to be furious, yet merely notes in his diary: "Thirty thousand livres* to Beaumarchais to suppress a scandalous publication."[6] The king was not unwilling to read the pamphlet even if it cast aspersions on his virility. He relished gossip about others, including his wife. Next to hunting, voyeurism is his favorite sport, and reading pilfered letters his constant occupation. It takes sharp eyes to watch at keyholes, and for that sole purpose he has hired a certain Pezay, a "minor poet" but a major scandalmonger, who "won the king's heart right off by telling malicious tales about several people."[7] That devilish fellow Beaumarchais seems to have a mischief-making tongue as well. A useful person. Two years later Turgot declares indignantly: "Beaumarchais and Pezay are the two arms of the government."[8]

In Vienna, Maria Theresa refuses to listen to another word about this whole incident, "which had made her blood boil." But an ill wind always blows someone good, and as she desperately hopes to learn that her daughter is pregnant, she writes to Mercy with a sigh on September 20: "If only the king's mettle could be roused in response to this scurrilous assertion of impotence. I don't know what to make of it."[9]

21

SEPTEMBER 1774

To Fashion a Prince Out of a Turd

Another liar, on a very different scale, will not get off so easily. Pugachev is captured during the night of September 14, 1774. His last, lingering agony begins. Yet his lies have set an empire tottering.

His newest officers have betrayed him. Catherine II had put a price on his head: ten thousand rubles alive; five thousand, dead. How many followers did he still have on that final crossing of the Volga? Three or four hundred perhaps, as compared to twenty thousand the month before. But the rebel army's rout on August 24 near Tsaritsyn** at the hands of that confounded German, Michelson, started a panic. Pugachev's artillery is gone now, abandoned by the Don Cossacks. Having given up his plan to march on Moscow, he is wandering over the steppes looking for an escape route to Persia or

---

*About 120,000 modern francs [$24,000].
**Later Stalingrad, now Volgograd.

Turkey. Loyalist troops moving up from the south have encircled the last rebel pockets; General Suvorov has plugged every hole.

For a week they drifted about, exhausted, famished, the hoofs of their horses sinking into seas of gray dust. No grass to feed their mounts: the steppe's burning heat had withered every blade. Forced to walk, they eyed each other furtively, in dismal silence.[1] In fact, His Majesty Peter III, Czar of all the Russias, was already the prisoner of his "courtiers." At Sarepta, not long before, he need not have bothered distributing those resounding titles: "Marshal" Utchinikov, "Army Chief of Staff" Perfiliev, "Lieutenant General" Tvogorov, and to Dubrovski, the only one who can write, "first staff secretary."

"No, Majesty, do as you like, but you might as well chop off our heads. We will not march into foreign lands. There is nothing to gain from it, Little Father. It is too far."

He flushed, blanched, urged desperately that they open a new attack— what about Iaïtsk?* They shook their heads. All they wanted was to catch him alone in his tent. Tvogorov had planned the whole thing and stirred up the others: "He can't even threaten to have us hanged anymore . . . "

By the morning of September 10 it was all over. A scene from Shakespeare. They had surrounded Pugachev, with his black beard and grizzled head, his piercing, "slightly frightening" eyes, his patchwork of scars or seams—no one quite knew which anymore. "Our Little Father Czar Peter": some of them might have believed that once, but not any longer. "Don't make us laugh, Yemelyan Pugachev . . . "

"Come now, my children, why should you want to harm me? You will destroy me without saving yourselves. What are you doing? Would you lift a hand against me? Really, my children, you must be joking."[2]

They were not. When guile failed, he tried force. Finally, they snatched his pistol and sword. He did in fact ride into Iaïtsk in a cart, but not as a conqueror; with hands bound, he was delivered over to the authorities. They chain his ankles and wrists, lock him in a cage, and ship him off to Moscow under heavy guard. Interrogated four times on the way, he confesses proudly at the start that he is not Peter III. The rebel Pugachev elects to suffer in his own name. "If I deserve death, it is best to die gloriously."

This belief cannot be shaken; he will never repent. His myth has very nearly served to cement a full-scale Russian revolt against the militant colonization (from Poland to the Urals) of Catherine, German usurper of "Piter,"** whose generals, victorious now in quelling the rebellion, are Reinsdorp, Brandt, Greiman, Korf, Wallenstern, Bülow, and Michelson.

The scenery unfolding before Pugachev from south to north for days on end is essentially that of the French Crusades, really no different from Mont-

*Now Uralsk.   **Popular Russian name for Saint Petersburg.

ségur and the White Mountain. Russia merely adds infinite distance and horrifying close-ups. Atop the crude stockade surrounding each town—heaven knows how many versts from the last one—sit impaled the heads of rebels, punished, on orders from Count Panin, "according to Christian canon, first by cutting off the hands and feet, then the head, and leaving the body exposed on the edge of the highway."[3] Monstrous creatures from the brush of Bosch or Brueghel crawl along remote side roads, lucky to have escaped merely with torn-off noses or gouged eyes. Villages which had hailed Pugachev just a few weeks ago now billet "units of repression," soldiers of "our beloved Little Mother" the czarina, who flog, hang, loot, and rape in the shadow of the gallows, the wheel, the pillory installed in the marketplace. On the gallows, victims hang by the neck; in the pillory, with iron hooks in their sides; on the wheel, human beings are reduced to a bloody pulp. Here is the purgatory of enlightened despotism.[4]

Pugachev's mythomania brought him success, then doomed him. A year earlier it had transfigured an ordinary Russian youth, a Cossack peasant from the Urals, helpless pawn of the nobility, tossed about at will from their fields into their wars. His back was scored by the knout. Alcohol had a way of loosening his tongue; he would spin out his hopes and dreams to enthralled listeners, inventing tales of sights and sounds in Poland or on the banks of the Don. One evening, in a ravished region, he mused aloud: suppose Czar Peter III, who was at least Russian, murdered ten years ago by his German wife, actually had not died? Suppose I were he? A few voices answered him: "And if you were he?" "I *am* he!" The nebulous vision ballooned and sharpened. Across thousands of miles, captive peoples, persecuted "Old Believers," runaway serfs and convicts needed only "their own czar" to lead them out of despair into revolt.

The clever ones were not taken in: "He is a Cossack, not the czar, but he will protect us as the czar would; what do we care as long as we win?" Others whispered: "What difference does it make whether or not he is the czar? We could fashion a prince out of a turd. If he can't take Moscow, we'll make our kingdom in the Iaïk.*"[5]

Pugachev, self-proclaimed Peter III, looked for support at first solely from Bashkirs, Kalmuks, Tatars, and Chuvashes. Eventually the Cossacks joined him, colonization's mobile arm, the only groups able to cover vast distances on their small horses. Turning against Moscow, they were becoming the liberation's chief weapon. But the Russians also entered the picture. "Holy Russia" had lost its meaning for peasants bought and sold in the marketplace, herded with cattle and fowl onto barges bound for Saint Petersburg; for the serfs of Count Rumiantsov, flogged for not going to church, given five thousand strokes of the rod for failure to take Easter communion. As to serfs in

*Urals.

factories adjoining mines in the Urals and the Upper Don,* they were deported for life to prison colonies and assigned to field, foundry, or mine according to the taskmaster's whim. Wages were unheard of.

By spring Pugachev controlled the entire Ural Basin apart from its major cities, threatened Moscow, and laid siege to the fortress of Orenburg linking European Russia with Central Asia. Defeated in battle, he recouped the loss on the heels of an uprising. In June he reappeared on the Volga, capturing Kazan. In July he was crushed at Tsaritsyn.

He had failed to consolidate the bits and pieces of his dream, the "Old Believers" eager to revive the past, symbolized by the wearing of beards, the rebels craving a future. After Catherine had arranged a hasty peace with the Turks, General Suvorov rushed northward to smash the revolt.

Riding alongside the cage, Suvorov personally escorts his prisoner, followed by two infantry units, two squadrons of "good" Cossacks, and two cannon. At Simbirsk he presents the captive to Governor Panin:

"Tell me, little Pugach, Yemelyan Ivanovich, have you hanged many nobles and boyars?"

"I've hanged 707,000** of you people. You're lucky I didn't catch you, Panin; I would have raised you a notch or two; I would have broken your back, I would have tied reins around your neck and, for your pains, hoisted you higher than all the rest."[7]

Count Panin's manicured white hand plants a righteous slap on the monster's face. Pugachev has no illusions; in the end, no one is more surprised than he to learn that Empress Catherine, in her great mercy, has spared him from being torn limb from limb and has commanded merely that he be beheaded.† She feared that his protracted suffering might trigger riots.

In contrast, the Iaïk River receives a life sentence: to be known henceforth as the Ural.

Before all his teeth were ripped out in the third session of "ordinary" torture, Pugachev boldly sang the song of Makarov, composed some twenty years earlier by a rebel in the Ismaïl regiment, on the theme of Russian army life:

> I am my country's shield
> And my back is covered with scars;
> I am my country's rampart.
> My reward is a whipping.

*Fifty-four new factories under Elizabeth; thirty-two under Catherine; thirty thousand tons of Russian iron exported annually to Europe.[6]
**He was bragging. The number of nobles and landowners killed in the rebellion was at most two thousand.
†January 10, 1775, in Moscow.

Poor wretched soldier
More miserable than the sole of a shoe,
The very worst of life is yours,
It's no secret.

They beat you, they hammer you
As if forging a bar of iron.
A dog is treated better.
They beat you on the face,
In the eyes, the mouth,
Even the teeth.[9]

DUPONT DE NEMOURS

22

SEPTEMBER 1774

What an Astounding Revolution!

On Russia's doorstep, Pierre-Samuel Dupont,* Turgot's friend, struggles desperately to shake some changes into one small part of the globe: Poland. Armed with enlightenment, can Dupont the reformer succeed where Pugachev, using force, failed earlier this year?

Dupont rates his own abilities highly but is honest about his looks. Smallpox has left deep ruts in his irregular features.[1] "Around the age of five, I managed to ruin my face by tearing the nasal cartilage." His engaging smile makes up for it: "I am naturally cheerful . . . My life was meant to be happy at all times and in all places." This is no indication of spineless inertia; in fact, twenty years before, he had cut himself off from a brutish father, "the royal clockmaker," when, after a female cousin had tattled about his irreverent parody of a tedious church sermon, the elder Dupont had locked his son in a cupboard. "I found an old hunting knife. I drew it and would have killed or seriously mutilated myself if my cousin's cook had not snatched it from me. They took it to my father, who slapped me about, grabbed me by the collar, and flung me to the floor. On the first Sunday after Easter, four months past my seventeenth birthday, I departed, taking nothing that belonged to my father, leaving nothing that belonged to me."[2]

---

*The biblical name Samuel indicates a Protestant background. Dupont's parents were Huguenots.

It had been a tragic blow, at the age of seven, to lose his mother, a
Montchanin of noble stock. The loss further embittered him against his "stern-
faced [father], in whose presence one dared not breathe." The breach between
them never really healed. He grew up learning to shift for himself, relying on
his own chiefly intellectual rather than manual resources. His determination
to marry the great love of his life, a girl from Nemours, "tall, chestnut-haired,
nymphlike, with gentle albeit dark eyes," Nicole Le Dée, had sent him to work
for two painful years as secretary to the intendant of Soissons in order to earn
enough to satisfy his fiancée's parents. In time he became affiliated with the
tiny emerging school of physiocrats. As a matter of fact, it was he who christened them with that Greek borrowing, denoting those who seek "the natural
constitution of government best suited to mankind."[3] Their spokesman, Dr.
Quesnay, liked him and introduced him to La Pompadour, who took "something of a fancy" to Dupont. "She told the doctor to bring me around some-
time when she was alone. She referred to me indulgently as 'our young
farmer.' "[4] According to the elder Mirabeau, Quesnay took Dupont in tow:
"He stripped away all the slag of polite society, thwarted him, drove him to
despair with unmatched bounty and zeal, and made him into a diver, the
swimmer that he was . . . Referring to Dupont, the doctor made this note-
worthy observation: 'We must look after this young man, for he will speak
when we are gone.' "[5]

Marriage ushered in several years of meager satisfaction during which he
edited physiocratic publications, proving himself equal to his masters. People
came long distances to consult him in Paris; certain chiefly agrarian states
sought trained personnel in this laboratory "of happier, more productive
countrysides and cityless regions," this school of physiocrats, neglected in their
homeland.

Warsaw had beckoned Dupont, or, more precisely, a magnate recently
come to power, Prince Czartoryski, cousin to "the King of the Republic of
Poland." Besides needing a French tutor to instruct his son in managing the
vast family estates, he wanted a secretary "to the king and to the republic" for
the high council of national education—another experimental laboratory (official this time) of utmost significance involving the first attempt to organize
public education.

Combined altruism and self-interest persistently motivated "enlightened"
Poles: the twenty-odd families who controlled their twenty million countrymen (possessed them, actually, for deeds of ownership specified thousands of
serfs as well as numbers of acres) faced the impending necessity of raising
additional taxes. If productivity were to be increased, it would require better
"instruction," meaning more efficient farming techniques on the part of the
tax-paying peasantry. This fundamental physiocratic doctrine gained endorse-
ment from penny-wise landowners such as the elder Mirabeau. "Fiscal reform

must be demanded by all as part of an orderly system and not decreed by a ruler . . . This brings me back once again to education . . . "[6]

In innocent good faith, Dupont walked into a hopeless situation. He set out for Poland "eager to test whether Enlightenment has not greater power to uplift a nation than have swords, cannon, and mercenary armies to tear it to shreds . . . It can never be said that a Frenchman schooled in the traditions of good citizenship and trained from childhood in the defense of liberty is not prepared to die in its cause."[7] He was hired, however, simply to design a machine for turning out taxpayers.

From the French standpoint, there was profit to be made in improving relations with Poland, whose crops lay rotting in the fields. French entrepreneurs could gain tidy fortunes from Polish grain and spirits despite the cost of carting or shipping them in. "There is grain here which will rot or be drunk up as bad beer and bad brandy, more than enough to feed the French kingdom for three years."[8] But to produce, stock, and exploit such assets requires education.

This is why they are paying selfless Dupont the magnificent salary of ten thousand francs [$2000] annually, with the promise of a hundred thousand [$20,000] in principal when young Prince Czartoryski comes of age in ten years.

On July 18, 1774, he set out with his wife and two sons, the younger named Eleuthère,* "in honor of liberty and peace," by his godfather Turgot, Limousin's intendant. "I go to Poland to flounder in a void, much as Milton describes Satan vainly thrashing about in space. I go to the land of intrigue, jealousy, conspiracy, despotism, slavery, pride and inconstancy, weak men and fools. I wager that I will make my fortune there, and nothing else. Indeed, I had higher aspirations and I grieve for my youth."[9] Self-confidence and firm convictions come to his aid, however, and off he goes to this aristocratic republic ruled by a king who had been Catherine II's lover. But who are the real liberals, the "republican" nobility behind the Confederation of Bar or the recent prizewinner among them, their urbane "king," Stanislas Poniatowski, reared in the salon of his spiritual mother, Madame Geoffrin? Poland's violent internal struggles had produced such "anarchy"** that Russia, Prussia, and Austria used this as an excuse two years earlier, in 1772, to carve her up: four million "souls" offered to the highest bidder. " 'Oh, Mama,' Stanislas Augustus complained to Madame Geoffrin, 'what a difficult and depressing task it is to rule Poland. Be patient, though, things will improve. Meanwhile, I am plastering as best I can.' "[10] The "plaster" meant wholesale reforms.

*Eleutherius, an epithet of Zeus, meaning "god of freedom." [*Trans.*]
**The word is used officially in the treaties covering the First Partition of Poland.

Stanislas welcomed Dupont warmly. "This prince has great intelligence, loftiness of spirit, and sensitivity. He appreciates decent things."[11] But apart from the king, Dupont finds little to admire. The dusty journey takes him through endless fields of grain, past hundreds of crosses bordering the stubble. A downtrodden people; praying beasts of burden. These peasants do not care who rules them. What difference would it make if he were Polish, Russian, Austrian, or Prussian? They are chattels of their lord, and their lord chooses the king. Dupont shudders to discover that Poland is a nation of serfs. He is expected to wave a magic wand and awaken a mass of slumbering, illiterate slaves. Their masters certainly cannot help him: he is appalled by the court at Warsaw, "this collection of French and Polish outfits, floor-length robes, long beards and shaved heads . . . As if two remote centuries stood side by side . . . A host of impoverished nobles cluster about the magnates, like swarms of famished insects bent on sucking an ox dry."[12] Dupont's bourgeois heritage has not prepared him to associate with aristocrats like Prince Radziwill, who rules "over estates vaster than Lorraine," yet sleeps on the floor; or Prince Sapiéha, whose immense landholdings rival those of an imperial elector and who eats off gold dishes that are never washed lest they wear out. In no time Dupont realizes that the Polish reality boils down to a desperate struggle pitting tradition-bound Radziwills and Sapiéhas against progressive Czartory- skis and Poniatowskis. The Poland melting the hearts of Frenchmen does not exist.

What about the educational program? Gritting his teeth, he plunges in. He must start almost from zero, for only a handful of "academies" exist in two or three cities, offering military training to children of the nobility. In the countryside, parish priests teach the catechism, then Latin to promising peasant sons, who go on to enter the seminary.

Dupont—and other French intellectuals who have collaborated on such a plan—envisions a four-tier pyramid designed to cultivate the Poles without disrupting the social structure. At the base are "parish schools" where, in addition to obtaining religious instruction, children at last can learn to read, write, count, and speak their native tongue. Why not also a smattering of rural economy, of natural science?

On the next level are provincial and urban grammar schools aimed chiefly at creating a bourgeoisie; above that, schools to prepare children of the nobil- ity for entrance into military academies and universities. At the very pinnacle is a court school.[13] Dupont's main interest lies in the parish classrooms, cradles of independent thought; he urges Polish leaders to accept them: "They will prove inoffensive to European eyes, but extremely valuable to the Republic as training grounds for a skilled and productive people, virtuous and patriotic, seasoned, governable, inured to the discipline of courage, a people whose strength can serve you, whom you may call your children and who will regard you as benefactors and their country as a true mother . . . " What greater reassurance could he offer? A flock instead of a pack.

But he goes too far. He dreams. For advanced levels of instruction he proposes bringing in the best European textbooks: mathematics, ethics, and social economy from Paris; chemistry and electricity from London; "practical agriculture" from Berne. He urges noblemen "to give schoolmasters either land or board and lodging in their own palaces." Their suspicions are well founded when he confides to his friends: "I thought it might just be possible to exploit the pride, justifiable or not, of the nobility." What is this M. Dupont really up to? Even when conniving he is hopelessly naïve. What prompts him to urge village squires to organize Sunday-afternoon sessions of "running, jumping, climbing, swimming for those living near rivers, military exercises for everyone"? He must be out of his mind even to suggest teaching young peasants to use firearms. Really! Is he promoting reform or Armageddon?

After a month he knows what he is up against. "It is practically impossible to do anything here but plan . . . " for the simple reason that the educational "commission" is penniless. A vicious circle: schools are needed in order to swell the tax rolls, but there is no money for the schools. The nobles are badly in debt, the king worst of all. "So I confined myself to a few plans for grammar and high schools, mere pipe dreams." "It is torture to live in an unrepublican republic where corruption is rampant and the tiny, infinitely tiny scattering of responsible citizens has a narrow focus, no influence, and nonexistent resources. Legislators, paid by the usurpers from public funds . . . are interested in only two things: lining their own pockets and wiping out any ray of light, any establishment, any institution that one day might lead . . . the nation to freedom. In such a country I could have served only a conspiracy or a revolution, which is scarcely the task of a philosopher." Pedagogy certainly did not attract him: "What a boring occupation for a man, especially a kind of statesman, to teach a four-year-old brat!"

Good news arrives just in time to raise his gloomy spirits: Turgot summons him to Paris. On September 27, 1774, he has received Louis XVI's formal approval of Dupont's appointment as inspector general of commerce. In the end, Dupont will look back on his Polish experience as merely a round trip to disenchantment; he stayed there less than three months. How foolish, he admits, to expect change anywhere outside France, where Turgot's presence now symbolizes prosperity and hope. "What an astounding revolution! . . . I am sure to find my country already transformed, with honorable men setting the tone and even scoundrels making a pretense of honesty, with decency reviving and luxury waning. I can barely wait to set eyes on all this . . . "

Just before leaving France he had bought the estate of Bois-des-Fossés in Gâtinais, between Nemours and Montargis, about five miles from Bignon, where his esteemed "Friend of Man"* makes his home. A "bourgeois house, with farmland, vineyards, meadows, and woods." It will provide "a needed refuge against the follies and idle dreams of ambition. Up to now I have gone about as something of a romantic hero, noble rather than well advised."[14] With Turgot as his guide, "the young farmer" is about to discover the satisfactions of tilling the soil; after thirty-five years in Paris he will start breathing fragrant country air. At this time he adopts the name Dupont de Nemours.

LOUISE DE MIRABEAU

23

SEPTEMBER 1774

Struggles in the Dark

Bignon was in fact the birthplace of "Mirabeau fils," well over two hundred miles from the ancestral Provençal château enfiefed to the Riquetis under Louis XIV. Unfortunately, Gâtinais's mild climate is out of bounds to him this summer.

His wife's docile surrender, in response to the "Gassaud affair," has not lasted very long. She cannot forgive his "pardon." Since June one angry scene has followed another in Manosque, increasingly violent because the pair is forced to live together with no distraction other than tearing each other apart. One day she explodes:

"Everyone knows that you slept with your mother and sister, those two trollops!"

He slaps her and refuses to apologize. She runs off to her parents at Marignane, staying just long enough to abort the child in her womb, a relief both to her and to Honoré, who thus will be spared the sight of a second baby resembling the musketeer. Emilie returns to Manosque in July, the breach between them wider than ever.

One August morning, unable to stand it any longer, he jumps into the saddle, his spirits rising with each mile of the long ride to the Nice district in southeastern France, where his dearest lady friends reside, including the Marquise de Tourettes and the Comtesse de Vence. But the dearest of all (notwithstanding their quarrels since his marriage) is his sister Louise.

In breaking his "ban" he has committed a serious crime. Defiance of the

*Mirabeau the elder. [*Trans.*]

lettre de cachet ordering him to remain in Manosque is equivalent to high treason. If caught, he will go to prison. And he is still penniless.

Well, it's done now. Besides, he had taken the bit between his teeth several times before in his youth. This irrepressible man with the oversize head is off for a day's gallop through tawny fields dotted with vineyards and olive orchards. On each hilltop perches a village proud as himself. All the scents of Provence, "that perfumed wanton,"* greet him at dusk as he slips inside the ramparts of Grasse, high in the hills not far from the sea. A profusion of flowers, but also the effluvia from tanneries and soap factories tucked in between the main waterway and an open culvert. He rides into the fashionable quarter of this "second capital of Provence, the only town besides Aix fit to house a great nobleman."[1] He waits for darkness to fall before knocking at the Cabris dwelling, set into an angle of the town ramparts,** and before alarming the porter. Who is this caller wrapped in a cape that conceals his face?

"Take this note to your mistress."

Louise de Mirabeau, the Marquise de Cabris, is in bed with a handsome fellow. Her husband? Her lover. Without further ado, she sends for her brother to join them in the bedchamber.

Emilie was wrong to call Louise a harlot. She is instead an attractive, "liberated," slightly dizzy young woman of twenty-two who has already learned the hard facts of life. Like her brother, she is wildly temperamental, lusty, spirited, and, on occasion, cynical. Had they slept together four years ago at the Château de Mirabeau, reclaiming each other after an absence dating back to their childhood, she still reeling from the effects of an arranged marriage with that degenerate simpleton, the Marquis de Cabris? Once before at Bignon, when they were ten and thirteen, the two had had to be separated. Upon rediscovering each other in 1770, apparently they loved indiscreetly. Honoré boasted of it, but if incest actually occurred, it could not have lasted more than a few days.

Tonight they greet each other as lovers rather than siblings. She has left her husband, who is slowly going insane in the Château de Cabris atop the hill, another nest perched high on the slopes above Grasse, and she is happy with her present lover, another musketeer: Jausserandy-Briançon, a Verdache landowner, good company in the salon as well as the bedchamber. Mirabeau and he get along even better when it turns out that Briançon was wounded in Corsica, where Mirabeau had also fought against Paoli† in Choiseul's time, the only pleasant episode of his youth. Louise orders refreshments and, with her lover looking on, shows her brother the baby daughter she has borne her husband. The party stretches far into the night.

*Expression coined by the French writer Charles de Brosses (1709–1777).
**Today the Fragonard Museum, which contains a death mask of Mirabeau.
†Pasquale Paoli (1725–1807), Corsican patriot defeated by the French, who fled to England and was welcomed in Samuel Johnson's circle. [*Trans.*]

Do money matters enter the conversation right away? They are one of the chief reasons for Mirabeau's journey, which is less impulsive than it seems. The family dispute that poisoned their childhood is now public. Their mother has gone to live in Limousin and communicates with the "Friend of Man" only through legal writs. It is one of the kingdom's permanent judicial spectacles. Louise sides with her mother. Honoré watches and waits; as a perpetual minor, he cannot challenge paternal authority. Moreover, his mother has just won one round in the legal battle, recovering possession of her paraphernalia:* 250,000 livres.[2] Honoré hopes to share some of the booty by ingratiating himself with her through Louise, and also may wish to prevent his beloved sister from inheriting the entire family fortune. Friendship, tenderness, lust, and gold: basic ingredients in the Mirabeau household. But all that can wait until tomorrow.

Tomorrow, August 5, dawns green and golden. Locusts begin chanting early in the morning. Why not picnic with Madame de la Tour-Roumoules, a childhood friend of theirs? Louise puts on her riding habit. Luncheon is served beneath a row of chestnut trees lining the main road. Mirabeau is nearly euphoric in this congenial atmosphere, after six dismal months with Emilie. Servants appear with demijohns of tangy Var, then full-bodied Italian red wines to accompany the fish course, the partridge, and the season's first grapes. They enjoy themselves. As yet, nobody broaches the subject of business. Conversation focuses on *the* scandal of Grasse.

And what a scandal! For the past few weeks local society has been rocked by the "affair of the verses honoring the ladies of Grasse," a highly irreverent lampoon posted all over the town walls and even distributed at mass. In it some seemingly well-informed rhymester painted the hidden charms of Grasse's most prominent matrons, including the wives of two high judicial officers, the *lieutenant général* of the criminal seneschalsy and the president of the court. Even priests came under fire for publicizing "one of the crimes that nature abhors and for lighting sacrilegious fires in holy places."[3]

At first Honoré bursts out laughing: such doings in the churches of Grasse! But, hothead that he is, his temper flares on hearing that Louise is accused of writing and circulating the piece, which is in fact the work of her husband. At times like these Mirabeau cannot stomach raw reminders of the crushing humiliations that filled their childhood. "He inclines to evil before knowing what it is or being capable of it," said his father when the boy was six years old.[4] So when anything goes wrong, blame it on Louise and Honoré, those rotten Mirabeaus.

Quite by accident, down the tree-lined path saunters one of the scandal-mongers, a neighbor of their hostess, followed by a line of workmen turning up the soil. M. de Villeneuve-Mouans, a gentleman in his fifties nicknamed

*Personal property, apart from dowry, reserved by law to a married woman: in cash, about a million current francs [$200,000].

"Lard Ass," "wears his paunch like the sign of his dignity." He typifies the notables who have reduced Honoré to the single identity allotted him: "Mirabeau fils." Leaping to his feet and flourishing his napkin, Honoré rushes forth to avenge twenty years of mortification. Collaring the man, he thrashes him soundly on the back with a parasol, wrestles him to the ground, and the two tumble over one of the low retaining walls known locally as *estauques.* None of the workmen budges; the more courageous peasant women try to intervene. Briançon steps in and proceeds to urinate on the path directly in front of the pair. The picnic party rocks with laughter. Villeneuve-Mouans is still stretched on the ground, more dead than alive only because he is scared to death, when Mirabeau gets to his feet, standing tall and triumphant in pale-blue breeches and waistcoat, his head a mass of ringlets, and tosses a handful of six-livre pieces at the onlookers:

"Drink to my health!"

He will need all the good health he can muster, for this escapade has just made him an outlaw.

Under the aristocratic code, "Lard Ass" should have challenged Honoré to a duel; under the law, he could sue him in the seneschalsy court of Grasse. Wisely, he opted for the latter, but this minor detail is nothing compared to Honoré's real peril arising from his broken ban, now public knowledge, which is an intolerable offense. In a kingdom where the "forces of order" command such feeble resources, the sovereign's absolute authority cannot function without contagious obedience. Hence the necessity for exemplary punishment.

Sheepishly, Honoré hurries back to Manosque the next day. He is forced to rely on the two people for whom he no longer cares, his father and his wife. He decides to send the latter to the former. He wants his father to obtain royal consent to substitute a "paternal" sanction for the administrative ban. But the elder Mirabeau is likely to reject the plea if he hears about the incident from strangers. Now the Marquis de Mirabeau has always had an eye for pretty women, and once, in a letter, he expressed solicitude for Emilie, whom he has never met. By taking the news to him, she can soften the blow; he in turn can mollify the king. An added advantage: this brief separation will ease the strife between the young couple. At Bignon, Emilie de Covet-Marignane will resume the manor life so dear to her. She departs gladly and hastily, delighted at this unforeseen vacation from a husband who, just three months earlier, tore a confession of adultery from her. A letter she writes to him from Aix conveys perhaps a glimpse of what might have been and never was. "Farewell, true and tender friend; I regret every moment I have spent with you; had I one of those moments now, I would put it to better use than I did."[5] Unknown to either of them, they would never see each other again.

The problems of her journey preoccupy Emilie. In Aix old friends vanish. The Marignanes will not contribute a sou to help their rascally son-in-law. She leaves with twenty-five louis—loaned by M. and Madame Gassaud—in a rattle-trap post chaise "hired from Rudolf the Jew." A tyrant to the last, Honoré forbade her to journey by way of Tain-l'Ermitage, where her musketeer is stationed. A "drenching thunderstorm" arranges the matter, however, "forc-ing" her to stop at Tain on August 23. First sign of her reclaimed freedom. Without lingering, she passes straight through Lyons, not even bothering to glimpse the Place Bellecour, forgetting her weariness and dizzy spells. On August 29 she visits the Dominican convent of Montargis, where the eldest Mirabeau daughter, Marie, has taken the veil. From Bignon, some seven miles away, another sister, Caroline du Saillant, arrives to greet Emilie and guide her to the château.

Who could possibly take these Mirabeaus for monsters? Louise and Honoré, the only clan members she has met thus far, must have been joking. The rolling landscape surprises her at first, it is such a stark contrast to rugged Upper Provence. Bignon is "a basket of vegetation so thoroughly blended with trees, woods, streams, and cultivation that you would think all the birds in the region had congregated there."[6] In the midst of this basket stands a handsome Renaissance structure, simple, square, two-storied, with nine win-dows. Around it, a patriarchal community, clusters of peasants doffing their caps, intrigued by the economist homilies of the marquis, whose applied theories have truly improved their lot. Feasts and entertainments, fountains of wine, fireworks, "flowering processions" to celebrate the opening of baths or "closets of greenery" as well as the feast days of master and mistress, who occasionally help bring in the harvest, churn butter, and haul in the shrimp nets. Minuets and contredanses on peasant fiddles. A melody from the nearby Loire.

Caroline is "a robust laying hen," as her father so elegantly puts it. A hulk of a girl, vain and garrulous, built like a rock, whose husband, "Mr. Slyboots," has a reputation for "warmth without fire, coolness without starch"; regularly once a year she bears him a child, but Bignon has room for all of them, and the Saillants are determined to use it. Why doesn't Honoré care for his father's mistress, Madame de Pailly, "the black pussy cat"? Like most Vaudoise women, she is "a born mother"; a lady and a sweetheart as well. And what of the great man himself, the master of this household, whom Emilie ap-proaches tremulously to deliver her message? Aristocrat to the core, with his cold, haughty manner, his impeccable dress which he changes before every meal. How can he have sired such an unorthodox elder son? Not that the younger one, Boniface, is much to look at with those unwholesome layers of fat, but he proves entertaining and attentive to his sister-in-law. It is love at first sight between Emilie and all those who made her husband's childhood a nightmare. She adopts the basic principle of life at Bignon, proclaimed by the marquis: "As you see, my children, I haven't a single tooth left that can handle even a pie crust; my eyes refuse to serve me; the rest I won't mention; my one ambition in life, therefore, which I'll never give up, is to hear laughter around me; otherwise I'll go off by myself to the banks of the Loire, where people laugh impulsively."[7]

Emilie's nature is to be cheerful, and all of those painful months of marriage were sheer accident. She was spoiled to death at home; here at Bignon her pleasing looks, her smiles and songs invite the same treatment. "A warbling monkey," comments her father-in-law, who in less than two weeks "is covering her with kisses all day long, from the roots of her hair to her chin." While pretending to be furious at Honoré and reluctant to help, he is secretly rejoicing: he has him. Now he will be able to "tighten the screw securely fixed in my heart." The "Friend of Man" has hated his son savagely, mercilessly, since the day he came into the world with that oversize head and a whole list of other defects traceable to his mother's side of the family, those confounded Vassans. The marquis is never happier than when Honoré justifies that hatred by putting himself in the wrong.

A series of four chatty and syrupy letters from Emilie conveys to her husband the fact that he can no longer rely on her and is bound for prison. On September 3: "I have met my father-in-law at last . . . he received me warmly . . . He is extremely irritated, and none of the arguments I gave him had much effect . . . He said he had no choice but to put you beyond reach of the law . . . When I suggested going back to you, he told me it would be improper; he keeps reminding me in front of all the others that I am to consider this my home." On September 5: "Your father has written to request an order shielding you from normal judicial procedure; he is obliged to ask this as a favor . . . Please, my angel, behave yourself in this affair, and perhaps it will turn out for the best . . . " On September 6: "They are furious at Madame de Cabris . . . they say she's a trollop who deserves to be crushed between two stones . . . " Finally, on September 13: "All my efforts have been vain, dear friend, and I have been unable to spare you the blow that prostrates me . . . I have been despondent ever since we learned that the administrative order had been issued . . . "

. . . The order consigning "Mirabeau fils" to the Château d'If,* a royal fortress** off the Marseilles coast.

The arrival on September 18 of Sheriff's Deputy Ouvière and two mounted officers comes almost as a relief; he had been expecting them all along, waiting for them to appear as part of the natural sequence of his father's hatred. On September 21, Sénac de Meilhan, intendant of Marseilles, informs the Duc de La Vrillière that Mirabeau is imprisoned at If and it will cost the Treasury 403 livres and 10 sous. "The amount may seem high, but you must

*Through arbitrary imprisonment.
**The Man in the Iron Mask, the Count of Monte Cristo, and other literary heroes survived its dungeons. [*Trans.*]

consider that there are a full fifteen leagues to cover and the deputy and his two aides had to be alert day and night in order not to bungle the operation."[8]

They do not want to break his spirit. They have not searched his baggage. They left intact the manuscript of his *Essai sur le despotisme,* roughed out at Manosque to pass the time. In this respect he is a bit like his father—even attempts to emulate him—for both turn out a constant stream of words. But may heaven prevent his father, the government, or the king from reading his latest statements. For example: "Despotism is a way of being terrifying and convulsive . . . A despotic state becomes a kind of menagerie ruled by a ferocious beast." And this: "Duty, self-interest, and honor call for resisting a monarch's arbitrary commands and even divesting him of power, the abuse of which gradually can destroy freedom, if there is no other way to preserve it." This as well: "All acts of despotism are struggles in the dark."[9]

CONDORCET

24

SEPTEMBER 1774

Watch Out for the Dévots*!*

The autumn of 1774 arrives early. Storms and torrential rains put an end to the fine weather shortly after the king's twentieth birthday and the Ministers' St. Bartholomew. Harvesting in the Ile-de-France is a fitful affair; grain may rot in the fields. Overloaded drains in Paris add to the city's noxious odor. Every street becomes a running stream. The stench invades the comptroller general's office, tenanted by Turgot.* Divine Providence is not looking out for him—not that he ever relied on it. Already his desk groans with pamphlets —one by the Abbé Galiani, for instance, a Neapolitan with galling wit: "He will not keep his place long enough to carry out his programs. He will punish a few scoundrels, he will rant and rail, try to do what is right, encounter obstacles, difficulties, thieves in every corner, his reputation will decline, people will detest him . . . he will retire or be dismissed."[1]

Possibly. Turgot is not too concerned for his own fate. He will do the best he can, without knowing just yet what that means, except for one principle on which he stands firm: despite adverse weather and pamphlets, the grain trade must operate free of controls. Only on that score is Turgot dogmatic.

*On the Rue Neuve-des-Petits-Champs, now an annex of the Bibliothèque nationale.

Symbolically, he has reduced his own yearly salary from 140,000 livres to 80,000. He has brought in a new departmental *premier commis* (an official somewhere between a secretary of state and a cabinet minister), appointing Jean de Vaines, a glutton for work whom he met in Limoges, to replace the corrupt official dismissed along with Terray. He changes two of the six intendants of finance, who are largely responsible for perpetuating diffuse fiscal control: six undersecretaries, each with a separate staff and offices in Paris or Versailles, independently regulate the budget, public works, trade, industry, and the Mint. One of the two discharged intendants is Joseph-François Foullon,* an upper bourgeois from Saumur "with a soul of bronze," according to Terray; his sole achievement was to have set a record for robbing the till.

Turgot turned his attention to current problems. The question of where to build the new Théâtre des Comédiens Français could wait. On the other hand, he insisted on testing at once the "ice-breaking machine" designed by someone named Parcieux, a "floating harbor boom" anchored with chains in the center of the Marne to combat winter ice floes. People call it "Turgot's machine." If it keeps the river from freezing over, they can install it on the Seine to ensure year-round barge deliveries of wood and grain for the Paris community.[2]

Aside from administrative responsibilities, he is building a staff, "musketeers of a free economy," reliable mouthpieces for opinions he dares not express openly. To bridge the gap until Dupont arrives in November, he appoints the journalist Suard "historiographer of coinage," and, more significantly, Condorcet to help run the Mint, with the Abbé Morellet in charge of liaison. Only in their company can he relax, or on occasion with the select circle of admiring ladies who love Turgot all the more, knowing that he has no taste for conventional love: the Duchesse d'Anville, Julie de Lespinasse, and that odd creature Madame de Marchais, so tiny that her long hair all strewn with blossoms and feathers, like a river flooding its banks, streams down to the ground, half concealing her furrowed features.

So Condorcet suddenly shifts from theory to social practice. The change leaves him undismayed; he is used to mixing geometry with sentiment. He felt old when he turned thirty. Human progress was his great passion: "If the people had bread and justice, freely given, one could put up with everything else and patiently await the inevitable decline of superstition with all it produces or protects,"[3] he wrote to Turgot in 1770. And in 1771: "Not until now have I understood the misery of being poor, jobless, helpless. I used to hate the persecutors and the legal murderers: now one must also include bureaucrats! Heretofore I merely despised them."[4] Suddenly finding himself in charge of these bureaucrats, he resolves to keep them in tow. Beneath his cold, judicious features, "the snow-covered volcano" (as Julie de Lespinasse called him) is

*A victim of the Paris mob on July 22, 1789.

perpetually erupting. He badgers Turgot, who may have wanted him around for just that purpose. He entreats him not to imitate Colbert, but Turgot is quite different from Colbert, "who lived from day to day, with no other concern, in order to keep his place and enhance his prestige, than to provide Louis XIV with the means for indulging his extravagant tastes."[5] Even Condorcet bears grudges, warning Turgot to beware of old De Muy, minister of war, "one of the stupidest, most designing men in the kingdom";[6] of Maurepas, whose casual manner alarms him: "I am afraid this petty, narrow-minded man will cause us great trouble." But the worst trouble will be the priests. Condorcet can never forgive his mother for dedicating him to the church and eight years in a white robe. His long, stubborn silences stem from that resentment: "Watch out for the *dévots*!" [7] he repeatedly cautions Turgot, whose tolerant outlook worries him: "Try to lack sufficient virtue to be taken in by hypocrites."

To this plea Turgot retorts: "For once good old Condorcet has become a raging sheep."[8] The Abbé Morellet provided welcome relief from such intransigence: priest he was, but a priest of quietude, unpedantic and naïvely —almost pathetically—self-centered. Not at all bad at pamphleteering either, and anxious to square accounts with Galiani. This combative spirit led Morellet's friends to nickname him *"Mords-les."**

In the end, however, the changes must come from Turgot; everyone looks to him for the first major decision. At last he has reached the enviable station coveted by so many of his ancestors, generations of Norman nobles who had founded hospitals, battled intendants, run schools, and published daring thoughts. His father, the *prévôt des marchands*** of Paris who had set up such a fine plan for the capital, would have been happy to see Jacques-Robert attain such prominence. This and many other matters run through his mind during his first months in office when, despite admonishments from Condorcet and Julie de Lespinasse, he insists on imposing his own peculiar blend of flexibility and determination. Right from the start he offends the physiocrats, especially the elder Mirabeau, by refusing to apply their system. He maintains that "partisanship calls down hostility and persecution upon useful truths. When a single individual modestly advocates what he believes to be the truth, people will listen if he is right, and if he is wrong they will ignore him. But once educated people have formed a body and begun saying *we,* thinking to dictate public opinion, the public rightly rebels against accepting precepts other than the truth from some arbitrary authority. Any such body soon finds itself sustained by imbeciles, madmen, and ignorant fools proud of an affiliation which makes them feel important."[9]

*"Snapper." [*Trans.*]
**High municipal magistrate with jurisdiction over markets, contracts of apprenticeship, local commercial enterprises and the like. [*Trans.*]

The elder Mirabeau complains: "The arrogant rascals* surrounding Turgot, and, in my opinion, the most noxious breed of wicked men, are constantly attacking economists. They begin to sound like our enemies. This is just as I expected, for nothing alarmed me more than the public acclaim they received along with us."**[10]

On September 13 Turgot makes it plain to friend and foe alike that he knows what he wants: Louis XVI puts his signature on a decree restoring freedom to the domestic grain trade.

"A pound of dark bread costs four sous. Can a wretched journeyman earning only twelve sous a day feed his wife and six children? . . . Six pounds of bread come to twenty-four sous; he earns twelve."[11]

A notary thus pinpoints the overwhelming issue of the day: the production, distribution, and consumption of bread, dietary staple for three quarters of the French nation. The bread was usually black, of variable mixtures of rye, wheat, and other cereals depending on the region. Hence all the talk about "grain" rather than wheat. A loaf of bread ordinarily costing four sous was selling for between eight and sixteen. Wage laborers on the farms and in the cities earned from ten to twenty sous daily, but worked only 200 or 250 days a year. The gap between those two figures depicts the visceral anguish of ten to twelve million Frenchmen whose future was hopeless. Over the past twenty years the price of bread has risen faster than wages. Producers, meaning that multiform, elusive class of "property-owners," face the recurring dilemma of whether to export surplus crops to other parts of the country and abroad if the harvest is good, or to store them for next year and risk falling prices. A series of crop failures would cut off the local grain supply and necessitate importing it from remote areas at great expense. Diastole and systole: grain distribution in France resembles a malfunctioning circulatory system, under constant threat of a clot from frozen rivers, bad weather, or capricious policies of intendants and local parliaments. Rural communities waged a perpetual struggle for food, further complicated by arbitrary decisions of local authorities. People eyed outgoing grain shipments with instinctive apprehension, crying famine where there was yet no shortage. In March, at Tours, crowds looted cargo ships: "It is not the cost of wheat that provoked the riot, but fear of a new rise in the price of bread occasioned by the provisions seen moving off down the Loire."[12] When asked what they were doing, citizens of Tours replied: *"Monsieur, je nous révoltons!"* ["We protest!"]

Turgot is familiar with the persistent problem facing dealers, who want to distribute sufficient grain to meet popular demand but also want a reasona-

*He means the Encyclopedists.
**In fact the public mistakenly lumped physiocrats—or economists, as they were generally known in 1774—with the Encyclopedists. Because he opposed sectarianism and assumed no rigid posture, Turgot had more in common with the latter.

ble profit. Exponents of a planned economy and liberals have gone on jabbing at each other on this question; the Morellet-Galiani bout is just the latest episode. Economists, most of whom were rich landowners interested in selling in volume at high prices, have stoutly maintained that France can feed her own people with enough left over for export, and that grain should circulate freely from one province to the next. Their view nearly prevailed in Madame de Pompadour's day, when Quesnay* became her physician. But disorder swept the provinces: oversupplies of wheat in some districts, shortages in others. The countryside was up in arms for all sorts of reasons—rightly or wrongly, who could say? Terray reversed the trend, immobilizing the circulation of grain. "In their hearts people cherish the ancient rule that the harvest is meant chiefly for the district that bore it."[13] Thwarted, the physiocrats retired each to his own Bignon and waited. Eventually, Terray's efforts to regulate the grain supply were universally rejected, including the flour mills at Corbeil and Poissy's "central treasury," an enormous government-run granary for storing wheat against possible shortages in the Paris region. And what about those mysterious purchases ordered in the king's name, though surreptitiously, by obscure agents in Lyons and Bordeaux, in Tours and Beauvais? Was it a well-intentioned attempt to regulate the market, or a "monopolistic" conspiracy to wring profits from the plight of starving, impoverished Frenchmen?** Foullon, for one, and Terray himself made millions from it. Foolishly, the government concealed the positive face of its controls: the idiotic secrecy shrouding state operations under Louis XV had prompted provincial governors to arrest agents—who turned out to be working for Terray, buying up grain clandestinely for public use.

Since August 24 no one doubts that Turgot champions freedom—for mankind perhaps, for grain certainly. By September 13 he is through sharpening his quills, scribbling notes to himself, and dawdling, all of which are his customary preparations for writing. In his office on the Rue Neuve-des-Petits-Champs he holds out his hand, expecting torrents of grain to descend on the kingdom. Faith, not fact, moves him; there are no statistics on French productivity. Free trade is the gospel of 1774—either you believe in it or you don't. Confident that prices will rise, however, Turgot frames a fairly flexible edict extending the export ban and maintaining certain controls over reserve stores. He also introduces an excellent device for bridging the gap between wages and prices: public works. Whenever a "dearth of abundance" exists somewhere, it can be converted into abundant cheap labor. Famine transformed into roads, inland waterways, and new towns.[14]

*In addition to his medical qualification, François Quesnay (1694–1774) was an economist, founder of the physiocratic school. [Trans.]
**After 1789 this gives rise to claims (all mythical) of a "starvation pact" between Louis XV and certain speculators aimed at swelling the royal treasury.

His approach, unlike Terray's, is completely open and aboveboard. Everything is clearly articulated, step by step. This explains the need for good writers—Condorcet, Morellet, and Dupont—in a finance ministry. Turgot has one other creed, stronger even than his faith in economic freedom: he believes in the power of men to convert their fellow men. "Sooner or later, the knowledge and understanding which men of letters can shed will destroy all artificial blights on the human race and teach mankind to enjoy the good things in nature."[15] His ordinance covers two pages; the preamble, twelve.

. . . Meanwhile, the Duc de Croy, pillar of the Catholic Church, records in his diary this reaction to Turgot's appointment: "It was, although mute and without fanfare, the hardest blow to religion perhaps since the time of Clovis."[16]

POPE CLEMENT XIV

25

SEPTEMBER 1774

He Savored His Own Death

The pope is dying, the one who suppressed the Society of Jesus. What a string of names for so small a man: Giovanni Vicenzo Antonio Ganganelli, son of the local "surgeon" (who tripled as barber and apothecary) of San Arcangelo in the Romagna district not far from Rimini; to the religious community he was Brother Francesco Lorenzo Maria in the "Conventual Franciscans" of Rome's monastery of the Holy Apostle;* and for the past five years His Holiness Clement XIV. This papal designation had not taken hold, however, and people continued to call him by his family name. "Ordinarily one rarely knows the names of sovereign pontiffs. One is familiar with them only by the name they assumed at the time of their exaltation [that is, their election]; but out among the people, out in the countryside, everyone knew that this pope was named Ganganelli."[1]

His (relative) popularity stemmed mainly from the fact that he was the first pope in ages not to come from one of the aristocratic dynasties which had expropriated the Holy See. Italian peasants and cobblers now could dream of their own sons mounting the papal throne. But his cruel death may give them pause: nearly six months of agony.

*The Franciscans had split into two major branches: "Conventuals," entitled to possess property of their own, and "Observants," obedient still to the rule of poverty.

What is killing Clement XIV? Poison? Or remorse for having outlawed the Jesuits? The Roman public remains divided on the issue, endlessly fascinated by this death in slow motion, the summer's main attraction. Not for a moment does anyone believe the pope is dying of natural causes, of a general skin disorder, "a herpetic disease attacking the inside of the mouth and throat glands."[2] Until then he had never been sick a day in his life; he radiated monastic well-being, stimulated by the blissful joys of consummated ambition. Why in heaven's name would the Jesuits risk poisoning him *now?* They are extinguished; the damage is done. Remorse? He feigned it to some degree the year before in issuing his brief *Dominus ac Redemptor.* With eyes probing the heavens, with pen and voice all aquiver: *"Questa supressione mi darà la morte . . . "* ("This suppression will be the death of me"). Among those witnessing this surrender to temporal power—perhaps the most abject surrender in papal history[3]—stood a handful of Jesuit sympathizers. It could do no harm to melt their hostility. Actually, he was well satisfied with himself, having done precisely what he set out to do. To that alone he owed his election. Anyway, who would expect a Franciscan to be truly conscience-stricken about the Jesuits? At last, after two centuries of global struggle, he had raised one order to victory over the other.

But no sooner had the word *morte* left his lips than it proceeded to wheel above his head like a buzzard. Though in the pink of health, he had summoned an evil omen—and in Rome this spells trouble. Other voices tossed the word about; unknown hands scrawled it on the walls of the Quirinal and the Lateran. In March, Ganganelli began noticing a set of impudent initials here and there in his travels: I.S.S.S.V. *In Settembre Sara Sede Vacante* (In September the throne will be vacant). Bernardina Baruzzi, a visionary in Valentano, took to trumpeting the same prophecy—divinely revealed, she assured—that heaven's wrath would descend upon the butcher of Christ's soldiers.[4] Though he bore all this stoically, Clement's temper began to fray. Behind him lay the best winter of his whole life, the result of having finally made that crucial decision. He was only sixty-nine. In 1775 he would preside over Holy Year celebrations and, with all Christendom looking on, make his regal entrance through the bricked-up and then torn-down portals of St. Peter's, transformed for the occasion into a symbolic Jerusalem. What was all this nonsense about death and repentance? "His health is superb and he is more cheerful than usual,"[5] reported Bernis, the French ambassador, after trading off Avignon for Jesuit hides. And Naples gave back Benevento.* Even now Clement walked in the footsteps of his hero, Sixtus V.

A warning, plain as could be, came on March 25 during the procession taking him to the Dominican monastery of Santa Maria della Minerva for the Feast of the Annunciation, when the glowering sky suddenly unleashed a

---

*In 1806 Napoleon appropriated this Campanian town from the Holy See and awarded it to Talleyrand with the title Prince of Benevento. [*Trans.*]

downpour, sending *porporati* (cardinals in long scarlet robes), *monsignori* (ordinary priests in a variety of colors), and their cavalry escort scurrying for cover. Smiling a sickly smile, His Holiness rode on, reaching the monastery virtually unattended and soaking wet. Added proof of his excellent health, right? Then why had people stared at him in fear or pity? He tended to panic. Instead of fasting on Holy Thursday, he indulged in a meal of chicken and gave the skin to his pet dog—who refused to touch it. Why? Ganganelli had felt a burning sensation in his stomach, chills along his spine. Shivers, distress. Nothing to worry about. Summertime would cure all that. He went off privately "to take depurative waters." On his return, everyone searched his face for signs. They were laying odds on his death or survival even before he fell ill. He could read their eyes and knew what they were thinking. By May "he was down to half his normal size, and his complexion, always dusky and a bit ruddy to begin with, had turned positively green."[6] Halting gait; stumbling speech; he had come around to their view. If he had been poisoned, it had been by the look in their eyes.

By August death stood waiting in the wings of the Quirinal Palace, where braziers smoldered day and night to keep him warm.* He shivered and shook while the palace baked like an oven in the Roman sun, yet it was the only bearable spot in the city, atop Monte Cavallo, traditional refuge of the popes "owing to its wholesome air." The windows, however, were kept shut. No longer did he stroll in the gardens designed by Le Nôtre; his legs would buckle. An inflamed throat caused his mouth to sag. He stuttered. He vomited.

Madness began to overtake him. He was dying because others had predicted his death. He imagined vials of poison, daggers, and nooses, all because others supposed a crime. He insulted his servants, leaped from his chair to prepare his own polenta, and in the end, having made a show of repentance, he felt it. He imagined himself damned. "Ghosts pursued him in his sleep; in the silence of the night he would kneel before a miniature of the Virgin detached from his prayerbook, in front of which, for the past forty years, two tapers burned night and day."[7] Yet he managed to recover his senses enough to put off the Archbishop of Bologna, who had forced his way to the pope's bedside to inquire if His Holiness desired to receive the sacraments.

"There is no hurry. I have already made confession and taken holy communion. I do not believe the end is so near."

Archbishop Malvezzi bent over the small, crafty face. Beneath its balding temples and thick brows, a pair of sharp, furtive eyes peered out like hunted rats. He protested roundly: no pope should die without the last rites—especially a pope who had outlawed the Jesuits. "Everyone would call it divine retribution."[8] On September 10 comes the announcement that His Holiness has received extreme unction "in the presence of cardinals and generals of

_____
*Or perhaps to induce heavy sweating—a sure cure for eliminating poisons, according to the pope's medicine men.

religious orders, his tranquillity and resignation doubly admirable because, in the words of St. Bernard, he savored his own death."[9]

For twelve more days he hung on, wearing everyone out. Having marked him for death three months earlier, Romans were astonished to find him still there. The prospective conclave aroused great excitement. A change of popes was the one event that could stir this city of cities, rooted in an ancient dream of stones and trailing weeds that Piranesi was then recording in his sketchbooks: churches rising from temple ruins, laundry strung between tottering pillars, a cypress pushing its way up among the paving stones flanking a baptistry. A living corpse two thousand years old. Who would become its new master? Question put by the ragpickers of Monte Giordano to the tinkers in the Piazza Navona, by the gilders of Vicolo del Fico to the mattress-makers of San Pantaleo. Agitation in the great wine and fruit storerooms at Ripa Grande, provisioned by buffalo-towed barges plying the Tiber. Craftsmen work outdoors in the narrow alleys, and gossip quickly reaches all 160,000 inhabitants.[10] No bourgeoisie is there to shroud or shape it, no middle class dividing the common people—handsome young men, pretty girls, robust, untutored, gesticulating, superstitious, and docile—from the fifteen or twenty leading families who run the city and create popes in the salons of their sumptuous palaces, unless it is the armies of black-and-white priests scuttling about (at least thirty thousand strong), whose priestliness no one can warrant, least of all themselves. Words or spectacle convey everything there is to know, especially the news. In place of news sheets there is an invincible satiric weapon with hosts of editors: Pasquino's statue, a damaged, pug-nosed marble bust standing on a street corner, the pedestal of which carries daily messages that no one dares utter aloud.

Master Pasquino* has a lot on his mind these days. Butchers, fishermen, bargemen, carters, tanners, shopkeepers, weavers, and laundresses mill about him, waiting for someone able to read and comment on the merciless inscriptions about Ganganelli. Rome has never cherished losers, and death is a loss no Roman can abide. Being a commoner, Clement XIV, unlike his predecessors, did not enrich or exalt his family. What of it? Instead, he installed at court two wretches, Father Bontempi (who whispers it about that the Jesuits have poisoned him) and a certain Nicholas Bischi. Now Bischi's wife, Victoria, seems to have spent much of her time, rather cozily too, with Father Bontempi —who knows, maybe even with the pope himself? Pasquino rails at this:

> E Roma soffre, e Roma può tacere?
> Ah tempi infausti! E che mancan le corde,
> Le fruste, forche, ergastoli e galere?

*The name probably derives from an acid-tongued tailor living on the Via Parione at the end of the fifteenth century.

[Rome suffers; can she be silent?
Oh, woeful times! Are there no ropes,
No lashes, gibbets, dungeons, or galleys?]

Rumors have spread so rapidly of late that Rome's governor grows alarmed and doubles the watch on all bridges. Rolling in with the tide of gossip comes the name of a Jewish banker, Coen, who has just spent a fortune buying up grain. A sensible precaution to meet the future needs of Holy Year pilgrims, or speculation on the part "of an extortionist commended to the pope as the world's most honest man, and who, secretly, took care to make his fortune at public expense"?[11] In any event, Ganganelli suddenly looms as the symbol of impending starvation; the populace grows restless in Rome and throughout the vast lozenge-shaped expanse of papal states dividing Italy in two, from the Tyrrhenian Sea up to Ancona and over to Venice via Ferrara. The hybrid agglomerate comprising "Peter's patrimony," this "miserable property" dependent on priests and police to hold it together, is Europe's worst example of underdevelopment, with its rundown roads, its noxious marshes, its fields lying fallow.[12] The people are hungry this summer, very hungry; in Rome there is even famine. Will there be riots like those of 1773 when the mob sacked Ripa Grande and looked for cardinals to hang? Things would calm down if only the pope would die; conclaves never fail to distract the crowd. What is Ganganelli waiting for?

He lies shriveled up on his deathbed. At peace. Now and then he hears prayers. He has always believed in God, or at least "the supreme being," and in the saints rather than Christ, whose name he rarely uttered once he had suppressed Catholicism's strongest pillar, the Jesuits, the only order still implementing its original vows to carry St. Peter's teachings throughout the world. He had sawed off the very branch on which papal supremacy rested. All because the Christian rulers of France, Spain, Portugal, and Naples had had their fill of these modern Templars of ultramontanism, these teachers who secretly instructed children to obey another master, and who all too often, right in the classroom, reminded their charges that "the Lamb is above any race, any nation, any tongue." Ganganelli had chosen between them and the secular powers. In the last conclave he had committed himself to destroy the Jesuits in exchange for the papal throne.[13] So, on July 21, 1773 . . . Do echoes of his decree *Dominus ac Redemptor* flit through his mind while "his bones exfoliate and diminish like a tree with its roots eaten away, that withers and sheds its bark"?[14] He has exfoliated the Catholic Church, his universe, reduced it, subjugated it to powerful rulers. Yet those rulers did not need him to outlaw and persecute Jesuits in their own kingdoms; they needed merely the justification for doing so. His consent. The right words from the pope would prevent Jesuits from becoming martyrs. He had earned his election. They called him "the sovereigns' pope." He had written (or simply affixed his signature—not that it matters when one has sole responsibility): "Our beloved sons in Jesus Christ, kings of France, Spain, Portugal, and the Two Sicilies, were forced to banish and expel from their kingdoms, states, and provinces all priests of this order, convinced that it was the only way to undo so many wrongs and to prevent Christians from offending each other . . ." His conclusion, as merciless as the sanies corroding his bones and flesh: "After mature consideration, out of certain knowledge and the abundance of our apostolic authority, we suppress and we abolish the Society of Jesus; we eliminate and we abrogate all and each of its offices, functions, and administrations, establishments, primary and secondary schools, retreats, almshouses, and all other places over which its authority extends in any manner, in whatever province, kingdom, or state they may be situated, all its statutes, customs, practices, decrees, constitutions, even if ratified by oath and by approval of the Holy See or otherwise."*

Christian education in Europe thus was deprived of eight hundred schools and fifteen hundred teachers, the best. Asian and South American missions hardly existed any longer. Adding his enthusiastic applause, Voltaire declared: "In twenty years there will be no more Catholic Church!"[15]

His Holiness Clement XIV expires on the morning of September 22, 1774, between seven and eight o'clock. "Artful hands summoned to embalm him found a pale, ghastly corpse with blackened lips, swollen belly, and withered limbs flecked with purple blotches. The size of his heart was manifestly shrunken; the tissues all along his spinal column were detached and decayed. Despite quantities of aromatics and perfume pumped into his body, it continued to reek. Clement's entrails burst the vessel containing them. When his pontifical garments were removed, there were strips of peeled-off flesh still clinging to them. His scalp lay intact upon the velvet cushion beneath his head; a slight jar caused all his nails to drop off one by one."[16]

The news reaches Paris on October 1. The Abbé de Véri and most churchmen welcome the event: "It will be of great cheer to Rome, a relief to imprisoned Jesuits, a boon to the papal states, and a minor loss to the church. Ganganelli's pontificate was unpleasant for him through no one's fault but his own. He made trouble for himself because of his distrustful, secretive, despotic, unbending, and excessively cunning temperament. His tactics in attaining a cardinalate and the papacy were singularly shrewd, but his administration as church leader and temporal ruler was a succession of blunders."[17]

Two years earlier, when Orthodox Catherine of Russia and Protestant Frederick of Prussia had united to dismember Catholic Poland, he never breathed a word to the empress either publicly or privately. Silent Ganganelli now is forever the prisoner of silence.

*Extract from the brief *Dominus ac Redemptor.*

26

Who Gives a Damn Now or Ever?

For Turgot and his aides, the main concern this autumn was the grain issue. Seven out of ten Frenchmen had to agree, not knowing how they were going to feed themselves from one month to the next. But court circles worried only about recalling the parliaments. Nothing else mattered.

The final uncertainty of this new reign: would Louis XVI recall the parliaments or not? There was no doubt that Maupeou's dismissal made recall almost inevitable. Still the king hung back. Like the public, he assumed—somewhat arbitrarily—that the old magistrates espoused Choiseul, having been discharged shortly after the duke himself was turned out. The king preferred the "new" men, greenhorns recruited by Maupeou as much for their compliance as for their political reliability. You knew what to expect from them. No trace of Encyclopedist curiosity. Some even sympathized with the Jesuits, whom his father revered.

For two months the matter hung in limbo, just as when His Majesty had been unable to make up his mind about dismissing his ministers. None of the judiciary—neither exiled judges nor their replacements—knew what to expect next.

Meanwhile four men had made a practice of closeting themselves secretly with Louis XVI: Maurepas, Miromesnil, Sartines, and Turgot. They constituted a kind of supreme council in which major policies were arrived at and the king was made to feel that he alone had evolved them. The court anticipated that a decision on the parliaments would emerge from these conferences, which Véri invisibly controlled through Maurepas: "The object was to persuade the king that the outcome would be his own achievement, encouraging him thus to inject the zeal and interest appropriate to operations of this nature. Determination, persistent and manifest, on the master's part is the true incentive for settling domestic problems. He must really possess it and not merely the appearance of it . . . This system had the desired effect of making him regard the adopted plan as his own."[1]

Meaning recall. This is clearly the case after October 15, when His

Majesty offers a cold reception to the "new" presiding magistrates who come
to pay their respects, while exiled judges, their ears to the ground, begin
returning to the capital from their estates without fear of breaking their bans.
Maurepas favored this; his oldest friends were former magistrates. Miromesnil
also. Slightly more cautious, Sartines merely wanted to join the winning side
early in the game—a freethinker with no love for the church party. As for
Turgot, he was totally absorbed in liberating the grain trade and paid scant
attention to the dispute. Let his friends argue it out: Condorcet fiercely anti-
parliament; Malesherbes fiercely pro, as might be expected, having presided
over the former Cour des Aides*—and because blind devotion to the English
system of parliamentary debate made him receptive to any type of assembly.
"Malesherbes is fond of organized bodies no matter how contemptible they
may be, from the imperial diet, the Polish diet, the French clergy, and the
English Commons on down to the the white- or blue-robed Penitents," Condorcet complained.[2]

The issue is serious, as Condorcet knows, for Turgot will be the first to
feel the degree of resistance or compliance of the reinstated parliaments. He
will adopt new measures, attack privilege. He intends to give France a taste
of the enlightened despotism now pervading Europe. But the law courts of
Catherine, Frederick, and Joseph II do not presume to dilute their rulers'
decisions, and Gustavus III has found ways to hold his own judiciary in check.
Louis XV had installed a device to simplify his rule; why not use it now to bring
about reform? Those gentlemen of the robe, a thousand strong, about to be
reinstated as a buffer between the people and the government, constitute an
aristocracy of wealth blindly devoted to perpetuating the status quo. Courts
of fear. But Turgot sees them differently; he is so keen on discussion and
explanation, so intolerant of tyranny, that he insists on reform by persuasion
and refuses to be put off. He favors recall, the same position adopted by the
king under concerted pressure from all his chief councillors except Vergennes,
from princes of the blood, and from the public. Louis XVI wants to win
popularity before the year's end, especially with Parisians. But the capital's
rejoicing over Maupeou's dismissal had turned to bitter denunciations of the
new crop of lawyers taking over the courts. Crowds near the Palace of Justice
hurled a projectile at a man named Bouteille, tax-exempt member of the legal
profession though not even a nobleman, whom someone proposed discharging. He died. When an arrest was made, a mob of eight hundred assaulted the
court president's mansion. Guards patrolled the Palace of Justice after that.
People called them "custodians of the tomb." "They await the resurrection.
Guardians of the peace and commoners laugh and drink together. For ordinary folk, it is a unique sight."[3] Parisians unconsciously associated rising bread

*Administrative court originally intended to enforce the allocation of taxes. Its function was to
interpret fiscal edicts, to examine and protest expenditures of the royal household. "The Cour des
Aides is responsible for hearing most litigations involving tax collection" (Véri).

prices with the presence of gowned and bewigged intruders who had never been welcome in the Ile-de-la-Cité. The same spirit prevailed that had prompted the posting in 1771 of a conspicuous sign next to the roster of lawyers and their charges: "Who gives a damn now or ever? Get out for good."[4]

Working men from the faubourgs and peasants with no use for lawyers heard gossip and began hoping that some good might come from the reinstatement of magistrates who had never done a thing for them. An official decision to recall the parliaments had been reached, though not one Frenchman in a hundred could say what their function was. The Abbé de Véri himself finds it difficult "to explain the precise and rational aim of these bodies. They were set in motion on petty occasions of no significance to the state. They sold their silence to the king in matters of taxation, the rights of the people, and the citizens' welfare. Yet they have made it a practice to cite the public interest in rejecting corporate privileges, personal jurisdictions, and private grudges."[5]

In any event, they are on their way back. It was inevitable. That's the way things are and there's no point discussing it. On November 11, proud of having decided an important issue "all by himself," Louis XVI faces the four men who brought him to that decision and rehearses the brief speech he will deliver the next day. Three sentences that cause them much concern, for it is to be His Majesty's maiden address. Will he stammer like Louis XV, whose morbid timidity paralyzed his delivery? Maurepas marks the rhythm with one hand:

"Too fast, Sire, too fast. We could not hear you clearly."

"If only I had the ease and dignity of my brother Provence, it would be marvelous. He would manage it beautifully, before the Great Council. But I mumble and won't be half so effective."[6]

The fateful day, November 12, dawns dismally gray; it is the feast of St. René. The king and princes have spent the night at La Muette to be near Paris. Promptly at 7:30 a flurry of colorful silhouettes pierces the mist, putting an end to the night. The royal procession tramples the autumn leaves on its way through Passy and the Cours de la Reine as if scattering to the winds every last reminder of Louis XV. Meanwhile a bomb scare sows panic in the Palace of Justice when Maurepas receives an anonymous warning that the premises have been mined. A likely story, he thinks, but alerts the watch all the same; a patrol with architect guides combs the cellars by torchlight, haunted by fear of another Gunpowder Plot.* They visualize Louis XVI, his brothers, cousins, ministers, and magistrates blown to bits. A Spanish prince inheriting the

---

*In 1605 Catholic conspirators secretly stored thirty-six barrels of gunpowder beneath the floor of London's Houses of Parliament and nearly succeeded in pulverizing James I and his government.

French throne . . . Not a speck of powder is found. The comic interlude turns out to have been a spiteful trick played by the political underdogs of the day.

These underdogs are assembled across the river at the Louvre, penned up for the crowd to jeer at in the Queen's Pavilion, where they will constitute a "Great Council," without any specific duties, and attempt to save face—not to mention their jobs. In gloomy impatience they await the king's brother, whose arrival follows a *lit de justice** restoring to them most prerogatives of the old Parliament of Paris, with one or two minor restrictions intended by Malesherbes to reduce frictions that had brought the machine to a halt five years earlier.

The returnees pay scant attention to this. In the Palace of Justice, a visual feast of red, black, blue, and gold in the great hall, which seems dwarfed by the multitude of robed figures seated on tiered benches, facing each other in a square: a mass of fleecy wigs with side curls, punctuated by the broad hats of the princes, the galaxy of decorations studding the king's chest as well as those of his brothers, the princes of Orléans, Conti, and Condé, for whom this is also a day of reckoning. Flickering tapers dispel the grayness, casting light down from the coffered ceiling. Sumptuous tapestries cover the walls, their bright colors adding warmth to the scene. A *lit de justice* is indeed one of the dazzling spectacles of the monarchy.

The "bed" is there, a heap of cushions embroidered with fleurs-de-lis upon which repose the elbows, feet, and haunches of His Majesty, in sparkling regalia befitting "the living sun of justice" who "dims the radiance of inferior celestial bodies"[7]—meaning that he is justice incarnate, God descended among the scribes to make their pens gallop: a ritual of obeisance, a liturgy of submission, each step as narrowly defined as those of a bonze or a talapoin. At the king's feet, his grand chamberlain; at the base of the throne, the master of the horse, the four captains of the royal guard, the commander of the Swiss Guards, and the *prévôt de Paris*** with his long white staff. The ceremony has not changed since the time of St. Louis except to become more artificial: three hundred years ago everyone gave his opinion aloud, after which the king decreed the law. Now, the chancellor passes among the members, polling each in a whisper, but the sovereign is free to ignore their sentiments. Miromesnil, "keeper of the seals and acting chancellor," performs this pantomime in lieu of the conspicuously absent Maupeou. Aiguillon, sitting among the peers of the realm, looks proud and determined.

The entire performance—two hours of whispering, bowing, and scraping —ends the instant a seated, nervous young man, the one member still wearing his hat, addresses the assembly in words intended to make history:

*Literally, "bed of justice," a solemn court session presided over by the king. [*Trans.*]
**An office not to be confused with that of the *prévôt des marchands*, who acted as mayor of the capital. The *prévôt de Paris* was head magistrate in charge of the Châtelet district with authority to issue decrees in its name.

"Gentlemen, the king, my highly esteemed lord and ancestor, driven by your repeated defiance of his commands, acted to uphold his authority and to carry out his duty to dispense justice to his subjects. I recall you today to functions which you ought never to have resigned. Be grateful for my charity and do not forget it."

To everyone's surprise, Louis XVI "comes across well" with this peevish schoolmaster's admonition lifting a collective sanction. The Swedish ambassador observes: "The king spoke in earnest, emphatic tones, stressing his final syllables and lending expression to each phrase. His resolute discourse impressed everyone."[8] Myopia came to his aid: unable to distinguish the faces around him, he was carried away by the churchlike setting and fancied himself a high priest. He is timid only in personal contacts on a one-to-one basis, not in public situations.

But sensitive ears discern the jarring note. "Be grateful for my charity" shocks even the Abbé de Véri, who writes: "It seems to me that this expression gives the sovereign a false notion of his authority. There are certain types of favors, like positions at court, which a ruler grants out of generosity. But his other relations with citizens can never be regarded by him as charity. They are his rightful duties. He cannot reward or punish, make laws, levy or abolish taxes unless based upon lawful principles, never upon the principle of charity." Malesherbes, however, will not come out and say so to the king's face when His Majesty formally reinstates the Cour des Aides, choosing merely to flatter him: "Yours, Sire, will be the reign of justice . . . After eight centuries of struggle and glory, it is time to achieve peace and contentment. That time is come, Sire, when wiser men understand that the virtues they ought to revere are the virtues of peace, benevolence, and justice above all, which is the true benevolence of kings. We awaited a lawgiver . . . "[9]

The feeble impact of this skirmish is lost in the universal chorus of acclamation accompanied by jibes from reinstated judicial officers at the "new ancients." Nineteen-year-old Jean-Jacques Duval d'Esprésmesnil, a "returning" lawyer who already calls himself a victim of persecution, roundly denounces those "traitors" sitting in the Châtelet,* some of whom are four times his age: "Gentlemen, meet some magistrates whose exile, perhaps unwittingly, you may have prolonged. The only vengeance they seek is to secure your position insofar as it depends on them, and all they ask of you is to emulate when necessary . . . their courage and perseverance and to instill those qualities in your children."[10] The echo rebounds from all corners of France, especially Aix, where Archbishop Boisgelin exults in the reopening of Provence's Parliament: "At last we see an end to the dispersion of the courts, the banishment of magistrates, and to this astounding revolution [sic] which seemed to have swept away like a torrent the entire judicial system! Thus,

*The Châtelet fortress (demolished in 1802) guarding the Pont au Change was the seat of criminal jurisdiction for the Paris district. [*Trans.*]

when all has surrendered to sovereign authority, public opinion remains, and prevails on that authority, never yielding to it . . . Respectable citizens have been observed growing secretly alarmed over the country's welfare. What is happening, they asked, to the sacred laws of property?* . . . Now let them learn to recognize the mild and pleasant government of an enlightened nation, and how a rushing river may peacefully reverse its flow, obeying the necessity to return to its natural course."[11]

Beaumarchais is jubilant. He counts on "not remaining the victim of the wretched parliament you have lately buried beneath the rubble of its dishonor," as he describes it in a letter to Sartines on November 15, just before embarking on his new career of spying for the throne in the salons: "I promised to keep you advised of what the princes are thinking: I dine tomorrow night with M. le Duc de Chartres and thus far have seen only M. le Prince de Conti . . . ."[12]

. . . But Condorcet is as depressed now as he was optimistic in September. The breach widens between himself and Turgot, whom he berates:

> All legal reform is impossible since our laws are excellent for those presiding at the bar and reprehensible for those brought before it . . . A profitable financial operation becomes impossible and an ill-advised one doubly ruinous when you include the price of those gentlemen's silence . . . [They] have the same ideas held by fools in the sixteenth century . . . They scorn all understanding, all philosophy, and being puffed up with pride equal to their ignorance, they will oppose enlightenment, persecute its sources, and try to plunge us back into barbarism . . . What is really hostile to the public interest is to allow a band of murderers to sit in judgment over the lives of citizens, when such murderers murdered the Chevalier de La Barre . . . They murdered Moriceau the *huissier* for criticizing them, and Ringuet the priest for calling Damiens a Jansenist. They murdered Lalli** for the sheer pleasure of humiliating the nobility of the sword . . .
>
> . . . Farewell,† sir, I cannot bear the idea that you are now a minister and that good becomes impossible; the more I expect from you, the more this idea torments me. Love me always, and if France ever is in a desperate state, save a corner of the colonies for me.[13]

The queen has observed this episode like a disinterested spectator. For the moment, she resists promoting Choiseul. On advice from Maria Theresa, she has silenced the gossip about Vergennes among her attendants and allowed his wife to be presented at court; to Turgot she is polite but distant. Other things are on her mind: she would use the transition from dauphine to queen to create a freer life for herself—having young persons around her, especially young

---

*The possession of offices is meant. Even at this point, the sanctity of the almighty franc outweighs the sanctity of anointed monarchs in the eyes of the parliamentary bourgeoisie.

**Baron de Lally-Tollendal. [*Trans.*]

†Conventional way to end a letter, neither dramatic nor indicative of a break-off in relations.

men, and no more dowagers . . . Ségur, a pompous ass whose pedigree assures him access to the queen, later recorded this demi-warfare: "Thus began to emerge, between the old and the new courts, the same rivalries and antagonisms which led from the first petty verbal skirmishes to those terrible ordeals that have since changed the world . . . The opening contest pitting old courtiers against new entailed an effort on our part to revive the dress, customs, and diversions of the courts of Francis I, Henry II, Henry III, and Henry IV. Before long we persuaded the king's brothers, Monsieur and the Comte d'Artois, to adopt those ideas . . . We encountered at once such remarkable success that the revolution in manners nearly swept the field."[14] Are we about to find Louis XVI sporting a ruff and Marie Antoinette a coif? Devastating "revolution" when the young devote themselves to resurrecting the fashions of another day. The king himself seems quite taken with the campaign. Marie Antoinette reports to her mother: "Before coming here, * we spent five days at Choisy. The king was in fine fettle, extremely polite to everyone, especially the ladies, to whom he paid more attention than one would expect from his upbringing."[15] Before long the gossips are saying that Louis XVI might even take a mistress—imagine that! A first affair! Another "revolution" in the making, as they see it. But the king's own remark puts an end to these fantasies: "M. le Duc d'Aumont, gentleman-in-waiting, asked him, according to custom, which lords His Majesty desired to accompany him on his journey.** " 'Put whomever you like on the list,' replied the monarch. 'It's all the same to me provided they are over thirty; I'm tired of looking at young men.' "[16] Goodby, plumes, petticoat breeches, mid-calf turn-down boots. Nothing will change for the present, even by turning the clocks back. Nor will icebound etiquette give way. "The queen has not yet managed to modify court ritual and permit men to dine with the royal princesses . . . When one of her ladies urged her to prevail upon her husband: 'What can you expect,' she retorted sharply, 'from a block of wood?' "[17]

Benevolence? Justice? One wonders sometimes how the "block of wood" himself interprets the lofty words that others put in his mouth or trumpet in his ears. "Having encountered on his way to Fontainebleau a woman blazing with diamonds, the king took her for one of the court ladies and greeted her with due respect. It should be observed that His Majesty is extremely nearsighted. Informed subsequently that she was merely one of the queen's women in waiting, this august spouse rebuked Her Majesty, declaring that as he no longer cared to let subordinates assume the footing of ladies of rank, he commanded that when on duty they must wear short aprons to single them out and identify their function."[18]

---

*Fontainebleau, where the court spent the last of autumn, the sixth château in six months for the young couple.

**Another brief escapade of his, at Choisy.

27

FEBRUARY 1775

If What They Say Is True

The search is on for Donatien-Aldonse*-François, the Marquis de Sade, born June 2, 1740, baptized on the 3rd in the parish church of Saint-Sulpice in Paris, son of the high and mighty Comte de Sade (deceased) and the noble Lady Marie-Eléonore de Maillé, former attendant to the Princesse de Condé. Every district throughout France, Navarre, Savoy, and Piedmont has been alerted to arrest and imprison him on sight. More than two years earlier, on September 11, 1772, the second criminal court of Aix-en-Provence's Parliament sentenced him to death *in absentia* "for the crime of poisoning and sodomy." He was already in flight. In the Place des Prêcheurs in Aix he was beheaded and burned in effigy. Arrested at Chambéry on December 8, 1772, by agents of the King of Sardinia; imprisoned in the fortress of Miolans, "Bastille of the dukes of Savoy," overlooking Saint-Pierre d'Albigny; escaped on April 30, 1773, and has been scurrying ever since all over France and Spain.[1]

Description: five feet three inches [five feet six inches on the modern scale, average height for those times], blond or light chestnut hair "gathered in a bag," "rather stout" of build, fair complexion slightly pitted by smallpox but with "attractive features," regular nose, small mouth, pale-blue eyes, high forehead, rounded chin, "well turned out" and usually in possession of a walking stick. The search also extends to his "familiar," Latour, valet and inseparable companion of his pleasures and escapades, like himself condemned to death and burned in effigy, taller, with hair worn loose, and similarly pockmarked.

These two men are dangerous. Reports say they are capable of murdering —namely by poison, bludgeoning, or sexual mutilation—any adolescent girl or boy, or any woman who falls into their clutches.

Actually, the "search" proves sporadic and limp. No efficient police system operates outside Paris, for provincial law enforcement is just beginning to adopt the organization installed by Sartines. There is a *lieutenance général* in

---

*Aldonse was an ancient Provençal name, so unfamiliar north of the Durance that people constantly transformed it into Alphonse in Sade's case, even on his birth certificate.

"each locality under royal jurisdiction" composed of a handful of petty administrators and tax-exempt officials; rarely do these bodies consult each other, being more interested in handling local matters than in working cooperatively, licensed to hunt in neighboring districts for their own offenders. And if they stir up no fresh scandals, these offenders can live peacefully in Bordeaux while Marseilles turns itself inside out hunting for them. Which is precisely what Sade has been doing all summer. But Sade courted disaster by seeking refuge in his Provençal estate at La Coste, where, instead of living quietly with his wife, he embarked on a singularly active winter in the company of five teen-age girls recruited in Lyons, a boy "secretary" of fifteen, and two or three riper prostitutes. The dubious reputation already attached to the Sade name from Marseilles to Lyons made it necessary to assure the "secretary's" parents that there were several branches of the family, in Eyguières, Saumane, and Tarascon, and they were not entrusting their son to the one who . . . [2]

Who *what?* When Inspector Goupil of the Paris police came poking around La Coste on a futile investigation in January 1774, what sort of information could he find in the "Sade dossier"?

Ancient noble blood. Flocks of ancestors with impeccable credentials dating back to the thirteenth century and beyond, including Petrarch's Laura. Because of their long-established roots in the south, the Sades were frequently called on to serve the popes in Comtat Venaissin.* Numerous relatives among the Provençal aristocracy, not the least distinguished of whom were the Mirabeaus. Donatien-Aldonse and Gabriel-Honoré were distant cousins, but virtual strangers.

Parents? A soldier and diplomat father who wound up his career as *lieutenant général* for the provinces of Bresse, Bugey, Valromey, and Gex. He had married a young girl as aristocratic as himself, related to the Richelieus and Condés through the Maillé-Brézés; in a crisis she can still ask a favor of the Condés. Upon her husband's death she took lodgings with the Carmelite nuns on the Rue d'Enfer in Paris. Donatien-Aldonse is their only child.[3] A dozen uncles and aunts, most of them in holy orders, are in no position to help him, except the Abbé de Sade with his rich benefices, now retired to Saumane in Provence, where he divides his time between courting the ladies (in verse or in the flesh) and scholarly pursuits.

Family fortune? "Adequate." Estates, châteaux, farm rents; the Comte de Sade had paid 135,000 livres for his lucrative office in Bresse.**

Childhood and adolescence? Nothing extraordinary about them save the luck of belonging to the privileged caste. He was born in the Hôtel de Condé.† His earliest education, petting and coddling by grandmother and

---

*A papal territory, along with Avignon, from 1274 to 1791. [*Trans.*]

**About 600,000 modern francs [$120,000].   †On the site of what was soon to become the Théâtre Français (subsequently the Odéon) and the streets radiating out from it.

aunts in Provence. Basic skills taught him by the Abbé de Sade, without much stress on religion. At ten, a day pupil at the Louis-le-Grand high school in Paris, still a Jesuit institution at that time. No punishments, no prizes. At fourteen, the preparatory academy for entrance to the cavalry, open to boys of "the oldest nobility," on the Avenue de Sceaux in Versailles.

Military career? Second lieutenant at fifteen. Captain at nineteen in the Bourgogne cavalry regiment. Three Prussian campaigns. Courage under fire but no exceptional exploits. The usual, more or less conventional, scrapes of a young officer sowing his oats for months on end during the Paris winter: gambling, women, and debts. His parents paid. After the war's end, return to civilian life until the army recalls him.

Marriage? Arranged between Donatien-Aldonse and Renée-Pélagie de Launay, daughter of the lord of Montreuil and former president of the Cour des Aides. Wed in the Church of Saint-Roch in Paris on May 17, 1763. A misalliance, for the Launays of Montreuil have purchased their name only recently along with their social station: petty nobility of the robe. They are rich, however, and the Sade fortune is starting to dwindle. Classic exercise in regilding family arms. A routine procedure for marrying off sons and daughters of the feudal aristocracy.

Domestic life? Nothing irregular. Husband and wife even seem to enjoy a more stable relationship than most such matches, at least when they share the house on the Rue Neuve du Luxembourg in Paris or the Château d'E- chauffour in Normandy, both part of Renée's dowry. As a wedding present, the Comte de Sade transferred to his son that peculiar office* he possessed in Bresse and neighboring provinces paying an annual income of ten thousand livres. She receives roughly the same amount from her parents. A rather tight budget for their elegant style of life, but each can look forward to a rich inheritance. In short, the young couple began married life in much the same fashion as the majority of their peers.

Sudden shock. A bolt from the blue. Donatien-Aldonse is clapped into Vincennes prison on October 29, 1763, four months after his wedding, "for wanton debauchery, blasphemy, and profanation of Christ's image." He stands on the brink of a new life, first as a suspect, ultimately an outlaw.

October 1763. Jeanne Testard, a prostitute, files charges against Sade with the Paris police. He has maltreated her, birched her brutally, forced her to commit sodomy; he made her trample on a crucifix and shout at Christ's image, "Bugger off, you rascal!" He uttered "countless blasphemies and dreadful oaths, declaring that there was no God, that he could prove it, that he had

---

*Officially designated as *lieutenant-général d'épée,* a rank more honorific than useful, entitling the holder to some control over certain local judicial and fiscal operations without any residence requirement.

masturbated and defiled a chalice which he kept more than two hours in a church chapel, that Jesus Christ was a slippery customer and the Virgin a strumpet."[4] Sade is arrested and imprisoned in the fortress of Vincennes. In 1766 the Chevalier de la Barre went to his death on far less serious charges, but the incident of the Abbeville crucifix created a public scandal* that the authorities resolved to silence by meting out the severest of indictments. The accusation against Sade rests solely on one girl's whispered tale. That plus the fact his father-in-law is a high-ranking magistrate suffices to bury the affair. Louis XV intercedes. Sade is released on November 13 and ordered to reside either in Paris or in Echauffour. They intended to watch him like a hawk.

April 1768. Second complaint against him, filed this time by the victim, a prostitute named Rose Keller, in concert with three women from Arcueil, a once pretty little town not far from Paris. They were the first to answer the plaintiff's cries; their names were Sixdeniers, Pontier, and Bajou. Sade locked himself up with his victim one afternoon in a rented cottage—he has two or three such "love nests" in and around the capital. Repeated flagellations until the blood flows, so terrifying to the girl that she finally leaps through a window, screaming for help. She is bruised all over. Impossible to hush up this incident. Parisian magistrates open an investigation. Simultaneously, undoubtedly at his family's request, Sade is arrested "by royal edict" to shield him from the law, like Mirabeau from his creditors, by the device of a *lettre de cachet.* Incarcerated first in the castle of Saumur, then the fortress of Pierre-Encise near Lyons. When the 3rd of June arrives, Louis XV has quashed proceedings by issuing *lettres de relief,*** but the "reprieved" man must remain in prison. Sade's fate henceforth lies in the hands of the wife of Montreuil's chief magistrate; she will be the instrument of decision in all proceedings for or against him. At first she is "for" him, and amazingly indulgent for a mother-in-law. She has just saved him a second time by winning his release on November 16. He settles down in La Coste—mandatory residence—with his wife. They already have one child. A second son arrives in 1769. The reins slacken: Sade is allowed to come back to Paris, to travel in the Low Countries, to serve in the ranks again for several months, though at court his presence is judged undesirable. Return to La Coste with his wife and children (three by now) at the end of 1771. A new morals charge, more damaging than any thus far, in Marseilles in June 1772. Instead of protecting him this time, his mother-in-law

---

*One night the wooden crucifix decorating Abbeville's main bridge received several slashes from a sword. The Chevalier de La Barre was accused of this because of his highly exaggerated reputation for impiety.

**The antithesis, in a sense, of *lettres de cachet.* They declared a crime abolished "by the supreme right of royal authority"—and the guilty party could not be investigated, even in prisons where His Majesty frequently decided to hold him.

does not lift a finger to halt proceedings that can hang him. He flees to Italy just as they sentence him to death. A year later they recapture him at Chambéry, on his last legs, desperate to re-enter France. The Savoyards will imprison him at Miolans until his escape the following spring.

Madame de Montreuil had good reasons for her change of heart. In La Coste during the winter of 1771–72 Sade openly became the lover of Canoness* Anne-Prospère de Launay, his wife's younger sister; not to mention having dishonored a daughter of the president of the court. Two daughters of hers! When the scandal reaches into the very bosom of her family, she draws the line: he must be punished. Too bad that he got himself into this mess.

What about the Marseilles business? On June 27, 1772, Sade had organized the nearest thing to an erotic orgy in the rooms of a prostitute of the Rue d'Aubagne. The cast included himself, his valet Latour, and four girls. A full day's arduous, elaborate gymnastics comprised their pleasure, laced with pain. The inexhaustible marquis then went on to spend the evening with a fifth girl. He had fed some of his partners lavishly on anisette drops filled with cantharides, a powder made from tiny ground-up beetles "of a lovely shade of green, shiny, finely striated, tinged with gold, which you find in summertime on the outskirts of Paris gathered on the leaves of ashes, rosebushes, and poplars." Cantharides, or Spanish fly, introduced and used extensively to spice up his seventies by the Duc de Richelieu, veteran connoisseur of erotic pleasures at the court of Versailles, was reputed to act as an aphrodisiac, though in fact it merely produced mechanical erections, "ulcers, a burning urethra, thirst, fever, blood in the urine, and stinking, ghastly body odors."[5] Those poor girls on the Rue d'Aubagne almost died of it. The charge of poisoning entered Sade's now classic record of sexual offenses. The lever of repression flipped out of control.

February 1775. Thick dossier. In addition to escaping from Miolans and further insulting French justice by playing hide-and-seek for a year, Sade, still (or rather increasingly) on the run, has just added one more—debit, should we say, or credit?—to his record: the affair of the young girls of La Coste. Perhaps because the throne and the administration had changed hands, he enjoyed some degree of tacit immunity in Provence during the early part of that winter. La Coste tolerated him provided he remained "out of sight." By December and January, however, even the sun-drenched castle walls could not hide what was going on inside. Rumors, terror. Alerted as far away as Lyons, parents of several victims filed suit. Three young girls named Berh, Desgrange, and Abadie fled the château, or were allowed to leave, "dismissed"

---

*The title of "canoness" has no bearing on the scandal. It was a faintly religious designation reserved for certain daughters of the aristocracy, committing them only temporarily to chastity. They wore no ecclesiastical habit.

by the marquise, whose blind loyalty to her husband defies comprehension. Now they are hospitalized or under treatment at home, savagely battered, ravaged, all of them under sixteen. Children of the poor.

Something worse than murder has visited La Coste, assaulting innocent flesh and minds. But it happened in the dull gray light of winter; the victims' screams melted into the swirling mistral. People are afraid to ask questions, reluctant to initiate a serious investigation. Writing to her son-in-law's business agent, Madame de Montreuil says that her hands tremble each time she opens a letter from Marseilles. "If what they say is true, anything could happen from one minute to the next."[6] As for the marquis, reports say he is on his way to Italy, where the papal conclave is drawing to a close and everyone's attention is focused on the issue of who will become pope. In reality, he has never left La Coste, though his wife insists he has vanished.

POPE PIUS VI

28

FEBRUARY 1775

Quanto è bello, tanto è santo!

This time Master Pasquino really hits below the belt. One icy December morning—icy even in Rome—the sun rises upon a public notice posted during the night on the base of his statue:

The coming carnival will feature a comic ballet:

THE CONCLAVE OF 1774
Lyrics by Metastasio
Score by Nicola Piccinni
At the Théâtre des Dames*

The cast listed every cardinal, and the corps de ballet every high dignitary, in the papal court. Within an hour the notice had drawn such a crowd of hilarious bystanders that the police called in reinforcements to break it up, yet dared not remove the offensive poster for fear of inciting a riot.[1] It ought to be said that Master Pasquino rarely indulged in this kind of insult; an offense against

*Pietro Bonaventura Trapassi, known as Metastasio, aged seventy-six, had already enjoyed fifty years of fame and fortune for his highly sensitive, almost effeminate poems and plays. Reputed to be the "Italian Racine," he was a pensioner of the Austrian court and a Viennese resident. Piccinni, forty-six, was living in Rome, but contemplated moving to France to eclipse Gluck. Their rivalry, needless to say, sharpened as a result of this prank.

the Sacred College, lord and master of Rome and the Catholic Church during vacancies of the Holy See, invited harsher treatment than a direct assault on the pope because of its accompanying threat to the ruling aristocracy. "During the interregnum the Sacred College demands even greater respect than the pope himself, being composed of all Christian nations and therefore represent- ative of the entire Church hierarchy. Thus ambassadors awaiting an audience of the Sacred College must remain on bended knee until the dean of cardinals beckons them to rise."[2] Passing itself off for a cross-section of "all Christian nations," the assembly of cardinals, closeted in the Vatican since October 5, includes about twenty Italians (mainly Roman aristocrats), two Frenchmen, two Spaniards, and a brother of England's king—pardon! of the Stuart pre- tender to the throne occupied since 1688 by that heretic Hanover dynasty— His Eminence Henry Benedict, Cardinal York. This parlor Christendom is engaged in a leisurely process of selecting St. Peter's heir. It is taking the whole winter, a blend of buffoonery and pageantry, a mock spectacle of secrecy elevated to the status of a holy rite.

Outside, the city of Rome lives and breathes only for this conclave. Clusters of young men stationed in St. Peter's Square are eyeing the tip of a long funnel expelling smoke from the ballots tossed into a stove in the Sistine Chapel after each successive vote. They are paid to rush news to their masters around the clock: in all, 220 reports of *sfumata nera,* black smoke from burning paper, signal that the bargaining continues. The rich are not the only specta- tors; commoners, eager to know whether their new master will be suave or uncouth, stare at the train of nobles gravely escorting litter-borne trays of food for the cardinals from their own palace kitchens. Laden platters mean that deliberations will drag on in the Vatican's single adequately heated wing "containing sitting rooms, bedchambers, and connecting corridors. The sitting and sleeping rooms are partitioned into a number of tiny cells for the cardinals; one such room may contain six sleeping units . . . Some serve exclusively as fireplaces, for the cardinals' bedchambers are unheated; all the rooms are furnished austerely with green or purple serge; a coat of arms [each cardinal's private heraldic device] hangs on the door of every chamber, nearly all of which are dark because the windows have been walled up except for the topmost pane . . . Each cardinal has two conclavists* . . . They are under oath not to divulge the secrets of the conclave."[3] A useless formality, considering the daily trickle of "secrets" leaking out through prominent visitors peeping at the conclave through the grating. Germany's empress and the French and Spanish kings needed no such eyes and ears, for their ambassadors to Rome were among the cardinals and sent regular dispatches. Louis XVI thus satisfied his appetite for gossip with Cardinal de Bernis's letters.

---

*Conclavists were "servant priests," actually aides of the cardinals. An important position leading to rich benefices and high office.

Guess who had written the following to a friend, seventeen years earlier, about the conclave destined to enthrone Clement XIII: "Here is Rome wide open to schemes and strategies, not to mention predictions. In a few days there will be as many popes as cardinals, owing to individual efforts to elect a patron or a friend . . . The conclave is a second firmament, especially for mortals not present. They use telescopes to observe it, discovering luminaries that eclipse each other, comets that vanish one by one." None other than Fra Francesco Lorenzo Maria Ganganelli of Rome's monastery of the Holy Apostle, next in line for the papacy.[4] Nothing has changed since then. The interval preceding the Holy Spirit's descent is filled with idle chatter in this improvised nunnery. About thirty prelates will huddle for whatever time it takes to come to an agreement, living like aged spinsters regulated by two daily rituals of dropping ballots silently—no discussion allowed—into the great gold chalice from which Christ's new vicar will emerge. Visits they pay each other throughout the rest of the day, to talk of matters in general, bear on the course of the election by shifting ever so delicately the thrust of political forces.

What political forces? The Jesuits, influential until 1770, now count for little. The recent Franco-Austrian coalition has ended the game of "veto," favorite device of the major powers for slapping down protégés of rival nations. Despite this, the French Bourbons have managed to promote Cardinal Pamphili (too young: barely forty-nine!); Spanish Bourbons prefer Negroni, veteran courtier and implacable foe of the Jesuits. A prominent clique of Roman aristocrats is sponsoring one of themselves, if only in response to the popular demand: *"Lo volemo romano!"* ("We want a Roman!") Maria Theresa stands behind Visconti, who caught her fancy when serving as papal nuncio to the court of Vienna. Nor are the "petty" powers to be outdone: Venice, the Savoy dynasty, and Tuscany all are advancing their pawns in the interim.

In a larger sense, the conclave is split into two camps, not necessarily apparent in the voting: defenders of temporal power and defenders of the faith. The independent *zelanti** are outraged by successive political intrusions in the religious domain, yet cannot seem to mold a homogeneous party. They constitute a reservoir of pious, upright, uninspiring candidates which supplied most of the past century's pontiffs once the ambitious designs of incisive personalities had lost their edge. Hence the series of seven mediocre (save the much underrated Benedict XIV) though honorable occupants of St. Peter's throne since 1700. Colorless individuals. The habit of supporting a nullity has become second nature to the conclave and is further encouraged by the voting procedure, which directs that the pope be elected by a two-thirds majority of cardinals.

*"The term *zelanti* has survived to the twentieth century, having undergone a fairly significant shift in meaning. As political pressures lessened, the term came to refer more and more specifically to conservative 'right-wingers' concerned exclusively with church issues and totally uninvolved with political or social problems."[5]

Essentially, two men are calling the tune here, or at least are in a position to boast such power: Floridablanca, on the outside, for Spain; Bernis, on the inside, for France.

Moñino, Charles III's ambassador extraordinary who was instructed to extort suppression of the Jesuits from Ganganelli, was made Conde de Florida-blanca* upon the successful completion of his mission. A poised and polished soldier, politicized, a man of calculated rages and iron diplomacy. Infinitely ambitious. Each day he stations himself at the grating to propagandize the cardinals: under no circumstances must they choose a Jesuit-lover. The very thought of resurrecting the Society of Jesus makes his blood boil. His weapons are intimidation and bribery.

Cardinal de Bernis, the French ambassador, has others: affability, flexibility, and a groaning table. Madame de Genlis said of him: "He was an inimitable host . . . He conveyed a blend of good fellowship and finesse, nobility and simplicity . . . " Every day for years he would hold open house in his palace on the Corso, making it "the center of French hospitality at one of Europe's crossroads" owing to a vast army of servants, a host of *maestri di camera, di capella,* pages, and footmen; a never ending series of entertainments, concerts, *conversazioni . . .* in brief, a court."[6] His friends never ceased to marvel at the heights to which twenty years of La Pompadour's favor had propelled "this affable, jolly, plump, and chubby-cheeked fellow, pink as a little doll . . . who could turn out elaborate, florid verses at the drop of a hat, genuinely fresh and fragrant bouquets lasting but an hour, but imparting an hour's pleasure."[7] They used to call him Babet-la-bouquetière [Betty the Flower-seller] and Pigeon-pattu [Feather-footed Pigeon], though now he looks more like a crimson bumblebee, buzzing from cell to cell, confident of making a pope or a poem with equal facility.

The Roman winter drags on in this fashion for the closeted cardinals, unconscious of the sun's timid rays along Bernini's colonnade. Which of them gives any thought to several thousand truly devout souls throughout the world who pray for the conclave? Catholicism, ravaged by the Reformation, corroded by the Jansenist controversy, must now withstand atheism's first concerted assault. It has jettisoned the Jesuits without allaying the hunger that produced them. God seems to be dying this year, along with Louis XV and Ganganelli. Rome's primacy begins to resemble a whited sepulcher. For ten years Catholic Germany has been grappling with Febronianism because a prelate of Treves, enamored of his cousin Justinia Febronia (whose name he adopted as the pseudonym Febronius), has published a kind of *Social Contract* for Christians, declaring that religious power belongs to the worshiping community, not to the pope, whose authority is purely symbolic. Where will it

*Nothing to do with the state of Florida. Moñino took the name of one of his ancestral estates in Spain, located in a rich and fertile region.

end? In Austria it is common knowledge that Joseph is simply waiting for his mother to die before imposing his own religious tastes on the empire. In France the reinstituted parliaments are laced with Jansenists, thus Gallicans . . . Where indeed will all this lead? Bishops are rich powerful princes, and curés petty provincial tyrants. No one takes communion at Easter. Priests say but five or six masses yearly. Liturgical rites border on spectacle, the principal attractions being the organ and the chorus. Audiences crave the excitement of the opera house in church, where the traditional verger has been replaced by Swiss Guards, who must be native Helvetians at least five feet six inches tall and maintain order in holy precincts. Their swords and halberds, once purely ornamental accessories, now serve as weapons of law enforcement. But even Swiss Guards cannot prevent the faithful from gazing up at ceilings decorated by pupils of Fragonard and Boucher with luscious Bathshebas in woodland pools, dozens of Susannahs tempting their elders, and Lot's daughters struggling with their father.[8] Certain anonymous Roman subscribers to the *Encyclopédie* whisper that this conclave will elect the last of the popes, destined to preside over the destruction of the "Beast."

Morning of February 15, 1775. *La sfumata bianca!* Wet straw mixed with the final ballots; the signal draws crowds into St. Peter's Square to acclaim the new pontiff—unenthusiastically at first: not even a Roman, he turns out to be a petty nobleman from Cesena in the Romagna, Giovanni Angelo Braschi. Still, he is not entirely unknown, having been treasurer to Clement XIII, the next-to-last pope. Anyway, after 141 days of suspense it is a relief to wind things up. "*Habemus papam!*" ("We have a pope!"—official wording of the proclamation.) A unanimous choice, according to rule, which developed from the last three days' balloting, as no cardinal would dare alienate the victor at the last moment. Tradition is sustained by the choice of a plodding personality, cautious, not unduly "drenched" in the Jesuit business, neither pro- nor anti-, and therefore in a position to calm the ferment. Bernis had supported the winner in the end, reluctantly, but only to make Louis XVI believe that Braschi was his man; Floridablanca also fell into line. In reality, however, this is simply one more apathetic pope, who, being only fifty-seven, may last a little longer than his predecessors. "His outlook is extremely narrow, but such is the current mood of Romans in comparison to the rest of Europe . . . He carries on an acceptable conversation within the limits of his intelligence."[9] Pius, the odd name he adopted, is probably the one small mark of his originality; breaking with the succession of Clements and Benedicts, he seems determined to turn over a new leaf, claiming kinship with a great militant pontiff, "Saint" Pius V, a rugged Dominican, notorious burner of heretics, architect of the victory at Lepanto against the Turks in the time of Mary Stuart and Philip II of Spain. Still, Romans are a trifle leery of this sixth Pius, the number six having already brought them bad luck with Tarquin, with Nero, with Alexander VI, the Borgia pope. Pasquino mutters.

But the women forsake Pasquino once they catch sight of this tall, well-preserved man in his fifties with barely a wrinkle on his face, "slender legs and sprightly gait"; "his forehead is bald, but a few pure-white tufts escape from under his tiara." Habitual arrogance serves him well when he deigns to bestow a blessing on the poor: his smile, his white hand raised aloft are acts of grace to the undeserving. He looked at us! He gave us his blessing! After that provincial lout Ganganelli, I guess we know a sovereign of Renaissance caliber when we see one. After one or two public appearances Braschi is solidly "in":

"Quanto è bello! Quanto è bello!" ("How handsome he is!") shouts a washer-woman right under his nose; and another echoes her:

"Quanto è bello, tanto è santo!"[10] ("How handsome he is, and no less saintly!")

In the euphoria of this happy epilogue, the author of the seditious notice, one Brother Gaetano Sertor, is pardoned, having been traced in the meantime, arrested, and cheerfully sentenced to death—a Florentine!

29

FEBRUARY 1775

Who Knows If the World Will Last Another Three Weeks?

During the same month of February another poster, another world. This time, the première of a real comedy. Paris:[1]

THE BARBER OF SEVILLE
or "The Useless Precaution"
prose comedy in five acts
by Monsieur de Beaumarchais
presented on the stage of the Comédie Française
Theater in the Tuileries
on February 23, 1775

It is a "comedy with songs"—a musical comedy in today's idiom. Baudron, first violinist of the Comédie Française company, had composed a theme for Figaro's entrance, a song for Almaviva, an arietta for Rosina, Bartolo's enticing *"Veux-tu ma Rosinette?"* and even a "thunderstorm with orchestra for the interlude between the third and fourth acts."[2] Beaumarchais's definitive title was a last-minute choice; the year before, he was still calling it by its ultimate subtitle, "The Useless Precaution," but subsequently decided against pirating the latter from Fatouville, who had written a *Précaution inutile* in 1692.* So it seems those mishaps of the previous summer have done him no permanent damage. He must be performing well as salon spy: even before receiving *lettres de relief* exonerating him of the 1774 indictment, he is allowed to produce the *Barber*. None too soon at that, for Parisians gossip about nothing else. The play had been "unanimously accepted for production" by the Comédiens Français on January 3, 1773, immediately went into rehearsal with the censors' and Sartines's blessing, was banned in March 1773 on the heels of the Chaulnes-Beaumarchais incident, resumed production in December, was banned again and reapproved in January 1774, only to be banned anew on February 10 under pressure from the Goëzman faction.[3] No dramatic creation since *Tartuffe* had known such birth pangs, or promised such timely success—provided it could ever reach the delivery room. Unlike Molière, however, Beaumarchais took an active interest in "promoting and publicizing" his works. For three years he had made the rounds of nearly every important salon giving readings of the *Barber* prefaced by derisive volleys to silence the anticipated sniping of critics:

> I should like to be among you in one of those blissful moments when, free of care, of worries about your health, your business, your mistress, your dinner, your digestion, you are disposed to enjoy a reading of my *Barber of Seville* . . . But if some mishap has impaired your well-being; if you are not in top form; if your mistress has deceived you; if your dinner sits badly and your stomach is in knots, pray then forgo my *Barber* ; it is not the right moment. Examine the state of your pocketbook; study your adversary's charges; reread the treacherous note to Rose that you intercepted, or glance at Tissot's** masterly treatises on temperance and meditate on politics, economics, nutrition, philosophy, or morals . . . What spell could a lighthearted piece cast upon your darkest depressions? And why indeed should you care if Figaro the barber has made a fool of Dr. Bartolo by helping the latter's rival steal his mistress? The merry pranks of others are not very funny when one is in gloomy spirits . . .
>
> But are you feeling cheerful? Is your digestion excellent, your cook reliable, your mistress honest, your repose imperturbable? Then you are just the person to attend my *Barber*.[4]

Parisians respond in droves—at least two thousand strong—to this invitation set for February 23 in the Tuileries, where Molière's heirs had taken

---

*Scarron also had published a novella by the same title.

**André Tissot, born in 1728, a Swiss physician practicing in Lausanne, was the current darling of both scientific and literary professions. In 1760 he published a treatise on onanism; in 1770 his study of the health of literary personalities appeared, followed by an "Essay on the Disorders of Socially Prominent Persons."

shelter while waiting for a new, permanent theater to be built for them near the Luxembourg. Four years ago they vacated their century-old quarters in the Saint-Germain district, opposite the Café de Procope; the machinery creaked unbearably and there were never enough seats for the audience. So they moved temporarily to the Right Bank, amid the mansions and gardens of the Noailles and the Orléans, who had just welcomed the Opera to the Palais Royal; close to the Tuileries and the Louvre, royal palaces deserted in favor of Versailles, empty now, so why not open a theater there? The "machinery room" in the Tuileries was a vast hall recently converted by the architect Servandoni into a stage for "spectacular pantomimes." "It stretched from the shrubbery in the Tuileries gardens to the entrance to the Cour du Carrousel. The king's and queen's loges faced each other on the right and left of the stage, looking out into the hall. Instead of directing actors to 'move toward the king' or 'move toward the queen,' monitors* began using more vivid language: 'move toward the garden' or 'move toward the court' . . . A new theatrical term came into being."⁵ Poor acoustics. "The hall is deaf!" complained one playgoer. "How fortunate!" retorted the Abbé Galiani.** "Modern" accommodations, thanks to innovations recently introduced (and funded) by the Comte de Lauraguais: wax tapers to replace reeking tallow candles, the stage cleared of benches reserved for the gentry, and a lounge where actors could warm themselves in cold weather.

The audience, too, is unconventional. Standees crane their necks peering up to admire, in the crescent of loges overhead, the beauties of the new reign with their outlandish coiffures, many the elaborate creations of that master hairdresser Beaulard: "The man racks his brain to depict, on the heads of young women, the major issues in the gazettes. On one bonnet† can be seen the reopening of Parliament, on another the Russo-Turkish pact, on another Henri IV at the Battle of Ivry, or an English garden, in fact every conceivable event from ancient or modern history."⁶ Gentlemen attired in white, crimson, and gold stand behind the armchairs out of which all this intricate scaffolding cautiously emerges. An exotic array of plumage waits to pounce on Beaumarchais and peck him to shreds. They forgave his attacks on Goëzman only because those attacks also struck at the rising legal profession, the *noblesse de robe.* Now they intend to settle accounts with this adventurer who calls himself a professional writer. Secret agent or pamphleteer is bad enough, but who ever heard of a clockmaker dramatist? "Monsieur de Beaumarchais will never achieve anything, mediocre or otherwise," Baron von Grimm declared in his

*The concept of stage director was as yet unknown. Actors got together and worked out gestures and movements, sometimes with the playwright's collaboration. Each week a different monitor (*semainier*) was responsible for keeping track of the stage directions and prompting the cast.

**The Convention met in this hall, after extensive alterations, from May 10, 1793. Scene also of the momentous decisions of May 31, 9th Thermidor, and First Prairial.

†A *bonnet* was simply a piece of fabric—satin, taffeta, or perhaps linen—shaped to suit the wearer and pinned to the hair as a base for further ornamentation. [*Trans.*]

private news sheet in 1767 following presentation of *Eugénie,* a dreary melo-drama about the seduction of a poor girl by an aristocrat. Beaumarchais missed the mark that time by abandoning his satiric vein for a fling at bourgeois tragedy, which Sedaine and Diderot were currently trying to launch. As usual, he was stubborn; two years later he represented a farmer-general for the first time on any stage in *Les Deux Amis, ou le négociant de Lyon,* a play about money —traded, invested, buried . . . An utter fiasco, though totally undeserved according to the author, who imputed it to the public's acute class-conscious-ness: "Depict persons of modest means on the brink of ruin and despair? Never! They must always appear ludicrous. Ridiculous citizens and ill-starred kings, that is the full range of today's theater."[7]

But this time he set out to do something different. The curtain rises "on a street in Seville where every window is barred." Count Almaviva, "alone, wrapped in a flowing brown cape and wearing a slouch hat, walks along consulting his watch"—the actor Bellecour, "well built, distinguished fea-tures, prodigious memory, keen intelligence . . . " Offstage, a voice bursts into this bold and lively song:

> Banissons le chagrin,   [Banish sorrow
> Il nous consume . . .   All-consuming . . .]

The man who enters "humming cheerfully, paper and pencil in hand, a guitar slung over his back tied with a large bow," is the great Préville, finest comedian of his day, "who seemed to be improvising the part, so totally absorbed was he in the spirit of it"—though Figaro already exists, in the person of Beaumarchais. "As for myself, seeking merely . . . to create an entertain-ing, untaxing play, a kind of *imbroille,** I made the machinist [in the sense of "machinator" or principal conniver] an appealing fellow instead of a villain, a jaunty soul able to laugh at his own triumph as well as his failures."[8] No youngster, Figaro has been around. He has grown "slightly jaded since the time his mother used to tell him he was charming; the count doesn't recognize the plump and prosperous fellow. He is not handsome . . . This rough-cut Figaro recalls Harlequins in the burlesque tradition and those impudent buf-foons serving as foils for the elegant gentry in the comedies of Marivaux."[9] He is about to lend Almaviva a cheerful hand in abducting Rosina (pretty Mlle Doligny) from Dr. Bartolo, who, like all amorous elders bent on guarding their youthful treasures, takes the ever useless precaution of locking her up. The entrance of Bartolo, played by rotund Désessarts, sets the audience laugh-ing: a marvelous actor, this former magistrate in the courts of Langres took up the stage as a hobby and found his corpulence a great asset. He has tried to re-create Figaro's detailed description (which vanished from the text after the play's première) of Bartolo: " . . . a handsome, fat, short, youngish old man, dapple-gray, beardless, blasé, spry and spruce, beribboned like lovers gone

*Etymological transition between *"imbroglio"* and *"embrouille."*

a-courting; yet wrinkled, gummy-eyed, jealous, foolish, gouty, and dispirited, who alternately wheezes and splutters, growls and frets. Kidney stones, one lame arm, two game legs . . . If his head still sprouts greenery, you know it must be like moss or mistletoe upon a dead tree." [10]

Beaumarchais had encountered his characters not in Seville but in Madrid, having gone to Spain in 1764 to seek his fortune and wound up in a dispute with Clavijo. This Spanish adventure headed a series of controversial incidents in which he "embroiled" himself periodically. His first resounding failure. It supplied the heroes of his revenge. Almaviva, Dr. Bartolo, Don Basilio, Rosina, and Figaro had hibernated for ten years in the back of his head, ultimately merging, as so often happens in the artistic process, with seeds of creativity generated around the age of twenty. Even earlier, at Etioles, where he used to entertain La Pompadour and some of her banker admirers, he would stage salon *"parades,"* a type of satirical farce adapted to the tastes of parvenus. One such burlesque, *Le Sacristain,* depicted a crabby old man hounded by "three or four devils flying through the air" and "deceived" by his young wife. Since that time the alchemy of experience and imagination had fused Germany to Spain, London to Vienna, Goëzman to Clavijo. And lo, after forty tumultuous years, up pops Figaro like a Jack-in-the-box: "Hurrah for gaiety! Who knows if the world will last another three weeks?" Laughter returns to the French stage, the people's laughter. Molière and Rabelais, after the half-smiles and genteel snickers of Marivaux. René Pomeau calls it "laughter sympathetic to youth, which triumphs over all obstacles." [11]

But this particular audience is no obstacle; it is sheer disaster. Faint titters in the first act give way to dead silence in the second. The third draws jeers. Later, in publishing the *Barber,* Beaumarchais actually recorded it as a "comedy performed and fallen flat . . . on February 23, 1775." That evening Caron de Beaumarchais achieved the distinction of a literary failure. Figaro was a flop; the audience found him insolent and crude. They balked at the image of a trusty valet as the indispensable source of girls and games. The author, gritting his teeth in the back of a loge, is our most reliable chronicler of this "saddest of evenings. You should have watched the *Barber's* fair-weather friends leaving, hiding their faces or just dashing off, the women, supremely bold when they choose to sponsor you, wrapped, plumes and all, in their cowls, utterly embarrassed, the men rushing up to consult each other, apologizing for ever having said a kind word about my play . . . It was sheer desertion, hopeless desolation. Some gazed to the left in anticipation of my passage on the right, ignoring me completely. Others, more courageous but making sure no one was watching, drew me into a corner: 'Say, how did you manage to pull the wool over our eyes? For admit it, friend, your play is the greatest platitude that ever was.'" [12]

Many of these people had attended and applauded readings of the *Barber.*

Individually, they like it; in a body, they oppose it with a wall of convention and offended dignity. Is it because, collectively, they feel threatened? Beaumarchais is not even angry. The stakes are too high. His existence, his very purpose in life hang in the balance. He pretends to drink in, to weigh, the advice of his critics. He reflects on an observation made by Diderot two years earlier: "A man of genius arises, yet few are clever enough to mark it; the public never suspects. But as this man essentially is a creator, far ahead of his times, disclosing a whole new system of things or unfamiliar beauties . . . he is judged; being unlike anything known thus far, he is indicted, and ought to consider himself fortunate if not made to suffer for the endowments of genius which fate chose to bestow on him . . . A lifetime may not be long enough to obtain forgiveness for his superiority."[13] In any event, Beaumarchais takes a drubbing, but is able to stage a comeback by acting upon the one valid criticism advanced by his admirers: why the devil did he expand a play which the censors had approved a year ago, a taut, lively *Barber* in just four acts, with the plot galloping along full tilt? Bowing to his demon Excess, he inserted another act between the third and last, packed with references to the Goëzman affair and the German interlude. Along with this newest crop of spicy irreverences came unwelcome touches of melodrama: Bartolo's complaining grows tedious, Almaviva and Rosina bill and coo endlessly, the action grinds to a halt, and anyone bent on finding the *Barber* a bore can do so in this uncalled-for fourth act that serves too obviously as a transition.

So that's the problem in a nutshell. Beaumarchais rises to the challenge. It is Thursday evening, with the second performance scheduled for the following Sunday. Parisians will come back—again and again—to plow the play into its grave. But they won't be seeing the same *Barber*—or rather, as the just reward for their snobbery, they will see the original "genuine" article they took to their bosoms in 1773 because it flattered their sense of being "in" on a secret.

In three days Beaumarchais "splits into four"—that is to say, four acts. Aided by the cast, who enjoy the play and believe in its author, he cuts, splices, weeds, tightens, and speeds up the pace. No great problem: he has only to delete nearly everything he added last year for the *Barber* to resume its original form. Having to remove some choice jibes at the ruling caste is admittedly galling, as, for example, the following exchange between Bartolo and his old servant, whose name does not just happen to be Youth.

> Youth: But when something is true? . . .
> Bartolo: When something is true? Well, if I don't want it to be true, I simply assert that it is not true. Once you start letting those rascals think they're right, you'll see what becomes of authority.[14]

And what a shame not to hear Figaro say *"Qu'es à co?"* or declaim on " 'Goddam,' pillar of the English language," a broadside at the current tide of

Anglophilia. But Beaumarchais is a patient man; whatever he strips from the *Barber* is not jettisoned, but stowed away, for future dramatic use. The important thing is that Figaro has not died—or succumbed to matrimony.

In any event, his most felicitous addition to the original text, Don Basilio's speech on slander, stays in: it was Beaumarchais's revenge on everyone and everything. As for the rest, his mind was made up: "Seeing rabid enemies out there, the public undulating, agitating, booming in the distance like the inrushing surf . . . I came to realize that many five-act plays [like my own], all well constructed, needless to say [like my own], would never have stirred up the devil [as mine did] if the authors had acted vigorously [as I did] . . . And so, giving the devil his due and ripping up my manuscript: God of hecklers, snorters, spitters, coughers, and brawlers, I wrote to myself, thou callest for blood; drink up my fourth act and abate thy fury!"[15]

"Despite everything, the *Barber,* collapsed at its première, raised and rearranged by its author, enjoyed a highly successful second performance. Everyone recognized the comedy's original plot revived, enlarged, refreshed, and yesterday's taunts became cheers."[16] He made them applaud their own performance—Figaro's last laugh. Stunned, Madame du Deffand writes: "Yesterday I went to Beaumarchais's play, which was in its second performance. The première was hooted, but yesterday it was an astounding success; the applause nearly brought down the roof." Yet this blind old woman's thinking remains fixed: "Nothing could be more ridiculous; the play is odious . . . This Beaumarchais, so engaging in his pamphlets, is deplorable in his play *The Barber of Seville.*" Madame du Deffand's sour pronouncements were beginning to pall on an enlightened Europe, whose oracle she had once been. Gluck's *Orpheus* had left her "bored to death."[17] Beaumarchais ignores the mutterings of his latest peevish critics. In fact, he is now a "prophet in my own land. This poor Figaro . . . nearly laid to rest on Friday . . . rose on Sunday."[18]

For the fourth time this year, the sixth or eighth in his lifetime, he stands to gain from a crisis. This latest triumph is precisely the one he has waited and prepared for since childhood: a chance to make some money. Money at last! Receipts for the première, the "fiasco," the "failure," have already set a new record for the company: 3367 livres,* roughly one sixth of which goes to the author. Each of the seventeen performances to follow this spring will nearly duplicate that figure. For the first time in history, a playwright is actually making money from his play. Begging the question: in what proportion shall actors, financial backers, and author divide up the profits? Who decides? Who must be consulted? Who is running things? Instead of meekly accepting whatever they deign to allot him, Beaumarchais begins to envisage a "definite arrangement" among dramatist, promoters, and artists—namely, "an accurate,

---

*Approximately 13,600 current francs [$2720]. Voltaire's *Mérope* held the previous record of 3270 livres. In 1781, after fifty performances, Beaumarchais's net gain was roughly equivalent to 45,000 modern francs [$9000].

reliable accounting system on which to base all future disbursements."[19] Is *The Barber of Seville* about to raise a second "revolution" in behalf of honest treatment for playwrights?

LINGUET

30

MARCH 1775

Start by Overthrowing Society

But the pre-eminent personality in the spring of 1775 is Linguet, not Beaumarchais. Paris demands one illustrious victim per annum. The public was quicker to acclaim Beaumarchais last year, after the Maupeou Parliament indicted him, than to appreciate his *Barber* now. Parisians currently are applauding the image of a grizzled Figaro, of a mournful, irate Beaumarchais, the vanquished hero of his day, Henry Linguet. He was formally disbarred on March 29 after battling the courts every step of the way against the concerted assault of his peers, who were resolved to rid the fold of this black sheep. "In favor of disbarment: 197; in favor of a deferred ruling: 13; not one vote for the accused; total number of votes cast : 210."* Linguet will cease to be a lawyer, will never again put on the black robes he wears in the hundreds of engravings that depict him pointing an accusing finger at judges of all parliaments, old as well as new. Actually, he has already unfrocked himself from a profession he never cared for. Since early February, in "a gray dress coat, gray waistcoat, black breeches, boots with spurs, and his hat cocked over one eye to convey an air of defiance,"[1] he has haunted the corridors and chambers of the Palace of Justice, finally gathering the courage to leave this city that acclaims yet refuses to help him—as usual. What has he left but his pen? He will go somewhere else and be a journalist, for here they are resolved to muzzle him. Whatever he writes for publication in Paris stands to be burned within three months at the foot of the grand staircase in the palace, which he now descends for the last time. He resigns himself to the life of a roving writer: Brussels, Amsterdam, London, dragging a small portable printing press with the rest of his luggage, not to mention a tiresome mistress, the imperturbable Madame Buttet, whom he hesitates to dislodge since she quit her husband's bed for his own. A galling start: ladies offering bouquets soon will remember him only

* According to the final ballot taken on February 3, confirmed by the Great Chamber of Parliament on March 29.

as having inspired fabrics and bonnets *"à la Linguet,"* in style for the past year
and bound to sell like hotcakes from now on. Following his disbarment,
fashion decrees that dress stuffs and bonnets named after him shall be
striped.*

The Morangiès case had brought him to prominence, stirring the public
conscience as vigorously as the Goëzman affair—he made sure of that, declaring that no opportunity had been missed "to turn the trial into a confrontation
between the Bourgeoisie and the Military, between the Common People and
the Nobility."[2] Linguet defended an officer of noble birth, the Comte de
Morangiès, a spendthrift who refused to repay debts of three hundred thousand livres to one Madame Simon, perhaps for good reasons. But his main
thrust, in the name of the "common people," bore down on the rising bourgeoisie, specifically the legal profession—to which he himself aspired, all the
same, as an escape from the aftermath of his deprived childhood in a shabby
district of Rheims. A petty clerk for a father, exiled from Paris to Champagne
for his Jansenist beliefs: "My father was a martyr to the tyranny of banishment
just as his son was to the tyranny of deposal."[3] A mother who died when he
was two. A plucky stepmother, Barbe Lallemant, remained a widow with ten
children. A scholarship for Henry, the most gifted of the brood; Paris, the
Navarre high school, which marked him for life: "its rules, as in most schools,
were aimed chiefly at imposing the cult of Latin, of regulating rigorously and
minutely the rites of this cult whose god was Cicero. Pupils had to address
servants in Latin or Greek and were forbidden to use the vernacular . . . the
masters, naturally, spoke only Latin to their students."[4]

Life began for Linguet with a series of paradoxes. At the University of
Paris he won three first prizes in those classical disciplines he found so tedious.
His classmates crowned him "the Emperor of Rhetoric," though writing gave
him more pleasure than speaking. He wanted to become a civil engineer and
ended up secretary to a German aristocrat, the Duc de Deux-Ponts, before
settling down to the law. He would have liked to be a great philosopher, but
became friends with Fréron, pre-eminent Catholic apologist of his day. He
championed the Jesuits against the tide. As a novice lawyer in the courts, he
refused to crawl: "I made my way without patronage, without backing; an
unfamiliar, unarresting face, a hesitant manner that could pass for shyness did
not destroy the impressions people tried to build up against me. I did not know
that to be successful in the law one had to dog the footsteps of an ancient, cater
to his decadence . . . sacrifice one's own youth in the hope of eventually
capturing another's; and ultimately, in the new Elysium, don the mantle of
some hoary Elijah."[5] He did just the opposite, aping David by challenging
Goliath in the courts, Gerbier the invincible, pride of the Paris bar. Any case
that Gerbier took—at astronomical fees—was a winner from the start. Such an

*A play on the word *"rayé,"* meaning both "striped" and "struck off" (the rolls of the legal
profession). [*Trans.*]

eloquent lawyer! "His long, sinewy neck supports a classic head such as one sees in the museums of Rome or Naples, but not ordinary, and possessing a rare purity of line. A delicate mouth, straight nose, alert eyes beneath the broad, elevated dome of this ancient philosopher or orator."[6] His discourse? A sea of solid boredom, a confluence of Latin quotations and legal jargon. But what an instrument, ladies, that velvety voice of his . . . Enough to make your head spin without having understood a word.

Then one day in 1767 Gerbier finds himself face to face with this shouting, gesticulating clown. "Linguet is ugly, short, thin, with a nervous, fidgety manner . . . broad, slightly balding temples . . . very high, bushy brows, straight nose, thin, sinuous lips and, below clenched teeth, a devilish jaw that was the essence of the man."[7] At thirty-seven, he had managed to alienate everyone save the illiterate public. Judges hated him—and with good reason: he told them straight to their faces that "the legal profession is about the most disgusting one there is, enough perhaps to make one ashamed of it."[8] After defending Aiguillon, he had angered the duke by submitting his bill, an intolerable display of bad taste familiar to persons who must earn a living: "Monsieur le Duc, I encountered you midway between throne and scaffold; I brought you nearer to one and rescued you from the other . . . Even if physical labor alone is all I am entitled to be paid for, you are in my debt, and heavily so* . . . As to stooping [to the practice of charging a fee], set your mind at rest, Monsieur le Duc, my business is to elevate my fees!"[9] Is M. Linguet just a trifle megalomaniac? Probably, judging from his habitual use of the third person: "In eight years the Comte de Morangiès's counsel has produced 110 written documents including memoranda as well as defense pleas, handwritten or printed."[10] Utterly intolerable fellow. Unpredictable temper. Whacks old Tesson, "concierge of the Conciergerie," on the back with his walking stick; calls his colleague "a fiend for formalities" in the midst of a civil suit; and bellows at Maurepas, loud enough to be heard outside the judge's chambers, when the latter tries to conciliate his dispute with Aiguillon: "They've set you against me, Your Honor. Well, now I stand informed of your bias!"

Fine thing to say to the king's adviser, the one man who could really help him and whom he proceeds gleefully to demolish: "What a farce it is to see him [Maurepas] a minister at fifteen, dismissed at thirty, reinstalled at eighty,** thus devoting only the two incompetent stages of life to public affairs and rounding out his years by combining the frivolity of adolescence with the apathy and mediocrity of decrepitude!"[11]

That did it! The ax fell on Linguet. Not content merely to champion his

---

*Meaning the time spent studying the record and preparing the La Chalotais case for trial. Linguet charged the duke a fee of 36,000 livres (7200 new francs).

**In the heat of his rhetoric, he exaggerates by six years.

own cause, he had insisted on publishing that impudent *Theory of the Law** in which he vainly defended the Chevalier de La Barre; had dared to attack not only Rousseau but the *Encyclopédie* as well; and had sided with corrupt nobles against prosperous bourgeois, thus involving himself in a mass of contradictions which he was either too insolent or too lazy to resolve. He was roundly criticized for his *Réflexions* dealing with a current trial in which he acted as counsel for the defense of another aristocrat, the Comtesse de Béthune, an excitable lady not afraid to shower abuse on everyone, including the prime minister, in support of her lawyer. No barrister should publicly air a case still undecided in the courts. Professional misconduct. The president of the bar fulminated against this reprobate, this insolent guttersnipe: "The repeated lapses of M. Linguet have necessitated his removal from our organization . . . Not content with attacking the fundamental principles of this kingdom, he has seen fit to slander its custodians and institutions . . . Nor does he show the slightest respect for the bar, which he has portrayed odiously . . . In his folly, he would force us to keep him among us when all the while he insults our administration,** our discipline, and our traditions."[12]

He had sinned against his own fraternity. So why expect a warm welcome from the bourgeois camp? Friends helped seal his fate by leading a student rabble into the law courts on February 3, date of the final pleading. A hundred or so troublemakers following or pushing Linguet from room to room, occupying "St. Louis's bedchamber in La Tournelle"† before the advocates had assembled; the latter wandering here and there in quest of a meeting room and ending up in nothing less than the Great Chamber, scene of the *lits de justice,* where they met the others head on, "canes raised," "hunting knives bared." Who was the flushed young man apparently in command of the attack? Lauraguais, of course. A lawyer barred his path:

"What's all this, Count? Do you mean to storm the assembly as a body?"

"Devil take that body!"

Behind Lauraguais stood Beaumarchais with his big nose sniffing the wind, who was just completing his tirade against calumny—the disbarment ruling charged Linguet with stealing two horses from the Duc de Deux-Ponts, his "patron" twenty years earlier—along with François, Linguet's secretary, lately sacked by Neufchâteau;‡ also the greenhorn law clerk recently arrived from Chartres who idolized Linguet, Jacques-Pierre Brissot; and a twenty-six-year-old Genevan fighting his first literary skirmish, Jacques Mallet du Pan.

A party of "short-gowned, privileged persons" had evicted the agitators,

---

*Théorie des loix civiles ou Principes fondamentaux de la société, which appeared in 1767.
**Nicolas Lambon, president of the bar, was really speaking of self-rule in the legal profession during the eighteenth century. "That pack had managed to become a law unto itself " (Valéry Larbaud).
†One of the towers in the Palace of Justice where judges of the Paris Parliament originally held court. [*Trans.*]   ‡Future member of the Directory and senator under the Empire.

the latter having sealed Linguet's fate by "violating the sanctity of this hallowed shrine," so President Lambon declared, clinching the matter with this irrefutable charge: "You have no liking for Roman law . . . Your attitude is not currently shared by the legal profession."[13]

Exit Linguet. Into his baggage go several copies of his *Theory of the Law*, also a departure from current literary practice. Nobody can understand it. Just what is the author trying to say? Does he really know? So-called liberals attack his ostensible defense of absolutism: "Why all this emotional pageantry, these programs for financial and fiscal reform? [So much for Turgot!] What good is parliamentary government or attempts to imitate the English political system? What good are these instrumentalities urged by Montesquieu, these grasping judicial bodies which, while professing to hold royal power in check, are merely protecting their own privileges? . . . What good is all that when the poor are destined forever to be oppressed by the rich, when workingmen must always serve property-owners? A single despot is better than a horde of petty tyrants!"[14]

That means he must favor royalty versus the parliaments. Renegade! In his *Essai sur le despotisme,* which he was then writing in a cell in the Château d'If, Mirabeau castigates "the ignorant and brash M. Linguet, advocate of Neros, of sultans and viziers, among the most disgraceful yet accredited proponents of arbitrary power."[15]

An odd kind of renegade, driven out of the courts "where, strangely enough, he is appreciated," by his own followers, his relatives, his clients, his readers. Banished by people who cheer him on as they run him out. "Nero's apologist" has calmly declared that if "all men were wise, perhaps they would re-evaluate the praise heaped upon conquerors . . . I doubt that any tyrant ever lived whose whims did more damage to mankind than Alexander or Caesar . . . A few historians have dared to extol Caesar for slaughtering a million men in his wars. If that were true, the human race has never known so cruel a foe. Caligula, Commodus, and Heliogabalus were by comparison shining examples of sweetness and mercy."

True enough, that is not "the attitude of the legal profession." Nor of the times. It is ahead of the times. Whether it bespeaks a prophet or a madman, it is, in any event, untimely when applied to problems that do not concern his audience, the literate public. To them he describes an unfamiliar world:

"All this weeping and wailing about slavery has not raised by a single penny the wage of laborers, or journeymen, or soldiers, or servants: the cheap labor provided by such persons is the basis of social wealth and the foundation of governments[16] . . . Can you not see that the obedience, and in reality the destruction, of a majority of the flock creates the opulence of shepherds? . . . Before you talk of protecting the flock, start by overthrowing the sheepfold, society itself! . . . In abolishing servitude, no one intended also to abolish wealth and its privileges. No one has thought of restoring the equality of primitive men; the rich man's surrender of his prerogatives has been purely nominal . . . Our cities and towns are peopled with a race known as journeymen, laborers, etc. They have no share in the abundance produced by their labor . . . A slave was precious to his master because of the money he had cost. But the laborer does not cost his rich employer a penny. In the days of slavery, human blood had value. Human beings were worth at least the price they fetched in the marketplace. Now that they no longer are traded, they have no real intrinsic value. In the army, a scout is less valuable than a dray horse because the horse is costly and the soldier can be had for nothing. With the abolition of slavery, such military reckoning filtered down into the community and, ever since, all well-to-do bourgeois calculate on the same scale as field marshals."

Why the bourgeoisie waited this long to reject him is a mystery. Off he goes in a blaze of glory, laden with dubious praise, for among his cheering supporters are the foes of Turgot, whom Linguet has been attacking mercilessly for the past seven months, calling him the spokesman of bourgeois privilege, dedicated to making the rich richer.*

Turgot was not the type and not in the mood to be swayed by Linguet's attacks. He had assigned the Abbé Morellet to defend him from that quarter. The final blow strikes Linguet on March 30, the day after his indictment, from old "Snapper" himself, whose *Théorie du paradoxe* appears in print, its title pointedly reminiscent of the *Théorie des loix*. The provocation was Linguet's recent pamphlet *Le Pain et le Blé* (Bread and Grain) arguing against a free grain trade, calling it an incentive to monopoly because "grain is a pitifully insufficient product that breeds more hunger than it drives away, in appearance, judging from its unwholesome properties, a gift of nature's wrath, the stalk of which contains far more misery than grain . . . Bread is a deadly drug the basic ingredient of which is corruption. We are compelled to alter it with poison [a leavening agent] in order to reduce its harmful effects."[17] What were people supposed to eat? Fruit, vegetables, fish, and quantities of that modern manna discovered among the Indians of North America and currently overrunning France from the north and east: the potato. "From Brabant, potatoes spread to neighboring countries and throughout Germany, Sweden, Switzerland, etc. . . . in Sweden for the past fifty years, Bayreuth since 1690 . . . in Saxony for thirty years. All these regions have made it a staple dietary item, and a nobleman serving in the French army assured me that when large numbers of his troops in Saxony had their food supplies cut off by the enemy, they lived for ten days exclusively on potatoes, called *artoffles, tartoffles*, or *tartuffes* there, and managed to survive."[18]

No idle daydream, this enthusiasm for the potato was shared by Parmentier, the agronomist and pharmacist, as well as scientists like Tissot and Buffon.

*The guillotine will claim Linguet on 7th Thermidor, Year II (June 27, 1794).

But here again Linguet went overboard in insisting that "sordid intemperance, criminal laxity which enervates* individuals and empires . . . have existed only in wheat-raising lands where there are mills and bakers."[19] A brash statement, plainly inviting Morellet to lower his horns and charge in his usual bullish fashion: "His mind, soul, and body, all equally athletic, shared, so to speak, the same muscular system . . . Passionate as well, headstrong, aggressive, opposed to any compromise . . . It was always a duel to the death . . . To the arrows of his critics, which merely whetted his courage, he retaliated always with a bludgeon, for nature left him no choice of arms: Hercules was his patron."[20] Plying his pen in the service of Turgot, Morellet feels called upon to perform a sacred mission—St. George battling the dragon. Long ago he had declared his "revulsion, shared by all sensible persons, at Linguet's passion for Oriental despotism . . . at his absurd ideas of liberty and his hostility to men of letters . . . I sent for everything he had written . . . after locking myself in my study, I read it all, pencil-marking the nonsense I found."[21] In other words, Morellet is out to destroy Linguet with his own fire; like a clever gambler—or simply a cautious one—the abbé waits for the court to hand down its sentence. "At last the day of reckoning arrived for Linguet: he was erased from the picture. The next day, after the seven-o'clock hearing, my *Théorie du paradoxe* went on sale in the Palace of Justice and with various booksellers. Amateurs, and especially lawyers, were so eager to get their hands on it that a week later I had to bring out a second edition of two thousand copies." Morellet was not a modest soul. He adds, "I can truly say that the *Théorie du paradoxe* dealt Linguet the death blow and did its share, in the view of rational humanity, to put a fraud and a bad writer in his place, a person whom the public never would have known but for the use he made of fame's most powerful instrument: impudence."[22]

Now everything is straightened out. Linguet "put in his place": exile, anguish, adventure; Morellet in his: a snug existence presided over by his unrivaled genius for detail. This "peculiarity of his contrasted sharply with the rough-and-ready coarseness of his features, of his discourse, of his voice and manners. His passion for the most infinitesimal commodities of life was so intense and so discriminating that he would stop at nothing to satisfy it . . . An obsession for comfort pervaded his every motion." "This inclination undoubtedly guided him more strongly than the church, to which he belonged by virtue of only half his faith, half his wardrobe, and one entire priory."**

He had even worn the martyr's crown when paying a providential visit to the Bastille in 1759 for having offended one of Choiseul's mistresses: "I saw literary fame flickering upon my prison walls: persecution would make me better known . . . Those two months in the Bastille would serve as an excel-

---

*In the etymological sense: to destroy the nerve, deprive of vigor, enfeeble.

**Actually, the income from a priory which paid him a benefice.

lent recommendation and were bound to make my fortune . . . The social set, who love satire, would welcome me more warmly than ever."[23]

These elegant aristocrats, whom he has defended so valiantly against a defeated man, greet him with open arms when he arrives for his annual holiday at Madame de La Briche's country seat, the Château de Marais. A fashionable crowd awaits him in the avenue lined with century-old elms, and a "spontaneous cry of joy" goes up as his carriage, of Falstaffian proportions, rolls into view; "drawn by a fat black mare, the huge green cabriolet is furnished with two seats, the forward one occupied by his manservant decked out in coachman's livery. Behind, in a cozy little nest well padded with commodious armrests, sat the abbé. A large traveling bag, trunks, crates of books, carpetbags, portmanteaus . . . completed the travel accessories. In stepping out of his carriage, the Abbé Morellet's first concern, after hastily greeting his hostess and residents of the château, was to have his luggage delivered to his rooms," while the guests rushed off to lock their doors, Morellet having developed a habit of dispatching "the château's floor-polishers" to confiscate from his neighbors whatever conveniences and comforts he found wanting: a chest of drawers, a desk, a candelabrum, an easy chair, a rug. And "no one felt secure in his own premises until the abbé had attained supreme local bliss, the secret of which he alone possessed."[24]

He was not one to waste time reading Linguet's remarks on laborers' wages. And how could they ever see eye to eye on the bread controversy when they were not even talking about the same commodity? Each day Madame de La Briche's private baker turned out mouth-watering, snow-white rolls made of milled flour, or a softer variety known as "chapter" rolls. At Sunday dinner, guests were served bread with the crusts removed, "made of fine, light flour seasoned with butter or milk."[25]

The bread consumed by seven out of ten Frenchmen, which Linguet denounced as a poison that breeds intestinal disorders and ulcers, is brown, the "worst kind of bread," made of whatever happens to be in the local grain supply, a variable mixture of white flour, "fine- or coarse-ground wheat flour," and, for Parisians since the famine of 1769, *recoupette* or bran, the third flour left over from partly milled grain husks.

The price of this common loaf of bread, which weighs about four pounds, is creeping up to twelve sous from last year's eight.

31

MARCH 1775

A Hero Is Always a Madman

"From Gilbert Romme, medical student, Rue des Lavandières, fourth floor, Paris;

"to Gabriel Dubreuil, postmaster of the town of Riom, seneschalsy of Riom, province of Auvergne, lodging in the house of M. Guymoneau on the Rue des Taules:

"I'm surprised at your chiding me for not having mentioned that I saw the king and queen.* I saw them and the whole royal family, and I also saw the gallery of Versailles, its gardens and zoo,** as well as the waterworks and the park of Marly. I wrote you about the last two because I enjoyed thinking of them again. Since you're ordinarily so choosy as to what things deserve attention from a practical man, why do you forget yourself at times and ask me such questions?"[1]

Not very accommodating, this twenty-five-year-old student who proclaims his indifference to the royal couple and takes his correspondent to task. But don't rely on this, for in the same letter Gilbert Romme exposes the tender heart beneath his tough Auvergnat hide. Dubreuil, a shy, sensitive, insatiably curious fellow with a childlike sense of humor, is his best friend, and Riom his "homeland," the ducal town that rates itself superior to neighboring Clermont-Ferrand. What luck that Gabriel became postmaster general, and so young, too. Gilbert can write him whatever he pleases at no cost† and send him gazettes and new books by the armload. Dubreuil distributes them to friends in town, who await news from Paris as if it were the gospel according to St. Gilbert Romme.

In 1775 Romme's every thought and gesture still proclaims his deep attachment to the rich yet mournful Limagne district, from which he feels

---

*In an earlier letter from Romme describing a visit to Versailles.
**The royal park of Versailles, adjacent to the Orangerie, included a well-stocked botanical garden and a small zoo containing wildlife from "the islands and the tropics" open to the public on certain days.
†In those days postal levies on letters, printed matter, and parcels were charged to the addressee.

utterly displaced. He lives only for his native soil, for his mother,* for his friends; in Paris he feels like a soldier in the field. What could be lovelier than Riom-le-Beau, where, owing to the Massif Central's volcanic rock, "even the houses dress in black, black waistcoats, black breeches," and each in this supremely judicial town "lodges at least one councillor, one judge, one lawyer, one clerk of the court, one bailiff"?

Riom's rugged landscape is reflected in Gilbert Romme's pride, which will go with him all his life and even now invests his stern countenance "carved out of wood, recalcitrant, pale, aggressive, and haughty, etched with melancholy and an incurable shyness" (according to biographer Alessandro Galante-Garrone).

He is ugly and knows it; he also knows that he is ill-tempered. He adapts to it, as does Auvergne to its black stone for building churches. "I'm annoyed at myself for asking prominent persons to take an interest in the career of a penniless little provincial."

He intends to manage for himself. Arriving in Paris to study medicine in September 1774 with two hundred francs in his pocket, he had nothing left after paying in advance for his lodgings and some essential expenses "to make myself presentable in society": a dress suit and sword, a hair-bag, a hat "to be carried under the arm," and face powder. His furnished room—more like a garret—on the Rue des Lavandières costs him six francs a month; counting the hairdresser three times a week, meals "brought up to my room," laundry and incidentals, he can hardly get by on less than forty francs a month. "I don't know whether in time I can learn to spend less, but at the moment it doesn't seem possible." It was a cold winter. "Two sticks of firewood are my andirons; I burn them when it gets very cold, which means I have neither andirons, shovel, nor tongs. Imagine what I go through to roast the chestnuts my mother sent me; putting them in the fire is easy, but I can't say the same for getting them out. I often laugh about the tricks I have to resort to, and that's the sole impression poverty leaves on me . . . A trestle bed, a mattress, a sheet, a blanket, no curtains, two straight chairs, a water pitcher, a tumbler: such is the inventory of my household furnishings."[2] He gets along by tutoring mathematics, though his days are crammed with sessions of anatomy, chemistry, physiology, pharmacy, and "the science of herbs," not just at the Ecole de Médecine, now in its decline, but also in private lecture courses, a great innovation of the period; students and amateurs were flocking to hear the young and renowned Dr. Vicq d'Azyr speak.

Reluctant spring, typical of the Ile-de-France, puts in a grudging appearance. Romme finds it milder than in Auvergne and breaks his monastic routine to make brief excursions to Versailles, Marly, Chantilly, and Yerres:**"A country lad eager for all kinds of beautiful sights, because he sees

*His father, a prosecutor, had died in 1763.
**Southeast of Paris; site of an ancient abbey. [*Trans.*]

them so rarely, marvels each step of the way in these enchanted wonderlands."
In his usual bristling manner, and armed with introductions, he calls on compatriots from Auvergne who have "made it" in Parisian society: Marmontel and the Abbé Delille. Neither of these literary personalities seems to inspire him; graceful language means nothing to Romme. "Marmontel's reputation is uncertain; the Abbé de l'Isle's [*sic*] is more solid." But "the couplets, the novels, the long or short epics, all the rubbish of our literature . . . are intolerably dull to me . . . They are mere words, sentences, words, sentences, and fine paper. That is my feeling about literature."[3] He prefers scientists, and thinks physicists are nicer than geometricians, whom he dislikes. "It appears that a geometrician is entitled to consider himself better than others because his function is essential to all other sciences." Even geometry's emperor disappoints him somewhat, despite the triumphant cry: "I have seen D'Alembert!" Ah, but wait: "He was with an artist who was sketching his portrait. His build and features seem to contrast greatly with the mind and endowments that have earned him so vast a reputation. If the artist had not been holding his pencil, I would have taken him for the scholar and D'Alembert for his servant."

Our impecunious provincial is sharpening his teeth. He tests them on another idol, Buffon, or at least on his writings. "M. de Buffon does not have as many admirers in Paris as you think and as I myself thought when I was with you. Every day critics are coming up with new errors in his work, especially his *Supplément à la théorie de la terre* . . . I can hear you shout 'Blasphemy!' There was a time when I would have shouted too, but I grew hoarse awhile ago."[4]

He went about tense and suspicious, unshakable as one of those blocks of basalt that turn up every now and then in the fields around Riom. A blighted childhood had marked him for life: his mother's premature widowhood. He clung to her still, through his chastity, his Jansenist ideals. No women. Fear of pleasure. Work and virtue. He endorsed Christian doctrine if not Christ: "Christianity places the soul at a sufficient distance from nature to permit enjoyment of it without involvement in it, to permit rejection of it when it alarms us."[5] The Christianity of Stoics, regarded as a discipline and a training ground for courage, was drummed into him during his schooling in Riom under the Oratorians, now Clermont's leading educators since the Jesuits had been banned from Auvergne as from everywhere else. A great opportunity for young Romme, the best scientific training in France. Jesuit instruction would have tormented him with its emphasis on rhetoric. Unawares, the Oratorians of Riom and their adjuncts in Montauban, Troyes, Rodez, Cahors, Montbéliard, and Bordeaux were slipping into the Encyclopedist camp by surrendering to "the triumphant explosion of mathematics and experimental physics within the culture, the pedagogy, in short the daily life of France."[6] Romme never regretted his schooldays; learning enchanted him, especially geography, which helped him relate what he observed in Riom to the larger universe: "Geography draws a man out of the narrow sphere of his environment and places him atop the whole world, making him its citizen."

Around the age of fifteen he had contracted a type of ophthalmia, possibly infectious and certainly dangerous, the worst of ordeals for a book-loving adolescent. It got to the point where he could neither read nor leave the house. His mother meekly shouldered this added burden: "My husband dead, my son blind . . ." Faith in science saved Gilbert Romme by prompting him to write to Janin de Combe-Blanche, the best eye specialist in France. Janin practiced in Lyons, curing rich and famous men from all over Europe—and he treated Gilbert for nothing, by mail, dispensing a series of extremely meticulous prescriptions. That was when Romme decided to become a doctor: knowledge of the human body, he perceived, enabled a man to save his fellow beings. But his vision remains weak, and the eyes he casts upon things will always be somewhat injured.

He had found it difficult to leave his birthplace and the nucleus of friends fast becoming his disciples; at the same time, and without admitting it, he found Riom dull. Paris symbolized the fountain of knowledge. He didn't really care whether he became a doctor or a scientist: "Learning is my one goal, my single passion. All modern discoveries rightfully interest me, and in I plunge. If that's a crime, I confess to it." His greatest delight was "the acquisition of one more item of knowledge," practical rather than abstract, in order "to comprehend reality, to transform and perfect it with the aid of scientifically improved techniques and instruments notably in the areas of animal husbandry, increased agricultural output, development of the tools of manufacture, of the means of transportation, of mills and mines."[7] He had no patience with "political history, the history of conquests, which is invariably a record of the slaughter, the injustice, the cruelty, the ambition of men in every era . . . As far as I can see, a hero is always a madman and too often a scoundrel whom people honor out of fear that they won't be able to convict him, and maybe also because . . . people applaud the vices for which they seek approval from others and like to celebrate a man who resembles themselves."[8]

Romme in Paris in the year 1775 is the *Encyclopédie* becoming personified in the flesh of a Jansenist.

A ray of sunlight pierces his dismal existence: he meets Count Golovkin in the course of tutoring his son. Golovkin is a "good nobleman"—like the proverbial "noble savage." A human miracle. A Russian born in The Hague and brought up in western Europe, with his back to his native land, to what is happening there behind all the hypocrisy and bloodshed—thanks to that wretched Catherine the Great. Golovkin vows never to return to his homeland until the two ruling dicta no longer rule: "I am guilty without having sinned" and "Everything belongs to God and my Sovereign." He avoids lectures and the salons, abstains from luxury, idleness, and affectation. He devotes his time to scientific pursuits and to educating his children along lines set forth by Rousseau, whom he knows and idolizes. Romme is completely taken with the man: "Yes, my dear chap, I have indeed paid frequent visits to M. de Golovkin. His forthright manner, not to mention his ability and character, inspire my deepest admiration and affection. He has neither the outlook nor pretensions of an aristocrat . . . Some people would question the compliment because it applies to a nobleman and might take me for a flatterer, but if it is dangerous to say something good, it is sometimes unfair to say nothing at all."[9]

As Golovkin is a friend of Turgot, Gilbert becomes a confirmed "Turgotist." In a letter to Dubreuil on March 25, 1775, he says: "This enlightened, truly objective minister doesn't promote his own views, which are judicious and invariably useful to the nation, until he has tried their efficacy himself. He has done away with the road service* in his own lands."** Gilbert's imagination suddenly runs wild as he fancies himself passing on suggestions to the king's chief minister via Golovkin. More than that, he sees a marvelous opportunity to advance his career. Turgot wants to found a chair of hydrodynamics in the Congregation of the Oratory in Paris and to systematize this new field of study: "M. Turgot takes most delight, next to the public welfare, in the arts and sciences, to which he extends his patronage and encouragement."[10]

Those whose confidence he has won look to Turgot not only for fiscal reforms but also for making science work to change the face of France. So Romme is inventing a hero after all, patterned after his own special design. And why shouldn't Turgot create a chair of mathematics and experimental physics in Riom in order to revive the Riding Academy, arm of Effiat's Military Academy for the sons of Auvergne's nobility, which is falling into disuse for want of a modern curriculum?[11]

And why not put Gilbert Romme in charge of it? Gilbert sees himself stepping from the coach, a combined physician and professor, and borne off triumphantly by his friends to transform the entire province. Auvergne, starting with Riom and Effiat, could be regenerated: "Once they become more industrious and informed, the inhabitants would make an effort to cultivate the vast marshlands infesting the region that surrounds Riom and Clermont." Manufacture would follow, and "for trade to flourish would simply require more roadbuilding or improved waterways."[12]

"All Auvergne would have wakened from centuries of slumber."[13] Gone forever the legend of a province buried among the dunghills, peopled by peasants in wooden shoes and spattered smocks. "Is there no desire for science

*The *droit de corvée* was a direct tax (though paid in service rather than money) on the peasantry which required them to supply labor and equipment for keeping local roads in repair over a given number of days each year. [*Trans.*]

**The lands he administered as intendant of Limousin, not his private estates.

there? Then those who feel the lack of it must implant that desire . . . We approach the decisive moment for molding the tastes of Auvergne either to embrace science or to reject it forever and thus invite the ridicule that has so infected our Parisian wits."[14]

Through the arts and science, Turgot will regenerate France and Gilbert Romme will reawaken Auvergne. What splendid dreams fill the springtime of 1775!

BENJAMIN FRANKLIN

32

MARCH 1775

Boar Versus Hunter

The old gentleman leaning on the arm of a youth "with alert, sparkling eyes and just the hint of a double chin,"[1] his grandson, and followed by servants bowed under the weight of his trunks is Benjamin Franklin searching for the launch that will row him into exile from the London docks on March 25, 1775. Biblical scene. The first great bourgeois of modern times, patriarch of the old and new worlds, is leaving England.

He will board a vessel on the Thames, above London Bridge. His tiny craft is harder to spot than a water rat in the chill night fog, among the thousands of ships moored side by side "five or six rows deep, in perfect order along the near or far bank, and which stand as an awesome symbol of the great might and prosperity of human industry."[2] Is that what he means to defy, this old fool, at the end of a prudent life? He's lucky they let him slip away quietly, that George III didn't have him arrested while all London was gossiping about his imminent banishment, that he wasn't clapped behind bars for high treason, sent to the block, and his head put on display at Temple Bar. Many Tories complain that the government is too soft on this spy. Rather than make a martyr of Franklin, however, Lord North and the king would prefer to have him vanish into the night. Excellent solution: send him back to his colonial cronies and let His Majesty's troops take care of the lot of them. Project for the coming summer. Franklin has stirred up Londoners, a persistent, symbolic reminder of a fiasco now thirty years old. Over there he'll be just one more rebel.

The old man and the youth book passage on Captain Osborne's *Pennsylvania Packet*. In the gray dawn breaking over this bustling port, no one suspects that the sturdy windjammer heading down the estuary carries with it the last hope of peace between Great Britain and America.

The crossing will be a long one, at least a month, over the North Atlantic, "the roughest sea in the world," aboard this solid packet built to ride the waves and to ply its stormy transatlantic route. A kingdom of timber, tar, canvas, and brine. A crew of thirty, all hardy as the ship they serve; Ben becomes attached to them. They remind him of the sturdy colonists among whom he grew up as a child in Boston. Here aboard the *Pennsylvania Packet* it's the sea rather than the land they must master, battling one storm after another from the west. The gale seems bent on anchoring Franklin's gaze in the direction of his once beloved England. Now, though, "when I consider the extreme corruption prevalent among all orders of men in this old, rotten state, and the glorious public virtue so predominant in our rising [America] . . . I fear they [England] will drag us after them in all the plundering wars which their desperate circumstances, injustice, and rapacity may prompt them to undertake . . . to unite us intimately [with England] will only be to corrupt and poison us also. It seems like . . . coupling and binding together the dead and the living."[3]

Look what he has come to, conciliation's champion, the man who always opted for compromise. Even yesterday, on the same page of his journal, he wrote: "Yet I would do anything, I would endure whatever one can endure without risk to our just liberties rather than engage in a war with such parents, unless driven to it." But why insist on moderation? He leaves England slandered and insulted by these "parents" with whom he is still determined to postpone a conflict. Baron Rokeby has just flooded London with a pamphlet declaring that "our colonies would indeed be peaceful but for Dr. Franklin, who, brandishing a torch fired by thunderbolts, has ignited all America."[4]

Logical deduction. The average Englishman is acquainted with only one American: Benjamin Franklin. Therefore he must be the cause of England's colonial woes. The man of peace is a warmonger.

He had fought tooth and nail to avert a struggle, even after losing his personal security when they deprived him of the postmaster-generalship. He had retreated into a life of scientific and literary pursuits—retirement, in short—peace at last, and let the world gallop on its own course without him . . . But the world came knocking at his door. Hardly had George III's Privy Council condemned him when the news from Boston sent England into a fury: on December 16, 1773, Bostonians disguised as Indians had jettisoned the tea cargo of three East India Company ships. A matter of principle: the captain had paid the crown's tea duty to which the colonists so strongly objected. Those tea leaves caused waves in the Atlantic. British leaders declared that after ten years their patience had run out; the Americans, their impatience.

Would-be conciliators looked to Franklin as their last hope for averting an impending clash. The elder Pitt, Lord Chatham, had sought Franklin's counsel on possible remedies. But the once glorious Chatham, conqueror of France, was only a shadow of his former self; sick, crippled with gout, given to drink and to maudlin sentiments, a faded political force. The April elections had strengthened Tory power and the king's hand. The great Whigs were in eclipse, like Pitt and Franklin. Lord Sandwich complained to the benches that the Yankees were just a bunch of rascals who could be taught to behave by an army of only ten thousand. Lord North carried his Boston Port Bill that paralyzed this key maritime center by closing it to all shipping. Other colonial ports stood solidly behind Boston. Dozens of vessels were drifting aimlessly up and down the American coast like weary seagulls.

The war hawks triumphed: they had evidence of planned rebellion in the colonies. "What do these shopkeepers mean by assembling to discuss politics? Let them mind their shops instead of acting like independent officials."[5] "We have a right to revoke their charters since the Americans are violating them; we have a right to govern them because they are incapable of governing themselves."[6]

One Whig, Edmund Burke, had pleaded for reconciliation; the Commons had hissed every sentence. But Burke, a born orator, was stimulated to even greater eloquence by the hostile shouts:

"Driven to desperation, the boar turns upon the hunter. If your sovereignty and their liberty cannot be reconciled, which will they choose? They will fling sovereignty in your face. Is there a man alive who will let himself be enslaved by an argument? . . . Do you now ask if these Englishmen of America are content with their servitude? . . . Do you ask how you are governing a people which believes it has a right to be free and thinks it is not? . . . "[7]

Burke had managed to sway only forty-nine members out of more than six hundred. In fact the House of Commons provided a reliable public-opinion poll. Long before his London friends did, Franklin had realized that the English people favored this war no less actively than their king. Burke admitted discouragement: "The insensibility of the London Merchants is of a degree and kind scarcely to be conceived."[8] And English farmers were fed up with the pretensions of colonists across the ocean who claimed to be their equals. "The only point in which the Administration seems to have the People on their side is in asserting the sovereignty of the Mother Country."[9]

In introducing to Parliament four restrictive acts which, along with the Boston Port Bill, came to be known in the colonies as the Intolerable Acts, corpulent Lord North trembled for once and stammered. At the Court of St. Jame's, George III had been moody all day. British leaders saw—rather belatedly—that the die was cast. But England did not tremble.

Franklin had published a pamphlet "on ways to pour oil upon troubled waters" during the month when General Gage landed in Boston with four regiments and held the city in a state of siege. Franklin's letters to America repeated over and over: "No violence! No blunders! We must play for time." But his voice grew fainter, as if he had shouted himself hoarse. From habit; like a conditioned reflex. He was still observing the teachings of Cotton Mather, the fiery Puritan preacher who had terrorized Boston when Franklin was a boy and who once had cautioned him, pointing to a low beam jutting out into the aisle of his church: "Stoop down, stoop down! You are young and have the world before you. Stoop as you go through it and you will miss many hard thumps."[10]

For forty years he has walked with a stoop. But lately the fearful prospect of violent rebellion was not all that saddened him as he prepared to leave England in disgrace; he sensed also that countless possibilities had withered and were dying. In bidding farewell to Burke, he said: "It is all over. America has known happy days under England's scepter, before this grievous dispute —perhaps she will never know happier ones."

What about himself? Will life ever be as pleasant again as it was in London with companions like Mrs. Stevenson? (Actually, his "good wife," Deborah, lies dying in Philadelphia. He may never see her alive. He thinks of this occasionally. Marriage killed their love; still, it doesn't make his life more cheerful.) Farewell to the relaxing company of Whig friends, English liberals amazed to hear an echo of themselves from the New World which Franklin brought to the coffee houses, the theaters, the salons where he was taken for an oracle, and all over ancient Europe where he felt at home because here and there people were installing his lightning rod.

But once back home, will he really *feel* at home? He plans ahead, realistically, during those nights on the ocean filled with endless games of checkers, under the swaying light of an oil lamp, with a grandson who does not bear his name. William Temple is indeed the child of Benjamin's son William, who has chosen not to acknowledge publicly the son Miss Temple bore him. Nor has he adopted his father's courageous views, for William Franklin is an administrator for the crown in America and wants to keep his job. The son's outlook aged as the father's was rejuvenated. "William remained faithful to the principle that the king can do no wrong. He sent polite letters to his father urging him to return to America and live out his last years in peace . . . He hastened to assure their mutual friends in England that he did not share his father's political attitudes. So they went separate paths."[11] The real Franklins were a grandfather and a bastard grandson.

To which America is Benjamin returning? There are many Americas. Is it the fish and onions of New England? The linseed and flour of Pennsylvania? The tobacco of Maryland and Virginia? The pitch, tar, and turpentine of North Carolina? The rice and indigo of South Carolina? "Georgia has sawdust to sprinkle over everything."[12] The thirteen colonies with separate governments and conflicting interests have been quarreling ever since they came into existence. There is no one America, the English keep saying, there are thirteen plus Canada. Franklin himself is the symbol of this division, tossed back and forth all his life between two major centers, Boston and Philadelphia: Puritan, mercantile New England; Quaker—and mercantile—Pennsylvania. Because he was a product—and a rare one—of those two cities, he became the unique citizen of two worlds. Yet he remains a Northerner and bristles at the arrogance of rich Southern planters with whom some degree of accommodation has to be reached. He will find them in Philadelphia, where the Continental Congress has been in session for several weeks. He isn't aware that they, too, have become wild boars. It is in Virginia on March 8 that Patrick Henry sounds the call to arms, in the Old Church in Richmond ("old" by virtue of its hundred years of existence!):

> It is natural to man to indulge in the illusions of hope. We are apt to shut our eyes against a painful truth, and listen to the song of that siren till she transforms us into beasts . . .
>
> Our petitions have been slighted; our remonstrances have produced additional violence and insult; our supplications have been disregarded; and we have been spurned, with contempt, from the foot of the throne! In vain, after these things, may we indulge the fond hope of peace and reconciliation. There is no longer any room for hope. If we wish to be free . . . we must fight. I repeat it, sir, we must fight! . . .
>
> They tell us, sir, that we are weak; unable to cope with so formidable an adversary. But when shall we be stronger? Will it be the next week, or the next year? Will it be when we are totally disarmed and when a British guard shall be stationed in every house? . . . Besides, sir, we have no choice. If we were base enough to desire it, it is now too late to retire from the contest . . . Our chains are forged. Their clanking may be heard on the plains of Boston . . .
>
> It is in vain, sir, to extenuate the matter. Gentlemen may cry: Peace! Peace! —but there is no peace . . . I know not what course others may take, but as for me, give me liberty or give me death![13]

A good five hundred miles separate Richmond from Boston, but the clanking of chains has reached there. Franklin will find America in a bellicose mood, on the verge of unification—Britain's final legacy. Is there still room for him? "Not in his wildest dreams had he anticipated colonial revolt until some time in the remote future after the general population had attained urban standards of living. That would have taken a century." His frequent advice to Americans in recent years has been: "Have as many children as possible as soon as possible."[14]

At the beginning of May, when at last his ship enters the Delaware's deep bay, he is toying still with notions of appeasement. Each day he had measured the ocean temperature on a large thermometer attached to a cord (he deduced the existence of the Gulf Stream); he also lectured his grandson, who wants to be a painter or a surgeon: No, no, William Temple, you must take up the law, for we are approaching a period of rampant chicanery.

On the evening of May 5 they reach Philadelphia. Balmy spring weather, the pungent odors of the riverside where trees seem to spring straight up out of the water. Franklin still feels the bite of London's winter between his shoulder blades. Here everything is green and fresh, the forest belt halfway between North and South. And over there at the foot of the bay, in the straits of the Delaware, lies the City of Brotherly Love founded by William Penn, with its low brick-and-wood houses to which Europe's persecuted have flocked for less than a century: Dutch and German Protestants, French Huguenots, Scotland's Irish and Ireland's Scots, Quakers, Masons . . . Benjamin Franklin became a journalist there, a scientist, a statesman. It was he who paved the streets. It was he who founded the university and the hospital. Crowds throng the dock waving scarves at the *Pennsylvania Packet*; musket volleys ring out. They wait to welcome the most eminent town father of a town no longer a tiny backwoods parish. Philadelphia has become the center of a continent. Congressional delegates mingle with Philadelphians: blond Virginians, New Yorkers in corduroy suits, Yankees with their New England twang. Amid the cheers for Franklin a new cry is heard: "America for Americans!" People rush up to tell him the news; their faces are tense, their excitement hushed: while he was at sea, the lid blew off in Boston—that second pole of his existence—when General Gage sallied out of the city to intimidate neighboring towns. On April 19 English soldiers were fired on by the militia first at Lexington, then Concord. The Massachusetts campaign had exploded like a string of dynamite. British troops retreated under withering fire from every house and hedge. They gave up 73 dead and 174 wounded. General Gage is now blockaded in Boston.

The American Revolution is under way.[15]

A cavalcade of five hundred well-wishers escorts Franklin to his house, which will be besieged for a week to come. And to think he worried about the sort of reception he might get! Having departed in the role of a rather dubious negotiator, he returns a martyr to the cause of liberty. Hutchinson, Wedderburn, and the rest of his persecutors chose the right moment to restore his credit.

A few close friends have embraced him with sober faces, murmuring condolences, for his wife is dead. He returns to an empty house. But who can think of Deborah at such a time?

33

They All Hold Hands

Turgot is settled in office, his staff nearly complete with the arrival in December of Dupont, whose ecstatic admiration provides a welcome relief from Condorcet's aggressiveness. Installed in the Hôtel du Contrôle Général, the seat of the fiscal administration in Paris, Dupont proclaims rapturously: "To win M. Turgot's affection, one need only be willing, honest, and sensible." And to his patron he expounds just the advice Turgot wishes to hear: "Let no one suppose that you have been elevated to this ministry for nothing. But don't do anything suddenly. Move only by undulation."[1]

Yet bread has cost twelve sous nearly everywhere in the Ile-de-France since early March.

"By undulation" is precisely the way Turgot would like to progress—that is to say, step by step, and without treading on either the king's bias or the queen's whims. He wants to hasten at a leisurely pace, pressed by Condorcet, curbed by Dupont and Morellet, to clear the hurdles one at a time; he has a strategy, but keeps it to himself. He has disciples, but no confidants; guidelines, but no hard-and-fast rules. He has already freed the grain trade and is confident that the economy will right itself. Once Louis XVI's coronation, this spring's main event, is past, he will attack the budgetary deficit by progressive cuts in court and military spending. He has planned his tactics and chosen the man he will produce at the last moment to carry them out. But that's his secret. Everything in good time. At any rate, it is imperative that France not go to war again, though there seems little danger of this at the moment. Ultimately, when financial and economic matters are on an even keel, he will attack the root of the problem by eliminating the farmers-general, by levying taxes with the consent of regional assemblies and by having government agents collect them. His dream is to see France rid of the *corvée,* the tithe, and the salt tax, her propertied classes flocking to contribute to the general welfare . . . By then it would be time for him to step aside: "In my family, they die of gout at the age of fifty." He is forty-seven and was racked with gout all last winter. He gives himself three years to reform France by undulation.

But by October 1774 bread was selling for thirteen sous in Caen. Normandy's intendant grew alarmed: "The populace, on finding the markets destitute of grain, blame the free trade . . ." he informed Turgot, who shot back: "There is no cause for heeding complaints from the people. In fact, they must be made to realize that their resistance, their disturbances, and their rioting will serve only to impose stricter measures of containment."[2] With respect to the general public, "undulation" is futile, a hurdle to be smashed, not cleared.

M. Necker, or Nèckre as everyone pronounces the name, sees things differently. Turgot dodges a surprise blow, winces, and shrugs it off. In fact he feels injured because the rebuff comes from bankers and economists, his own tribe. An academic dispute involving the whole country. And what prompted this confounded Genevan son of a German, who made his fortune in the banking business in Paris, to leave his Château de Saint-Ouen and attack Turgot in an essay entitled *Sur la législation et le commerce des grains*? Political ambition? A literary itch? Necker, on the threshold of retirement, was telling the world that his remaining years would be devoted to his wife, his daughter,* his friends, his salon . . . Then he went and published this piece on March 12, a firebrand tossed at Turgot's feet at the worst possible moment: when poor harvests combine with certain drawbacks inherent in a free grain trade. He had even indulged in the luxury of politeness by poking his big, puffy face into Turgot's office to inquire whether the minister wished to read the manuscript "and decide if it should be permitted to appear in print." Morellet was there, beaming, the perennial gossip, about to witness an important debate. "What I have to say here is not the word of someone else but what I saw and heard with my own eyes and ears. I was in M. Turgot's office when M. Necker appeared with his notebook . . . M. Turgot retorted rather curtly that he could print whatever he liked, that there was nothing to be afraid of, for the public would pass judgment by refusing to read it; all this in the scornful tone he frequently reserved for attacking ideas in conflict with his own . . ." There is a certain type of contradiction that Turgot cannot abide, especially when it is muffled. "M. Necker went away bloody but unbowed."[3] Another declaration of war. Yet Necker was soft-pedaling the affair, knowing that Turgot, champion of free speech, could censure him only at the risk of forsaking his own ideals.

His essay calls to arms all opponents of Turgot, aristocrats and bourgeois alike. Necker had accommodated Choiseul by acting as "the banker of bankers to the king" and lending him a paltry million and a half** during the war

*Madame de Staël. [*Trans.*]
**Nearly 600 million modern francs [$120,000,000].

against England.[4] Anything that had to do with money aroused his interest; most members of Parliament support him. His wealth and his vast correspondence have won him a broad following in Switzerland, England, Germany, and Sweden. He offers philosophic direction to the assorted fraternity of those who, from fear of progress, from jealousy, from bigotry, or from sheer ignorance, would bar Turgot's way. Ultimately they will adopt for their gospel an essay which none of them ever bothered to read. Opposition to Turgot undergoes its Pentecost, its enlightenment emanating from Geneva.

Necker's essay is not a pamphlet—nothing like Linguet's diatribes. The arguments are subtly balanced, the style is eloquent, Rousseauesque: praise for economic pragmatism over and above planning; a whole list of specific proposals tailored to fit the needs of various regions. The second part gains widest attention, where the author denounces the speculations of "monopolists"—he, the millionaire banker!—and warns that they will send prices soaring.

Voltaire is stunned: "It infuriates me to find a banker defending such an unworthy cause."[5] What will happen if the entire banking establishment turns traitor? As a rich landowner at Ferney and Tournay and virtual lord of the Gex region, Voltaire is a stanch convert to Turgot's policies. He stands ready to fight for freedom of the grain trade as vigorously as he fought to vindicate the Calas family. Necker, on the other hand, has the bulk of his fortune invested in speculative stocks; his financial interests are not dependent on the market price of crops. Unhampered by necessity, he can afford to think imaginatively of the economy, nearly as imaginatively as Marat in denouncing the misery of the peasants, the threat of inflation, and the selfish motives of landowners: "If one day someone were to discover a food less tasty than bread which could sustain human existence for forty-eight hours, people soon would be compelled to eat every other day even if they preferred their former habits."[6] Heavy-handed sarcasm from this Swiss. Currently, however, it is he, rather than Voltaire and Turgot, who is right on that particular point, and a few people won't forget it.

A *setier* of grain costs twenty francs on March 31 in Pontoise, which sets the price of a loaf of bread at twenty-one sous. Pointoise prices affect those in Paris, a two-day journey, since commodities shipped by barge down the Oise and into the Seine reflect prices in the north inflated by transport charges. When the Abbé Terray was finance minister,* large stores of grain in the Paris region allowed municipal authorities to amortize price fluctuations and to stabilize the cost of bread locally at between eight and ten sous by supplying flour (often of inferior quality) to bakers at a fixed price. But Turgot—in the name of freedom, sacred freedom!—sold those reserves last autumn at a profit to the state. Now nothing can stop the cost of bread from skyrocketing to as

*Turgot's predecessor. [*Trans.*]

high as twenty-four sous in April—twice as much as three out of five citizens can afford.

April 17, 1775. Dijon, capital of Burgundy. Commotion for the past two days up and down the Cours de l'Arquebuse and the Cours du Parc, public promenades as broad and fine as Parisian boulevards. Restless groups mill about in the main square around the equestrian statue of Louis XIV.* Mostly workingmen and a scattering of women: the city is becoming industrialized. They come from mills and factories sprung up in the suburbs where they make velvet, cotton, muslin, printed cloth, and wax. For a week they haven't had enough to eat. And there is no one on the balcony of the town hall to explain why. Their new intendant, "the gentleman who represents the king," hasn't yet arrived. His deputy, La Tour du Pin, lieutenant general of the province, mumbles some inane remarks and treats them like naughty children:

"Look here, all you good folk, grain isn't up to twelve livres *yet* . . . "

Not true. A *setier*** costs eighteen livres. To prove it, here comes Janty the miller in a cart piled high with sacks of flour that he refuses to sell for less. Fishwives leave their stalls at the public fish market to rush after him, flailing the air with dead carp. Somehow he manages to fend them off. People are still able to laugh.

The next morning, Tuesday, April 18, there is no more laughter in Dijon. It is market day and people from five miles around flock here to buy their flour and meal and grain. But who can afford eighteen francs? They lash out at the richest "monopolist'" of them all, Carré, whose mill on the Ouche grinds a flour so white that everyone suspects it of being laced with powdered beans. Women take the lead, as on the previous day, only this time they brandish sticks. Carré barricades himself in a lawyer's house. The crowd breaks down

*Toppled in 1792.

**The following elements are provided as an economic primer to the Grain War, all relative to the Paris region—in Lyons, Toulouse, or Bordeaux, for instance, weights and measures varied from those in Paris. In the pages that follow:

A loaf of *bread* generally weighs four pounds (1.8 kilograms).

The most common unit of grain measure is the *setier* (1/12 of a *muid*; a *boisseau* is 1/12 of a *setier*). The modern equivalent of a *setier* is approximately 156 liters (21 pecks).

The tolerable price for the general public, meaning the consumer who lived off his daily wage or profit, called the "fair price," was twelve francs per *setier* of wheat, which worked out to eight sous per loaf. The sou (or sol) was 1/20 of a franc.

What might be termed the "fixed price of misery," according to calculations of Edgar Faure,[7] is the fourteen-sou loaf of bread. Above that level, the wage-earner "found himself compelled to cut into the bare necessities vital to family existence. From then on human beings face the threat of bodily damage."

Bread played so fundamental a role in the daily existence of ordinary persons that a laborer bringing home an average annual wage of 200 francs spent 108 of them per year for bread at eight sous (based on the average family's consumption of three pounds daily), but 192 if it cost fourteen sous. In modern terms, on an income of $800 a year, $440 would go for bread at eight sous and $767 at fourteen sous. In the last instance, that would leave a person drawing the minimum legal hourly wage only $32 for the rest of his annual needs after purchase of bread.

the door. He escapes over the rooftops. In revenge they wreck the house and toss all the furniture out the window. The crowd then heads for his mill on the city's outskirts, where they destroy everything in sight except the mill-stones, "the sheer weight of which protects them."[8] And it's plain to see that the grist here is spoiled: it reeks and is gritty. They dump it into the Ouche.

La Tour du Pin arrives, brave but inept as ever. He stands virtually alone, surrounded by the local militia. He has already sent for troops from Auxonne, Dôle, and Besançon, but they won't come for another day. At first the people treat him respectfully; but why does he beat those poor folk with his walking stick and call them looters? They haven't stolen anything, only taken revenge. He shouts at them: "The grass is starting to come up. Go graze, my friends!"

The next minute he's in full flight and spends the night in hiding, waiting for those reinforcements to arrive, while other rioters pillage the house of Sainte-Colombe, a parliamentary counselor in league with Carré. They expect to find his cellar stacked with grain. And if they ever lay hands on him . . . They don't, for he's burrowed under a dungheap. No grain in the cellar, but plenty of casks—and they don't contain holy water, this being Burgundy. There is plenty to keep the attackers occupied and put them to sleep.

Upon arrival the next morning, His Majesty's troops have merely to scoop up the whole drunken lot of poor devils from the magistrate's cellar. On the way they also pluck some forty-odd residents of Dijon from their beds, both men and women, calling them "agitators" when in fact they were named more or less haphazardly by informers who subsequently went underground the day before the arrests.

Not even an insurgence, it was no more than a spontaneous billow of popular unrest. But Dijon's authorities, not proud of their actions, promptly inform the finance minister that "the riot was sparked by his enemies"—and Turgot repeats it to the king. How convenient! The fault lies not in the price of bread but in the idiocy of sheep who let themselves be led astray by wicked shepherds. From Turgot to La Tour du Pin on April 20: "I am not surprised, sir, at the tumult occurring in Dijon. To indulge the fears and, worse still, the prejudices of the public is only to encourage unlimited excesses." On the 24th, Turgot, whose icy exasperation begins to thaw, writes again to Dijon's vis-count mayor: "It is not the people who should govern you, it is the law. It is up to you, who are responsible for maintaining public order, to conduct, to direct, to contain the populace, and to exact obedience to the law."

The Dijon incident established a stock interpretation of what came to be known as the Grain War: a government acting in behalf of its brainless subjects by allowing the price of grain to soar temporarily; agitators linked to a vast conspiracy against Turgot; and the sole outcome: repression. At least Dijon is back to normal. No reason to get alarmed.

But wait, what are these reports that begin to pour in from Tours, from Metz, from Rheims and Montauban on April 20? A chorus of intendants complains of "much ferment and upheaval among the populace."[9] It doesn't occur to anyone in Versailles or Paris that the elementary conspiracy afoot is hunger.

On April 27, in Beaumont some twenty-five miles from Paris, things get worse.[10]

Beaumont-on-the-Oise, between Chantilly and Pontoise, is a major port through which Paris-bound grain barges pass coming from the north before they enter the Seine. A thousand inhabitants, many of whom make their living from the river. Surrounded by the great forest of Carnelle with its oaks and Celtic rocks, it is a cool, damp region where life is not easy and the Prince de Conti owns the land and all hunting rights. Alarmed at one point by the disturbances, he shuts himself up in his Château de l'Isle-Adam, yet public gossip persistently ranks him with the "conspirators."

In Beaumont, city magistrate Nicolas Bailly* runs up against the wrath of haulers exhausted from unloading provisions for the weekday market, who find they cannot afford the new prices for bread and flour. They collar a grain merchant, dunk him twice in the public fountain, and drag him, well roughed up, before Bailly:

"The bastard is selling wheat at thirty-two livres! Give us justice! Come regulate the market and lower the price of grain."

The magistrate does no such thing. From his window he watches the haulers release the grain dealer with a flurry of kicks in the rump and, aided by women "of the lowest order," seize sacks of grain or meal and run their own market, selling at "the fair price": twelve francs per *setier* of wheat, twenty sous a *boisseau* for meal. No looting. No one helps himself without paying. Spontaneous popular price-fixing is born this day, Thursday, in Beaumont-on-the-Oise: the improvised distributors deliver cash receipts to Bailly for him to give the merchants, who have taken to their heels in terror.

The merchants reappear next morning, thinking the disturbance ended. They pry the magistrate out of his house and drag him about to search for and recover their underpriced wares—foolish fellows! More growls of protest. A crowd closes in and jostles Bailly:

"Villain! If you won't fix or lower the price of wheat, we'll do it ourselves."

He beats a hasty retreat behind bolted doors "since he had no power of enforcement and no help from a single soul."[11]

---

*No relation to the astronomer Jean-Sylvain Bailly, future member of the electoral assembly and mayor of Paris.

The virus of revolt will follow the course of the rivers, conveyed by barges laden with grain now costlier than gold. Pontoise and Beauvais on April 29. Poissy, Saint-Germain-en-Laye, Saint-Denis, Gonesse on the 1st of May. Versailles on the 2nd. Paris, the 3rd, and on up the Seine into the Marne as far as Chelles and Gagny. Choisy-le-Roi on the 4th; the 5th, Fontainebleau; the 6th, Meaux and Corbeil. At this stage, roads relay news from the river, accompanying (though often preceding wagons traveling to market from the docks) bands of men and women eager to report the anger or joy in their own parish to neighboring townspeople. And each hamlet ignites on contact with the nearest village when it comes time for the sale of grain. East of Paris, the whole Brie region is astir—each individual locality—from May 3 to 8, from Lagny to Melun and Valenton to Crécy.

False alarm: yesterday's blaze seems to have died out, though today's fires rage. No slogans; no politicking. No one is denouncing the government, much less the king. And even though local magistrates and police lieutenants have taken a mild cuffing, the event is brushed off as merely a marketplace affair, a dispute between buyers and sellers which explodes into violence only over the controversial item itself: sacks of grain, loaves of bread in the bakeshops. Really and truly, it's the Grain War and nothing else.

April 28. Town officials grow panicky. The job of maintaining peace and order rests almost universally with the local "watch," who are likely to be relatives or friends of the demonstrators. From Beauvais, a certain M. de Beaumesnil calls for government troops: "Yesterday in Méru a large crowd pillaged and carried off more than a hundred sacks of grain after ripping some open with knives and manhandling several proprietors." So things are getting rougher. Pilfering does in fact occur. "Over a hundred persons armed with sticks set out from Méru and its vicinity for Noailles, two leagues away . . . Farmers are apprehensive, reluctant to take their grain to market. The public is alarmed."[12] To cheer him up, they dispatch an armed brigade—of four cavalrymen.

April 29, Pontoise: pivotal town along the victualing route for districts north of Paris because the bridge spanning the Oise marks the convergence of land and river traffic. M. Saffray de Boislabbé, "king's counsel and attorney for the town," deals as best he can with "the crowd descending on the harbor to loot ships" while the tocsin tolls in the ancient belfry of Saint-Mallon, whose bell bears a Latin inscription that explains the tocsin's sound: *Unda, unda, unda, unda, unda, unda, accurrite cives!*[13] (Eddy, eddy, etc., hasten, townsfolk, hasten!) The gates are shut. "The bourgeoisie is called to arms," but the next day, when this fails to discourage "every peasant in the neighborhood from assembling to carry on yesterday's looting," Boislabbé takes it upon himself, contrary to Turgot's official orders, to advise merchants to sell their grain for twenty francs—until the soldiery arrives.* The looting stops. Peace returns to Pontoise on May 2.[14] But Demonthion, lieutenant general of police, sows panic among his superiors in Paris by reporting: "The crowd has gone to the flour and grain merchants . . . Few pay and all pilfer . . . They all hold hands . . . Some are overheard saying that the same thing will happen in Paris. I thought you ought to be warned."[15]

Monday, May 1: Leclerc and Sauvage,** well-to-do millers, alert the soldiery of Triel: several peasants "from neighboring villages" have crossed the Seine at Poissy and told them "in a threatening manner that they were bound for Saint-Germain to obtain flour."[16] At eleven o'clock, "having been informed of a riot in the grain market," Saint-Germain's police lieutenant appears there and declares that "persons of both sexes, from the town as well as the suburbs, were browbeating [sic] the merchants" and that "the main party was overturning stacks of merchandise, ripping open sacks with knives, seizing goods and dragging them off without paying."[17] Here, as in Beaumont, women have radicalized the unrest: flour at the "fair price" means life or death now, today, for their children and husbands. When dealers refused to be bullied—that is, declined to sell their flour at forty sous a *boisseau*—"the women began saying they would get it for nothing, whereupon they pounced on the sacks and slit them open."[18]

That same day the people of Nanterre compel Madame Jarry, the baker's wife, to sell fifty-one sacks of flour at forty sous per *boisseau* instead of fifty-five. In Gonesse, Pierre "the Swineherd" Cadet (so nicknamed because he threshes corn) leads the mob to cries of "Twelve francs a *setier*!" In Goussainville, Jacques Hazard, laborer, incites the crowd against the local garrison, shouting: "Give those fellows a drubbing! They're only flesh and bone like yourselves!"[19]

Tuesday, May 2: "Versailles is under attack," Louis XVI writes to Turgot at eleven in the morning.

The king is left virtually by himself. Turgot, Sartines, Miromesnil, and Lenoir, lieutenant general of police, rushed off to Paris the day before to prepare for the expected "demonstrators" and to maintain order. Since Versailles is under the jurisdiction of Paris, the ministers have assumed that any action will break out in the capital. No such luck. Rioting erupts to the east and southwest of Paris where the Seine and the Marne form loops. Louis XVI has only De Muy at hand, his decrepit old minister of war, plus the palace guard. What about Maurepas, his mentor and fount of wisdom? Vanished. He also is in Paris and seems to shun all responsibility—on principle, not out of cowardice. Let Tur-

---

*To punish his complacency, Turgot later claps Boislabbé in the Bastille for seven weeks.

**Sauvage will be hanged as a hoarder by the residents of Saint-Germain fourteen years later, on July 15, 1789, in one of the riots linked to the taking of the Bastille.

got run the risks; he's the one who promoted this free grain trade in the first place. Tonight Maurepas goes to the Opera.

In Versailles the rioting begins at daybreak and is not affected by the king's presence.[20] The same pattern as in Nanterre and Gonesse—as if Louis XVI never existed. He is mistaken to say Versailles is "under attack" when in fact what is is the marketplace of Poids-le-Roy. This astounding conglomeration of fetid, unsanitary stalls (without running water or latrines) had sprouted on the rigid checkerboard designed by Mansart to form a grid around the Parc aux Cerfs, a thickly wooded game preserve in Louis XIV's day, which evolved as a geometric caravansary in the last fifty years, a great bazaar offering frivolous wares to "transient guests"—such as the king and his court, his army, and his domestic or foreign visitors—in addition to supplying the necessities of life for fifty thousand inhabitants of a village accidentally sprung up on the grounds of a hunting lodge. It was the place to go when you wanted a prostitute or grain —but only the grain was costly at Poids-le-Roy,* a millstone about the necks of the village poor and peasants from the countryside.[21]

The peasants arrive at dawn from Saint-Germain, Montesson, Houilles, Crécy, Sartrouville, Puteaux, Bougival, and Carrières, gathering neighbors in their wake and instilling them with courage. "Between eight and nine o'clock numerous audacious persons burst tumultuously into Poids-le-Roy . . . There they punctured and slashed numerous sacks of flour . . . Some headed for the bakers of this town, whose bread they pilfered; others, when encountering flour carts in the streets . . . forced them to turn around and plundered their goods."[22] In one morning more than half the nine hundred *setiers* stored at Poids-le-Roy is ransacked or spilled. There is flour to wade in. Many insurgents are Limousins who come rushing out from the Rue du Bel-Air, a nearby ghetto into which they are packed like animals. They don't think twice about enjoying this sudden windfall.** And if the onrushing human tide deflects in the direction of bakeshops, it's because of a rumor that the authorities have just reduced the price of bread to two sous a pound. The fair price. But bakers don't know what to make of it: a loaf for eight sous when only the day before they were getting fourteen? It must be a lie. Then the looting starts—for the "lie" is true.

Versailles's military governor has indeed ordered the sale of eight-sou loaves. This is the Prince de Poix, a pretentious, puckish poseur with elevated heels designed to augment his lilliputian stature, popularly known as *"le petit Poix."* His appointment to this sinecure was construed as a great favor, for it put him in charge of parades and festivals. Assuming that rioters have taken over the town, he panics and capitulates in a wink, playing for time to assemble the royal guards and musketeers. A good tactic, though shortsighted: Poids-le-

---

*The Parc aux Cerfs district, encircling the parish of Saint-Louis, is to the right of the Avenue de Sceaux as you stand with your back to the palace.
**The term "Limousin" was loosely applied to masons, many of whom, though not all, did in fact come from that province. Similarly, chimney sweeps were called "Savoyards."

Roy, deserted by the crowd, is reoccupied by noontime. Danger ahead: the bakers won't comply and the mob may resort to violence if it thinks it has been cheated.

Yet Louis XVI remains perfectly calm. One might even say content; it relieves the boredom. Stolid composure and apathy, his Bourbon heritage, prompt him to behave in kingly fashion, firmly and sternly. He welcomes the chance to dispatch letters to Turgot—several during the day—and thus to exercise his right to rule a nation with blows on the back: "I have just sent the guard to march on the market [his eleven-o'clock bulletin, the one announcing that Versailles was "under attack"] . . . You may rely on my firmness. I am pleased with the safety measures you have taken for Paris; that was my great-est worry. You may indicate my pleasure with his conduct to M. Bertier*
. . . You will do well to arrest the persons you mention. . . " meaning the mysterious, protean "agitators" who are now permanent characters in Tur-got's head.

At two o'clock the king sends off a victory bulletin to his minister: "We here are undisturbed. The rioters began to grow boisterous; troops dispatched to the scene calmed them and made them settle down . . . They left afterward, and units of the guard followed to see which way they went. I don't think much damage was done. I have ordered troops stationed along the road to Chartres and the mills in the Orsay and Chevreuse valleys, and have alerted the markets in Neauphle and Rambouillet . . . I advised the intendant to try to identify those who were paying,** whose apprehension I would strongly welcome. M. de Beauvau interrupts to inform me of a foolish step that has been taken to let them have bread at two sous [per pound].† He insists there is no choice but to concede that or else force them at bayonet point to pay whatever is the current price."[23]

So much for bayonets; since yesterday Turgot has been firing off note after note urging use of them. Louis XVI can sleep with a clear conscience: order reigns at Versailles, where relatively few bakeries have been raided and where, unlike most other areas in France, a sizable army can be mustered on short notice. "But," Turgot warns, "we must take every precaution to make sure they do not return to lay down the law."

That is precisely what Turgot is doing for Paris, where THEY are expected to arrive on May 2 and to demonstrate on Wednesday the 3rd.

---

*Bertier de Sauvigny, intendant of Paris, has just sent troops to the major ports along the Oise and the Lower Seine. He will be butchered by the Paris mob on July 22, 1789, the same day as his father-in-law, Foullon.
**That is, whoever is paying the people to revolt. Agitators, eternal agitators, hired presumably by rebel princes or foreign powers. Not a single such recruiter of hired hands was discovered.
†The Prince de Beauvau was duty captain of the guard that day. His failure to name the Prince de Poix as the person "guilty" of price-fixing stems from the fact that the latter was his son-in-law.

Who are THEY? One is a young gardener from Colombes, "arrested for seditious statements about bread." Another, a grape-grower from Boulogne who, on the evening of the 2nd, appears "with numerous persons" in two bakeshops, where, "without threat or violence," he orders loaves at eight sous —because the news is out that Versailles is selling bread at that price. A cartwright and a joiner from Epinay, "followed by a prodigious assembly," who meet up with a carter on his way to deliver twelve sacks of flour to the Paris market and relieve him of his goods at twenty-five livres and five sous per sack. A man named Guérangé from the Petite-Pologne district of Paris, who helps himself to bread at two sous (per pound) from two bakers, and at three sous from a third after hearing that "they had cried bread at two sous a pound in the Pologne."* Or Rémy Girier, ragpicker from Bougival, who demands the same consideration from bakers in Ruel, saying "he will pay the difference if they can prove to him that a loaf is worth more."[24]

"They all hold hands," as someone puts it. Meaning that though they live five or six leagues apart and are strangers, they need no cue to act and speak as one when hunger stalks, and they are scrupulously honest, paying, not pilfering—until they discover the lies that have been told them. Wednesday is market day in Paris, and Turgot, enraged by the Prince de Poix's surrender, orders price controls lifted from bread, which promptly rises from thirteen and a half sous to fourteen in the course of the morning. Six sous above yesterday's price in Versailles. It doesn't make sense. Except to someone whose babes will go hungry if bread costs more than eight sous. No one gives a damn about him or whether he starves. He was a fool even to think of paying. He loots. THEY loot.

Paris stood ready for them at strategic sites in the battle for grain: in other words, the forces of order (grenadiers of the French and Swiss Guards and mounted royal dragoons) had taken stations around the new grain market on the Right Bank and at barge landings along the Seine, one of which, also on the Right Bank, was Port-au-blé. However, all those arrangements were canceled on Monday night and Tuesday morning by Turgot, who assumes the functions of a prime minister in issuing direct orders to the police via Lenoir and to the army via the Maréchal de Biron, colonel of the French Guard. No royal or administrative authority permits him to do this; he simply is stepping into the shoes of Maurepas—who had no more official sanction than he to call out the army. Turgot's spontaneous self-promotion is his response to this invasion of the economists' turf by "persons of the lowest order." A mini-coup d'état against the micro-revolution.

Turgot receives encouragement from his staff, all of whom are indignant. Do that to us, after we've bent over backward to help them? Treat us as if we

*Near the convents of Saint-Lazare, on the Right Bank.

were Terrays or Maupeous? On this score even cautious Dupont and hot-headed Condorcet see alike. Later, when the rioters pass in front of the administrative-services building brandishing hunks of greenish bread ("Look at the bread they want to give us for fourteen sous! It's poison!"—"Come now, you know perfectly well that that bread has been tampered with by agitators[25] in their laboratories; they've used some compound to make it look moldy and blackened"), Dupont will personally lead "a vigorous sortie of Turgot's friends and servants" to turn back those louts.[26] And Condorcet, who, true to prophecy, has become a "raging sheep," dashes off a note to Turgot: "It seems to me that written instructions ought to have been issued to municipal police officers . . . The troops in Soissons stand rooted to the spot, looking on calmly while the countryside is ransacked . . . The military also should have received orders . . . The public will not rest easy until it hears that some of these thieves have been punished. Meanwhile the disease spreads." And a few hours later: "I am not exhorting you to be courageous, only not to show indulgence."[27] Yet six months earlier he was writing thus to Turgot: "Yesterday, on my way back from Choisy, I found myself between the poorhouse and Bicêtre,* and as I glanced at that prison confining twenty thousand miserable souls, I said to myself: because they cannot stifle all feelings of compassion in the human heart, priests have invented poorhouses in order to wreak misery on mankind under cover of a humanitarian impulse."[28] How pleasant it had been to revile the priesthood and dream of a happier human race—and how galling now to see those wretches pouring out of Bicêtre by the thousands without anyone's leave! Enemy number one is no longer Necker but public impatience.

"The populace," Hardy the bookseller narrates in his diary, "stirred up by bands of thieves and robbers [we now know they are peasants] who entered Paris chiefly through the Saint-Martin, the Conference, and the Vaugirard gates [indicating movements from north, south, and west], are agitating in Les Halles [because on an ordinary market day they find Biron's soldiers barring their way to the stalls]. The insurgence is spreading through the city into the suburbs . . . Since the markets have been stripped of bread, that same populace is now trying to force open one bakeshop after another in different districts, banging with rods and clubs and sometimes iron tongs on the doors of bakers who seemed bent on resistance."[29]

By noon the whole city is in turmoil, though hardly in a state of rebellion or civil war. It is "not a revolt or even a riot but a case of thievery, of rampant pilfering, of widespread disorder in one segment of the lower class."[30] Three factions: the terrorized bakers, protected by troops. The "neutrals," namely artisans, bourgeois, domestic servants, gentlemen of the robe and of the

---

*Bicêtre's poorhouse was more like a concentration camp for the impoverished of the Paris region, who were herded there to await death. Prisoners also were kept there.

sword, who retire behind locked doors—to laugh: "Windows were opened and people gathered to watch the crowd as one watches a procession."[31] And lastly the restless throng of marchers in this hunger "parade," which does indeed resemble an unwonted celebration, laughter like a clap of thunder from five or ten thousand voices before the shuttered entrances to twelve or thirteen hundred Parisian bakeshops, some thirty of which would be raided but not a single owner slain.*

In the "parade," suddenly lifted out of their misery by a converging tide of humanity at the street corner, jostled and jostling, laughing and shouting, chewing or brandishing hunks of greenish, barely edible bread—the immediate cause of this eruption but fast becoming an excuse for it—are the following, cited at random: Marguerite Germine, shopgirl in the faubourg of Gloire; Jean-Claude Lesguillier, sixteen years old, apprentice gauze-worker; Jean-Denis Desportes, twenty-eight, porter in Les Halles, domiciled in the Rue Mouffetard; Louis Fillandre, twenty-seven, handler of "floating timber"** along with his two brothers Etienne and Pierre; Vincent Hamon, twenty-three, silk weaver; René Priette, fifty-six, carding-machine operator in a mattress shop; Philippe Cordelois, twenty-six, journeyman cobbler; Pierre Fontan from Avignon—what's he doing here?; Jean-Baptiste Joyeux, twenty-three, journeyman saddler, "unemployed itinerant"; Pélagie Caumont, twenty-one, "homeless female wage-earner"; Marie-Anne Roudinet, only nineteen; Julie Narbier, only seventeen; Jean-Baptiste Sahonne, "beggar who calls himself cobbler"; Louis-Guy Moreau, forty, master locksmith on the Rue du Faubourg Saint-Denis; the brothers Charrois, forty and forty-one respectively, knackers; Jean-François Huot and the woman Letronc, both *gagne-deniers*;† François Thiéry, thirty-three, thresher; Jacques Chapotin, eighteen, quarryman; Jean-Baptiste Laborde, fifty-seven, laborer; Victor Quintel, apprentice gilder, fourteen, accompanied by a boy of ten, Thomas Péquinot, son of a porter in Les Halles; Jean-François Jovis, twenty-two, chairmaker; Elisabeth Forgerot, twenty-four, greengrocer; Jean Bedeau (or Bideau), journeyman baker, "homeless and unemployed"; Joseph Blondeau, twenty-eight, shellfish vendor; Pierre "Jean-Jacques" Gloria, forty-eight, unemployed manual laborer; Pierre Lenoir, employed by the customs agent at the Conference Gate; and five poor journeymen hatters peacefully seated round a table in a Bercy tavern when the Châtelet police pick them up (Sergeant Lahaye will report they were

---

*Only the richest of these bakers, those who supplied bread to religious institutions, purchased several *setiers* of flour at a time, usually two or three, for an average daily output of 600 to 700 pounds of bread. The overwhelming majority of bakers were as poor as their customers and could afford to buy only one *setier* per day (200–250 pounds of bread), so any increase in the cost of flour was immediately reflected in the price of their loaves.[32]

**That is, unloading log trains that were floated down the Seine to supply Parisians with their fuel.

†A trade similar to that of a commission agent. The ordinary commission amounted to one denier, the smallest coin in circulation, one twelfth of a sou.

"rioting"): Jean-Baptiste Le Gat, Pierre Roche, Guillaume Flageollet, Joseph Tronchet, Jean Bonnet, the first three natives of Lyons, the fourth from Chambéry, the last "from Pont-Saint-Esprit in Dauphiné" [*sic*]; their ages range from seventeen to thirty.

More? Yes, more. Why shut the window on a tale far too trim and tidy thus far? Let the breezes blow in. This is an invasion by the "populace": the real men of liberty, men whose labor kept others alive. Every urban trade of the times, every age, every mode of suffering. Alexandre La Crèpe, "self-declared master craftsman of pasteboard snuffboxes"; Jean-Baptiste Collier, known as Baptiste, water-bearer for the carriages in the Rue Mazarine; Marie-Catherine Dupuis, wife of Bertin, water-bearer for carriages in the Rue des Quatre Fils; Antoine-Joseph Longchamp, "runaway pupil at La Pitié, from which he escaped ten months earlier wearing the church habit"; Joseph Gaché, enameler, domiciled in Belleville; Guillaume Saint-Eustache, deserter from his royal infantry regiment; Jacques Roux,* thirty-four, "homeless laborer sleeping in the Saint-Gervais poorhouse"; Michel Desandre, native of Paris, "unemployed itinerant tailor"; Nicolas Depuis de La Vaux—why the aristocratic name? Was he the bastard son of some nobleman?—age thirteen, "homeless *gagne-denier.*" And those seventeen boys, a few of whose names follow, arrested "at the Palais Royal market" by Commissioner Goupil (the one who went to Provence to investigate the Marquis de Sade at the beginning of the year), "some armed with clubs, the other vagabonds insolent and disorderly": André Lheureux, Simon Loreille, Florent Beuvré, Daniel Ferret, Jean Robinet, and even a Salomon Lévy among them.[33]

The movement gradually swells from eight o'clock until noon, leaderless, rudderless, swirling aimlessly through the city center to the Left Bank and out to the suburbs, until at four o'clock it confronts the royal Gray and Black Musketeers dispatched from Versailles, a never failing instrument of repression. Municipal peace officers would have fraternized openly with the insurgents. In fact, some units of the watch look on curiously, without lifting a finger, while bakeshops are ransacked. And when musketeers corner a band of youths in an alley and charge the watch to round them up, the latter reply: "We have no orders to make arrests."[34] The mounted musketeers are forced "into action" around seven in the evening in order to break up the last demonstrations. The Grain War is practically ended in Paris. It will continue to spark sporadic explosions all over France for a week or so. In Joigny, on May 10, a "letter" is found bearing a red wax seal imprinted with the design of a horse and containing a single sentence: "We are twenty millyun men who dys of hunger—thats why we bak the revolt."[35] After May 15 analysis and rhetoric succeed the event while the price of grain fluctuates wildly, but what does it matter to those who can afford to pay? The punishment about to be

*Not the Jacques Roux of 1793.

visited on Parisians will serve as a warning to all their countrymen "of the lowest order" to behave themselves from now on.

Extraordinary council of ministers during the night of May 3 or 4. Turgot continues to dominate the stage: from necessity, since everyone else takes cover behind him; from impulse as well, as he finds it difficult to regain his composure, like a cool-headed person who suddenly flies off the handle. This council takes on the complexion of a polite squaring of accounts, with Turgot exploiting his emergency powers as acting prime minister to dismiss both Laboureur, commander of the watch, and Lenoir, lieutenant of police, whom he blames for weak and improvident conduct. He replaces him with his own man, D'Albert. He "short-circuits" old De Muy by putting another graybeard in command of the Paris forces: Biron, colonel in the French Guard, no better able to comprehend the day's events than was Lenoir and who spends most of his time raising exotic flowers in the greenhouse of his splendid Paris mansion. Biron, however, has the ear of the queen and her coterie, thanks to his nephew, handsome Lauzun. He has a knack of hopping about in frenzied excitement and giving the impression of great activity. For two months he turns the Hôtel de Biron into an active field headquarters with fleets of couriers radiating out to the twenty-five thousand men who will protect water-supply lines to the capital, where oil lamps are kept burning through the night, set low on the ground "as during uprisings when there is fear of a sudden attack . . . You set up invulnerable defenses, as if an invading army were about to besiege the Bastille or the Arsenal," its cannon visibly trained on the battlements.[36] Parliament's mounting opposition to military usurpation of civil authority is quashed by a *lit de justice* hastily arranged for Louis XVI on May 5*: "I must and I intend to put a stop to this wave of banditry that could degenerate into rebellion . . . I forbid you to remonstrate." Miromesnil, keeper of the seals and Turgot's implacable foe, is compelled to support this version of a conspiracy: "It appears that a plan was put forward to devastate the countryside, to intercept shipping, to halt the movement of grain . . . Its aim? To starve the major cities, principally Paris." Miromesnil cannot forgive Turgot for that statement, nor can Maurepas for casting him into temporary, though unintentional, oblivion. Sartines will never forgive him for discrediting his friend Lenoir. Even Louis XVI begins to think Turgot is going "a bit too far." As for the "conspirators," no one makes any real effort to apprehend them. Names are whispered about: the Prince de Conti for one, since his château at L'Isle-Adam is so near Beaumont; and Necker of course, whose essay appeared on April 27, opening day of the riots. No one is terribly serious. Or persistent. Except Voltaire at Ferney, who has followed events like an astronomer observing an eclipse through his telescope, and who promptly dashes off a short *Diatribe* (the first word of his title), his own scenario for the

*Exactly fourteen years to the day from the opening session of the Estates General.

conspiracy, that simply adds grist to the mill of repression: his agitators are churchmen, parish priests, fanatics who pounced on the chance to provoke attacks on triumphant rationalism symbolized by Turgot's ascendancy. Voltaire invents the framework of an "imaginary documentary" which treats— sometimes by raw exposure—his enlightened European readers to a dismaying view of the Grain War. "As we approached Pontoise, we were all astounded to see ten to fifteen thousand peasants [*sic*] rushing along like crazy fools and shouting: 'Grain! Markets! Markets! Grain!' They stopped at each mill, wrecked it in the twinkling of an eye, and dumped grain, flour, and bran into the river. A little priest proposed to them in stentorian tones: 'Sack everything, friends, God wills it. Let's destroy all the flour to be sure we have something to eat!' . . . This cleric explained to our travelers that he, like some of his colleagues, was one of the leaders of the mob: 'We were paid for our good deed.' "[37]

As peace returns in and around Paris, police move in to arrest, at home or in the street, thousands of persons designated at random by informers, the great majority of whom are the poor and destitute: two thirds cannot read— even what Necker tells them. A "provostal court"* with emergency powers is constituted in four days, composed of "eleven gentlemen from the Châtelet" (eleven police commissioners) authorized not to investigate but to condemn, invariably on some petty charge, a few poor wretches from the lot. The whole hasty performance betrays only token concern for due process. Sentence is passed upon:

Jean Derive, water-bearer: "took bread from a bakery on the Rue Tire-Chappe; paid for it the next morning."

Ignace Derive: "was merely inside a bakeshop when the baker of his own accord handed him a roll."

Jean-Denis Desportes, twenty-eight: "on leaving work, he and his wife entered Jardin's bakeshop on the Rue Mouffetard, where his wife took three four-pound loaves for which she paid thirty-six sous."

Jean-Claude Lesguiller, apprentice gauze-maker: "kicked the door of a bakeshop to demand that it be opened."

We met the latter two a week ago in the May 3 riots. They are sentenced to death on the morning of May 11 and hanged that same afternoon. Charges against the former two are dropped—meaning they will be kept hostage in case further examples need to be made.

May 11, three in the afternoon. Buds are bursting all over the capital. Louis XV has been in his grave for a year. Turgot became the hope of France just nine months before, the gestation period of two gibbets.

They stand on the Place du Grève atop an unusually high scaffold, eighteen feet above the ground. Today's event is unlike other public executions

*Temporary criminal court without appeal. [*Trans.*]

traditionally held on this site, for the square has been cleared. Two lines of soldiers back to back, one facing in, the other facing out toward the public, keep spectators on the perimeter of this vast, more or less rectangular area bounded on only two sides: by the window-dotted façade of the Hôtel de Ville and, beyond a serpentine wall, by the strip of grimy sand and mud where Seine barges come to rest. A clutter of housefronts forms the other two sides, and the view from their windows commands top prices on such special occasions. Something odd about this execution: the crowd will get only a distant glimpse of the hanging pair. Do authorities fear an insurrection? The tumbril carrying the two victims in their shirt sleeves has had a very short distance to cover coming from the Châtelet along the Seine. And why should they complain? They were spared both ordinary and extraordinary torture and were not even required to kneel on the steps of Notre Dame to make public confession of their crime and accept punishment. The city fathers are in a rush.

A group of men waits at the foot of the scaffold: almoners bearing the crucifix, the hangman's assistants, and a tall, robust, and elegant gentleman still in his prime, wearing a well-cut suit of green* and a sword: Charles-Henri Sanson, "executioner of criminal judgments, hangman for the viscounty of Paris" over the past twenty years, having succeeded his father at the age of fifteen.[38] An honorary rather than an active office; it would be beneath his dignity to lay a hand on these victims, around whose necks his deputies pass three separate nooses: two *tortouses,* each thick as your little finger, and the *jet,* a narrow loop that will merely serve to jerk them off the ladder. A deputy is the first to climb backward up this ladder, and while the priest below intones prayers for the dying, he attaches the *tortouses* to the gallows arm. The *Salve Regina* begins and reaches out to the four corners of the square, chanted by clusters of curious onlookers kept at a distance. Custom obliges: who ever heard of hanging someone without first singing the *Salve? "Vita, dulcedo et spes nostra, salve."* The two poor wretches grow pale, knowing what follows the amen. They try, each in his own tongue, to shout a message to those faraway figures who marched with them just a week before and are now jostling each other to get a better view of the final agony, singing prayers in the meantime. "The condemned pair begged the crowd for help, shouting that they would die for their sake."[39] Jean-Denis Desportes again swears he has committed no crime or incited anyone to loot. Jean-Claude Lesguiller sobs like a child. He cries out "that he never should have left work and gone out that day, that he is sober and industrious, qualities his employer can confirm . . . "[40] *"Ad te suspiramus, gementes et flentes in hac lacrimarum valle."** No use darting desperate glances westward to the Quai Pelletier in the hope of seeing a

---

*When the public prosecutor at the Châtelet forbade him to wear blue, "the color of noble blood," Charles-Henri opted for green, thereby launching "the Sanson style" so much the rage in Madame de Pompadour's day.

**"We who pray to Thee weep and wail in this vale of tears . . . " [*Trans.*]

dust-covered rider suddenly appear. Until the *Salve* is ended, clemency may yet arrive from Versailles. But someone would have had to petition the king, who would certainly have refused under pressure from Turgot. And who at court would have pleaded the cause of a porter and a sixteen-year-old apprentice?

Sixteen.

"O clemens, o pia, o dulcis virgo Maria." The hangmen yank the *jets* and, with their knees, kick the victims off the ladders, which are thrust aside. The hanging bodies writhe and pitch, strangling in the two slip nooses. "Then the executioners, each holding fast to the beam of a gibbet, step onto the bound hands of the dying men and, by jabbing them in the stomach with their knees and jerking them, put an end to their agony."[41]

JOSEPH II

34

APRIL–MAY 1775

Even If the Rains Were to Fail

"Our Father, father of peasants, look what is happening to us . . . Father, we can bear it no longer, they take away our daily bread . . . "

Whence this new version of the Lord's Prayer, like an echo of the *Salve Regina* sung just lately for those two victims of the Grain War in Paris? It comes from the east, from the mountains of Bohemia, where fresh shoots are poking up through patches of blood-flecked snow. No Parisian will hear this echo; no gazette will inform its readers of the peasant rebellion that has shaken the Hapsburg empire of Maria Theresa and Joseph II. At least one person has seen the connection between the Paris riots and the threat to Prague: Mercy-Argenteau, Austria's ambassador to the court of Versailles and adviser to Marie Antoinette, receives a letter from his sovereign dated May 4, 1775—the day after the Paris "event": "For the few days left to me I ought to enjoy some measure of repose. I have sacrificed thirty-five years to the public; I am so weary, so troubled, that I do more wrong than good. The latest Bohemian revolt has been crushed but is far from snuffed out . . . The emperor [Joseph II], who carries popularity* too far, has spoken too openly to the people—without making any formal pledges to them during his tours—both as to their freedom of worship and their freedom from their masters; on top of that,

*Today Maria Theresa would have said "demagogy."

conscripts and their officers have talked too much, holding out promises and stirring up the public. All this has sown confusion throughout our German provinces since 1770, the predicted and predictable outcome of which we can now see. Yet it was all treated as idle nonsense, empty words. It is not just the Bohemian peasant we have to fear but the Moravian, Styrian, and Austrian ones as well; on our doorstep, right in front of us, they dare to commit the most insolent acts, the results of which are to be deplored as much for themselves as for other innocent peoples. The boldest and worst of them now command the field."[1]

The Bohemian rising, covert from 1770 to 1774, which finally unleashed itself this spring of 1775, was not just "a simple rebellion against poverty."[2] Protestant victims of religious persecution from all walks of life had united with peasants reduced to serfdom. Both groups had had their eyes opened to their own plight by imprudent remarks dropped by Joseph II as he toured the empire making all kinds of rash promises merely to dissociate himself from his mother's policies. But people took him at his word. Matthew Chovjka, something of a Czech Pugachev, had assumed command of a peasant army; they were already calling him "Emperor of the Peasants." He looked so much like Joseph II that some people took them for brothers. Fifteen thousand rebels laid siege to Prague, only to be flung back. In April the insurgence had been crushed in Bohemia as in France, and Joseph, while not admitting it to his mother, regretted having fostered the peasants' hopes for freedom. He wrote to his brother Leopold: "The miserable Bohemian rebels, who have committed countless crimes and looted many châteaux, were cut to pieces by the army. We took a great many prisoners. Eighteen leaders have been put to death."[3]

A popular song records the Bohemian uprising, stifled this spring at the very gates of Prague while Maréchal de Biron was bringing Parisian mobs to heel: "Even if the rains were to fail forever and the skies dried up, our lands would be watered; the sweat of oppressed peasants, the tears of broken serfs would moisten them each day. Poor peasant, your throat is parched, your clothing in rags, your leggings in shreds; stand up, raise your scythe and remember your Czech ancestors. They would not have allowed the people to be oppressed; they rendered unto the king his due and nothing more."[4]

35

MAY 1775

If Ever I Glimpsed Happiness

May 25, 1775. Ascension Thursday. François-René de Chateaubriand is not yet seven. He leaves his grandmother's house in the hamlet of Abbaye, "a house whose terraced gardens descend in tiers to a valley at the foot of which stands a fountain encircled by willows,"[1] and with the dignity of a born aristocrat leads the family procession along the single paved road leading to the chapel of Notre Dame de Nazareth, ministered by the Dominicans of Plancoët, "a pretty village situated between Dinan, Saint-Malo, and Lamballe."[2]

Northern Brittany, carpeted with hawthorn and broom. The sea is near; the tangy air, the sky, the breeze tint each hour of the morning with pastel hues. Gray stone crosses mark each crossroads. The strange ritual about to inscribe itself permanently in the child's memory and saturate his mind with indelible religious awe is also typically Breton. "I had on a white gown,* white shoes, gloves, and hat, with a blue satin waistband." He is bewildered by his own outfit, for the little aristocrat has grown up like a wild thing with no more concern for cleanliness than the sons of his father's tenants. "It was the first time in my life that I had been properly dressed. Ultimately I would owe it all to religion, even cleanliness, which St. Augustine calls closely akin to Godliness." His kindly grandmother is not along: "she had trouble walking but, apart from that, none of the hindrances of age; she was a pleasant old lady, plump, white, tidy, with a proud, dignified manner." Chateaubriand senior chose to remain in gloomy seclusion at Combourg. But I had "my mother, my Aunt de Boisteilleul, my Uncle de Bédée and his children, my nurse, and my foster brother." "The convent, standing on the rim of the road, looked as old as its quincunx of elms dating back to the time of John V of Brittany . . . The monks were already seated in the choir stalls; an array of candles lit the altar . . . Mace-bearers met me ceremoniously at the door and conducted me to the choir. Three chairs had been placed there: I took the middle one; my nurse sat on my left, my foster brother on my right."

*Like the albs worn nowadays by choirboys.

The nurse was not there by coincidence: when François-René was but hours old, she had made a vow to the local patron saint, Our Lady of Nazareth, to dress him in blue and white in her honor until he came of age, this half-frozen babe they brought her from Saint-Malo more dead than alive. "I had nearly expired before I saw the light of day"—actually, it was the night of September 3, 1768, with the moon approaching its fourth quarter, in "a dark narrow street of Saint-Malo called the Rue des Juifs" during an unforgettable storm, unforgettable even for these shores where storms are part of the setting along with heaths, calvaries, and hobgoblins. "The booming surf raised by a squall heralding the autumn equinox stifled my wails; people have recounted these incidents to me; their sadness is ingrained in my memory." In fact a stubborn rain persisted for almost two months. The wet spell caused widespread alarm . . . The awful effects of the storm were felt throughout the region, especially along the Sillon Causeway,"[3] a kind of umbilical cord connecting Saint-Malo to *terra firma,* "battered on one side by the open sea, washed on the other by the tide that shifts to enter the harbor."

Our Lady of Nazareth had answered the old peasant woman's prayers; the region around Saint-Malo was dedicated to her. Madeleine Morice, a much respected local mystic, died the year after François-René's birth—from the devil's torments, it was said—and the statuette of the weeping Virgin whose tears Madeleine had often brushed away was duly installed in the church of Porcaro.[4] The boy, now six and a half, had grown sturdy and pugnacious. It was time for a solemn ceremony to lift the vow made in his name and to permit him to wear colors other than blue and white.

François-René is overjoyed. It marks the rapturous climax of his childhood, that fleeting moment when the conscience awakens in concert with the joy of living and being loved. Having been reared in the Chateaubriand house at Saint-Malo, he is as yet unexposed to the gloomier side of his family: Combourg and his father. He has never set foot inside a schoolroom and amuses himself instead with lessons from the Couppart sisters, "two elderly hunchbacks dressed all in black who taught the children to read." His grandmother's house and his Uncle de Bédée's nearby Château de Monchoix, "high on an open hill," are his paradise. "Joy bloomed there: the mirth of my uncle," a former naval officer brimming over with tales of sea fights and adventure, "was inexhaustible. He had three daughters, Caroline, Marie, and Flore . . . who shared his lightheartedness. Monchoix fairly burst with local relatives; there was music and dancing and hunting and festivities from dawn to dusk." François-René moved from this château filled with young girls to the house in Plancoët peopled with old spinsters, all of them equally fond of him. "If ever I glimpsed happiness, it was certainly in that house."

Now pride enters his life. "In view of my ancestral titles, I would have been justified, if I had inherited my father's and brother's conceit, in ranking myself as cadet branch of the dukes of Brittany." On this Ascension Day he is honored like a prince of the realm, as indicated by the posture of tenant peasants along the way who doff their hats of boiled leather, bowing low, greeting the young gentleman in a strange tongue, the dialect of this region which his ancestors were born to govern and to preserve through the intermediary of "rectors."* No chance of their having heard of the Grain War. Their diet consists of black bread, turnips, and fish; with that they are content. Do you hear them complaining?

Chateaubriand is more familiar with Latin than with Breton. "The mass began. During the offering the celebrant turned to me and read prayers; after which my white garments were taken from me and fastened *ex voto* beneath an image of the Virgin. They dressed me in a purple robe. The prior pronounced a sermon on the efficacy of vows; he recounted the story of Baron de Chateaubriand who accompanied St. Louis to the Orient. He told me that one day, in Palestine, I too might visit the Virgin of Nazareth to whom I owed my life as a result of the prayers of the poor, to which God always listens."

TALLEYRAND

DANTON

36

JUNE 1775

I Felt Persistently Rejected

June 11, 1775. First Sunday after Pentecost; high feast of the Trinity. At Rheims, Charles-Maurice de Talleyrand-Périgord and Georges-Jacques Danton attend the coronation of Louis XVI, each according to his station: the former close to the stage of honors, the latter lost in the crowd.

It is the French monarchy's supremely breathtaking rite. This lavish pageant has been seen only four times in two hundred years. The *Encyclopédie* scarcely needs to remind its readers that "the investing of the king confers on him no new privilege: he is king by birth and by right of succession"; also that "the aim of this pious ceremony is no doubt to inform the peoples, by means of an overwhelming spectacle, that the royal person is sacred and no attempt shall be made on his life, for, as the Bible says of Saul, he is the Lord's anointed."[1] Despite these directives, actors and spectators alike behave as if the coronation elevated Louis XVI to the status of a demigod.

More practical-minded and offended no doubt by the religious side of the

*The Breton term for priest, still in use there today.

event, Condorcet, true to his economist principles, had been trying since
September to focus Turgot's attention on the colossal waste: "Don't you think
that, of all useless expenditures, the most useless and ridiculous would be the
coronation? Trajan was not crowned."[2] He hammered at the point again in
his New Year greetings: "People have suggested using the coronation funds
to relieve misery in provinces devastated by epizootic disease. This seems so
just, so Christian, that opponents of it strike me as more unfathomable than
government officials."[3] Yet he knew that preparations had been under way
for six months and that Turgot, though basically in agreement with him, would
be committing political suicide if he subverted a thousand-year-old tradition.
At best the minister had sought to temper customs with innovation—as always
by undulation—and heeded the proposal of Paris merchants that the ceremony
could just as well take place in the capital as in Rheims. Hadn't Henri IV had
himself crowned in Chartres cathedral? They offered to defray a generous
portion of the expenses . . . Turgot had explained the advantages of this
alternative to the king: the journey to Rheims would be costly and provisioning the drastically swollen population of that city difficult; the whole affair
would be far more manageable if played out between Versailles and Paris, as
the event would surely attract flocks of foreigners. And what a chance to
conquer the hearts of Parisians who had been sulking since the Fronde!

Louis XVI had listened in silence and then commanded that the ceremony
take place in Rheims. This complicity between Turgot and Paris carried a stale
whiff of sulfur. Better rely on tradition than tamper with innovation.

The busiest, most harried man at court these past six months has been Papillon
de La Ferté,* "chief steward and comptroller of silverware, petty disbursements [menus plaisirs], and expenses of the king's bedchamber"—in reality a
permanent head bookkeeper in charge of His Majesty's "personal budget"
under jurisdiction of the minister of the king's household or the first gentlemen of the bedchamber. The latter changed from time to time and viewed
matters philosophically, whereas the intendant des menus, as Papillon was
known, kept the office he had purchased for three hundred thousand livres and
grappled with day-to-day fiscal realities. A job that would give anyone ulcers.
On July 3, 1774, Papillon nervously began to write up his accounts: "I have
turned over my work on the coronation to M. le Duc de Duras** so that he
might receive the king's orders, and tomorrow I send off accounting inspectors
to Rheims to take all measurements and dimensions needed for work to begin
when they return."[4] On August 15 he was there on the spot with a miniature
battalion of chamberlains and scribes to decide "what had to be done in the
archdiocese as well as in the cathedral, whose choir will need to be expanded

*He will go to the guillotine on the 19th Messidor, Year II, twenty days before Robespierre.
**Duras, one of six "first gentlemen of the bedchamber," was "on duty"—meaning in charge
of the daily schedule at court in 1775, the coronation year.

over two additional bays to accommodate the court and audience. We have inspected the vestments, offerings, and gifts of the former king as a guide to previous practice." Since Pepin the Short* sat upon the throne, thus had the snowball of tradition mushroomed from a simple episcopal unction marking baronial approval into a lavish four-day pageant with a cast of ten thousand. "The chapter [of the cathedral] has formulated various requests, in consequence of which I have composed a memorandum to the king," who, obligingly, had consented "to supplement the vestments with twelve tunicles and four *chappes* [*sic*]" and to add "to the usual gifts a special offering consisting of a gilt ewer, two paxes,** one silver, one gilt, and two gilt altar cruets. The king's [extra] gift will be a fine gold ciborium. He has also approved requests for additional lace."[5]

By December 1 the estimated cost of the coronation had climbed to 760,000 livres (nearly $800,000 today) "covering robes for the king, peers of the realm, major officials of the crown, the chancellor, and others, as well as adornments for the cathedral of Rheims, embellishments for the reliquary of St. Marcoul, the canopy surmounting the crown at Aix-la-Chapelle,† lace and linens, royal offerings, medals, remuneration of ceremonial officials, church fees, the cost of transporting monks from the Abbey of Saint-Denis to escort the crown and sword of Charlemagne . . . expenses and wages of the king's officers and musicians, lighting, construction costs in the archbishop's palace and the cathedral as well as the covered walkway between them . . . " On top of all this, the Duc de Duras insisted on "decorative structures, colonnades, sculptures and paintings."[6] Enough to give Condorcet a stroke. Papillon de La Ferté himself was on the verge of collapse by May 22: "I had sharp words with the provost of Rheims cathedral over the substantial extra lighting he wanted for the church, but I stood my ground and he was none too pleased about it. I do battle almost constantly over each and every estimate. M. le Maréchal [de Duras] sends everyone to me, and though I am up at five in the morning, the days never seem long enough to complete what has to be done."

June 5 brings the final blow. Having just paced off the length and breadth of the cathedral interior, he is struck by "the immensity of the task at hand";

---

*First Frankish ruler whose coronation is historically confirmed. Clovis is always said to have been crowned after his baptism, but this is pure legend.

**"Pax": a chased plaque depicting a scene from the Passion, which the priest gave the general public to kiss, replacing the "kiss of peace" formerly exchanged by worshipers. At the end of the seventeenth century this ceremonial kiss of peace had been declared conducive to "countless indecencies."

†To provide a link between Capetian and Carolingian traditions, there was an additional ceremony at Aix-la-Chapelle in which someone representing the monarch being crowned at Rheims—in this case it must have been Papillon de La Ferté—appeared with great pomp to convey, and later to return, Charlemagne's sword, normally kept at the Abbey of Saint-Denis. The canopy mentioned is a huge decorative hanging ordinarily on prominent display in the cathedral of Aix.

the builders have admitted "that in the course of working they came across many things which it would have been impossible to anticipate on the estimate . . . and which consequently will raise the cost substantially. Those few words stung me with greater distress than I have ever known."[7] Papillon de La Ferté claimed to be descended from Molière, whose great piercing eyes he did indeed possess. And in fact it was like a scene from a comedy—the gentleman decked out in his frills and laces, covered with plaster in that cathedral transformed into a construction site, struggling desperately against the army of parasites overrunning the coronation city. Even the bittersweet ending is there in which everyone makes up: Papillon is consoled by the king and made to forget excess spending with "the promise of a share in the gunpowder monopoly* or other financial investments. This favor is even more flattering to me in that it marks His Majesty's satisfaction."[8]

So everything turns out all right after all. The hell with grubby money matters! How beautiful the Champagne district looks when the grain is high, especially to thousands of coronation-bound visitors who, with Louis XVI, discover it for the first time as they arrive in successive waves from Versailles or Paris between June 7 and 10. The heat is stifling, the first spell of the year, reflected off chalky roads back up to the white-hot sky along with clouds of dust that never gets a chance to settle before the next coach passes. Mornings are clear and fresh: the forests surrounding Rheims purify the air and pour out repose. The king left his beloved Compiègne on June 7. A much overworked master of the horse, the Prince de Lambesc, had twenty thousand horses in harness on a staggered schedule, having scoured all livery stables within a ten-mile radius of Versailles for available carriages. Every servant wore new clothes, from pages down to the humblest coachman. "It would be improper for my outrider** not to have a fine suit of clothes for the coronation."[9] Lambesc travels in the royal berlin with the Comte d'Artois; another carriage follows with the Prince de Beauvau, captain of the guard; the Duc de Bouillon, grand chamberlain; the Duc de Coigny, first equerry; and the Duc de Fronsac, son of old Maréchal de Richelieu. At noon Soissons witnesses this invasion of blue, red, and gold, these splendid horses, these graybeards decked out with gold braid and medals, surrounded by wheeling, dashing, aristocratic young cavalrymen flaunting their brand-new uniforms. Hunched in the corner of a coach, a sulking figure: the king.

Overnight stop at Fismes, a small town transformed into a two-hundred-room inn. Later, by moonlight, Marie Antoinette arrives inconspicuously in an ordinary coach to join her husband, who will dominate the scene. She is merely a privileged member of his retinue.[10]

Friday, June 9, marks the triumphant approach to Rheims and first

*Today it would be a share in the profits of the national armaments industry.
**A liveried servant who rode ahead of the coach to prepare relays.

glimpse of the royal city "from the tip of a hill overlooking the slender valley of Epernay on one side and the great plain of Rheims on the other. The initial view is magnificent from this hilltop just beyond the suburbs. The cathedral rises splendidly and the church of Saint-Rémi proudly designates the city limits." Recent arrivals instantly notice the difference between Rheims and most other French cities, which, though seemingly alike when seen from afar, "turn out to be, when one enters them, merely a maze of narrow, dirty, dark, and winding streets. Rheims is quite different: nearly all its streets are broad, straight, and well paved."[11] The weather stays dry and clear. A league outside the stately city gates, Louis XVI climbs into a new conveyance, a mirrored state coach with an extraordinarily high roof, further adorned with paintings and brocades and crowned with waving plumes at each corner, like a hearse for the living. The solemn entrance at five in the afternoon bears out the promise of the cathedral's great bell and all others that chime in. The procession of coaches slowly weaves its way between rows of glittering grenadiers and cavalry officers "in battle formation." The crowd is dense and enthusiastic in the ancient square "with its Gothic houses," where the king alights at the foot of the cathedral steps, mounts them at once, and, kneeling upon a velvet stool, embarks on a prayer marathon. A hundred hours' worth.

How remote the Grain War seems. Though it spilled over less than a month ago from Brie into Champagne, who thinks of it here?

Certainly not Georges-Jacques Danton-Camut,* a lad of fifteen going on sixteen who had scrambled over the wall of the Richard pension in Troyes, where he is finishing his classical studies. His rhetoric teacher had assigned a written speech on the coronation as a "topic for amplification," intimating that detailed, graphic accounts would earn higher grades. But how do you describe the crowning of a monarch when you have never set foot outside Arcis-sur-Aube and Troyes? The only king Jacques knew was Girardon's full-length statue of Louis XIV** in the public square at Troyes, a semi-nude gentleman wearing a crown of laurel. Rheims, in a remote corner of Champagne, was like the end of the earth. Danton saw his chance to get away with a great piece of mischief that no one would dare punish: truancy in the name of rhetoric and the king. He scampered off with money borrowed from schoolmates and took four days to cover roughly seventy-five miles, sleeping in barns along the marvelous road to this spectacular adventure, a road that unfolded like a green-and-white carpet beneath his feet and the feet of other marchers flocking like pilgrims to the coronation. He slept in the streets of Rheims without even glimpsing the things he had hoped to see, for only notables were admitted to

---

*He was called Jacques at the time, the second of his two first names. In high school they had added on his mother's maiden name, (Marie-Madeleine) Camut, to distinguish him from a tribe of cousins.

**Toppled during the Revolution.

the cathedral. Perhaps he caught sight of Louis XVI before he disappeared through the entrance. The purpose of constructing that surprising canopied walkway between the cathedral and the archbishop's palace was in fact to shield the king from the public and the threat of an assassin's blade. Louis XVI, whose myopic gaze flickers vaguely over the crowd, is not apt to single out this homely face peering up at him, the uncouth features of a schoolboy amid a sea of uncouth faces: adolescent Danton.[12]

Good Lord, he really is ugly! Ugliness that is not inherited but acquired through a series of mishaps. Healthy and robust, his compact little body and broad chest give promise of an impressive carriage once he fills out. But wicked sprites must have rocked his cradle and saddled him with an irredeemably unruly temperament that would invite disaster. With the tip of its horn a bull had ripped off his upper lip. A subsequent bullfighting engagement resulted in a crushed nose. Then he slipped on a path surrounded by a herd of pigs he had been tormenting with a whip; they left him scarred for life. He was so fond of swimming stark-naked in the Aube that he nearly drowned. After they fished him out half dead, he contracted a raging fever; smallpox followed, "accompanied by the purples," which turned his pitted skin into a speckled mask."[13]

It doesn't faze him at all; he has befriended his ugliness. He continues to barge ahead boldly, inquisitive, blundering, ill-tempered, but a decent fellow. His family makes no effort to check him; there are too many brothers. His father, *huissier* of Arcis-sur-Aube, died when Jacques was two, the fifth child of seven. His mother then married Jacques Recordain, owner of a spinning mill, and continued to bear children. With each new arrival, they sent the eldest out to make his way. Jacques took the usual route of a petty-bourgeois son—toward the law courts. He was taught first by a schoolmistress at Arcis, then by the local schoolmaster. He was not a model pupil. "Anything involving habit was alien to my nature."[14] He enjoyed reading and was not averse to learning, but he and his book kept wandering off along the banks of the Aube to a cool, shady glen rare in the heart of barren Champagne. When back at school, he spent most of his time playing hide-and-seek and fighting with his classmates, a habit he transplanted to the Troyes secondary school,* to which he was "siphoned off" in 1772 not with the idea that he should enter the church—though his parents would have been delighted at the prospect of securing a living for one more son—but to improve his Latin. There he and his fellow students took classes in science and philosophy with the Oratorians of Troyes. After two years he left the school, whose bell grated on his nerves. "It will still be tolling for my funeral!" He was a good student** who couldn't adjust to the stifling clerical climate, unloved and unencouraged. He chafed

*Staffed by priests. [*Trans.*]

**Fourth among eighteen in general studies and ranked *inter bonos* in the records of the Oratorians for 1774.[15]

at the bit. His classmates used to call him the "anti-superior," or "the republican" long before he knew what the word meant.

His mother provided unfailing moral support, sometimes indirectly. She understood and forgave him, feeling partly responsible for his erratic behavior. He never uttered a word against her. He loved this broad-cheeked woman with a warm smile who slyly managed to exert her will over her sprawling brood. She had never made him conscious of his ugliness. Neither did his stepfather attempt to thwart or humiliate him. Thus, Danton is not soured. He won a battle before the age of fifteen, in 1774, when they said to him calmly: "You don't like the school, son? Then we'll send you to board with M. Richard in the parish of Saint-Nizier. You can go on studying at the Oratory."

A "secular" boarding school! Sheer paradise—as schools go. From there he "escaped" to Rheims and, without the slightest trepidation, expects to go back to school in a few days to boast of his adventure and all the sights he saw. Life is not unbearable in Troyes, where colonies of cousins invite him to visit and have already cultivated in him a taste for the wine of Champagne, chilled, sparkling, and so good for every ailment. Besides the magistrates Danton-Bécet and Danton-Cuisin on the Rue de la Levrette and the Rue du Coq, and the *huissier* Danton-Flamet, there are Danton-Marguenat the laborer and Danton the priest, curate of Barberey-Saint-Sulpice a few miles outside the town, who gave up some time ago trying to guide his nephew's fortunes. No class-consciousness among the Dantons. No urge to meddle or manage. No family quarrels. Georges-Jacques likes Troyes, with its bustling activity when the cotton mills and pin factories let out, its amazing butcher shops "where you never see a fly, owing to the type of wood used in building them." The one trouble with Troyes doesn't really bother him too much: "This town lacks good drinking water."[16] But who cares about water in Champagne?

On his return he gets a scolding as a matter of form, but no beating. He "will display superb gifts in French rhetoric, Latin composition and poetry," all on the subject of the coronation which he was privileged to witness. His work earns him a public citation on August 18—to a flourish of trumpets from the school band. It turns out "to be perhaps the happiest day in his life."[17]

Danton will never abhor his boyhood.

Talleyrand vomits his. He will nurse a single, unrelenting rage against his parents. "I was born in 1754;[18] my father and mother were not rich;* they had positions at court which, if properly managed, could open doors to them and to their children."** Yet here he stands on a Sunday in June in the

*An income of 15,000 livres (3000 new francs) at the time of their marriage.
**Charles-Daniel de Talleyrand-Périgord traced his ancestry back to the Comte Adalbert de Périgord, reputed to have defied his suzerain Hugh Capet with the famous insolence: "Who made thee king?" An ancestor on his mother's side was Chamillart, one of Louis XIV's best

cathedral of Notre Dame de Rheims, just steps away from a king the same age
as he and from his father, who, if his forebears had been luckier during the
Middle Ages, might himself have been sitting on the Bourbon throne instead
of in attendance as one of the four dignitaries escorting the dais protecting the
rosy vessel of holy oil used to consecrate French sovereigns: Charles-Daniel
de Talleyrand-Périgord is "hostage for the Sacred Ampulla." Charles-Maurice, his eldest son, attends the ceremony brimming with resentment, feeling
worse than a failure: one of a host of near-failures tossed from the aristocracy
into the Church as a result of fortune's cruel twists.* On January 16 he became
"titular of the Chapel of the Virgin in the parish church of Saint-Pierre in
Rheims"[19]—not yet ordained and only a sub-deacon, but already an un-
believer. Scorn is all that allows him to hold his head high.

He is good-looking, tall, very blond, very elegant in the black silk mantle
covering his satin cassock, mark of a future bishopric. Several ladies in the
audience are distracted by his handsome face with its amusingly uptilted nose
that sets a mischievous stamp on his rosy, doll-like features, which react impu-
dently if the lady is pretty. Eyes that do away with introductions. And he limps
so charmingly! "Women adored him. They whispered that he was depraved,
and other women were eager to test the truth of it."[20]

The 10th of June was given over to rehearsals and prayers. Solemn
vespers. An interminable sermon from the Archbishop of Aix on the duties
and privileges of kingship. The cathedral was half deserted; many people were
preparing for the next day, Sunday, which promised to be an ordeal.

Some of them slept hardly a wink on the night of the 10th, especially the
canons, who must be dressed in their copes and lined up in the chancel by six
a.m. The flood of "guests" arrives soon after: all must be ready by seven in
the beleaguered cathedral, whose exterior has acquired a false wooden façade
by whimsical order of the Duc de Duras, a classic appendix planted like a
screen over the ancient stones, and, inside, a colonnade of gilded timbers
which narrows the nave and transforms one of the most beautiful Gothic
interiors into an opera hall. In this colossal boxlike setting the ceremony is
about to unfold for seven consecutive hours.

It begins with a meeting that represents the first act of the coronation and
constitutes its uniqueness: the encounter between the king and the Sacred
Ampulla. Along with the Comte de Talleyrand, three nobles whose ancestors
all managed to capture a rock—La *Roche*foucauld, *Roche*chouart, and La
Roche-Aymon—leave at dawn in quest of the miraculous vessel from the Abbey

---

ministers. His wife was a Damas d'Antigny. The Talleyrand-Périgords thus descended from the
most ancient French nobility.

*Charles-Maurice was the second son of the Talleyrand-Périgords, but his elder brother, Alexan-
dre-François-Jacques, died at the age of five. The right of inheritance then passed over the head
of this middle son with a crippled foot to the youngest, Archambault-Joseph, born in 1762.

of Saint-Rémi. A special ceremony is enacted there to the chant of Benedictine monks: the four gentlemen "in short mantles of gold cloth" swear upon a Bible that no harm shall befall the Sacred Ampulla and pledge their lives to safeguard it. They become its "hostages" until they return it to the abbey.[21] An echo of times past when hostile dynastic factions tried to steal the vessel en route in order to anoint their own leader. There go the four "hostages" riding through the streets of the city, whose citizens at least can enjoy that part of the spectacle, like a parade preceding a feudal tournament with banners flying, tiers of shields and halberds and damask stuffs, while "knights of the Sacred Ampulla" surround the "hostages," and the prior of Saint-Rémi, like an ancient, wrinkled gold tortoise, sits astride a white charger with silver trappings. In his hands is "a golden dove covered with white enamel, crimson beak and feet, and wings outspread, containing in its gullet a minute red-tinted glass vial about an inch and a half high stoppered with a wad of scarlet damask."[22] It holds a speck of ointment, more or less rosy and solid, which an angel (or a dove, depending on the text) brought from heaven in A.D. 496 to Saint Rémi, who had no magic oil with which to anoint Clovis.

When the Sacred Ampulla reaches the cathedral, out to meet it waddles a rotund human doll wearing long silver robes over a scarlet spencer. The Bishop-Duke de Laon and the Bishop-Count de Beauvais escort the doll—in procession, of course—along the covered walkway: it is the king. A great burst of song and shouting meant to convey that though the king needs the church, he also needs to feel needed by the people. An echo of the Palm Sunday rite when the celebrant knocks at the church door. This time it is the Precentor of Rheims striking the ground with his staff and the grand chamberlain who responds:

"What do you wish?"

"We wish the king."

"The king sleeps."

The same response is repeated three times before the doors of the cathedral are thrown open and the prelates approach the canopied bed of state, bow "very low," then hoist the overstuffed doll to its feet and conduct it to the central nave.

Priests of lesser ranks must also brace and all but carry the principal officiant, who is barely able to walk: venerable Monseigneur de La Roche-Aymon, Cardinal-Archbishop-Duke of Rheims, trembles and totters with every step. With each word he expires. It was generally assumed that he would never make it and that the office and the honor of exercising it would devolve upon his coadjutor, Alexandre de Talleyrand, Charles-Maurice's uncle. But as La Roche-Aymon managed to win the struggle—with the aid of stimulants and coffee—here he is shuffling up to meet the prior of Saint-Rémi, who addresses him solemnly:

"I entrust you, Monseigneur, with this precious treasure sent down from

heaven to our great Saint-Rémi for the consecration of Clovis* and his successors upon the throne; but I entreat you, in the ancient custom, to pledge yourself to return it into my hands after the anointment of our King Louis XVI."

The stage is set now for the great sorcery to begin. Priests may confer
absolute power on this Bourbon ruler because Clovis had bowed to the precedence of Rémi. Final formality: the vows. The red-and-white doll is permitted
to speak: the voice sounds strong, resonant, seemingly resolved to keep its
oaths:

"I swear to devote myself sincerely and with all my power to annihilating
heretics condemned by the Church in all lands under my rule . . . ."

Then follows the vow "to maintain and uphold the Orders of the Holy
Ghost and of St. Louis, and to wear forever the cross of the latter on a
flame-colored silken ribbon." Standing among the clergy of Rheims, Charles-
Maurice de Talleyrand watches every motion of this historic sanction of aristocratic privilege which extends the hand of God, right down to the fingertips,
into every corner of society and makes it a mortal sin to entertain the notion
of change, be it only the color of a ribbon. By now he has developed protective
armor for his thoughts, that faint wry smile on his drooping lip that locks his
features in an impassive mask.** He can safely think whatever a dedicated
womanizer may think at the sight of Louis XVI being anointed from head to
toe (through special apertures in his spencer) with dabs of balsam mixed with
chrism. He never winces when they set Charlemagne's mammoth sword in
Louis's flabby hands, or when, during one of the twenty sermons that follow,
the archbishop exhorts the sovereign "not to abandon his dominion over the
kingdoms of the Saxons, Mercians, Northumbrians, and Cimbrians"—that is,
the English.

Never will he admit what he was thinking as he watched this undistinguished cast of characters perform, rigged out in the regalia and with the
names of bestial seigneurs who, a thousand years earlier, had set the pattern
of Western civilization: two degenerate oafs, Louis XVI and Monsieur his
brother, plus an insignificant fop who looked like a "dazed sheep" owing to
"the peculiar arch of his nose which overhung his sagging mouth,"[23] the
Comte d'Artois. The latter represents the "Duc de Normandie" and Monsieur, the "Duc de Bourgogne," while the other so-called "secular peers"
standing in for the barons who once chose the king are the paunchy

---

*A coronation known never to have taken place. The sudden appearance of the Sacred Ampulla
in Benedictine hands, giving them a comfortable supremacy in the Rheims region, goes back to
Merovingian or Carolingian legend. The first mention of this *ampel* (Saxon word meaning vial or
cup) occurs in Hincmar, around A.D. 815.

**In 1804, twenty-nine years later, Talleyrand will attend Napoleon's coronation as grand cham-
berlain and, in that same office, fifty years later, in 1825, the enthronement of Charles X. And
if Louis-Philippe had been crowned . . .

Duc d'Orléans, his acne-cheeked son the Duc de Chartres, the Prince de Condé,* and his son the Duc de Bourbon, each temporarily rechristened the "Duc d'Aquitaine," the "Comte de Toulouse," the "Comte de Flandres," and the "Comte de Champagne." These princes of the blood have but one common bond: their contempt for the brother or royal cousin whom they are enthroning on bended knee.

The only personal remark Talleyrand will record in his memoirs is that "his relations with several women singularly gifted in different ways, the Duchesse de Luynes, the Duchesse de Fitz-James and the Vicomtesse de Laval," date from the coronation of Louis XVI.[24] His roving eyes have habitually lighted on pretty women since the day three years before when they came to rest, "in a chapel of the church of Saint-Sulpice, on a lovely young girl," Dorothée Dorinville, an actress seven years his senior.[25] "I attended mass more punctually. One day as she was leaving the church, a sudden downpour emboldened me to offer to accompany her back to her rooms . . . We shared my umbrella. I escorted her to the Rue Férou, where she lodged. She invited me upstairs and, unabashed, like a very innocent young girl, urged me to return again. I visited her every three or four days at first, then more often." The Sulpician** fathers were tolerant of this seminarian with the prestigious name of Talleyrand-Périgord who was being forced into the priesthood merely because in infancy he had fallen off a chest of drawers while in the care of a wetnurse.† The Rue Férou was a short walk from the seminary. "Her parents had made her enter the theater; I was at the seminary against my will . . . All the grief in my life, all my resentment, and all her own troubles filled our talks. I have since been told that she was not very bright; though I saw her almost every day for two years, I was never aware of it."[26]

All things come to an end, even coronations. It is past noon. Louis XVI swelters under the heavy ermine robes that cover his dalmatic and the layers of sacerdotal vestments. Is he a king or a priest? Peers of the realm perform a complex ballet as they raise Charlemagne's crown, which La Roche-Aymon sets on the royal head, praying "that the king shall possess the strength of a rhinoceros and, like a gust of wind, drive enemy nations to the ends of the earth." Talleyrand walks out with two thousand others, his torso stiffly braced to counteract the pain of each step on a foot so deformed that it resembles a horse's hoof. He will be wined and dined by friends of his own generation (with ladies present, of course) while His Majesty, still costumed to the hilt, returns to the great hall of the archbishop's palace for a sumptuous feast. Two duchesses and a viscountess: that was Charles-Maurice's prescription for blot-

*Future commander of the émigré army that will invade France in 1792.
**The seminary stood on what is now the Place Saint-Sulpice.
†Leaving his right foot crippled for life. [*Trans.*]

ting out "all the grief in my life, all the resentment" which must have welled
up afresh out of the childhood he had been cheated of at the sight of his father
in the procession. "Some distressing recollections gripped my heart. I felt
isolated, helpless, persistently rejected . . . " "I am perhaps the only man of
distinguished birth, member of a large and pre-eminent family, who never for
a single week has known the sweet pleasure of living beneath his father's roof
. . . " "But I was defenseless; I was alone; around me everything had its own
fixed pattern and gave no hint of a way to escape the plan my parents had
designed for me . . . " "Youth is the time of life when we have the greatest
integrity. I could not yet understand what it meant to enter one profession [the
priesthood] only to carry on another [statesmanship] . . . to attend a seminary
in order to become minister of finance." But "this accident [his clubfoot]
influenced the rest of my life. It was the decisive factor, after my parents
realized that I could not join the army, which inclined them to steer me toward
a different profession. They thought it would better promote FAMILY* interests. For among the high nobility one loved the FAMILY above its individual
members, especially the young ones whom nobody really knew. I prefer not
to linger over this topic . . . I say no more of it."

Ever. Not a word of protest after that. Was it protest, or simply an effort
to shrug off his own private burden? "Gods knows I was neither arrogant nor
scornful; I was simply a nice young man bitterly unhappy and resentful."[27]

CHOISEUL

37

JUNE 1775

The Poor Fellow

The coronation built to a final sweeping climax, a great surge of emotion
unleashed by the superb singing of the choir, the swelling organ, the rustle
of silks and satins behind clouds of incense. June sunlight, like a rainbow, pours
through stained-glass windows of the apse; the archbishop escorts the king to
his throne set high above the cathedral floor between four lofty columns so
that everyone may see him:

Vivat rex in aeternum!

The doors swing open, trumpets sound, the restless crowd outside now
is free to mingle with the guests, while fowlers from Compiègne loose not just

*The emphasis is Talleyrand's; he underlines the word twice.

pigeons but a flurry of various species of startled birds to symbolize "the bestowal of royal grace upon the people."[1]

Carried away by the tide of excitement, Marie Antoinette had wept. Mercy-Argenteau, who scrutinized her every movement in the gallery, for once found something to report to her mother that did not reflect discredit on the queen: "During the enthronement, in a rush of affection, the queen wept copiously to the point where she was obliged to withdraw from the gallery, and when she reappeared minutes later, the whole church burst into cheers and applause and demonstrations that would be difficult to describe. Everyone was in tears; people noticed that when the king looked up and saw the queen, his face assumed an unmistakable air of contentment. The queen's emotion made such an impression on the king that for the rest of the day he smiled in utter adoration at his majestic spouse. Every few moments he would mention the queen's tears to his courtiers; he kept returning to this subject."[2]

Marie Antoinette is so proud of her conduct that she boasts of it to her mother: "I could not hold back my tears and this made everyone glad. I did my best all during the journey to respond to popular acclaim, and though it was hot and crowds were dense, I don't regret the fatigue I suffered, which has not impaired my health. It is both a surprise and a relief to be so well received just two months after the revolt and despite the high cost of bread, which persists unfortunately. It is amazing how easily the French are led astray by bad advice and then quickly return to their senses. Seeing people in distress who treat us so well surely obliges us to work even harder for their welfare. The king appears to have been struck by that same fact; as for myself, I know that never (even if I live to be a hundred) will I forget this coronation day."[3]

By the next morning she will have forgotten all about it; her husband, who rejoices when she weeps, will manage to provoke tears of frustration and rage to which she grows accustomed. The other side of the coronation coin is the widening breach between the royal couple. Not only is there no love between them, but they are now beginning to clash. An hour's euphoria cannot change things: Marie Antoinette is not happy—and never has been. But her unhappiness is turning into rebellion.

With a cold as her excuse, she took a private bedchamber. For both of them, sleeping together meant endless vexations. Worse than the absence of desire was their mutual repulsion, a nightly humiliation. They had never succeeded in consummating the marriage and no one tried to help them do so. Now the Comtesse d'Artois, one of two homely Piedmontese imports at court, had been parading a ballooning belly for the past few weeks; it did not enhance her looks, but would make her husband (the only one of three brothers whose virility went unquestioned) father of an heir to the throne.

All around her Marie Antoinette began to sense a growing lack of respect.

The little history she had learned—under prodding from the Abbé de Vermond, her official reader but actually a maternal pawn instructed to lecture and
spy on her—warned incessantly of the disastrous fate of barren queens. She
kept hoping for a visit from Joseph II, her favorite brother, who shared her
background and whose advice she could trust. Maximilian came instead, her
bulging clod of a younger brother, so ugly and so dull-witted that at court, in
February, no one could resist making cruel sport of his jutting jaw, his cross-
eyed stare, his harelip: living proof of Hapsburg degeneracy.[4] The queen's
insistence that this blighted creature be honored as a visiting sovereign
erupted into a duel of protocol between herself and the princes of the blood,
who refused to pay the first call on her brother. This issue merely fueled the
fires of hostility against the queen; Marie Antoinette found herself isolated at
court, her only protection the casual friendship of the Comte d'Artois, who
amused himself by amusing her.

Wholly innocent indeed were those rare moments of relaxation shared by
the young man of eighteen and this young woman of twenty. But Mercy-
Argenteau's dispatches to Vienna alarmed the Hapsburgs: "On May 11 there
was another outing and hunt in the Bois de Boulogne. M. le Comte d'Artois
accompanied the queen there and back in an open carriage called a *diable**
driven by the prince himself. Paris is still whispering about this promenade and
the highly informal conveyance used by the queen so close to the capital. It
is certain that such things leave a bad impression and the king frowns upon
them."[5]

The carriage ride . . . The separate bedchamber . . . Enough to send
Maria Theresa into a rage. The old widow hated the notion of her children
enjoying themselves. She had written Marie Antoinette a scathing sermon
reflecting Mercy's complaints, as if he were guiding the empress's pen from
Versailles. As he was not privileged to rebuke the Queen of the French, he
simply confronted her with a wall of stony silence and, once back in his
embassy, poured out his objections to her mother. On May 18, for instance:
"I should be wanting in zeal and lax in my duties if I did not humbly entreat
Your Majesty to stress forcefully the following points in her forthcoming
messages to the queen: First, that the public voice** has informed Your Sacred
Majesty that the queen (of her own free will) had slept apart from the king
for several weeks,"[6] and secondly . . . and thirdly . . . Maria Theresa readily
snatched up the cudgel: "I have received your letter [of June 2], Count de
Mercy . . . I shall write to my daughter along the lines of those three points
you mentioned . . . I shall make it appear that through rumor and the press
I have learned of her leaving the king's bed and the scandalous impression this
has made . . . not to mention the disapproval of her participation in the Comte

---

*A light, fast, two-wheeled carriage that could be driven standing up. The mounting interest in
speed was introduced from England.

**The "public voice" was his own, naturally, conveyed in his dispatch of April 20.

d'Artois's pleasure parties."[7] That same day she dispatched to her daughter the promised tongue-lashing, which arrived at Rheims during the coronation festivities. The spring riots add fire to her arguments: "Our subjects in Bohemia" have spoken out like the French, "except that yours were for the high cost of bread and ours for the *corvées.* * They also claimed there was a law abolishing them. In general, this mutinous spirit begins to spread everywhere: it is the outcome of our enlightened century."

Now on to the hard facts: "I complain of this often enough, but it is depraved morals, it is indifference to the tenets of our holy religion and this unending dissipation that is causing all our ills. I was most distressed, I must confess, to read in the gazettes of your growing addiction to all kinds of races in the Bois de Boulogne with the Comte d'Artois, at the very gates of Paris and in the king's absence. You ought to know better than I that this prince is not highly esteemed and you do injury thus by association to your own reputation. He is so young and so irresponsible, deficiencies which are bad enough in a prince but far worse in a queen of riper years . . . A princess must invite respect for her every action and not behave like a paramour either in her dress or her entertainments. Because the public is quick to find fault with us, we cannot afford to slacken our guard.

"There is a matter that distresses me even more: letters from Paris all say that you have left the king's bed and are rarely privy to his confidence. This dismays me more, I confess, since I know that by day, engaged in dissipation and away from the king, this friendship, this habit of being together will likewise erode, and I predict nothing but grief and misery for you . . . We are brought into the world to do good unto others; your task is among the most essential; we are not here selfishly for our own pleasures but to seek our reward in heaven, our ultimate goal, which is not freely given: it must be earned."[8]

Indirectly then, from Versailles to Vienna to Rheims, as in a billiard game, they played upon the French queen, treating her like an overgrown child. Failing to notice that she is becoming more womanly and less childish. She begins to understand that she is queen. She rejects the gilded cage to which they consigned her as dauphine, when her letters and messages were spied on. Once again circumstances are luring her into political entanglements.

It was not her natural inclination; she simply wanted a measure of personal freedom. As for politics, she was content to transmit the desires of the Austrian court. The Duc d'Aiguillon's dismissal a year earlier marked the beginning as well as the end for her. Finding herself bullied and defenseless not only as a woman but also as a queen, she develops new interest in her ministers. Not their ideas, to be sure, for what would she know about such things? She neither spited nor encouraged Vergennes and Turgot, who, for safety's sake and when it suited them, occasionally kept her informed. She

*Maria Theresa means "against" the high cost of bread and "against" the *corvées.*

knows this. Now she longs for another minister who will be loyal to her alone, another Mazarin for Marie Antoinette of Lorraine-Austria, a sworn liegeman, as if all courtiers didn't owe prime allegiance to their queen!

A combined minister and courtier, there's the answer. Like the one she once had, who arranged her marriage and cajoled her when she first came to France. No one could ever replace Choiseul.

Her desires, thwarted as a novice ruler the year before, rise up now and precipitate her maiden political maneuver. When the king and she first mounted the throne, Louis XVI ignored her wishes and chose his own set of men to run the country. But haven't the bread riots given him second thoughts? Doesn't he need someone to lean on? She thinks she has sized him up; she despises him thoroughly, both his public and his private image. She is convinced that he is unwilling to rule alone. Around her, Choiseul's allies (the friends and relatives of La Pompadour's protector) spring to life and regroup as Louis XVI appears to tire of Turgot. And Maurepas is too ill to attend the coronation.

But Choiseul is among the invited guests. The coast is clear.

It will be a close game, with thousands looking on. Try to involve the king, using the tactics his ministers use: get him to make *their* decisions. Marie Antoinette innocently asks permission to receive Choiseul; on the eve of the coronation she tells the king that "she would like to speak" with the duke but doesn't know how or when to schedule the audience—couldn't you, dear and clever husband, arrange a suitable time?

Delighted that she has asked his advice—and isn't it commonly known that women have no sense of time and need to be told everything?—Louis XVI replies: "Why, naturally, the day after tomorrow in the morning." This places the royal seal of approval on the proposed audience. Whispers gallop. Maybe the king will be there to receive Choiseul; maybe he will return from Rheims a minister . . . Two days of feverish gossip, time to blow a colossal soap bubble.

Choiseul, who has never given up hope, feels it is now or never. For a year he has been living sumptuously as a prime minister, without the means to do so. He has Chanteloup, near Amboise, to maintain, another Versailles. But Chanteloup was the only palace he had to worry about when the old king ordered him into exile there. The new king has allowed him to winter in Paris on the Rue de Richelieu, in the mansion* built during his "reign," which boasts "a superb gallery, palatial rooms" with ceilings decorated like those in the Medici Palace, candlelight receptions five nights a week where "great and petty nobles" rubbed elbows with magistrates, writers, and bankers. Gatherings like those in the Salon de la Reine** around "the great central fireplace

*Located on what is now the intersection of the rues d'Amboise and Saint-Marc.
**At Versailles. [*Trans.*]

with a huge fire burning," reinforced by stoves at each end; in the middle of the room stood a table large enough to accommodate an assortment of games called *la macédoine* [medley], alongside which were card tables for whist, piquet, *comète, macao, tré-sept* "and three or four backgammon boards going full tilt . . . At a quarter to ten Lesueur, the majordomo, glanced into the various rooms and, with practiced eye, ordered forty, fifty, or sixty places set for supper, always a lavish meal."[9] He could not do otherwise, for Choiseul had made up a list of 210 persons who had risked their careers to visit him openly at Chanteloup during his disgrace. "There were standing orders to receive them at all hours and always to treat them as guests." With an income of eight hundred thousand livres a year,* he was ruining himself.[10]

More than aristocratic extravagance, it was an investment, a race between his rising credit and his fading fortune.

Marie Antoinette and Choiseul have only an hour. They waste it. It was wasted before it began, since, anointed or not, Louis XVI remains stubbornly wedded to the memory of his father. Besides, the conversation is stilted; they don't seem to recognize each other. The duke is surprised not to be greeted by an awkward child; the queen is disappointed to see him grown depressed and puffy. They talk of this and that mutual acquaintance, of the Breteuil, the Broglie, the Guines, the Beauvau tribes. A knightship here, an ambassadorship there. Trifles. As neither is willing to expose himself, they both lose the chance to sow their conspiracy. From timidity, and perhaps from pride as well. For Choiseul's ambition lacked political content: he had neither plan nor platform. He wanted his old job back, simple as that. And equally obvious.

Louis XVI had discovered late, but not too late, that his wife meant to trick him, and he made it his business to attend the audience. The next morning finds him in the presence of Choiseul and the hundred other Knights of the Holy Ghost, called *cordons bleus,* flower of the nobility since Henri III founded the order to thank his Maker for propelling him from the Polish to the French throne one day during Pentecost. Scuffle of sweeping mantles embroidered with the fleur-de-lis as all kneel to kiss the king's hand—then, sensation! Louis XVI, nodding good-naturedly to this assembly of notables, snubs only Richelieu, whose dissipation he abhors, and Choiseul, on whom he pins a schoolboy's sneer that will send the duke packing from Rheims before the day is over. Superficial perhaps, but Choiseul was touchy and could neither bend nor crawl. He proved a good courtier to those who appreciated him. Not quite enough for a stable career. Second rebuff in a year, second rejection. Smiling, with rage in his heart, he goes off to defeat and boredom.[11]

*Three million francs today [$600,000].

According to Mercy-Argenteau, the duke had had time, "either on his own or through friends, to convince the queen that she had only two choices: to conquer the king with honeyed words or to subdue him through fear. It is apparent that the queen seems partial to the latter alternative."[12] Mercy is correct, and she is about to corroborate him by launching her own little spy ring. She refuses to admit defeat despite this latest affront to Choiseul. Proud of the way she tricked the king into granting an audience, she boasts of it—to Count von Rosenberg for one, a childhood friend. From time to time she corresponded with him, recounting all kinds of insignificant items, whatever trivia happened to cross her mind, though occasionally she would insert a meaningful remark, as on April 18: "My tastes are not those of the king, who enjoys only hunting and mechanical contraptions. You must admit that I would look out of place by the forge; I could never play Vulcan, and the role of Venus is apt to offend him . . ."[13] She wants to show Rosenberg how clever she is: "You have probably heard of the audience I gave the Duc de Choiseul in Rheims. There has been so much talk about it that I wouldn't be surprised if old Maurepas trembled in his sleep last night. You may well imagine that I didn't receive him without first consulting the king, but you can't imagine how cunningly I acted so as not to appear to be asking his permission. I told him that I felt like speaking to M. de Choiseul but couldn't see how to go about it. I behaved so convincingly that the poor fellow arranged it for me himself and set a convenient time. I think I effectively exercised my woman's prerogatives."[14]

Alas, her dear childhood friend Rosenberg turns out to be an ordinary spy. To curry favor with the court at Vienna, he turns over Marie Antoinette's letters to Maria Theresa and Joseph II, who promptly castigate the unhappy queen. Double dose of ice water. Joseph's letter* shifts from nastiness to cruelty—a demi-emperor bent on reducing a queen to the position "that every woman should accept in her household":

"Is it possible to write something more imprudent, more irrational, more unseemly than what you wrote to Count von Rosenberg regarding the way you arranged a conversation at Rheims with the Duc de Choiseul? . . . What business is it of yours, my dear sister . . . to speak of affairs and to express yourself in terms most ill-suited to your position? Did you ever pause to ask yourself what right you have to dabble in affairs of state and of the French monarchy? What education do you possess? What training have you acquired to make you think that your advice or opinion is of any consequence, especially in matters requiring extensive knowledge? You, a nice young lady who thinks only of frivolity, of her clothes and her pleasures all day long; who neither reads nor listens to fifteen minutes of rational talk in a month; who never reflects and never meditates, I am sure, and never calculates the effects of what

*Watered down somewhat in transmittal by Mercy-Argenteau.

she does or says?''[15] He made a habit of venting on his sisters his hostility to his mother.

The lecture has an impact, but not the one Joseph intended. Marie Antoinette is stung to the quick. The rebuff reaches out from the safe, sheltered world of her childhood, a world to which she still retreats spiritually. Renegades. Spoilsports. The umbilical cord stretches and threatens to snap. On August 6, 1775, after the Comtesse d'Artois gives birth to a son,* the queen will write her mother the shortest, curtest note of their entire correspondence (when read between the lines):

"Madam, my dear mother, the Comtesse d'Artois was delivered on the 6th at 3:45 as easily as possible: she had only three severe labor pains and only two hours of labor all told. I stayed in her room the whole time: I needn't tell my dear mama how much it grieved me to see an heir to the throne who is not mine; yet I managed to give my full attention to the mother and baby. I am, with respectful filial affection . . . ''

Rosenberg's "betrayal," her brother's harshness, and her husband's cunning combine to leave her distrustful of younger men. Marie Antoinette's need for affection transfers itself to the only persons likely not to traduce her: close friends much older than she or else those two plaintive, cherub-faced contemporaries who share her griefs: her beloved Princesse de Lamballe and the still gentler Yolande de Polignac. The period of consoling handmaidens is begun.

Festivities have tapered off. Each day brings a little less praying; parades and crowds are thinning out. A final flourish on June 14: Louis XVI sets out with great pomp to "touch the scrofulous" at the Abbey of Saint-Rémi. Astride Vainqueur [Conqueror], his favorite mount, he who is so clumsy on foot seems surprisingly young, agile, and relaxed. He was born to hunt and ride—only in the saddle does the King of France look like a youth of twenty. Behind him, grooms lead his two other best horses, Fier [Proud] and Monarque. Next come musketeers, pages, the Hundred Swiss Guards, the light-cavalry guard; the pageant of history's most spectacular monarchy arrives at a contemporary Court of Miracles. More than a thousand victims of goiter and scrofula constitute a vast reservoir of charity for the Benedictines of Rheims, who care for them, lodge and maintain them for years in a dozen poorhouses, awaiting the day when the king will come to inspect their good works—an orderly regiment of well-trained, well-scrubbed souls—and touch the forehead of each, saying: "The king touches thee, may God cure thee." Those afflicted with scrofula in the Rheims region are lucky; instead of castaways, they become charity's cast of characters.

Scrofula is not a disease; it is the clinical result of poverty. You don't find scrofula among the rich. Victims develop "hard painless tumors which tend

---

*The Duc d'Angoulême, future husband of Madame Royale and the ephemeral Louis XIX of the "events" of 1830.

eventually to suppurate . . . The disorder is also known as *strumae a struendo*, 'to pile up in a lump,' because the swellings usually comprise several lumps collected or packed one atop the other . . . Scrofula comes from an inflammation of the lymphatic gland caused by bad food such as salted meats, unripened fruit, raw milk, tainted water . . . These inflammations commonly develop under the ears and lower jaw, in the armpits, the groin, and around the joints. Although these lumps are hard as scirrhi, they suppurate rather easily and never become cancerous." They were not considered incurable; remedies included "purges, baths, beef or chicken broth in combination with thirst-inducing plants like watercress . . . and soap pills, reputed to be highly effective,"[16] in addition to the magic virtues of French sovereigns who, since Philip I's reign, made a practice of dispensing cures by infusion of the Holy Ghost.* "It is an ancient human disorder to believe that one's ruler has exclusive power to cure certain victims of disease by touching them," the Chevalier de Jaucourt had dared to state in the *Encyclopédie,*[17] which did not dampen the joy in Rheims that Wednesday when the king played thaumaturge, the monks cast themselves as Good Samaritans, the poor were visited and fed, and the bill was shared by the state, the Benedictine community, and the bourgeoisie of Rheims. Years of observation will follow, and anyone cured after June 14 will be proclaimed a miraculous case.

Total cost of Louis XVI's coronation as entered in the bookkeeping records of Papillon de La Ferté a year later: 835,828 livres, 12 sols, 10 deniers.**

The long caravan winds its way back by the same route: Fismes, Soissons, Compiègne, and, inevitably, Paris. They are resigned to having to pass through the capital, under one of those diluvian downpours that frequently strike the Ile-de-France in June. Marie Antoinette and Louis XVI travel together this time, wearied by the endless series of halts at the gates of each town to hear official speeches, to receive bouquets, to fondle babies. Their spacious coach enters the Saint-Martin Gate, crosses an arm of the Seine, and draws up in front of Notre Dame, whose head canon appears to kiss the king's hand. As they roll up the Rue Saint-Jacques on the Left Bank, approaching the Montagne Sainte-Geneviève, the sovereigns' sole desire is to be done as quickly as possible with the waiting crowd of students and to head for the Enfer tollgate en route to Choisy for a rest. The streets are flooded, a sulfurous symphony of streaming, splashing gutters. Paris broods and reeks; few citizens elect to brave the deluge. Only delegations, committees, craft corporations,

---

*Scrofula probably corresponded to what we now call chronic adenitis, tubercular in origin, often accompanied by abscesses; it developed in constitutions weakened by lack of calcium and vitamin C, both highly deficient in the diet of eighteenth-century peasants.

**About $700,000. His marriage to Marie Antoinette in 1770 had cost more than twice that amount.[18]

official organs. A large group, men in stiff collars and young students in black, is gathered in front of the austere edifice housing the Collège Louis-le-Grand, "seat of the University" since 1763. They are there to represent the entire teaching community: an island of lay persons in a sea of cassocks. "The king and queen consent to delay their progress" or, rather, that of the coach.[19] One of a dozen such scheduled "consents." But it is getting late. Rain and fog blur the train of resplendent coaches and dull the rich leather trappings of the cavalry. All is gray. Let's hurry on. A seventeen-year-old schoolboy, an orphan attending the Louis-le-Grand high school on a scholarship from the Arras diocese, kneels by the royal coach, from which the king and queen are directing mechanical, benevolent nods. He recites a "compliment in French verse" composed by his literature instructor, Monsieur d'Hérivaux, who has designated this boy, his best student, to parrot his own pedantry.

Soaked to the skin and totally ignored, since everyone has eyes only for the royal pair, Maximilien de Robespierre pours out platitudes he has learned by heart and watches resignedly, without a syllable of "his" compliment having been preserved for posterity, while the royal procession embarks on its final mission: to receive the homage of priests on the Left Bank in the sparkling new church* that crowns the hill of St. Geneviève.

SOPHIE DE MONNIER

38

JUNE 1775

With You, Love Began

The first exchange between Mirabeau and Sophie de Monnier[1] takes place at a banquet given by the notables of Pontarlier on Sunday, June 25, 1775, to mark the coronation. On that day the whole country tunes to the pitch of Rheims: by royal decree dispatched to every governor and intendant in France, a *Te Deum* is to be sung, followed by celebrations strung out over a week in some cases, including balls, theatrical productions, receptions, and fireworks. Local color sets them apart: in Pontarlier, a bailiwick of Franche-Comté, which had been under the imperial boot less than a hundred years earlier, the dominant tones are crimson and gold, seen in the brocades of the bourgeoisie "in their Spanish dress" and in the massive banners. Festivities as rigid and solemn as a mass. This tiny community of three thousand on the

*Which later became the Panthéon.

eastern border of France, tucked between forests and mountains, relaxes woodenly, awaiting official sanction for every step it takes. The influence of nearby Switzerland is plain.

The *Te Deum* following high mass ended well past noon. The banquet will drag on for five hours, but neither Honoré nor Sophie minds: the current of attention and delighted surprise flowing from one to the other transports them to a world of enchantment far beyond the horseshoe table in the hollow of which bewigged valets stagger under the weight of whole boars, a side of beef garnished with three chickens and six pigeons, a haunch of venison ringed with small game birds. The style of cooking in this backward province is more Regency than Louis XV: meats have simmered communally in huge kettles dotted with onions and herbs; roasting and stewing chickens and turkeys have bubbled gently for twelve to fifteen hours.[2] Wineglasses are filled with chilled, sparkling white Arbois. Mirabeau is not indifferent to the menu, a far cry from his prison fare over the past nine months; he simply assigns priority to a different kind of game: the young girl not yet twenty on his right whose rosebud lips have barely tasted life. Everything about Sophie is at once proffered and withheld; though married, she is still a virgin—the one and only feature she and the queen share. He, an experienced rake, reads her character instantly, for she makes no effort to hide it. He reaches out to her eagerly, bent on making up for a year of misfortune. Why should he hesitate? She's no raving beauty. The least he can hope for is an afternoon's pleasure; at most, a summer affair.

She is neither ugly nor pretty, an intriguing inconsistency ripe with promise. Her wounded air, the sadness and mystery about her attract this frustrated man so sensitive to injustice. Wouldn't it be interesting to seduce someone nice and at the same time champion the cause of this overgrown girl just a shade too tall, which gives her a forward tilt while enhancing the arch of her bosom? "From timidity and not flirtation, she constantly bit her lip, which had the added effect of narrowing her face; it was too round and doll-like to begin with, having irregular, somewhat plain features, a large flat nose, and prominent cheekbones; her voice was rather loud and low-pitched." Identification marks: a mop of dark, curly hair atop a well-rounded forehead; milk-white skin.[3]

It is open season: Sophie, focus of all eyes in this tiny society, has swarms of admirers, all graybeards or prententious fools. Her husband, the Marquis de Monnier, an old man fifty years her senior and honorary president of the court of accounts in Dôle, sits stiffly at the far end of the table, laced into the corset of his magistrate's career. Not once does he glance at her. He looks only at his past. He didn't even buy her from her family to appease a yearning for tender young flesh, but rather to get back at an unruly only daughter by his first wife who had wed the musketeer Lebeuf de Valdahon against his wishes. He wanted another child in order to disinherit the couple; that was proved to be impossible on his wedding night with Sophie. Now he asks nothing more of his wife than to act as hostess at his whist or reversi parties.[4]

But the Comte de Saint-Mauris seated at the head of the table, who is governor of Pontarlier as well as warden of the fortress prison of Joux and Mirabeau's permissive jailer, is ogling Sophie and clucking like an old pigeon. At sixty-five, he is lively, robust, alert, and doesn't look his age. The ladies eye him appreciatively. He has been courting Sophie for months, but she is tired of village elders. If only he were handsome! Mirabeau later writes: "We were both equally ugly, but I was forty years younger than my rival."[5]

His own ugliness simply stirs Sophie's boundless compassion. He arouses pity, yes, but not repulsion. Her gaze fastens on this odd stranger at once ceremonious and spontaneous, a courtly aristocrat if ever there was one, an eagle among the local crows. Never will she forget his broad, puffy face pitted with smallpox, his hair, a riotous mop like her own, his bold, probing stare that pounces on a woman like a scouting party swooping down on its prey. What a pleasant surprise in the midst of this mandatory gathering. But what the devil is he doing here "among the bears of the Jura," a southern aristocrat, son of a modern-day Montesquieu and, so they say, a future minister of the crown? Why is he forced to live, but is not locked up, in the fortress of Joux, the sprawling edifice that looks down on Pontarlier about a league beyond the valley of the Doubs? He is a political prisoner; he has insulted the king and confesses to, even boasts of, a young life burdened with more suffering and adventure than the combined lives of all Pontarlier's soured elders. What a splendid voice he has! Soft, mellifluous, caressing; music to thrill a woman's soul.

Honoré has spent just over one winter in the Château d'If, which twenty-five years earlier his father, the Marquis de Mirabeau,* had celebrated in the following verses:

> Nous fûmes donc au Château d'If:
> C'est un lieu peu récréatif
> Défendu par le fer oisif
> De plus d'un soldat maladif . . .
> . . . Sur ce roc, taillé dans le vif,
> Par bon ordre, on retient captif,
> Dans l'enceinte d'un mur massif,
> Esprit libertin, coeur rétif,
> Au salutaire correctif
> D'un parent peu persuasif . . .
> . . . Nous sortîmes d'un pas hâtif,
> Et rentrâmes dans notre esquif

*Or a friend of his, Lefranc de Pompignan.

En répétant d'un ton plaintif:
Dieu nous garde du Château d'If.[6]

[So there we were in the Château d'If:
Not the most amusing spot
Defended by the idle blades
Of many a sickly soldier . . .
On this solid slab of rock
Legally they've imprisoned
Behind massive walls
A wayward soul, a rebellious heart
Impervious to the remedial urgings
Of an unpersuasive parent . . .
We left in haste
And re-embarked
Murmuring plaintively:
God save us from the Château d'If.]

God could do little to save the son from detention since the marquis himself
had been responsible for putting him there. Honoré nearly choked with grief.
Once before, in 1768, he had tasted insular prison life on the Ile de Ré
following his first run-ins with the authorities, but it never broke his spirit and
afterward he scoffed at the experience. The Château d'If, however, was the
trap that clamped shut over his youth. He had arrived there ill and irate in a
flimsy little boat rocking in the autumn mistral. He saw nothing bucolic about
the scene, only the dreary, hostile aspects of a seascape which in fact is strikingly beautiful, dotted with colored sails, off the Marseilles coast. He felt
indifferent to the waves lapping about "the desolate rock," to the play of light
and shadow up and down the rugged coastline as far as the eye could see; and
on the adjacent islands of Pomègue and Ratonneau he observed only the
absence of trees. Nor was there a single patch of green on his own island,
where, behind high limestone walls and by special dispensation, he was authorized to walk a hundred yards along a circular watch corridor, knowing that less
"favored" prisoners were crouching in their cells: "Men whose only crime was
having a pretty wife who had caught the fancy of some of those base flunkeys
called the high nobility, apparently for purposes of antithesis"—in other
words, like himself, most of them were victims of a *lettre de cachet*. Out of thirty
inmates, only one, "from the dregs of society," was a common criminal, and
six others could hardly be called dangerous subjects. The rest, however, were
well on their way to becoming so—which is simply another advantage of such
august precincts where one bad apple contaminates the whole lot.[7]

At the outset, he had won the warden's heart: Monsieur d'Allègre, whose
opinion alone counted, was delighted to find such good company. Just as
rapidly, Honoré had taken charge of "the one woman with a woman's face"

in that dismal place: Lazarie Mouret, wife of the prison canteen-keeper. "I was twenty-six. It's an utter lie for anyone to have suggested that I found her pretty."[8] Temperament drove him to it (had she not been available, he would have fornicated with the rock itself); also necessity, for Lazarie went on frequent errands to Marseilles or Aix and would mail secret letters from him to his sister and mother. Desperate to get away, once again he only made things worse for himself.

His younger brother informed on him. Boniface, a wine-drenched ectoplasm and syphilitic already marked by "the gifts of Venus," had come to work off his boredom in Provence, having progressed from the army's eastern garrison to the island of Malta, whose knights threw up their hands in despair at a hopeless fellow who did "thirty-eight dozen inept things every day,"[9] to Paris, where he tried to wheedle from his father the estate abandoned by Louise and Honoré. In November he set out for the Château d'If, ostensibly to pay a friendly call on his brother but actually to "report" to the marquis on the situation there. He couldn't wait to tell everyone at Bignon, including Emilie, about Lazarie Mouret: what a treat to advise his sister-in-law that her husband was two-timing her with the canteen-keeper's wife! Boniface relished such pleasures. Another came his way three months later, after he had rejoined his regiment to help put down the bread riots around Paris, when he defended the Charenton mills against the "mob" and even diverted some of his troops to guard Bignon just in case . . . His uncle, the Bailli de Mirabeau, another great philanthropist, had written thus to the marquis about the Grain War: "Nothing astonishes me so much as the savagery or stupidity of those who would teach crowds the secret of their strength; I don't know what gives people the conviction that intellectual ferment will be halted; if I am not mistaken, however, such disturbances have always preceded revolutions."[10]

Emilie welcomed her revenge with open arms. Seven months earlier Honoré had ranted and raved about her affair with young Gassaud. Now, on December 13, 1774, she was in a position to write the prisoner: "The chevalier [Boniface] told me all about you in great detail, especially, and at some length, about a certain canteen-keeper's wife, who takes up a lot of your time, from what I hear. Well, sir, here's to your greatest commodity! . . . It helps pass the time."

Final shock wave through a correspondence that was bound to explode. Emilie was the prisoner's sole guarantor; the marquis had specified this to avoid having to deal personally with his son. This left Honoré entirely dependent on a woman who had proved superficial and false to him and to whom he had already acted cruelly. Three months intervened between the wild cries emanating from If and cautious responses from Gâtinais. Lightning bolts coated with honey: "My dear friend . . . my beloved friend . . . my good angel . . . The picture of your present situation gave me a severe headache

[October 7] . . . I was obliged to buy myself a little white-and-black satin gown for the house, since my father-in-law cannot abide scanty attire [October 18] . . . We spent the night at Fontainebleau. We saw the palace on the way through, and the king and queen, etc. . . . It was all very beautiful, as you can imagine [November 5] . . . Try to control your imagination, which in your case is like the mind wearing out the body, as they* say [November 8] . . . I hardly have time to turn around; my whole morning is taken up with breakfast in your father's room. After that I have to listen to some of the servants who chew my ear off; or else there's mass to attend, for around here they celebrate every saint's day on the calendar; then there's shopping to do, hats to buy, and so time flies [November 11] . . . I was taken to the opera and yawned my head off [November 18]."

Gradually she drove him to fury. Once in a while a vague sense of guilt struck her, a gnawing fear that she had gone too far. Instead of harping on the canteen-keeper's wife, she tended to avoid the subject and prattled merrily about nothing at all. On January 3 she wrote him: "I have seen Dupont;** he spoke of you with the greatest warmth. I liked everything about him. They say that M. Turgot will not treat him as he deserves; we'll see."[11] But her change of heart came too late, for Mirabeau's anger had reached the boiling point, as in Manosque and again in Grasse with M. de Villeneuve-Mouans, and nearly drove him out of his mind. He had settled accounts on January 14 in a fairly terrible letter: "You're a monster. You showed my letters to father . . . I refuse now or ever again to be deceived by you. Go trail your infamies somewhere else. Go far away, as far as possible, with your perfidious duplicity. Good-by forever."[12] She swallowed this, feigning surprise and pity. "You [tu] mean to break up over a hint of suspicion?" (January 29). Honoré remained silent. She in turn resigned herself to using the formal mode of address which ruled their correspondence ever after: "Your [votre] father received a voluminous letter from Marseilles on Sunday . . . " (February 22).

And who was telling tales to Bignon's masters? Not only the warden of If, who lamented his lax treatment of Mirabeau, but also Mouret, the canteen-keeper, informing them that Lazarie had disappeared with four thousand livres of household money.[13] She was known to have taken refuge with a Captain Briançon in Grasse—in other words, under Louise de Cabris's roof. Mirabeau would follow her in short order—but this the informers did not know. To escape alone without funds would have been foolhardy, and here was Lazarie offering to provide money for him to live on for two or three months. He felt the urge to burn his bridges and start afresh. Louise dissuaded him at the last moment. Who would believe him? "Only on her own account did she behave

*"They" presumably means her father-in-law, whose opinions she begins to parrot in a familiar tone.
**Dupont de Nemours had known Honoré as a boy at Bignon, where he turned up frequently as a starveling disciple of the marquis.

preposterously. To others she was the very soul of wisdom and reason."[14] It simply wouldn't do for her brother to run off with such an ordinary woman. Patience! Local authorities were beginning to side with the prisoner; public opinion showed signs of shifting in his favor. Don't spoil it all by some rash act. In any event, surely they won't confine him too much longer at If.

She misgauged only the timetable, for the marquis was not anxious to surrender his prey at one fell swoop. The canteen-keeper's complaint plus the open rift between Emilie and Honoré gave him an excuse to transform his son's eventual discharge into a purely nominal "release."

Ideal solution: a transfer. It would nip in the bud this harebrained fellow's ancillary love affairs and snatch him away from that confounded sister of his who was about to become his tool. Without actually soliciting any cabinet official, the "Friend of Man" possessed excellent connections at the highest levels of power. He could obtain whatever *lettre de cachet* he wanted from the Duc de La Vrillière. For Gabriel-Honoré he hesitated between several royal fortresses: Pierre-Encize, near Lyons, or Doullens in the north, providing it was out of touch with Paris or Provence. He had asked La Vrillière to send his son "some place not within reach of a large city that would encourage him to exercise his wits in some harmful fashion, but where at least he could expect certain amenities from the commandant if he earned them."[15] By May 25 the affair was arranged: "I have had my son transferred from the Château d'If to the fortress of Joux on the Franche-Comté border, where he will not be so closely confined." That wasn't how the poor captive saw it. He was beginning to see welcome signs of spring in Marseilles: "I leave a prison where at last they were treating me with some consideration, only to enter the dreariest, coldest spot in Europe . . . I arrived dressed in camlet in a region where linen is too light a fabric for summer, where snow blankets everything by October 30 and in early June not a leaf is showing."[16] The Château d'If took on the status of a luxury inn when, after miles of bumpy roads, one glimpsed "that nest of owls enlivened by a handful of army pensioners . . . the Château de Joux atop a rocky mountain, one end of which forms a loaf on which the fort perches . . . This château is divided into five sections joined by fortifications . . . ditches, three drawbridges . . . Every gate is locked and bolted . . . The walls are about twelve feet thick with triple rows of crossbars for openings. . . ."[17] Carriages could not climb the steep approach to this fortress on Mount Jura (the same as Mount Joux). Overlooking both Pontarlier and the pass leading to Switzerland, it served as a state prison now that the Germans and French no longer were at war over the region.

But the first impression did not last. In those days Honoré collected a following of tender-hearted prison wardens—tender-hearted to him alone because of his noble ancestry. M. de Saint-Mauris cheerfully announced: "Up to now the fortress of Joux contained one gentleman [himself]; henceforth it will have two." How kind of the king to send him an aristocrat. He had received instructions in advance to treat him leniently, unlike a dozen or more smugglers who were gradually freezing to death "in seven vaulted stone dungeons where the light never penetrated."*

"Provided, sir, that you give me your word to return each evening to the quarters I am charged to assign you, there will be no prisoner and no jailer. You will be free to move about the countryside at will, to hunt, to make friends . . . "[18]

By easy stages, that is: the countryside, yes, but not nearby Pontarlier as yet, and the right to hunt applies only to the Joux preserve—like a caged squirrel, Mirabeau can chase his tail for a thousand paces in any direction. Still, it meant a lot to be able to stretch his legs, and he wasted no time doing so. Spring finally burst in the early days of June, like a pretty girl coming out of hiding. All the blossoms of the Jura, flowering raspberry, cherry, and wild rose. Even the pretty girl, pretty as all those flowers, waited to be plucked at the very edge of the fort within the prisoner's bounds. Jeanneton Michaud, a sister of Pontarlier's royal magistrate, was spending the summer in the family house at La Cluse, a tiny hamlet perched midway up the river between Joux and Pontarlier. Appetizing, hot-blooded, only twenty-five and well experienced, she had already showered her favors on most of the acceptable local bourgeois. Why not Mirabeau as well? Clearly, he wasted no time between his arrival at Joux and the coronation banquet.

But Jeanneton is just a pleasant passing fancy on the afternoon of June 25, as he leans toward the neighbor at the right and begins rattling on to Sophie, unaware that the dialogue will continue for six years. How well she listens. She is like a sympathetic vibration, an invitation to narcissism on the part of any companion. She seems bound to induce "these poor devils, these smart fellows, to pour out their hearts, to talk, to weep, to vaunt their noble courage, their sufferings, their good looks . . . "[19] "Nothing from my lips was lost on you," Mirabeau later writes to her; that afternoon she begins to piece together the tangled strands of his life. As Mirabeau surrenders, Jeanneton Michaud dissolves and with her a host of others: Lazarie Mouret, the canteen-keeper's wife; Emilie de Marignane, his lawful spouse; the daughter of the town watch in Saintes, his first conquest as sub-lieutenant, which sent him to prison on the Isle of Ré; Louise de Cabris, the sister he loves too passionately; the big girls, little girls, nymphets, or just plain sluts he manages to sandwich in between prison terms; the "two sisters from a respectable family in Ajaccio" during the Corsican campaign; and that nun, also on Corsica, "pretty as a picture, but whom his still stammering genius had not succeeded completely in thawing out"; not to mention the yards of powder, brocade, and satin he claimed to have captivated at Versailles: Mesdames de Marigny, de Genlis, de La Tour du Pin, and even de Lamballe. What harm could it do to boast about it? But

*Under Napoleon in 1802, Toussaint L'Ouverture was left to perish in one such cell.

until this encounter in Pontarlier "I had dealt only in flirtation, which is not love but is simply the illusion of love."[20]

"With you, love began . . . " Even now the words take root in Mirabeau's head.[21] He is a flame that cannot smolder; he burns. She, too. He realizes this at the end of several hours, too late to undo the damage. This young country miss may not turn out to be just another female. Desperate alarm. Suppose he were to seek voluntary imprisonment in the fortress of Joux; suddenly the world seems topsy-turvy. He will not treat Sophie like the others. He will not pounce on her. For the first time in his life he will flee a woman. He is afraid.

THE MARQUÊS DE POMBAL

39

JUNE 1775

There Is No One to Take His Place

This month of June 1775 has witnessed ceremonies in another country, not in connection with any coronation. Joseph I has been ruling Portugal for twenty-five years, a reign not unlike that of Louis XIII in France: Pombal was his Richelieu. And the gala event in June to celebrate the rebuilding of Lisbon marks Pombal's apotheosis.

Rheims and Paris will ignore Lisbon as if its festivities were taking place on the moon, and vice versa. Spain interposes its shrouded mass between France and Portugal, whose limited intercourse is more by sea than by land. The average Frenchman knows nothing about this tiny country at the end of nowhere, this land of two million souls and two hundred thousand priests; informed persons are aware simply that England has staked it out as a private preserve.

Some of the Portuguese themselves will shrug off events in the capital of this kingdom shaped like "a spider whose enormous body [Lisbon] contains its whole substance, with long, feeble, spindly legs which it has trouble moving."[1] The legs are roads or, rather, cow paths which turn the two-hundred-mile trip from Lisbon to Oporto into a seven-day excursion. In any event, on the 6th of June, Lisbon celebrates her resurrection. Alleluia for three hundred thousand souls.

In 1755, twenty years earlier, the city had expired in exactly nine minutes on All Saints' Day, the eve of Marie Antoinette's birth in Austria. Europe's worst disaster since Pompeii struck one of the world's most picturesquely positioned capitals, nestled in the mouth of the River Tagus, Olisipone or Lixbuna; the Roman and Arabic names mean nothing to the inhabitants, for Lisbon is a city that cannot say where it got its name.[2] Such tranquil beauty, this hillside facing south and sloping down to the Tagus, which mirrors houses and sailboats in the ocean breeze. The scenery is antiquated, "a medieval town peopled by a court with baroque tastes."[3] Sixty churches; a sprawling royal palace like the Louvre, wedded to the Tagus instead of the Seine; the Terreiro do Paço or palace terrace, a vast esplanade to which the public flocked at dusk to watch the running of the bulls or heretic burnings; monasteries, towers, statues by the dozen; a quay converted to a boulevard bordering the Tagus and extended over the centuries, like a seagull with outstretched wings greeting merchant vessels from India; "Lisbon, the seat of explorations, a city that ultimately based its existence on the sea."[4]

The sky was clear. On that 1st of November the sun beat down as warmly as the August sun in Paris—sixty-four degrees at 9:40 in the morning when the earth began to roar like a wild beast, then to tremble vertically (as if thousands of hidden mines were exploding all at once), then horizontally, making the whole city shake from north to south like an enormous pancake on some celestial griddle. A minute and a half of those two tremors; a minute's relief; more quakes for two and a half minutes; another minute's respite; three minutes of shaking, by which time it was generally thought that the end of the world had come. The Tagus receded, exposing the bare river bed, then rushed back to submerge the Terreiro do Paço and houses along the banks under sixteen-foot waves. Fires raged for six days. The death toll reached ten thousand, "including fewer than eight persons of rank": the churches, all reduced to rubble, had not been expecting the main throngs of worshipers until eleven, and the first shock, the lightest of all, had sent everyone into the streets. But the worst casualty was Lisbon itself, which was all but destroyed, while Portugal lost twenty billion reis.*

The tremors continued for twenty-four hours. Everyone who could do so fled: the royal family, princes, prelates, priests, rich men, and state officials—except one. Sebastião José de Carvalho e Mello, a petty nobleman still unsure of his power since his appointment as secretary of state for foreign affairs and for war in 1750, stayed on, fortified by his courage and ambition. He became virtual dictator: "secretary of state for affairs of the kingdom" (the Portuguese equivalent of prime minister) on May 5, 1756; Conde d'Oeiras in 1759; Marquês de Pombal in 1770.

How did he do it? By deceiving the king; by clamping down ruthlessly on the poor and the grandees; by elevating commerce to the pinnacle of

*About 500 million francs, three or four times what we now call the country's then gross national product. English merchants lost even more: 25 billion reis.

national ideals. In other words, a combined Richelieu and Colbert: Pombal was born at the age of fifty-six in the glow of fires smoldering in the wake of Lisbon's earthquake, which catapulted him to fame and fortune. For years he allowed the king and his household to go on living in a string of wooden barracks in Ajuda, for no one would set foot any longer inside a stone dwelling. Without meaning to surrender his capital, Joseph I was compelled to give him a free hand in rebuilding it. Pombal reassured his sovereign by keeping him at a distance. "The king never knew how serious the earthquake was; he was told at first about some houses crumbling, then some churches . . . One may safely say that he was the only person in Europe who never found out the full extent of a disaster that occurred just a few miles away."[5] Similarly, Pombal saw to it that the ruined palaces were not rebuilt, for he wanted the grandees to wither away on their remote estates and die off. To keep the populace in check, all he had to do was round up a few hundred "looters" and panic-stricken "alarmists," hang them publicly, and maintain martial law amid the ruins. This left him free to reconstruct Lisbon as a temple of commerce.

June 1775. It's finished. At least that's the impression he wishes to give, and what better way than with a three-day inaugural celebration? A procession of symbolic chariots, fireworks, military parades, illuminations, a public ball and banquet at which four and a half tons of cake are consumed. The court banquet alone costs forty million reis, including a special commemorative porcelain service imported from China.[6] On the 6th of June the celebration converges on the old Terreiro do Paço, appropriately renamed the Praça do Comercio. It's only half finished? No matter, for in two months' time over three thousand workmen have laid out its final dramatic outline. The long and colorful procession of dignitaries winds its way like a golden serpent along the esplanade to the platform on which, concealed presently under rich hangings, stands a monument to victory over destiny: the equestrian statue of Joseph I. The towering, elderly man who grins like a demon and is about to unveil the piece is Pombal; shifty-eyed as ever, impressive in stature. The person helping him, second in command among the "official representatives of merchants and craftsmen," is another Pombal, his eldest son, president of the municipal senate.

Ringing applause. A second Venice is born. No one pays attention to the pseudo-heroic bronze group emerging from its wrappings, a man on horseback three times larger than life, the king disguised as some tragic Roman conqueror in a toga and plumed helmet over a suit of armor which never in his life had he worn. He lists permanently to the left: Machado de Castro, the sculptor, was banished from the city for protesting the way they were aligning his piece, so they did it without him—askew.

No one really cares: the monument is merely a backdrop for the imposing, almost man-sized medallion set into the gigantic pedestal bearing the bewigged image of Pombal. At the king's feet? What a joke! And come to think of it, where is that rat-faced Joseph I with his protruding upper jaw, his glassy stare, his warty features?[7] A train of common coaches has crept unnoticed through the crowd to the customhouse, bringing the king, his wife, his four daughters, his brother (who became also his son-in-law by marrying the eldest princess, Maria), his grandchildren, the whole Braganza tribe, bastard sons of bastards, their bloodlines hopelessly entangled, a sorry crew of deranged and demented degenerates. Unheralded, His Majesty attends the unveiling of his own statue; like the mikado, he is not permitted to appear in public—not that he would want to in the first place. Pombal has drained his power of all substance: the tablet dated June 6, 1775, on his statue officially marks the advent of the "Pombalian bourgeoisie" who have financed the reconstruction and assumed the proprietorship of the new Lisbon beneath its crumbled façade of baroque nobility. The Latin inscription on the pedestal makes it quite plain: *"Restauraverit auspice administro ejus marchione Pombalio et collegio negotiatorum curante"* ("Reconstruction completed under the guidance of the Marquis de Pombal and the council of merchants"). Unannounced, the third estate has seized control of Portugal through an army of masons and builders, a third estate which not only admits but loudly proclaims its monetary aims.

At last Pombal is taking time out to examine the country as a whole, after twenty years of furious, pragmatic, but uncoordinated activity. "His leisurely, speculative, and rather diffuse temperament matched that of the nation."[8] Seventy-six years old. For the first time perhaps since the earthquake, he is wondering how much longer he will continue to function as *de facto* ruler who extends his hand to be kissed, whose subjects withdraw backward from his presence, before whose wife one must kneel, that fat, wild-eyed German woman who snubs the queen. In June 1775 he is composing his *Observaçoes Secretissimas* for the edification of his phantom sovereign and posterity. National pride in the reconstruction is his keynote: "The merits of these highly demanding labors, all achieved by Portuguese hands, demonstrate vividly to foreigners that their own draftsmen, their painters, their most renowned founders, their ablest expert mechanics cannot arouse envy in Portugal."[9] Pombal boasts of this spontaneous outgrowth of organization and development which he attributes to his single-handed efforts: a hernia of enlightenment at Europe's edge. The judicial system "recast in the interests of immediate repression"; a standing army of forty thousand men exposed to Prussian discipline under Count von Schaumburg-Lippe; the Inquisition "converted" to a political police force—and controlled by Bishop Paulo de Carvalho, Pombal's own brother, whom he appointed grand inquisitor. The Junta do Comercio or council of merchants set up and run by him, covering seventy new industries, "refineries for sugar, metal, woolen goods, hats, textiles, pottery, clothing, paper, hardware, glass, etc."[10] Tobacco imports from Brazil increased 110 percent; the export of port wines rose steadily; Portuguese America (Brazil) was organized for systematic exploitation, like a dairy cow or maybe the hen who laid the golden eggs.

And what about the treasury deficit that had tripled owing to constant tapping for Lisbon's reconstruction? Or the soaring cost of sugar, not to mention Negro labor?* What about those new industries that struggle along for want of good roads and communications? Or idle peasants in the *latifundia,* where five sixths of the land lies fallow? "The Portuguese peasant is the poorest in western Europe. Without wheat from the Azores, Lisbon would have no bread."[11] If a physiocrat should happen to wander into Portugal, he would be shocked to find virtually no farming there. Like the spider mentioned earlier: a limp body attached to a colossal head gazing out to sea. Pombal's Portugal, a product of colonial more than mercantile thinking, caught between two conflicting economies, is symbolized by this image of Lisbon, half virgin, half cadaver, which "truly represents *the* phenomenon of eighteenth-century urbanism, situated at a historical crossroads where past and future clasp hands." True, but only for the newly rebuilt Baixa district behind the Praça do Comercio, which has just been inaugurated with great fanfare while the rest of the city, the majority of it, has revived in hit-or-miss fashion. On one of his obscure missions to Lisbon several years prior to the inauguration, Colonel du Mouriez complained of a "dreadful heap of crumbled palaces, of burned-out churches, of debris resembling the wreckage of a fortification that has been blown to bits . . . In many places you walk upon the foundations of houses, along roads paved with rubble . . . " Elsewhere are "ruins as bizarre and as grotesquely beautiful as relics of Roman and Greek buildings." Italian** and English travelers had further tales to tell: in 1771 great quantities of stones, "piled high, divided and aligned like tenanted buildings," were still to be seen in the vicinity of the central city. In 1772 "Lisbon is in the approximate state of destruction inflicted by the earthquake. Though they are putting up new structures every day, a great many streets are still choked with rubble."[12] This study in stark contrasts is one experiment in enlightened despotism, carried out in isolation, unrelated to others. To Pombal and to the class he represents and which supports him, the truly significant gains are a thousand or so "income-yielding structures" built over a period of three or four years, more than existed before the earthquake, the total value of which came to two billion reis.[13] These houses cannot collapse, being braced by a *gaiola,* a wooden structure designed to support the floor and roof in case the walls give way. So Portugal will survive as long as God spares Pombal. Van Loo's portrait of him, seated stiffly in an armchair facing the panorama of his new city, shows a pile of plans spread out on his knees, plans covering "not only the central city but the whole of Lisbon as well, whatever then existed and whatever ought

---

*Pombal ended slavery in Portugal. [*Trans.*]   **Alfieri in this instance.

to exist, nay, must exist."[14] Other cities in Portugal and Brazil will take shape from these blueprints: even Goa in Portuguese India is due for reconstruction.

In dealing with the national budget, there again he needs just a little time. The Lord helped him by destroying Lisbon; he helped the Lord by sweeping human obstacles aside. In 1759 he carried out a campaign of slaughter among the nobility—after all, didn't the Marquis de Tavora fire a pistol at his wife's lover? The offending lover happened to be the king, who found himself with two bullets in the arm. Joseph I had a plaster model of his punctured limb placed *ex voto* in the cathedral. His revenge he assigned to Pombal. The injured husband, his family and relatives, the Tavoras and Aveiros, as well as his servants were tortured, decapitated, burned, or hanged in the public square of Belem, overlooking the Tagus: the gibbet rose eighteen feet in the air. The Duke d'Aveiro was broken on the wheel "and suffered endless agony before he died, filling the square and river front with dreadful shrieks and groans. Then they set fire to the whole works: in a flash, wheel, scaffold, and corpse went up in flames and were pitched into the Tagus,"[15] a symbol of the Lusitanian nobility which had set out to conquer the world two centuries earlier and now was simply a yoke about the neck of the rising merchant class. Pombal, an ardent admirer of Richelieu, eliminated his enemies. With one exception: an indulgence he has offered himself lately by forcing the grand-daughter of his victims, a Tavora, to marry his son.* Meanwhile he is the first in Europe to have gone after those other mischief-makers, the Jesuits, packing them off by the hundreds in filthy, rotting old tubs to be either drowned or cast ashore in Naples and the Roman states. Another treat he has allowed himself was to send their most celebrated spokesman, Father Malagrida, before the Inquisition. "I want the world to see the utility of this tribunal," declared the enlightened Pombal. Malagrida was slowly strangled to death, then burned in the square of Belem.**

There are those in the crowd surrounding the equestrian statue who would hasten the Marquis de Pombal's demise. Witness the Genoese arrested with pistol in hand. But the foiled assassination also proves that Providence is watching over him. He has rid the world of troublemakers and jealous husbands. "Civilization shall be the legitimate daughter of despotism."[16] He has a monstrous appetite for work. The heads of Europe wish him well, for it is to their interest to see Portugal remain stable. "All agree that if this man goes, the country will plunge into disorder because there is no one to take his place," writes Count Scarfanigi, Turin's minister to Lisbon.[17]

---

*They lived unhappily and produced a flock of children. Some of their many descendants are still in Portugal.
**Outraged, Voltaire denounced "this excessive ridicule combined with excessive horror" and refused ever to admit Pombal to the ranks of enlightened society.

40

JUNE 1775

A Revolution in Physics and Chemistry

This was in fact the great epoch of bronze equestrian statues, ever since 1699 when Bouchardon had succeeded in anchoring his figure of Louis XIV in the Place des Victoires in Paris. Now Falconet was agonizing in Saint Petersburg over the problem of how to make Peter the Great plunge skyward in defiance of the laws of gravity. Twelve years before the inauguration of the new Lisbon, the equestrian statue of Louis XV (also by Bouchardon) had been installed with great to-do in the midst of a sprawl of bare ground, sand, and new constructions bridging the gap between city and suburbs in the western part of the capital, linking the Tuileries to the Cours de la Reine and the Champs-Elysées.* It was meant to commemorate the peace treaty of 1763 that left a defeated France at England's mercy. But Parisians were so elated to get the war over with that they turned that June 20 into a victory jubilee. Antoine-Laurent de Lavoisier was nearly twenty, like Condorcet, and would never forget those illuminations in the Place Louis XV, where he wandered about lost in the crowd, peering up at the sky like the fabled astronomer: he was preparing recommendations for improving the lighting system in the capital. [1]

Eleven years later, in February 1774, a flash bulletin from Baron Grimm in his *Correspondance littéraire* informed enlightened society that the young man sauntering about in the Place Louis XV had not been wasting his time: "M. de Lavoisier,** of our Academy of Sciences, has just translated and compiled in a single octavo everything printed and articulated during the past two years on the subject of *The Discovery of Fixed Air*. People call it a most unusual treatise highly significant to the history of chemistry." [2]

It was, of course, simply "a collection of various papers that have ap-

*It is the Place Louis XV (Place de la Révolution in 1792), which ultimately became the Place de la Concorde (under the Directory).

**He acquired the nobiliary title two years earlier; his father, like Beaumarchais, had purchased the office of royal "councillor-secretary," a purely honorific function which, combined with knighthood, conferred hereditary nobility.

peared in England on this question," but it served to introduce a new personality and name. Wisely, Lavoisier chose to launch his first offensive under the protective shield of English research. A year later, in June 1775, he opens a full-scale war, fighting for his life. He knows what the stakes are: by undertaking a series of bold experiments "on elastic fluids released by fermentation and distillation in order to analyze the nature of air absorbed through combustion, he meant to gather sufficient data to constitute a body of theory. He was the only European scientist to foresee development of the chemistry of gases."*
His laboratory records for February 20, 1773, had borne the following heading: "The importance of this object seems likely to cause a revolution in physics and chemistry."[3] Modesty will never mute his strings. Being the first to know that France has a second Newton, he has no desire to bury the news.

And what if fire were not an element? The world would tremble with doubt and apprehension. Where are we? In what do we move about? Previously it had been so simple to count them on your fingers: air, earth, water, and fire. Whatever exists is a combination of those four. Apart from the elements, there is only void, space, the angels, or blind chance. The aim of scientists boils down to determining which elements compose each animate or inanimate object, even if it means pursuing the quest for the elixir of life or the philosopher's stone; in fact, only two centuries earlier, alchemy and chemistry were more or less lumped together, the latter remaining the preserve of specialists. Dr. Alexandre Denyau opened his medical lectures at the Collège de France in 1683 with this grim admonition: "I believe there can be no doubt as to how chemistry threatens the state; it should be taught behind closed doors to doctors only; women ought to be excluded, as well as priests and anyone curious to learn about poisons and counterfeit coins."[4] Of course this was just three years after the Affair of the Poisons.

Lately, however, a great many irresponsible persons seem to be opening their laboratories to the public at large and handing out their diabolic powders to schoolboys. The nature and composition of bodies, long a trade secret of God and scholars, is entering the public domain; the dogma of the four elements is crumbling. A host of rash souls with thinning hair and eyes grown dim from peering into test tubes are about to launch a frontal assault on the phlogiston theory. That's the name of this adventure. The controversy over Lavoisier is the war on phlogiston. Esteem for the word is dying. Becher and Stahl, two Germans out of the previous century, invented the impressive term; what better warrant of credibility? Skeptics who asked why fire appeared in various forms and what made it so different from the other three elements needed to be silenced. People had been conditioned to accept phlogiston as "the inflammatory principle" that all combustible bodies were said to contain. "When a combustible burned, its phlogiston was released and escaped."[5] But

*The term "gas" does not appear for another ten years.

now England's Priestley—that troublemaking scientist and Whig-sympathizer —has just produced (1774) air that is singularly suited to respiration and to combustion, which he calls 'dephlogisticated air.' " Yet Scheele, a Swede, recently proved that "atmospheric air," defined since ancient times as a single indivisible fluid, is in fact a combination of fluids.[6] There is not *one* air; there are two, ten, even twenty different airs. These various discoveries all hang in the air, so to speak, and Lavoisier is engaged in comparing and coordinating them, with an eye to attempting far more daring experiments. What if phlogiston simply did not exist? What if fire resulted from a combination of several flammable elements? Then what is true (or rather what was not true) for fire would perhaps be confirmed in other ways. Good Lord, what if air and water turned out not to be primal elements? That would still leave earth. But if the earth itself . . .

The universe would burst into splinters. Our universe. And leave man floating like a gnat in a sea of dust. Easy does it! Remember that only 130 years earlier Galileo nearly went to the stake. So if explosive ideas of this sort begin to romp about in Antoine-Laurent's head, he proceeds cautiously, unprepared to storm the bastion of accepted beliefs. Besides, he considers himself a scientist, not a seer or poet, and bases his convictions solely on accumulated evidence.

Louis-Bernard Guyton de Morveau,* a Burgundian scientist, visits Lavoisier in the spring of 1775 to compare experimental findings and try to apply them to the metallurgical industry, which is of special interest to Buffon, who owns several blast furnaces between Dijon and Montbard. Though five years older than Lavoisier, Guyton appears to be his pupil, but a stubborn one who does not easily accept Antoine-Laurent's strikingly novel concepts. He clings to the phlogiston theory like a priest to the written word. It even explains, he says, the single "cure" discovered to date for pox: mercury applications. "Because of its ready absorption of phlogiston, this metal attracts that which inflames the lymph with venereal virus."[7] Intelligent and hardworking, Guyton de Morveau has just discovered the disinfectant properties of chlorine and saved an entire district in Dijon from a threatening epidemic spread by the stench of rotting corpses piled up in the cathedral cellars. Nothing worked: neither lime nor clay nor perfume, nor "detonations of saltpeter," nor vinegar fumigations. Guyton had the idea of releasing "hydrochloric air" in iron kettles "heated on a bed of coals" from the reaction of sulfuric acid on sea salt. After forty-eight hours Dijon's good citizens finally were able to breathe again. But Guyton is still too tentative and too dedicated to Stahl's principles to accept Lavoisier's audacious theory that in the process of combustion, matter, specifically phosphorus and metals, instead of giving off something presumed to be phlogiston, actually acquires "something additional" which must be a component of the atmosphere. Air that becomes

*Future delegate to the Constituent Assembly and member of the Committee of Public Safety.

matter! Guyton panics: "I must confess the pain I suffered to see these phenomena happening before my very eyes . . . This aspect threatens to destroy the bulk of our knowledge."

Lavoisier had teased him good-naturedly: "You put crayfish to steam and when they are done, you take them out the loveliest red . . . Where is the phlogiston that gave them that color?"[8] Still, he knew that Guyton voiced the skepticism, not to say alarm, of most of the scientific community. Arrayed against him: Fourcroy, Berthollet, Macquer, Baumé, Sage, and virtually all foreign scientists (Priestley and Scheele lack the courage to follow up their own research). In his favor: his intellectual integrity, his patience, his systematic approach. "The achievements of a variety of sources have presented me with separate links in a great chain. Some have joined together in sections, but a vast series of experiments remains to be done before we attain continuity" (from his laboratory notes for February 20, 1773).

For two years Lavoisier has been engaged in this snail-paced revolution. "If, in his *Discours de la méthode,* Descartes set out to modernize philosophy, Lavoisier now is doing the same for chemistry."[9] Feverishly, but in control of the fever. He strikes his first blow in a treatise published in January 1774 under the unarresting title *Opuscules physiques et chimiques,* which he sends to every learned society of note from London to Saint Petersburg, from Stockholm to Basel. After the Easter recess in 1775 he delivers a paper three quarters of an hour long before the Academy of Sciences in Paris on "The Nature of the Ingredient Which Combines with Metals During Their Calcination and Increases Their Weight." Added precaution: he calls this "eminently breathable air" and the other, in which a flame dies and human beings choke to death, "mofette."* As for the phlogiston theory, "Why take for granted an element that we can do without?"[10]

Not only the scientific community but the economic and industrial ones as well will have to learn to think in this man's terms.

Turgot constantly seeks to attract talented men. Lavoisier is just the type: he has physiocrat friends, money, a seat in the Academy of Sciences; he is industrious, famous, and controversial, a quality not frowned upon by this minister, who writes him on June 18, 1775: "It is with great pleasure, sir, and based on my opinion of your abilities and your unselfishness, that I have chosen you to fill the office of which M. d'Ormesson has apprised you in my behalf."[11]

The office of chief of the state gunpowder commission.

Turgot also was making slow but steady progress. The creation of this commission was part of his overall strategy. One of the reasons France had lost the last war probably had something to do with the poor quality and short supplies of gunpowder, made and furnished exclusively by a company of prominent

*Guyton de Morveau later christened it "nitrogen."

scoundrels who enriched themselves and kept production far below demand. They angered the citizenry by constantly sending search parties into cellars, stables, and private dwellings, wherever saltpeter-gatherers were authorized to enter and scrape from the ground and walls the precious niter needed for gunpowder, blasting powder for mining, sporting powder for hunting, and "select" or "royal" powder. These searches became such a nuisance that the rich made a practice of paying off the gunpowder concession instead, which enriched its principals and left the country more vulnerable. "Gunpowder-farming filled to overflowing the coffers of the 'farmers' rather than the royal arsenals with gunpowder." The king should not have paid more than three hundred thousand francs annually for a million pounds of gunpowder, yet it cost him six times that amount. In 1760 it had been necessary to import saltpeter from Holland. Lavoisier shares Turgot's sense of outrage. Does he speak as a scientist or a politician when he says: "A country the size of France, surrounded by neighbors jealous of her power . . . compelled by her very position and far-flung possessions to take an interest in events in Europe, America, and Asia, ought to have access domestically, independent of outside sources or circumstances, to all the saltpeter, all the gunpowder necessary to arm its fleet, to supply its troops, to defend its borders, to protect its crops, to operate its manufactures, its mines, its public works"?[12] Rather windy rhetoric, typical of Lavoisier; still, one can tell that he had thought the problem through. Following issuance of a royal edict putting him in charge of a state commission to replace private concessionaires, Lavoisier sets about curtailing searches of "stables, sheepfolds, dovecotes, empty barns, and other low-lying premises that are natural niter beds." His plan is to stimulate the manufacture of gunpowder by increasing and perfecting the refining process under competent technicians. Methodical testing and experimentation will eventually give France the best and cheapest product in the world. Quietly, behind the scenes, Antoine-Laurent de Lavoisier is fulfilling the role of an undersecretary of defense.*

He is rather tall and dark, with the narrow, pale face of men who lead sedentary lives; thin lips, a prematurely bald dome of a forehead, and gray eyes with uptilted pupils, like a mystic. His manner bespeaks the quiet self-confidence of those to whom success comes as a matter of course, who have never suffered.

Lavoisier was born in the Saint-Merry district of Paris; his forebears came from Soissons and had been hired laborers, journeymen, and postilions risen to become bailiffs, legal officials, and attorneys, gaining great wealth along with social status. His mother, daughter of a lawyer, died when he was five, leaving a large fortune. Antoine-Laurent and his only sister (who died at

*Three other commissioners besides himself are appointed, but his fame and expertise place the burden of responsibility on him.

fifteen) were raised by an ideal mother: an aunt devoted to the two children and, to a lesser extent, their father. No anguished adolescence; pampered but not spoiled, he grew up in a fine house on the Rue du Four-Saint-Eustache and attended classes at the Collège Mazarin, also called the Collège des Quatre-Nations* (the most popular in Paris, owing to its science curriculum). In fact, when Antoine-Laurent was a pupil, no other high school in the capital gave the sciences equal footing with history and the humanities.[13] There he acquired "a passion for learning" that nearly killed him—they had to "build him up with gruel." Nothing else mattered. He studied law, of course, and philosophy to learn how to express himself; he absorbed mathematics; geology under Guettard, the best naturalist in Paris; botany under Jussieu, the best of the botanists; and chemistry with the best chemist, Rouelle. The only significant events of his youth had been field trips into the country with one or another of those teachers. At twenty, he made notes morning and evening on the weather outside his house on the Rue du Four-Saint-Eustache and continued to do so the rest of his life, no matter where he happened to be. At twenty-three, he traveled all over France studying the different varieties of gypsum. At twenty-four, he was romping through the Vosges, Alsace, and Lorraine with Guettard and a servant laden with thermometers, barometers, serometers; he was compiling a mineralogic atlas of France and Europe. He bombarded his father and aunt with letters about the "analysis of water," of soils, mines, and plants. Meals along the way never caught his interest. As for girls, where would he find time for them?

At twenty-five, he was elected to the Academy of Sciences purely on the strength of his scientific ardor—and his colossal fortune.** He polled more votes than Jars, who introduced iron-smelting to France, the discoverer of minium commissioned by the king to study mining techniques throughout Europe. In their tight, cozy little world, however, the academicians favored rich men. Lalande, the famous astronomer whose head was not always in the clouds, innocently gave away the secret: "I helped to elect Lavoisier, though he was younger and less famous [than Jars], because a young man of learning, culture, and industry whose fortune allowed him to take up another profession would naturally be very useful to the cause of science."[14]

There was some truth in this. Lavoisier had not taken the election for a sinecure. In those days an academy worked. Antoine-Laurent had deluged his colleagues with quarterly, even monthly, reports on Carlier's aerometer, Dufourny's lantern, a water-driven bellows, the conversion of water from the Yvette River to drinking water for Paris, and the "rouge women use to color

*The four French "nations" of that date: Alsace, Flanders, Roussillon, and the Pignerol region, all acquired by Louis XIV's conquests. The school was intended to serve boarding pupils from those areas, but also took in paying day pupils.
**His mother's legacy alone came to over 170,000 livres (700,000 modern francs [$140,000]); his father advanced him double that amount when Lavoisier married.

their faces." Considering "that this adornment had been adopted by entire social classes and especially by ladies of high quality," he will investigate ways "to make rouge that contains nothing harmful either to the skin or to the general health."[15]

A voracious appetite for keeping busy. Instead of wearing him out, new posts or functions simply slowed him down. Was it this craving for extra work that prompted him, while still a very young man, to become a farmer-general?* Foresight also, perhaps. Lavoisier had no time for pleasure, but managed to set aside a few moments for making money: it was the nerve center of his war. He knew there was no such animal as a poor scientist, so if he intended—and he did—to become the French Newton, he would have to rely on his own purse strings. His father and aunt had no real understanding of his research, but resolved to help him get ahead. They had raised and educated him to believe that making money was a duty just as essential for him as labor for the peasant. At the right moment they had bought him a place among the sixty millionaires who were charged with collecting the bulk of indirect taxes and who exploited the country shamelessly, presumably in the king's behalf but actually for their own pockets. This called for a large initial cash outlay, "which was 1,560,000 francs for each farmer-general. This expenditure actually did not represent an advance payment to the state coffers, for almost all of it covered the cost of buildings, storehouses, raw materials, mostly salt and tobacco over which the tax farm exercised a monopoly, and which were transmitted from lease to lease as inventory. Thus, for each year of his lease beginning in 1774, a farmer-general received dividends of nearly three hundred thousand francs, meaning a twenty-percent annual return on his capital investment."** In five years Lavoisier and his fellow farmers could expect to recover their money; in twenty, to triple their fortunes.

But Antoine-Laurent would have found it unseemly to applaud his situation; like bodily imperatives, one simply did not speak of it. He was satisfied that his money proliferated faster than rabbits. He took pleasure instead in an incredible list of activities: in 1775 he is a member of the tobacco commission, the customs commission (to regulate and collect tolls at the gates of Paris), the salt-mining commission of Franche-Comté, the commission of excise collectors, of the bureau of accounts and personnel . . . The lucrative delights of tax farming! Most of the time he is traveling around to check on collection of

---

*In 1768, still only twenty-five. He and his father had advanced 520,000 livres to buy him a share in the "farm" of old François Baudon, which covered a mere third of the total cost of the office. An individual lease for a farmer-general in 1775 ran as high as a billion pre-1970 francs [$200 million].

**According to Mollien, finance minister later on under Napoleon, who was just entering the tax-farming bureaucracy in 1775.[16]

the salt tax, to exhort the farm's agents (there are thirty thousand of them in France), and to inspect tobacco shipments along the Marne.

One almost had to grab him by the coattails in order to drag him to the altar on December 16, 1771, in the chapel of the finance-administration building in Paris, where he married the daughter of farmer-general Paulze, a nephew of the Abbé Terray, who was then at the height of his prosperity. Antoine-Laurent regarded the experience as inevitable and not unpleasant. Marie-Anne-Pierrette was fourteen (half his age), a nice wisp of a girl with merry eyes and long brown hair. She was very fond of him, admired his work, and liked to help him in the laboratory. She became his first and last pupil. As for the business side of the contract, it was acceptable, not lavish: a dowry of eighty thousand livres. The husband was far richer than the bride, who wasn't exactly a pauper. And Paulze had long arms.

Now that he has been appointed to the gunpowder commission, they will move from the twelve-room wedding gift bought for them four years earlier on the Rue Neuve-des-Bons-Enfants into a handsome "official" mansion in the Petit Arsenal district near the Bastille. This gives Lavoisier a four-story house with large, sunny, high-ceilinged rooms in which to install a modern laboratory. He is already making lists of the instruments he will need to equip it. He has decided to spend six hours there every day: mornings from six to nine, evenings from seven to ten, and one entire day a week reserved for experiments, aided by his closest friends. The rest of his time will go to the gunpowder commission and tax farming. But what really obsesses him is the urge to find a simple, succinct name for that "eminently breathable air," that "vital air" he is in the process of discovering, a name to which his own shall be attached.

MALESHERBES

41

JUNE 1775

I See That We Must Think of Living

Though Maurepas did not attend the coronation, Turgot, racked with gout, dragged himself there, like a good soldier unwilling to desert his regiment. He could not ignore signs of interest from the court when Choiseul made his bid to regain power. Turgot understood at last that time was working against him, a realization reinforced by the stabbing pains in his legs which, by the day's end, turned his whole body into a mass of pain. He grew vigilant because he couldn't sleep. When the festivities ended, when the lights went out and the king returned to Versailles, he wasted no time launching his plan and summoning his "surprise man" to help promote reforms he feared might not otherwise succeed.

Alone, he cannot hold his own on the royal council. Sartines is bent on destroying him; Miromesnil raises formal obstructions; Maurepas is evasive; De Muy openly detests him; Vergennes ignores him. He is "in a bind." And somehow he must progress to the second stage of his plan, the purely fiscal part, for he remains convinced that freeing the grain trade was the first step toward economic sanity. But budgetary balance can be no more than a pious vow so long as no one is willing to tackle the real problem—that is, to curb and gradually reduce royal spending. "All ministerial reforms would prove useless to counteract a court teeming with princes, officials, and favorites who lived on memories and to whom the future meant nothing."[1] The king's household was a blight on the treasury: an incredible proliferation of offices, prebends, pensions, and purchased privilege; fifteen thousand individuals and five thousand horses dependent on the king's bounty, not to mention the "households" of the queen, the king's aunts and brothers, and princes of the blood. The man who for fifty years had managed this mountain of parasitism finally came to be identified with it: but fifty years are enough. The Duc de La Vrillière, now deaf as a post, is simply a doddering emblem of the worst excesses of Louis XV's reign and is to be replaced after the coronation. This leaves one vacant seat on the Council. Turgot intends to fill it with the antithesis of La Vrillière and Choiseul, someone not afraid to stanch the nation's gaping wounds.

The miracle man of June 1775 whom Turgot would summon to purge the royal household is Malesherbes.

More than a change, it will be a dramatic thunderclap—and Turgot is counting on this. In place of the tottering toady bent in two from having bowed his way to fortune—this Phélipeaux advanced by royal favor to become first the Comte de Saint-Florentin, then the Duc de La Vrillière, three names for one nullity—he will install France's most prestigious magistrate, first president of the Cour des Aides, a rock of fortitude, an independent mind, a man! Lamoignon de Malesherbes. The *Encyclopédie's* defender will succeed the author of *lettres de cachet.* The public official who once presented remonstrances to the king will henceforth distribute his favors.

His friendship with Turgot dates back over twenty years.

Act quickly. Intrigue this once if you must, for the issue is critical. Turgot resolves to do so. He exploits Maurepas's fear of Choiseul's bid for power to bring old Mentor into the act. Miromesnil, a stanch parliamentarian, cannot oppose Malesherbes. These three ministers, joined at the last moment by Vergennes, obtain royal consent to summon Malesherbes on the morning of June 26.

And nothing happens.

One, two, three solid days of waiting. A snag somewhere. Turgot's tactic has run up against two obstacles that he had anticipated but underestimated: the queen's opposition and Malesherbes—who backs off.

The Abbé de Véri, who watches these maneuvers over Maurepas's shoulder, is not surprised: he thinks Turgot has been playing the apprentice sorcerer for several months, trying "to be the first to bring the queen into affairs. He did not realize that the frivolity of this princess would carry it away from him* sooner or later owing to the necessity for a finance minister to resist the court's excessive demands. He wanted to persuade her and to win her support. This meant granting her power with which the king's weakness already overloads her."

On the evening of June 27 Véri observes: "We are reaching the point where the unseen struggle of the two factions is about to take on color."[2] Meaning that the high sign given to Malesherbes will act as a disclosing solution to reveal the contours of these two parties, which up to now have been indistinguishable amid the general euphoria of the new regime: the party of reform pledged to Turgot and the party of privilege. New fact of life: this latter group is aware of having found a champion in Marie Antoinette. She returned from Rheims toughened by Choiseul's defeat and Vienna's reproaches, feeling slightly soured toward everyone. She still looks for a "comeback from Chanteloup." She has her own ideas as to who should replace La Vrillière: docile, corrupt, and entertaining, Sartines is the man she wishes to promote from the naval ministry to the royal household. He would not try to end the traditional "gavage" of court favorites. The next best choice after Choiseul. On learning that Malesherbes is about to be appointed, she takes issue openly and forcefully with her "poor fellow" of a husband; prior to this, her objections always had been circumspect and devious. On the evening of June 29 she lets Maurepas know that she has asked the king to reconsider and name Sartines instead. This is the queen's official political debut.

Maurepas smells danger. Sartines's promotion would open the way for Choiseul's return. Joining with Turgot, he tells Marie Antoinette that things have progressed too far to be reversed without discrediting the king. He is bluffing, of course.

For even on June 29 he knows that Malesherbes plans to refuse the appointment. The key man in Turgot's game plan is slipping off the board.

---

*"Carry it away"—sooner or later she would deny the support that Turgot expected from her.

It might have been sensible to consult Malesherbes sooner. But Turgot's *modus operandi* is to pounce without warning after too long a delay. He realizes now that he doesn't really understand one of his oldest friends. Chrétien-Guillaume Lamoignon de Malesherbes will not be pushed around.

He is only fifty-three, though people say he looks older. The Sage of France. Was Nestor ever young? Since Henry IV's day has any Lamoignon not worn the scarlet robes of the magistracy? The men in that family seem to have read the law in their mother's womb. Chrétien-Guillaume has been ostracized to Malesherbes near Pithiviers, not far from Bignon, where the elder Mirabeau is his neighbor. The exile is not very neighborly; neither is he fond of visitors. Solitude and banishment have patterned his life since 1771, when the mounting audacity of his remonstrances so angered the throne that Louis XV banished him to this Gâtinais estate acquired by his father at the turn of the century.

> Monsieur de Lamoignon de Malesherbes, by this letter I command you to remain at Malesherbes until further notice from me. I pray the Lord to watch over you, Monsieur de Malesherbes.
>
> Signed: Louis—countersigned: Phélipeaux.[3]

Precisely the same Phélipeaux-La Vrillière he is commissioned to replace four years later. But Chrétien-Guillaume, better known now as Malesherbes than as Lamoignon, doesn't relish this spicy situation. Become a minister and be in a position to sign such letters? God protect him from his friends! He has had all the revenge he wanted six months before, when the old king's death ushered in a "new order" that he might otherwise never have seen: he presided over the reinstated Cour des Aides, and the Lamoignons triumphed over the Maupeous. Reinstalled as first president, he is in a position to teach the young sovereign his civic duties publicly. What more could he ask for? Only on state occasions does he return to court at Paris or Versailles. And since Turgot and Maurepas began feeling him out, he has barricaded himself behind the simplicity (mildly ostentatious, yet appropriate to his station) of the "little" country house to which he retired two years earlier when financial ruin atop his disgrace prevented him from occupying his immense Louis XIII château.* He dismissed all his servants "except two plus a *chartier* [*sic*], and a woman from the village does my cooking."[4] This is the man they mean to put in charge of the royal household. The thought of it truly upsets him. He comments (for himself? for Turgot?) on June 25: "We have reached the critical and decisive moment of the king's rule . . . It is the queen's desire to appoint M. de Sartines to M. de La Vrillière's post . . . Her wishes already

---

*The two dwellings still exist, but remodeling of the château has made it more eighteenth-century in style. As for the "little" house, now a photography studio, it faces the Place de la Mairie along the extension of the main street in Malesherbes, about three hundred yards from the château's entrance.

are known to twenty or thirty persons and in a week everyone else will know them . . . If I were to assume the office desired by M. de Sartines, who is still a powerful member of the Council and, what's more, exerts incalculable influence on the Paris police, which influence is doubly dangerous for being invisible . . . and since everyone knows it is against the queen's wishes, no one would really obey or support me . . . In a few months I would be dismissed and in even shorter time I would have deserved it for the errors I committed, errors forced upon me by my subordinates . . . I would leave the government, and I would leave in disgrace . . . The queen wants her way . . . Far be it from me to argue whether or not the king ought to yield . . . The fact is that such is her wish and she will have it. Hence it is inimical to the public interest and to the peace of the realm to appoint any minister of whom she does not approve."[5]

That is Malesherbes to the core. Possibly his foes know him better than do his friends, who fail to recognize the existence of two Malesherbes and are discovering it too late. There is the Rock of Gilbraltar, the magistrate who remonstrated fearlessly against Louis XV and risked his neck in defense of a certain concept of "civic welfare and order": "The people are crushed by taxes, and when faced with new ones after several years of peace, when told that costly loans are a necessary source of funds, they lose hope of ever seeing an end to their misery."*

The Great Judge.

Also a slippery, undefinable man, "director of the library" from 1750 to 1763, the liberal yet tyrannical grand censor; meddlesome and great-hearted; quick to anger or else timid; obstinate or tentative; placed by that thankless yet prized office at the very axis of all the great controversies of his day: summoned by the critic Fréron to ban Voltaire and by Marmontel and Voltaire to ban Fréron when the latter maligned them. "But how can he** say this periodical enjoys my patronage because I don't ban it? Can't he see that it's like holding the chief of police responsible for every case of pox contracted in the brothels because he tolerates them and reserves his police units for combating cutthroats?"[7]

The man who fostered the *Encyclopédie* yet nearly caused its publishing license to be revoked because he hid some of the articles in his house. "Friend" of Diderot, whom he managed to vex with a single frown. Malesherbes is "a *philosophe* who does disservice to philosophy, who thrives on controversy," Voltaire lamented when unable to decide for himself whether to love him or tear him apart—and who did both periodically.[8] Malesherbes adores a good

---

*Opening statement of the "great public remonstrance" addressed to the Duc de Chartres (the future Philippe Egalité) on January 16, 1769, when the young prince was dispatched to the Cour des Aides by Louis XV to compel registration of a new twentieth-tax.[6]
**"He" refers to Marmontel. The quotation comes from a letter sent to Turgot by Malesherbes in June 1759.

wrangle, there's the point; he looks for it, yet dreads it; he derives from it his own morose pleasure. For nearly fifteen years he protected all those writers and made them suffer; now they line up like whipped children asking for more.

He is the very spirit of controversy. A skeptic and a believer. A rebel dedicated to public order. His mother died when he was thirteen; his father was a typical starchy magistrate who tyrannized the boy uneasily. From childhood, Guillaume learned to outsmart him and to tell polite half-truths. Brought up to scorn wealth, he was never really without it. As a magistrate, he vilified the bankers, but managed to marry a farmer-general's daughter, Marie-Françoise Grimod de La Reynière. Twenty-two years of wedded silence until the day in 1771 when Marie-Françoise strapped a pistol to a tree in the forest of Malesherbes, tugged on a ribbon attached to the trigger, and disemboweled herself with a single shot. That was the only sound she ever made. Malesherbes never mentioned her suicide to anyone after the funeral. His private life henceforth would concern only himself. He didn't mourn the loss: with two daughters to care for, he made every effort to give them the happiness his wife never knew.

The night of June 29? It was agony for Malesherbes. On the 27th, Turgot, Maurepas, and Véri had invaded "the little house." They arrived together, a solemn trio, and began at once to harass the rotund, bulb-nosed Burgundian, majestic only in his judicial robes, who threw up his hands in dismay, waving a pair of soiled lace cuffs above his disheveled bobtail wig, stuck on askew, and his tobacco-stained collar.[9] "Me a minister, and in the worst possible job? I'm not cut out to be a minister, not even keeper of the seals. To discourse, yes, or to write and read and criticize, but not to administer, not to supervise and direct valets!" They hammered away at him by turns, hardly giving him a chance to breathe. Like the three petitioners before Job, who sprawls not on a dungheap but in a roomy Louis XIII armchair behind a desk covered with neat piles of papers, the window open to the peaceful sounds of the harvest· in 1775. Hordes of wasps signaled a good summer. Malesherbes would have liked to rid himself of the trio, as he would wasps, with a flick of the wrist. Unfortunately, they stayed, advancing arguments with which Boisgelin, Archbishop of Aix, had lately armed them:

> "It is not the mind, nor the virtues, nor superior ideas that make a good governor, it is will power."
> "How right you are! That's what makes it impossible for me to be a good minister: I have no will power."
> "What's that? You think *you* have no will power?"
> "That's right, I really have none."
> "Yet I see that you uphold your convictions when they are firm."
> "But there's no assurance that I have firm convictions about most things!"[10]

They went away exhausted. "Three hours of pleading produced that and no more!" A virtual refusal. Yet they could not accept defeat. If Malesherbes rejected the office, it would constitute a palace revolution in the eyes of Europe instead of the dramatic event intended, with the queen gaining a voice in domestic affairs through Sartines, and Turgot left helpless or forced to resign. On the 29th, Maurepas and Turgot send an ultimatum to Malesherbes via special messenger: "Your decision involves the welfare of twenty million souls." Awakened by the courier, he does not go back to bed, but paces his candlelit study, then dashes off page after anguished page to Turgot. Do they take him for the country's savior? Yet he himself is drowning, his head barely above water. "I am awakened, sir, and am told that you require an immediate answer . . . The queen has obtained what she wishes from the king, and I believe this was so before you even knew it." He reiterates his position: "You seek to bring me in contrary to the will, to the choice, of an all-powerful queen. Is that at all realistic? You bring me in today in order to have me driven out tomorrow . . . And you want an immediate reply, in the dead of night . . ." The honeyed, starry Gâtinais night just after the Feast of St. John, the myriad enchanting sounds of silent June. And here is this man struggling desperately, half-beaten. Still seeking a way out, he asks to have a "conversation with the king *and one with the queen*" (the emphasis is his own) before accepting the appointment—his anxiety reaches its pitch now—because "I know how dangerous it is to hold that conversation" . . . in which he would talk to Marie Antoinette "as I would talk to someone forty years old with a solid head on her shoulders." "I feel that if, after such a perfectly forthright conversation, the queen persists in supporting M. de Sartines, then you are lost, you and M. de Maurepas . . ." Let them be lost; Malesherbes doesn't care. He continues to pour out page after page, trembling with emotion,[11] the first case of insomnia in France over the role Marie Antoinette is preparing to play. "Here is my answer, since you insist on having it . . . But don't take it as final, for it is folly to decide such a matter impetuously. I shall turn it over in my mind, stroll a bit . . ."

About time! The sun is already baking Versailles at ten on the morning of June 30 when the courier rides up to deliver this rambling reply to Turgot, who takes it at once to Maurepas. They have what they want now in black and white. Quick! Malesherbes must be besieged and overwhelmed on the spot. Maurepas grabs Turgot by the arm and they both go before the king. Using an ancient god that still proves effective, they needle his masculine vanity. Who rules his household, he or she? Louis XVI reaches for his pen and dispatches these lines to Malesherbes: "I believe that your devotion to the public welfare must overcome your resistance, and you cannot imagine how pleased I would be if you were to accept, at least for a short time [this strategy of a "provisory" acceptance was Turgot's] . . . I believe this is absolutely essential for the good of the nation. Louis."[12] The Abbé de Véri leaps into a coach and dashes off to deliver the letter, coupled with a long, confident message from Turgot: "I am assured that the queen is not personally opposed to you [which is not true] . . . I am sorry to have disturbed you in the middle of the night. You know me well enough to realize that I wished neither to surprise you nor to abuse your good name . . . Your idea of a conversation [with the queen] might have worked if the situation had been as you saw it. Actually, it would have made things worse rather than better . . . Good-by . . . May our friendship persist despite the distress I have caused you."[13]

The "distress" amounts to rape. Véri knows this as he hands the two letters to their victim: "It grieved me to see him subjected to this violent turmoil."

"Short of a fatal disease, nothing more disastrous could happen to me," Malesherbes tells him excitedly. "But no one can resist a longing far more potent than a command."[14]

Thus he becomes a minister. They've tricked him. Just under the wire.

On July 14 Voltaire writes to a friend: "France must be quite glad if M. de Malesherbes has become a minister! Truly now, in all respects we are ruled by reason and virtue. I see that we must think of living."* Julie de Lespinasse exults: "Never, no, never have two more virtuous, unselfish, and vigorous men been brought together and inspired by loftier interests. You will see, their tenure will leave a lasting impression on the human spirit** . . . Hard times are here for rogues and sycophants!"[15]

They believe the battle is won, that the advocate of progress seconded by the advocate of enlightenment will finally restore the nation.

But Marie Antoinette is unforgiving. "To her, in the language of intrigue, it comes as a slap."[16] For this slap she will make Turgot alone pay, Maurepas having managed to extricate himself deftly from the affair. She will not be too hard on Malesherbes, if only to avoid another lecture from Vienna, but for the comptroller general she reserves a frown that is permanent, overt, and contagious. Worse still, Louis XVI agrees with her. He has not forgotten that his father, the dauphin, considered Malesherbes an accursed Encyclopedist. The pressure of having to plead with this man to serve the monarchy has been humiliating. His Majesty, too, feels "violated" by Turgot and on July 1, in an aside to Maurepas, mutters: "Did you hear that? [Speaking of Turgot] Only his own friends deserve notice, only his own ideas have value . . . "

---

*Figuratively in general, but also in a particular sense, for Voltaire was very ill during the summer of 1775 and believed himself at death's door. The news revived his spirits.

**Letter to Guibert on July 6, 1775. She refers, of course, to the Turgot-Malesherbes "tandem."

42

It Is the Final Struggle for Freedom

La Fayette has been utterly bored for a year. At least, whenever he happened to be home with his child bride in the little gilt schoolroom set up in the Hôtel de Noailles for the young couple to play house. He found the game less than amusing with her: she was innocently unresponsive. Gilbert found himself bound in wedlock to an adolescent girl who was expected to bear him a child before she had even learned her catechism. She didn't object, of course, for everything about the handsome, carrot-headed lad of sixteen delighted her. She was the first person in Gilbert's life to treat him with respect. She went along with the game as if it were just another lesson in deportment, so what more could he ask? They had been married on April 11; by May 15 she was pregnant. In July she miscarried. He was already far away, Louis XVI's accession having licensed his escape from this silly nursery tale. His army career had been helped along by members of his own family: the Duc d'Ayen (his father-in-law) had prevailed on the queen through "Madame Etiquette," the Duchesse de Mouchy (his great-aunt), to put him in charge of a company in the Noailles Dragoons Regiment commanded by the Prince de Poix (his cousin). La Fayette thus became a captain at sixteen and divided his time between home and his unit; he was expected to remain in garrison for part of the summer, in this case Metz, and to appear regularly for military training. To amuse himself he chased girls, who interested him enormously, and entertained his own circle of young officers, all more or less related, at leisurely, talk-filled luncheons. He went from one idle pleasure to the next, longing for a war.

Adrienne had returned under her mother's wing and spent afternoons with her sisters, the "nest of doves," in a spacious gilt-paneled drawing room hung with crimson damask, where she resumed the lessons presided over since her earliest childhood by the Duchesse d'Ayen. Family instruction, like a bedtime story, could be picked up where left off the night before: a bit of this and that, by turns amusing or starkly Jansenist. The Bible, Corneille, a taste of Voltaire—his tragedies. Never a harsh word: "My mother felt she had accomplished nothing if she failed to persuade the child to whom she was speaking.''[1] Adrienne's marriage had changed nothing, except that now their discussions frequently touched on the responsibilities of motherhood, and, blushing, she would read aloud the insipid letters that arrived regularly from her Gilbert, whose every other word was "dear heart":

"How can you ask if I was happy to hear of your pregnancy? . . . It is a mutual gift, dear heart; that's how we ought to think and feel about it. I swear to you that my joy was greater than I imagined . . . You are acquainted with the vicomte's* delightful footman, a fellow much superior to the ordinary run of servants. His master gave him to me because I have more use for him and wanted him very much; they parted tearfully, and now that I possess [*sic*] him I have the best servant there is.''[2] This was the type of news he wrote her, and a sample of La Fayette's philanthropy at age seventeen. In May 1775, however, echoes of the Grain War alarmed him: "You have had rebels [in Paris]; here [in Metz] it is peaceful. But they say we would march on Rheims during the coronation if there were any signs of disorder. Perhaps this is just a barracks rumor. If you would please me, dear heart, write me in detail what is happening, what they predict and what they say at court." So he worried a bit about things that had no one else worried, at the close of a typical winter of gay parties with his peers the Dillons, Ségurs, Coignys, Durforts, or Guéménées at the Epée de Bois, a fashionable cabaret on the edge of the Porcherons district between the boulevards and Montmartre hill. He had danced at carnival time, desperate, like the rest of his set, to revive old customs. He had even been invited informally by the queen with "the little group from the Epée de Bois" to perform some quadrilles, out of "Madame Etiquette" 's sight. Yet they mocked him. "He made a point of cultivating whatever seemed fashionable about people or things. His manner was always awkward; he was very tall, with bright red hair; he was a clumsy dancer, a poor rider, and all the young men with whom he lived proved far more agile than he at physical exercise.''[3] Once he missed the beat and Marie Antoinette burst into laughter. Mortified, he tried even harder to excel in the few areas of competition open to haughty sons of the feudal aristocracy, principally drinking and womanizing. "Ever since the Duc d'Orléans introduced English customs at Mousseau,** society had taken to drinking heavily," and the young Noailles, Gilbert's inseparable companion, "succeeded regularly in keeping up with aristocratic English visitors to the continent." What they wouldn't do in the name of honor! One evening Gilbert got sick as a dog on champagne. He had no talent for that either. Friends stuffed him into his carriage and packed him home to bed, while over and over he kept muttering: "Don't forget to tell Noailles how much I drank! Don't forget . . .''[4]

Chasing skirts seemed to give him better results. By now he could spot the attackable women and did so industriously, perhaps by emulation at first,

---

*Another Noailles, this time his brother-in-law, who was garrisoned at Metz.

**A tiny hamlet for which the Parc Monceau later was named.

but soon by choice. The fact that he was married to a young girl who adored him never entered the picture. No one could ever accuse him of that ridiculous foible, marital fidelity. For months he had vied with the Duc de Chartres and others for the favors of Aglaé d'Hunolstein, the season's smash hit. Vainly, it appeared, though Aglaé had not locked him out; she gave him a rain check. Gilbert had nearly won his spurs in the attempt, for he came close to fighting the theatrical duel without which no aristocrat could call himself a man. He had set out one evening, sword in hand, to visit young Ségur, a close friend (though bluebloods of his day were not averse to cutting a friendly throat), and challenged him to a duel over Aglaé. Ségur had a terrible time convincing the would-be swordsman that he was not among the favored recipients of Madame d'Hunolstein's attentions. The older generation underestimated the fiery passions glowing beneath that mop of red hair. "A few days after our quarrel and reconciliation," Ségur writes, "I nearly burst out laughing to hear the Maréchal de Noailles and other members of his family begging me to use my influence to melt his reserve, to rouse him from his indolence, and to put some fire in his spirit."[5]

Must he, like the rest of them, throw away his youth gambling and flirting until it came time to retire? Luckily, the smoldering fire found worthy fuel on August 8, 1775, when Gilbert Motier de La Fayette learned of America.

The news sheet of "Public Notices, Announcements, and Miscellanous Information for the Trois-Évêchés* and the Duchy of Lorraine" carries the following advice on August 17: "For the past week Metz has been host to his Royal Highness the Duke of Gloucester, his wife the duchess, their child, and a large retinue. Their Royal Highnesses have attended several dramatic performances and toured the city. His Royal Highness the Prince de Poix and several noble lords in Metz have given dinners in their honor."[6] One such affair was hosted on the 8th by the Duc de Broglie, commander of the regional army. His was the privilege of being first to entertain the King of England's brother, which he did at a luncheon extending far into the afternoon at the governor's palace. To honor his guest he invites the cream of local society, including the youngest members of the illustrious Noailles d'Ayen family, the Vicomte de Noailles and the Marquis de La Fayette. Seated near the Gloucesters, young La Fayette stares admiringly at the princely couple, who have just chosen to exile themselves from England, and drinks in their every word. He has always believed himself born to mingle with royalty, a conviction that not even Marie Antoinette's burst of laughter could shake.

Metz: a world apart, caught up in its military and urbane preoccupations. A city that never had a chance. The ancient capital of Austrasia has been

*Former territorial district comprising Verdun, Metz, and Toul, independent of the Duke of Lorraine. [Trans.]

reduced by a thousand years of warfare to serve either as the principal French stronghold against Germany or as Germany's buffer against France. Each time it tried to live and flourish, an army intervened, razing its suburbs, dismantling its churches and monuments, confining Metz behind her battlements like a woman squeezed into a corset. The imposing citadel of 1556 had been built by French troops under Henri II—to intimidate the townspeople, who still cherished the memory of their proud "republic" in the fourteenth century.

Republic indeed! The dream of another Florence died under the heels of invading armies. In 1775, if Versailles is the theater of the monarchy, then Metz is the true repository of monarchic power. Thirty thousand inhabitants, one third of them in uniform, tripping over each other in the narrow corridors between curtain walls, bastions, ravelins, and counterscarps. To enter the city you must cross three drawbridges. The barracks are Europe's finest, but Voltaire complains that Metz has twenty eating houses for one bookshop. The troop commander in the Trois-Evêchés, a vast military camp that includes Toul and Verdun, is a key piece in the monarchic machine: within a few days he can shift his regiments from the Moselle to the Rhine or the Sambre, threaten the Hapsburgs, the Dutch—or Paris and Rheims, for that matter, as was proposed three months earlier. And when it comes to keeping order, Louis XVI can rely on the Duc de Broglie to maintain stern military discipline and mete out floggings at the drop of a hat.

But today the mood in the great banquet hall is festive and urbane. The soldiers are outside, the footsloggers, who get beaten to death, hanged, mutilated, and broken on the wheel if they rebel or desert.[7] They cover the city, they mount the guard and present arms by the hundreds in their blue-and-white uniforms, an impressive array of force. Among them are the eighty fellows La Fayette is supposed to drill every day and who actually are teaching him the ropes. Others come and go in the palace proper, converted to footmen, cupbearers, and master cooks because the Governor of Metz is a petty sovereign for the day: might as well make merry if you can't make war. Victor-François de Broglie, third marshal of that name, presides over the table with the solemnity of a man well pleased with himself. Woe to anyone who recalls his ancestors—humble Piedmontese, those Broglios (the word means "intrigue" in Italian) who slid into the French court in Mazarin's wake just four generations before. This man's grandfather went on to prove himself a decent Frenchman by slaughtering the Camisards.* Victor-François himself** took part in all the glorious surrenders of Louis XV's army: Rossbach, Filing-

*Protestant peasants of the Cévennes mountains who waged guerrilla warfare against Louis XIV in retaliation for the persecutions that followed the revocation of the Edict of Nantes in 1685. [*Trans.*]

**His younger brother, Charles-François, the Comte de Broglie, played a key role in Louis XV's secret diplomacy, for which he was rewarded with exile to his estates. Some historians of the "luncheon at Metz" have confused the two brothers.

hausen, and Minden are just a few of his military honors. That string of defeats is his crown of laurels.* Gilbert feels privileged to serve under him.

But the real focus of attention now is the Duke of Gloucester, who shares the limelight with his pretty, slender, young wife—isn't she the daughter of a seamstress?

Yes, but also of a Walpole, one of those Whigs who have actually been ruling England for the past ninety years and brought to the throne (since someone had to sit there) those fat Germans from Hanover with bulging eyes and clumsy manners. Gloucester is an actor born to play bourgeois dramas who has wandered onto the set of *King Lear* or *Les Frères ennemis*. His marriage struck the final blow to six years of deteriorating relations with his brother George III. He refused to submit to the Royal Marriage Act that George had promulgated three years earlier expressly to prevent his brothers and sons from "derogating" or losing caste. Poor Gloucester would have had a hard time obeying it, having already secretly wed the "illegitimate" daughter of Edward Walpole without daring to tell his brother. A fine mess, which the "gossip columns," Europe's salons, reported in full detail: the birth of a daughter had called forth Gloucester's confession, George III's wrath, and awkward gymnastics at the court of St. James's.[8] Riddled with debts which the British treasury refused to pay, discouraged and embittered, the Gloucesters set out for Italy in hopes that the climate would improve the duke's health: he does in fact look sickly, with his ashen features, his skin falling in folds like an oversize garment. His speech, however, is not the least infirm. La Fayette is stunned by the prince's open hostility to his brother, which he expresses in fluent French. The Hanovers, still newcomers to the English language, are more at home in French or German. Hostility toward his policies, of course, not his sacred person. Metz pays tribute to Gloucester because of his royal descent and because indirectly they are honoring the English ruler, and never a word is breathed about those things everyone knows and no one speaks of: his illicit marriage and self-imposed exile. The French may know how to live, but in politics these English are genuine connoisseurs of freedom!

"Do you realize, you Frenchmen who have made a mountain out of those few beggars you strung up in May, that England is about to lose her Colonies? Colonies with a capital C, overseas settlements, subjects who are also equals, towns named for our kings, Georgetown, Williamsburg, Charlestown? We have it coming to us; we are reaping what we have sown: revolt. We had no right to tax them without their consent. One principle is sacred to the English; Charles I ignored it and lost his throne as well as his head: no taxation without

*Being fairly shrewd, he had managed, in advance of those disasters, to win several substantial victories over the Prussians, which earned him a promotion to the rank of marshal at the age of forty-two. They called him "the victor of Bergen." He lost favor sooner than his brother for getting involved in intrigues with the Soubise family in the midst of the Seven Years' War.

consent. We've tried to play cat-and-mouse with them for ten years. If they protested too loudly, we pretended to yield, only to grab with one fist what we were holding out with the other. When we abrogated the Townshend Acts, that series of levies which they resisted so violently, why did we have to maintain the tea tax, a quasi-symbolic tax on tea, just to humiliate them? We pressed them to the wall. No longer is it a mercantile dispute between London and the Colonists over the issue of high profits; it is an affair of honor. And don't fool yourselves, gentlemen, the Bostonians are as solid Englishmen as our own Londoners or Bristolians. An Englishman will always fight back when you pin him down. That's what they've just done at Bunker Hill. Did you know that even the farmers are shooting at our troops? They're holding a congress in Philadelphia and have appointed a general to lead them, a proper Virginia gentleman, George Washington, who fought you over there in the service of my grandfather. Now he's out to give us trouble. By 'us' I mean those scoundrels in my brother's government . . . . "

The Duke of Gloucester drones on about people he calls Insurgents, Bostonians, or Colonists, but never Americans. A number of guests find his speech insufferably tedious; in fact his eyes have a strange glint, and his normally ashen cheeks are flushed from the Duc de Broglie's sumptuous wines and delicacies as well as from anger, which is too plainly obsessive to disguise his sympathies for the cause of England's colonial citizens. Freedom is the issue, even if princes are apt to call it pride or honor. One person, whose eyes also sparkle, has grasped its meaning, or rather the word has fired his imagination. In 1828, fifty-three years later, La Fayette trembles with emotion as he recounts the Metz luncheon to Jared Sparks, a biographer of Washington, like St. Paul recalling the journey to Damascus.[9]

It is his own journey to Damascus. This tall, gawky lad who dances badly and married too young, a clown of an army captain, suddenly hears the gospel preached, "that fastening of destiny's wing to our innermost desire." Happy the man who plucks a comet before it passes. Within a few hours La Fayette was turned from boredom and found something to live for. His emergence in history dates from this August 8, 1775.

"Never had such a worthy cause caught men's fancy; it was the final struggle for freedom, and defeat would have left it homeless and without hope."[10] This is his immediate reaction, and he will stand by it always. Does he also resolve to join the "Bostonians" this same night? Probably. In any event, he has made a decision grave enough to inspire the courage to dissimulate it. He asks a few questions respectfully, without excitement or insistence, and disappears in the throng of guests at the end of the meal, no one but himself the wiser that France now possesses one Insurgent.

The days ahead are for gathering information, for reflection. Where is this place called Boston? Who is this Washington? Every scrap of knowledge about

America, from the moment La Fayette emerged as the individual we know, came to him from an English prince.

TOM PAINE

43

AUGUST 1775

The World Is My Country

Another European has just discovered America, this time firsthand. Thomas Paine, an Englishman thirty-eight years old, is ahead of La Fayette and can't contain his amazement. "Today America has emerged from infancy. Its strength and its commerce are rapidly reaching maturity . . . Yesterday's cottages have become villages, and villages, cities . . . Degeneration is a meaningless word here."[1] Ecstatic reaction of a man at the end of his tether, who has fled England in desperation. The New World does not disappoint him: it is *his* new world, something he sorely needed.

Much as he would like to forget his Quaker upbringing, it clings to him like a glove. The long, narrow, furrowed face, the loose-hanging gray hair free of powder and side curls framing a high forehead, that perpetually defensive, almost haunted look—such is the appearance of the "young [*sic*] man of intelligence and merit" whom Franklin encouraged to go to Philadelphia in November 1774 and commended to his son-in-law. "He goes to Pennsylvania with a view of settling there . . . If you can put him in the way of obtaining employment as a clerk, or assistant tutor in a school, or assistant surveyor, you will do well."[2] A nice gesture that cost nothing. A good-will letter in behalf of a man facing middle age in sorry straits, a potential schoolteacher like the many others Franklin had been sending across the Atlantic for years to remake their lives. But on his own arrival in May Franklin was amazed to find that this protégé had done quite well for himself since the previous November. Tom Paine so advised him personally:

"Your countenancing me has obtained for me many friends and much reputation, for which please accept my sincere thanks. I have been applied to by several gentlemen to instruct their sons on very advantageous terms to myself, and a printer and bookseller here, a man of reputation and property, Robert Aitkin, has lately attempted a magazine, but having little or no turn that way himself, he has applied to me for assistance. He had not above six hundred subscribers when I first assisted him. We have now upward of fifteen hundred, and daily increasing."

A short fling at teaching, then, just long enough to get his bearings, followed by the dream of his lifetime: journalism. Six months in Philadelphia have advanced him further than thirty in England. The only drawback is the need to choose sides, to pledge his pen in his new country's struggle against his motherland. The grim situation allows no time to pour out elegies. It's war, Tom Paine! "It grieved me to watch the country bursting into flames almost the very moment I arrived . . . ."[3]

How peaceful the world had been till then. Thetford, his birthplace, tucked among the fields of Norfolk, was a region of salt marshes, of murky skies clouded by the North Sea, of poor soil which the farmers turned into common pasturage. Thetford itself, perpetually serene, had been known as "the holy village" in feudal times because of its many priories. Anglicans took over peacefully from the monks, leaving a Quaker minority, a sect without dogma at that time, without Christology, more or less without ritual, non-conformists of whom Joseph Paine the corset-maker was one. "As my father professed to be a Quaker, I had the good fortune to receive an excellent moral education coupled with a decent amount of practical instruction." A decent level of comfort also, in a solid brick house too close to the pillory and gallows of Cage Lane—the local place of assembly where thieves were hanged and acts of impiety punished—for it not to trouble the mind of a sensitive boy. At the "age of reason," Tom Paine had discovered the truth about priests of the established church: "I was barely seven or eight when I heard a sermon read aloud by one of my relatives, a Church of England fanatic, on a subject known as the Redemption through the death of the son of God. When the sermon ended, I went into the garden and as I walked down the steps (for I recall the spot perfectly), I felt a sense of revulsion at what I had just heard and thought to myself that it made Almighty God into a passionate man who killed his only son because that was his only means of revenge . . . At present I think no differently; what's more, I believe no religious system that in any way offends the mind of a child can be valid."[4] Even the god of Quakers, meek as he was, seemed too rigorous, for in addition to proscribing the taking of a human life there was also a ban on dancing, card games, the theater, cosmetics for women, and non-black clothing for men. "Though I reverence their philanthropy, I cannot help smiling at the conceit, that if the taste of a Quaker had been consulted at the creation, what a silent and drab-coloured creation it would have been! Not a flower would have blossomed its gaieties, nor a bird been permitted to sing."[5] Tom Paine's cheerful temperament rejected whatever was contrary to nature. He threw over the family traces and, after three years of apprenticeship in his father's corset business, felt he had had enough. He longed to travel after discovering a book on the exploration of Virginia in his schoolmaster's house. "On that day the dream of visiting the Atlantic's western shore was born and never left me." At seventeen, he went to sea; at twenty, he came home sheepishly, having tasted the bittersweet lot of a cabin boy aboard clippers and merchant ships. Back to the corset trade, though not in his father's shop; in London this time, where ship sails loom at the foot of every street. On to Dover and Sandwich. Then a stint gauging beer casks in the bars of Grantham, followed by a job in Alford inspecting for contraband. He wanted to be a pirate and ended up a customs agent. Blacklisted, dismissed for unruliness or negligence; tutoring, odd jobs, improptu sermons on all sorts of subjects here and there, in remote hamlets where his audiences listened wide-eyed; married, widowed, unhappily remarried to the daughter of a "grocer-tobacconist" whose shop he took over, making him half "tobacco-grinder" and half customs agent once again, more or less forced to behave himself, ill at ease, not liking the situation one bit. He even took it into his head to organize an informal little neighborhood union of customs inspectors aimed at pressuring Parliament to improve their lot. However, "a rebellion of customs officers, who rarely enjoy popular support, was not viewed as much of a threat by their superiors."[6] At thirty-five, he lost everything: bankrupt, washed out. "To be sold by auction on Thursday the 14th of April [1774], and the following day, all the household furniture, stock in trade, and other effects of Thomas Pain, grocer and tobacconist, near the West Gate, in Lewes: Also a horse tobacco and snuff mill, with all the utensils for cutting and grinding off snuff; and two unopened crates of cream-colored stone ware."[7]

It was election time, the year Wilkes won the London mayoralty and Marat published his *Chains of Slavery.* The brutal mechanization of English labor cast thousands of unskilled workers like Paine into the gutter. On June 4 he left his wife:* "It is nobody's business but my own; I had cause for it, but I will name it to no one."[8] Though he will never speak of it, his *Reflections on Unhappy Marriages,* written in June 1775, says all he has to say: "As extasy [*sic*] abates, coolness succeeds, which often makes way for indifference, and that for neglect. Sure of each other by the nuptial bond, they no longer take any pains to be mutually agreeable. Careless if they displease, and yet angry if reproached; with so little relish for each other's company that anybody else's is more welcome . . . "[9] Besides, she was a strict Calvinist, convinced that most human beings were damned from the start by divine whimsy; he was tolerant, tending toward rationalism and an evolving notion of universal good will. God had punished him with bankruptcy; no woman stays married to a doomed man. At the close of 1774 Tom Paine found himself alone and helpless as a newborn babe.

What then? Franklin, and America.

---

*They had no children.

Was it really paradise? He shouted it from the rooftops, as if to convince himself. In fact he had found his one true happiness: a feeling of usefulness. Though repelled by violence, his heart went out to the American rebels. His youthful spirit revived. But over the years, to meet the blows life had dealt him, he had developed a permanently critical attitude. Amid all the splendors of life in Philadelphia, one aspect of the American scene shocked him deeply. Late on the morning of May 9, 1775, Colonel Washington of Virginia, a hero of the colonial cause, makes a dashing entrance into Philadelphia, handsome, dignified, and sad-eyed in his blue-and-brown uniform studded with brass buttons. They say the Congress will appoint him commander-in-chief of the army. He arrives on horseback, surrounded by liveried servants and a great many oddly dressed Negro slaves.[10] Delegates from Virginia, the cradle of slavery, have a generous proposal to put before the Congress to encourage the raising of an army: Virginia will offer three hundred acres and a slave to anyone who enlists.[11] Tom Paine is stunned by this everyday spectacle of American life; not merely in Washington's train or that of his fellow Virginians, but behind all these fine gentlemen and lovely ladies about to discover the right of self-determination stands an army of slaves: men, women, and children, household objects as common as dogs or parrots. Tom Paine is the kind of man who feels totally committed to aiding the Americans in their struggle and at the same time compelled to castigate them. He fights for them against them. In June 1775, Dr. Rush, one of his first friends in the new land, a liberal opponent of slavery (something of a phenomenon in those times), reads "a short essay with which I was much pleased . . . against the slavery of the Africans in our country, and which I was informed was written by Mr. Paine. This excited my desire to be better acquainted with him. We met soon afterwards in Mr. Aitkin's bookstore, where I did homage to his principles and pen upon the subject of the enslaved Africans. He told me the essay . . . was the first thing he had ever published."[12] This American of four months, a writer with ten pages to his credit, expressed himself like a Philadelphia Rousseau: "We [*sic*] have reduced multitudes to slavery, we have shed innocent blood, and today we are threatened with the same peril . . . How just, how fitting to our crime [*sic*] the punishment that Providence has in store for us!" The article was entitled "Justice and Humanity" and bore this device: "The world is my country; my religion is to do what is right." The absence of any signature left some readers believing that it was the work of Ben Franklin, who had already professed abolitionist views, though far more discreetly. In fact it was Tom Paine's noisy opening bid for admission to the ranks of civilization's great moralists.

August finds him championing the rights of women. America indeed had taken in a Don Quixote:

Affronted in one country by polygamy, which gives them their rivals for inseparable companions; inslaved in another by indissoluble ties, which often join the
gentle to the rude, and sensibility to brutality: Even in countries where they may
be esteemed most happy, constrained in their desires in the disposal of their
goods, robbed of freedom of will by the laws, the slaves of opinion, which rules
them with absolute sway, and construes the slightest appearances into guilt, surrounded on all sides by judges who are at once their tyrants and seducers . . .
who does not feel for the tender sex? Yet such I am sorry to say is the lot of woman
over the whole earth. Man with regard to them, in all climates and in all ages,
has been either an insensible husband or an oppressor . . . When they are not
beloved they are nothing; and when they are they are tormented. They have
almost equal cause to be afraid of indifference and love. Over three quarters of
the globe Nature has placed them between contempt and misery.[13]

Events rush forward. The guns around Boston are never silent. In July 1775,
Massachusetts, soon followed in turn by the other eleven colonies,* establishes
its own government independent of the crown, and the traditional shout "God
save the king!" changes to "God save the people!" Unperturbed, pioneers
continue to thrust westward through the wilderness and claim new territories
"in the name of the great Lord Jehovah." Northern colonists defer to southerners by electing Washington commander-in-chief—of fifteen thousand or
three thousand men, depending on the season, for the American army is still
something of a dream, though a painful one for the British when it consoli-
dates, as at Bunker Hill on June 17, behind fighting militiamen—irregulars
without uniforms or direction, who fire from behind improvised defenses.

No one talks of independence yet, least of all Washington. In Philadelphia, a jumble of conflicting motions and amendments put forth by partisans of rupture or of last-minute negotiations. Not to mention the bitter
struggle emerging between federalists and anti-federalists. Steadfast, strad-
dling the fence, stands Franklin, to whom all turn, who yields to his natural
inclination to conciliate, holding both ends of the chain, paying it out evenly,
wanting so much to continue thus for weeks on end until George III finally
understands . . .

But on August 23, 1775, England's ruler formally declares the colonial
governors "rebels" and forbids "his loyal subjects" to have anything to do
with them. Gloucester was right, two weeks earlier in Metz: his brother
chooses the path of violence. He would crush the insurgents. He decides to
"devastate America." In surprise attacks the English fleet bombards two open
ports, Falmouth in the North and Norfolk in the South.[14] Then Tom Paine,
who had never written a single syllable against the crown, but spoke out, along
with all America, against the excesses of "ministerial troops" in order not to
offend the king, resolves to publish a book, his first, in which he will collect

*Georgia, where Wesleyan influence contributed to making the people obedient and submissive
to the established powers, didn't join them until a little later.

a series of four or five articles he plans to write between September and the following January. No more skirmishes: what we need is a solid offensive. No more appeals to the intelligence of our adversaries: they are too stupid. An appeal to common sense, yes, but our own. Today reason means war. He decides to call the book *Common Sense.*

Meanwhile Franklin the peacemaker takes up his pen and writes to one of the last of his correspondents in London:

> Mr. Strahan,
> You are a member of Parliament and of the majority which has voted to destroy my country. You have begun to burn our cities and slaughter our people. Look at your hands; they are smeared with the blood of your neighbors. You and I have been friends for a long time; you are now my enemy, and I am yours.[15]

GONTAUT-BIRON

44

OCTOBER 1775

A Passion for Racehorses

From all appearances you would think France hopelessly in love with England —if you take infatuation for love, and if two thousand snobs constitute the French nation. At noon on October 6, 1775, Louis-Armand de Gontaut-Biron, the Duc de Lauzun* for these past nine years, stands saucer-eyed at the entrance to the Plaine des Sablons. French society is setting its clocks by English time. Even at Newmarket, in his beloved Britain, Lauzun had never seen such an impressive display of bluebloods assembled for a horserace. It will go down in history, he is convinced, and become something of a tradition, which he and his friends have worked since 1766 to establish and finally succeeded in 1775 after winning the queen's patronage. Enormous crowd. Save for the king, the entire court is there; coaches leave Paris and Versailles starting at eight in the morning. In the center of the field stands a pretty gazebo, like a vine-covered arbor dotted with flowers, from which the queen and her ladies may follow the race without ruining their delicate complexions in the baking sun. Trees are starting to turn in the Bois de Boulogne along the distant flank of this vast

*At the death of his uncle the marshal in 1788, Lauzun inherits the title of Duc de Biron. He is known by that name during the Revolution and will go down in history simply as Biron.

open space between the hamlet of Ternes and Neuilly, where the king used to review his guards once a year. The Plaine des Sablons has just been consecrated as racing's hallowed turf, Anglomania's chosen land. Among the spectators, the anonymous editor of the *Correspondance littéraire* prepares to inform Europe of the accelerating osmosis of two societies, which began when the persecution of French Protestants lessened, to the dismay of British ladies, who no longer can hire all the pert maidservants they want from the influx of banished heretics. "A frightful thing! Religious persecution has ended in France; you can't find decent French help anymore . . . " "Nothing is more amusing than the exchange of odd and absurd little habits that has taken place recently between France and England . . . Today we treasure our English footmen as highly as the English our poor Huguenot girls; we have acquired the same craze for their horses, their punch, and their philosophers as they have for our wines, our liqueurs, and our music-hall artists . . . We have no use for any steel but theirs, they adore our money; we insist on English coaches, gardens, and sword blades; they prize our craftsmen, especially our cabinetmakers and cooks; we send them our fashions and adopt theirs; our philosophers extol republican* government while theirs quietly champion the tenets of monarchy . . . It seems therefore that we have set out to ape each other so completely as to erase all traces of our ancient rivalries. If the cost to each kingdom were but an added tinge of the ridiculous, surely it would be a cheap price to pay for permanent peace."[1]

The race will start at one o'clock and last six minutes, "though the prescribed course was a long one, three times around the field."[2] Everyone has wasted the whole day for those six minutes, and some will end up losing a lot more than their time, for the betting mounts steadily. Rutledge, the English traveler bent on discovering Louis XVI's France, moodily watches "the quadrupedal hero" on which he has just wagered 150 louis (more than $2000 today) to please his friends. "Midway in the last lap our fate was decided: the superannuated Pegasus bearing our fortune, winded and weary, was on his last legs and breath."[3] Goddam! Rutledge is furious. "I've always been warned against such wagers . . . Most of the time one is at the mercy of the rider's venality."[4] Still, he had one chance in four of winning, since only the Comte d'Artois, the Duc de Chartres, the Marquis de Conflans, and Lauzun were competing with their horses and their *jacqys* —or is it *jacqueis* or *jockeis*? No one is quite sure how to spell the word. "We copied them from the English. It is the animal that wins the prize. We oblige the jockey to fast or we give him a purgative the night before the race to make him weigh less. The betting starts and a lot of money gets lost . . . Unfortunately, we are not the only ones to have adopted a ridiculous practice and have also tried to create a dazzling

---

*Meaning a ruling aristocracy tempered by the joint control of Lords and Commons, yet dominated by a few families, including royalty. This use of the word "republican" is said to have drawn a sneer from Marat.

reputation for our jockeys. Now all you hear is talk of the 'Barbary horse' or the *petit duc,* and the horseracing craze has replaced the spirit of chivalry, which is nowhere to be found. We go out to the Plaine des Sablons to watch gaunt, rawboned animals* race each other, rushing by like streaks of lightning, all covered with sweat after ten minutes; and we inject into the discussion arising from these races an air of profundity and significance that is all but ludicrous."[5]

Lauzun is exultant. His entry from Lower Normandy has won the "sweepstakes" under the skillful handling of his little English jockey in the green-and-black-striped cap. "The queen appeared to take a lively interest in this spectacle; she complimented Lauzun warmly and asked to meet the jockey" . . . "She was as lovely as the day itself, which was indeed delightful." She has changed a good deal in the past year and become quite charming. Horace Walpole has this to tell his English friends back home: "One has eyes only for the queen. The Hebes and the Floras, the Helens and the Graces are but common streetwalkers next to her. Standing or seated, she is a very statue of beauty; when she moves, she is grace personified."[6] But today isn't her splendor partly the effect of Lauzun's victory? He is an "old-timer" at twenty-eight; she finds him reassuring and agreeable. Few courtiers can match his easy conversation with women, including this queen, still so unsure of herself, who welcomes the tasteful blend of effrontery and respect in his bold eyes. Maturity is beginning to erase Lauzun's fatuousness; his advancing baldness already reaches from his high, narrow forehead down to a neatly rolled and powdered fringe. Drooping lips accentuate this seasoned roué's listless smile set beneath a large aquiline nose. Behind him stretch endless tales of love and money. His exceptional charm rests on a precocious air of world-weariness that every woman vows to dispel.

Ancient family, its roots steeped in history . . . In 1602 Henri IV had had the duke's great-uncle Louis-Armand beheaded for conspiring with Spain. To relatives who begged him to spare Charles de Gontaut, admiral and marshal of France, duke, peer, and governor of Burgundy, forty years old with thirty-two wounds in the king's service, Henry IV had awarded the customary type of consolation: "Such punishments do not dishonor a family. I am not ashamed to trace back my ancestry to the Armagnacs and the Comte de Saint-Pol, who perished on the scaffold."[7] For six years in turn, Louis XIV had persecuted and imprisoned the first Duc de Lauzun, related by marriage to Louis-Armand, for the unpardonable crime of having been loved by a recalcitrant Orléans cousin, Mlle de Montpensier, known as "La Grande Mademoiselle." The Birons regained their status and wealth during the Regency and under Louis XV by chipping away at salt deposits along the Languedoc coast, a lucrative monopoly obtained through royal favor. Louis-Armand's uncle, the

*This passage is from the pen of Louis-Sébastien Mercier. Whether he pirated it from Rutledge or vice versa is still a matter of debate. Both men were acute observers.

fourth Maréchal de Biron, has just been made chief law-enforcement officer over the Paris populace, which he has held tightly in check since the bread riots.

His nephew is of a different cloth. Lauzun wouldn't hurt a flea, but thinks nothing of losing a fortune in six minutes at the racetrack, or his heart nightly when he courts all those lovable ladies—whom he so truly adores that it takes him exactly a week to recover from each. He is recuperating now on his return from Warsaw in the wake of a passionate tryst with the Princess Czartoryska, "who proved that without being pretty a woman could be charming." Can the child she has just borne be his? The journey that took him across northern Europe and back again the previous winter is no evidence. Two years earlier the English ladies caught his eye. Sixteen-year-old Marianne Harland took over from twenty-year-old Sarah Bunbury "with a dazzling white bosom and the freshness of a rose."[8] Meantime there had been Madame Dillon among ten or twenty others ard, long before, that *ménage à trois*—or was it *à quatre?* Louis-Armand had been snapped up at a tender age by the singular Choiseul-Stainville family. "I was fourteen at the time and a rather attractive boy. Mme la Duchesse de Grammont* took me under her wing with the aim, I believe, of molding a young lover all her own and an unlikely target for gossip."[9] Hence the enmity of Choiseul, who himself, after one of his mistresses died in childbirth, had married her sister. The name of the mistress? What difference does it make? Or maybe it does make a difference, for history ought to be told as it happened. The mistress of this fine gentleman who became the Duc de Choiseul was Antoinette-Eustachie Crozat du Chatel, wife of Charles de Gontaut-Biron. And the child whose arrival took her life is no other than Louis-Armand, the present Duc de Lauzun. At the age of fourteen, then, he lost his virginity to the sister and mistress of his mother's lover, who had married his own aunt.

Confusing? Let's sort out the occupants of those beds. The partners support either the throne or the church. Identification marks: a Stainville, destined to become the famous Choiseul, and a Gontaut-Biron. These two men married a pair of sisters named Du Chatel. Choiseul took up with his sister-in-law behind his wife's back in the midst of an affair with his sister, who was not averse later on to taking up with her nephew through marriage, who may yet have been her blood nephew since there is good reason to believe Lauzun was an illegitimate son of Choiseul. Illuminating, yes?

Beaumarchais currently was working up the themes of his *Marriage of Figaro* and inventing Cherubino. Invention also indicates discovery.

To crown an adolescence that flowered on a dungheap, Lauzun was set

---

*Béatrix de Choiseul-Stainville, sister and mistress of Etienne-François, who later became the Duc de Choiseul. At the age of twenty-nine, she had married a drunken degenerate, Antoine-Antonin de Grammont, in an attempt to cover up her poorly disguised incest. She did her best, but in vain, to unseat Madame de Pompadour from Louis XV's affections.

upon one night by three armed men just outside the palace of the dukes of Bourbon. He was lucky to escape with his life and thought he knew who had instigated the assault: "M. de Choiseul concealed his rage [against me], but the effects of it were dreadful." Then follows an account of the attack. "The next morning I went and told my story to M. de Sartines, who was then lieutenant general of police. He said they were probably drunkards and advised me not to mention the incident . . . " Lauzun blames Choiseul for trying to kill him not out of jealousy over Béatrix but over another sister-in-law, the Comtesse de Stainville, with whom Lauzun was carrying on an affair in proper Cherubinesque fashion, much to the annoyance of his rival Choiseul. "So many obstacles, so many perils unnerved Madame de Stainville. We began seeing each other less frequently. Her attraction to me lessened, and in a few months I was nothing more than a friend . . . The king made me a duke in the meantime, and in order not to take the name of either my father or my uncles, I became the Duc de Lauzun." [10]

By 1775 this is ancient history. Choiseul is in exile. Lauzun has wooed so many other women since La Grammont and La Stainville that the whole episode seems lost in the soft autumn mists of Les Sablons, out of which emerges his newest radiant idol and potential thousand-and-first conquest: Marie Antoinette. One small problem: he is practically bankrupt, despite vast landholdings and a fistful of shares in the East India Company. Since the age of fifteen he has been spending an average of a million livres* annually, and his chief steward laments the horde of creditors. [11] Well, that's the steward's worry; he's being paid for the job. No Gontaut-Biron ever racked his brains over money problems. An insouciant but unhappy childhood much like Talleyrand's shaped his philosophy: "I was like all children of my age and background: the prettiest clothes when I went out; naked and famished at home. At twelve, I was entered in the royal guards regiment, a commission which the king declared subject to reversion, and I knew then that I was destined for a great fortune and the highest offices in the land without needing to be a loyal subject." [12] Temporarily, to economize for a few months each year, he puts up with the boredom of Mouzon in the Ardennes, the same type of boredom that La Fayette endured at Metz, drilling three thousand blue-clad recruits to march back and forth between the Meuse and the Sarre—Germans exclusively: fusiliers, grenadiers, dragoons, and hussars of the Royal Legion, in which he had just bought himself a colonelcy from the Comte de Coigny for a trifling 150,000 livres.** Evidently one needed vast resources even to

---

*In 1774 he spent 1,187,576 livres and 47 sols (about five million current francs). Half a box at the Théâtre des Italiens cost him 1500; a box at the Comédie Française, 1500; half a box at the Opera, 1337 livres and 10 sols. He spent a kingly 74,000 livres of *rentes* and pensions annually.
**On March 16, 1774. It was a veritable "foreign legion" like the one established in 1743 by the Maréchal de Saxe.

contemplate saving money in this fashion! At Mouzon he plays at war for lack of the real thing and learns his ancestral trade, but only here at Les Sablons, or on the gleaming parquet floors of Versailles, does life truly unfold. With her customary imprudence, the queen has just taken his arm despite the fact that he has had the gall to appear before her in boots and *chenille,* the braided vest worn by men in the privacy of their chamber before making their toilet. When will she learn to mask her enthusiasms? Will the gossips report a new favorite? For the past two months she has had eyes only for Besenval, who now casts reproachful glances at her; an old-timer of fifty-four, this lieutenant colonel in the Swiss Guards, Swiss by birth. "He possessed the artfulness so common to his countrymen, who, behind a stony, lumpish exterior, usually turn out to be far shrewder than the French."[13] A handsome, white-haired man, dignified but cynical, with an endless store of spiteful tales that feed Marie Antoinette's penchant for mockery. All of a sudden Besenval's credit is plummeting and Lauzun's soaring since the latter's racing triumph an hour earlier. Much gossip about this among the boisterous group of young courtiers who have enjoyed the queen's presence, though not her confidence, since the coronation: Ségur, Coigny, Vaudreuil, Guines, and that mincing little gigolo Montfalcon, who has just landed a wife twice his age, a widow with an income of forty thousand, and thereby acquired the title of Comte d'Adhémar.[14]

In fact Lauzun is also married, to a shy, skinny, awkward* miss named Boufflers, a respectable nine-year union of nobility and wealth. "My father prided himself on finding me a woman who neither cared for nor suited me."[15] Where is she? People tend to forget about her, he first of all. Probably in one of their châteaux, or at Chanteloup with the Choiseuls. She has never bothered him and never will.**

Besenval takes heart after hearing Lauzun's remarks to the queen, while the rustic cluster of conceited men and ladies trample the yellowed grass as they head for their carriages. Louis-Armand won't last too long; his manner is a bit too arrogant. He talks of Poland, of Russia, of England, and sounds altogether like Vergennes. Eternal ambition of the Birons, who lose their heads in the rush to display their valor. Lauzun won't last six months if, instead of scandalmongering, he insists on trying to interest Marie Antoinette in an alliance with Russia or, worse still, with England, his obsession, his great design—indeed, he talks of it too readily and rationally, like a would-be ambassador or minister. Besenval relies on his natural allies to protect his standing with the queen: the two or three dolls whose "angelic faces" (that is, totally vapid, sexless faces) contrast sharply with the overprominent Hapsburg features of Marie Antoinette, whose beauty derives from her figure and bearing. Twittering as they twirl their parasols, the Lamballe, Polignac, and

---

*Rousseau thought she had "a virginal face and sweetness . . . The feelings she imparts are utterly tender and chaste" (*Confessions,* Part II, Book X).
**The guillotine will claim her on June 24, 1794.

Guéménée ladies decide who shall mingle with the queen, and they look on dispassionately now, as they did when watching the race, with the serene confidence of insiders. Indeed, the transition at Versailles is proceeding smoothly all along the line, from jockeys to court beauties. "The ladies attend the races and show not the slightest compassion for these adolescents with shorn hair made winded or asthmatic* to win a race for a duke, who accepts his prize in bed. When the ladies have seen a race in the morning . . . they gush with emotion. They spend all their time fixing their hair. They wear *altars to friendship,* they recite *odes to friendship.* The portrait of their *charming lady friend* is carried about in a locket; they rhapsodize over the delights of friendship. This display of *mawkish sentimentality* comes into being along with the jockeys."[16]

Lauzun is apt to be disqualified and lose the race on account of his best quality: a belated interest in serious matters which tends to dominate his exchanges with the queen. She does not care to be courted with talk of Europe's balance of power—and is too alert not to anticipate it.

But today the handsome duke happens to please her; she has nothing to lose, the game has just begun. Marie Antoinette and her court return gaily to Versailles, having admired the cascade of "puce-colored" satin revealed by the shapely leg of the season's most talked-about actress, Mlle Dervieux, as she curtsied to the queen. Ladies start to wear the same purplish-brown tinted with tones of "flea's belly, flea's back, flea's thigh, young flea, and old flea."[17]

The year 1776 promises to be the "puce-colored year."

ILLUSTRATION
FROM LE PAYSAN PERVERTI

45

NOVEMBER 1775

Where Next Will Genius Nest?

On All Saints' Day, 1775, the first edition of *Le Paysan perverti* comes off the presses of Quillau, a bookseller in whose printing house the author has type-set and run off three thousand copies. They will go on sale in ten Paris bookshops.** Full title: *Le Paysan perverti, ou les Dangers de la ville, histoire récente mise au jour d'après les véritables lettres des personnages* [The Perverted Peasant, Or the Perils of City Life, a Recent Tale Brought to Light from Authentic Letters

---

*From sudden gains or losses of weight.

**Le Jay, Merigot, Duchesne, Dorez, Valade, Esprit, Humblot, Durand, De Hansy, and Quillau.

Exchanged Among the Characters]; by N. E. Rétif de La Bretone [*sic*], eight parts in four volumes in 12mo. One thousand sixty pages in all.[1] The public will buy out the edition in a month at six or seven francs a copy.* The author is stunned. "In the third week of sale, around the 25th of November, I met Le Jay in the Rue de la Vieille-Bûcherie. 'I think your *Peasant* is catching on; it's moving fast,' he told me. My normal response ought to have been joy, but fear gripped my heart instead, and I was distressed to emerge from my anonymity."[2]

Typical reaction. The prospect of joy, not to mention pleasure, sends Edme-Nicolas Restif de La Bretonne** into a fit of panic. Like an emotional cripple on whom happiness acts as an irritant, he has little use for pleasure. But the bookdealer, being a less complicated soul, is gleeful and not the least ashamed to have a "best-seller" on his hands. Moving at the rate of a thousand copies a week in the capital alone! The event has excited Parisian literary circles almost as much as the spring première of *The Barber of Seville.* Restif had already published fourteen books, all practically unnoticed, including *Le Pied de Fanchette* and *Le Pornographe,* attracting little more than the scornful comments of a few critics. A laboring man, a former peasant who has the gall to turn out books and even to philosophize! No wonder his work was so tasteless and rambling. No one read him.

Now all of a sudden this fictional autobiography, half imagined, half lived, of a workingman becomes the topic of the day. The *Correspondance littéraire* gives it as much coverage as the great horserace at Les Sablons the previous month: "To convey the sensation caused by *Le Paysan perverti,* suffice it to say that several persons have ascribed the work to M. Diderot and the majority to M. de Beaumarchais . . . Admittedly, even after learning that it is by the chief compositor of one of our leading publishers, the same M. de La Bretonne who gave us *Le Pornographe, Le Mimographe,* etc., it is impossible not to suspect M. de Beaumarchais† of having lent his pen and talent on nearly every page to the said compositor . . . It is a highly original work. Full of unlikely incidents . . . frequently indecent, the book provides a glimpse of the tawdriest, most loathsome scenes of life"—all this because Restif describes peasants making love at harvest time in the fields of Burgundy—"yet it grips and compels us . . . We find it absorbing. Much as we may find fault occasionally with the tone, we cannot put it down and feel bound to finish it."[4]

On the other hand, Julie de Lespinasse raves about the book. This triggers another passionate outburst to her lover Guibert, who will have to

---

*Today about thirty-five francs [nearly seven dollars]. Restif will make only one or two francs per copy, even less, depending on the seller.

**He misspelled his own name on the book's frontispiece, for which he later took the blame: "We spell our name either Restif, Rectif, or Rétif. Still, I prefer the first on account of its derivation."[5]

†Groundless suspicion. Beaumarchais, who later becomes slightly acquainted with Restif, had nothing whatever to do with the book.

weather her hysterical fits through the winter; but her days are numbered—
only to books and affection does she now respond. "Midnight. I've just
finished volume one of the *Paysan perverti.* Didn't the final page delight you?
Didn't you feel the urge to tell me about it, to read it to me? Soul of ice! It's
sheer bliss, divine words! And to think we spent last evening together; the
book was there, you had read it and never told me so. My friend, a tiny corner
of your soul could be compared to a large part of your conduct in a manner
that would not please you. Indeed there is a trace of Edmond in you; the
resemblance is not so much in your face as in your profile . . ."[5] Many a lover
will never forgive Restif for providing his mistress with the comparison to
Edmond.

    Edmond is the pure-hearted peasant, born and bred in the rugged Morvan
region, wherein—God forbid!—one must not confuse the fresh air of Nitry
with the unhealthy climate three leagues away in Sacy.* The Restif family
moved from Nitry to Sacy, where Edme-Nicolas was born and where he tilled
the stubborn soil and herded animals for La Bretonne farm. The bad air
made Sacy's men rude and nasty and the women far more shrewish than in
Nitry . . . In any event, for all its harshness, Morvan became paradise lost to
Edme-Nicolas, who is Edmond in the story, his double, his projection, as much
a victim of his emotions and senses as of his desperate search for work (in the
book he is a painter, but the image of a typesetter driven from one printing
house to the next is clearly suggested), which finally drags him into the slums
of Paris from the dance halls of Auxerre. "His throat burning from strong
liquor, and bleary-eyed from insomnia," he came "to drink iniquity like water" in "the flood of filth" to which he is exposed by his evil spirit, Gaudet
d'Arras, an unfrocked friar and master of every vice. Edmond struggles and
slowly succumbs; in Paris he searches for another image of lost innocence, his
sister Ursula, who had been seduced and carried off by a marquis. He finds
her, to his grief, hopelessly corrupted by libertines; Ursula has taken Gaudet
as a lover, and he urges her to seduce her own brother. It would suffice for
"a breast to pop out of its bodice" at the right moment—which comes to pass
and is triumphantly announced by the guilty girl in letter No. 253. Edmond
has been perverted to the point of incest. Yet when he returns to die at the
edge of his village, too ashamed to set foot there, an escaped convict with only
one arm and nearly blind, he finds divine inspiration in the sweet voice of
Fanchon Berthier, a childhood sweetheart and his Samaritan for the day:
" 'Edmond, would you happen to have some water? I'm dying of
thirst . . .' 'Yes, Fanchon, it's here under the nut trees . . . ' I went without
it for her sake, for I too was thirsty, and held the barrel while she drank."[6]

    "Restif de La Bretonne is a people's writer."[7] The first communist novel-
ist of record makes his appearance in November 1775, between the Rue
Saint-Jacques and the cloister of Saint-Séverin, in this book which female

*About twenty-eight kilometers from Auxerre, twelve from Tonnerre, and sixteen from Vézelay.

enthusiasts of pastoral revels claw one another to obtain. Ultimately, when eyes have dried, the *Paysan perverti* advances a code of life in a "communal town" where farmers, by banding together, could protect themselves from the immoral pressures of urban society "and from poverty, which is all too common in the country."* Land, tools, and livestock would belong to the community. "Each person owns only his household furnishings, his linen and clothing."[8] But few readers take note of this; the majority are content to follow the adventures of Edmond, "that young man who is almost always guilty despite unflagging virtue,"[9] in whose sentimental meandering Julie de Lespinasse finds "the residue of passion and warmth that animated Saint-Preux and Julie."** The *Correspondance littéraire* reports with mounting bewilderment "the prodigious success of the *Paysan perverti* among the widest audiences, even women," and admits "that not for some time have we read a French literary work of greater perspicuity, originality, and genius. Where next will genius nest?"[10]

This one nests in a lusty but unwieldy frame "with a chest as hairy as a bear's," temporarily perched on the fifth floor of what used to be the Presles high school, now fallen into decay, where Rapenot the bookseller, one of its "concessionaires," lodges Restif in a garret furnished with a bed and three wobbly chairs, high up under the roof, "as near the angels as possible."[11] This is printers' and booksellers' row on the Left Bank, where he is close to his job and, according to Marc Chadourne, "thirty sous carry him through the week, three to launder a shirt, one for a collar, twelve for an occasional theater seat, and the balance for a bottle of wine on Sundays. Two half-sous' worth of pancakes on the Pont-Neuf and a gulp of water from the Trahoir fountain answer his daily needs."[12] But sometimes this wretched frame shakes all over. Restif de La Bretonne is forty, and looks fifty. Robust as he is, poverty and disease have taken their toll: he has stomach ulcers brought on by anxiety; a touch of epilepsy or some other nervous disorder; blood poisoning caused by a dozen cases of clap contracted from a string of streetwalkers. Above all, he suffers from the daily despair of a married man chained like a galley slave to his mate, Agnès Lebègue. Months in advance he begins making preparations to escape this woman, who is still young, excessively neat and proper, rather prim, and forever scolding him for his untidy appearance in contrast to her undeviating stocking seams, her impeccably groomed hair, her white hands, and a flood of rebukes that streams from her pouting lips. She never misses a thing, whether at La Bretonne farm, where she complains about him to his brothers and sisters, or in shrewdly planning her extramarital adventures with

*The word "communism" does not appear in the *Paysan perverti*; twenty years later, however, it will occur frequently in the last volume of *Monsieur Nicolas,* in which Restif attempts to sum up his life and philosophy.
**In *La Nouvelle Héloïse.*

shopkeepers, writers, and members of the gentry. Clever woman, that Agnès. She always manages to lay hands on the pitifully scant royalties occasionally paid to her author husband. She is an expert at coaxing what she wants from him through her daughters, eleven-year-old Agnès, whom he adores, and Marion, seven, whom he knows he did not father. He has packed the three of them into one room on the second floor to ensure the peace and privacy of his garret. His wife looks after him during severe illnesses, as she had three years earlier when he developed gangrene, erysipelas, and serious skin eruptions compounded by "painful inflammation of the mucous membranes," which Agnès cured by abusing him so mercilessly that "his anger cut the pain."[13] That was when the idea of writing the *Paysan perverti* first came to him, as he lay in bed for three weeks devouring English novels like *Pamela* and *Clarissa* which then were flooding the boudoirs. Through them he saw the tale of his own life unfolding and vowed to tell it if he recovered. He did, kept his word, and managed to sandwich in one of the spiciest episodes of his life: a whirlwind affair with Louise and Thérèse, two attractive lesbians on the Rue Bourbon-des-Petits-Carreaux. Thérèse was attracted to him, but he slept with Louise. "My whole soul passed into that delightful body." He loved her passionately enough to break off the relationship forever. "That was the only time in my life when I behaved so virtuously . . . ." "Until 1776 no woman caught my eye."[14]

He went back home for a while to the farm at La Bretonne, where, on his parents' death, he had inherited a dovecote set into the ancient, austere buildings between thick and silent walls. But the rural setting stifled him; he hurried away and would write about it later: his beloved valley of Bout-parc; the roof tiles "tinted with shades of Beaune wine"; and his sole idyllic love, Jeannette Rousseau, whose white, fleeting profile glimpsed at mass in Courgis he had once hungrily devoured. All those memories were painful.

In his forties, then, M. Nicolas reaches a somewhat shaky, uncertain peace with the inner turmoil that drives him back and forth from Burgundy to Paris and turns his emotional life into a constant tug-of-war between the father image and the whore's, between his yearning to see the sun rise over the pastures of Nitry and a compulsion to stand for hours at night in the gutters of the Rue Saint-Jacques peeping up at half-shut windows, listening for the laughter and plaintive sighs which he feels are now denied him. One steadying influence, one pleasant scene: Quillau's printing house, where he regains self-confidence amid the smell of ink and moist paper, standing in front of the large cases that slope like school desks, where he meticulously picks out letter after letter and fits into the composing stick the elegant, unrivaled type of his century. He has lived and breathed the printer's trade ever since he began sweeping out and emptying water buckets for Maître Fournier in Auxerre. His only friends now are the planer he uses to even the type before securing it in the case, the gimlet, the gripper, the shooting stick, the burr—all tools that enable him truly to say he is *making* a book, his own or someone else's, just as the next-door cabinetmaker produces a table or the watchmaker a timepiece. An assemblage of wood, lead, iron, and paper forged in the creaking press, which he likens to the groaning of ideas a-borning. When Restif completes a composing frame, packs it with wool batting, tightens the band around its circumference, and secures it under the press, he could pass for a baker at his oven.

That was how he worked *Le Paysan perverti* out of his system: it became the loaf that contained every serious idea in his head. But even this isn't satisfying, and the simmering persists under the bald crown of this little man (five feet one inch) "whose posture is so awkward and contracted that he looks hunchbacked, stout yet skinny, with a clumsy walk, alert eyes under bushy brows that make him look grim, a long face with a slightly hooked nose, a thick graying beard, in short, a man whose sole attraction is a pair of ruby lips,"[15] of which he has been vain ever since he was taught to use them before the age of twelve by a young girl cowherd on his parents' farm.

So the *Peasant* is causing a stir? And he is becoming quite a celebrity? This spurs him to launch a fleet of tracts on social reform. The world as it is doesn't suit him. It has made him suffer too much and and ought to be changed. If people will just listen to him, he, Edme-Nicolas Restif, will tell them what to do about everything. *Le Pornographe* advocated laws to regulate prostitution; *Le Mimographe* set out to reform the national theater; next we have *L'Ecole des pères ou le Nouvel Emile, L'Educographe, Les Gynographes, Le Glossographe, L'Andrographe, Le Thesmographe** . . .

**Les Gynographes,* "or ideas of two respectable women on a proposed measure affecting all of Europe to put women in their place and ensure the contentment of both sexes"; *Le Glossographe:* a plan to make spelling conform to sound; *L'Andrographe,* "or ideas of an honest man on a proposed measure submitted to all nations of Europe to amend morality for the benefit of mankind"; *Le Thesmographe* appears later, in 1789, and urges the Estates General to pursue mass legal reforms.

46

NOVEMBER 1775

Clinging to C(h)aron's Ferry

In London on November 4, 1775, history's strangest "transaction" (its precise title) is signed in duplicate, "without seal or witness," between "Pierre-Auguste [*sic*] Caron de Beaumarchais and Charles-Geneviève-Louise-Auguste-Andrée-Timothée d'Eon de Beaumont." In it the former is identified as "acting on special orders from the king issued at Versailles on August 25, 1775"; the latter (pardon—it should be ladies first) is described as "an adult female formerly known as the Chevalier d'Eon, equerry, captain of dragoons . . . (former) French minister plenipotentiary to Great Britain," etc.

It is an agreement between an official representative of the crown and one of its secret agents, who is committed thereby to change clothes and call himself a woman. The chevalier changes sex.[1] One might take this for the epilogue to a lengthy tale of bribery, deceit, blackmail, slander, and violence that has gone on for over ten years, "the D'Eon affair," but it is only one of the closing chapters. Confronting each other are two mythomaniacs of continental dimension. Who is tricking whom? Or have they both conspired to dupe their contemporaries and posterity?

The contract, fifteen pages dotted with marginal initials like notarial seals wherever a word has been deleted, seems to leave nothing to chance. Actually, it could pass for a dialogue or set debate. "I, Caron de Beaumarchais" commences the opening section, demanding "in the name of the king" the return of "all public and private documents dealing with various political negotiations which the Chevalier d'Eon has been handling in England," specifying the method of return, ordering D'Eon to desist from "any further attacks" on the memory of the Comte de Guerchy, former French ambassador to London. This brings him to Article IV, the crux, wherein "it is demanded absolutely that the ghost of the Chevalier d'Eon shall vanish completely and a clear, precise, and unequivocal public announcement of his true sex be made . . . together with his resumption of feminine dress to fix his image once and for all in the public eye." In return, His Majesty agrees to pay him an annual income for life of twelve thousand twenty-sous francs* and promises "larger sums" (unspecified, therefore open to violent debate later on) to "settle his debts in England."

In the second part of the document, "I, Charles-Geneviève" has his say and submits "to all conditions herein above named . . . solely to prove my respect for and obedience to His Majesty, although . . . "

Although: D'Eon's long list of reservations suggests that he is harassed and under pressure to yield, but still proud, still his own master. He asks to be allowed to dress like a man on certain occasions, to receive written citations of his outstanding military and diplomatic service to Louis XV, to wear his Cross of St. Louis** "on whatever clothes I put on," and finally to be paid an additional sum "to buy my feminine wardrobe since this unanticipated, extraordinary, and mandatory expense is due not to my own acts but to my submission."

It sounds like a coded message from a hostage writing at gunpoint. The Chevalier d'Eon had gone to Jesuit schools in his youth and knew the value of mental discipline.

Final section: Beaumarchais bares his claws and pounces. Three pages of hemming and hawing about the Cross of St. Louis, an item of considerable significance instead of a mere trifle: earned under fire by a captain of dragoons, it would make a travesty of the gown on "the Lady Knight d'Eon" and affirm his manhood. Good king, "I take it upon myself therefore" (after much beating about the bush) "to let the lady C.G.L.A.A.T. d'Eon de Beaumont keep the Cross of St. Louis and wear it with female dress, though His Majesty is not bound by this decision and may disapprove of my conduct" . . . "As to the request . . . for money for her wardrobe . . . I am allotting her the sum of two thousand écus† provided she brings none of her arms or male attire from London so that the temptation to revert to them may not be aggravated by their presence, and am allowing her to keep a single regimental uniform, including helmet, saber, pistols, musket, and bayonet, as souvenirs of the past, just as one preserves the treasured effects of a dear departed soul."

After suffering so cruelly at the hands of powerful aristocrats, how can Beaumarchais in turn mete out such cruelty to a woman? Is he taken in? The savagery of their negotiations runs through every line of the contract. Yet this is the time when it is seriously rumored at court that Beaumarchais is going to marry "La Chevalière d'Eon." He even writes the following to Vergennes:

---

*A sizable amount, nearly 5000 francs [$1000] a month. D'Eon had been receiving this sum since 1766 but in the form of a yearly pension subject to arbitrary reduction or cancellation. The contract now guarantees him the irrevocable right to this tidy little fortune.

**The Order of St. Louis, founded by Louis XIV in 1693, was the only royal decoration given for real military achievements and valor. The Cross of St. Louis therefore was the nearest thing to the modern French military cross or medal of honor. It was never debased—neither was it awarded to commoners.

†About 30,000 francs [$6000].

"Everyone tells me that this madwoman is mad about me. She feels I have slighted her, and women never forgive such an offense. I certainly do not slight her; but who the devil would have guessed that to serve the king in this affair I would have to play gallant knight to a captain of dragoons? The situation strikes me as so ludicrous that I can barely keep a straight face."[2]

And what a dragon the "lady" is, "with a ruddy-black [*sic*] complexion in which heavy, dark brows shade a pair of glowing eyes"[3]! Britons, who peer at D'Eon with indecent curiosity and lay odds on his true sex, think he looks "even more manly since becoming a woman. In fact, one cannot attribute femininity to an individual who shaves and has a beard, who boasts herculean muscles, who leaps into carriages and descends from them without a footman, who dashes up steps four at a time, and who, to get closer to the fireplace, advances his chair with one hand thrust between his legs . . . "* He is flat-chested; the only indication of his female sex is a falsetto voice ill suited to the foul language it utters: he curses, calls a spade a spade, smokes a pipe, drinks from the bottle, and goes out of his way to pick a fight with either sword or cudgel. When Beaumarchais informed him of the royal decree commanding D'Eon to dress as a woman, the chevalier began to swear "like a German trooper."

Another ambiguity: women don't interest him. Neither do men, for that matter. They say he has never had a love affair with either sex. The Marquis de L'Hôpital, his first "patron" at the French embassy in Russia twenty years earlier, never failed to remind his "fair damsel de Beaumont" or his "dear little D'Eon" of the one oddity about himself: "Your head and arm are solid. Only one thing bothers me: your *terza gamba*!"[4] One of many popular ditties of 1775 inspired by him takes up this theme:

Très brave capitaine,	[O brave captain
Pour un oui, pour un non,	For a yea or a nay
Chacun sait qu'il dégaine . . .	He will gladly disrobe . . .
Quel malheur s'il est fille!	What a disaster if he's a girl!
Que ne serait-il pas,	Just think what he'd be
S'il avait la béquille	If he had the crutch
Du père Barnabas?	Of old man Barnaby.
. . . Qu'il soit fille ou garçon,	Whether he's a girl or boy,
C'est un grand personnage	He's an important person
Dont on verra le nom	Whose name will be handed down
Se citer d'âge en âge.	From generation to generation
Mais pourtant, s'il est fille,	But if he's a girl,
Qui de nous osera	Which of us will dare

---

*This description appears two years later in a "confidential" gazette called *L'Espion anglais* [The English Spy] when D'Eon begins implementing the contract by wearing skirts. In 1775 no one in England has yet seen him in female dress.

| Lui prêter la béquille | To lend him the crutch |
| Du père Barnabas?[5] | Of old man Barnaby?] |

In any event, D'Eon enters into the spirit of this new game, or at least partly so. He dresses as a man while awaiting his "maiden's trousseau" and also the settlement of his debts, but he pads about like a doddering bachelor, or spinster, in his library containing some eight thousand books and two hundred manuscripts at 38 Brewer Street, Golden Square. He dashes off pages at a frenetic pace "on all kinds of subjects . . . He works fifteen hours a day and receives no visitors during the week. Only on Sunday does he see any-one."[6] No longer does he stroll down to Lloyd's coffee house near the stock exchange and thrash whoever wages a farthing on his sex with a cane "previ-ously insured under that very roof for two thousand pounds sterling."[7]

He surrenders. He can't go on. He has trapped himself in lies, blusters, confusion, and slander ever since the Comte de Guerchy's arrival in London in 1763, when astonished Englishmen watched two French ambassadors, the acting one, D'Eon, and the titular, Guerchy, fly at each other's throats in pamphlets and in lawsuits over apothecary bills, a financial dispute that turned violent when Guerchy tried to have D'Eon poisoned with opium, according to the London Grand Jury's indictment of March 1, 1765.[8] Guerchy, as it turned out, was the one to die—of rage, soon after his inevitable return to France. But D'Eon found himself in an untenable position, "in limbo," out-wardly snubbed by his country but secretly retained to bribe British officials for the King of France* and denied regular payments of his pension, expert blackmailer whom they in turn blackmailed, planting themselves with drawn swords over the floorboards in his flat where secret papers lay concealed, including plans for a French invasion of England which Louis XV could never decide whether to buy at an outrageous price or to capture by force. "You know that D'Eon is a lunatic and may be dangerous . . . I loathe and detest lunatics" was all the king could murmur when Broglie asked for his or-ders.[10] They tried to wear him down and starve him out, so he took his grievances to the gazettes. Never was a secret agent so public.

Prior to 1770 it had been a man's quarrel. No one questioned his sex until the day a Russian princess visited London and disclosed that she had met the famous D'Eon in skirts during his first secret mission at the court of Empress Elizabeth.** Rumors about his doubtful classification spread from London to Paris and became a public joke. D'Eon, angry and embarrassed at first, gradu-ally came to accept this unaccustomed notoriety—to the point where he could

---

*Undated letter (1773) from D'Eon to the Comte de Broglie: "Would you like to see a revolt when Parliament reconvenes after the coming elections? We'll need so much for Wilkes, so much for the others. Wilkes costs a lot to keep, but the English have Paoli the Corsican, whom they have taken up and are supporting with us in mind. Let's match bomb for bomb."[9]

**Actually his penchant for disguises and his youthful appearance were being exploited to send him on spying assignments dressed as a girl.

not bear the idea of sinking back into his former obscurity. Two years passed, then three, during which he found out that that deficient *terza gamba* of his, which had always been a source of humiliation, could in fact raise him to extraordinary celebrity. The silent anguish of self-doubt turned to self-assertion. As a man, people made fun of him; as a woman, he was the object of unqualified admiration.

In May 1772 he "confessed" privately to Drouet, a secretary to the Comte de Broglie, "that the suspicions raised as to his sex were well grounded."[11] By the same token he could hope to avert the harassment, or even murder, in store for him at the hands of the Guerchy family, among the most prominent in France, if he returned home. You don't draw swords against a woman, not publicly anyway. He longed to be back in Tonnerre, to revive "his vines devastated by ten years of absence," to quit the "land of Milord Sterling and Milady Guinea," where his debts were skyrocketing. Initial discouragement when Louis XV would not go along. The king's death kindles new hope: in utter amazement Louis XVI and Vergennes explored the labyrinths of "the King's Secret" and discovered that Louis XV's reign had been an interminable game of hide-and-seek involving the monarch, his ministers and ambassadors. Louis XVI responded sensibly: "These clandestine relations serve no purpose and might even jeopardize my administration. Undoubtedly it hampers the minister of foreign affairs not to know what is going on, and is potential for chicanery if he does."[12] In other words, they meant to close down the secret service and pay off its agents—through a fresh batch of agents. And everyone agreed that D'Eon , whether man or woman, would cost too much to salvage.

Still, to muzzle D'Eon, Beaumarchais had contacted him in April 1774 through Morande when he was first sent to London. "I gather there is still a man in Paris," D'Eon had observed to Morande, referring to Beaumarchais's pamphlets. He intended it as a compliment. A year went by. Having survived his Viennese adventure and become famous for the *Barber,* Beaumarchais was back in London in May 1775, fully at home as a professional spy. There were still a great many scents to pick up in the "nest of Frenchmen"—as well as those being carried over by the tempest gathering across the Atlantic. D'Eon, thoroughly winded by now, was in no mood to run: "We met, impelled no doubt by the natural curiosity of rare animals to examine each other." Not long afterward Charles-Geneviève admits his true feelings: "Like a castaway whom the late king and his secret minister [the Comte de Broglie] have abandoned, so to speak, to a flood of corruption, I clung momentarily to Caron's ferry, as if to a bar of molten iron. Though I shielded my hands with gantlets, there was no way to avoid burning my fingers."[13]

Fingers that ultimately will pen the Comte de Broglie a letter of unconditional surrender on December 5, 1775, a logical conclusion to the "transaction" of November 4:

"Monsieur le comte, it is time to open your eyes to the facts. You have as captain of dragoons and aide-de-camp in war as in diplomacy just the semblance of a man.* In reality, I am only a woman, and would have functioned as such forever if politics and your enemies had not made me the most wretched of females."[15]

"Caron's ferry" was the boat that brought Beaumarchais from France back to England, where Figaro is now thoroughly at home, one foot in each country, assigned to clean out the royal gutters first with Morande and the self-styled "Angelucci," next with D'Eon. Gudin de La Brennellerie, his raving admirer, accompanies him like a Sganarelle who has taken leave of his critical senses, not to mention his poetic ones: "We set sail from Calais at sunset; calm sea, cloudless sky, not a breeze; the ebb tide drew us along. The spectacle of night was new to me. A few diving birds still frolicked on the water; others hastened to return to shore . . . Silence was all around, but not so deep as in the country; you could hear the waves lapping, the sound of the ship's wash; the prow slicing through the water sent electric sparks flying round the vessel . . . All we needed was music to make the voyage seem like a pleasure cruise."[16] Gudin strolled through England as blissfully as he navigated the Channel: "We visited the famous factories of Birmingham,** coal mines, and other sights; we admired the countryside dotted with livestock, unguarded by herders or dogs as in the Golden Age." He cast an equally serene eye on the scarred legs, "grim reminder of wounds inflicted when a cavalry squadron rode over them," which "the lady knight d'Eon" showed him, confessing tearfully that she was a woman."[17] A fine respondent, Gudin is, for the two sly foxes who, from August to December, negotiate to exchange Louis XV's papers for petticoats on "the lady knight," who go through the motions of trading off compromising letters, hating each other more and more, resolved to cheat each other, D'Eon withholding a number of documents and Beaumarchais keeping part of the payoff from Vergennes.

Distant events already preoccupy Beaumarchais. Compared to America, how important is D'Eon? "No one else may have felt as deeply as I the frustration of seeing everything on a magnified scale when I am the smallest of men." In September, Pierre-Augustin began bombarding Louis XVI with reports on the scene in Boston and Philadelphia as if he were an eyewitness, as if he already knew what was going to happen in the next ten years. "The Americans are determined to suffer whatever they must rather than succumb . . . I tell you, sire, that such a nation must be invincible . . . Realistic Englishmen are

---

*Not true. The report of an autopsy performed on the Chevalier d'Eon in London on May 28, 1810, by the surgeon T. Copeland, and certified by eleven prominent persons, states that he possessed "male reproductive organs perfectly normal in all respects."[14]
**Where children from the age of six worked a twelve-hour day.

convinced therefore that the English colonies are lost to the mother country, and that is my belief also" (as of September 21, 1775). His exaggerated, exgravagant statements are intended to have an impact on the king. The "realistic Englishmen" turn out to be few and far between in London. Yet he goes on preaching for a good cause and for his own interests: "A superior, vigilant man would prove indispensable in London today."[18]

Gudin chimes in like a loyal choirboy, buttonholing Londoners and exhorting: "Give up your colonies and preserve your freedom!"[19]

Is Caron's ferry westward bound?

MANON ROLAND

47

JANUARY 1776

Revolutions of Entire Nations

The first weeks of 1776 are exciting, eventful ones for Marie-Jeanne Phlipon, known as "Manon" to her friends and family.* She is almost twenty-two. Her mother died recently, on June 7; Manon still mourns her. On January 4 she advises Claude Pahin de La Blancherie that her father has forbidden her to see him privately. The next day, January 5, she writes him a repentent, affectionate letter, the kind a dozen other aspirants had hoped vainly to receive: "Surely my heart will never belong to another."[1] On the 10th, from her window, she sees a fire break out in the Palace of Justice in Paris. On the 11th, Jean-Marie Roland calls on her for the first time. She sees him again on the 23rd, with little enthusiasm. On February 19, already beginning to put La Blancherie out of her mind, she is thinking in terms of a romantic friendship with "old" Sainte-Lette.

Let's go back and see what she is up to as the year opens. She, her engraver father, Gratien Phlipon, and a maidservant occupy the apartment over the engraver's studio in one of the exquisite red brick houses built in Louis XIII's day to ornament the Place Dauphine.** But the view from the windows looking down on the Quai des Lunettes ignores that little square tucked in between the shops of goldsmiths and spectacle-makers [*lunetiers*]; it sweeps out over the muddy banks of the Seine and, slightly to the left, domi-

*The future Madame Roland. She was born in Paris on March 17, 1754.
**Now 37 Quai de l'Horloge, in a row of houses, and not No. 41 at the corner of the Pont Neuf, where a historical plaque has been put up.

nating the far side of the river, over the massive façade of the old Louvre palace, abandoned by royalty. By leaning out, she can watch, still farther to the left, the bustling throng on the northern stretch of the Pont Neuf between the downstream tip of the Cité and the Samaritaine, those hydraulic water pumps built in the form of a small Gothic chapel dedicated to the Good Samaritan who provided water from the Seine to the citizens of Paris. Far beyond, a clump that is dark or green, depending on the season: the Chaillot rise, behind which she can see the sunset. To her right, along the quay and very hear her house, rise the stone walls of the Palace of Justice.

She was born and raised here in the Cité, on the Rue de la Lanterne; she grew up and played in the Place Dauphine, chattering away to adoring artisans, who raved about it when she confused soup tureens with chamber pots.[2] She made her first communion in the church of St. Bartholomew,* just before going off, at the age of twelve, to sample the thrills of mystical fervor and exclusive friendships in the convent of the Dames de la Congrégation on the distant Rue Neuve-Saint-Etienne in the Faubourg Saint-Marcel—remote enough to be a foreign country. She returned home at fourteen after a year with the nuns and another year at her grandmother's house in the Ile Notre-Dame (now the Ile Saint-Louis), an unknown world right next door to her own; residents of the two islands had little to do with each other. She was back just in time for her cheerful, wholesome mother to spare her the panic of discovering her womanhood; Manon likes to think of it later as "a fresh, growing rose opening its blossoms in the spring sunshine."[3] But a year later her mother could not spare her a double shock inflicted by one of M. Phlipon's apprentices, who took her aside when they were alone in the shop "to have her measure what nice boys usually don't display to young girls"[4] and, a few days later, seduced her on the workbench. The trauma clung to her—or she to it—and turned her against men, especially young ones, who were beginning to buzz around her like flies. It also marked the onset of rebellion against her father. She was a typical only daughter, doting on her parents and expecting the same treatment from them, but smart enough to realize that, of the pair, her mother adored her more. Gratien Phlipon, a handsome, rather conceited man, resented his wife and took no consolation in his daughter or his work. He had several mistresses and drank. As a result, his business deteriorated. "My father went bankrupt by degrees." His wife suffered in silence; his daughter, upon her mother's death, persists in criticizing him, politely but implacably. Their domestic life is grim: "I never get up at that time of year [winter] until nine o'clock; mornings are given to household matters; in the afternoon I do needlework while daydreaming and inventing whatever suits me: verses, arguments, plans, etc. In the evening I usually read till suppertime, which varies depending on the schedule of the master, who is always out, except for meals, without my having any idea where he is or what he is doing,

*Later destroyed. The Ile-de-la-Cité had seven churches at the time, in addition to Notre Dame.

and all too often leaves me to deal with callers seeking business with him. Normally he comes home at half past nine, sometimes ten or later. Supper is over in a hurry, for if the food is light and you eat quickly without exchanging a word, it isn't likely to be a festive affair. Then, to amuse him, I bring out the cards and we play piquet. All the while I try to shape some kind of conversation; laconic responses promptly interrupt it. I work like a dog for minimal results. I sweat, but in vain. By trying my best, I manage to make the time pass; eleven o'clock comes around: my father falls into bed and I shut the door of my room and write till two or three o'clock."[5]

Her "room," a cubicle converted into a sanctum, is "an alcove to one side of the parlor fireplace that had been set off and pierced with a small window for light . . . There was a bed, so jammed in that I had to climb in at the foot. A chair, a small table, and several shelves: that was my refuge." There wasn't even space for a stove, so her heat comes from a clay pan of charcoal fitted into a wooden footwarmer with slits on top. This is where she writes for hours on end, insensible of the chill, nervous but robust, dressed in a "cambric dressing gown," even in winter.[6] Reflections on her reading, essays on manners or the arts that were extremely serious for one so young (she "would have cut off an arm rather than show them to anyone"), but mostly letters by the carload to her dearest and best friends, her looking-glass, the Canet sisters, Henriette and Sophie, whom she had met in the convent and who, like herself, had returned home—to Amiens, in their case—to await a Prince Charming. For ten years now these letters* have been bringing to Amiens a detailed weekly chronicle of the emergence of this solitary hothouse plant at once wild and cultivated: in her "refuge" Manon Phlipon eagerly devoured the *Lives of the Saints* as well as Plutarch before she was ten; Scarron, Tasso, and Fénelon by the age of fifteen; Locke and Voltaire's *Candide* at sixteen; Buffon at seventeen—followed by Rousseau, who has become her gospel.

Through reading she generated an artificial life for herself filled with the experiences of others and her own inexperience; also a tendency to tiptoe about, a fear of men coupled with a yearning for *the* man. "From fourteen to sixteen, I wanted a refined man; from sixteen to eighteen, a cultivated man, and since eighteen I have wanted a true philosopher. If my demands kept increasing at that rate, by the age of thirty I would doubtless require a humanitarian sage. For all I know, excessive fastidiousness may drive me to outright rejection of the human race."[7] She hasn't reached that point and, as a matter of fact, has been trying hard to convince herself for the past few days that she has found "a true philosopher." Her desperate search for love seems to lead to the doorstep of Pahin de La Blancherie.

Is it for him that she drove her suitors on the Place Dauphine to despair?

---

*At substantial cost to the addressees, who had to pay six sous on receipt of a plain letter (a single folded sheet) and seven sous [about twenty cents] when it came in an envelope. The Canet sisters wrote back just as regularly.

"They came in crowds . . . All the young men in the neighborhood paraded by. My refusals caused, for the most part, no ill feeling, but my father cared only for money." After a jeweler, a goldsmith, a haberdasher, and a clothes merchant were eliminated, Phlipon had the gall to promote a butcher. Another reason to scorn her father. The second wave fared no better than the first, the self-styled "intellectuals": petty nobles, low-ranking army officers, lawyers, and doctors. Slaughter of bashful lovers. More strongly than ever, she began to turn toward the "philosophers"—men older even than her father and, wherever possible, of noble extraction.

La Blancherie was only twenty-one when she met him in 1773 at a concert. To his credit, however, he was far less handsome than Gratien Phlipon. "Short, dark, and rather ugly, in no sense did he stir my fancy, but I liked his way of thinking and could tell that he was much taken with me."[8] Unlike her father, he was articulate; also literate, having just published L'Extrait du journal de mes voyages ou histoire d'un jeune homme pour servir d'école aux pères et mères[9] [Extracts from my travel notes or a young man's story told as a guide to mothers and fathers], a topic of interest to Manon. Also to his credit: Phlipon disapproved of the man because he "had no social standing" and no pecuniary "hopes." From his mother, the widow of a magistrate in Langres, he stood to receive very little when he finished his legal training, unsure of where it would lead him. He had asked for Manon's hand in the autumn of 1773. When Phlipon put him off politely, Manon did not object, having no strong feelings about him one way or the other. Pahin returned to his books at Orléans; from time to time he would turn up on her doorstep, neither pressing his courtship nor renouncing it. Madame Phlipon's death triggered an emotional crisis in her daughter, who found herself utterly alone, disliking her father to the point of hatred, ready to seek any port in a storm. In December, Phlipon had all but shut the door on her suitor, who was beginning to appear too regularly. The stage is set for Manon to fall in love.

To Sophie Canet (the younger sister, Manon's favorite), January 5, 1776: "Sophie, Sophie, my friend! Without you I am lost; I am going through the most dreadful crisis, struggling desperately with myself . . . Another instant, one more minute, and the letter I enclose [to La Blancherie] would have gone off direct to him. I restrain myself only with the greatest effort. I want to fool myself by sending it to you . . . Oh, sentiment acknowledged by nature and reason, why must I conceal you from those who have borne me? How I yearn to open my heart; I think I must for the sake of what I love, and because of bias, convention, my father . . . Oh God, how I suffer! . . . Poor D.L.B.* is desolate, defeated, dying; he can't seem to get better, can't sleep, his strength sapped by anxiety, grief, and compassion. Alas, when he received that command from the stairway, his health was improving, he was cheerful

*Abbreviation for La Blancherie used in all her letters.

and seemed to feel better. I never saw him afterward; he has changed fearfully . . . A single word from me could restore him to life, to health—I know it, I feel it, and why shouldn't I say it? . . . I send you the letter I have written him; I dare not tell you that I desire you to forward it from Amiens in a fresh envelope. Yes, I desire it, I would like it, yet I hesitate to command you . . . Love has conquered me: I can't control myself, but . . . I place in friendship's hands the authority that I no longer can keep. Unseal the letter, read it . . . and decide whether you ought to send it.

"In any event, don't burn a thing. If my letters ever become public, I would not want to conceal the sole monuments of my weakness, of my feelings."[10]

Sophie does what anyone in her place would have done: she forwards the letter to La Blancherie, but its roundabout route from Paris to Amiens and on to Orléans takes time, and by January 11 Manon is still without news: "What are you doing, dear Sophie? Why the silence just when I need friendship's hand? . . . I haven't gone out all week in order to be here to receive your letter. God keep it from arriving in my absence . . ."

Life was not entirely dull for her, because one night the Cité nearly burned down. "I was awakened by the tocsin tolling most ominously from several places. I leap out of bed to the window. I see a terrible glow; I waken the household, I dress, and Papa does the same. The sky seemed on fire above our yard, with sparks falling. My father goes out; it was two in the morning. I settle down by the fireplace with my needlework, expecting him to come back and tell us to leave . . . He returned to say the fire was in the Palace [of Justice], so we were not in danger . . . Help came from all around, but always too late in time of disaster. The fire had made great headway . . . They transferred prisoners who were trying to escape. One entire gallery burned down along with the Cour des Aides, the chancellery, and several record offices." Early in the afternoon of the 11th she writes, "the damage is not diminishing, though it is less conspicuous from the outside; six hundred masons, carpenters, soldiers, firefighters, Capuchins, 'recollects,'* and Jacobins are working everywhere . . . The Sainte Chapelle is threatened, the first president is afraid . . ."

Her letter was interrupted by the arrival from Amiens of a friend of the Canet sisters who was visiting the capital for a few days and had been urged by the sisters to call on this most unusual twenty-two-year-old social philosopher in a white cambric dressing gown. With unaccustomed foresight, Manon notes the date and hour of a meeting to which she devotes little more than a perfunctory comment. Those who believe in precognition will rejoice: "Another more important visit I have had just now (Thursday, January 11,

---

*"Recollects": reformed Franciscans. Jacobins: the name commonly applied in Paris to Dominican preaching friars from the abbey of Saint-Jacques.

1776, at five in the afternoon) is from M. Roland. I was writing to you when
Mignonne* came in to say that someone was asking for me. I went into the
parlor and waited next to my needlework, where your note was handed to me
by the gentleman" with a sharp aquiline nose set in a long, mournful, priestlike
face, a balding forehead, long unpowdered hair, a jaundiced complexion
resulting from liver trouble, but whose smile, though rare, is discerning and,
like her own, eschews the commonplace. Jean-Marie Roland de La Platière,
a factory inspector from Amiens, is forty-two and looks much older. Definitely
a *philosophe*. Manon reads the letter of introduction from Sophie. "Papa came
in at that moment; we were talking of things in general; the conversation
became interesting . . . M. Roland stayed with us for a good hour and a half.
I stuttered a bit, but wasn't too shy; I received him in my ordinary house cap,
with a white camisole under the négligé you liked for summer wear." He isn't
the least put off; fond of women and a confirmed bachelor, he responds at once
to this attractive girl who has no impulse to cover up, being familiar with every
inch of herself in the mirror. Several years after that first encounter, she recalls
that she was "about five feet tall, with well-shaped legs, graceful bearing,
slender hips, a well-developed bust, narrow shoulders, good posture, and a
light, rapid step . . . There was nothing striking about my face except a
marked freshness, a gentle expressiveness: the description of these features
makes one wonder where the beauty lies. None is regular; all are pleasing."
And if having a nose "a bit too broad at the tip" distresses her, she is proud
of her ruddy complexion "often reinforced by sudden exuberant flushes."[11]

As yet no exuberance has been summoned. They barely know each other.
"M. Roland must have inferred that I was delighted by his visit and indeed
he was right, for I liked him; he asked if he could return and I readily
consented; we will see if he does anything about it . . . We argued about the
Abbé Raynal,** Rousseau, Voltaire, foreign travel, Switzerland, government,
etc., but in a friendly fashion, as if sounding each other out." Momentarily at
least, it is enough to make her stop thinking of Pahin de La Blancherie: "Once
I get involved in intellectual matters, in science and study, good-by love!
When I get worked up about my philosophy, I tend to find D.L.B. rather
trivial."[12]

Compared to Roland? No, merely through the effect of distance—between the start and close of the letter.

On January 13 Manon learns that Sophie has forwarded her "confession"
to La Blancherie. Fresh hope: "At last I am committed, Sophie, committed
forever. D.L.B. has loved me for a long time; he knows now that I feel the
same way; if I cannot be his, I shall never belong to anyone."[13] But Claude
doesn't seize his chance. Now it's too late. He was vexed, to begin with, by

---

*The Phlipon maidservant, nicknamed after her departed soldier husband, Pierre Montmignon.
Her annual wage was 100 livres (500 current francs or $100).
**The Abbé Raynal's *Histoire des Deux Indes* made him as great a celebrity as Voltaire or Diderot.

Phlipon's attitude, and a trifle dismayed by the sudden enthusiasm of the young girl he had been courting in vain for two years. Furthermore, after adding up his prospects, he found that Manon's dowry would amount to very little compared to a certain young lady named Bordenave, ten times richer than Manon, who was his for the asking. Manon, now soft-pedaling the whole affair, is relieved when he doesn't come running. Roland returns on January 22, not as a suitor but out of sheer curiosity. She is contentious and things don't "click" as they did the first time, even on the simplest social level. They quarrel over Buffon, over Raynal, whom she adores and he doesn't. The breach is partly mended by their mutual regard for the Ancients, for the "virtues of the Greeks," for the Roman Republic, which they both agree has never been equaled "for its vitality, its heroism, its patriotism . . . We see great men around us, but not nations of great men. Modern times do not produce these interesting revolutions of entire nations actively struggling for freedom, for the common good. They are subjects who kill each other and do battle for the interests of princes. They are slaves in chains fighting for the amusement of their masters."[14]

On February 19—and with continued neglect for La Blancherie, whom she rarely mentions anymore—a new set of initials appears in her letters: "I saw the man from Pondicherry again. His name is M. de Sainte-Lette, and I shall refer to him as D.S.L."[15] She had made his aquaintance a few days before Roland's call; he had received Phlipon's address from one of his friends on military duty in the French Indies. Sainte-Lette "looks to be over sixty; his demeanor suggests the austerity of a philosopher, the reflection of a sage, and the utmost simplicity."[16] He was a civil servant at Pondicherry recently assigned to Versailles to protect "the affairs of the colony." Manon takes a fancy to him: here's a man easy to love without passion, who courts her persistently without trying to snare her. Besides, his conversation is so interesting and informed. His professed atheism fascinates her at a time when she longs to stop believing in God but hasn't quite found the courage to do so: after all, Rousseau himself is a firm believer. "Monsieur D.S.L., a man brimming with humanity, feeling, and warmth, is an out-and-out atheist. I think no less of him for it; each time I find him more gifted, more cultured, the very essence of integrity . . . I have felt remarkably close to this old man; I can say that our souls are in unison. Yet I believe in God."[17] For the moment, he outsprints Roland by several lengths, that Roland "on whom, to be honest, I haven't looked too favorably. When I compare him to Monsieur D.S.L., I find him merely well informed . . . M. Roland strikes me as faintly biased; the fact that he utterly repudiates the Abbé Raynal prevents me from accepting his attentions"—on top of which the bungler speaks most unkindly of the *Histoire des Deux Indes*: "He calls it neither a story nor a philosophic narrative but instead a romantic tale, undistinguished in style, a book for women, fit for the dressing room!—I can't stomach such a coarse opinion."[18]

48

You Would Please the People Greatly

The winter of 1775–76 is severe in France. Rivers freeze over. Olive trees wither and die in Languedoc, where rampant epizootic disease decimates livestock. Destiny slips a bad card into Turgot's already hard-pressed hand. How much longer can he survive? Europe begins to catch sounds of daggers being whetted in the halls of Versailles.

By autumn's close, the stage was set for a drama in the classic tradition:

> THE FALL OF TURGOT
> A Play in Two Parts:
> 1. The Capitoline Hill
> 2. The Tarpeian Rock*

Cast (in order of importance): *Turgot,* impersonating the spirit of reform, aided by *Malesherbes* the Sage and two acolytes, *Dupont* and *Condorcet.*

Opposing him, the enemy of reform, in her first appearance: *Marie Antoinette,* with her confidantes *Lamballe, Polignac,* and *Guéménée,* and her prompters: *Lauzun, Besenval,* and *Coigny,* supervised by that distinguished fox *Mercy-Argenteau.*

Midway between the two camps stands the unpredictable Louis XVI, torn by indecision, tyrannized by brothers, aunts, and cousins who hate each other and end up collaborating with their mutual enemy, Marie Antoinette.

Among princes of the blood, a first-class rascal, the aged Conti, who is nearing his end. In the middle ground, a shifting crew of high officials, all more or less spineless, who ultimately wriggle into step with *Maurepas.*

Two key members of the supporting cast: *Necker,* the bankers' weathercock, and *Guines,* an urbane diplomat whose surprise entrance will provide a sudden twist that triggers the climax.

And in the background stand twenty-three million peasants, laborers, and bourgeois, invisibly pursuing their daily tasks, whose destiny hangs in the balance.

---

*A rock on Rome's Capitoline Hill from which traitors and criminals were hurled. [*Trans.*]

The opening scenes are acted out in January, when Manon Phlipon receives a visit from Roland on a different planet yet less than a mile from the finance ministry, where Turgot, who is also the ultimate boss of factory inspector Jean-Marie Roland de La Platière, has taken to his bed with a severe attack of gout.

Once before, a tragi-comic crisis had involved the minister of war. Maréchal de Muy had been unable to urinate. To remove his gallstones, the celebrated Father Côme was called in, a competent but overconfident surgeon-priest lately given to botching one out of four operations. The patient's wife, uninformed as to when the impending surgery would take place, learned of it only when her suffering mate began to howl under the scalpel and continued thus for two days. Who would replace him? The Choiseul faction, ever ready to stanch a breach, sponsored Maréchal de Castries, the Comte de Broglie, and the Baron de Breteuil. Turgot and Maurepas, united still in time of crisis, back "a virtuous man," a known reformist, the Comte de Saint-Germain.* After repeating the same tactic used in July for Malesherbes, they had steered him into place by October 22 just before the queen blocked the maneuver by pressing for Castries's appointment. But their haste proved risky, for only by hearsay were they acquainted with this sixty-eight-year-old individual with rigid ideas of the best and worst sorts on military matters: he hoped not only to reduce the royal budget but also to compel army attendance at Easter mass. An obstinate fellow who could not be moved, and who lived like a misanthropic recluse after serving his country in every European capital from Austria to Denmark.

"M. de Saint-Germain received word of his appointment at his country estate. He went to Fontainebleau [where the court was gathered] and stayed at an inn under an assumed name. His accommodations were wretched.

" 'Have you no more comfortable rooms than this?' he inquired.

" 'No, because all others are reserved for retainers of the new minister of war, who will arrive momentarily.'

"He did not press them."[1]

Maurepas and Malesherbes reached the "tavern"** shortly thereafter and managed to pick out of the astonished crowd this pale, tow-headed, "rather nasal-voiced" old gentleman already ensconced in his new role: "affecting to fret over the weight of his task and to regret the loss of his philosopher's hermitage . . . " despite "vibrant, ill-concealed joy over his promotion."[2]

---

*Not to be confused with a contemporary adventurer of obscure ancestry who had usurped the same name and title and went about insisting that he was as old as Christ. This Saint-Germain probably made a fortune as a spy and retired to Germany, where he died in 1786.

**The Hôtel du Cerf in the Place du Charbon. The incident took place on October 26, 1775.

Another tableau one month later, to fix the date. Brief dialogue between Malesherbes and the king, who commends his new minister for introducing various minor economic palliatives. Louis XVI adds that, instead of anticipated hostility, Malesherbes enjoys "widespread approbation." He refers to the court, of course, that being the only forum with which he has daily contact. This type of compliment distresses Malesherbes:

"It proves, sire, that I am not performing the task you set me. If I were, I would be stirring up a storm of complaints."

The king replies: "That sounds like the comptroller general, who cannot manage to ingratiate himself."[3]

This happens on November 25. Louis XVI is becoming convinced that Turgot is unpopular.

Malesherbes, on the other hand, is no longer taken for an ogre by the court. Little wonder: the reformer is not reforming. He himself had predicted this disappointment. "I may lay the groundwork for reform, but it is a great mistake to expect me to carry it out. Temperamentally, I am incapable of it . . . I am too inclined by nature to agree with whoever enters my office."[4]

So the cornerstone of Turgot's plan, the design of which is beginning to emerge—reform of the king's civil household (Saint-Germain can be relied on to reshape the military one), without which all else is hopeless—now is in the process of being discarded by Malesherbes. The King of France spends thirty-three million livres* annually for his housekeeping expenses, his stable, his servants, and the maintenance of his palaces. This is nearly equal to the Prussian national budget. In contrast, England's king gets only twenty-three millions (a million pounds sterling) for his civil expense, out of which he must pay his personal bills as well as his ministers, ambassadors, and judges.[5]

The French court continues to be a bottomless pit of debts. In August a faint attempt was made to hold down wedding expenses for Clothilde, the king's younger sister, a fat oaf known as "Stout Madame," who married the Prince of Piedmont. Yet each of the king's aunts had been awarded a household, thereby tripling the cost of supporting them and their hangers-on. The birth of the first Artois heir diverted a stream of gold into the Duc d'Angoulême's cradle. The total outlay for another royal brother, the Comte de Provence, was 855,194 livres and 6 sols (four and a half million francs) for the year 1774—and of course the Comtesse de Provence has her own household as well. Monsieur, the king's eldest brother, has spent 6000 francs (30,000 modern francs) "on washing for servants in the bread pantry, the butler's office, the kitchen, household and servants' quarters, as much for laundering His Highness's table linen as for that of the chief steward and all

_____
*160 million francs [$35 million].

the other tables, for the pages and generally for all the offices,"[6] and 500,000 annually "for the first secretary's livery."*

The point of intersection between this unending scandal and Malesherbes's good intentions had been the resurrection, in September 1775, for the Princesse de Lamballe's benefit, of the office of superintendent of the queen's household (eliminated during Marie Leczinska's time). In Marie Antoinette's scheme of things, it was the most elegant way to compensate for the loss of a friend. She had taken a fancy to Madame de Lamballe five years before, in the early, frustrating days of her marriage, but tired of her before she became queen. A Polignac and a Guéménée might try to occupy the vacant place. Marie Antoinette did not want to hurt the women she had been fond of and sought to console them the only way possible: materially. Urged by her entourage, Madame de Lamballe chose the right moment to beg for her consolation prize. As daughter-in-law of the Duc de Penthièvre, the richest man in France after the king and the Duc d'Orléans, she asked for "a purely ceremonial and costly office, with overwhelming prerogatives." Turgot hoped to get by with an annual settlement of "only" 70,000 livres (350,000 francs [$70,000]) —enough to support an elaborate household. But the last superintendent, the Duchesse de Bourbon, had received 150,000 livres. The Penthièvre clan protested: to accept less than half that amount would have been insulting to Madame de Lamballe. Among the very rich, money is synonymous with honor and to give up money is to debase oneself. Malesherbes yielded, if only to conciliate the queen, of whom he continued to be deathly afraid. So let the woman have her 150,000 livres! Turgot couldn't help frowning; another demerit for him in the eyes of the court.

By springtime the "Malesherbes experiment" seems to have fizzled out. Malesherbes spends all his time gathering information about the injustices he was authorized to eliminate, but wearily, like an opposition leader unable to focus on the facts. After voicing indignant protests against *lettres de cachet*, he proceeds to sign them, heaving sighs fainter only than La Vrillière's. He frees seven inmates of the Bastille, leaving behind thirty more for whom he claims nothing can be done: captivity has "turned them into prisoners." Hopeless cases: "In the Bastille and Vincennes, I found that more than half of those who had been locked away for over fifteen years had gone mad or were in such a state of frenzy as to make their release impossible."[7] His opinion is based not on what he has seen but on what he has read in the files of prison wardens, meaning the testimony of jailers or even clerks in his own ministry, both obtained effortlessly.** In fact, he retreats before the surge of hope aroused

---

* 25,000 francs today; a "clothing allowance" of sorts for the prince's chief secretary, whose yearly salary (on the modern scale) was 30,000 francs.

** To my knowledge, no record exists suggesting that Malesherbes, as minister of prisons, ever interviewed a single captive.

in the hearts of desperate men by his appointment. "We have yet to discuss the feelings generated by hopes of freedom in the prisons . . . To counteract the dangers of this, which are real enough, you suggest* sending a military inspector into each prison to hear complaints and take depositions from the inmates . . . I think this would be the best approach because it accomplishes two things at once . . . [the first of which would be] to calm the restlessness of prisoners."[8]

As to cutting royal spending, "it is a task unlike anything I have ever done. It is so far beyond me that whereas the prospect of going to my office once made me cheerful, now I must force myself to go there and even to get out of bed in the morning."[9]

His protean jurisdictions include keeping a watchful eye on indigents and beggars, notably in the capital. He would prefer not to meddle in such matters: "Is it known that the police cannot keep track of all the beggars in Paris and that nearly 91,000 persons are without fixed abode,** forced to sleep in hovels, and get up each morning uncertain whether they will survive the day?"[11] What solution does he have in mind? Deportation or charity: setting up concentration camps for the impoverished. He will give it further thought: "The main thing is to have an island, or some other piece of land, where people could be put to work under supervision and where the majority would consent to go . . . In cases for which the king meted out long sentences—which would have to be preceded by an investigation and a reasonable, written charge duly executed—these persons would themselves choose exportation [sic] to this work colony over harsh prison detention."[12] Others put forward remedies of their own, including the Archbishop of Paris, who suggests something like social security, or perhaps unemployment insurance for the needy, funded by a general levy on the rich. Malesherbes opposes this idea: "If it [this tax] is ever adopted, there will be no more charity . . . " "I believe England's mistake is to feed jobless, able-bodied beggars, to make the lot of welfare recipients the same as if not superior to that of the man who lives by his labor."[13]

Nagging and grumbling at himself and everyone else, Malesherbes goes his way, anxious to resign, regretting only "two or three things I would like to have settled before leaving: Protestant marriages, for which I see ample opportunities† without serious impairment of our legal system; and an end to the oppression still visited on former Jesuits . . . " Such are his modest dreams.

---

*Letter from Malesherbes to Saint-Priest, Languedoc's intendant, dated October 7, 1775.
**Out of a population of approximately 700,000 inhabitants.[10]
†After the Edict of Nantes was revoked, Protestant marriages performed by a minister were treated as concubinage under the laws of the French kingdom. Malesherbes refers to "opportunities" to ease those laws.

Meanwhile "a snowfall heavier than anyone remembered seeing for years" blankets the Paris region, where, to amuse Marie Antoinette, the younger set at court launches a fad for Austrian sleighing parties. "We ride in sleighs in the Viennese manner . . . and today [January 14, 1776] there is to be a great sleigh race in Paris."[14] The wintry weather doesn't let up until early March, taking a severe toll of the poor. On February 28 "the bitter cold did not prevent the queen from making numerous outings in her sleigh, some in the park and neighborhood of Versailles, others in the Bois de Boulogne . . . The queen rode to the very boulevards of Paris and even through several city streets," Mercy-Argenteau reports to Maria Theresa with marked disapproval, as if the royal couple were hazarding a jungle expedition by entering their own capital. "At such times when the frost-covered ground is excessively slippery and could cause many a dangerous spill, the queen, out of the goodness of her heart, dismissed her guards and reduced the customary size of her mounted escort . . . It was felt that the queen displayed herself publicly in a manner unbefitting her rank and dignity."[15]

His gout aggravated by the cold, Turgot takes to his bed and tackles current and future problems from under the blankets. He puts an end to the vehicular transportation monopoly enabling certain private companies to provide public road service that is both incredibly slow* and disorganized. A number of bulbous berlins and lumbering mail coaches are replaced by light, well-balanced *turgotines* seating four to nine passengers. Turgot's efforts will convey Parisians to Bordeaux in six days. In the process, however, he alienates one more group, the private-transport profiteers, who howl with rage despite fair offers of compensation. Undismayed, he lays plans for an elaborate system of inland waterways designed by the Abbé Bossut, a hydraulics expert: "One of the most effective ways to spread abundance through the land and supply the people's needs would be to create a chain of water routes from province to province, making rivers navigable wherever possible and linking them by canals."[16]

He takes over the postal system with intent to curb the censorship of private correspondence by secret agents of the crown and its officials. This merely raises the queen's dander, as she had planned to award that office to one of the Montmorency tribe. "She was so upset that when the comptroller general appeared before her, she never addressed a single word to him; but he, being a man of simple habits, paid scant attention and told his friends how pleased he had been with the queen's reception."[17]

Unlike Malesherbes, Turgot loses no sleep over the royal sulks. He has too much to do and too little time to do it. The standards he sets for the manufacture and distribution of pharmaceutical products will serve as a basis

*Ten days from Paris to Strasbourg, fourteen from Paris to Bordeaux.

for national legislation two hundred years later. He lays the groundwork for the establishment of a metric system. He requires all provinces to adopt certain preventive measures to combat epizootic disease. He organizes an official loan agency to regulate credit, to ease demands on the royal treasury, and to pave the way for a Bank of France ultimately empowered to mint money. He frees the shipment of wines from Bordeaux and Marseilles, and eventually, as with grain, removes all restraints from the wine trade; he abolishes the tax on deep-sea fishing; he revokes an exorbitant concession granted to the Hôtel-Dieu or hospital in Paris to sell meat on fast days. He designates Rochefort and Saint-Brieuc as ports of re-entry for merchant vessels returning from the Indies and Antilles, a privileged status formerly enjoyed only by the port of L'Orient (now Lorient).

So far none of this has caused a great stir. People tend to excuse it as the work of a conscientious official—an oddity, to be sure, though there have been one or two before him: Vergennes was known to hound his subordinates mercilessly, and Saint-Germain appeared to be trying to earn his reputation by initiating a broad spectrum of reforms, from the most practical to the most outlandish, from organizing the army into divisions to instituting corporal punishment for recruits in the form of beatings with the flat of the sword* and attempts to assign the training of career officers to ten colleges of Benedictines and Minims. Saint-Germain did not neglect himself in the process, having set his own salary 250,000 livres above that of any other official; he was vexed when Turgot rebuked him for overspending. Another adversary—just at the time he least needed it. "On the Ides of March," in fact, Turgot precipitates matters and shifts his activity from current to future concerns. The first three months of 1776 are the Time of Edicts.

What is he after now? How far does he intend to take his reforms? One of the reasons for the sudden concerted opposition to him is that "they" have no idea where Turgot is heading. He still has no program, but he has ideas, which are at least clearer now than they were when he came to power eighteen months ago. A few of these ideas will motivate the edicts he presents for the king's signature in February. Ideas alarming enough to terrorize the moneyed community and call down its wrath on Turgot's diabolic head.

With nothing less than abolition of the tax farm in mind, he sets to work negotiating a royal loan in Holland aimed at compensating the farmers-general for cancellation of their leases—ninety-three million is the sum he must produce.** Fiscal stability would then depend on the cooperation of regional assemblies, perhaps even a national one. An embryonic constitution begins to stir in Turgot's scheme of things, a pyramid of voters on several levels culminating in an elitist group of "proprietors," rural landowners—practitioners of physiocracy, which works to sustain the mass of urban dwellers—and there-

---

*Flogging with a stick already existed, but only at the personal whim of a regimental commander.
**500 million modern francs [$100 million].

fore sensible persons loyal to the established order, yet who would act as *representatives* of the moneyed interests and would *consent* to the annual tax collection, two sacrilegious concepts in this kingdom without a written constitution, where the ruler's will is law and the only "consenting" taxpayers are the clergy. Turgot has asked Dupont to think about creating such a "general municipality for the kingdom," which would "gather together in the sovereign's hands the reins of control over the tiniest and remotest parts of his land."[18] But what if one day the situation reversed itself? Dupont, a confirmed optimist, refused to consider the possibility and calmly proceeded to draft a memorandum from Turgot to Louis XVI stating that "the trouble,* Sire, lies in the fact that your nation has no constitution. It is a society composed of various ill-assorted classes and a populace whose members have few social bonds to link them. There is no public spirit because there is no visible, recognized common interest."[19] Pressing his case, Dupont revived the grand design for Poland that he had promoted two years earlier, trying to persuade Louis XVI (still via Turgot) that public education ought to be organized on a rational basis and not left to priests, religious institutions, and village schoolmasters. "If Your Majesty were to accept this plan, in ten years this people would be unrecognizable in their learning and their informed zeal to serve the crown as well as the nation; they would be infinitely superior to all other peoples."[20]

"Learning" and "nation" are concepts that raise the hair on Louis XVI's head. Still, without a murmur, he approves the six edicts submitted by Turgot for his signature in early February, cornerstones of the edifice to come. They represent a substructure too vague and formless to alarm the crown. However, two edicts carry great weight: one to abolish the *corvée* or mandatory road work, and one to do away with *jurandes*.** Impoverished peasants will no longer be required to pay a tax in the form of backbreaking toil to maintain the roads, work which turned them into forced laborers for anywhere from six to forty days a year, depending on the district—a levy institutionalized in France only a half-century earlier. The logic of this step is economic as well as humanitarian: time given to such labor means time away from the plow, which disrupts agricultural output. As to abolishing the guilds, it prepares the way for occupational mobility, a component of commercial freedom: the fact that in 1776 an artisan or laborer could not lift a finger unless authorized by the rules of his trade paralyzed initiative and ossified the ranks of skilled craftsmen.

In this domain, and with habitual ardor, Condorcet has put his shoulder

---

*This "trouble" is the absence of a civic-minded taxpaying public.
**The term *"jurande"* ordinarily referred to a craft or trade guild, generally urban, tightly controlled by statutes which severely restricted freedom to work. The other, less significant, edicts served to regulate grain distribution, to lift restraints from tallow manufacture, and to improve the supply of livestock in Paris.

to the wheel. Since autumn he has toured the country, braving snow and ice, to reinforce Turgot's resolve with concrete facts, arguing endlessly with public-works officials, whom he denounces categorically as "adjutants of the *corvée*": "Just think that here [in Flanders] you have to deal not only with their greed but also with the arrogance fostered by a sense of power that the administration of *corvées* allowed them to exercise over the people . . . Perronet,* who heads this whole crew, is a highly ignorant and conceited man who instituted the civil-engineering *corps* [the emphasis is Condorcet's] and would rather see the country perish than eliminate such a glorious organization . . . "[21] "I don't know whether the corps of civil engineers is as ancient as the monarchy, but it treats you just as it treats the parliaments and, I fear, will undermine your campaign against the *corvée* . . . unless you reform it at once . . . By destroying their clan spirit, which gives these people greater credit than provincial governors . . . you will be doing an immeasurable service to the public. Furthermore, total impunity for all those gentlemen would create something of a scandal."[22] Condorcet also applauds the proposed suppression of guilds: "The servitude of the rural masses was broken,** but the urban masses had chains of their own which needed breaking."[23]

But while Condorcet and Dupont are cheering, the vast majority of court nobility, members of parliament, and privileged society grow agitated: probably they feel anger triggered by fear. Compulsory road service is replaced by a monetary tax imposed on road-owners for the upkeep of their property. Easing guild regulations threatens the *de facto* supremacy of the most prosperous artisans and a thousand petty local dynasties. "A parliamentary explosion long gathering beneath the surface sent up its first blast on January 29," Véri reports. "The Prince de Conti, whose restive spirit will go with him to the grave, was daunted neither by the bitter cold nor by the signs of death etched on his brow. He has gone to Parliament wrapped in furs"[24] and there he leads the resistance to Turgot, backed by that talented young barker Duval d'Esprémésnil, who took the stage once before during the recall of the parliaments and, secretly, by the royal council in the person of Miromesnil, keeper of the seals, who, "like a loyal Norman, nurses deep hostility† against Turgot and will not forget it when an opportunity presents itself . . . He is the mainspring of parliamentary agitation against M. Turgot's operations."[25]

Louis-François de Bourbon, the Prince de Conti, resolutely plays out the last act in a long, depraved career launched at the age of twenty. A man who murdered prostitutes for pleasure, who paid two thousand women to sleep with him and kept a ring from each locked away in a coffer into which his bruised hands plunged now and then to stir a sea of memories; the "Grand

---

*Whose name has just become permanently associated with construction of the Pont de Neuilly.
**Through abolition of the *corvée*.
†Since the Grain War.

Prior" of the Temple, who scoffed at religion, rises again to attack reform. His features are grotesquely livid, almost cadaverous; only his savage eyes still burn. Racked by gout, smallpox, and nervous disorders, he cannot find strength to make the traditional "grand tour" of the court expected of members when Parliament is in session and cuts diagonally across it instead— carried in a sedan chair, inspiring respect and demanding it lest anyone forget that he is a cousin of the Condés. His presence adds special luster to the great remonstrance addressed by the Paris Parliament to the king on February 26 "in the name of the French nobility" who protest replacement of the mandatory road service by direct taxation of property-owners: "Every man in the kingdom is your subject; all must contribute to the needs of the state. But within this contribution itself order and harmony are forever present. The personal duty of the clergy is to perform all functions relative to education and religious worship, and to share in the alleviation of suffering through charitable works. The nobleman pledges his blood to defend the state and aids the sovereign with wise counsel. The lowest order of persons, who cannot render such distinguished service to the state, pay their debt in tribute, in industry, and in manual labor. This, Sire, is the ancient rule governing the duties and obligations of your subjects . . . The service of nobles is as noble as they . . . These institutions are not random products of chance which time can change."[26]

These remonstrances opened wide the breach between Parliament and Turgot. For the edicts to take effect, they have to be "registered"; Parliament refuses to do so. Turgot is not alarmed; the king need only hold a *lit de justice.* * Louis XVI does not object and, as a matter of fact, he rather enjoys such ceremonies. Surprisingly, however, his Council solidly opposes forced registration with the exception of one lone dissenter, Malesherbes, who appears reticent and embarrassed: for thirty years he has remonstrated against the sovereign and now feels disloyal to his class and to his party.

For the first time Turgot is physically aware of his isolation. It doesn't bother him much, for the king is on his side—or at least so he firmly believes. The others will come around sooner or later, provided Louis XVI persists in behaving like an enlightened despot.

The king holds the *lit de justice* on Tuesday, March 12, in the Great Guards Hall of Versailles, to which the magistrates have been summoned. The ceiling is not coffered, and the wall hangings are immense Gobelin tapestries depicting biblical scenes with people wearing animal skins that contrast oddly with the lavish regalia of this august assembly. Apart from such details, the ritual is no different from a *lit de justice* in Paris. From the "bed" dominating the scene, atop a six-step riser surmounted by a dais, Louis XVI looks out across the hall, over a fleecy field of heads powdered white or capped with "mortar-

---

*A solemn court session presided over by the king. [*Trans.*]

boards," to the gallery* where the queen is observing, if not scrutinizing, him, surrounded by her ladies, who have been asked not to wear farthingales in order that everyone can squeeze onto the benches.

No longer tense and fidgety, the king speaks without a stammer and appears determined. But he is visibly dismayed to find a wall blocking his already failing determination. This icy wall of respect is worse than dissent. Conti, on his last legs and too weak to address the gathering, submits his protest in writing. For the first time in public, Provence and Artois, the king's brothers, disapprove of his actions. D'Aligre, first president of the Paris Parliament, opines that the suppression of the guilds "leaves unguided and unchecked a restive, licentious body of young people which will regard itself as independent," and that "depressing gloom is to be seen everywhere by His Majesty. If he deigns to cast his eyes on the people, he will discover public consternation . . ." As a matter of fact, a mood of cheerful optimism hovers outside the palace, in the taverns of Versailles where city workers, with an ear to the gossip of government clerks or servants of the magistrates, better informed than most of their brethren as to the relative freedom promised by the edict, have piled eight or ten strong into hired carriages "and are putting on a spectacle of genuine delirium" like an impromptu carnival.[27] Antoine-Louis Séguier, chief public prosecutor, drums into Louis XVI's ear: what does it matter if "the lifting of restrictions has invariably occasioned or motivated the worst disorders," because "independence is a vice in the body politic since men are tempted to abuse freedom" and "constraints, obstacles, and interdictions constitute the glory, the security, and the immensity of French trade"?[28] Despite the royal presence, applause greets the close of this diatribe, and ladies of the court "call attention to themselves by their clapping." The queen never stirs; her companions have spoken for her. And the words heard by the king echo those of his father, the dauphin, whose memory fills him with guilt whenever he yields to the innovations of this godless minister they have saddled him with, whom he alone now supports.

Louis XVI departs in majestic pageantry from his *lit de justice,* unable to disguise his distress, and having granted one concession by promising that "if experience brings to light certain drawbacks in these provisions, I shall take care to correct them."[29] On that same afternoon, March 12, Turgot orders the seals affixed in all the principal guildhalls in Paris. He ignores the general discontent, having won the most significant victory of his tenure. He has every reason to visualize himself atop the Capitoline Hill.

In fact he was only two months from the Tarpeian Rock.

---

*A private box on the second floor, reached by a stairway within the hall itself.

49

His Name Was Turgot

The alarm sounds in early April—April Fools' Day, 1776[1]—with the appearance of handwritten copies of an anonymous pamphlet, *Les Mannequins, conte ou histoire* [The Straw Men, fable or history], the faint acidity of which is generally taken to be the trademark of the Comte de Provence, favored contender for leadership of the nobiliary opposition. He rakes Turgot over the coals: "Once there was a stout, burly man in France, more brash than brave, more stubborn than stolid, more impetuous than tactful, a charlatan in administration as well as virtue, brutal out of vanity, aloof out of arrogance. Day and night he dreamed philosophy, liberty, equality. People thought him profound; he was shallow. His name was Turgot."[2] Not even the king is spared: "Mindless integrity, when informed, is more disastrous politically than outright corruption." This brand of humor suggests Monsieur, whose rancor ripened at the age of twenty. Marie Antoinette, his momentary ally, describes him accurately to her mother: "He lacks the mixed blessings of the Comte d'Artois's vivacity and turbulence, but, in addition to his spinelessness, he takes an underhanded approach and stoops very low at times; to achieve his ends and to obtain money he resorts to petty schemes that would make an honest man blush . . . Unfortunately for Monsieur, his tactics are becoming familiar and earn him neither esteem nor public sympathy."[3]

All the same, Provence adds considerable clout to the anti-Turgot camp, along with Conti. The queen barely has time to cue her leading man in the emerging coalition. As early as February 12 the Abbé de Véri began to worry about this: "I cannot yet tell whether the queen has undergone a change of heart. A chorus of voices says she has, and her conduct leads one to believe it."[4] The change did not stem solely from the February edicts. Beginning with her return from the coronation, Marie Antoinette's intrusion, not to say invasion, of politics, which Malesherbes warned against in August, had become a reality as the court settled in for the winter at Fontainebleau.

Emotional release. A burst of self-assertion that no human being subsequently can retract. Triggered probably by news that the Comtesse d'Artois was pregnant* for the second time as wintry snow and grippe confined Fontainebleau's tenants to their stoppered vessel and focused attention more pointedly than at Versailles on the royal couple's sexual malaise. Casting aside the modesty she had shown as dauphine, Marie Antoinette no longer made the effort to conceal her husband's inept performance between the sheets. Recompense? The costly stewardship of Madame de Lamballe and the first of many lavish gifts bestowed upon the Polignac clan. In December, Maurepas had stolen the Swiss ambassadorship from under the nose of Vergennes's own brother and given it to the Vicomte de Polignac, Yolande's brother-in-law. On December 15 the court and its vast baggage train left Fontainebleau and its "dismal mists" which accounted for "widespread grippe that starts with a headache and progresses to fever and coughing."[5] Having survived Lapland, Marie Antoinette reinstalled herself as mistress of Versailles and her own style of life. Horseracing replaced sleigh rides once the snow melted. "The queen's balls have resumed; they are given on Mondays from six until ten in the evening. Ladies come masked in fancy dress; men dance in ordinary clothes and are not required to wear their uniforms."[6] The names of these men and women were beginning to interest the rest of Europe, and Maria Theresa plied Mercy-Argenteau with questions about her daughter's court, the image of which gradually was emerging. Exactly what role did the Lamballe woman play? And who were all those Polignacs? Or Besenval, Coigny, and Lauzun, the men around her? Mercy did his best to answer, more often with groans than with perceptive insights.**

Madame de Lamballe? Pretty in a way, if you happen to like that type. Something of a giraffe. Her stubby hands contrasted oddly with a long, elegant neck. Narrow, angular nose; jutting lower jaw; a vapid smile. "She never had an opinion of her own and, when conversing, invariably adopted the opinion of whoever sounded most intelligent," Madame de Genlis observed affectionately.[7] Borderline hysteria, developed in childhood and undiminished by marriage to a human wreck or subsequent widowhood at age nineteen.† "The sight of a bunch of violets made her swoon as readily as the sight of a crayfish or a lobster. She would shut her eyes and remain motionless for half an hour."[8] It was contagious: in October the "court gondolas" glided along the Seine from Choisy "to the arsenal that forms one boundary of the city of Paris. Several boatmen decided to put on a little show for the queen and began diving into the river. At first the queen thought they had fallen overboard and were drowning. [What an assault on the senses of those two frustrated women to watch handsome young men splashing about half naked!] Fearing this, Her

---

*With the future Duc de Berry. This would make Artois father of two heirs to the throne.

**The thumbnail sketches that follow come chiefly from him, corrected subsequently by diarists and historic perspective.

†Her name derived from the town of Lamballe in Brittany, one small part of the vast Penthièvre landholdings over which her husband was lord.

Majesty was taken ill, and the Princesse de Lamballe fainted dead away."[9] How Maria Theresa pounced on that! "I find something odd about the excessive terror displayed by the Princesse de Lamballe at the sight of boatmen plunging into the water."[10] Never forgetting that by birth she is the Princesse de Savoie-Carignan, Madame de Lamballe insists on equal status with the king's two sisters-in-law—both of whose marriages she managed. Newly installed now as superintendent of the queen's household, she takes on the airs of a royal princess and "inflames some of the queen's attendants, who protest the tyranny of the first lady in waiting. Disputes continually break out involving the lady of honor, the wardrobe mistress . . . Her Majesty grows impatient, the household is badly run and everybody out of humor. The Princesse de Lamballe, usually at fault, is gradually losing favor with the queen, and the time is approaching [Mercy-Argenteau writes on May 16, 1776] when I wager that Her Majesty will be distressed and embarrassed to have revived a thoroughly useless position in her household."[11]

Lamballe, then, belongs to the past, much as she complicates the present. Paralleling her decline is the "rise of a new favorite whom court oracles predict will eclipse all others before her":[12] the Comtesse Jules de Polignac, née Yolande de Polastron. Beauty, sweetness, candor. Seventeen and not extremely rich. A pretty child for Marie Antoinette to pamper, a young girl without airs or any inclination to snub the Austrian-born queen; a handful of clay to be molded as desired. Indeed, the hint of Pygmalion in all this disturbs Mercy—and many others—who judge the little angel far too malleable to withstand the queen's influence; behind her hovers a grasping family and, candid as she is, a lover "who ruled her completely and manipulated her as he wished; their liaison was public gossip."[13] The Comte de Vaudreuil had a facile tongue with the ladies and a special flair for handing out bounties while he himself wallowed in debt. He and his friends—Besenval, Noailles, Coigny, Luxembourg, and Adhémar—who attend the races and gamble nightly in the queen's apartments, are all more or less linked to the Choiseul faction, whereas Madame de Lamballe's support comes from the Orléans-and-Artois camp. Mercy-Argenteau and the Abbé de Vermond, joint masters of the king's household, feel the queen slipping out of their fingers. She listens to them politely and does exactly as she pleases. In the end they try to play off one faction against the other, to offset a Lamballe with a Polignac and one other entry in the race: the Princesse de Guéménée, daughter of the Maréchal de Soubise, slightly older than the other two, tied to the Rohans and the "fast" set at court. The queen was much taken with the spirited La Guéménée: "she attracts a lively crowd and many young people."[14] For protocol's sake and in order to visit her in the Château de Montreuil just outside the gates of Versailles, Marie Antoinette has just appointed her "governess of the royal children"—who have yet to appear.

The main attraction in the queen's playhouse at Versailles this April, in the puce-colored year, is the silent struggle of three "angels" with pearly, mordant smiles: Lamballe, Polignac, and Guéménée. Still out front in the men's race is this fall's outsider, Lauzun. He'll lose in a close finish.

Lucky man to have queens fighting over him! On January 10, knowing of the duke only at second hand, Catherine II tries to hire him by mail: "As I have planned for some time to train regiments of Cossacks, Tatars, and Bashkirs for my army, I offer you command of these forces and of the cavalry guard regiment I shall raise from these nations. You may recruit as many foreign officers as you choose. This position, among the highest in my empire, will guarantee you the esteem of my successor if God should call me from the earth."[15] This would have left the nephew to subdue the Cossacks two years after Pugachev's rebellion while his uncle kept Parisians in their traces. It was no sudden fancy of Catherine's to enlist the services of "this enterprising young nobleman, brimming with initiative, whose reputation with the ladies cannot have discredited him in her eyes."[16] They have corresponded for nearly a year; Lauzun cherished the vision of a grand Franco-Russian alliance fashioned from his conquest of two sovereigns. Vergennes, having no desire to see his authority short-circuited, has warned the duke to keep his nose out of such matters. Catherine in turn assured Lauzun that by serving Russia he would serve her as well.

Marie Antoinette did not agree. The virtues of competition threatened to cost her the virtue she had thus far preserved through no effort of her own:

" 'No, Monsieur de Lauzun, our cause is inseparable; your ruin would mean my own.'

" 'Ah, Madame, how can you compare the interests of a subject to the momentous interests of a queen?'

" 'A subject like yourself, Lauzun? Don't abandon me, I beg you. What shall I do if you forsake me? . . . '

"Her eyes filled with tears. Deeply moved, I flung myself at her feet . . . She extended her hand and I kissed it passionately again and again without changing position; she bent over me tenderly; she was in my arms when I rose to my feet. I held her close, my heart beating fast; she blushed, but I saw no trace of anger in her eyes . . . "[17] This conversation, after which they both collected themselves, by Lauzun's own admission ("in the privacy of my room, all the risks I had just run came to mind"), might seem trivial if the duke had not been at the height of favor, a potential party leader, just at the time when the Guines Affair is about to explode under Turgot's feet.

The Comte de Guines? A seasoned sybarite, extremely clever from all accounts, wry and politely derisive. But "how does he show his cleverness?" commented the Duc de Lévis: "For every suit of clothes, Guines had two pairs of breeches, in different sizes. When he was dressing, his valet would inquire gravely: 'Shall Monsieur le Comte be sitting down today?' If he intended to remain standing and could get into breeches that made him look thinner, he would climb up onto two chairs and drop down into his pants, which two servants spread for him."[18]

Under Choiseul's patronage, he had cruised the diplomatic channels from Berlin to London. The London embassy proved to be a real hornets' nest. Like Guerchy and D'Eon ten years earlier, Guines had quarreled with his secretary, a certain Fort de La Sonde, in 1771 over some murky business resembling a stock swindle. Running battle of insults for two years which kept Europe amused. Guines's fortunate choice of the ideal moment to charge Aiguillon, then minister of foreign affairs, with misconduct earned him the queen's gratitude. He had already managed to ingratiate himself with the Polignacs— a decidedly clever man. Louis XVI had given in to his wife on this score in 1774, against Vergennes's counsel, and the secretary was dismissed.

But the real Guines Affair explodes in March 1776, at the time of the *lit de justice* and the edicts. It rips aside the decorative curtain of court life and sets fans fluttering. Not just by chance do the activities of this oversize dung beetle suffice to bring down Turgot, for the issue of war or peace looms. Over the winter, Guines commits a series of diplomatic blunders grave enough to have cost him his head under Richelieu. He attempts to undermine French interests in the covert struggle between Spain and Portugal over their colonial possessions by conveying unauthorized hints to the British that Louis XVI will not enforce the "family pact"* by supporting Spain. Simultaneously he warned the Spanish (falsely) of an imminent English attack on Mexico and heightened the confusion by his written assurances to England that France would never aid the American rebels.

Fine ambassador! He could have set the continent afire if people had believed him. He was aiming for that, more or less, toying with war, yearning for it as did most other men in his circle, from La Fayette to Lauzun. The result partly of aristocratic idleness, partly of design: a general feeling that Choiseul alone was capable of conducting a new war. Against whom and for what no one cared particularly. Just return their idol to his temple and send them off to fight somewhere. Beyond that they couldn't see.

Though Turgot and Vergennes stood poles apart, neither wanted war. Nevermore for Turgot, whose entire economic and ideologic framework rested on a prolonged period of peace. Temporarily for Vergennes, until the flimsy fabric of European alliances eventually gave way.

Peace versus war. Turgot versus Guines. At the Council of January 22, 1776, when Louis XVI awoke to his ambassador's imposture, he had no choice but to recall him—if only to discredit Guines with the English.

But behind Guines stands Lauzun, and behind Lauzun, the queen.

The queen versus Turgot.

*Pact of mutual assistance binding the French, Spanish, and Neapolitan Bourbons.

News of Guines's recall reaches Madame de Guéménée in Montreuil one
February evening during the "queen's ball" given each Saturday of the carnival season. Two rooms are reserved for dancing, the rest for gambling. Lauzun
sits at a "fifteen"* table with the Comte d'Artois and the Duc de Chartres.
Madame de Guéménée approaches "looking like someone who has just
learned of a dreadful disaster." She informs Lauzun "that the Comte de Guines
has been recalled from the London embassy in the most humiliating fashion."
Instant mobilization. We can't allow this to happen! The queen arrives, escorted by Coigny, who seems to possess the only calm head in the room and
offers her good advice: "Stay out of this." But Lauzun gets excited: "I dared
to contradict [this wisdom] vigorously and to suggest that the queen ought not
so readily to abandon a man for whom she had shown a marked interest." Brief
but lively skirmish between two cocks of the salon: their honor—that is to say,
their standing with the queen—is at stake, against a background of card tables
heaped with coins glittering in the candlelight. Lauzun wins the hand: his
suppressed love scene with Marie Antoinette happened just the week before.
She is all the more vulnerable for not yet having slept with him, whatever else
the gossips may report. She strutted about one day wearing a single white
plume from his helmet in her hair. She had taken a fancy to it after seeing him
once in uniform and sent Madame de Guéménée to claim the trophy: "Never
have I felt more splendidly adorned, as if I possessed the rarest of treasures."[19]

She cuts short the debate:

" 'Enough. My mind is made up. I shall take Lauzun's advice. Yes,' she
assured me in a charming manner, 'I shall be glad to do whatever you recommend in this matter.' "[20]

What Lauzun—and his friends—recommend is that Louis XVI should
lavish on Guines the highest award any diplomat could hope to receive for his
blunders: a dukedom. And while they're at it, why not press the "poor fellow"
to dismiss Turgot? Even dismissal is too good for him; the queen envisions the
Bastille for this man who will have peace at all costs.

Why did he force their hand with the edicts when he might have gone on
progressing "by undulation"? Why adopt the "Condorcet manner"? Malesherbes chides him severely:

" 'You could postpone a certain project . . . and you could lead up to
another by degrees, imperceptibly, over a period of three or four years, in one
form or another that would arouse no protest . . . '

" 'With the ailment that runs in my family, will I have time? The disease

---

*A ruinous game of chance something like poker: players drew cards in turn, raising the stakes
each time around. The first player whose cards totaled fifteen won the pool.

gets worse each day I work. By using my time profitably, at least I will have delivered the people from these tribulations.'

"This family ailment is gout, which killed his father and brother," and from which "he suffered violent chest pains" throughout the winter and on into the spring.[21] Pain and fatigue have shortened his life. He is afraid not of dying but of having left so much undone.

Turgot spends hours stretched on a sofa, dictating or writing with his arm propped up on pillows, but the spasmodic pain is so intense, so excruciating, so unbearable as to plunge him at times "into a state of despair." For years now, January has signaled the onset of his torment "that begins with a grinding and a wrenching in his left big toe, rises to the ankle and heel, and creeps upward to the fingers of both hands." It wakens him punctually "at two in the morning" with a vision of all the wrongs in France that he will never have time to right. "It reaches to the tarsus and metatarsus, fans out to the malleoli, knees, hips, and vertebrae, while advancing in like fashion from the fingers to the metacarpus, carpus, elbow, arm, shoulder, and eventually invades the jawbone and neck joints." "It gets worse in the morning, intensifies in the evening, and slackens—temporarily—around dawn the following day." At the height of an attack the victim seems to be on fire. He glows: the heat thrown off by his inflamed joints sometimes "resembles a smoldering log that warms the hand from quite some distance." A year of overwork had paved the way for this winter's fierce siege. Turgot's gout has become "anomalous" or "intensified," judging from his sensation of a burning stone lodged in his chest. It is the "type that attacks the intestines or inner organs . . . induced by the gouty leaven which travels to the brain, throat, lungs, and intestines."* Realistic about the state of medicine in his day, he rejects the advice of doctors, who prescribe abstention from sex (in which he has never indulged) and "fine old wines, liqueurs, alcoholic or other, and nourishing foods." He refused poultices of bread and warm milk, plasters of sheep's whey or "still-pulsating beef or calf's brains," not to mention plain egg yolks.[22] At the peak of his torment he would ask simply for a grain of opium, which no longer put him to sleep but allowed him to work and to keep abreast of events.

And events start to look grim by mid-April. Unintimidated by the *lit de justice,* the Paris Parliament raises endless obstacles to enforcement of the edicts. The king, having spent his energy and endured the queen's nagging importunities in behalf of Guines, goes off to hunt in peace at Meudon or Marly. No cause for alarm if only the ministers would unite to help Turgot act, since the edicts now provide the tools for action. They do indeed unite —to oppose him. On April 16 a threatening letter from Saint-Germain about a fiscal matter opens a rift between the minister of war and Turgot: "I am

---

*Gout, now on the rise in consumer societies with poor dietary habits after dropping off significantly at the beginning of this century, was widespread at the time. Basically, it involved deposits of uremic acid ("gouty leaven") in certain tissues, chiefly around joints.

aware, sir, that people are trying hard to turn you against whatever I do . . . "[23] Miromesnil refuses to vote enforcement powers. Typically, Vergennes retreats from a confrontation and avoids offending the queen by maintaining that he had sanctioned Guines only out of official necessity and has no objection to his dukedom.

Minus three. Four counting Sartines, an antagonist from the start. This leaves Maurepas, the "principal minister," who camps in Madame du Barry's apartments and sees the king daily.

Maurepas is switching colors. He has come out all but openly for the queen and against Turgot, whom he deserted at the time of the Grain War. He is jealous of him, of his prestige, his energy, his ability to get things done. A hint of malice wells up from the frustrations of a wrecked career. Resentful, bitter old age. The Abbé de Véri, who served as link between people of Maurepas's stripe and Turgot, sniffs the breeze and repairs to his country seat just when he could be most useful. He, too, finds Turgot tiresome, uncompromising, laconic, unbearably self-confident—enough to dismay any ambitious churchman.

And what about Malesherbes the Just? He backs off. In fact, he lands the blow that sends Turgot reeling: on March 19 he had resigned his stewardship of the king's household and remains in office pending the choice of a successor. The controversy over this successor sparks the first overt antagonism between Louis XVI and Turgot.

Malesherbes is thoroughly disgusted with everything and everyone, himself included. Wedged between past and present; professional and class loyalties have always guided him. Now he refuses to preside over the compulsory registration of any edict, whatever it is, by his former colleagues. "I found that I was getting nowhere and actually was losing face with the king, whereas M. Turgot had been and continued up to the last moment to be convinced of his favor. Never did he doubt that he had transferred his own feelings to the heart of that young prince."[24] Furthermore, he will "break his neck for taking the very steps I had been urging him for six weeks not to take and which were really a fit of madness on his part, as it is just that to try to force the hand of one's master [sic] by importunities . . . and just that to risk appearing ungrateful to an all-powerful patron." In short, Malesherbes confesses that he, too, is through with Turgot and tired of being treated by the king "as the unremitting champion of a man who went out of his way each day to offend him." How? Horseracing? Gambling away a fortune every night? Sex orgies at the Palais Royal? Slave trading? Peccadilloes all. No, Turgot's offense was to have made a practice of dealing honestly with his sovereign. He had called in Malesherbes in order to have at least one pillar of support. One too many, as it turned out. "My position is untenable; in a week I shall return to my books and my friends."[25] But Chrétien-Guillaume Lamoignon de Malesherbes will depart on tiptoe. Only "well-informed circles" know in April that he has resigned.

It is generally assumed by the enlightened that if Turgot is dismissed, Malesherbes will be dragged down with him and then cheerfully turn against Turgot "the very evening of his dismissal, in the home of a mutual lady friend," showing only the tip of his rancor in this equivocal comment: "Did you think yours was a passion for the public good? Not for a moment! It was sheer madness!"[26]

Louis XVI probably decided to cashier Turgot when Malesherbes resigned. If not, it would have involved a singular display of loyalty to a minister whom he clearly disliked and whom everyone else had rejected. Madame du Deffand is jubilant; the smell of death hangs in the air: "One thing is certain, Turgot will not give in; there is no one more enterprising, more stubborn, more presumptuous than he. His associate Malesherbes does what he is told. Of our three ministers, they say that Turgot doubts nothing, Malesherbes doubts everything, Maurepas doesn't give a damn, and all of them feel that such a government can't survive."[27] Still, an excuse was needed for the final act. Louis XVI abhors decision-making; every official dismissed since he took the throne—and the list is growing—knew the torment of uncertainty, not to mention hope. Turgot's case is different: he hasn't the slightest interest in knowing what everyone else knows. He has a job to do and nothing to be ashamed of; openly, the king has expressed no displeasure. So Turgot goes on working as usual from March 19 through the end of April. The others shuffle their feet; how can they make him understand that his influence is zero—that Turgot no longer exists? Maurepas, repeating a maneuver that preceded the dismissal of Maupeou and Terray, presses the king:

"Here are two men [Malesherbes and Turgot] whom I myself represented to you as being highly virtuous and loyal servants. One of them is leaving you . . . The other keeps threatening to leave unless you follow his counsel to the letter. I see now, regretfully, that neither one is devoted to you."[28] In the end, Maurepas triggers the parting shot by proposing Amelot, his incompetent nephew, to replace Malesherbes. Turgot, who had Véri in mind (before the latter skipped off to the country), feels compelled to protest: if the royal household falls into the hands of a flunkey, adieu fiscal reform. One whole section of his plan collapses. He tries to convey this to the king several times during their regular work sessions in the last week of April, but encounters a wall of silence, a reaction so evasive that it jolts him belatedly into awareness of the crisis, of his imminent peril. Well, if he must fall, he will do it gracefully. Denied the king's ear, he will write to him. Three times that same week. His letter of April 30 alone is both a hara-kiri[29] and a severing of relations, the cries of a man who believed in his sovereign's good will.

> Sire, no longer can I conceal from His Majesty the gaping wound in my heart inflicted by his cruel silence last Sunday after I had described in great detail in prior letters my own and his position, the threat to his sovereignty and to the

glorious record of his reign, and the futility of my continued service if deprived of His Majesty's support. He has not seen fit to send me a single word of reply. I cannot imagine, Sire, that you would consent lightheartedly to surrender your throne and your people's welfare . . .

Sire, there are men who cling to their positions for prestige and profit. They can endure the neglect which His Majesty has heaped upon me. A minister who cares for his sovereign needs to be cared for in return . . .

His Majesty sees that I cannot fight those who would harm and prevent me from doing good by fouling my every effort, yet His Majesty gives me neither help nor comfort. How am I to believe that he esteemed or cared for me? Sire, this I have not deserved, I must confess . . .

You need experience, Sire. I know that, at the age of twenty-two and in your position, you lack the means to judge people which ordinary men acquire from living among their peers. But will you develop more experience in a week, or a month? . . .

Think, Sire, that in the natural course of events you will rule for fifty years, and think of the progress disorder can make, having reached the point it has in twenty. *Oh, Sire, do not wait for such disastrous wisdom to overtake you and learn from another's experience . . .* *

Now, Sire, do you honestly realize how weak-willed M. de Maurepas really is? How vulnerable to the dominion of those around him? It is common knowledge that Madame de Maurepas, who is infinitely less intelligent but far more courageous, tells him what to do . . . that public opinion exerts far too strong a grip on him for an educated man who ought to form his own opinions. I watched him change his mind ten times about the *lit de justice* depending on whether he was with the keeper of the seals, or M. Albert, the lieutenant of police, or myself. . .

Never forget, Sire, that it was weakness which brought Charles I's head to the block; it was weakness which made Charles IX cruel; it generated the League under Henri III; it turned Louis XIII, and today the King of Portugal, into crowned slaves. It is responsible for all the ills of your predecessor's reign . . .

And what if domestic strife were compounded by war, Sire, which a thousand reckless acts could incite or circumstances force? How will the hand that cannot steer the ship through calm seas prevail against the storm? How can any war be fought with such fluctuating doctrines and motives, with the indiscretions that customarily accompany weakness? . . .

Truly, Sire, I cannot understand you at all. No matter how often you have heard me called a hothead and a dreamer, I cannot believe that what I write you is the thinking of a lunatic. It seems to me that the measures I have adopted, despite the protest and resistance they have provoked, have had the success I predicted. And if I am not altogether insane, if the perils I warned of have an element of reality, Your Majesty cannot, without betraying himself, yield to them for the sake of pleasing M. de Maurepas . . .

Finally, if by misfortune this letter should warrant His Majesty's disfavor, I beg that he will so inform me privately . . . In any event, I rely on his discretion.

*Underlined by Turgot.

The tone of his letter suggests that Turgot is courting a dungeon on top of dismissal. He flirts with disfavor like a moth circling a light bulb—the light that ultimately illumines his life. As to being informed "privately" of his fall, if he really expects this to happen he is even blinder than he appears. A pattern of moral anemia has been built up by three kings: the process of cashiering a minister suddenly, without warning, on the heels of an ordinary work day, is now ritual. Louis XVI avoids registering any reaction to this message. He receives Turgot two or three more times, routinely, and expresses "vague things that leave him hanging in the air,"[30] not so much as to the reality of his dismissal as to its date: Turgot assumes he will have several weeks to put his files in order and even "submit for the king's perusal a program to reform his household."[31]

Now the meanest blows rain down on him. Who would have expected one from Lavoisier? He intervenes during the month of April, not as a member of the state gunpowder commission, which continues to enact Turgot's policies, but as an agent of the farmers-general at the tollgates of Paris, where he openly flouts Turgot's edicts, as does every other farmer-general throughout the land. At the Saint-Jacques tollgate Lavoisier imposes a tax on peas, beans, lentils, and rice from outside the city, contrary to an edict of February 5 establishing free entry for foodstuffs. And when the Cour des Aides objects and tries for once to enforce the law, Lavoisier declares that the chief of police and Turgot himself have sanctioned this assault on free trade. Turgot remains silent. It is May 8. The magistrates are outraged: is he really as stringent as he makes himself out to be, this controller general who is not controlling things?

Condorcet has known all along where Lavoisier stands, and by the end of April he abandons hope of Turgot's survival. His letters to his friend during this period bristle with anger: the farmers-general "want their usual plunder from this year's grape harvest. My colleague* Lavoisier has behaved predictably in this affair like a true nephew of the Abbé Terray and son-in-law of M. de la Pauze [*sic*] . . . Instead of using his knowledge of such matters to enlighten his colleagues,** he seeks only to inflame them. Good-by! This rabble makes me sick."[32] Soon his morale touches bottom: "Stay in bed, do no work unless it benefits the nation, and, if you can, leave yourself a little energy for summer, when you always feel better. No longer am I sure that it is worth your while to suffer from gout for humanity's sake. Having got to know humanity during your administration, I am disgusted with it. All that should concern us is the common good, as with a herd of animals responsive only to pleasure and pain. The rest are vicious wild beasts."[33] Marie-Jean-Antoine-Nicolas de Caritat, the Marquis de Condorcet, is decidedly not cut out for politics, and his concept of the public welfare partly explains why Turgot's

---

*In the Academy of Sciences.
**Here he means the farmers-general.

dismissal provokes no reaction from the "common herd," a few members of which had been singled out the year before to hang as examples to the public.* The "informed" crowd of reveling laborers gathered in Versailles for the *lit de justice* on March 12 had no counterpart elsewhere in France. The working class, barely conscious of its existence, did not feel liberated. Nor was it. "Turgot the 'liberal' equates wage-earners with domestics and compels their masters to register them on lists available at all times to the police; in fact the chief of police is authorized to settle all employer-employee disputes apart from matters under the jurisdiction of common law tribunals."[34] Moreover, the banning of labor or employer associations, in place of the guilds, tended to favor small shopowners "by disadvantaging groups whose dispersal exposes them to the will, not to say the whim, of masters."** Turgot, Condorcet, and Dupont truly believed they were struggling for the common people, but on a philosophical plane. They fought for an intelligent redistribution of the privileges enjoyed by their own class. Yet "the man who knows contentment and who suffers, the man eager for life who is forced to abandon it—he is my brother; with him have I joined forces, and for him are the laws made. I am left cold by this icy intellectual compassion for future generations which shuts our hearts to the cries of ten thousand miserable souls all around us."[35] A year later Necker put his finger on the central weakness of Turgot's effort: its absence of popular roots.

As to the ruling class in France, it is beginning to defy all rational rescue attempts. It rejects Turgot like diseased tissue rejecting a graft that fails to take hold—faster and more aggressively than he expected. On May 10 he learns that Amelot will be named to preside over the king's household—something he had spent five pages in his letter of April 30 trying to stave off. That same day Marie Antoinette extracts from the king not only a dukedom for Guines but a handwritten note as well from His Majesty announcing this honor— which she makes him rewrite three times because the opening lines are not sufficiently flattering. Turgot is beaten on all counts. On the 11th he sends a brief message to Véri: "M. de Guines has the title of duke, consequently white as snow. The appointment of M. Amelot may be announced today. Judging from this news, you can form your own political speculations about the country . . . "[36]

Also on the 11th he tries several times to see the king—and finds the door barred. Little does he suspect how real his peril is: Marie Antoinette, exultant over her triumph, would have him condemned to the Bastille and relents only under pressure from Mercy and Vermond.

On Sunday morning, May 12, Louis XVI sends Turgot orders to vacate his office and the court. At the same time Malesherbes is informed that his

---

*At the time of the Grain War. [*Trans.*]   **According to Braudel and Labrousse.

resignation has been officially accepted. The two men leave Versailles at noon; their baggage has been ready for days. Turgot feigns relief, but departs a broken man, fatally wounded in spirit, "sorrowful to see a beautiful dream vanish"[37] while they sip champagne in the apartments of the young queen to whom Joseph II had written eleven months earlier: "What business is it of yours, dear sister, to make and unmake ministers?" Caraccioli, the Neapolitan ambassador, calms the fears of an anxious correspondent: "Basta! Don't you fret: those are only the king's baby teeth."[38]

And for Madame du Deffand, writing to Horace Walpole on June 5, it is one of the last great pleasures in her life: "The truth is that Turgot would have upset everything . . . Except for the economists and the Encyclopedists, everyone agrees that he is a lunatic . . . They are delighted to be rid of him. Let us hear no more of that foolish creature."[39]

JULIE DE LESPINASSE

50

MAY 1776

We Will Have Lost Hope

May has another treat in store for Madame du Deffand: the young woman she most despised succumbs to tuberculosis during the night of the 21st, and the blind old lady can scarcely contain her satisfaction: "Mlle de Lespinasse died at two o'clock this morning. Once it would have been an event in my life; now it means nothing."[1] Madame du Deffand's utter rejection of Turgot expressed her scorn: "I used to see him every day [in her salon] fourteen or fifteen years ago. The Lespinasse woman set me against him and the rest of the Encyclopedists . . . " "If she goes to heaven, let the Holy Mother beware, for she will rob her of the Holy Father's affections."

Julie has lain dying since May 15. Turgot's dismissal is not what kills her, because she has been expecting it and because her infinite capacity for self-torture focuses on the shifting barometer of her love for Guibert. Still, this final political setback was depressing enough. She had little else to live for, not even the hope of seeing conditions improve for others. "If no good comes of Turgot's efforts, we will be far worse off instead of back where we started, for we will have lost hope." And so it is. She might just as well drift away to the death she has awaited like a lover, the death she summons, she romanticizes, she has savored now for months: the start of a voyage "out from this mournful land called life." Her death throes have lasted four or five years. She, rather than the agony of passion, is killing herself.

Heavy doses of opium induce pleasant fantasies of death and veil its terrors. Madame du Deffand is responsible for her opium addiction, which dates back almost twenty years to the time when Julie served as handmaiden in the salon of this older woman, who was gradually going blind (though many of her guests had eyes only for Julie), and who flew into a jealous rage one day over an Irishman—what was his name? It seems so long ago: 1758. The Chevalier de Taaffé. The whole incident was so innocent, until her benefactress and social sponsor showed her true colors and ordered Julie to remain in her room when Taaffé came to the house. "In a fury, the young girl swallowed sixty grains of opium, which, instead of killing her as she intended, brought on agonizing convulsions and permanently damaged her nervous system. Madame du Deffand wept bitter tears at her bedside: 'It's not time yet, Madame' . . . said Mlle de Lespinasse, who believed she was dying."[2]

Her rendezvous with despair took place under the tearful gaze of that dragon of social patronage with whom she finally parted company in 1764— also in May. By then Julie used opium regularly, more to ease spiritual than bodily aches. She took it while her beloved Mora lay dying a hundred leagues away, in 1773. "He spat blood; they bled him twice . . . Some comfort that is! Pain has dulled my spirit and I surrender to it. At five this morning I took two grains of opium [June 20, 1773]. It brought me peace of mind, more precious than sleep." She worked up to several daily doses of four grains* each beginning in January, when she felt chilled, so chilled "that my temperature is twenty degrees lower than the Réaumur reading . . . I freeze, I shiver, I die of cold, I bathe [in sweat] . . . When taken at this strength, opium calms me as it calmed Medusa's head . . . My faculties won't function; what I see is a mere projection, and for two hours this afternoon I was unable to identify a single face. How strange it feels to be lifeless and yet alive!"

She lives out her last hours in this her home for the past twelve years, a typical eighteenth-century three-story townhouse opposite the convent of Belle-chasse, with its entrance on the Rue Saint-Dominique, the two upper floors of which she had rented** from the carpenter landlord just after her break with Madame du Deffand, a next-door neighbor, largely to infuriate her. Friends of the feuding pair invented elaborate ruses to pass from one salon to the other.[3]

---

*These "grains" were tiny pills of opium mixed with sugar or marshmallow, the morphine of her times. Opium abuse was not uncommon, since the pills could be bought, for a stiff price, at all the fashionable perfume shops.

**For 950 livres plus a donation of 42 livres and 10 sous toward the concierge's wages, or about 5000 francs [$1000] on the modern scale.

Confined for the past month to her spacious bedstead four feet wide, she suffocates under a canopy of red damask which matches the damask-hung walls of the bedroom overlooking a quiet street. Gardens and cloisters surround the house; opening the window brings in the sound of bells and birds chirping. The faces that blur when her fever mounts are familiar ones, the four servants who look after her, try to make her eat or drink something, change her nightclothes when she coughs up blood: Geneviève Beaujon, the cook; Marie Plainchant, the housekeeper, nicknamed "La Joinville"; Agnès Saint-Martin, the chambermaid; and Eloi Raimbault, her coachman and valet.* Two men came to sit at her bedside: D'Alembert, who loved her, and Condorcet, a loving friend. "I cannot express my affection for M. d'Alembert and M. de Condorcet except to say they are part of me; they are as necessary to me as the air I breathe; they do not trouble my soul, they occupy it completely." She felt freest with Condorcet, whose love was platonic. A good, if faintly crotchety friend whom she scolded like an older sister: "You drink too much coffee; it doesn't help the state of your nerves . . . You ought not to work at geometry like a slave, to dine like a hog and then barely sleep a wink . . . " "I would advise you to stop biting your lips and nails; they are highly indigestible . . . Take care of your ears, which are always full of powder, and your hair, which is cut so close to your scalp that your head may end up poking through your cap." But not even to Condorcet would she open up completely.

D'Alembert's compassion and affectionate nonsense irritated her. What good did all that erudition do him? He enlarged the horizons of human knowledge, yet failed to see what was under his own nose. A deceived lover who had never even loved. The fact that he couldn't was not his fault; his high, shrill voice told the story. Julie made no demands on him during the eleven years they lived together (she sublet three rooms to him on the top floor), a relationship which provoked as much gossip as that of the king and queen. But his penchant for playing watchdog annoys her, though he looks more like a trained monkey with that small, wizened face of his. She feels guilty for ordering him about so much; glued to her bedside, he compounds her suffering with remorse. "If it didn't make me appear so ungrateful, I'd tell you that I look forward to M. d'Alembert's departure with a degree of pleasure. His presence weighs on my mind; he makes me feel uncomfortable."

She confesses this to a third man, *the* man in her life, whom she will not consent to see again because a convulsion twisted her mouth at the beginning of May and she would like Guibert to remember her as beautiful. "Her features, though somewhat irregular, were attractive on the whole, despite pockmarks: a small head atop her supple neck; thick brown hair; snub nose;

---

*Julie de Lespinasse had an annual income of 12,000 livres (60,000 francs [$12,000] today) from pensions contributed by friends and from an estate secretly left to her by her natural father. She spent money freely not out of prodigality but because she found it impossible to budget herself. At her death, some forty silk and satin gowns hung in her wardrobe.

rosy lips on the full side; dark, pensive, oddly expressive eyes." Men, even the lustiest, rarely gave a thought to her figure; her sparkling mind was a rampart that only Guibert had scaled.

He is close at hand, this Guibert, just beyond her bedroom door, trotting in and out of her little white-paneled drawing room with its crimson silk draperies where Mlle de Lespinasse has helped to elect so many academicians and placed her stamp on ten years of Parisian cultural life, in the footsteps of Madame du Deffand, who cannot forgive her for it, and kindly Madame Geoffrin, who was carried in for a visit just the other day in a sedan chair, weeping real tears of grief.

Guibert winds in and out among the hassocks, the settees, the easy chairs, seats designed for the sitter to ignore his comfort and sharpen his mind; he wanders from the rosewood writing table to the small cherrywood chest of drawers and the roll-top desk displaying busts of Voltaire and D'Alembert, who thus could contemplate eternity nightly in his own image. Does Guibert ever suspect that posterity will remember him only as Julie de Lespinasse's lover? Surely not, for Jacques-Antoine-Hippolyte, the Comte de Guibert, a colonel in the royal guard when he has nothing else to do, thinks of himself as a great writer—an opinion widely shared since he published* his *Discourse on Tactics*. At last the ladies have a military manual for their bookshelves! A serious, scholarly treatise to guide French officers for the next twenty-five years. The ladies have never read it through, for what they really enjoyed was Guibert's preface [*"Discours préliminaire"*], in which he likened himself to the Friend of Man and condemned absolutism. "High society fancied itself loosing a colonel against the whole tide of literature." Guibert's friends firmly believe that posterity will set him on a pedestal beside the elder Mirabeau and Montesquieu. His celebrity worked to great advantage in courting women writers; open sensuality did the rest. A Don Juan of the salons, he had "a broad forehead framed with thick hair, a heavy-set jaw, a large mouth with fleshy lips, head set high above a muscular neck, and something adroit and deliberate about his manner." His crowning asset: "a gift for eloquence that was nothing short of prodigious," aided by "an incomparable organ," as the saying went, and it said a great deal. Madame Necker, another of his adoring women, witnessed a mass swoon in her salon one evening when he read a tragedy from his own pen, an indigestible, unstageable bore: "All by himself this young man reads a play better than the finest cast of actors, and dead or dying women are carried out at the close of his performance."

Having long craved a motive for dying, Julie de Lespinasse found it at last in Guibert on June 21, 1772, at the Moulin Joli, the country seat of farmer-general Watelet near the Bezons ferry, where they first met. Groves, meadows, rocks, and rock gardens, artificial hills which Horace Walpole lik-

---

*Anonymously in 1770 in the Lowlands; under his own name in France in 1773.

ened to "grass puddings"—a ready-made setting for romance. She held him at bay until February 10, 1774, when together they "sipped the cup of delicious poison" in a "chamber" adjoining her box at the Opera. Yet Guibert was not the man she really loved, she said; it was Mora, a handsome Spaniard dying of consumption like a respectable romantic, in Madrid, whose family intended to keep him from marrying Julie de Lespinasse or any other illegitimate daughter. She had refused to sleep with him, yet professed to adore him; all the more reason for her to take up with Guibert, an act which had killed Mora by telepathy. He died at the very hour on that memorable 10th of February, Julie insisted, sighing rapturously. To Guibert: "February 10, 1775. Midnight tolls, my dear; I have just remembered something that chills my blood . . . Good heavens, a year ago at this same hour M. de Mora suffered his fatal illness,* while I at that very moment, three hundred leagues away, acted more cruelly and remorselessly than the ignorant savages who killed him.** I am plagued with guilt . . . Good-by, my dear, I should not have loved you."

The situation had grown even more complex: Guibert, though he loved Julie and fell under her spell, was a lusty fellow unwilling to settle down with any one woman. He continued seeing his former mistress, Madame de Montsauge, and made plans to marry a ravishing young heiress of seventeen, Louise de Courcelles, on June 1, 1775. Considering all the blows Julie has dealt herself, this last probably is the decisive one. But nobody knows it. D'Alembert and her friends all believe that Mora's death is killing her when in fact it is Guibert's marriage,[4] which doesn't prevent her from writing delirious messages to Mora—care of general delivery beyond the Styx. Still, most of her letters go to Guibert during this long, crushing year of inner strife, the closing chapter of one of history's saddest, most incoherent love affairs. Day after day she would heap abuse on him, tear him to shreds, only to relapse suddenly into abject entreaties. Ten ruptures. Ten rediscoveries. "No longer do I know what I owe you; no longer do I know what I give you. I know that I brood over your absence, yet I cannot say if your presence does me good. What a dreadful situation it is when pleasure or consolation or whatever it is turns to poison. Tell me, what shall I do? Where am I to find peace of mind? How many times must we die before dying?" Guibert was not a bad chap. He braved the storm and shared her bed when she bade him, girding himself for the hail of abuse certain to follow. He never deserted her.

They were in love.

On the last day, however, he is left to himself in the drawing room. Together on that 21st of May the two bastards await death in the crimson bedchamber:

---

*A critical attack of hemoptysis. He actually died on May 27, 1775, in Bordeaux, on the way home to Madrid.

**His parents? His doctors?

Julie, daughter of Lady d'Espinasse and Gaspard de Vichy, Madame du Deffand's brother;* Jean-Baptiste Lerond, called D'Alembert,[5] newborn and still wailing when deposited in 1717 by his father, the Chevalier Destouches, on the steps of the outer baptistry of Notre Dame in Paris.** D'Alembert himself observes: "Both of us having no parents or family, having been exposed at birth to abandonment, neglect, and injustice, nature seemed to have sent us into the world in search of each other, to be one another's all . . . like two battered reeds that survive the storm by clinging fast to each other."

Have they so much as kissed? D'Alembert is there, which speaks for itself. He has always been there, since the age of seventeen when obsessive independence earned him the nickname "Liberty's Slave." But to Guibert he delivers unread the last message she scribbles painfully at four in the afternoon. A cry for help? To end her suffering? Life is crushing her: "My dear, I love you; it is the balm that numbs my pain. You alone can change it to poison, the most active and violent of all poisons. Alas, living is such grief that I am tempted to implore your pity and charity to do me this favor. It would end a painful agony that soon will weigh on your conscience. Dear one, let me owe you my repose. Out of virtue, be cruel this once. I am dying. Farewell."

The last words are barely legible. Guibert is at a loss to reply. Julie still has strength to murmur a message for D'Alembert, a plea that he "forgive her ingratitude," but he cannot understand what she means and questions her vainly; she lapses into a coma as night falls, bringing two vultures to her bedside: Abel de Vichy, a half-brother who gallops in from Mâcon province with a priest at heel just as she is slipping away, enabling him to announce the next day that he was "fortunate enough to see that she received the sacraments in the face of and despite the whole *Encyclopédie.*"[6] "The whole *Encyclopédie*" referred to grief-stricken D'Alembert, who, by writing the "preliminary discourse" to mankind's first great scientific endeavor, had raised the curtain on modern civilization. "She died in Christian piety," Vichy promptly proclaimed of a woman who had not set foot in church for twenty years. Her "Christian piety" takes the form of feeble, incoherent murmurs, a prolonged fainting spell, and one final, astonished gasp at midnight:

"Am I still alive?"

She was forty-four.

------

*Who therefore had exercised her "duty" as aunt to take Julie under her wing and sponsor her without ever publicizing the family tie.

**His mother, the Marquise de Tencin, refused to have anything to do with him. The circular baptistry, like a wart flanking the left side of Notre Dame's façade, had been built as a church called Saint-Jean-le-Rond (after which Jean d'Alembert was named) and was destroyed in 1748.

On May 23 she is laid to rest in the ground, or more precisely, in the crypt of Saint-Sulpice, with its towers newly completed, a church where there is room to spare for coffins.* A tiny cluster of men and women, unbelievers for the most part, attend the low mass and simple funeral rites. Julie wished to be interred "like the poor, without public display of the casket in the church vestibule." Guibert remains inconspicuous in the funeral procession led by D'Alembert and Condorcet. The latter seems to stoop and looks more bewildered than usual, like a forlorn sandpiper. Who will remind him now not to bite his fingernails? The Abbé Morellet tries to distract him, mentioning Turgot and reminding him of Julie's prophecy on the eve of Louis XV's death: "My dear Abbé, the worst is yet to come . . . " Tact never was a virtue of Morellet's; he doesn't realize that to his grieving neighbor the remark implies lost hopes on top of a lost friend. Condorcet keeps repeating: "We had such a beautiful dream . . . ," a refrain he will echo in the years to come. The funeral cortege at Saint-Sulpice is putting to rest Louis XVI's first twenty years along with the most intelligent and sensitive woman who graced them. Voltaire will have to modify his advice: "We must think of living," he had said, but now it is a question of surviving. Ahead of the mourners stretch another fifty years or more of Louis XVI and Marie Antoinette, who have become the personification of their disappointment. The king who recently dismissed Turgot will be seventy in 1824.

51

MAY 1776

My Name Is Mirabeau

Gabriel-Honoré de Mirabeau will burn his bridges behind him during the night of May 24, 1776, by disappearing from Dijon. He will involve himself in an adventure of unpredictable dimensions. He will accept the curse hanging over him since birth. He is twenty-seven; Sophie de Monnier is twenty-two. This is the wildest year of their romance, and the longest: a year that stretches out, like a fat picaresque novel, to fourteen months, from June 25, 1775, to August 24, 1776, a few dates from which Mirabeau himself has singled out.[1] "Month of July [1775]. Festivities for the coronation. I ought to stop

---

*Persons "of quality" often were buried in the cellars of Parisian churches, a practice not discouraged until 1808.

calling at the marquis's [de Monnier] house." It all begins with this candid, tactical retreat. "I was afraid of myself from the first flutter of emotion."[2] In any event, he would not have been able to see Sophie during the summer, as she and her husband went off to the Château de Nans, their country estate deep in the forest of Fresses, near Champagnole and roughly twenty-five miles from Pontarlier. More to the point, he has just learned that the Dowager de Marignane is dying, the rich old lady for whose fortune he had seduced Emilie. Upon her death, Emilie will receive an additional sixty thousand livres of dowry.* Enough to refloat the stranded couple, provided that Honoré can obtain his release from the fortress of Joux. He could enter the army or serve Turgot. He sends out a desperate call for help to his uncle, the Bailli de Mirabeau: "Times are getting better. Ambition is acceptable today. Do you believe the emulation which inspires me is totally sterile and that at age twenty-six plus your nephew can do no good? . . . Help me to escape the terrible ferment I am in, and perhaps to erase the effects that mental and physical suffering have had on me. Some men need to be kept busy."[3] An attempt to move his wife to pity also, for this letter will make the rounds of the whole Bignon tribe, including Mirabeau senior, the Friend of Man, from whom a single word to Malesherbes would release his son. Legally speaking, Honoré is "guilty" only of having once disobeyed a royal decree and of roughing up Villeneuve-Mouans; his debts do not count as crimes. He is answered evasively. Whereupon he agrees to humiliate himself before Emilie and pens an eight-page billet-doux to her, a last-ditch effort to patch up their tattered marriage. He asks her to join him in Franche-Comté and flee with him to Germany, where he can serve some German prince for a year or so to clear up his debts. Then they can return home with a clear conscience (to collect her inheritance, if you read between the lines). August; September. He waits a long time, too long, for the answer that will set the course of his life. From high up in his "owl's nest" he watches the distant meadows of the Jura turning green below him, tucked between mammoth forests of pine, like animal pelts topped here and there with fleecy white clouds. Once in a while, to break the monotony of his increasingly symbolic confinement, he rides down toward Salins or Arbois. There he finds inspiration for a pamphlet on salt-mining, a basic industry for the entire region: salt is the poor man's currency and essential to his survival, enabling him to preserve forage, meat, and fish and to cure animal hides. It is "white gold," the measuring standard used by the king's men in levying the extortionate *gabelle* or salt tax. The town of Salins derives its name from salt—as well as the term *"salaire"* or salary. North of Salins, along the final ten-mile stretch of the River Furieuse just before it empties into the Loue, Mirabeau comes in contact with a growing industrial community: hundreds of "wage-earning woodcutters" and ironsmiths are digging canals,

*About 300,000 francs [$60,000] today.

working pumps, stoking enormous wood fires to mine the great ignigenous*
salt bed extending from Lons-le-Saunier (Lons the Saltmaker) to Besançon.
Along the Loue it is even busier: stone-breakers, masons, and carpenters keep
pace with loggers to construct, midway between the villages of Arc and Se-
nans, the foundations of the strangest town ever to come off the drawing
boards: the utopian community designed by Claude-Nicolas Ledoux, royal
architect. Because it is cheaper to bring timber to the salt beds than raw salt
to the furnaces, forty thousand acres of pine from the forest of Chaux will be
consumed here; there is enough left to last for centuries. They will heap up
mountains of white gold among the pyramidal forges, the "grading building,"
the directors' residence on the riverside, the "four-family houses," the church
that resembles a Greek temple, the "milliner's dwelling," not to mention the
"author's dwelling," the stock market, public baths, the underground cemetery in the form of a half-buried sphere, the "sanctuary of all virtues" or
panaretheon, and the "house of pleasure" also known as the "Oikema," with
a private toilet for every prostitute in a building shaped like a horizontally
erect phallus. As work has started on this ideal community only in April,
Mirabeau gazes at an eyesore. Having no time to rhapsodize on the projected
temple and brothel, he confines himself to gathering information about salt-
mining: mini-thesis for a doctorate in industry that may land him a job in
Turgot's administration. [4]

Emilie's crushing reply from Bignon, dated October 11, must have reached
Joux about the 21st: "To begin with, Monsieur, I apologize for not having
written sooner, but I confess that the proposal contained in your last letter
upset me so that I didn't know what to say, being unable to carry it out
. . . I believe I would do you irreparable harm by consenting to accompany
you in an adventure which would make you look like a fugitive and embroil
you worse than ever with your father."[5]

"I made a mistake to look for fruit on a tree that bore only flowers,"
Mirabeau sighs.[6] But what kind of fruit did he expect? The golden apples of
the Hesperides. Emilie's letter also apprises him of the old dowager's death,
the grandmother to whom she feels "obligated for all the joys of childhood"
and from whom she now inherits a fortune, not one cent of which does she
intend to share with her spouse.

No more wife. No more money. The Marquise de Monnier has just
returned to Pontarlier. Mirabeau notes in his diary: "October 25, on her
return from the country, I go there."

---

*Salt produced by evaporation, after heating, from the interaction of salt water upon subterranean
beds of rock salt.

He goes with the greatest ease, his captivity at this stage being pure fiction.
His status has changed color with the autumn landscape. From prisoner of the
state he has graduated to the rank of impromptu notable in Pontarlier society,
whose magistrates assign him the task of chronicling the coronation festivities.
"Worthy indeed is the rush of revelry to honor the king."[7] Shrewdly, he
praises the Comte de Saint-Mauris, governor of the prison, for his civic leadership, and the Marquis de Monnier for distributing grain to the poor. Released
sur parole [on his word of honor] by the former, he will proceed to court the
latter's wife after ingratiating himself first with her husband—classic maneuver. He takes a room—on credit, being still penniless—at M. Bourrier's inn
at the far end of the main street, near the bridge spanning the Doubs. It is only
a short walk from there to the Monnier house,* where the old gentleman
eagerly awaits his entertaining visitor, a lively conversationalist who can also
read and knows how to live—a gust of fresh air through stuffy provincial
society. But the retired seventy-year-old president of the law courts goes to
bed early and leaves his guest to entertain the marquise in the drawing room.
What good fortune to have such a pleasant chap on hand to amuse his young
and rather starchy wife. Mirabeau talks to her of books, of herself, of himself.
His talk progresses to herself *and* himself, neither too soon nor too late,
around the end of October, with the confidence born of strong passions and
past experience with "hundreds of women," whereas her sole exposure to love
has been the dismal advances of an impotent old husband. She has yet to decide
whether or not she is still a virgin. A blank page, marked only by Rose-
Gabrielle de Saint-Belin, her childhood friend who partly takes the place that
one day a man will occupy: Sophie feels "compelled at times to repress her
feelings" when the two lie side by side.**[8] Closer questioning reveals also an
infantry captain stationed in Vesoul, a certain Montperreux, whose courtship
she has encouraged out of boredom. He has some letters and a portrait of her,
enough to spark a show of jealousy from Mirabeau and thus advance his cause.
"Jealousy is a disease to which I am always subject."[9] Prodded by her conscience and her sense of honor, Sophie resists him strenuously, fearing the
abyss that threatens to swallow them both. Prodded also by a maidenly instinct:
two steps forward, one step back. But she loves him already, viscerally, down
to the pockmarks on his puffy face: "I have a certain weakness for tool-
ing."[10] Falling in love is a leisurely journey for her, even if Mirabeau prefers
the short cuts. Inch by inch she surrenders. He is not used to prolonged female
resistance: "Modesty no more consists in refusing all things to a lover than
does temperance command us to die of hunger."[11] Final delaying action: a trip

*The Monnier house stood on the corner of the main street where it bisects the Rue des Trois-Sols.
Transformed and heightened, it is now the Hôtel de la Poste.
**Mirabeau to Sophie in 1777: "You yourself wrote me that you were stricken by ideas which
drove you out of the bed you shared with her."

in November to Neuchâtel, where the "prisoner" is free to roam, all expenses paid by Saint-Mauris, and to contract for the printing of his salt study and report on the coronation festivities in Pontarlier. Barely twenty-five miles away, but in Switzerland, where the illusion of freedom persists. Unknown to his jailer, he takes with him a third manuscript, his *Essay on Despotism.*. Neuchâtel, on the shore of its great lake that steams in the chilly morning mists, is an enclave of Prussian discipline among the cantons, where Frederick the Great gives certain printing houses leave to publish subversive literature, which occasionally proves useful against his relatives. The pamphlet's title as well as the author's name and nerve induce Fauche the bookseller to pay fifteen hundred livres* for the right to print (anonymously, of course) the *Essay on Despotism* . . . the first money young Mirabeau has ever earned.

On his return to Pontarlier in early December, more confident and swaggering than ever, he wastes no time. On the 13th he and Sophie meet secretly, out of habit by now, for a "chat" in the parlor of one Mlle Barbaud (locally known as "the Trollop"), who lives opposite the Monniers. And when the Trollop receives callers, she hustles the amorous pair into her bedroom. They go there willingly. "December 13: I was happy."

"The Marquise de Monnier then made a slip, or you might say that nature made it for her by suddenly imprinting on her rather stern features the signs of contentment. Ladies of Pontarlier at once assumed that Sophie had a lover."[12] The ladies perhaps; the marquis not yet; the swarm of Sophie's other admiring swains for certain. Chief among these, the engaging Marquis de Saint-Mauris regards himself as having been doubly tricked: by Sophie, whom he still hoped to catch, and by Mirabeau, his prisoner "on parole," who certainly had wasted no time. But how was he going to raise a row? A Pontarlier shopkeeper furnished the excuse by turning up at the fortress with an IOU from Mirabeau made out to Fauche the bookseller, a subversive publisher, having nothing at all to do with pamphlets Mirabeau had been authorized to print. It must be a joke—or else an act of rebellion. Saint-Mauris is frantic: his career is doomed if the court should ever think that he aided, wittingly or unwittingly, the printing of this *Essay on Despotism,* where it is said that the "king is a paid worker, and whoever pays has the right to fire the paid. Other Frenchmen may have thought this before me, but I am probably the first who dared to print it . . . Long-established rulership has corrupted the prince, long-established submission has corrupted the people."[13] The prison's governor summons Mirabeau to Joux for a dressing down. No more escapades: from now on the prisoner stays put. Instinctively, Mirabeau pounces on an excuse to avoid separation from Sophie. In four days he is expected to attend a great ball at the Monnier house; not to appear would cause a scandal. Let him

*A little over 6000 francs [$1200].

have this last dance. Saint-Mauris grudgingly relents and will regret it: "On January 14, 1776, I hide at Sophie's house to avoid returning to the fortress."

Mirabeau's conduct as a young man is consistent: driven to commit senseless follies that only fulfill everyone's worst predictions, he tries desperately to avoid them and finally succumbs. For twenty years his father has declared that he sired a rebel; now it is finally true: Honoré has sinned against the king's "hospitality." Guilty of "willful and perverse high treason," he becomes an outlaw. The escape that took him from Manosque to Grasse is no more than a prank by comparison.

The reality of his situation does not dawn on him immediately. He is too busy keeping safe and having fun, playing detective and thief at the same time. How easy it is to baffle those thick-witted Francs-Comtois with the help, for once, of a loving woman. He spends two days in a tiny, windowless closet two feet square adjoining Sophie's bedroom. Only a parlormaid knows the secret. But the valet Sage, the coachman Pellerin, and other maidservants soon spot the soiled linen and vanishing food. "On the 16th I went to the Trollop's house," where they arrange to hide him in the cellar in a large washtub in case the house should be searched. Friends in Cluse and Jeanneton Michaud, who bears him no grudge, offer sanctuary: a court bailiff, a carpenter, a laboring man. Mirabeau's adventure becomes an open secret in Pontarlier. To save face, Saint-Mauris reports that his prisoner has fled to Switzerland and he does not press a local search. Sophie comes to Honoré nearly every day, wherever he happens to be hiding, and the two spend hours together. Soon he urges her to stay overnight, and one evening, wrapped in a scarlet cape with silver trim, he appears before old Monnier.

"I come from Berne on my way to Paris to see the minister and arrange things. Let me stay over till daybreak and be sure your servants keep silent . . ."

"Why, of course!"

The magnificent cuckold even provides him with money.[14] This farce continues through mid-February.

Mirabeau know that it cannot last. He never plays out a role; there is an element of calculated risk in everything he does. In hiding, he writes to Saint-Germain, minister of war, asking to enlist: "I belong to the king as a subject, as a gentleman and an officer. I am French; my name is Mirabeau, and I am a captain of dragoons . . ." He appeals to his mother, now settled in rooms at the convent of the Trinity in the Faubourg Saint-Antoine district of Paris, from which address she proceeds to harass her husband through legal channels. "Your own distress overshadows mine, mother dear . . . Never doubt that your son is honorable and deserves your compassion."[15] Above everyone, he turns to Louise, his sister and accomplice, and has Sophie write to her also, asking for money and someone to help the two of them escape—Captain Briançon, for instance.

But Louise has her hands full at Cabris and is soon to leave her husband, who has gone mad. Endless bickering. She toys with the notion of joining her mother and bringing the Friend of Man to his knees. The Mirabeau clan, like the ill-fated House of Atreus, seems torn by endless strife. Louise reacts ambivalently to the news of her brother: like a rational woman and a possessive sister. She is solicitous, cautious, and jealous. January 11, 1776: "I am more upset, more overwhelmed than you. I feel your pain more than you do, I foresee perils that have not yet befallen you. My worries began when you left me . . . I sense that you could make excuses and plead innocent to me. I also sense that you have done yourself irreparable harm . . . Your mistress's letter is matter-of-fact and prudent; it would have reassured me but for the knowledge that the aftermath of ecstasy is often serene. Only in retrospect do we recognize the follies of passion." Six bittersweet pages culminating in: ". . . perhaps you would do better to slip over into the Savoy states and come to me via Nice . . . My honorable friend [Briançon] will rush to your side if I can find the money to give him."[16]

Briançon will not have to travel all the way to Pontarlier; Mirabeau's tightrope walk is about to end. "M. de Saint-Mauris put all his spies to work . . . He was out for vengeance against my mistress and myself. He sent messengers to the husband: a priest, the most devout of his breed, rushed to M. de Monnier and informed him point-blank of everything he had thus far ignored."[17] The old man is forced to hear the very thing he dreaded. Sophie merely cites the fifty-year gulf between them and announces that she is returning to her mother in Dijon. Mirabeau vanishes again: Rose de Saint-Belin has arranged for him to follow Sophie like a shadow. "Ash Wednesday, February 21, I leave for Vitteaux. Friday 23, Sophie leaves for Dijon."

A large town, closer to Paris—perhaps the dawn of freedom? In fact they are rowing from Scylla to Charybdis.

Because Sophie returns home and the Ruffeys turn out to be the very model of a tyrannical family. An irritable father (magistrate, naturally); a mother who is "tall, dried up, wrinkled, her hands full of prayer and her bosom brimming with satire";* a canoness for a sister, a real harridan, forever hounding Sophie with visions of hell, and two churlish brothers who spend their time either taking her to task or pelting her with vulgar innuendos. Only one thing counts to these people: money. That was the reason they sold Sophie to old Monnier, after ruling out Buffon. They are clannish, too; they stick together. "Mirabeau produces a marvelously comic effect by introducing them always en masse: my father, my mother, my sisters, my brothers."[18] Informed of the situation by Monnier, they erect a human prison around Sophie. To prevent her from

*The description is Mirabeau's.

loving seems to be their main obsession, but they are up against an irrepressible force. Mirabeau comes to Dijon and rents a furnished room in a shabby street named for one of the city's tollgates, the Rue Portelle. He arranges to cross paths with Sophie, whose family drags her, like a convict, to social affairs.* Nowhere can he slip by unnoticed. He is going to be caught. Flight that sends him charging ahead. And one evening the game is up, at a ball given by the grand provost of Burgundy, who commands the local militia, when Mirabeau is announced under a Rabelaisian pseudonym, "the Marquis de Lancefoudras." Madame de Ruffey recognizes him sight unseen and has him arrested. It may have been just what he wanted and provoked. To make the ministers face their responsibilities. To prove his undying love to Sophie—and perhaps to get rid of her before it was too late, thinking she would have no grounds for complaint if they were forced to separate. "I cannot understand why you would make me into the one man in all the world who is not a mixture of good and bad," he writes very shortly to his father.[20]

If guesswork, it was good: that arrest brings Mirabeau very near to deliverance. The grand provost, M. de Montherot, has his heart in the right place and an open mind. He detests the bigoted Ruffeys. He simply stations a guard in the young man's lodging, allows him to come and go freely, and transmits his petitions to the proper authorities, Saint-Germain and Malesherbes, describing to them a repentant, chastened Mirabeau. Panic in the Ruffey household: the canoness moves into Sophie's bed and every night ties her sister's ankle to her own with a ribbon. But once she gets sick: "Thursday, March 14, I spend the night *à la perspective* with Sophie," referring to a long passageway in the ramparts near the Vauxhall or festival hall where townspeople come to dance and walk about. Sophie and Mirabeau make passionate love, promiscuously, clandestinely, against all the rules of their class and background. For the first time she enjoys it: "that encounter greatly increased my love."[21] Her childlike abandon captivates and moves him: "The possession of my mistress delights and transports me. I am the most voluptuous and ardent of men, but I do not corrupt. Erotic pleasure is not corruption. Yet pious women, who attain piety only after they cease to be whores, do not know this."[22]

That night of bliss turns out to be their last folly in Dijon. They must try to outwit Sophie's pious jailers. Malesherbes's response to the grand provost is mildly encouraging, but insists, for the sake of formality, on Mirabeau's return to prison pending deliberation of his fate. "Orders to put me in the fortress of Dijon arrive on Thursday [March] 21; Sophie leaves for Pontarlier on Saturday 23 . . . ," flanked by the ineffable canoness. Back under her husband's roof, she will be confined more closely than her lover in Dijon, but she accepts that sacrifice: all gossip about them must cease if Honoré is to win

*Sophie to Mirabeau, August 16, 1776: "Do you recall how upset you were when we saw each other at the Comédie in Dijon for the first time? How I trembled as I approached you?"[19]

his freedom. They swear to rejoin each other later; she relies on this. Does he? If all goes well, he might be in uniform before summer.

Nothing happens for two months. Mirabeau is invited to take his meals with the fortress commander, M. de Changey, and is generally treated as "a royal guest," free to wander off into town. Each day he looks for a letter from Malesherbes and the chance to go to Paris and clear his name. He is not aware of Turgot's precarious position or the fact that Malesherbes has resigned on March 19 and is conducting business with a limp hand. Yet this is a matter the minister would like to settle before leaving office. He is all the more inclined to pardon the overgrown, persecuted truant after Madame de Mirabeau intervenes energetically in her son's behalf: "His father, who has treated him just as severely as he has treated me unjustly, has forced him for the past ten years to expiate faults that warranted more indulgence than they received, as they involved merely the squandering of money so common to children of his age and background."[23] But Malesherbes cannot openly defy the head of the house, the Friend of Man he has known for so many years and whose temper, especially when family affairs are concerned, is enough to frighten anyone. Now the Marquis de Mirabeau distrusts him and bombards him with threatening messages, copies of which go to the king via the Duc de Nivernais. "The minister to whom I have the honor of addressing this memorandum [in early April 1776] is charged with having ruled, in most matters involving fathers and sons, against the fathers." Nothing was surer to irritate Louis XVI, who worshiped his father, and to turn him against Malesherbes, whose career is nearly ended, and against young Mirabeau. The rest of the memorandum tears his son to shreds: a twelve-page infanticide. If they release the young wastrel, "what will become of him? He will join the ranks of lunatics and rabble-rousers bent on borrowing, plundering, stealing . . . He is twenty-seven years old and has been in prison since the age of eighteen, and when he was free he did more harm, and to more persons, than anyone could imagine. In prison or in exile, no peace, no submission, not a moment's rest for him or for others . . . His contempt for royal decrees is manifest, for he was at liberty the two times he escaped.* If he is to be free once more, I wash my hands of him before God and men, and I hold the minister responsible for whatever offenses result."[24] That was the kind of respect Malesherbes inspired in the spring of 1776. He swallowed it without a murmur three weeks before his retirement. Still the fate of the young prisoner haunts him, for it symbolizes abuses that cry for reform. He calls in the elder Mirabeau, but manages only to incite his wrath: "That Malesherbes, with his philanthropic drivel and his fine republican sentiments, has the gall to tell me that it was natural to want to escape."[25] He files an official demand that his son be imprisoned in still another fortress, at Pierre-en-Scize near Lyons, "and be forbidden any communication with the outside, either verbal or written." He requests Lyons because it is far from

*From Manosque in 1774; from Pontarlier in 1776.

Paris and therefore from his wife, the mother of this "criminal." Honoré
accepts the plan, thinking it will bring him closer to his sister, and asks merely
to travel there via Paris. Still hoping for clemency . . .

Last and fatal episode: Louise de Cabris deserts her husband on April 1 and
travels from Grasse to Lyons, where she settles down as a "lay boarder" in the
distinguished convent of La Déserte. Perhaps she expects Mirabeau and even
Sophie. On hearing of this, the Friend of Man promptly changes his mind and
wishes to send his son anywhere but to Pierre-en-Scize. On April 8 he dispatches a second memorandum to Malesherbes canceling the first one: "His
sister suddenly informs me that she is taking rooms in a Lyons convent . . .
Her head is even cooler and more conniving than her brother's . . . If they
should get together, all hell would break loose."[26] Malesherbes consents to
issue another *lettre de cachet* consigning Mirabeau to the fortress of Doullens
in Picardy, where he will be kept "under observation" for six months, closely
confined. He is ordered to go there directly, not via Paris. And on May 12
Malesherbes quits the government, the same day as Turgot. Just beforehand,
had he perhaps gotten word to Mirabeau to flee the country rather than submit
to his latest sentence? Mirabeau states that he did, but offers no evidence,
whereas Malesherbes was not wont to give such advice.

  One piece of bad news after the other reaches Honoré: he is trading the
snowbound Jura for the mists of Picardy; no one in Paris will listen to him,
for every minister who ever supported him has been forced out. "Malesherbes's resignation was a shock to me." Pleading a "pain in the chest," he
takes to his bed for several days to plan his escape, there being no other
recourse. The grand provost and the fortress commander, who have tried to
help him for two months, share his disillusion and will shut their eyes. The
Dijon prison lodges other sons of the nobility, all more or less "outlawed" like
Mirabeau, meaning that they have refused the station in life assigned to them
by their families. Young men said to have "turned out badly" because a father
or mother rejected them: the Marquis de Saint-Huruge* and the Chevalier de
Mâcon, among others. The latter, once a member of the royal guard, joins
forces with Mirabeau, whose flight takes place without much difficulty "on the
night of Friday [May] 24 with the Chevalier de Mâcon."[27]

Gabriel-Honoré de Mirabeau makes his first conscious break with those who
have prevented him from living ever since he came into the world afflicted
with an oversize head. This escape is real, from everything and everyone
except Sophie—and his sister Louise.

  He starts for Pontarlier.

---

*Who becomes one of the "aristocratic rabble-rousers" in the Revolution's simmering stage. We
will hear more of him, chiefly during the summer of 1789.

52

JUNE 1776

A Horse Broken to the Bit

On June 11, 1776, by decree of the ruling duke, Johann Wolfgang Goethe is appointed privy councillor to the court of Weimar, making him an unofficial minister* in this micro-Germany at the geographic center of the German states. He takes office and settles in. Two months short of twenty-seven years old. The peak of his career in terms of material success. "You would say that the strings on which my destiny hangs, and which have tossed me back and forth like a pendulum for so long, are about to knot."[1] Still, he has just broken his engagement to Lili Schönemann, cannot exist without Charlotte von Stein, and pens passionate letters to Augusta von Stolberg, on whom he has never laid eyes. In this respect the swinging motion from woman to freedom continues: "Not long ago I thought I had reached home port and was planting roots in real terrestrial joys and sorrows, but once again I find myself plunging out to sea . . . Thus do I watch my life dancing on the element called *fatum congenitum*: the destiny that rocked my cradle."[2] Is he dancing or flying, this strapping young man with "Apollonian" features, this engaging, somewhat dandified fellow whose excesses rock the tiny capital like a tempest in a closet? Perhaps, in the fashion of 1776, he is sledding: "Like a sled on the ice, my life swerves back and forth at breakneck speed, setting the bells a-jingle . . . From dawn to dusk I am swept along by an assortment of entertainments organized on a grand scale, but all goes well for me despite the inexplicable sensation this is causing here."[3]

Birth of a third Goethe on June 11. There were already two others: the irrepressible bear and the popular young writer. *Werther* had appeared two years earlier,** making Wolfgang the undisputed arbiter, at once tame and untamed, of reckless passion; author of a best-seller, probably history's first. Young men dress *"à la Werther"* in a blue dress coat over a yellow waistcoat; an epidemic of suicides *"à la Werther"* breaks out, the main features of which

*He attains ministerial rank officially in 1815, but performs all the duties thereof onward of 1776.
**In Leipzig. Numerous translations are in preparation throughout Europe. A French one, among the last to appear, comes out in 1778.

call for blowing out one's brains before an open window bathed in moonlight with the book conspicuously in view turned to the penultimate page: "The clock strikes twelve. So be it. Charlotte! Charlotte! Farewell! Farewell!

"A neighbor saw the flash and heard the shot; but, as everything remained silent, he paid no further attention to it."[4]

Delighted yet infuriated by his sudden celebrity, Goethe grumbled privately and submitted. "When a writer attracts wide attention with a work of genuine merit, the public does all it can to prevent him from writing a second one . . . Success is obtained, but independence lost; a budding talent is dragged reluctantly through the social whirl because people fancy they can pluck and plunder a particle of his personality."[5] He has already begun *Faust* and is pondering a *Prometheus,* a *Ganymede*, a *Satyros.* He feels and knows himself to be the bearer of a poetic universe embracing the whole of human destiny. Will this slender novel keep him from becoming a Homer or Dante? Will mankind ever hear the ode that "ferments in his heart,"*Alles geben die Götter?*

> All . . .
> The infinite gods give all to those they love:
> All joys, infinite;
> All sorrows, infinite;
> All![6]

Now this high dignitary, His Excellency Johann Wolfgang Goethe, member of the supreme council, takes an oath to uphold the institutions of a state about which he knows next to nothing, and appears at the first council with a sword at his side and silver buckles on his shoes, dressed in black as the court is in mourning for the Grand Duchess of Russia.* He is watched for eagerly, peered at, envied, mocked. How will he handle his high office? He is the duke's "favorite" and spent all last night in his company. "In this tiny Weimar no one can take a step unnoticed. Will he dive headlong into his work, will he attend all the debates?"[7] Is he affecting resignation like Werther in the face of passion: "I shall improve my ways. I no longer wish to go on savoring down to the last bitter dregs whatever destiny assigns. I shall enjoy the present and let the past remain the past"?[8]

He is, and has been for some time, his own best audience, lucid, skeptical, perplexed by his own performance: "If you can imagine, my dearest, a Goethe beribboned from head to toe, illumined from all sides by garish candlelight and torches, bound to the gaming table by a pair of lovely eyes . . . you have the current picture of Goethe the reveler, who lately mumbled some confused and profound words in your ear . . .

"But there is another Goethe, dressed in gray beaver, a brown silk

*Louise of Weimar, daughter of the Landgrave of Hesse-Darmstadt, was the first wife of the czarevich, who took the throne as Paul I.

foulard, and boots, who feels a touch of spring in the tingling February air*
and watches his vast, beloved universe opening up once more beneath his eyes;
who, always self-sufficient, struggles and works, trying as best he can to convey
his youthful candor in these short poems and the glow of life in his plays
. . . who asks no one's approval of what he has done because the act of
working always carries him one step higher, because he does not aspire to
attain perfection in a single bound but would rather let his feelings, through
their interplay, transform themselves into faculties."[9]

Out of which at times rises an explosion of anguished laughter: "Oh, my
brother,** I am racked by sentiments that may have a name but no limits
. . . Oh, Fritz, this pitiful collapse into the dust! These wormlike contortions!
I swear to you, it is infantile babbling, an absurd gnashing of teeth, *Werther*
and all that goes with it, in response to my intimate revelations about myself."[10]

These sober, unemotional Germans all stare at him in dismay. The Swiss
philosopher Lavater offers a diagnosis: "He is all energy, sensibility, imagination. He acts not knowing why or how. He seems swept along by a
flood."[11]

Whence this flood? Where is the sled taking him?

Goethe has "performed" all over Germany, sowing his oats early and wildly,
at the cost of a "weak chest." He was born in the west, at Frankfurt-on-Main,
grandson of a burgomaster on his mother's side, an innkeeper on his father's,
but he traveled east to study at Leipzig. His faith in God was shaken at the age
of seven because of the Lisbon earthquake ("How can a kind and loving deity
condone such disasters?") and his sensibilities bore the impact of war since
1759, when the Maréchal de Broglie's army occupied Frankfurt during the
Seven Years' War.[12] He had rejected instantly the stifling climate of Saxon
universities, where obedience was the chief topic taught in classrooms strung
with princely portraits and genealogical trees of the reigning dynasties. "Students were divided strictly according to social class. The nobly born alone had
the right to occupy the upper tiers on both sides of the lecture amphitheater.
Down below stood the ordinary students, without so much as a bench to sit
on, unless they had the cash to rent chairs."[13] His indignation still simmers
in *Werther* and adds a distinct social dimension to this love story whose hero
"nurses in his heart a fondness for freedom,"[14] professes that "every regula-
tion, whatever you may say, will extinguish a true feeling for nature and the
expression of it,"[15] and rails against "moral men" who are "marvels of inscru-
tability. You curse drunkards. You turn from lunatics . . . I myself have been
drunk more than once; my passions never have been very far removed from
madness, and yet I feel no remorse."[16] Along with his unrequited love,

*Letter to Augusta von Stolberg, February 13, 1775.
**To Frederick von Stolberg, Augusta's brother, October 26, 1775.

Werther comes to know the despair of a peasant shackled to his miserable existence whom he tries to rescue from the gallows for a crime of passion. Once Werther realizes that human justice inevitably crushes such poor creatures, he begins to toy with the notion of suicide. "He went away grief-stricken after the bailiff had repeated over and over, 'No, nothing can save him! . . .'

" 'Poor man, there's nothing to save you now. I see it plainly, WE shall not be saved.' "[17]

From Leipzig back to Frankfurt, then on to Strasbourg, where he had received his law degree by tripping blindfolded through an exam that tested little more than the ability to spout a few pompous aphorisms. Advocate Wolfgang Goethe promptly decided to live for something other than study: for songs perhaps, and women. A Margaret at age fifteen; an Annette at sixteen; a Friederica at eighteen. A host of others by the age of twenty-two, when he arrived as a probationary lawyer at the imperial court of Wetzlar and found Charlotte in the neighboring township.

Contrast. At Wetzlar, the magnificent corruption of the Reichs-Kammergericht, the court which litigated disputes involving any of the three-hundred-odd states in the empire, established in a busy farming town with narrow, dung-littered lanes. Corrupt judges. Thousands of issues under deliberation that will drag on unresolved for years. Complaints set forth in grotesquely comic fashion, such as the curate's suit against the elector of Württemberg: "Your most serene sows have deigned to devour my humble potatoes."[18] Symbols of the targets of his youthful outrage. The encounter on June 9, 1772, with a vision he had dreamed of always: two unforgettably blue eyes rested on him at a country ball in Volpertshausen. He waltzed away the night in the arms of Charlotte Buff, burning with desire for this blonde and robust, yet somehow vulnerable miss, not yet twenty, who finally, at daybreak, confessed her engagement to another man, though she was visibly smitten by Wolfgang. A nice enough fellow, that fiancé planted there by fate, whom neither Goethe nor Werther really disliked. Albert in the book; Kestner in real life: a human-size obstacle impossible to ignore. He had done Goethe a favor by rejecting him, casting him into melancholy gloom during the famous "moonlight scene" that actually took place on August 28, 1772. Wolfgang played the part of Werther that night. Charlotte assumed that their parting was temporary; he decided it must be final. " 'We shall see each other tomorrow, I suppose?' she said, smiling. How I felt that tomorrow. Oh, she was unsuspecting when she drew her hand away . . . I looked after them . . . and could still glimpse her white gown shimmering in the shadow of the tall lindens near the garden gate. I stretched out my arms, and it vanished. *End of Book One.*"[19]

The bullet that Werther fires into his own brain at the close of Book Two may have saved Goethe's life. "Oh, if you could only express what you feel, if you could breathe onto paper the warm, full life flowing within you, so that the paper becomes the mirror of your soul . . ."[20] He will survive even if some of his readers decide not to. He will travel to shake off his melancholy. He will become acquainted with German men of letters not as a disciple but as a peer, *Werther*'s creator, all except the great Herder, whom he had met previously in Strasbourg and who, "like a cranky, nagging midwife, [had] brought into this world the true Goethe" by converting him to the elastic and vaguely pantheistic deism of Spinoza.[21] Inspired by Beaumarchais's Spanish adventure in the latter's anti-Goëzman pamphlets, Goethe writes *Clavijo,* a dramatic failure. An elaborate fake. Beaumarchais's dazzling wit naturally appealed to Goethe, those barbed innuendos that shredded convention. On his return to Frankfurt he becomes engaged to Lili Schönemann, another blonde. "She was really the first woman I loved purely and profoundly [poor Charlotte!]. I might also say she was the last."[22] What he means is that never had he come so close to attaining normal happiness—which causes him to panic and flee, without any excuse this time, driven by an uncontrollable yearning for freedom. "Ransom for a false situation. One silences doubt. One emphasizes only what is favorable. One hardens outwardly and melts inwardly, yet passion never wanes. My servitude was total."[23] He left for Switzerland with the Von Stolbergs in May 1775, without a word to Lili. "It is to test my heart . . ." In fact it was to shake off his yoke. The theme of freedom began to transcend the theme of love. *Egmont** overcomes *Werther.* Even Frankfurt, his birthplace, had grown intolerable: "a nest just big enough to shelter birds and, at the same time, figuratively, a *spelunca,*** an odious hole. God help me out of this misery. Amen!"[24] The cavern was the shell he finally fought his way out of like a shaggy eaglet reaching for the aerie of his maturity: Weimar.

Providence assumed the image of Charles Augustus of Weimar, far too young at eighteen to rule over the "provinces of Weimar" though they comprised a mere forty thousand subjects distributed throughout Eisenach, Jena, and Ilmenau.† Also married, at eighteen, to Louise of Darmstadt, a highly cultivated but frigid and unappetizing bride. Gay young blade tethered to bookish prude. Charles Augustus traveled about Germany hunting for men of letters to govern his state. And in doing so he had to compete with three

---

*Lamoral, Count of Egmont, related to the dukes of Guelder, served Philip II of Spain in the Low Countries, but was suspected by the Duke of Alba of fomenting rebellion against Spanish rule. His beheading in 1568 made him a symbol of liberty and plunged the Netherlands into open revolt. Goethe wrote the first version of *Egmont* in 1775.

**"Cavern" or "cave" in Latin.

†An area thirty-two by sixteen kilometers, smaller than present-day Luxembourg.

hundred other princes also in search of competent administrators to challenge
the tyranny of pedants. This is all to the benefit of German writers, who are
forced to work or starve. Not even the most famous of them can live off his
pen. Klopstock draws a pension from Denmark; Lessing is a librarian, Wieland
a tutor, Herder a Protestant pastor and councillor in the Consistory. Goethe
will occupy the post of unofficial "favorite" at the court of Weimar, then
become chief minister of state. Confusion and indecision have prompted him
to play hard-to-get with this prince, who woos him persistently. It is almost a
love story, beginning with the honeymoon, a passion on the part of the young
duke for his new friend, a combined mentor and companion ten years his
senior, not one to raise an eyebrow when the two of them go boozing together
and piss on the front doors of respectable townsfolk, when they spend nights
together in the same room—far from the duchess—talking of women and
God.

It is Werther's revenge. Charlotte von Stein's mother, also named Charlotte, writes that "Goethe has disrupted everything here . . . Our peace of
mind has vanished. Our court is not what it used to be . . . A master discontented with himself and the world, who ruins his health daily when he has so
little health to spare . . . A vexed mother,* an unhappy wife. Good people,
all of them, and nothing runs smoothly in this dreary family." Goethe is
working on *Faust* and acting the part of Mephisto. Drink up, my lad, drink to
their health! He has always been drawn to young men, on whom he exerts a
spell verging on homosexuality, but short of it, as he is too fond of women.
"At Weimar, things are dreadful.²⁵ The duke goes about town with Goethe
like an unruly schoolboy. He gets drunk and both share the favors of any girl
who comes along. A minister daring enough to warn the duke "against such
licentious behavior as being detrimental to good health was informed that he
did it deliberately to build up his strength."

At first Charlotte von Stein rejects this provoking side of Goethe: "The
way he acts, he cannot go through life unscathed . . . Why does he indulge
in these incessant pranks? . . . And why the oaths, why all those vulgar, trivial
expressions? . . . The duke has reached the point where he cannot bear
the company of anyone who lacks a trace of vulgarity. All this is Goethe's
doing."²⁶

Even the majestic Klopstock complains from Hamburg, where he combines a bit of preaching with poetry, and would not be averse to censoring
German morality as well, having lived in a cloud of incense since publication
of his epic *Messias,* a Christian *Iliad* that everyone talks about and no one has
read.** He lectures Goethe: "If the duke continues to drink . . . it will affect
his health and shorten his life . . . Goethe, would you cause the Duchess

---

*The "Dowager Duchess" of Saxe-Weimar, Charles Augustus's mother, is thirty-six.
**"Who would not praise Klopstock? Yet no one reads him. We prefer to receive less praise than
he and to be read," Lessing commented.²⁷

Louise to suffer?" How will a man react who, four years earlier, had linked Charlotte's confession of love with the Great Man's name? "She laid her hand on mine and said, 'Klopstock!' I recalled instantly the sublime ode she had in mind . . . Divine Klopstock!"[28] Well, there's been a lot of water under the bridge since then. Goethe dismisses the Divinity with a curt: "Spare yourself such letters in the future . . . " The Master chokes with rage: "I declare you unworthy to receive that letter of mine." Parting of the ways. "I despise Goethe!"

Goethe cares very little. He has made his choice. The salary he will draw, twelve hundred thalers a month,* is the highest at court after the prime minister's. "Sometimes I have wanted to be a wage-earner so that, upon waking each morning, I might have a perspective on the day ahead, a motive for acting, a hope." He becomes a wage-earner of sorts, a privileged one. "Sometimes I feel the urge to devote myself to some occupation. But after further reflection, and when I recall the fable of the horse which tired of its freedom and allowed itself to be saddled and bridled, and was eventually worked to death, then I am not so certain . . . "[29] That was Werther speaking. No more such talk now. But Goethe finds a whole new vocabulary to plead his cause before Augusta von Stolberg, who is indeed posterity's ideal tribunal and vanguard, a woman not to be touched, or seen, or deceived, a woman to whom one only wrote letters: "When once more I begin to feel that amid this void so many feelings slip from my heart like dead skin peeling away . . . that my view of the world becomes more serene, my relations with others more secure, more solid, more fruitful; that my secret self remains consecrated to that single sacred element which is love, and that gradually that love expels all foreign bodies through its own cleansing essence and eventually renders my soul as pure as beaten gold—when once again I feel all those things, I can relax.

"Perhaps I deceive myself."[30]

---

*About 15,000 francs [$3000], an enormous sum.

53

JUNE 1776

The Outlook of an Independent Spirit

Alfieri also turns twenty-seven in 1776, when this Italian "is converted to the Italian tongue" and experiences a passion fierce enough to drag him back from the brink of ruin following *childhood* ("including nine years of vegetation"),* *adolescence* ("eight years of pointless education"), and *youth* ("about ten years of travel and dissipation"). Like Goethe, he has reached *manhood*: "over thirty years of compositions, translations, and original studies."[1] The great Italian poet of freedom matures as late as the German poet. In those days men aged twice as slowly as women.

Eight years earlier, during the summer of 1768, he almost became a second Werther with a vengeance—that's to say, he lived and nearly died for love in The Hague, on one of the dreary journeys he was in the habit of making all over Europe, angry, scowling, blind to everything in sight, a driven man. He had "fallen under the spell of a young bride of just a year, beautiful, sweet, innocent, shy, and endowed with great natural charm." "What struck me as very odd at the time, and I have since come to understand, is that the urge to study and a certain effervescent creativity gripped me only when I was deeply in love." But the idol's husband liked to move about: in contrast to Batavia,** his birthplace, he found the Dutch scene stifling and resolved to take his wife traveling, a decision she made no effort to protest. Brokenhearted, Alfieri tried to commit suicide in the only honest fashion: secretly. He had himself bled, then tore off the bandages. His alert servant found him in time.

All of which is past history today. He feels rather embarrassed about it now, in this eventful year of 1776, when at last he is his own master, solid and secure in the saddle as if astride the horses that were his first childhood passion. He feels destined to become a writer, a wordsmith, but in a new style, one who will communicate, who will commune with his readers in their own

---

*This label and the parenthetic remarks are Alfieri's, taken from his *Memoirs*, which he began in 1790 at the age of forty-one and kept until 1803.
**Now Djakarta, Indonesia. [*Trans.*]

idiom, the Italian dialect of Siena, cradle of the purest Italian that exists. For the past year Count Vittorio Alfieri has been hard at work in northwestern Italy, mainly Tuscany and Piedmont, building a vocabulary of popular language. In Turin, on June 16, 1775, he staged *Cleopatra,* his first tragedy, for an audience of friends. He spent the autumn and winter in the Alps relearning Italian, which heretofore, like all self-respecting aristocrats, he had abused and misused as a vehicle fit only for communicating with servants. He rejects French and takes up Latin purely to absorb the roots of the Tuscan dialect. In Pisa, where he spent the spring, he began work on his *Orestes.* In mid-June 1776, after settling down in Florence to do research in its archives, he meets the Countess of Albany. A bolt from the blue, still secret. In three weeks he produces another tragedy, *Philip the Second.* But his real desire is to spend several months of the coming year in Siena and create an Italian drama on an Italian theme: the Pazzi rebellion against the Medici. No more classical subjects—send the Romans and Greeks back to the museum! He wants to write about the here and now in modern idiom. He will "people his tragedies with characters like himself, with tyrants and their slayers, with supermen and rebels, united by one driving impulse: anxiety. He will create a theater so unconventional as to be provocative, which will negate any concept of the stage as entertainment."[2]

Not easy to get on with, this tall, skinny Piedmontese beanpole "with a mop of nasty red hair" who, as a child, resembled "a glowing candle stub," and who carries inside him "the horrid sadness that nature gave me at birth"—he says. Actually, it developed out of the fact that he grew up like some wild, untended plant in a luxurious greenhouse, a peculiar blend of affluence and neglect. His father died when Alfieri was very young; his mother was not unkind, she simply remarried. He grew up in want of nothing except attention, looked after by priests and servants. The deep scar on his left temple dates from a fall onto a pair of andirons. He is not one to make friends easily: "My surly nature kept me from reaching out, and since this was stamped on my face, no one sought my company." "This unsociability resulted from an inflexible temperament undisciplined by education, and from a nearly invincible aversion to the sight of new faces." His manner is stern—meaning stiff—even where pleasure is involved. "I create order, even out of disorder. Whenever I have done something wrong, almost always I have done it deliberately." But look out for sudden gusts that churn up the stillness of that seemingly placid lake. He nearly killed his favorite servant, Elie, the one who saved him from suicide, by hitting the valet across the face with a candlestick for having yanked his hair while curling it. "That good fellow, whose magnanimity matched my own[!], sought no revenge other than keeping the two blood-soaked handkerchiefs used to mop his wound and for several years afterward showing them to me from time to time. One needs firsthand knowledge of the Piedmontese temperament to understand this blend of savagery and generosity on both sides."

The temperament of Pied-des-monts (Foot-of-the-mountains), collar of the Italian boot tucked up against the Alps, the Piedmont of the dukes of Savoy, who call themselves kings of Sardinia because for fifty years, through a proliferation of treaties, they have ruled that vale of misery as absentee lords. Alfieri is a native of Asti, "a town that has fallen markedly from its former splendor," according to the Marquis de Sade, a recent visitor who apparently was not moved to linger over its ocher and pink housefronts: "One sees the abandoned ruins of several fortresses. In July 1775, when I passed through, the King of Sardinia had no garrison there."³ Alfieri's only memories are of "the first stirrings of his amatory faculties" in the Carmelite church next door to his home, which he attended daily—not out of piety but to contemplate at leisure "the faces of young Carmelite novices, boys ranging from fourteen to sixteen in their white rochets, who attended various liturgical rites of the church," which Sade finds "so tastefully painted and adorned that one could mistake it for an opera set instead of a house of worship."⁴ Those boyish faces, "not unlike female ones, had left on my tender and innocent [Alfieri, not Sade, is speaking!] heart the same impression and the same desire to look on them as had the face of my sister"—his only sister, sent off to a convent at the age of nine, whose absence left him broken-hearted.

At ten, he discovered Turin, a sprawling new city with streets laid out at right angles, for Sardinia's princelings, bent on aping Louis XIV a century after his death, resolved to have their own Versailles and Paris. He entered the academy as a boarder: "a stately, rectangular edifice built round a vast inner court. Two wings of the building were occupied by students, the other two by the royal theater and archives." "No moral instruction, no practical learning was offered there." Vittorio had to put up with the annoyance of "eleven boys crammed into one room" presided over by "a stupid, crude peasant in priest's robes." Years of waste, "an ignorant boy, among ignorant boys, taught by ignorant men." At least he began to step out a bit and to become exposed to the beauty of the Italian language, "which is practically contraband in Turin, this amphibian city."* In 1763 the death of his uncle and guardian delivered him—and made him a millionaire at fourteen, virtually independent, with his own carriage and horses and servants, and a tutor who, for a small sum, would yield to the boy's slightest whim. Sheer idleness. He managed to forget everything he had never been willing to learn. A first, groping sexual encounter saved him from homosexuality, but gave him the habit of visiting prostitutes, whom he treated distantly and with disdain. "The remembrance of that first experience, which had no sequel, has never left me . . . It remains an inner consciousness guiding my entire life." "I was perfectly free to do nothing, the

---

*French was the chief language of "high society."

only occupation I really wanted." Still, like a loyal subject, he did his three mandatory tours of duty in the army of his petty sovereign. "I was never able to accept the yoke of gradual dependence known as subordination, which is the essence of military discipline but would not occur to a poet." To broaden himself, he decided to travel. But even that required permission from Charles Emmanuel, the aging king who kept a firm hand on this decorative adjunct to the Piedmontese court, where scions of the aristocracy—meaning any young man able to read, write, count, express himself, and issue commands—were followed about like colts on a stud farm. "The king, who kept an eye on the petty affairs of our little realm, was not inclined to let his nobles travel, especially a boy just out of his shell and with a distinct streak of independence. I was obliged to bow and scrape [to get permission to travel], but fortunately this will not keep me from straightening up afterward."

Twenty trips just for the sake of traveling about, "seeing nothing at all, or glancing hastily and dimly at what deserved to be seen." Milan, Florence, Bologna, Venice, Rome, Naples, "Italy erased from the ranks of power; Italians divided, weak, servile, enslaved. I was ashamed to be and to look Italian." But in Siena "a ray of light pierced my soul: my ears and heart were thrilled to hear the common people speak in such pleasing tones, with such elegance, such admirable clarity and precision." He would still have to "live a long time outside Italy to know and appreciate the Italians." Paris, Versailles, London, Amsterdam, The Hague, Vienna, where, in the gardens of Schön-brunn, he is so outraged to see Metastasio "execute the customary little bow to Maria Theresa with such a slavishly self-satisfied and adoring smirk on his face, that I, with Plutarch fresh in mind and fiercely idealistic, would never have consented to associate with a poet who had capitulated to despotism and whom I detested so heartily. Thus did I assume the outlook of an independent spirit" who began to be his own instructor, to devour Plutarch and travel about with Montaigne, whose *Essays* in ten slender volumes "alone filled the pockets of my carriage."

Berlin, where cultivated society flocked as if to philosophy's promised land. To him it was just the opposite. "Upon setting foot in the states of the Great Frederick, which appeared to resemble a vast barracks, I felt added horror for the military profession. I was presented to the king. When I saw him, I felt no thrill of surprise or awe but instead a rush of anger and rage: impulses which were building up and multiplying daily inside me at the sight of anything that failed to do what it was supposed to do, of so many falsehoods wearing the mask of virtue." He is twenty years old. We are watching the genesis of a man of liberty. "The king spoke the customary four words to me. I looked at him attentively, eyed him respectfully, and thanked heaven for not having been born his slave." In Copenhagen, like Goethe, he takes up sled-ding, "the all but imaginary speed of which stirred and enlivened my racing imagination." He felt instantly attracted to Stockholm, where "Sweden's mixed form of government" (a relative division of authority between the nobility and the throne prior to Gustavus III's coup d'état) seemed to imply "freedom of sorts" before he realized that the "extreme corruption of the two classes of nobles and bourgeois, who had been bought by French and Russian gold* . . . was destroying their resolve and crushing any notion of a just and enduring freedom." He had seen enough to "form an idea of it in my own little head," which developed into "an odd blend of philosophy, politics, and skepticism."

In Saint Petersburg he did not want to meet Catherine II and was thoroughly disgusted with everything "except the beards and the horses . . . among those barbarians masquerading as Europeans." Then off again, like a traveling circus, for a three-year tour of the continent: Spa, Rotterdam, return visits to London and The Hague, new women, several duels; "the loveliest, pleasantest part of France," the Loire and Aquitaine regions, which he crossed "without a single glance"; Barcelona, where he read Montaigne, and Madrid, to buy horses; Lisbon, where, fifteen years after the earthquake, "masses of stone were piled high, divided and aligned like tenanted buildings"; Seville, Cadiz, Montpellier—Turin.

Turin, where in 1773 he bought himself "a magnificent house on the Piazza San Carlo." Finally. Alfieri is going to settle down, be himself, cultivate some real friends and enjoy life. Finally, one night at the bedside of an ailing mistress, he takes up "five or six sheets of paper that happened to be handy" and begins "to sketch out at random, with no plan in mind, a scene from a play which I hardly know whether to call a comedy or tragedy, whether it would have been a single act, or five, or ten." A few more ripples ahead, then the jubilant cry of the watch sighting land: "Here I am at last, at twenty-seven, committed publicly and privately to becoming a playwright." For this he will always be indebted to the Countess of Albany,** a pretty German-born woman of twenty-five residing in Florence, where, with tact and taste, she has organized the likes of an English "counter-court," being the wife of Charles Edward Stuart, Bonnie Prince Charlie, the Young Pretender of the 1740s, who at one point had galvanized Scotland against the Hanoverian rule, but by this time has been reduced to a drunken, dissolute derelict and is three times her age.† They were married in 1772 and separated in 1774. "My first impression of her was infinitely agreeable. Dark, sparkling eyes combined—which is rare—with very fair skin and blond hair . . . a strong feeling for literature and the arts, an angelic disposition, a large fortune [Alfieri always maintains great respect for such things], and an exceedingly distressing domestic situa-

---

*The Hat and Cap parties.
**In his *Memoirs*, the chapter in which Alfieri mentions their first meeting (Fourth "Period," Chapter V) bears the heading: "At last I fall truly and nobly in love—forever."
†"Count of Albany" was a "royal incognito" he adopted during his Italian exile.

tion which made her miserable: how was I to resist so many reasons for falling in love?"

He has no desire to resist; he is trapped. "I realized that here was the woman I was searching for, who, instead of dwarfing my thoughts, stimulated them, encouraged them, and set an example of all that is good."

54

JUNE 1776

They Were Ferocious, But They Were Great

The Marquis de Sade was also enchanted, in 1776, by the beautiful Countess of Albany, who offered a pleasant contrast, he tells us, to the ugliness of Florentine women. "Three foreign ladies held sway, to whom not a single native could compare. One was the Countess of Albany, wife of the Pretender . . . who, once a hero whose tribulations made him interesting, has sunk to the level of a common debaucher, a glutton for daily wine and women. He married a Princess von Stolberg of the Palatine House,* a former canoness in Flanders. She is fair and plump, with very agreeable features."¹ On the other hand, the marquis remained skeptical as to the linguistic primacy of Siena, "which is to Tuscany what Beauvais or Mantes is to Paris. How can it be that the purest tongue is not spoken in the capital [Florence] but is relegated to a half-forsaken town?"²

In early June 1776 Sade is winding up his second trip to Italy. For the past year he has been exploring a number of towns on the peninsula after escaping from his château in Provence, where, even with his wife's connivance, he could not convince the magistrates "that he was not there" and ran the constant risk of arrest. He had spent the winter in Naples, often under an assumed name, accepted by society but not by the court. No one knew exactly what his legal battles were about, but Béranger, the French chargé d'affaires, had him placed under surveillance by the Neapolitan police. His dubious reputation had leaked out. He grew bored. On March 15 he alerted his wife that he intended to return to La Coste via Marseilles. Foolhardy plan as usual; he should at least give the authorities time to forget him. Did he want to get

---

*A cousin of Augusta von Stolberg, Goethe's epistolary Egeria. In reality the Wittelsbach family, who rule Bavaria and had inherited the title "Palatine" through extinction of other "Palatine houses." The Rhenish Palatinate was their chief ancestral fief.

himself hanged? Madame de Sade sent a flunkey, La Jeunesse, to dissuade him. Hopeless cause. Once he gets an idea in his head . . . He set out for France from Naples on May 4,[3] having sent aboard a tartan* two heavy trunks "full of old bric-à-brac and curios" weighing six quintals** apiece. The 1st of June found him in Rome for the third time in his life. "On the approach to Rome, from six miles away one can see the cupola of St. Peter's rising above all else. From there on until you reach Rome, the road improves slightly, but is horrid before that. They are beginning to clear the land," owing to the efforts of Pius VI, who encourages large-scale agricultural and urban development, "and heavily cultivated areas are springing up all over. Blood runs coarse in these parts, and peasant women are very round and stout."[4] Sade is not anxious to linger in the pearl of cities, whose churches and monuments he has already plundered. He wants to reach Bologna before the end of May, and yields to his wife's urging that he return home via Grenoble to avoid recognition.

Rome itself is scarcely recognizable, like a city buzzing with excitement on the eve of a carnival. Pius is resolved to make a great splash with this year's presentation of the palfrey, a ritual celebrated annually in the Church of Sts. Peter and Paul. He, a Braschi, intends to go down in history as a builder on as lavish a scale as any Farnese or Borgia pope. In deference to his wishes, triumphal arches span each street. The palfrey will get a royal reception.

A political message is implied: the pope is tired of playing second fiddle, tired of being treated like a dozen other Italian princelings since Louis XIV's day. The palfrey ceremony serves as a symbolic reminder that he considers himself the rightful ruler of the Kingdom of the Two Sicilies and therefore of the whole southern portion of the Italian boot. He intends to trumpet this reminder to the skies.

That is why, on June 28, the two banners of the Holy See flutter over Castel Sant'Angelo,† massive papal fortress surmounted by the figure of an angel sheathing his sword in memory of a vision of St. Gregory. Sade complained: "It would be a hopeless task to try to record all the monuments erected in Rome to so-called miracles. This statue suggested nothing other than the state emblem. The angel is the pope, and the sheathed blade is the Vatican's thunderbolt."[5] A nostalgic reminder of times not so distant when Italy was a battlefield, when cannonballs sailed out from the fortress and shook the city from dawn to dusk.

A colorful procession streams from the Colonna Palace to the Vatican, where the pope awaits the high constable of Naples and the palfrey. The marchers must slice their way through giant crowds gathered in front of

*Small sailing vessel peculiar to the Mediterranean, used for fishing and coastal transport.
**The quintal was then equivalent to 100 pounds, not the 200 it is today. The pound itself varied from place to place, but generally represented 500 grams on the current scale.
†Originally Hadrian's mausoleum, converted to a fortress in feudal times.

ancient palaces hung with gold cloth and tapestries. From every balcony, splendidly dressed women peer down on the pageant of Western civilization decked out in uniforms that date back more than a thousand years. Light cavalry, "baggage porters of their eminences the cardinals," their mace-bearers, their tailors, bakers, and barbers . . . The extramural chamberlains in scarlet, chamberlains of honor in black, Roman patricians, each resembling a Henry II of France, surrounded by his own private court, Swiss Guards with halberds, an endless train of multi-colored prelates swaying gently astride their caparisoned mules, a swarm of pages (sons of the nobility), and then the drummers, the trumpeters, the armed and armored attendants, and on and on. Focus of the procession: Prince Colonna on horseback representing Naples, dressed in scarlet and gold, preceded by some fabulous beast so laden with rich trappings that no one can tell if it is a mare or a gelding. The dignified palfrey ambles along, docile enough to be ridden by any woman or priest. It carries the annual tribute of seven thousand gold écus* which the Bourbon ruler of Naples pays the pope for his throne. The whole procession advances in random order, intersected by moving islands of humanity, where mothers fling out their babes at arm's length to kiss the feet of cardinals—guaranteed to spare them a hundred days in purgatory. And because Rome is still Rome, on arrival there is a mad scramble for precedence among three "gentlemen of honor" who draw swords, each insisting that he proceed first: a Cimitile, a Grimaldi, a Cornaro. Prince Colonna is compelled to intervene: "Gentlemen, hold your tempers and your swords! Ride in any old order and I will hear your arguments later."[6]

"*Il papa bello! Il papa bello!*" A great shout goes up in St. Peter's Square as "the pope with the shapely legs," Pius VI these past sixteen months, appears at the entrance to the basilica upon the *sedia gestatoria,* surrounded by *flabelli*** busily engaged in driving off giant flies. Here is the high priest in splendid trappings handed down from Thebes and Babylonia and further embellished by the Romans. No other individual in the Western world is so exalted. It is a costly rite. Gian Angelo Braschi beams. These are the halcyon days of his pontificate, before the incense wears off and the cares multiply. He still feels confident, at ease in his gold-encrusted shell. Unabashed, he has sent for his two Onesti nephews, sons of his sister Giulia, and has given them his name. Now they, too, are Braschi. He plans to make one a cardinal, the other a duke. How he relishes the combined delights of nepotism and vengeance: he has brought charges of extortion against Nicholas Bischi, Clement XIV's favorite, who ignored him during the previous reign. He has revoked the emoluments and privileges of all those who had shown reluctance to support him at the conclave.[7] But far beyond such petty diversions, he longs to dazzle

---

*Neapolitan currency is hard to translate. Very approximately on the modern scale, 100,000 francs [$20,000].

** "*Flabello*": fan made of feathers. [*Trans.*]

Rome and the papal states. He wants to finish construction of the museum of antiquities, to build the sacristy of St. Peter's, to raise an obelisk in every public square, to drain the malarial Pontine marshes. Money? He takes it from wherever he can find it. The House of the Holy Family, a shrine which, as everyone knows, angels transported from Nazareth to Loreto,* will be stripped of thirty-six thousand livres' worth of silver objects that undoubtedly never cluttered it during the tenancy of Joseph and Mary. And think of all the precious metals waiting to be scraped off church ceilings and walls! Posterity must speak of Pius VI in the same breath as Paul II, the Farnese pope whose name radiates from the façade of St. Peter's.

Braschi had wagered his career and won at the age of thirty-seven, when he chose between the church and a rich wife. Clerk, on his way to becoming a priest, and secretary to Benedict XIV, he was "in the business" but not subject to the rule of celibacy. Roman matrons threw themselves at this handsome man, then offered their daughters. A marriage contract was being drawn up at the notary's when Pope Lambertini offered more: a canon's post in St. Peter's. The path to a bishopric, a cardinalate—why not the tiara? predicted Leonard of Port Maurice, a tall, spindly monk with glowing eyes, known to all even then as St. Leonard.**

Yet he was not an ambitious cleric, Leonard, the gaunt Franciscan, founder of the "Company of the Lovers of Jesus and Mary," who had planted no less than 573 crosses in Rome and neighboring districts. But did Pius VI recall the fiery speeches of this holy man who rocked the pedestals of the mighty and made them hear "the trumpets of the Holy Spirit"?[8] "Dust! Life into dust! Young man, where is thy boyhood? Gone, returned to dust. Adult, where is thy adolescence? Gone, returned to dust. Old man, where is thy prime of life? Gone. Returned to dust." But the era of killjoys who haunted mid-century Rome is past now. St. Leonard died in 1751; his successor, who carried on his penitent streak, Paul Danei, known as Paul of the Cross,† has just died conveniently at the Mother House of Passionists, the order he founded. One less troublemaker around, that bent, rheumatic old man barely able to control his obsessions in the presence of worshipers who would crowd around to touch his rags: "Suffering! Redemptive suffering!" When he could no longer speak, he distributed little black crosses.[9] As long as Paul of the Cross was able, he enacted the Passion during his sermons, flagellating himself raw, stabbing his palms with rusty nails, inciting his audiences to great waves of mass hysteria. He stopped short of piercing his heart with a lance, but fainted in the arms

---

*The feast commemorating this "miracle" was Italy's patronal festival until the time of Pope John XXIII.
**Beatified by Pius VI in 1796 and canonized in 1867; Pius XI later proclaims him "patron of missionaries within the Church" in 1923.
†Beatified in 1852 and canonized in 1867.

of the *Addolorata,* the Virgin of Sorrows who appeared to him weeping blood-red tears.

Pius VI's Rome welcomes other spectacles. The pope's deep, melodious voice rings out across the square: "We are receiving the *cens** justly due the Roman pontiff for the direct exercise of dominion over our Kingdom of the Two Sicilies, on both sides of the Faro . . . "

In the Vatican, while awaiting the palfrey, Pius VI has accepted a few trifles from petty vassals: a live buck from Galicia, a hawk from Montecapiello, a white horse from Terracina, two thousand écus and a chalice from Sardinia.[10] That night Michelangelo's dome will be lit up by a thousand torches and lanterns, like a beacon shining out to all Italy.

Such is the Italy that Sade leaves near the end of June 1776, without a trace of scandal in his wake: his police file is none the bulkier. His baggage contains ten fat notebooks filled with his neat, regular, elongated calligraphy, among the finest of his time. It is the manuscript of his first sustained, though unfinished, literary undertaking, the *Voyage d'Italie,* in which the reader may meet "a real Marquis de Sade at liberty."** It is suitable reading for almost everyone, being chiefly a tedious catalogue of churches and art galleries. The qualifying "almost" covers that occasional fugitive bubble that breaks the mirrorlike surface, revealing fantasies that are already part of the author's permanent baggage, blasphemous or erotic bubbles slight enough not to offend the censor in the event of publication.† They merely signal the presence of two Sades, one of whom writes like the people of his own social milieu but now yearns to create something different once the bubbles take shape. Throughout this journey suspended between two lives—and, he fears justifiably, two prison sentences—he has looked about him with a more or less arrogant, dispassionate eye. The eye of an aristocrat who has already seen all there is to see. He concedes for the moment that Turin is "beautifully laid out, with superb churches, fine streets, nearly all straight, and houses built to the same height,"[11] but when it comes right down to it, he ventures the opinion that *"nowhere in Italy is there a duller, more symmetrical city: persons of rank are tiresome, the average citizen gloomy, and the common people pious and superstitious."*‡ In Florence he finds something praiseworthy in young Grand Duke Peter Leopold, Hapsburg brother of Joseph II and Marie Antoinette, who is said to

---

*Under the feudal system, a money payment owed by a tenant to his lord. [*Trans.*]

**According to Gilbert Lély. Sade had already written several fragments or "miscellanies," a one-act prose play of minor interest called *Le Philosophe soi-disant,* and a short *Voyage en Hollande* in epistolary form. The *Voyage d'Italie,* however, is his first important piece in terms of sheer bulk.

†The *Voyage d'Italie* was not published until 1967 by the Cercle du Livre Precieux. See note 3, chapter 53.

‡Italicized quotations in this chapter are taken from Sade's *Histoire de Juliette,* where, twelve or thirteen years later, the obsessions that haunted him in Italy surface along with his acid opinions. He draws on his Italian manuscript for certain settings and characters in *Juliette.*[12]

be "full of wit and learning; he is fond of the arts, but does little to patronize them." He points out approvingly that Leopold has "shaken off his mother's yoke" to the point of exiling to Tuscany all persons suspected of dealings with Maria Theresa.[13] Yes, but *"Leopold's tastes are despotic and cruel like those of all rulers."* Is he not *"the great successor to the Medici, the celebrated brother of France's leading whore?"*[14] Sade refuses to spare even the Ponte Vecchio: the Arno "divides the city into two nearly equal parts joined by four bridges that form a beautiful vista, if only one of the four, the one called Il Ponte Vecchio, had never been built up.* It spoils the prospect and creates a bad effect."[15] And the women of Florence are "haughty, impertinent, ugly, unclean, and greedy."[16] At the Florence opera the marquis learned of the castrati, and the scandalous practice of turning young boys into eunuchs trained to sing female roles, as the church forbade women to appear on the stage. "It was the first time I had ever seen this breed of half-male creature in a theater . . . And what does it achieve? Doesn't Rome, which first set them on the stage to avert any scandal that the presence of women might cause, commit a far worse crime by debasing Nature or encouraging the perverted desires of its subjects [by the presence of] beardless young men with the prettiest faces in the world? . . . I was revolted. One cannot get used to hearing emerge from a stout, mountainous, and misshapen male body a thin little voice much higher than a woman's." Of greater interest to him, however, he learns that the castrati are great at holding an erection: "These fellows are acrobats. The star soprano of the Opera in the fall of 1775 was crazy about the star castrato. He in turn was crazy for her . . . Their performance, according to reports from women who know, is highly appreciated because it lasts longer. Ardor never damps their fires."[17] Florence, in any event, is a sink of vice: sodomy, "incest and adultery, and generally all forms of defilement are licensed there . . . The thick, secluding palace walls of the nobility conceal many a horror, they say . . . Shortly before my arrival, an eight-year-old girl lost her life as a result of being violated two weeks earlier in one of those palaces."[18]

He wrote that with feigned indignation only a year after having raped "the young girls of La Coste"; but, for all the wickedness he finds there, he hates to leave a city which *"once possessed a remarkable law. No woman could refuse her husband an act of sodomy on the Thursday before Mardi Gras . . . Blessed be the nation wise enough to dignify its passions with the force of law!"*[19]

Rome's pervasive pietism turned his stomach. He reacted as Voltaire would have done. In the chapel "known as the Sanctum Sanctorum are kept a number of those holy trinkets which superstition unashamedly palms off on the credulous and the weak, whereas a wise man, knowing their value, scorns them utterly. The most remarkable is an impression of the face of Christ . . . which He sent to King Abgar, who had asked for His portrait."[20] "Let's be done

*That is, did not have houses on it.

with such trivia . . . They are too much of a disgrace to mankind. Leave these trifles and absurdities to the masses they nourish, and let's pity them for it. All children need toys."[21]

M. de Sade would never stoop to show compassion for the poor he treats so contemptuously. He either despises or ignores them. You would think he had traveled the face of Italy and seen only works of art or a handful of prominent persons. In recalling the history of the Forum, he vilifies "the people, who are today merely a brutish rabble," and who once, in that spot, "chose their leaders, enacted laws, declared war or peace. What changes, merciful heaven! The mistress of the world has become the slave of nations, and the people who once made the universe tremble are today selling oxen where their ancestors kept kings waiting."[22] The answer to such degeneracy is a good thrashing. Not, by all means, charity. The tradition of the popes feeding ten beggars [*sic*] is "a custom that controverts all the laws of good and judicious government and simply perpetuates apathy and idleness in the mass of people, who, on the contrary, require the most aggressive handling to be driven out of their sloth and natural indifference."[23]

Sadism came into being quite accidentally, unknown even to its creator, in a diatribe composed inside the Coliseum, a mass of ruins surrounded by bramble patches on the outskirts of Rome. "That structure presently serves as a storage depot for niter. They also keep a good deal of manure there . . . What a difference there is between our spectacles and the ones that used to be given here, when a crowd of over a hundred thousand would witness the event. Barbarism, I admit, characterized the bloody scenes that went on, but at least those entertainments did not undermine courage as do our modern ones, when the mere gestures of an actor dying suffice to bring on tears. A sterner, militaristic outlook accustomed those heroes of the universe to watch death with composure. They were ferocious, you say? Granted. But they were great, and we are, I admit, remarkably humane but also remarkably inconsequential."

The meeting of the two Sades took place, therefore, in that Coliseum, which was "long abandoned, yet its remoteness and solitude made it a setting for crime and debauchery. Benedict XIV resolved to sanctify this profane site by putting a hermit in charge, only to have him murdered a few years ago; then the cross standing in the center was erected and the circle of little chapels which succeeds in ruining the arena."[24]

Donatien-Aldonse is mistaken: the cross standing in the center of the Coliseum, flanked by the saltpeter and the dung, was planted there on Christmas Day, 1750, by St. Leonard. This emblem of torment and suffering is one of the few sights in Italy which the marquis did not view indifferently. One other object that caught his notice was the monumental papal altar in St. Peter's, where only the pope may officiate, directly under the cupola: "Nothing is as superb as this isolated altar supported by four spiral columns, three quarters of the way into the church, over the tomb of St. Peter, who, incidentally, never set foot in Rome or died there. Oh, what a divan to get buggered on!"[25]

BARRAS

55

JUNE 1776

I Had an Urge to Travel

On June 30, 1776, Jean-Nicolas-Paul-François de Barras turns twenty-one. Most people call him Paul to distinguish him from his father, the "high and mighty" but impecunious seigneur François de Barras. Paul sets sail from Marseilles on his birthday aboard the three-masted schooner *Duc de Duras* to begin his military and colonial career in India.

A handsome, blond young man, rather conceited, rather shallow, proud of his brand-new blue-and-white uniform of second lieutenant in the royal infantry. Oval face tapering to a pair of thick, sensual lips beneath a Roman nose, which punctuates his air of gluttony. Blue eyes so bright that one instinctively, but vainly, seeks the thoughts behind them. Yet thoughts of what apart from women and adventure could one expect to find there? "Neither the pleasures nor occupations available in France suited me: I had an urge to travel."[1]

He journeyed there on horseback in a single day from Fox-Amphoux, a tiny village perched atop a red clay hillside where the Barras property* begins and where he has just taken leave of his parents on the fragrant, wooded slopes of Upper Provence: the garden of his childhood in the center of an irregular triangle whose points were Manosque in the north, Aix and Draguignan at the base. Once again he leaped over Crayfish Brook, where he used to swim naked with the peasant boys on his father's estate, and flirt with the shepherdesses. On through Barjols, where he "made a poor record as a boarding student"[2] who once a week took the five-mile journey home. He reached Marseilles via Saint-Maximim, Roquevaire, and Aubagne, bypassing La-Sainte-Baume. This region grows progressively bleak and barren as one nears the sea, with fewer and fewer trees other than pines, more and more creepers "that

*Today there are bauxite mines nearby. In the town of Fox one can still see the house where Barras was born; though it has fallen into decay, a fine carved door survives. On the plain, a road leads from Route D32 to these remains.

resemble powdered heads."[3] "Despite the beauty of the climate, nine tenths of the region is arid slopes or hillsides dotted with single forlorn pines, scrub, and aromatic plants." The road to the main harbor "is paved with finely crushed white stone." A steady stream of vehicles passing over this limestone surface has ground it to a powder, and "one walks in a constant cloud of dust that coats the houses and trees with a white film as in a flour mill."[4] Too bad, for the choking, blinding effects spoil the approach to the outskirts of Marseilles, "dotted with a multitude of small country houses called *bastides*." Over four thousand of them in 1776, not to mention the host of others throughout Provence, and Paul de Barras can recognize his house at every turn of the road, his own boyhood home, not the one on the narrow main street of Fox, below the tiny fountainless public square with its four-hundred-year-old nettle trees, to which his parents seldom climbed along the twisting stony path except for social affairs or official ceremonies, including the birth of their children—but instead the "Château de Barras," as the family fondly termed it (though everyone else called it "the Barras place"), a mile or so down on the flatlands, facing Amphoux, on the edge of a forest of holm oaks and creepers.

He had a normal childhood, growing up in that solid, square Provençal house kept cool by the thick walls, crowned with its curved tile roof, surrounded by yew trees, with the familiar terrace facing east and the wrought-iron gate. On this journey at the end of June, marked at every stage by these *bastides*, one would think that not just his childhood but also his own class walks with him along the last lap of an expedition into a new life: the eight thousand or more nobles of the robe or the sword who own property in the towns and at least one small country house, and who hold every last inch of Provençal soil, at the expense of a million landless peasants.[5]

He leaves behind a father who always allowed him to do what he wanted, and was treated reciprocally. François de Barras is withdrawn and misanthropic, happiest in the company of his books; he did a short stint with the army in Corsica for the sole purpose of writing an account of it.*[6] Yet he is no misogynist: on a hillside a hundred yards from the Barras house stands a sign for which he is probably responsible, A L'AMOUR, painted in red on a stone jutting out over the "grotto of the rendezvous."[7] And surely it was he who had a lodge built deep inside the park—ostensibly for his gamekeeper, on condition that he himself might use it for an occasional tryst.[8] In any event, he and his wife had ten children, a normal-size family, six of whom in turn maintained the norm by dying at an early age. Paul became the eldest surviving son; his two brothers will follow him into the army; one sister is already married to a shopkeeper in Marseilles—times must be hard when a De Barras stoops to marry a Gauvin! Paul does well to head for the colonies: in the Barras tribe, every opportunity ought to be seized, for they are proud people but

---

*He also wrote several unpublished treatises on municipal government, the system of *corvées*, etc.

nearly as poor as their tenant farmers, in the sense that they cannot live off income for the year ahead. To make money or just to get along, they must rely on civil or military or clerical offices, not the income from their "estates."

If Paul de Barras is sorry to leave anyone, it is his mother, the good woman who opened his eyes to life, a Pourcelly by birth and therefore bourgeoise like her son-in-law; but the fact that she was also the granddaughter of a Castellane-Montpezat reflected credit on her future husband.[9] "My childhood, solely in the hands of the best of mothers, was bound to bring me affection . . . She possessed great virtues: beautiful, modest, extremely sensitive, popular,* charitable, devoted to her family and to managing a household on limited means."[10] He loved her deeply and will look for her image in the women he meets, a subject that interests him considerably. "My heart was in the right place, but one's state of mind is closely dependent on one's physical condition: I enjoyed vigorous good health. From the age of fourteen, a sense of independence and exaltation developed in me [his mother's Hungarian ancestry probably had something to do with this]. Active and courageous in the face of danger, if tranquillity seemed to damp my energy, the lure of pleasure took its place and often distracted me from my duties . . . I realize that even then I was ill-suited to intellectual tasks and had difficulty adjusting to them ever afterward."[11] Modest avowal: he is ignorant except when it comes to girls and horses. He even had trouble understanding basic military strategy. He writes out words almost phonetically. He knows absolutely nothing about history. The only instructor able to teach him something appears to be the famous La Poterie, riding master to a generation of army cadets sent to him by the ministry of war—at Cambrai, in Barras's case, where he "drew" a five-year assignment after boarding school in Barjols and further studies with the Carmelites under the tutelage of a certain Brother Gaëtan, so frail and sickly that the boy came to feel he was teaching his teacher, and a childish affair, rather too intense for a fifteen-year-old, with a female cousin of the Bishop of Viviers.

What about the court, or Versailles? He had given it some thought, of course, and had been presented during the reign of Madame du Barry. M. Talaru, one of his father's relatives, had offered to sponsor Paul as a page in the Duc d'Orléans's household. "I was disgusted that anyone would think me willing to wear livery, even that of a popular** prince . . . My father kissed me and said, 'You are right. Better the army.' "[12]

This Roman response was pure romance. In reality, Barras felt too poor in spirit and pocket to try his luck at the court of Versailles, an option he had had the good sense to turn down earlier. Better Pondicherry, India, rich

---

*Nowadays Barras would have said: "tactful and democratic-minded."
**The Duc d'Orléans was no more democratic-minded than anyone else. Barras, whose *Memoirs* are hopelessly confused and confusing, mistakes him for his son Philippe Egalité.

fabrics, spices, diamonds, the treasure of Golconda, even if he has no idea what the latter means.*

He is happy, eager to taste life. In Aubagne, for twenty-four sous,** he ate a six-course dinner with dessert and a bottle of wine.[13] And here is Marseilles, with its incomparable vista of the harbor boxed in by the city, with moderate-size vessels crammed like herring into a barrel, "products from the four corners of the globe, people from all over the earth in native costumes, every flag that sails the seas."[14] Notice of the *Duc de Duras*'s sailing is posted at the exchange, but this East India Company ship has not been able to enter the port, where the mooring is only three or fathoms deep.† With sails furled, it lies out in the giant bay, "which offers unlimited anchorage even in among the tiny islands in its center. There is safe passage between all those islands."[15] A longboat takes Barras out to the vessel, which sits alongside a dozen others in the chief moorage just off the islands of Saint-Jean and Ratonneau. Something of a bastard, this ship that is half man-o'-war, half merchantman, with gunholes for eighty cannon, though now, in peacetime, it carries only twelve. It bears the name of one of the company's major shareholders, who provided funds to outfit it. A rough welcome aboard is given to the young officer without a regiment, as Barras will be second in command of a company of Sipahis,‡ native Hindu recruits serving the King of France. Select passengers and top officers are assigned elegant staterooms in the stern, with its fine carved gallery, along with the captain and his aides. But the others, "lieutenants as well as second lieutenants, are lodged in the gunroom with the master gunner," meaning a general storeroom in the steerage between decks, near the powder magazine. "Aside from the place being very cramped and very dark, as lanterns provide the only light, only when lying down is one safe from the continual shifting to and fro of the tiller. Not to mention that the gunroom is more or less uninhabitable in the daytime."[16]

Barras spends the days up on deck. It helps him escape the first whiff of adventure he encounters, nauseating to the novice voyager, though it takes more than that to discourage him: the smell of pigs, sheep, horses, fowl, and their excrement, which rises from the hold. On those long ocean trips each vessel resembled a Noah's Ark. "Add to that the pungent odor of tar, coupled with cooking smells, and it will give you an idea of the discomforts men must endure the first time they go through this."[17]

A strong easterly wind drives the *Duc de Duras* out to sea. The Château

---

*Golconda, overlooking the ruins of the ancient village of that name, was the fortress of the Nizams of Hyderabad, traditional allies of the French. They kept their treasure there, chiefly certain colossal diamonds.
**Six francs [$1.20].
†Five to seven meters, too shallow for a three-master.
‡Earliest French version of the Portuguese word *"sipay,"* which the English rendered as "sepoy" and the French later on as *"spahi."*

d' If, blindingly white at midday atop the white cliffs, soon fades to a pinpoint on the starboard horizon. Mirabeau was imprisoned there the year before. Among these three eldest sons of Provençal nobility whose destiny shifts markedly in 1776, Mirabeau, Sade, and Barras, only Barras seems to have come out ahead.

56

JULY 4, 1776

Liberty and the Pursuit of Happiness

Four days away, on the other side of the ocean, an entire continent is casting itself adrift. July 4, 1776, will be Independence Day. John Adams, along with Franklin, Jefferson, Roger Sherman, and Robert R. Livingston, has finished drafting the Declaration of Independence. On July 3 he writes to his wife, Abigail, in the biblical style that marked every act of their lives, not excepting the most intimate: "Yesterday, the greatest question ever debated in America was decided, and a greater one, perhaps, never was nor will be decided among men. A Resolution was passed without one Colony's dissent 'that these United Colonies are, and of right ought to be, free and independent States, and as such they have, and of right ought to have, full power to make war, conclude peace, establish commerce and do all other acts and things which other States may rightfully do.'

"... When I look back to the year 1761* and recollect ... the series of political events, the chain of causes and effects, I am surprised at the suddenness as well as greatness of this revolution. Britain has been filled with folly, and America with wisdom ... It is the will of Heaven that the two countries shall be sundered forever. It may be the will of Heaven that America shall suffer calamities still more wasting, and distresses yet more dreadful."[1]

In fact nothing happens on the 4th of July. The principle of independence had been adopted by twelve states out of thirteen during the congressional session of July 2, John Adams having omitted to mention that New York temporarily abstained owing to the absence of a quorum. On the 4th, John Hancock, acting president, and the secretary sign and thereby authenticate the text of the

*The year he regards as the "commencement of this controversy between Great Britain and America."

Declaration submitted by Jefferson, Adams, and three others. Delegates of the United Colonies, from two to nine for each depending on the circumstances, around sixty altogether, placed their signatures in random order, whenever they happened to be present, and over a period of more than a month, at the foot of a single, giant, exquisite sheet of parchment on which a calligraphic expert managed to crowd a running text that normally would have filled seven or eight pages.* The date of the first two signatures prompted the secretary's solemn insertion: "In Congress, July 4, 1776." The United States came into being with the scraping of penpoints, without fuss, without riots or parliamentary hysterics, with the unhurried signing of a document that ranged from sermon to polemic. The first few sentences of the second paragraph give a typical example of Jeffersonian style:

> We hold these Truths to be self-evident:
> That all Men are created equal;
> That they are endowed by their Creator with certain unalienable Rights;
> That among these are Life, Liberty, and the Pursuit of Happiness;
> That to secure these Rights, Governments are instituted among Men, deriving their just Powers from the Consent of the Governed;
> That whenever any Form of Government becomes destructive of these Ends, it is the Right of the People to alter or to abolish it . . .²

At the close of this lengthy preamble comes a disillusioned statement of men who had been trying for over ten years to rouse their fellow citizens:

> Experience has shewn that Mankind are more disposed to suffer, while Evils are sufferable, than to right themselves by abolishing the Forms to which they are accustomed . . . Such has been the patient Sufferance of these Colonies; and such is now the Necessity which constrains them to alter their former Systems of Government.

It was all debated systematically for three months, in the spirit of a town meeting or a municipal council, by these sixty solemn and faintly pompous gentlemen with deliberate gestures and modulated voices. All are soberly dressed, careful to avoid oratorical effects, and never once interrupt each other. The Congress debates with the secrecy of a papal conclave, having turned away all would-be audiences in an effort to make its resolutions appear the unanimous choice of Northerners and Southerners, Boston Presbyterians and Maryland Anglicans, giant Virginia and lilliputian Rhode Island. Morning and evening found them gathered at Carpenters Hall, Philadelphia, in a room more like a parlor than a meeting hall, with barely enough chairs to go around. Only the president sat at a table covered with a green cloth atop a small platform. We are in the geometric center of the colonies, the city designed by

---

*Trumbull's huge painting in the Capitol rotunda, the *Signing of the Declaration of Independence,* in a style anticipating the whole school of revolutionary realism which inspired thousands of engravings, thus is wholly imaginary. The scene never took place.

William Penn's architects in 1680 to become "a green rural city" at the mouth of the Delaware, ten thousand acres of earthly paradise for the delectation of "Philadelphs," those advocates of brotherly love driven out of England and Sweden, Germany and Holland, thousands of resourceful and prolific saints who believed in helping heaven to help themselves. There are thirty thousand of them now, more than the Bostonians or New Yorkers. Brick has replaced wood; the earthly paradise has mushroomed. Sawmills, tanneries, tile factories, and glassworks have sprung up adjacent to the shipyards. What better, more centrally located capital could the new country have, a two-week journey on horseback from either New Hampshire or the Carolinas? The finest American city, the best dressed, the best fed, "practically one of the wonders of the world." Sober John Adams observes remorsefully: "Another guilty feast!" the morning after a banquet whose menu he noted in great detail, confessing that the wine was "admirable."[3] How could he have sipped such wine in Boston, where he touched nothing stronger than water? New England Puritans were fascinated by the stout, wigless Quaker merchants, who addressed everyone as "thee," were pacifists, looked upon childbearing and money-making as duties, tolerated Catholics, and lived like feudal princes in their country houses.[4]

But members of Congress complained bitterly about Pennsylvania's weather, "a composite of the worst of all possible climates: the dampness of an English spring, the summer heat of Africa, the autumn skies of Egypt, the cold of a Norwegian winter, and, what is far worse, the occurrence now and then of all these in a single day."[5] In Philadelphia the question is quickly settled as to what month will mark the Declaration: "after the summer solstice, the city is so fearfully hot that the streets are deserted from midday to five o'clock and most of the residents sleep after lunch.* What makes the heat even more intolerable is the absence of any breeze, especially after three in the afternoon, and the heavy humidity over this whole coast."[6] Nevertheless, on July 12 the city turns out for a joyful celebration after sundown, with drinking parties, balls, and fireworks. Free America's first birthday. Members of Congress participate with much the same stupor and pride that troubles John Adams: did they really do it all by themselves? They can hardly believe a compromise was reached. "The thirteen clocks chimed in unison,"[7] though each read a different hour. Will Patrick Henry's utopia become a reality? "All barriers are cast down; all frontiers are erased; the colonies have melted into a single whole; distinctions between Virginians and Pennsylvanians, New Yorkers and New Englanders have vanished. I am no longer a Virginian, I am an American. We are in the natural state!"[8] In the gas-lit streets of Philadelphia this would seem to be true. But inside Carpenters Hall the clocks grind on behind closed doors, and Patrick Henry, who had hoped this "state of

---

*Philadelphia is located on the fortieth meridian, which touches Lisbon and Madrid and passes through Sardinia and Ankara.

nature" would translate itself into voting rights proportionate to America's two-million-odd inhabitants,* hears his motion defeated: it is decided that each state shall have one vote, and that Georgia's population of 15,000 shall carry as much weight as the 280,000 residents of Massachusetts. Bitter battles lie ahead. To delay them, it was agreed not to begin drafting a constitution for the new nation right away. Independence, yes, and war, since independence demands it, but let's not rush to pin things down, for the new country is still faceless, its image blurred.

Thomas Jefferson is unhappy about this. It leaves him with a vague sense of uneasiness which keeps on growing until his last years, when he voices regret for the lost opportunity: "We imagined everything republican which was not monarchy. We had not yet penetrated to the mother principle, that 'governments are republican only in proportion as they embody the will of their people, and execute it.' Hence, constitutions had really no leading principles in them."[10] The silence from his pursed lips, and his cheerless, faintly sarcastic countenance vex his colleagues. John Adams asserts that he never heard Jefferson utter more than two words in succession. Jefferson the lawyer is a tall, spare man with sharp features and red hair that falls loose about his stubborn forehead. He is thirty-three. His plainness is not displeasing to the ladies, nor is his silence to the public: his pen pleads well enough for him with both. He is a man of letters rather than an orator. He cannot tolerate the "morbid rage of debate,"[11] but afterward, in the quiet of his study, has a talent for summarizing and channeling the arguments.

In a wheedling exchange John Adams had persuaded him the month before, apparently without too much effort, to draft most of the Declaration of Independence:

"I don't want to draft it myself."

"You ought to," Jefferson replied, as if to say, "Gentlemen, you have the first shot . . ."

"I don't want to."

"Why don't you want to? Go ahead."

"I don't care to."

"Why not?"

"For reasons of my own."

"Which are?"

"First of all, you are a Virginian, and a Virginian ought to be in charge; secondly, people don't trust me, I am unpopular; thirdly, you write ten times better than I do."

In a flash Jefferson had snatched up his pen: "Well, if you really insist, I will do the best I can . . ."

---

* 1,640,000 including slaves in 1763, an approximate census.[9] The figure had increased by ten to fifteen percent by 1776.

[Belated tug on the reins by Adams:] "Good. When you are finished, we'll go over it together."

"That is exactly what we did," he recounts sourly.[12] "On reading it, I was entranced by the tasteful surges of eloquence that abounded in Mr. Jefferson's text. His passage against slavery delighted me especially; I was aware that his southern colleagues would never allow such words to obtain congressional sanction* but I made no attempt to attack them. He used several terms I would never have chosen if I had been writing it, notably the word 'tyrant' as applied to the king. I found that too personal, too impassioned, too aggressive for such a solemn and dignified document. However, since Franklin and Sherman would be going over it, I saw no point in deleting the word and I approved the Declaration for presentation to the five-man committee . . . We were extremely pressed and the Congress impatient, so the document was presented in Jefferson's own handwriting just as he drafted it. The Congress rejected more than a quarter of it, as I expected, struck out some of the best parts [including the paragraph condemning slavery], and left in everything that was debatable . . . The Declaration of Independence contained no concept that had not been hammered out for two years in the Congress."**[14]

The text therefore is almost exclusively Jefferson's and was presented more or less intact by John Adams. The two men were the real "Founding Fathers." One silent, the other tempestuous; one withdrawn, the other highly emotional. A southern graduate of William and Mary College in Williamsburg, a northern alumnus of Harvard. Yet, contrary to all expectations, Jefferson the Virginian is by temperament the "radical," and John Adams the Bostonian, despite his acrobatics, the moderate.† By then Franklin had read, observed, listened, and written too much to add more than a word here and there. He watched those two fiery swordsmen whetting their blades for what promised to be a momentous duel and was amused by their attempts at compromise. These two symbolized the North and the South, for better or for worse: a marriage of convenience hastily arranged without a contract by the men of the Center, those pragmatic Pennsylvanians.‡ Philadelphia stood to

---

*Jefferson's reply: "Our northern brethren also, I believe, felt a little tender under those censures; for though their people had very few slaves themselves, yet they had been pretty considerable carriers of them to others."[13] Jefferson himself owned a number of slaves.

**The original document in Jefferson's handwriting does contain several deletions and additions supplied by Adams and Franklin.

†John Adams succeeds Washington as second president of the United States (1797–1801). In 1801 Jefferson will run against him and win, at which time Adams's supporters label him "an atheist in matters of religion, a terrorist in politics." Jefferson is re-elected for a second term in 1805. By a strange coincidence, these old feuding blood brothers both die on July 4, 1826, the fiftieth anniversary of Independence Day.

‡The term "middle colonies" meant something quite different from the present central states. The colonies extended westward only to the Allegheny Mountains. "Middle" refers to the Atlantic

gain by it. Besides, to Pennsylvanians the war is still an abstraction; they hope it will stay that way. George Washington, a Virginia delegate, has not signed the Declaration of Independence. He is too busy elsewhere. Named commander-in-chief of the colonial forces on June 15, 1775, he is now consolidating his defenses in New York, where Admiral Howe's mighty fleet is blockading the harbor. Although the British finally evacuated Boston on March 17, 1776, after a year's siege, they are gathering strength for a major strike, and Washington has scarcely ten thousand men to meet them. The alarming letters he dispatches almost daily to the Congress contrast with the serene mood in Philadelphia. From there, New York, a hundred miles away, seems like another planet. As long as New Jersey separates Manhattan from Philadelphia, why not be comforted by the lulling speeches of John Adams?

John Adams is forty. He is shorter than Jefferson by a head and stouter, his forehead more bulging, with only a few clumps of graying curls left. His broad mouth does most of the talking in Congress and makes its owner a lot of enemies. His sense of superiority rests on the conviction, premature, that his life is wasted. Which gives rise in turn to a persecution complex reinforced by the hostility of those who reasoned correctly from the start. In taking issue with Jefferson, his understanding was that it would be better to involve Virginians or Carolinians in drafting the Declaration as well as Pennsylvanians, since Franklin was to sign it. They were the ones who had been loudly protesting the notion of independence just the year before. When Adams arrived in Philadelphia with his cousin Samuel, Robert Treat Paine, and Cushing, "all four of them delegates from Massachusetts to the Continental Congress, all four penniless,"* they found themselves deluged with admonitions: "Friends of Britain in Boston have pictured you as reckless adventurers and fools . . . You are taken for poor devils who depend on their popularity. All of you are suspected of advocating independence. Be careful not even to whisper the word . . . You are representatives of the state which has suffered; Boston and Massachusetts are under an iron rod . . . You have long been persecuted; your feelings are hurt, your passions aroused. You are thought to be hotheads . . . Don't presume to take over the government . . . "15

Tom Paine's friendly interest did not help them any, although his behavior continued modest and unassuming. He was not a delegate to the Congress, yet his name was a tinderbox. People thought of him as the Jeremiah or Isaiah of the newly chosen people. On January 10, 1776, the *Pennsylvania Journal* had announced "the publication and sale by Robert Bell, at the price of two

---

seaboard; the middle states (New York, New Jersey, Pennsylvania, and Delaware) stood midway between North and South.

*Not exactly true, although as delegates they were short of money. John Adams relates the following incident.

shillings, of *Common Sense,* addressed to the inhabitants of America." The pamphlet was so bold that for three months it was generally ascribed to Samuel or John Adams or even Franklin. But people soon learned that Mr. Paine, a poor immigrant cast up on American shores, had written the first best-seller: 150,000 copies are overwhelming America,* spreading the prophecy of independence. Tom Paine at last has put in print what everyone was beginning to suspect. "It is the true interest of America to steer clear of European contentions . . . One cannot conceive of anything more absurd than three million persons** rushing down to the harbor each time a boat arrives to find out how much freedom they still have . . . Freedom has been hunted round the globe. O! receive the fugitive, and prepare in time an asylum for mankind." To say plainly what he thought of the British was bad enough, but he went much further. His cry of rage recalls the humble customs inspector at Lewes, crushed by society: "Society in every state is a blessing, but Government, even in its best state, is but a necessary evil . . . Government, like dress, is the badge of lost innocence; the palaces of kings are built upon the ruins of the bowers of paradise . . . Of more worth is one honest man to society, and in the sight of God, than all the crowned ruffians that ever lived . . . In free countries, the law is king; no other is needed . . ." In a few weeks Tom Paine has achieved the celebrity of a Franklin, especially among ordinary folk, who respond instantly to his plain, unvarnished speech. An agent of the British government writes to London at the end of July: "His pamphlet has set the public thinking and raised the ferment leading to the Declaration." At the same time he is becoming the most vilified man in England, where gentlemen have nails driven into their boot soles in the form of a letter "T" or "P" in order to trample the traitor. And in America also there are those who think this demiurge has carried matters too far. Slaveholders primarily, who have just succeeded in stripping the Declaration of Jefferson's eloquent antislavery clause. Didn't Tom Paine take it upon himself to lecture the plantation owners? "Can America be happy under a government of her own? The answer is short and simple, here it is: she will be as happy as she wishes. She has a blank page to fill. Do not wait too long to do it. Do not forget the unfortunate Africans."[16] Even in Philadelphia, Tom Paine gets his share of abuse. Recently he was sent sprawling in the gutter by a certain Matthew Slough, who was on his way home from dining with some wealthy landowners.

"Well, what do you know! There goes Common Sense . . . "

"The devil take him! I'll knock some common sense into him . . . "

So Tom Paine lands in the gutter at the hands of a group of gentlemen

*He could have earned thousands of pounds sterling, but ceded his royalties instead "to each state which prints him"—ultimately the thirteen colonies. He did not collect a penny even when the printing reached the million mark.

**The figure is inflated by one third, in good faith. At that time the colonies were generally assumed to be more heavily populated than was the case.

who have just dined with no lesser personage than the quartermaster general of the colonial army. Proving that it is unwise even in Philadelphia to talk too much or too loud.

Such reasoning accounted for John Adams's unwonted surrender to Jefferson in the hope that, with patience and tact, an "unnatural" emergency alliance could be forged between the patriots of Boston (where Samuel Adams has been preaching independence since 1768, long before his cousin) and the "proud sultans of the South," Washington, Jefferson, Lee, and Patrick Henry. Winning them over to the Bostonian cause has just tipped the scales of congressional sentiment in favor of independence, aided by a minor legal coup d'état engineered by Dr. Franklin and his Pennsylvania colleagues. But John Adams was heavy-hearted: "This continent is a vast machine difficult to set in motion . . . Up to now we have waged war only half way. You will see that after this we will probably venture to do so three-quarters of the way . . . "[17] Yet hope lay behind his acrimony: "Silence! Patience! Time will bring forth, with the usual wailing and labor, a fine child, a handsome, vigorous, and healthy son,"[18] the United States of America.

John Adams was unfair to Jefferson, who admitted that he had made every effort to avoid leaving his personal stamp on the document: "Neither aiming at originality of principle or sentiment, nor yet copied from any particular and previous writing, it was intended to be an expression of the American mind, and to give that expression the proper tone and spirit called for by the occasion."[19] There lay his genius: the capacity to voice America's still timid aspirations. Without a constitution, or a capital, or a leader, or borders, the United States begins to exist now on the strength of a document written by an individual as modest as the God of Moses, that great silent soul who communicated with his people only by the written word and founded a nation based on the Ten Commandments. Genesis haunts the minds of those three skeptics of July 4: Jefferson, John Adams, and Franklin were neither pious men nor atheists, "not intolerant, not arrogant, not openly scornful though quietly and all but secretly so, for the majority of citizens remained devout. To make a vivid impression on them calls for an appeal to religious sentiments; prayers and public fasting are a wise path of action for popular agitators."[20] "I do not agree with Christ on all points," Jefferson admitted to friends: "I am a materialist; Christ opted for spiritualism."[21] He also admits that to develop a tone in unison with influential preachers of his time, he looked for help to Rushworth,* "whom we rummaged over for revolutionary precedents and forms of the Puritans of that day, preserved by him, we cooked up a few resolutions, somewhat modernizing their phrases, for appointing . . . a day of fasting, humiliation and prayer . . . "[22] The founding fathers treated the newborn

---

*Author of an anthology on the English Revolution in which Puritan writers modeled their texts on the Bible.

nation like non-churchgoing parents who send their children to Sunday school
for the sake of convention.

On his own, however, Jefferson inserted three words into the Declaration
that belie his modesty: he and he alone is responsible for shaping the new
American Trinity, whose device, like a litany, captured the imagination of all
his congressional associates: life, liberty, and property. He crosses out "property" and lists as man's essential rights: "life, liberty, and the pursuit of happiness." Jefferson had devoured *Common Sense* and clung to this phrase of Paine's:
"The first, the foremost question, the one which determines all the rest and
from which all the rest flow, is Happiness."[23] To Jefferson and John Adams
in the year 1776, what does "happiness" mean, *their* brand of happiness,
which, like a drug, they wish to hand out to the rest of mankind? Essentially,
it means sharing power, wielding influence, the joy of becoming "a participant
in the government of affairs,"[24] happiness that is public rather than private,
that values admiration above love. "The burning desire for distinction," John
Adams wrote, "is the most basic and most remarkable human quality . . .
Wherever there are men, women, and children, old or young, rich or poor,
noble or humble, wise or foolish, ignorant or educated, it is apparent that each
individual is strongly motivated by a desire to be seen, listened to, discussed,
approved, and esteemed." Ambition, "which aims at power in order to excel,"
can become a worthy quality; it is "the desire to be better than someone
else."[25] Political activity, then, can bring contentment to everyone, not just
the select, powerful few. A new and startling concept, or else a very ancient
one rehabilitated after centuries of neglect from which the term "politics" has
yet to recover.

Jefferson took a wife in 1772, a young widow who keeps house for him
and bears him a daughter from time to time. He rarely speaks of this, however,
as if he had no private life. That kind of happiness belongs to the past, when
he fell passionately in love with Rebecca Burwell, his "Belinda." He proposed
to her and had sworn that "if Belinda refused him, he would never offer his
services to anyone else." "My fate depends on her resolutions. By her, I shall
fall or stand . . . If she consents, I will be happy; if not, I will make the effort
to be so."[26]

She rejected him. He went ahead and "offered his services" to another
woman. He "made the effort," loyally. But his ideal lies elsewhere. "And for
the support of this Declaration, we mutually pledge to each other our lives,
our fortunes, and our sacred honor"—the final sentence of Jefferson's version
of the Declaration. John Adams, who gives evidence of some degree of domestic contentment, takes the same tone in another letter dated July 3 to his wife,
Abigail:

> [The day on which the Declaration of Independence is adopted] will be the most
> memorable epoch in the history of America. I am inclined to believe that it will
> be celebrated by succeeding generations as the great anniversary festival. It ought

to be commemorated as the day of deliverance by solemn acts of devotion to God Almighty. It ought to be solemnized with pomp and parade, with shows, games, sports, guns, bells, bonfires, and illuminations, from one end of this continent to the other, from this time forward forevermore.

You will think me transported with enthusiasm, but I am not. I am well aware of the toil and blood and treasure it will cost us to maintain this Declaration and to support and defend these States. Yet through all the gloom, I can see the rays of ravishing light and glory. I can see that the end is more than worth all the means. And that posterity will triumph in that day's transaction even if we should rue it, which I trust to God we shall not.[27]

57

AUGUST 1776

Gabriel or Die

Mirabeau is not fool enough to bolt straight for Pontarlier. The Chevalier de Mâcon, his confederate in flight, finds him a hideout in Orgelet, a hamlet perched in the foothills of the Jura not far from Burgundy, midway between Saint-Amour and Lons-le-Saulnier. The place is a nest of smugglers, several of whom have been promoting his affair with Sophie by helping the lovers to exchange letters. This clandestine postal service operates for five days. Mirabeau, who dares not show his face for fear of arrest, remains in Orgelet while Mâcon heads for Pontarlier disguised as a peddler, accompanied by a hired servant and henchman named Le Gay.[1] The two attempt to abduct Sophie, actually to spirit her swiftly to Pontarlier before Monnier gets wind of Mirabeau's escape from Dijon. Their plan collapses, however, when Bourrier, the innkeeper to whom Mirabeau owes money, denounces him. Sophie can rely only on a chambermaid. Failure number one on May 29: the canoness, who watches her sister like a hawk, locks her in her room when she finds her "wearing a man's hat." Mirabeau's diary reports: "The Chevalier de Mâcon returns [to Orgelet] on Friday the 31st. I leave on Saturday, June 1, for Verrières, arriving there Sunday the 2nd. Sophie was supposed to leave that evening."[2] Evidently he is trying to rush things. He slips over into "Swiss Verrières" in the province of Neuchâtel, beyond reach of the police in Verrières de Joux on the French side of the border. A smuggler named Jeanret will take Sophie on muleback from Pontarlier to Switzerland over the back-

roads of Mount Larmont. The weather is cold and rainy. Soaking wet, Mirabeau waits out part of the night of June 2 at the French border. Sophie has
sounded another alarm at home by slipping into a pair of velvet breeches and
heavy-soled shoes in anticipation of the foul weather. That same morning she
ordered laudanum from Pontarlier's apothecary, intending to swallow it if her
escape failed, after first drugging or poisoning the household. She had half an
ounce.* Her frenzied excitement frightens everyone, including the lover waiting for her in the bone-chilling mist, who temporarily abandons the escape
plan on learning the next morning that a second Cerberus now guards her:
Richard de Vesvrottes, one of Sophie's brothers, who has come to reinforce
the canoness. The laudanum has been confiscated. "Monday the 3rd, I leave
Les Verrières. Richard arrives that day." Sophie scribbles a hasty note to her
lover promising not to kill herself and to wait a few endless weeks until her
husband takes her to Nans, where she will be free of her watchdogs. She begs
him to look after himself and to avoid recapture.

No real need for her to be alarmed. Mirabeau never drops his guard
completely. He is already en route to the Lake of Geneva in a hired carriage,
there being no mail coaches in Switzerland. He races toward the one other
woman who can help him, his sister Louise. At Morges he boards "a small
three-oared boat with a canvas top" and expects to perish in one of those
sudden squalls for which the lake is famous. "Wednesday, June 5, I reached
Geneva," that immaculate, unsmiling citadel of Calvinism which frowns on
lawless individuals like himself. He settles down in a small inn and, with hearty
appetite, attacks the eight or ten courses on the menu, "delicious dishes,
excellent preserves, but the cheese and butter are horrid and no heavy cream
is available because the natives prefer to use their milk for cheese-
making."[3] He has almost no luggage and less linen, yet he tips generously,
for Sophie has sent him several thousand francs** unabashedly "lifted" from
her husband—one installment of her dowry, so to speak. Honoré is recovering
from all the excitement and his imprisonment, awaiting word from Louise.
Where will they see each other? Should he meet her in Lyons? She suggests
a safer place: the Kingdom of Sardinia, where police are virtually nonexistent.
Thonon, for instance, on the edge of Lake Geneva, in the Savoy district.
"Sunday the 9th, I arrive in Thonon," and, calling himself the Comte de
Montchevrey, puts up at the Ecu de France.[4] This tiny fishing and farming
village on the shore of the lake is blind and deaf to the world; an oversize head
causes no stir owing to the current emergency: a frog invasion worse than the
Egyptian plague. One entire district becomes uninhabitable because of their
croaking, triggered, the residents complain, by the chiming of clocks. On June

*Nearly ten grams of liquid opium mixed with aromatic herbs and sherry, but quite as lethal as
granular opium.
**According to Ruffey, 12,000, which amounts to nearly 50,000 current francs [$10,000]; but
Mirabeau cannot have received it all at once.

13, four days after Mirabeau's arrival, a committee of public officials decrees that all clocks shall be silenced.* The ideal spot to go underground. How could Mirabeau know that the police are already on his trail and that his father, the Ruffeys, the Marquis de Monnier, and the Marignane clan will learn momentarily of his presence in Thonon?

They are furious and fearful. Having said so often that his son is a scoundrel, the Friend of Man finally persuades everyone of the fact. Emilie has returned to her family's estate in Provence and the Marignane household quakes: what if the prisoner tries to abduct her? Marignane writes to Mirabeau senior to urge apprehension of his son-in-law, and volunteers to contribute fifty louis toward the hunt.[5] Madame de Ruffey also informs the Friend of Man that she has intercepted a letter from Louise to Sophie and has learned that the wretch is in Thonon. The next step is to have Vergennes extradite him. "Your son is ruining a family and a well-born, well-bred woman whom he has bewitched to the point of making her forget all demands of duty and honor . . . You cannot doubt his capacity to induce her into one crime after another."[6] Their fears are ill-founded, for the marquis wastes no time. Malesherbes is not there any longer to pry into private family matters. The Friend of Man asks Police Chief Lenoir a favor which prominent aristocrats occasionally could obtain—at considerable cost. Two sleuths from the Paris force are "detailed" on a semi-private, semi-official basis to hunt down the escaped prisoner, whose father must pay them each twenty-five livres daily for wages and expenses.** Their names are Mouron, who is "unique in all Europe at this sort of thing," and Bruguières—*Monsieur* de Bruguières, if you please, one of twenty inspectors for the city of Paris, and who was not idle during the grain riots. The Marquis de Mirabeau spared no expense to teach his son a lesson: "The scoundrel is leading a wild chase. His odious talents baffle the best agents. But were he to run them around the globe, I'll get him."[7] When and if he is caught, they have picked out the ideal fortress for him, midway between the women he loves and who love him: Mont Saint-Michel, from which no one has ever escaped "because first there is the fortress, then an enclosure surrounding the hill, then a path through the dunes, rather long, requiring a guide if one is not to perish in the quicksand." The dogs are picking up the scent now, a week behind the quarry. They reach Geneva when Honoré is in Thonon. They cannot arrest him in a foreign country, but official status entitles them to cooperation from local law officers. Mirabeau will find himself struggling in a spider web that is drawing tighter and tighter about him.

---

*Savoy is a tradition-bound province: the partial prohibition of chiming clocks in Thonon lasts over a century, even after the town becomes French and long after everyone has forgotten the reason for the ordinance.

**A mammoth sum. The skin of "Mirabeau fils" begins to cost its weight in gold. To apprehend him, his father pays nearly 800 (current) francs [$160] daily for months. The 5000 francs [$1000] contributed by Honoré's father-in-law barely covers one week of the hunt.

Why does Louise keep him waiting? A week without a woman, without a shoulder to weep on in this frog-infested land, is intolerable. He writes to his sister, mostly about Sophie. "If I am to be separated from her, I prefer dungeons, death, and torture. Here I am banished from my country, separated from you, without hope of seeing my son again, lost to all my friends . . . I have made every sacrifice to love and done nothing for love. I shall never dare set foot in my native land, even if I should desire to. Object of insulting pity to poor creatures who pat themselves on the back for being incapable of passion . . . condemned by insects who call their bigotry morality, what would I do in France? And what would I want to do, far from Sophie? . . . I suffer an intense illness that is tearing my soul apart, corroding my physical energies . . . Love is the only remedy," of course, but is it love for Sophie alone? The letter ends with him turning hopefully to the woman whose arrival he awaits more and more breathlessly as the days pass: "Write to me! Write to me! Never have I needed you so . . . I am certain you must have written to me, but the mails can't keep pace with my head or heart." He could have saved himself the cost of that letter, dated June 15. Louise de Cabris arrives in Thonon the next day for a reunion not prescribed in any social manual. The past year has punished them both, emptied them. Two creatures stripped bare, dying for revenge on life, knowing that their hours are numbered. They grab all they can. Louise is not alone? That's all right, too; the more the merrier.

Louise has brought along her inseparable friend Briançon and a newcomer, Jeanne de La Tour-Boulieu, a delectably innocent-looking maid of twenty, the sort that Mirabeau never can resist. The face of an angel contradicted by the shape of her lips. Ironic touch: Mirabeau had slept with her older sister* ten years before when his regiment was stationed at Saintes, and he recalled meeting Jeanne, then only a child but not the least bashful. She is curious to see her sister's lover again. She also lodges at the convent of La Déserte in Lyons and has followed in Louise's footsteps, which suits Briançon admirably. The fact that she is betrothed to one Sieur de Villedieu is just another reason for indulging in a little fun. Mirabeau loudly declares himself to be Sophie's "fiancé" by all the laws of nature. What of it? Louise has planned things carefully by bringing along Jeanne; knowing her brother's inclinations, she orchestrates the affair expertly. The Mirabeaus cannot wait. Jeanne and Briançon register at the Ecu de France as servants of Louise, but the "ingenue" slips into bed the very next night with the "Comte de Montchevrey." At once the climate of Thonon feels unwholesome, for these are the mountains of Savoy, where the women wear black and the men have been domesticated by their priests. Sex outside of marriage is inconceivable. Villagers eye this unconventional quartet suspiciously. Sensing danger, the four of them depart. "We all leave together on Thursday the 20th [of June] for Geneva," where Mira-

---

*Who has since married the elderly Marquis de Saint-Orens, but still has a fond spot in her heart for Mirabeau, whom she writes to now and then.

beau passes himself off as "the Chevalier de Vassan," a name borrowed from his mother (foolish fellow!) which identifies him instantly to his pursuers when they make inquiries in Geneva a week later, after a mix-up that sends the agents from Geneva to Thonon and back again to Geneva, where the trail gets warm.

In Geneva are they reacting to the pervasive puritanism? The four suddenly go wild, doing all they can to attract attention. They sell some of Sophie's jewelry and fling the money right and left. The riding costume in which Louise goes about will baffle inspectors a week later: the authorities have been watching the borders since June 4 for Mlle Raucourt, the French theater's most notorious lesbian and wild eccentric, who has taken to her heels to escape a pack of creditors. Louise is mistaken for her, and because Mirabeau cannot avoid being recognized, even in disguise, wherever he goes, rumors reach the families and the police that the scoundrel has taken up with a she-devil of the same breed: "Mirabeau fils" and La Raucourt are reported in Geneva with two servants between June 20 and 22, joined by a fifth accomplice, which all but plunges the detectives into a fever. He is the Chevalier de Mâcon bringing ardent letters from Sophie, but also warning that they have been spotted and are being trailed. Up and away! Geneva suddenly feels unhealthy. Oh well, they had to pass through some big city or other in order to sell the jewelry. Mâcon returns to Pontarlier armed with equally passionate letters, in none of which is there a word of Jeanne de La Tour-Boulieu. Meanwhile the other four melt away on Sunday the 23rd, completely and totally. A week's "grace" before the law picks up their trail. The search continues in Switzerland, Savoy, and Germany; they reach France just in time . . .

The La Tour-Boulieu family owns a château in La Balme, on the banks of the rushing, still untamed Rhône, where boats venture cautiously. To the north, in France, is nearby Belley; eastward, in Savoy, lies neighboring Yenne. All they have to do is drift down the river from Geneva. They are alone with Jeanne, who presides over the household in her parents' absence, and a few discreet servants in the peace and quiet of the country, secure behind walls and moats that give the little castle a fortresslike air. No one would think of looking for them there. It is the kind of solitude *à quatre* that Mirabeau has longed for. Quiet, yes, but not repose, for in less than a week he falls ill from exhaustion. Fainting and choking spells suggest epilepsy. The doctors of his day call it "an attack of satyriasis." Indeed, the Friend of Man had predicted that if sister and brother ever got together, all hell would break loose. But was that the kind of hell he meant?

How far away Sophie is! She writes to him on June 24:* "Every evening I read your declaration of love . . . Yes, I swear to be yours alone, that nothing in the world can change the love I have pledged; I have told you a thousand times that I cannot live without you, without your love. Never fear,

*From Pontarlier she addresses the letter to Thonon, thinking he is still there.

hard as they may try to ensnare me, I shall not give in; I have already told them I will have to read in your own handwriting that you no longer love me . . . I would take it for forgery, such is my faith in you, such my confidence in your vows, in your love."[8] What is she after? He still loves her and is merely faithless, in the fullest sense of the word, behaving like a cad of a husband. Perhaps he is simply struggling to hold back the torrent of stifling, possessive affection that has suffused Sophie's letters over the previous two months, a flood of "baby mine, dear love, little one, my dearest love, sweetheart, Mimi, beloved, Sophie's better half, cherished little one, lover, dear one, dearest one, dearest of friends, husband, Fanfan, loving sweetheart, cherished lover," and especially "Gabriel" or "Gabriel mine," as apparently she has chosen to reshuffle the order of his name. To her he is Gabriel rather than Honoré, an additional form of possession. For herself she has invented a double first name and signs her letters "Sophie-Gabrielle."[9] On top of this, her obsessive association of death with passion installs defeat, like a worm, in the fruit of their love. "Let us live together or die" (August 1). "This must end, or else I cannot bear it any longer; your health and mine will not withstand it. I repeat to you: Gabriel or die!" (same day). "Let us be reunited or let me die! I shall not see another year, I cannot, nor do I want to" (August 3). "Oh my husband, yes, Sophie will be there at the end, unless she breathes her last before you and in your arms. At least we are almost certain to die together, and that in itself is a lot" (August 16). "I often remind myself that neither of us was born fortunate enough to see our hopes materialize, but at least let us be sure of dying together" (August 20). He disagrees, trying bravely enough to play Romeo to this morbid Juliet, though Don Juan is far more suited to his talents. Mirabeau has many failings, but morbidity is not one of them. He wants to love and be loved with a minimum of problems. He has no desire to exploit the romantic attraction of his ugliness: "I used to say, like Duguesclin, [who was] at least as ugly as I am: 'Never shall I be loved or welcomed, and thus forever rejected by the ladies, as well do I know that I am exceedingly ugly in form and feature. But as I am so ugly, the braver do I wish to be.' And as time passed, I grew less and less afraid of myself; I realized that ladies were so nice that the ugly men had quite as many as the handsome ones."[10] He cultivates a casual Rousseauism, without which the women of his set would shun him, Sophie included; besides, he appreciates the liberating philosophy of Jean-Jacques, whom he claims to have met at the age of seventeen when his father let him use the family's country cottage at Fleury-sous-Meudon. "I knew him, and I know several people who have practiced his teachings. He was always the same, a man of integrity, candor, and simplicity."[11] And "Gabriel," like a pilgrim in the Holy Land, did indeed commune with nature on the banks of the Lake of Geneva, recalling scenes of love between Héloïse and Saint-Preux: yet he refuses to identify with them. "Nothing seems so flat to a person in love as most love stories," he tells Sophie. "You will hate Rousseau when you reread Héloïse . . . Besides, none of those great writers seems so great when love is at hand. We are the ones who possess the key to this god."[12]

The more Sophie carries on about death, the fonder Gabriel becomes of life. After a week at La Balme, why does he risk returning to France and hiding in Lyons? To be nearer Sophie? No, for Louise has won out. He accepts her plan, a plan that locks him into dependence on her. The two have written their mother, asking her to locate a sanctuary for her son in Paris with some relative or trustworthy friend—one of the Noailles, for instance, who have great influence at court. From Lyons he will attempt one last secret journey to Paris to confront the king and his ministers. Let them arrest and interrogate him openly. Public opinion will defend him, so how could they possibly outlaw him again? By seeking justice in this fashion, he will expunge the record of his principal "act of rebellion," his escape first from Pontarlier, then from Dijon. The other matters, his debts and that business in Grasse, are mere trifles. And no one has any serious complaint against Sophie now that she has gone back to her husband. "Sunday [June] 30, Briançon and I go to Lyons." Sophie has just written to him: "Don't try to return home; go away; I keep telling you that I will join you no matter where."[13]

The two men hired a "mail boat" that arrived from Seyssel, took them aboard at the château, and is now heading down the Rhône for Lyons. By playing with rudder and tiller, the two boatmen drift along "at the pace of a carthorse." The shoreline shimmers in sunlight; the grassy banks seem to be choking the river. It's midsummer, which annually seems to spell madness for the man with the oversize head. Instead of passing unobserved, Briançon and Mirabeau behave like students on a rampage. At Cerdon they point their pistols at customs inspectors, and in docking at the port of Grange-Rouge below Lyons, they wave aside the normal invasion of transient stevedores—Lyons has twenty thousand beggars—with the legendary arrogance of English travelers. Are they drunk or what? The angry mob of dockers mills about the pair brandishing clubs and fishing spears.

Briançon takes to his heels and vanishes; Mirabeau will never forgive him. So that's the courageous Captain Denis-Augustin de Jausserandy-Briançon, seigneur of Verdache, officer in the Royal Roussillon regiment, with whom he is forced to share his sister's affections? The man Louise has been dragging about for three years? Predictably, Gabriel faces the mob head on with a four-round pistol in hand and manages to slip out. The pistol nearly figures in a duel once he catches up with Briançon. Explosive scene. End of the friendship. They never had much in common anyway, except a certain inertia; this will continue for several days to mask a breach that is like a crack spreading through plaster. They patch up their differences long enough to take lodgings "in a furnished hotel without signboard" on the corner of the Rue du Petit-

Pizay, swarming with prostitutes. Seventy-two livres* payable in advance is a
month's rental for "accommodations with two double beds" in which Louise
and Jeanne join them the next day, this time without fear of shocking the
neighborhood. This is a far cry from Thonon. The tallest buildings in France,
some of them six or seven stories, choke the narrow, dismal, stifling streets.
Foul odors and the July heat of Lyons. Half naked, for ten days or so the
foursome carry on their revels with windows wide open. Meals are brought
up by a maidservant, for whom the door is always left ajar. Louise finds all this
very stimulating, a welcome change from convent life, but the city is too hot,
too dirty, and too depressing for Jeanne de La Tour-Boulieu, who begins to
miss her fiancé, and for Mirabeau, whose choking spasms return. Spiritual
rather than physical strangulation this time. Briançon has been getting on his
nerves ever since the dock episode. Not just Briançon either, for by siding
with him against her brother, Louise has stirred Honoré's resentment. Not just
Louise either; he feels ashamed of himself. More than ever he longs for Sophie,
a longing that is more than sensual. He yearns to trade the gutters of Lyons
for the bracing mountain air of the Jura.

Mirabeau feels a certain sense of relief when told that the grim-faced
hunters are closing in. Time to move on. They must split up. Shall it be Paris?
Too dangerous without help from the Marquise de Mirabeau, who refused to
become involved. Briançon, partly to make amends perhaps, but mostly because Louise seeks to alienate her brother from Sophie, suggests that they flee
south to Lorgues, his birthplace in Upper Provence. The women will return
to the Benedictine convent in Lyons and wait for further word. Brother and
sister must say good-by—forever—promising falsely to meet again in two
weeks. "Sunday [July] 14, we leave for Provence." On Tuesday the 16th the
stagecoach races into Lorgues; he arrives after dark so as not to be seen.

Lorgues lies about seven miles from Draguignan and looks like the twin
of Barras's next-door native town. A speck on the map, a dozen whitewashed
houses and a church, where everyone knows exactly what his neighbor is
doing. No place for Mirabeau to hide other than a second-story room in the
house of Briançon's notary, who leaves for Grasse that evening. Here "Mr.
Hurricane" finds himself more closely confined than ever: four walls and
perpetually closed shutters through which street gossip filters. The shock of
sudden calm after the whirlwind. Sophie is his only hope and he writes to her
daily, huge letters (twenty-four pages on July 17) which the notary forwards
to Pontarlier through intermediaries. He replies to messages she sent him in
Lyons, brave displays of epistolary lust, which he knows are forced and chides
her for it: "Why is your mood so overwhelmingly amorous? At times this
really annoys me." Understandably, in the light of his own activities. And on
July 20, precisely because he had begun to live again, his letter to Sophie
contrasts in great detail her and his sister's sexual attractions. For Sophie's

*360 francs [$72] in 1970.

benefit he passes this off as memories recalled from his adolescence, when in fact it is a piping-hot chronicle of incest: "Her mouth [Louise's], though spoiled, is still splendid, but that dazzling feature is lost in bed when not complimented by fine skin and a fine figure, and in this respect you have the advantage. She has pretty arms and hands, but yours are prettier, a gift so rare among women, and here again you have the advantage because yours are infinitely whiter. Louise's thighs are too stout and bulging. Yours are merely plump but perfectly straight, which is far more desirable for walking properly and making love . . . As to describing her distressing qualities, things that pain me to recall, I can only say that you are infinitely superior to her in the quantity of your attractive features as well as your use of them; remember, dear Sophie, that a man of refinement can tell if a woman is more preoccupied with herself than with him when they make love, and that sexual transport is itself a delicate thing. Remember, too, my adorable wife, that a woman who may pass as the greatest beauty in society is far from being the most pleasing to her lover in bed." And on and on, then a blank sheet with several lines of writing in lemon juice* that provide new instructions for her flight, as he reaches out to Sophie in his solitude. He gives up the idea of Paris and promises her "supreme happiness in a refuge hidden from the world where we can be everything to one another." But she never receives this letter. Mirabeau addressed it, for some unknown reason, to Charlotte Bonjour, who tended shop for Charnaux the apothecary in Pontarlier, the same man who had reported Sophie's laudanum purchase. Charlotte has more to gain by selling the letter to her employer than by slipping it to Sophie, and Charnaux promptly hands it over to her parents. In no time all of Pontarlier, including the church establishment, is whispering about the Monnier household. An abduction is in the wind; villagers have a nose for such things, and the apothecary is reluctant to lose clients. Mirabeau's enemies now hold a dagger at his throat: evidence of his corruption signed in his own hand.[14]

Sophie is slow to see the storm gathering. Early August finds her still in Pontarlier—the trip to Nans is delayed from one day to the next—in a benignly feverish state. Her provincial life runs like clockwork: "I spend most of my day reading your letters or writing to you . . . The rest is taken up with books, meals, social calls, receptions, walks, sleeping, etc."[15] In the evening, like a dutiful wife, she plays reversi** with her husband, who finds her far more tractable now and would have no complaints were she to share his bed occasionally, if only to still local gossip. That she refuses to do, however, and reacts oddly when the poor man laments his enforced masturbation: "The day I arrive [at their house in Nans, which has a master bedroom] I shall refuse

*Which emerge when the paper is held up to heat.
**A card game played "in reverse," so to speak, since the player who picks up the fewest tricks wins.

to go to sleep unless given my own bed. Today he told me I would bear the burden of the sins he was committing, but I doubt that he is stealing many souls from God.''[16] Beneath her composure, she is all afire with plans to escape that alternately die and flare up a dozen times a week at a word from the smugglers or peddlers who constitute her chain of communication with her beloved Gabriel. She meets them in the only places a well-bred woman can expect to enjoy any privacy: the churches of Pontarlier. By August 10 she is ready, still waiting for word of their departure for Nans, where she expects Mirabeau's messenger to be Briançon disguised as a peddler, "but muslin is not the sort of thing he ought to bring around, for the marquis does not like opening his door to tradesmen with expensive products for sale; instead he can offer ribbons, needles, coat sleeves, pomade, or small artificial flowers. It will cost him less than twelve livres* to collect such an assortment.''[17] By August 14 she has improved on the plan and will slip into a compartment of the tradesman's cart, "which, unlike the average peddler's rig, will be a carriage with two roomy trunks . . . one of which will be closed and presumably empty. The other will contain a few pairs of gloves and some ribbons that he will insist on selling me. They will be 'Muffled Sighs' and 'Telltale Moans' the same shade as the queen's hair . . .''**[18] She grows anxious as the days pass. She is beset by worries because of the sizable time gap imposed by the slowness of their clandestine mail system—one to two weeks to transmit a letter: she begins to suspect that Gabriel has partly forsaken her, that he is not what he seemed to be, that Louise is tricking him, that Briançon will not come. On August 1: "But, my dear, is Louise false-hearted? How contradictory her behavior is . . . Well, we won't have her in our refuge!''[19] Next day her anguish focuses on one thing only: "Friday, August 2, 1776, dear love, I am greatly concerned about the letter you promise me containing the blank sheet . . . I shall keep looking for it until Saturday, but if it does not arrive by then, I fear it may be lost. Besides, it was not a good idea of yours to send it to a different address.''[20] August 6: "I received your letters of the 25th and 28th, but still not the one with the blank sheet.''[21] By now the "letter of incest" is in her parents' hands. Its seizure, which would terrify her if she knew about it, will shortly precipitate her "happiness."

Sophie's alarm over this letter sends Mirabeau into a panic around August 9. He realizes how foolish he was to send it and can imagine how someone might use it against him. He knows that his sister will never forgive him for dishonoring her if she hears about it—and his father is sure to see that she does. Besides, he is fed up with Louise. He rejects her. Instead, he will take the bull by the horns, make a dash on his own to Switzerland, and carry out the plan, thwarted last June, to meet Sophie at the border. Sophie, only Sophie can give him the love he wants and the money he needs. He informs her of his decision

---

*About fifty francs [$10] today.
**"Muffled Sighs": a type of brocade; "Telltale Moans": a type of dress trimming.

on August 10, but in a sour, ill-tempered note that projects all his self-hatred onto her. Nor does he spare her a fit of jealousy—hard to imagine in the wake of his own bedroom feats at La Balme and the Rue Pizay. He greets her not jubilantly but like a whipped dog. She receives this letter on August 20, having put to rest the doubts of family and friends by celebrating communion on the Feast of the Assumption. All Pontarlier whispers of her conversion while she frets her heart out: "Am I free? Alas, shall it be forever? Why do I have such gloomy forebodings?"[22] She replies to him with dignity, her head high, and rather archly: "It is not easy for me to accept harsh words from you . . . It was my understanding that Gabriel thought highly enough of his wife not to entertain offensive suspicions. Alas, will you not let me die secure in the knowledge of your love and your esteem? Such a death would have been sweet compared to what I am suffering . . . Oh Gabriel, how do you find the courage to write me those things, when only a short while ago you spoke of my sensibility?"[23] So now she is not happy about the situation; he has already managed to spoil their reunion. The die is cast, however; she feels a certain obligation to go through with the plan and, like a good soldier, awaits his signal. It is the last letter she writes from Pontarlier.

From Mirabeau's diary: "I leave [Lorgues] on the night of Tuesday August 13 for Les Verrières and travel through the mountains of the county of Nice [*sic*], Turin, the Great St. Bernard, Valais, etc." A mad gallop, practically non-stop, spurred by impatience and prudence, for the police are trailing him from Lyons to Lorgues. They have just learned his address from Louise's own lips: she would rather send her brother back to prison than into Sophie's arms.

Neuchâtel; the Val de Travers, also rich with memories of Jean-Jacques. A deep green springtime lingers into August, setting the scene for the abduction of another Héloïse. On August 23 Mirabeau puts up at the Monkey Inn in the town of Saint-Sulpice. His arrival seems to flush out an army of go-betweens: business-minded tradesmen like Lambelet the innkeeper and his wife; Jeanret the smuggler; Rosselet the quarrier; Cabasson the watch vendor; reliable young D'Aubonne; or Parguez, son of the local administrator. They besiege the Monnier house, they run a chain of messages between the lovers. Rain pours down, as in June—a piece of luck, for it keeps the townsfolk indoors. Another piece of luck: servants' vespers. The Marquis de Monnier, like most provincial aristocrats, observes the practice of assembling his domestics for a brief lesson based on Sunday's scripture reading. For one whole hour Sophie is not spied upon. She slips into man's dress, including, for the fun of it, one of her husband's hats. She "does the garden wall" with the aid of a rope ladder supplied by Cabasson, whom she joins, aided by Rosselet. The three traipse blithely down the deserted, rain-sodden main street of town. A horse is hitched at the entrance to the mountain path. For an hour Sophie winds her way along a muddy trail in the darkness, guided by the two men. Mirabeau awaits her, soaked to the skin just as he was two months (or two centuries?)

earlier—at the border, the foot of the slope, the other side of his life—
prepared for whatever may come, with only Lambelet the innkeeper at his
side.

"On Saturday 24, Sophie reaches Les Verrières at eleven-thirty at night."

"*Here* [editorial note to the first edition of his memoirs, published the year
after Mirabeau's death] *he has sketched a blazing heart.*"

ROUSSEAU

58

OCTOBER 1776

I Watched the Blood Flow Out of Me

On February 29, 1776, Manon Phlipon* had fled the stifling community of
the Place Dauphine and its swarm of aging admirers to try to contact Jean-
Jacques Rousseau. Her excuse? She needed his advice, possibly about her
reading or her love life, though we shall never know the contents of the letters
she sent him via "a good Genevan," sixty-year-old Augustin Moré, a "philosophic and republican clockmaker," one of the few persons who still had
access** now and then to Rousseau's house on the Rue Plâtrière. What exactly
did she want? To see "this man so celebrated for his endowments, his virtues,
and his misfortunes"?[1] Or to let him see her? She is tired of being ignored
and he is her idol, chiefly for having written *La Nouvelle Héloïse.* How can she
bear it, living so close to him? "I knew it was extremely difficult to get to talk
to him, and even then, rather than appear himself, he would have his wife
reply." So she settled on the letter; "that is why I decided to carry out my
mission in writing, and then go fetch the answer myself."

"Two days after sending my letter, this morning at nine o'clock I take
Mignonne [her maid] by the arm and set out for Rousseau's house, uncertain
of what the outcome will be." The two women have a short way to go under
leaden, wintry skies. Half the Pont Neuf; the Trois Maries crossing that leads
to the Right Bank; Rue de La Monnaie; a short stretch of the Rue du Roule;
then around the bulging Hôtel de Soissons and its garden onto a straight,
rather attractive street lined with four-story houses on either side of the St.
Agnes convent school for girls. His wanderings over, Rousseau has returned

---

*The future Madame Roland.
**And could thus deliver letters to the great man, who for three years had systematically refused
all postal communications, if only to avoid paying the postage.

to settle down with Thérèse next to the Hôtel du Saint-Esprit, where they had lived twenty-five years earlier.

Manon enters "the alleyway of the cobbler on the Rue Plâtrière; I climb two flights and knock at the door. No one enters a house of worship with a greater feeling of reverence than mine before that humble doorway; I was possessed, but not with my usual timidity toward ordinary people, for whom I really have no respect; I hovered between hope and fear. What useless anxiety. Is it possible, I wondered, that I may say of him what he said of scholars: 'I took them for angels; I never passed their doorstep without some respectful acknowledgment; I met them—the only disillusionment they ever caused me'? Thinking thus, I saw the door open; a woman in her fifties stood there in a little cap, a plain but fresh housecoat and apron, with a serious and rather grim look on her face."

Thérèse Le Vasseur is fifty-four. Thirty-one years before, Rousseau had pledged "neither to forsake nor to marry her." He kept his word, though now he insists on calling "wife" the woman whom not so long ago he called his "servant." She was not bad-looking at twenty-three, when the musician from Geneva, who was just starting to lecture on music, singled out in the ropemakers' hall in Paris "this innocent-looking young girl who was mending linen and waiting on table." She had "a modest air, an alert, gentle way about her, and an agreeable disposition."* Though not easy to get along with, she was eager to love and be loved. Penniless; compulsively tidy. Perpetually sick, he thought of himself as old before his time and longed to meet the dream woman of all misogynists: a lifetime servant to share his bed and spare his emotions. Each lived up to the bargain: she became his nurse, gentle mistress, and fierce watchdog; he was a conscientious provider, also demanding and disdainful by turns. "I had facing the windows [he narrates at this particular period in his *Confessions*] a sundial on which I tried for over a month to get her to tell the time. She can barely tell it now [thirty years later]. She has never been able to name the twelve months of the year in proper order and cannot count despite all my efforts to teach her."[3] Even now the "grim look" is not unbecoming. Her face simply registers thirty years of her companion's scorn, toward her as toward others—and to others she returned that scorn with interest. So Manon Phlipon, like others before her, can expect a warm welcome!

> "Madam, is this not Monsieur Rousseau's house?"
> "It is, mademoiselle."
> "May I speak to him?"
> "Why have you come?"
> "For the reply to a letter I wrote him recently."
> "Mademoiselle, no one speaks to him, but you may tell the persons who

---

*According to Rousseau himself, as quoted by Jean Guéhenno.[2]

prompted you to write him . . . for such a letter surely did not come from you . . . "

"Excuse me, but . . . "

"The writing is plainly a man's."

"Would you care to watch me write?" I asked, grinning.

She shook her head. "All I can tell you is that my husband has renounced these things forever; he has given up everything; though he wishes to be helpful, he has reached the age of repose."

"I know, but at least I would have felt flattered to hear this from his own lips; I seized this opportunity to pay my respects to the man I esteem above everyone else in the world: kindly tell him this, madam."

She thanked me, with her hand still clutching the bolt, and I went downstairs happy in the knowledge that he found my letter too well written to be the work of a woman, and faintly annoyed at having wasted my time.

So that was how the world and pretty young girls banged their heads in vain against Jean-Jacques Rousseau's door in 1776. Behind the door, in the inner room (there were only two), straining his ears, stood the bundle of nerves cursing and blessing Thérèse for carrying out his orders. He could not bear callers; the slightest human contact made him ill. How closely she guarded his lair! "Near him was a spinet* on which he would try out a melody from time to time. Two single beds with blue-and-white-striped cotton coverlets, the colors of the room; a chest of drawers, a table, and a few chairs completed his furnishings . . . A canary sang in a cage suspended from the ceiling; sparrows came to peck bread crumbs on the window sills overlooking the main street, and in the vestibule were flower boxes and pots of greenery . . . There was a pleasing air of tidiness about the house, of peace and simplicity."[4] All this observed by one of the few persons Rousseau still consented to see, a thirty-five-year-old wanderer still undecided between a scientific or a literary career, but well acquainted with poverty, Bernardin de Saint-Pierre, whose recently published *Voyage à l'Ile de France* has had no success. Sometimes they took walks together, praising God and cursing mankind. " 'My heart tells me that I am owed something,' Rousseau confided to him, 'but it is beyond human power to give it to me.' "[5] His appearance at the Opera during a rehearsal of Gluck's *Iphigénie* and the blessing he bestowed on its composer had caused a sensation two years before: the theatrical effect solemnized the event. He counted on that.

No more "events." No more men or women in his life. Eight months after Manon Phlipon's attempted visit on October 24, 1776, Jean-Jacques Rousseau goes out on one of the rambles he has been incorporating into a book: *Les Rêveries du promeneur solitaire.* He lives like a perfectly regulated clock. Rising early, he has copied music all morning to support the two of them, his daily

*Small keyboard instrument with strings plucked by quills. Though passing out of fashion, it remained Rousseau's favorite instrument.

occupation. If the weather had been bad, he would have gone back to work after lunch, but the sun is out. "I am just the opposite of the little man on my Swiss barometer: when he stays in, I go out, and when he goes out, I stay in."[6] The Rue Plâtrière brings him to the Rue du Mont-Martre and on up to the windmills and a sweeping view of Paris. He walks only as far as the boulevard dividing the city from its suburbs, which is climb enough even for the solid legs of this slightly squat fellow with one drooping shoulder, who considers himself an old man but actually is still quite attractive at sixty-five,* with his delicately chiseled lips, "well-shaped nose, high domed forehead, and sparkling eyes . . . His face bore several traces of melancholy in the deep-set eyes and sagging brows; profound sadness in the furrowed forehead; a lively, somewhat caustic sense of humor as seen in the thousands of tiny creases at the outer corners of his eyes, the pupils of which would disappear when he laughed."[7] He wears a gray dress coat which is comfortable for walking, and a short, round, slightly powdered wig; each shoe upper has "two little holes" cut out to relieve bothersome corns; he carries a walking stick and, slung over his shoulder, the box in which he collects plants for his herbarium.

Jean-Jacques Rousseau strolls unnoticed, as he wants to be, through this poor neighborhood. Never has anyone written the way he does. Never has anyone lived as he has. By simply writing and suffering, he is in the process of changing the world for everyone, and people are beginning to realize it, wondering whether he is dead or still alive. Fifteen years before, almost in the span of twelve months, a new concept of love: *La Nouvelle Héloïse*;** a fresh approach to education: *Emile*; a new plan for mankind: *Le Contrat social.* He became as famous as Voltaire. The pinnacle, then the pit of persecution that drove him to despair. Twelve years roaming like the Wandering Jew, escaping himself, too, a man constrained by his own genius. He came to hate the world after loving humanity. He suffered from a fairly common type of schizophrenia characterized by a distrust of persons who cared for and wanted to help him. His friends became his worst enemies. The inner world of this man who had changed the world gave way under pressure from the gulf between what he advocated and what he was. Thirty years ago his first child was born and carried to the orphanage, like the four who came later, by Thérèse's parents. Only his most intimate friends know this. In the eyes of some fifty thousand readers in three or four languages, including Manon Phlipon, Rousseau is Virtue Incarnate.

Now at last he lives according to his own commandments. He accepts his neuroses. The period of drifting is over; he is what he wanted to be; the

---

*Almost. He was born on June 28, 1712.

**Grimm writes: "Women spent nights reading him when they had nothing else to do, and sobbed their hearts out. He has the audacity to attempt what no other writer of fiction would ever dream of: bringing two lovers together before the close of volume one, with three more to go, when no one else would have known what to do with them."[8]

framework of his life, isolated from the lives of others, allows him to indulge peacefully in self-worship, a latter-day Christ sans miracles for the new times. Being his own Messiah is enough for him. He enters the final stage of his life's work: to create his own legend, Jean-Jacques-Jesus. "No longer will I have anything to do with things that take me from myself or tend to rob my mind of the peace my conscience now enjoys."[9]

He goes his way feeling content and secure, safe from further perils. He thinks himself shielded from the world and everyone in it. Twenty years before,* he had written a few lines that anticipate what would happen to him: Is it not the case that all the advantages of society belong to the rich and powerful? Are not all lucrative employments filled solely by them? Are not all bounties, all exemptions reserved for them, and does public authority not function wholly in their behalf? Let a man of rank rob his creditors or otherwise conduct himself like a scoundrel: is he not certain to go unpunished? The thrashings he hands out, the violent crimes he commits, the murders for which he is responsible, are these not suppressed and forgotten in six months' time? . . . Does the crowd disturb him? With a sign, he puts the world in its place. Is a carter in his path? His retainers promptly strike him down; and fifty pedestrians going about their business are more likely to be swept aside than a single idle, useless rogue in his train."[10] In their menacingly swift and massive coaches, the rich did indeed travel about Paris before the era of sidewalks, when persons on foot had to leap over gutters to cross the street. In Louis XV's day a rich man's arrival in town was preceded by "runners" hired for their speed and endurance, who would clear the street with shouts. In recent years some "progress" has been made: "Coach owners have given up this impertinent and dangerous luxury, but instead of a man, they send ahead their hounds, whose sole function seems to be to knock people down and subject them to the peril of being trampled by oncoming horses or crushed under the wheels. Pedestrians in those narrow streets had a hard enough time keeping clear of heavy carts, stagecoaches, and light carriages. Now there are giant dogs plunging at them, barking, leaping, and dashing about in the middle of the street, making enough racket to blot out the sound of hoofbeats and the coachman's warning shout."[11]

The Marquis de Saint-Fargeau appears in history books because of his dog. Jean-Jacques has made his way to the heights of suburban Mesnil-Montant by following the boulevards, then climbing up the Rue du Chemin-Vert. A gentleman named Montant once had a *mesnil* there, "which meant a small country house, on the hilltop overlooking the Temple; his name became attached to the spot."[12] "From there, along paths winding through vineyards and meadows, I made my way to Charonne across the cheerful countryside that separates the two towns, then took a detour in order to retrace those same meadows by a different path."[13] He is not far from Bagnolet, at the edge of

*In an article for the *Encyclopédie* entitled *"Economie," "*by M. Rousseau, citizen of Geneva."

which "stands the town of Charonne, where most of the land is covered with grapevines in the midst of which lies a small pond formed by the run-off from fountains you see on the way to Mesnil-Montant . . . The hillside location of this town explains the presence of pretty cottages there."[14] Rousseau goes herb-hunting and finds two specimens "I seldom came across in the Paris neighborhood but which grew abundantly in that township." No one can describe better than he what happened next, both inside and outside himself:

"The harvest had been in for several days; city strollers were gone, and farmers were leaving the fields until winter chores would call them back. The countryside, still green and beckoning, though partly defoliated and nearly deserted, was the picture of solitude and approaching winter. Its appearance conveyed a blend of sweet sadness too suggestive of my own years and situation for me to ignore it. I saw myself in the declining years of a blameless, unhappy existence, my heart still full of warm feelings, my mind still adorned with a few flowers though now they are faded by sadness and withered by care. Alone and forsaken, I felt the chill of approaching frosts, and my waning imagination no longer peopled my solitude with creatures after my own heart. Sighing, I asked myself: what have I done here on earth? I was born to live, and I die having never lived . . . My thoughts drifted back pleasantly to past affections, to attachments so tender but so blind, to ideas less sad than consoling which had nourished my spirit in recent years, and I prepared to recall them sufficiently in order to describe them with nearly the same pleasure I had experienced originally. The afternoon passed in the course of these peaceful meditations, leaving me quite content with the day, when I was rudely thrust from my musing by the event I am about to narrate.

"At about six o'clock I was descending Mesnil-Montant, just opposite the Galant Jardinier, when some people walking in front of me suddenly dove aside and I saw a Great Dane, followed directly by a coach, racing toward me, unable to alter its course or swerve aside as it caught sight of me. I felt my only chance to avoid being knocked over was to leap up while the dog dashed under me. This idea flashing through my head, which I had time neither to reason nor carry out, was my last before the accident. I never felt the impact or my fall or any of the aftermath until the moment I regained consciousness.

"It was nearly dark when I came to my senses. I found myself in the arms of three or four young men who told me what had happened. Unable to check its spring, the Great Dane had bounded at my legs, the full impact of its thrust and speed knocking me down head first: my upper jaw, with the weight of my whole body behind it, had hit the uneven cobblestones, and what made the fall even worse was that, on landing, my head sank lower than my feet.

"The coach* to which the dog belonged followed instantly and would have run over me if the driver had not reined his horses sharply. All this I learned from the men who had picked me up and were still holding me when

*Belonging to the Marquis de Saint-Fargeau.

I came to my senses. The state in which I found myself at that moment is singular enough to warrant description.

"Night was coming on. I glimpsed the sky, a few stars, and a patch of greenery. This first sensation was enchanting. I was aware of that and no more. I drifted into consciousness at that moment and felt as if I, with my unsubstantial existence, were breathing life into all the objects I could see. Wholly in the present, I remembered nothing; I had no clear notion of my individuality, not the slightest idea what had happened to me; I could not tell who I was or where I was; I felt neither pain, nor fear, nor anxiety. I watched the blood flow out of me as if it were a running brook, without once thinking that the blood belonged to me. I felt blissful rapture pervade every vein in me, which, each time I recall it, compares to nothing else in the scale of familiar pleasures.

"They asked me where I lived; I could not tell them. I asked where I was; at the High Milestone, they told me; they might as well have said Mount Atlas. I had to inquire in turn the province, the town, the district I was in. Even then I could not identify myself; it took me from there to the boulevard to remember my house and my name. A stranger who was kind enough to accompany me for a while, on being told how far away I lived, advised me to hire a carriage at the Temple to take me home. I strode along quite freely, feeling no pain or injury, though I spat a good deal of blood. But an icy shiver caused my smashed teeth to chatter most unpleasantly. When I reached the Temple, it occurred to me that, as I had no trouble walking, it would be better to continue on foot than to risk freezing to death in a carriage. So I covered the half-league between the Temple and the Rue Plâtrière at a steady pace, avoiding obstacles and conveyances, picking my way along as if in perfect health. I arrive, I spring the secret lock on the front door, I climb the stairs in the dark, and at last I am home with no ill effects other than my fall and its consequences, of which I was yet unaware.

"My wife's cries at the sight of me gave me to understand that I had suffered worse treatment than I thought. I spent the night still ignorant of my injuries and feeling no pain."

But he will never recover completely from the shock. From now on his walks become shorter and less frequent. The rhythm of his life has been broken.

59

OCTOBER 1776

Gunpowder and Engineers

On December 12, 1776, Jean-Charles Lenoir, counselor to the criminal courts reappointed chief of the Paris police,* the eyes and ears of the monarchy throughout the kingdom, writes to Vergennes: "Dr. Franklin's arrival in Nantes has caused a great stir, not to mention the departure of M. de Beaumarchais, who, from all reports, has gone to Le Havre."[1] Franklin? Beaumarchais? Are there two less likely candidates for acclaim in 1776 than the Sage of the New World and the Madman of the Old? The month of December will bring them together, not haphazardly as in the police files, but through the workings of international politics. Each becomes indispensable to the other, like France to America and vice versa. How has Beaumarchais managed to achieve such prominence?

He prepared himself well in advance, at the end of the past winter, by venturing far outside the bounds of his official mission to London involving the "Chevalière" d'Eon. Perhaps even in 1774, when negotiating for Madame du Barry's honor with Théveneau de Morande, he was thinking of the American cause. He never could do only one thing at a time. Beaumarchais is always thinking of something else. Methodically, he had cultivated the *"beau monde,"* the cream of London's gentry; he had met the celebrated Wilkes and renewed his friendship with Lord Rochford, a connoisseur of music and pretty women whom he had first met in Spain twelve years earlier, when this favorite of George III had been ambassador there. Then Rochford advanced to the foreign ministry, and after a few months Beaumarchais began to assume that he had learned all the secrets of English foreign policy. Figaro and Janus rolled into one. An evening with Whigs, a dinner among Tories, confident that he had become chief adviser to the French court. Secret agent? Nothing of the sort: the power behind the throne.

    Not quite so confident, Vergennes kept hands off. The fellow might

*He had been discharged by Turgot for "incompetence during the grain riots" and reinstated after Turgot's fall, in May 1776, through the efforts of Sartines, his patron.

prove very useful. Sartines continued to act as Beaumarchais's go-between with Louis XVI, to whom he handed reports glowing with an ineffable blend of braggadocio and insight such as the following, dated September 21, 1775:

"I slipped out of England claiming I was off to the country, and rushed from London to Paris to confer with Messrs de Vergennes and de Sartines about matters too crucial and too delicate to be entrusted to any courier, however loyal . . . Here is an accurate account of the English situation in America; the details were provided by a resident of Philadelphia transplanted here and freshly emerged from a conference with the English ministers, whom his story had thrown into utter confusion and panic."[2] The man in question was actually a young Virginia law student, not a Pennsylvanian, named Arthur Lee, a brash, acid-tongued fellow who would have said almost anything in the interests of self-advancement. Because he was among the last partisans of independence in London after Franklin's departure, Lee made himself out to be the colonists' official spokesman. As so often happens when two myth-omaniacs meet, he and Beaumarchais began to fabricate falsehoods, each eager to believe the other in order to delude the many. In September 1775 Arthur Lee was writing even more outrageous reports to a clandestine committee of Congress than was Beaumarchais to his sovereign: "M. de Vergennes has just sent a secret agent to inform me that the French court cannot undertake a war against England but is prepared to ship five millions worth of arms and supplies to Cap Français* for forwarding to the United States."[3] Vergennes would have thrown a fit if he had ever read that. Especially if he had known that in less than a year the lie would come true. Beaumarchais needs only nine months to obtain the mandate and assignment that he claimed in advance.

All winter long he had prodded Vergennes and his sovereign. On February 29, 1776, "To the king alone," ten pages on "peace or war": "The famous dispute between America and England is about to divide the world and change the system in Europe . . . Now that a violent clash is rapidly approaching, I am obliged to warn Your Majesty that the preservation of our American possessions [the "Sugar Islands"] depends solely on this single proposal: we must aid the Americans . . . Mr. L. (M. de Vergennes will provide his name to Your Majesty), colonial secret agent** in London, frustrated by my failure to obtain pledges of gunpowder and munitions from the French ambassador, asks me today: 'For the last time, is France firmly resolved to refuse us aid and to become England's victim and the laughingstock of Europe because of such incredible apathy? . . . We offer France as the price of her secret aid a secret commercial pact which would favor her exclusively for a given number of

---

*Santo Domingo's busiest port at the time, on the big island's northwestern coast. Today it is called Cap Haitien, second largest city in the republic of Haiti after Port-au-Prince.
**Arthur Lee is of course meant.

years after peace is restored, just as we have favored England for a century* . . . Sire, in the name of God! . . . There would be no risk if we adopted the plan I have proposed so often, to aid the Americans secretly without jeopardizing ourselves . . . And if Your Majesty has no one more competent at hand, I can arrange and answer for the pact without dishonor to anyone."[4] Feverish insistence that rises another degree on May 3 in a letter to Vergennes: "Monsieur le Comte, I beg you for gunpowder and engineers! I believe I have never desired anything so ardently!"[5] Vergennes showed signs of weakening. A slow-witted man, he shared Louis XVI's need to deliberate over matters and was the more highly regarded for it. Apparently he was nibbling at the idea: "I have submitted your letter to the king, sir. True to his principles of justice, His Majesty has no desire to take unfair advantage of England by adding to her difficulties, yet he cannot deny his subjects protection for their commerce, which it is his duty to provide."[6] Like a seasoned diplomat, he had perfected the art of saying what he didn't believe with utter sincerity. Neither he nor Louis XVI, nor the Bourbon ruler of Spain who had signed the "family pact" with France, supported the colonial cause. Why, indeed, would these absolute monarchs sustain rebellion, which might prove contagious and threaten France's "Sugar Islands"? And in turn rob Portugal and Spain of their South American holdings? No, it would never do to encourage subversion in half the globe. The ideal solution would be to isolate the colonies behind an effective cordon sanitaire so that England could finish them off—and lose a few of her own feathers in the bargain. The very principle of "taking unfair advantage of England by adding to her difficulties." A diplomatic game as old as diplomacy: "Let us hope that the Americans and the English wear each other out," wrote Spain's Conde de Floridablanca.[7] To French advantage, of course. And since this clockmaker's son was ready and willing to work and, indeed, had boldly volunteered, why not use him? Which of the two, Vergennes or Beaumarchais, finally took the bait? Vergennes reserved the right to disavow Beaumarchais if the situation threatened to become embarrassing—a distinct advantage in such undercover activities, which they had exploited to the hilt in dealing with D'Eon. Does Figaro need cash to generate this clandestine traffic? He will get it, neither too much nor too little, from the right hand, while the left, which swears on Bibles, will ignore him utterly.

In any event, an adventurer's scheme had turned into an affair of state. On June 10, 1776, Beaumarchais could pride himself on reaching the pinnacle of one of his many careers: this time the banking trade:

---

*The Congress offered no such favored-nation status, of course, nor could it, as it was trying to obtain supplies from five or six other powers, including Spain, the Netherlands, and Russia.

I have received from M. Duvergier, pursuant to instructions dated the 5th from M. le Comte de Vergennes, which I handed him, the sum of one million for which I shall render account to the said Comte de Vergennes.

Caron de Beaumarchais
Draft in the sum of one million *livres-tournois**
Paris, June 10, 1776[8]

Two months later, on August 11, the Spanish court paid him the same amount out of the French royal treasury through a tortuous feat of fiscal acrobatics. Never had Beaumarchais laid his hands on so much cash. Why not try for more? Tally ho!

The very next day, June 12, he gets off a letter to Arthur Lee, who is still in London. They had already worked out a method of correspondence. A fictitious Rodrigo Hortalez wrote Miss Mary Johnston an innocuous note which, when decoded, read: "Because of problems in my negotiations with the ministry, I have decided to form a company to forward munitions and gunpowder to your friend in exchange for tobacco deliveries to Cap Français, also addressed to your servant, R. Hortalez & Co."[9] Not a word of the funds he had received: the accounts of Rodrigo Hortalez (a name borrowed from his Spanish adventure, along with others in the *Barber*) were Beaumarchais's private business. Lee at once grew annoyed and replied on June 14: "This is no business transaction we are conducting, but a far-reaching matter of foreign policy." Even then he had visions of negotiating face to face with Vergennes. Those visions were politely quashed. This was business, strictly business, under the table, if you will, between a firm of gunmakers and clients in need of guns. Besides, Arthur Lee found himself short-circuited when Congress appointed Silas Deane to act as "agent of the United Colonies" in France—less than an ambassador, since none was officially recognized, but far better than a secret agent. An unofficial official. He was a merchant from Connecticut, where he had built up a thriving business selling timber, lead, and copper to England. Like countless other patriots, he acted from a mixture of selfish and unselfish motives. They had this in common with Beaumarchais. Deane landed in France at the beginning of July. His round, solid features, his plain, straight nose, his air of unquestionable honesty gave the impression of reliability—as well as gullibility. He was wildly, hopelessly optimistic.

At the outset, unfortunately, Deane wasted the few words of French he knew in a significant dispute. His host in Paris had been Dr. Barbeu-Dubourg, long-time friend of Franklin's, from whom Deane carried letters. Botanist, Rousseauist, though not too unworldly to organize a small committee of bankers and merchants willing to support the patriot cause at reduced rates.

---

*In 1767 the *livre-tournois* (so called because it was minted in Tours for the royal treasury) became the official currency for all transactions. It was beginning to be known popularly as the "franc" and was equivalent to twenty sous. In modern terms, one could say that Beaumarchais pocketed a billion old francs [$200 million], half from France, half from Spain, in the year 1776.

Among the members were Le Ray de Chaumont, a prosperous sugar-importer; Panchaud, a Swiss banker with connections all over the globe; Saint-James, the millionaire with sumptuous "follies" financed by his flourishing armament business; Grandclos-Mêlé, slave trader in Senegal; and several shipbuilders in Nantes and Saint-Malo. Solid, respectable citizens with government connections: Vergennes courted Dubourg and nurtured his hopes. In the light of this, the doctor had tried to take charge of Silas Deane on his arrival, had put him up at the neighboring Hôtel du Grand-Villars, and introduced him privately to Vergennes at a friend's house. For his pains, he found that Beaumarchais was already cueing Deane. "Address yourself to him. Cooperate with him . . . ," Vergennes urged, without much explanation. The bankers shuddered: in their view, Beaumarchais was a savage. It was all right to commission pamphlets from him, but not to treat him as a peer in the business world. Perennial debtor if there ever was one! Dubourg had acted as a screen between Deane and him, then had summoned him, only to have his condescension melt into dismay upon learning that Beaumarchais had been appointed adviser by Vergennes as well as exclusive agent for supplying the Americans secretly with arms. That very day Dubourg sent off a letter to Vergennes denouncing Beaumarchais: "Your lordship, I saw M. de Beaumarchais this morning . . . I believe him to be a man supremely qualified for political negotiations, and at the same time perhaps one of the least qualified to conduct commercial transactions. He is fond of display. They say he keeps young mistresses; he has a reputation for throwing money about, and in all France there is not a merchant or manufacturer who would behave thus or would consent to deal with him. Also it surprised me greatly to learn from him that you have charged him to aid us with advice and have made him solely responsible for coordinating all commercial transactions, including outgoing and incoming shipments, whether military supplies or ordinary commodities going from France to the United Colonies and from the Colonies to France, for directing all negotiations, setting prices, signing contracts, fixing terms, collecting monies, etc. There may be a hundred, there may be a thousand persons in France who, though far less gifted than M. de Beaumarchais, could better achieve your aims and inspire greater confidence . . . "[10]

To Vergennes, the diatribe could only confirm his choice: these prominent and obtuse merchants would saddle him with a war against England inside of three months. Why should he expect them to understand that Beaumarchais would be useful precisely because no one would take him seriously at the start? But, having an aristocratic streak of cruelty in him, Vergennes found it amusing to watch what happened when, as if tossing tidbits to a jester, he handed Dubourg's letter to Beaumarchais. The result reminded the good doctor that Beaumarchais did not believe in turning the other cheek and, since the Goëzman affair, was dangerous to tangle with: "Now, what difference to business can it make if I am active socially, ostentatious, and keep women? The mistresses I keep, sir, are indeed your humble servants.* There were five of them, four sisters and a niece. Three years ago, much to my grief, two of these women died. Now I keep only three: two sisters and my niece, which is ostentation enough for an individual like myself. But what would you have thought had you known that I courted scandal to the point of keeping men as well, two very young and rather good-looking nephews, not to mention the wretched parent who fathered such an outrageous provider?** As to my ostentation, this is even worse . . . The finest black suiting is not good enough for me; I have been known on occasion to stoop to silk when the weather is very warm. But I entreat you, sir, not to write these things to the Comte de Vergennes, for you should end up ruining me in his estimation . . . You are an honorable man, sir, so inflamed with the desire to do a great deed that you have allowed yourself to commit a small wrong in order to do it. This morality is not precisely what the Bible teaches, though it seems to satisfy a good many people. In order to convert the heathen, thus did the Church Fathers resort now and then to rash interpretations, to saintly calumnies which, among themselves, they called pious frauds."[11]

No Dubourg was going to intimidate him. He had already pocketed his first million, from France. On July 19 he met Silas Deane and won his confidence in an hour with the aid of an interpreter friend, Beaumarchais's English being no better than Deane's broken French. The next day Deane wrote him a letter establishing relations on the flimsiest of grounds, mutual trust: "Regarding the credit we shall require for the armaments and supplies that I expect to receive from you, I hope no long-term credit will be necessary. A year is the longest my colleagues are in the habit of taking, and since the Congress has bespoken large quantities of tobacco from Virginia and Maryland as well as other commodities which will be shipped as soon as vessels can be found, I see no reason why substantial remittances in trade should not reach you within six months and the balance before the year is up. This is what my letters are urging the Congress."[12] A Congress wholly uncommitted, which could always claim later on that it assumed Beaumarchais's shipments had been gifts of France. Once back in Philadelphia, Arthur Lee wasted no time warning the delegates that Silas Deane's agreement with Beaumarchais was not to be relied on and was merely an attempt at personal gain.

Figaro fell headlong into the trap innocently prepared by Silas Deane. "This political-commercial business will grow gigantic!" he wrote to Ver-

---

*What follows is a description of "the social circle on the Rue de Condé," where Beaumarchais provided living quarters, in a mansion purchased early in his financial career with funds received from Paris-Duverney, for his sisters Julie and Jeanne-Marguerite, plus three children of a third sister, Marie-Josephe. The latter, a widow, had just died in the convent of the Dames de la Croix in Roye almost at the same time as a fourth sister, Lisette, the unhappy heroine of his "Spanish adventure" twelve years earlier, who also had retired to a nunnery in Picardy.

**Beaumarchais supported his retired clockmaker father for twenty years. Here he simply "overlooks" the fact that old Caron had died on October 23, 1775, at the age of seventy-seven.

gennes, who by now enjoyed pulling the strings. This way Beaumarchais would at least work to clear his record. On August 12 the king had issued "letters patent" virtually expunging the years between Beaumarchais's public censure in February 1774 and the rehearing of his case, much as priests gave indulgences to shorten a sinner's passage through purgatory. Except that Beaumarchais had paid his fare in advance. Louis XVI was compelled to grant this favor if the new Parliament was to overturn the former Maupeou Parliament's sentence, as if the trial had advanced from one hearing to the next. Meanwhile there had been the Morande affair, the German incident, the transaction with D'Eon, *The Barber of Seville* . . . Two years of anguished adventure, like two seconds in the annals of power. On September 6, 1776, by formal decree of Parliament gathered in the Great Chamber, the charges against Beaumarchais were annulled and his civil status restored along with his duties at court. For how could they continue legally to outlaw a man who had just written thus to the Continental Congress sitting in Philadelphia: "I plan to send you about two hundred bronze four-pounders, two hundred thousand rounds of ammunition, twenty thousand excellent muskets, a few bronze mortars, some bombs, cannonballs, sheets, tents, gunlock plates, bayonets, etc."?[13]

60

OCTOBER 1776

He That Stands It NOW

It's about time. Or is it already too late? Things are going from bad to worse in America. Louis XVI and Vergennes begin to feel their fears are confirmed, that they have poured a million francs down the drain by backing a hopeless rebellion of ten to fifteen thousand ill-armed, ill-equipped farmers against an armada of four hundred supply ships escorted by thirty men-o'-war dispatched from Britain to end this nonsense. Thirty-two thousand infantry and ten thousand sailors with twelve hundred cannons were preparing to pluck New York like a ripe fruit, then sail 150 miles up the Hudson to Albany to join their Canadian regiments. Once the northern colonies were in the pincers, the middle and southern ones would have to collapse. One or two battles should suffice, a very modest paragraph in England's military annals . . . But what a strange idea it was for George III to place the expedition under the command of the Howe brothers, an admiral and a general, two mild-mannered, down-to-earth Whigs who were sympathetic to the colonial cause and had not been afraid to say so in London. They seemed reluctant, not to fight (that is, to send their men into battle), but to fight that particular enemy. A month wasted on Staten Island, facing a long spit of land called Manhattan where Washington had set up his defenses in an effort to block the Hudson. Then on August 22, in an obvious move, the British landed on Long Island, took Brooklyn, and nearly overran Washington's Manhattan headquarters. The American general knew that New York was lost and that he might be trapped there, but the residents begged him not to abandon them. They never guessed that General Howe wanted to play peacemaker, not conquistador, in America. He halted his armies once again on Staten Island and Long Island, two sentinels off the coast of New York, and waited for the Congress to send delegates to a conference he had proposed. There was still time to iron things out. After all, not much blood had been shed thus far . . .

Howe awaited Franklin.

What an autumn and winter for a man of seventy! Ben Franklin leaves Philadelphia on September 9, flanked by John Adams and John Rutledge. His stagecoach lumbers through desolate Pennsylvania and New Jersey. Straggling bands of militiamen stream southward, warning every hamlet that the British are coming before they are even on the march. The philosopher discovers soldiering, the utopian comes face to face with the grim reality of war in the squalid New Brunswick inn where he and Adams must share a bed and spend the night arguing about whether to keep the window open or closed. Wounded men covered with filthy bandages, weeping women . . .

Is it possible, on the following day, to repair a fractured world over a cup of tea? They hardly expect to on Staten Island, three ordinary men surrounded by thousands of redcoats drawn up in perfect formation, America like a nut in the fist of the British. General Howe had arranged a polite welcome and excellent refreshments. He treats Franklin as an old friend from London; after all, having known each other for years, are they not basically of one mind? Howe is empowered to act in the king's name. But while he was on the seas to the New World, the signing of the Declaration of Independence had changed the whole picture.

"Are you empowered to acknowledge the independent United States of America?"

Howe raises his arms helplessly. Anything but that. They would hang him, just as they will undoubtedly hang these three gentlemen who talk belligerently of "England's thirst for conquest" and "the mother country's passion for domination." What has happened to the cheerful Ben Franklin of those pleasant evenings at the Tavern? They rise and take icy leave of one another, like duelists. The English see the trio off with a sense of pity: their vulnerability, coupled with stubborn determination, has already persuaded

Howe that he need not hurry. The conference has given Washington a breathing spell and a chance to plan his retreat.

But Washington is running out of supplies. What's the matter with that Silas Deane in Paris? Is he asleep? The representative there really ought to be a personality of international stature. Franklin is appointed by the Congress on September 26, with Arthur Lee, who has managed to convince them of his utility, as deputy.

Although Franklin had stated publicly that he was retiring to Philadelphia, his cheerful acceptance of this mission betrays the vital spark that drives him still. "I am old and good for nothing; but, as the storekeepers say of their remnants of cloth, 'I am but a fag end, and you may have me for what you please.' "[1] Gossip says that he is only too happy to leave after seeing the size of the redcoat army. He knows what lies in store for Pennsylvania. How cozy Paris will seem next to Philadelphia. On the other hand, he runs the risk of any soldier: if caught by the British, he can count on being shot as a traitor to the crown.

But will they even find a ship to take him across the Atlantic? The American "fleet," which a "naval committee" in Philadelphia is trying to develop out of a handful of poorly armed commercial and fishing vessels and whatever the New England shipyards can provide, numbers all of two twenty-four-gun frigates, two brigs, two sloops, and two schooners, without ammunition to speak of—like swift minnows fit only to glide stealthily past those monster British whales patrolling the entire seaboard. A great effort is made in Franklin's behalf: the *Reprisal*, a merchantman designed for the tobacco trade, is armed. Godspeed! He packs while calkers make the ship seaworthy. Two worn and battered Saratoga trunks contain the cast-off effects of a peaceful life swallowed up by war. He settles his affairs: civil matters are disposed of promptly by leaving all his property to the Congress. Paternal obligations are settled even faster—and ruthlessly—by denouncing his son, now in prison for pro-British leanings, and taking grandson William Temple away from him once again, though the lad yearns to be reconciled with his father. Those who would follow in Abraham's footsteps never make tender-hearted parents. On the arm of this heartsick youth, a latter-day Abraham is "going out of the land of his birth" in search of the Promised Land of military aid. On October 9, 1776, Beaumarchais—actually the firm of Rodrigo Hortalez & Co.—rents a vacant mansion, former residence of the Dutch ambassador on the Rue Vieille-du-Temple in the Marais district, for sixty-six hundred livres* per annum from the architect Le Tellier. Three stories, spacious quarters, prestige. Beaumarchais pre-empts the lion's share, installing himself on the top floor with plump and pretty Marie-Thérèse de Willer-Mawlaz,** whom he thinks of marrying

---

*About 30,000 francs [$6000] today. The mansion still stands at 47 Rue Vieille-du-Temple, with its original oak door carved with bas-reliefs of Romulus and Remus, and traces of a sundial.

**She became his "official" mistress shortly after his return from Germany.

when time allows. She proves to be an excellent housekeeper and hostess, and even supervises the clerks when he is traveling. There are a dozen of them working in offices on the two lower floors, carrying on correspondence with Le Havre, Nantes, Bordeaux, Rochefort, La Rochelle, Marseilles, wherever supplies are to be secretly assembled and cargo vessels chartered. Beaumarchais will begin combing the four corners of France. He was getting rusty at that sort of job. Now he rarely appears at the Rue Vieille-du-Temple and leaves Gudin de La Ferlière in charge, the brother of his close friend Gudin de La Brenellerie, who reluctantly resumes the familiar role of Figaro's roving shadow and prepares to accompany him to Le Havre, where a December sailing is scheduled for the *Amphitrite*. Just the beginning, for a dozen five- or six-ton vessels will be chartered before the year's end in the name of Rodrigo Hortalez.* Beaumarchais has wasted neither his time nor the two million francs from France and Spain, which were soundly invested over a period of four months. He is not a man to let money sit idle.

November 3, 1776. Franklin boards ship in Philadelphia in a drizzling rain. The shores of the Delaware stretch out for two or three miles to meet the open sea, as if the images of his triumphant homecoming in the spring of 1775 were running in reverse, in dull, washed-out tints. Many of his friends have come to wave handkerchiefs on the dock despite warnings not to tip off English spies. How those faces have changed! Lined with anguish. Will he ever see his homeland again? Will America be free in a year? The wintry blast that drives the *Reprisal* forward, her sails nearly bursting, saves him from worry about British warships. A west wind plus the Atlantic's mighty current promise that the crossing ought not to take more than a month, even if the old man and his grandson get tossed about and battered in the captain's quarters. They huddle against the icy spray that frosts the sailors' clothing and salt-burned skin. Ship's bells, gusting winds, slapping ropes and yardarms set the mood and tempo for this old man adrift between two worlds. Behind him may lie the end; before him, the unknown. Howe has taken Manhattan. Washington's attempt to close off the Hudson has failed. The rebels have lost five thousand men and all their artillery—as if they had a single gun to spare. By sheer ingenuity, Washington has managed to march four or five thousand troops southward, but they are deserting right and left. New York has surrendered and the redcoats are advancing on Philadelphia, confident they can take it before returning up the Hudson. By the time Franklin reaches Europe, all the papers will be saying that the Americans have lost the war. Tom Paine showed him an article the day he sailed, an ode to the final hour: "These are the times that

---

*The ships were simply hired out by their owners to the exporter, who then had to recruit the crew and perform all other captain's duties for the period under contract. Cargo was measured in "freight tons," each equivalent to 979 kilos on the modern scale, as well as "measured tons," translated as the floor space occupied by four barrels of Bordeaux wine.

try men's souls. The summer soldier and the sunshine patriot will, in this crisis, shrink from the service of his country; but he that stands it NOW deserves the love and thanks of man and woman."[2] As a precaution, the Congress prepares to retreat to Baltimore. A single, frail hope: the iron resolve of George Washington, now supreme military commander, who refuses to admit defeat. But what sort of welcome will the French give Franklin as representative of a nation dissolving before it has even taken shape? How will he navigate the rapids between his old friend Dubourg, aided by Arthur Lee (who follows Franklin on another ship), and the Silas Deane/Beaumarchais tandem he will have to deal with? Does Beaumarchais speak for France?

On one of the rare days he ventured out on deck for a bit of exercise, a gust of wind plucked off his wig and flung it overboard.

December 3. The wind has died suddenly off the French coast, bringing the *Reprisal* out of choppy seas into calm water. Now it is tacking in the harbor of Quiberon, sheltered by the long tongue of land that projects southward and looks from a distance like gray houses afloat. Fishing boats approach warily to inspect this old British vessel at war with the British, which has just fired on two brigs offshore, the *Success*, bound for Cork with wine and timber, and the *Vine*, carrying spirits and linseed to Hull. Two seizures that create a nuisance for Louis XVI: he will not allow them in his ports for fear of offending the British and orders Franklin's ship on her way with the captive vessels in tow. With or without fair winds, on to Nantes they go, from where Franklin will continue overland by coach. He goes ashore not far from the church of Saint-Pierre-Quiberon, the first steeple they had seen from the ship, and talks to a group of long-haired peasants with broad-brimmed black hats, short jackets, baggy breeches, and tight gaiters. They speak neither French nor English, but Franklin knows them to be Britons more ancient even than the English, their musical dialect going back into the mists of time. This hardly facilitates the exchange, however, and a priest comes to the rescue in Latin. A cart is brought to take Franklin to Auray for the night, ten miles of woods and thickets, untilled acres, fields of stubble, and rampaging streams that defy fording. One night in Auray. Three days to reach Nantes via Vannes, a region dotted with marshes and ponds, watered by the Vilaine, and with very few roads. As the barouches available in Vannes have no springs, Franklin is obliged to buy his own gig and in this jaunty conveyance, better suited to spines of lesser vintage, enters Nantes on December 7. Here, he is back in his own element; apprised of his coming, the local bourgeoisie greets him with mixed sympathy and concern. Nantes is in the midst of a building boom, with splendid, sparkling-white mansions mushrooming all over the business quarter on both sides of the Bras de la Madeleine, a tiny branch of the Loire given over to the slave trade, between the Pointe de la Poissonnerie and the Bassin de la Fosse. Franklin might well wonder what continent he has come to, for the swarm of blacks and mestizos in rainbow-colored rags and kerchiefs lends a touch of the Carolinas or Virginia to the Quai de la Fosse. Slaves in France? Yes indeed, for the prosperity of Nantes rests on the slave trade, which in a century has tripled the fortunes of the upper bourgeoisie. Nantes has become a major turnstile for the export of African slaves. The shipowners had a practice of grabbing a commission in trade—a few black children in transit, little boys and girls who might strike the good ladies of Nantes as irresistible. Bringing them ashore and baptizing them did the trick. They became part of the household, received no wages, acquired a Christian name in the civil register, a dog's or cow's name around the house. Why complain if they were thus spared the ordeal of plantation life in America or the "Sugar Islands"?

Louis XV's death seemed to have put a curse on the slavers. The trade began to slump during the Seven Years' War and has been hopelessly stagnant for the past two years. Fourteen crossings officially reported to the admiralty of Nantes for the year 1774, thirteen for 1775—compared to the halcyon 1770 and 1771 when they numbered twenty-three, and twenty-five in 1767.[3] Now they handle an average of only four or five thousand slaves annually, barely enough to make ends meet, instead of the ten to twelve thousand shipped in 1750. But the slavers were counting on Vergennes and Sartines to boost the trade, for those two ministers had vested interests in the business. The Treaty of Paris of 1763 was wearing thin: Louis XVI intended to construct fortresses along the African coast to pen up captured blacks until the slave ships arrived. Now the Americans come along and threaten to ruin a flourishing trade! Reports say that a handful of demagogues in Philadelphia want to abolish slavery. Nantes is not anxious to revive hostilities with England and endanger the safety of French merchant vessels. Unless, as certain far-sighted shipowners think, the situation were to change radically. To defeat the British and, in the process, profit tidily from arms shipments to the colonies could lead to reopening the slave trade with America on an even grander scale. Beaumarchais's associates have that in mind now. So does he. One more reason to distrust Franklin, a notorious idealist. Pillars of the business community flock to the country house of Jean-Louis Gruet, a rich shipowner who is Franklin's host, in hopes of learning what the old man thinks of the situation in America. Two years in the Continental Congress, after twenty in England, have taught him to say little when answering questions. His odd appearance is all they can talk about: that great dome of his, ovoid and bald, which he covers with a fur cap to keep from catching cold. Among Parisian ladies, the high and bushy "Franklin hairdo" will be all the rage this winter. Once he realizes that it serves as a "status symbol," Franklin will wink at the tale going around that he tossed his wig to the waves in homage to simplicity and rarely will wear one afterward. But this is no dotard, this is a man whose activity has kept him young, with his stern, unruffled gaze, his large, thin-lipped mouth above a bottomless chin.[4] A man in full possession of his faculties, especially the one faculty he can exploit: his silence. Franklin has come to France to keep silent.

December 12. "Monsieur Durand" travels by post from Paris to Le Havre: Beaumarchais's latest pseudonym, far from foolproof. He does not linger in Rouen, where bourgeois families are "wise to own country houses in order to get away from this oversize, overcrowded, ill-designed, ugly, foul-smelling, stifling city strewn with refuse and industry."[5] Rather than sit idly by until Franklin reaches Paris, he will get to work now on cargoes for America; he will not face Franklin empty-handed. Twenty miles from Rouen to Yvetot, through apple and pear orchards stripped of their last leaves by December gales; "enclosures are towering parapets of thick hedges, oaks and beeches."[6] Twenty-five miles from Yvetot to Le Havre. Country houses, seats (not surprisingly) of the Rouen gentry, many of which are still in construction. Numerous farms, cottages, and cotton mills. The approach to Le Havre from Harfleur discloses a bustling port—which would be busier still were it not for the prying eyes of English spies. The Seine spreads out at last to a width of five miles between chalk cliffs and promontories "that seem to draw back to allow it to carry its vast tribute to the Ocean."[7] The harbor entrance is extremely narrow, however, and has to be dredged constantly, but beyond it is access to two large oblong basins with space for hundreds of ships. Only a dozen or two now ride at anchor there. The *Amphitrite* is loading up at dockside. Farther on, the *Romain*, the *Andromède*, and the *Anonime* [*sic*] are also taking on cargo. But whose ships are these? Figaro's activities are public knowledge. English spies watch these vessels, having been tipped off by irate merchants in Le Havre and Nantes. Irate not because they fear an adverse impact on the slave trade (slaves rarely are shipped across the Channel anyway, if only to avoid excessive losses from the cold) but because they wonder what will happen to our leather goods, our livestock, our cottons, fruits, and spirits. Jean-Louis Mistral, royal naval commissioner for Normandy in charge of all ship sailings, expresses what is on everyone's mind when he tells Sartines, his superior in Paris, that "the business community prays unceasingly for safety on the high seas, upon which its prosperity depends. It fears that the expedition [of boats chartered by Rodrigo Hortalez] will drive the British to extreme measures which might prove dangerous."[8]

Beaumarchais has not been burning up the roads for his health. On arrival, he prods the *Amphitrite*'s captain to set sail at once since its cargo is in the hold: sixty-three cannons, 20,160 cannon balls, nine thousand uncharged grenades, ten tons of ammunition, and 6132 muskets. From Commissioner Mistral he obtains authorization to take aboard forty-nine volunteers, the first French forces to come to the aid of the patriot army. Twelve officers and nine artillery sergeants; eight infantry officers; servants for the aforesaid gentlemen; and, most important, twelve engineers, highly useful persons since an engineer, "in the military world, is the officer in charge of fortifying, attacking, and defending positions . . . The word *'ingénieur'* emphasizes the knowledge, skill, and talent which these officers must have to be inventive. They used to be called *'engeigneurs,'* from the word *'engin,'* which means machine . . . An engineer has drafting experience. He has to have studied physics in order to assess the nature of construction materials, of bodies of water, and the different qualities of air in places that are to be fortified."[9] He is the architect of position warfare. Also the technician most needed by the patriot forces, since the majority of American engineers, trained in the mother country and enlisted in Britain's army, are loyalists. Washington had needed them desperately when planning the defense of New York.

Beaumarchais found few such men to recruit among French army rejects. The Comte de Saint-Germain* barely lifted a finger to help him. Silas Deane has been obliged to offer tempting bonuses; at last, with some pulling and pushing from Vergennes and Sartines, "Captain Nicolas Fautrel, commander of the vessel *Amphitrite*, is hereby ordered to take aboard with all their possessions, to provide passage to Santo Domingo, and to sit at his table, the following officers [including Major L'Enfant**] bound for service in that colony . . . as well as to take on board with their luggage and to transport to the said colony and provide with rations the non-commissioned officers, soldiers, workmen, and servants attached to those officers."[10]

In charge of this group is a prominent officer, Philippe-Charles-Jean-Baptiste Tronson du Coudray, artillery commander-in-chief for the French colonial forces on the American continent, who is highly indignant at having to rub elbows with this lowborn crew. Article Five of Captain Fautrel's orders specifies that "because most of the officers have never been to sea and are not familiar with shipboard discipline, we urge that in the event of any difficulty with these military passengers, [the captain] should inform M. du Coudray at once and rely on him in all matters not directly related to the ship's crew. We commend this officer to [your] special care and pray that he be shown every courtesy . . . "[11] owing to his rank as much as his foul temper. No one in the war department will lament the absence of this cantankerous gentleman who had volunteered to go teach the Americans how to fire a cannon. Coudray was confident that in a week they would put him in charge of the whole army, an impression no one has thus far managed to dispel. As to the ship's fictitious destination, the Windward Islands (Santo Domingo), this precaution was taken in the event of British inspection of the ship's papers. Once they reached Cap Français, the *Amphitrite* would receive new orders dispatching her to some port still in "rebel" hands.

---

*Minister of war. [*Trans.*]

**"Major" was a function rather than a rank, midway between captain and colonel. Pierre-Charles L'Enfant was born in 1754. He settles in the United States and, in 1791, designs the plan for its capital, Washington.

"Le Havre, December 14, 1776, at two past noon," from Commissioner Mistral to M. de Sartines: "Sir, for your *confidential* information, the *Amphitrite* has just left this port bound for her destination and is presently in the anchorage prior to taking on gunpowder.* She will then be on her way under an east-southeast breeze, fresh and favorable to the course she will steer."[12] Beaumarchais stood on the embankment until the ship left port; he could gloat for twenty-four hours. France finally had answered his appeal of last spring for gunpowder and engineers. From Mistral to Sartines again on December 16: "I have absolutely no knowledge of any instructions, either written or verbal, from M. de Beaumarchais to the ship's captain. M. de Beaumarchais left yesterday morning for Paris."[13]

Twenty-four hours. Not a moment longer. Before he had even reached Rouen the whole project began to unravel behind his back. A royal decree delivered to Le Havre on the night of December 16 enjoins the three vessels still anchored in the harbor from sailing. Informed by his spies, England's ambassador, Lord Stormont, had lodged bitter complaints with Vergennes. So now Le Havre's shipowners can relax, and the Rodrigo Hortalez & Co. is left with a messy dispute on its hands. Luckily, an easterly wind already has nudged the *Amphitrite* out beyond the English Channel. Apart from this one ship, the whole affair has collapsed.

To begin all over again will be the task of Ben Franklin, who leaves Nantes on December 18 and arrives in Paris two days later to meet Beaumarchais.

NECKER

61

DECEMBER 1776

I Shall Die a Child Who Never Grew Up

Voltaire and Diderot rarely write to each other anymore, once or twice a year at most. Each is immersed in his own persona. Diderot does not share the old patriarch's deistic leanings. The philosophers' universe is too small to hold them both. Still, like proud conquerors, they hail each other grandly. On August 14, 1776, from Ferney, Voltaire to Diderot: "A wholesome philoso-

*Gunpowder was never loaded at the docks for fear of an explosion; it was barged out to the ship's anchorage.

phy is gaining ground, from Archangel to Cadiz, but our foes can still rely on dew from heaven, the fat of the land, the miter, the strongbox, the sword, and the rabble. All we have been able to do is let the decent people of Europe know that we are right, and perhaps to ease and humanize social standards a bit. Yet the Chevalier de La Barre's blood still smokes . . . The dreadful part is that philosophers have not united, whereas the persecutors forever shall be. There used to be two sages* at court, but ways were found to remove them; they were out of their element. Ours is seclusion; for twenty-five years I have clung to this haven . . . Long life to you, sire, and may you strike mortal blows at the beast** whose ears alone I have managed to nip! If ever you should return to Russia, kindly pass by my grave."[1] The letter reached Diderot in Paris, where he had returned on October 21, 1774, after a far longer stay in Holland than suited his family. Since then he has been trying to regain his health and intellectual vigor, which the Russian winter had sapped. He kept up with events in France and America somewhat casually, as if reluctant to spend his limited energy. "Amid the general unrest," he advised Wilkes,[2] "look after yourself; be gay, drink fine wines, and when the urge to be tender comes over you, approach ladies who do not keep you dangling." Yet he sympathized with this English champion of popular rights, ten of whose speeches in defense of "American provincials" had just been published: "I have read with great satisfaction your various speeches on the subject of the provincials. I found them eloquent, dignified, and compelling."[3]

He also gave moral support to the efforts of his good friend Beaumarchais to supply the colonists with arms.

All well and good, but who was going to put up the money for those arms and supplies, for those volunteers and transport vessels, which the Americans would repay later on in trade items? Who had advanced the original one million? The French king. And which official would authorize and account for those expenditures? Until recently that was Turgot's province, and he would not have made Beaumarchais's task any easier. Now a wine-bibbing fellow named Clugny took over (briefly, as it turned out) the reins of finance—a refreshingly mild-mannered nonentity after Turgot's overwhelming presence. Maurepas has pushed for his appointment, thinking that a government of nullities will enhance his own prestige in the Council. However, M. de Clugny, the official "in charge of naval and colonial affairs," returned from the colonies without sobering up. Forty-six and a drunkard. He barely had time to install a trio of mistresses (three sisters) in the Hôtel des Finances, to reward a few sycophants with high posts, and to issue edicts revoking most of Turgot's reform measures. In an effort to replenish the treasury, he established a lottery. For six months he held on to his prize, the last six of his life. On November

---

*Malesherbes and Turgot.
**The "beast" which Voltaire bids Diderot crush is intolerance more than superstition.

17, 1776, a month after the fact, Diderot broke the good news to Grimm in Saint Petersburg: "A revolution in public affairs has taken place . . . Clugny, the finance director, has died and is succeeded by a certain M. Taboureau in company with M. Necker: the latter, who is foreign-born, a foreign representative,* and Protestant, was ineligible for the office. His deputy, then, is merely a figurehead . . . The public has applauded M. Necker's promotion. The rapid rise in value of government bonds also has inspired panegyrics for M. Necker and a virtual funeral oration for his predecessor. They say that in the latter's final hours he kept muttering 'Bankruptcy! Bankruptcy!' M. Necker is intelligent, fair-minded, firm, and unselfish, and I join all honest folk in wishing his administration well. I trust that the impossibility of doing good will not turn him away from the simple duty of preventing evil."[4]

When Diderot speaks of "the public" he is concerned only with the successive salons—Madame Necker's, which succeeded that of Julie de Lespinasse, also that of Madame Geoffrin, who lately had suffered a stroke. For years Diderot had met Grimm, Suard, Marmontel, D'Alembert, Beccaria; the Abbés Raynal, Morellet, and Galiani; and the ambassadors of England and Naples at this Friday salon, usually held in the miniature château built for the Marquise de Pompadour on the banks of the Seine at Saint-Ouen. Necker purchased it when he "retired from active business" in 1772 after making a fortune of seven and a half millions** in the flourishing Protestant bank of Isaac Vernet & Thelusson on windfall profits from shares in the French East India Company. Jacques Necker actually retired? He is forty-four and lets his wife do as she pleases while he embarks on a new life. The climate of the salons is changing: Julie de Lespinasse cultivated poverty; Madame Necker's cult was money. As court opinion gradually tilted in favor of the American cause, it was understood that "the cannon's opening roar could touch off bankruptcy,"[6] the threat of which had haunted Clugny. If anyone can ward it off, Necker will, being one of Europe's richest men. He won't find it necessary to load the government payrolls with his friends, as he is already supporting them. Necker after Turgot, clearly a prestigious tradition which even Diderot can back without losing face. Voltaire also takes courage from the knowledge that fiscal policy will be handled by a product of Calvinist finance, one of those "converts to money-making" whose money-lending, contrary to the teachings of Luther, had been condoned by Geneva's despot. Integrity within the framework of money-making: there's the theme of the rising generation.

Louis XVI's touchy Catholic sensibilities had not facilitated the change,

---

*"Foreign representative"means that Necker officially represented the republic of Geneva in France. Being a foreigner was no blemish or drawback; Mazarin and Law, after he became a Catholic convert, had been full-fledged ministers. "Protestant," however, was as dishonorable a blot as "Jew" or "Negro."

**Around thirty-seven million francs [$7,400,000] of capital on today's scale, which prompts Lady Blennerhasset, Madame de Staël's eminent biographer, to assert calmly that "with Necker, the disdain for money is a lofty quality which atones for many a frailty."[5]

but Necker's Protestantism proved less difficult for His Majesty to swallow than Turgot's atheism. The Swiss at least is a believer. And a millionaire. He had waited for the right moment to step forward and oppose Turgot's intransigence; he was a reputed "pacifist," a "reformer" perhaps, but within the system and not given to idol-smashing: he declared that frequently there was "more truth in general opinions than in new systems" and that "moderation is the essential condition of judicious administration."[7] That sufficed to ease the trauma which twenty months' exposure to Turgot had inflicted on the king. Madame du Deffand sums it up thus: "The Abbé Terray did a bad job well; Turgot did a good job badly; Necker will do a good job well."[8] To steer him into office, they hit on the scheme of appointing Taboureau des Réaux, an obscure parliamentarian, as titular finance chief, while the Protestant, that leper, will actually pull the strings.

Diderot is ready and eager to embrace the eminent financier whose wife has been pining for him over the past five or six years: "There is a Madame Necker here, an attractive, intelligent woman who is mad about me; she endures torment to invite me to the house."[9] She had set out to convert him to Calvinism, and he obligingly put up with her innocuous Friday sermons even if Suzanne Necker,* née Curchod, had never really managed to cast off her Swiss manners for Parisian ones. "Before creating her, the Lord soaked her inside and out in a basin of starch."[10] Why not let high finance have its Madame de Maintenon?

Diderot embraces Necker all the more readily for offering an alternative to Turgot's inflexibility. In fact he did not believe that a sudden shift in the established order was possible. The news of Louis XV's death reached him in Holland and left him utterly unmoved. On his return from Russia, all his hopes focused on reviving his literary projects, especially a new edition of the *Encyclopédie,* for which, as early as June 1774, he had thought of recruiting "Dr." Jean-Paul Marat as a co-worker.[11] In Holland it took him seven months to realize that the help he expected from Catherine II would never materialize. Lack of funds compelled him to abandon work on the project, and he made his way home to Paris shattered by this disillusionment more than by his trying experience crossing the icebound Dvina. Resignedly, he returned to his wife; tenderly, to Sophie Volland; blissfully, to his adored daughter. His "chest ailment still has not cleared up."[12] Actually he has developed heart trouble and can no longer walk upstairs without discomfort. Resolutely and with good humor, he itemizes the symptoms of impending old age: "My teeth wobble; my eyes fail me at night,** and my legs have grown sluggish, forcing me to use a cane more and more frequently. Yet I am gay . . . Normally I secrete

*She is twenty-seven in 1776.
**That is, when reading by candlelight.

either phlegm or aqua vitae. I pay no attention to the weather and go along as usual confusing the days, weeks, years, and months—thus there is no lessening of my conformity to eternity. Add to that the fact that though my legs tremble and my back is becoming tortoise-shaped, I can raise no less high my augur's wand.* So all is well."[13]

"The time of counting by years is past; now it is time to count by days . . . I have perhaps ten years left at the bottom of my bag. Of those ten years, swollen joints, rheumatism, and the rest of that tiresome clan will claim two or three; let us try to spare the other seven for repose and for the small pleasures one looks forward to after sixty . . . I used to think the heartstrings hardened with age. It is not so. I am not sure that my capacity for feeling has not increased. Everything moves me, everything affects me; I shall be the most notorious old sniveler you ever have known."[14]

In the spring of 1776 he had arranged a suitable retreat by renting part of the house of a certain M. Belle in Sèvres (or Sève, as it was still generally known at the time), on a lonely wooded hillside overlooking the Seine, facing Saint-Cloud.

"Disgusted with city life, where louts are commoner than ever, I have repaired to the country. There I live like a hibernating bear, off my own flesh, by licking my paws." He prefers this diet to the "lavish banquets" at D'Holbach's house which he had enlivened so often with his brilliant conversation. Now "the racket of eighteen or nineteen guests in extravagant plumage makes my head swim and leaves no chance for me to coax a single timid cheep from my throat." In Sèvres "I eat and say sweet nothings to little Pauline [his landlord's daughter]. It is delightful how innocently little girls behave with old men. They play freely around the decrepit cat whose teeth and claws are gone,"[15] but whose "augur's wand" still rises on command.

He writes persistently to the Neckers, husband and wife, pressing to obtain the lease on a royal ironworks at Senonches, near Chartres, for his son-in-law, Caroillon de Vandeul. Indeed, there is little likelihood of his children starving: the Vandeul brothers, one of whom married Marie-Angélique Diderot, are first "royal ironsmiths, then go on to become ironsmiths to M. le Comte D'Artois. They have a private income; property rights in Langres and in various ancestral estates; the inspectorate of the duchy of Nevers; a monopoly of the ironworks in Senonches and in Chateau-Roux. Not bad for a young couple just starting out,"[16] he comments to his sister on December 18, 1776. He had brought all this about by soliciting offices for his son-in-law first from Sartines, then Necker, while writing the *Supplément au voyage de Bougainville,* one of the most scathing anti-clerical publications to come out of the eighteenth century. Shame to him who thinks ill of it: the

---

*Staff with a curved handle which the ancient soothsayers used to carry. Diderot, of course, has another image in mind!

philosopher relates to grandees "as an aerialist to his tightrope: midway between servility and arrogance."[17] But for a good cause.

On December 13 he declares: "I shall die a child who never grew up.
A few days ago I cracked my skull against a block of marble in Pigale's [sic]
studio* . . . My three-year-old granddaughter,** seeing me with an enormous lump on my head, exclaimed, 'Oh Grandpa, do you bump your nose
against doors, too?' I laughed and thought to myself that I have done nothing
else since the day I was born."[18]

FABRE D'EGLANTINE

62

FEBRUARY 1777

This Intolerable Stability

Wherever he went, Diderot, who had written *Le Paradoxe du comédien* shortly
before his trip to Russia, was a keen observer of conditions in the theater. In
Holland, unlike the Catholic nations, he noted that actors were not treated as
social outcasts. They "have professions and carry on some sort of trade. Actresses dress moderately well and are respectable. A respectable actress would
refuse to share the stage with a wanton. Yet frequently they are heard to utter
statements that are an offense to common decency, to religion, to rational
politics, and to accepted social standards"[1]—and one may well assume that he
listened intently to all such shameless utterances. But south of the United
Provinces lay the Austrian Netherlands (Belgium under Hapsburg dominion),
where an acting troop, unless permanently attached to a nobleman's
household, was viewed as no better than an itinerant whorehouse. The social
aristocracy found it more entertaining to undress the performers visually, male
and female alike, than to hear what they had to say, and must have imagined
the cast as tenants of a one-night stud farm. Nonetheless, since Molière's day
a handful of rebels had continued to seek out the stage as an escape from
society, just as others went to sea. The promise of social exile did not bother
them; as a matter of fact, they rather welcomed it.

One such young scamp is Philippe-François-Nazaire Fabre, actor, musician, and operatic singer with an astounding range from baritone to counter-
tenor, already something of an author and journalist, and one of the few

*Pigalle's famous bronze bust of Diderot (1777) is now in the Louvre. [*Trans.*]
**Marianne de Vandeul, called Minette, was Pigalle's godchild.

characters in this long story whose first name never appears because he chooses to call himself Fabre d'Eglantine. The closing days of 1776 find him in Namur, Belgium, attached to the household of the Prince-Bishop of Liège. There a letter* from Chalon-sur-Saône dated November 29, 1776, reaches him from his fiancée, Sophie Poudhon: "Sweetheart, I am so happy . . . If one can die of joy, I will surely perish. Your letter, such a charming letter, promises that before St. John's feast day my dear sweetheart will be mine. How I shall count the days . . ."[2] Poor girl; he might as well have pledged to marry her by Easter or Trinity Sunday, like the four or five other "fiancées" he had deserted at each stage of his gypsy wanderings since quitting his family and trade four years earlier. A Jeanette in Grenoble, a Marie in Versailles, a chestnut-haired beauty in Bordeaux, a blonde in Troyes. Sophie of Chalon is "passée" now; in Namur, Fabre is giving his full attention to "Catiche."

Namur is a small town at the confluence of the Sambre and Meuse rivers, boxed in by ramparts whose deep scars bear honorable witness to the day when, with sword drawn, old Louis XIV led the assault at the head of his troops, though confined because of his gout-ridden feet to a sedan chair borne by six grenadiers. Namur's eight thousand inhabitants are used to warfare and submit helplessly to the battering visited on them every ten years or so, from one direction or another, like a cyclone sweeping over the Walloon plains. A "stronghold," the generals call it, licking their lips; a crumb for the French king or the Hapsburg empress to gobble up. Town life keeps pace with the rhythm of the garrison, which, for the moment, takes orders from Maria Theresa. The officers want to be entertained. This is Fabre d'Eglantine's reason for spending the winter here, a long distance from Carcassonne, his native citadel, where, on July 28, 1750, he came into the world in the parish of the Blue Penitents.

City born and bred, he comes from a line of landless townsfolk of recent bourgeois pretensions. At the beginning of the century Philippe Fabre, his grandfather, had moved his family from Montréal in Languedoc to Carcassonne, a mere three leagues away but an exodus nonetheless, and had shifted from farming to the draper's trade. Philippe Fabre also had managed to inch his way into the "aristocracy of clothmakers," to hobnob with the Pinels, the Airolles, the Laporteries, great cloth-manufacturing families who, through intermarriage, had ruled Carcassonne since Colbert's day and built fortunes by exporting their wool to the East. A closed society, hard-working and apprehensive: the clothmakers of Lower Languedoc bribed industrial inspectors who were in the habit of setting arbitrary, fluctuating production ceilings in order to protect the royal manufacture monopoly.[3] Their profits, like tides in the Mediterranean, varied from year to year according to the level of piracy, the slump in Italian trade, or the endemic war among Austrians, Russians, and Turks. Marseilles served as their umbilical cord.

*With every other word misspelled. [*Trans.*]

Philippe Fabre, a rough man, had carved himself a niche in the community and managed to marry his son François to a certain Anne-Catherine Fonds, daughter of one of the most prosperous wool merchants in Limoux. The son, however, would not follow in his father's footsteps, and in 1757, immediately after Philippe's death, François Fabre left Carcassonne for Limoux, a village farther south where the swift-running Aude River supplied energy enough for a dozen mills. In this period of diminishing harassment from royal inspectors, a savage rivalry sprang up among the cloth merchants of Languedoc. François Fabre preferred to work for his in-laws rather than to struggle.

He took his two sons with him; of six children, they alone survive.* Fabre d'Eglantine, the elder, was unloved by his father and despised by his mother. To his great relief, she died when he was nine:

> Jamais, le croiras-tu? ses yeux ne m'ont souri;
> Et neuf fois, oui, neuf fois notre dieu favori,
> Du Bélier aux Poissons a fini sa carrière,
> Sans qu'une seule fois la bouche d'une mère,
> Sur ma bouche enfantine ait daigné se poser.[4]

> [Never—can you believe it?—did she smile on me;
> And nine times, yes, nine, our favorite god
> Made his rounds from Ram to Fish
> Without those maternal lips
> Having once kissed the lips of this child.]

Carcassonne? He hardly remembers it. Of Limoux he seems not to recall the proud charm of a town whose houses plummet straight into the wharfless river, and rarely has he explored the surrounding countryside, where, six months out of the twelve, the Corbières sun bakes golden brown the stony soil thick with blackberry brambles. Limoux had a secondary school run by Doctrinarians, successors to the Jesuits. He attended it from the age of seven to twenty-two, hardly noticing the transition from student to teacher. Childhood and adolescence merged into pale shadows in this land of sunshine: Latin verses to grind out, humanities to cram down, a deluge of theology, in whose surf he struggled—hard enough to resist a career in the priesthood, though he perpetrated a sonnet to the Virgin that must have edified his masters.

> C'en est fait: l'Esprit Saint dans les flancs de Marie
> Produit le germe heureux qui me donne la vie;
> Mon Rédempteur paraît sous les traits d'un enfant.

---

*Four daughters die in infancy. Joseph, Fabre d'Eglantine's younger brother, will be a brigadier general in the Year II under the name of Fabre-Fonds.

Du berceau de ce Dieu naît le bonheur du monde;
L'oracle s'accomplit; une Vierge féconde
Ecrase pour jamais la tête du serpent.[5]

[It's done now: the Holy Spirit in Mary's womb
Produces the happy seed that gives me life;
My Redeemer appears in the guise of an infant.

In the cradle of this God is born man's joy;
The prophecy is fulfilled; a fruitful Virgin
Crushes forever the serpent's head.]

For this gem he was awarded a "silver lily"—today we would call it "honorable mention." This trivial trophy his boastfulness promptly converted to a gilded eglantine or sweetbrier, a rare distinction conferred by the Academy of Toulouse for exceptional oratory (at which he never excelled). He needed a fanciful name, one that would turn a Poquelin into a Molière. Imagine signing the name "Fabre-du-Lis" [Fabre-of-the-Lily]! No, he rechristened himself: Fabre d'Eglantine, his first brilliant invention, and went on to declare officially his father's profession as that of lawyer rather than draper. Rewriting the facts became his way of escaping the first twenty years of nonexistence.

His patience gave out. School bored him to death; he hated teaching. At home he could never stand those endless discussions among his father and grandfather and their friends over the difference between prime *londrins* in Segovian wool and common *londrins* in the wool of Languedoc and Roussillon, or the number of threads in a weave, the length of a bolt or half-bolt, the baling of woven goods.[6] Rather than a teacher or draper, he yearned to be a poet and an actor. In school he was fond of music and skits improvised for special occasions. A company of traveling players provided the chance to test his skills. Then and there he chose to make a living doing what he wanted to do.

"I was twenty-one, an actor for six months, full of talent, or so I thought, unpracticed in all aspects of the theater as I later realized, though it must have been apparent to my audiences and behind the scenes . . . Mild-tempered and solitary, a rich, lustrous imagination that will not be fettered by social strictures, a decided talent for a great profession, a passion for studying the arts and sciences related to the stage, a memory bulging with poetry, with heroic deeds of old that recall my schooldays, and that most prized possession of all: sweet, enchanting liberty; no social calls, no ceremonies, no unbearable relatives or possessive parents, no domestic stability, by that I mean the kind of stability which, to a proud and passionate youth, imposes an intolerable burden of conflicting demands, supposedly for one's own good . . . So many things, so many advantages, so many opportunities enjoyed or contemplated in a thousand different guises, have always drawn me to this profession, which is not respected, I grant, but which everyone would adopt if it were."[7]

In Namur this winter he turns twenty-six. To the girls he is the image of that freedom to which they hope a man will lead them. There is something fiercely attractive about him: "Hair swept back off his brow, deep, dark eyes, a strong, slightly hooked nose, jutting chin and prominent cheekbones."[8] An actor in life as well as on the boards, he tailors his costume to the occasion: casual dress for courting maids at the inn, starch and satin for the bourgeoisie. Like a professional, he maintains his role right up to the final curtain. People listen and believe because he believes.

Maybe he was never so sincere until he met Catiche: Catherine Deresmond, daughter of the rather shifty couple who manage the road company. For two months he is hopelessly in love with her—a long time for him.

He met her at Christmas; by New Year's he courts her steadily.[9] The fact that they play together every evening makes the task simpler, and she is eager for adventure. The resistance comes not from her but from her parents, who are less moralistic than calculating. Catiche is fifteen, the age at which a girl of her background becomes ripe to "repay" a pair of pandering parents for all the trouble they have taken to raise her. "St. Jeanne Bécu, pray for us": Madame du Barry's glorious career kindled wild hopes in the breast of every shop-owning family with a desirable daughter. To sell for the right price, a Catiche, like a Du Barry, has to be a dazzling beauty who is not at all prudish and even somewhat broad-minded, if possible, but still a virgin, which amounts to a guarantee that she won't give you the pox. Catiche is all those things. No one is going to ruin this marvelous piece of goods, least of all a Fabre without title or fortune, when even now some local army officers are beginning to ogle her.

Fabre d'Eglantine seduces Catiche, quite naturally between two backdrops. January 15: her parents hear of it and lock her up. He is furious: "My dearest love, your mother is your worst enemy. Yes, she will destroy you, sell you, deliver you into slavery and, like a slave, you will forfeit your health and beauty, your talent, your voice, and your lover's hopes, only to reap dishonor . . . ," the dishonor which our bold champion now uses as a weapon to "rescue" the poor girl, who, in any event, is not allowed to open her mouth.

The mother confiscated this letter and all others. January 20: Fabre d'Eglantine storms into the Deresmond house with saber and pistol, but what good are they against a harpy who comes at him flailing a stick? They throw him out. Namur's citizens are content: these actors certainly can perform at the drop of a hat.

The next morning Fabre takes up where he should have begun, with a formal declaration to the mother: "I love Catiche, Catiche loves me; she told me so, promised and swore it to me, has given me every token of it (I would not hide what you already know). For all these reasons, and chiefly the last, love justifies my asking for her hand; yes, I want to marry her, that is my intention . . . " His lack of fortune is surpassed only by a lack of modesty: "Without flattering myself, and aside from the dramatic talents which I can develop as fully as anyone, I believe that few men combine birth and education with such diverse gifts, all admirable, all useful, all related to each other, all independent of one another, and which, under proper cultivation, may lead to security and advancement."

Madame Deresmond was not about to let her daughter be hustled. No reply. Fabre abandons the role of Don Juan for that of Scapin.

February 5, to Catiche: "Today, if at all possible, I shall try to see you and hope to succeed. Don't be afraid. Here's my plan. I'll hide in your room, under your bed, and stay very quiet until the right moment, I mean the time your brothers go to bed . . . " The scheme unfolds whereby Catiche will drug her guardian with "a vial of liqueur laced with opium." "Peacefully, then, I promise you, we will spend the most enchanting night together." A servant girl named Catin spoils their plan; but though she, Catin, is opposed, the garrison commanders are in favor. A Lieutenant Maye arranges for Catiche to call on him. Her mother is only too delighted to have the girl pay him a visit on February 10. Fabre d'Eglantine waits at another door, and one hour later the two lovers are galloping toward Liège with a week's pocket money generously contributed by the officers.

Five days before, Fabre d'Eglantine had received another letter* from Sophie Poudhon harping on her favorite theme: "Let us love each other, oh let us love each other even more, if possible, than we do already; but what am I saying, for this I could never do, no, my love cannot deepen, it is stronger than the strongest, no one has ever loved as I love, dearest sweetheart who shall be my husband, yes, you shall, in spite of all."

63

FEBRUARY 1777

It's Just as It Ought to Be

It seems that the Marquis de Sade decided to become a professional writer at the close of his Italian travels when faced with the fact that the courts barred him from pursuing a military career. From scholars he had met, chiefly in Rome and Florence, he was able to obtain documentary material on "peculiar

*Spelling and punctuation equally eccentric. [*Trans.*]

aspects of luxury" drawn from the records of antiquity or from observers of contemporary Roman manners. Enhanced with those and countless more recondite pungencies, the amorphous manuscript of his *Voyage d'Italie* would have been the initial work of a highly original mind.

But those documents rarely reached him in La Coste. To begin with, he was prudent enough to bide his time incognito in Grenoble. When he finally returned home, toward the end of July 1776, the marquise had spread the word of his conversion and papal audience—wholly imaginary, to be sure, since the true pattern of his devotions was all too plain. He found his wife more submissive and cooperative. All summer long, in "heat too oppressive to overexert mind or body"* (the same hot spell which forced Mirabeau and his three companions in Lyons to live with the windows wide open), she fought against gossip and the written judicial inquiries respectfully delivered to her front door. No one would think of crudely hauling a lady named De Sade before the magistrates. But "the young girls of La Coste" continued to talk and their parents to storm. One of the few who stayed on at the château to volunteer for whatever "services" were required, the young cook, Marie, died on August 30 of "malignant fever" shortly after Donatien-Aldonse's unpublicized return. Pure coincidence, which simply fueled the legend of Bluebeard's Castle. It was sheer insanity to stay in La Coste and wait for someone to betray him, a man they had burned in effigy four years earlier in the Place des Prêcheurs in Aix, ten leagues south. The capital of Provence, the seat of government and privilege, is beyond the Lubéron, whose alpine ridge seems to form a natural protective barrier for the hilltop manor of the lord of La Coste, who still receives homage "on bended knee" from his vassals, a one-eighth tax on "grain, vegetables, olives, hemp, and acorns, and a one-tenth tax on grapes"[1] in addition to the rights of high, low, and middle justice.** Defaulter outside his own domain, sovereign judge within it, but only on principle, for he could never count on protection from the king's men, from "these villains, who were," according to him, "a bunch of rascally beggars fit to be roasted one atop the other, for which, without batting an eyelid, I would furnish the kindling."[2] The stares of his tenant farmers began to sear him, however. He was home but two months, like a ghost, "being there and not there" before taking off again. His choice of destinations was limited: he needed a spacious, luxurious inn for his comfort and pleasures; it had to be in the Midi because he was used to the climate and wanted to be near his wife. Aix and Marseilles were out of the question; Toulouse and Bordeaux too far away; leaving Montpellier.

The Hôtel du Chapeau Rouge seemed quite comfortable for a while. Montpellier is the Paris of Languedoc: one can move about unobserved. Being

*The phrase is Madame de Sade's, in a letter to her notary.
**High justice was the right of condemning to death after criminal investigation; middle and low justice involved jurisdiction over what are currently known as minor and civil offenses.

a well-organized soul, Sade kept an address book and inside a week was in touch with a certain Rosette who had spent two months in La Coste in 1775 and proved to be the cooperative type. Rosette introduced him to Adelaide. A recollect* friar named Durand, one of the real horde of priestly pimps who people the stories of Restif de La Bretonne and actually lurked in the shadows of every kitchen, whether an inn or a château, had procured a "young cook" named Catherine Trillet for La Coste. The Sade manor seems to have suffered chronically from a shortage of cooks. This one set out—with Father Durand as her escort and, not far behind, Sade himself, who returned home on November 4. Was he trailing this new cook, whom he described as homely? A better reason, surely, was that life in Montpellier without funds had become intolerable. Meals at the hotel, plus Rosette, plus Adelaide, plus heaven knows what else, were too costly for an outlaw whose rents had been impounded, whose wife was begging her mother to see them through the winter. They are short of firewood; some windowpanes are missing, and Madame de Sade stays in bed to keep warm. Her mother generously contributed twelve hundred livres,** in installments, through a notary. After a month of such deprivations, which he never could tolerate, Sade broke down.

Another nervous seizure. They were becoming increasingly uncontrollable.

Father Durand, a veteran recruiter by now, returned to La Coste one wintry mid-December evening when the icy mistral buffeted the château like a potter's vessel. He brought with him from Montpellier a relief squad, as Sade could not afford to hire local help. A secretary, a barber-valet, a chambermaid, and a scullery girl. The marquis put the quartet in four separate rooms, then proceeded to assault one after the other, male and female, throughout the night, "insisting that they submit to his desires." Only the kitchenmaid complied. The others fled at four in the morning and spread their tale all over Montpellier. Father Durand was banished from his monastery. Another city that is now off limits for Sade.

One poor fellow, a respectable weaver, took a dim view of all these aristocratic refinements—the father of Catherine Trillet, who had been cooking for the marquis since November. She was twenty-two, still a minor, and in danger. A danger that seemed to bother her hardly at all. In any event, Catherine's father arrived in La Coste about noon on January 17, 1777, and located his daughter only after considerable difficulty. Because the Marquis de Sade and his wife had rechristened her Justine.†

---

*Recollects were "orthodox" Franciscans who, in many cases, became corrupted by greed, ambition, and truckling to the vices of rich and powerful men. They multiplied for a century in Spain, then moved north into Languedoc in the wake of banished Jesuits.

**About 6000 francs [$1200] today; only one third of what the Sades normally would have spent for the winter.

†Four or five years later, while in prison, Sade was to write *La Nouvelle Justine ou les malheurs de la vertu.*

Old man Trillet was furious. He dived for his pistol. In refusing to give up the girl (apparently he had taken a liking to the "homely creature"), Sade ran a tremendous risk. The term "sadism" and the marquis's life hung on a damp cartridge cap which kept Trillet's gun from firing at close range. For that act —repeated later in the afternoon—the fellow could have been strung up on the spot. However, the "rascally beggars" of La Coste had helped him to escape and reach Aix, where he brought suit on January 21 before the royal prosecutor.[3]

January 30, 1777. Once again things get too uncomfortable for Sade and he feels compelled to leave La Coste. Like a gambler, he plays for double or nothing, just as Mirabeau had tried to do six months earlier. He will go to Paris and hide; try to regain his mother-in-law's good graces; at least he can count on help from his mother, Marie-Eléonore, née Maillé de Carman. Though ill and a retired pensioner lodging with the Carmelites on the Rue de l'Enfer, she is only sixty-five and could well bestir herself to put in a good word for him with the Condés. Does Donatien-Aldonse still dream of commanding a regiment? Four of them set off on roads so muddy that their carriage keeps breaking down: Sade takes along his valet, La Jeunesse, and the marquise takes Catherine Trillet, now called Justine, who insists on running away from her father. On February 8 they reach Paris exhausted, mud-spattered, aching in every joint, with all their hopes pinned on the old Comtesse de Sade . . .

. . . Only to learn that she had died and been buried on January 15 in Saint-Jacques du Haut-Pas. News of it must have crossed them on their journey. "M. de Sade was feeling confident of success all during the trip, and the blow struck him hardest."[4]

But at this point no grief or discouragement could change his habits. He lodges for a few days with his old teacher, the Abbé Amblet, on the Rue des Fossés-Monsieur-le-Prince, between the Luxembourg Gardens and the construction that has been going on for three years on the site of the Hôtel des Condé, where he was born thirty-six years earlier. They are clearing ground, laying out streets, planning to put up a theater. Sade promptly contacts an old companion of his Parisian revels, another priest of the same stamp as the Franciscan from Montpellier. He seems to know a multitude of dissolute priests. He writes that he would like to see him at once, to trade experiences, and of course to go on a spree together some night, not having chased girls in Paris for six years. Does he sense that time is running out? Probably not. More than ever now he relies on his wife; she will arrange the time and money he needs to chase girls. Meanwhile he takes rooms at the Hôtel du Danemark on the Rue Jacob.

Having no one but her mother to turn to, Madame de Sade breaks the news of their arrival on February 10. She has not yet digested the fact that her mother will never forgive Sade for dishonoring her two daughters and has no intention of letting him do further damage. Her younger daughter, the canoness, "recovered" now from that wild affair with her brother-in-law in 1772, is also in Paris under watchful eyes, "protected." Suppose the wretch tries to court her again? Maternal intuition is infallible. Madame de Montreuil knows that Anne-Prospère de Launay is the one woman whom Donatien-Aldonse de Sade really loved. For that sin he deserves to be punished far more than for torturing and poisoning prostitutes.

She informs the police at once. Two days later, on February 13, 1777, Inspector Marais, one of twenty in charge of the Paris region, arrests the Marquis de Sade in his hotel. By half past nine that evening he is locked in a dungeon at Vincennes. Cell number eleven. Madame de Montreuil heaves a sigh of relief and in a note to Gaufridy, her notary, remarks: "All is for the best and for safety's sake. About time! It's just as it ought to be."[5]

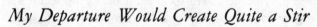

THE MARQUISE DE LA FAYETTE

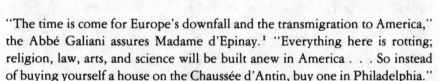

64

MARCH 1777

My Departure Would Create Quite a Stir

"The time is come for Europe's downfall and the transmigration to America," the Abbé Galiani assures Madame d'Epinay.[1] "Everything here is rotting; religion, law, arts, and science will be built anew in America . . . So instead of buying yourself a house on the Chaussée d'Antin, buy one in Philadelphia."

Shortly after daybreak on March 15, 1777, La Fayette bursts into the bedroom of his friend Louis-Philippe de Ségur. "At seven o'clock he marches into my room, locks the door, and sits down at my bedside to inform me: 'I am leaving for America; no one knows it, but I am too fond of you to go without telling you my secret.' "[2]

CUR NON? "Why not?" La Fayette has just decided to inscribe this motto above his coat of arms. But why should he go alone? Why not take Ségur and the third musketeer, Louis-Marie de Noailles, as they had agreed to sail together? Because of money, money which La Fayette had the good fortune to inherit early in life from a tremendously rich father whose sole heir he was. The exact opposite of what happened to Mirabeau, now a social outcast hounded by an abusive parent. Though Mirabeau is nearly ten years older than La Fayette, his personal independence has been denied consistently, as is also the case with Ségur, who complains sadly that "the Vicomte de Noailles and I were dependent on our parents and possessed only the allowance they gave us. Yet here was La Fayette, younger than we and of inferior rank at the age of nineteen, yet, through a stroke of luck, master of his destiny, of his person, and of an income of a hundred thousand livres."*

Ever since the "luncheon at Metz" in August 1775 the idea of America had settled in the back of La Fayette's mind, quietly at first, like a fond hope. His life went on as usual, divided between home and his regiment. A daughter, Henriette, was born in December 1775; her mother was fifteen. His main interest had been Aglaé d'Hunolstein, whom he tried to woo away from the Duc de Chartres,** but in the end she neither spurned nor favored him. A puce-colored heartbreak. During the summer his fond hope became an obsession. On December 8, 1776, a certain Dubois-Martin wrote to a certain Kalb: "Our young marquis does not despair; he still yearns to depart. M. de Noailles, who has abandoned the project, will probably try to dissuade the marquis from persisting in his own right, and the whole family will back him. The latest sensation is word of Mr. Franklin's arrival in Nantes. He will set out for Paris tomorrow."[3]

In fact the Noailles were not anxious to defy Louis XVI's ultra-conservative policy by pledging one of their own tribe to the rebel cause. Yet the above quotation is significant because of the writers' identities: Kalb is a well-traveled officer and former spy for Louis XV in America. Dubois-Martin is secretary to the Comte de Broglie, director of the same spying agency until Choiseul's disgrace sent him into semi-retirement. He spent most of his time with his brother, the Duc de Broglie; born in the same year, the two were nearly twins. He had met La Fayette at Metz. Barred from all diplomatic activities by Vergennes, he is bored and restless. Though the Duc de Broglie had done nothing to encourage Gilbert's contact with the Duke of Gloucester, he and his brother were privy to the young officer's excited urge to go overseas, which fed the ambitious schemes of these two embittered aristocrats.

At first the Duc de Broglie, number one in the family, feigned reluctance: "No, I watched your uncle die in Italy; I commanded the army when your father was killed at Minden;† I think you must devote yourself to your family.

---

*Ségur exaggerates. La Fayette had an income of 146,000 livres in 1777 (about 750,000 current francs [$150,000]). The Vicomte de Noailles (b. 1756), second son of the Comte de Noailles, who was also the Duc de Mouchy, belonged to the cadet branch of that all-powerful clan. He has just married his cousin Louise, sister of La Fayette's wife, one of the five daughters of the Duc d'Ayen, who heads the main branch of the family. Noailles figures prominently in the events of 1789, chiefly on the night of August 4, will emigrate and perish in a naval battle against the British at the end of the Consulate. The Comte de Ségur (b. 1753) goes to Russia as ambassador under Catherine II, then becomes grand master of ceremonies at the court of Napoleon.
**The future Philippe Egalité.
†In fact Colonel de La Fayette died at Hastenbeck two years after the Battle of Minden.

You are newly married and about to become a father . . . I would not dream of letting you risk your life."[4]

Fine, but then why does he go along so readily when, on June 11, 1776, La Fayette applies for discharge from His Majesty's forces, thus leaving himself free to join another army and not be labeled a deserter? Why does Broglie number two, the count, put him in touch with Kalb, his former agent, a man intimately acquainted with the situation in America and about to return there? Why does he tell his secretary, Dubois-Martin, to keep in touch with Gilbert and help him? Because La Fayette's eventual departure for America is a key factor in the younger Broglie's designs. This brother has so poisoned the mind of Silas Deane in Paris that the good fellow thinks he has unearthed the one and only champion of American independence. After all, a Broglie is worth far more than a Beaumarchais. In December, in order to steal the march on Franklin, Silas Deane dispatches a memorandum to the Congress in Philadelphia, the contents of which speak for the Comte de Broglie. Deane writes practically from dictation: "My aim is simply to find a man whose name and reputation alone will demoralize the enemy . . . Such a man is available, and I believe I have found him . . . The question is to win his confidence; which can only be done by heaping sufficient honors upon him to gratify his ambition, as, for instance, naming him commander-in-chief and awarding him a sizable sum of money in order that his numerous children may be cared for while he is overseas."[5] The younger Broglie aspires to rival his brother's battle record and claims to have no less military talent than he. But who would expect the Americans to accept his offer on the spur of the moment, or Louis XVI to take the initiative and propose it? The thing to do was send over a batch of officers to form the nucleus of a general staff and to create an atmosphere favorable to Broglie's leadership. In Europe there existed a clique of great generals from the Seven Years' War—whose defeat supposedly qualified them to lead the assault on any battlefront in the world. The name of George Washington made them laugh: with luck, he might last a year. Besides, it was all too apparent that sooner or later the Americans would need a real leader, an expert. Rather than an Austrian, a Prussian, or a Russian, why not the Comte de Broglie? Kalb knew of this scheme and would lay the groundwork. La Fayette, though naïve, was presentable, the perfect bait. Once he and Washington met defeat, he would summon a real champion.

In January 1777 Broglie and Kalb, with some assistance (gingerly accepted) from Beaumarchais, were preparing to send a group of about fifteen noble officers to America. This little plan also bespoke the rivalry between the idle landed aristocracy, the *noblesse d'épée,* and the rising class of foreign traders represented for the moment by Beaumarchais. Who would pull the chestnuts from the fire, the princes or the gun merchants?

Kalb was all set to sail on one of the armed vessels chartered by Beaumarchais in Le Havre and immobilized by royal decree on December 16. Furious, he returned to Paris to wait for another ship and was available to help speed the departure of La Fayette, who was eager to be off. They needed to act fast, before discouraging battle reports and the recriminations of England's ambassador further terrified Louis XVI, who was back-tracking almost before he had taken a step forward: by order of the Paris police, it became an offense to talk about America in the coffee houses and taverns of the capital.[6]

By request of the Comte de Broglie, Silas Deane had received La Fayette in mid-December and been stunned by the young officer's cheek: "In presenting to Mr. Deane a face barely nineteen years of age, I spoke more for my enthusiasm than for my experience; but I made him see that my departure would create quite a stir."[7]

He had found it necessary to delay for three months, the price of having talked too freely at the Epée de Bois. The Noailles and Ségur families had called a halt to the plans of Gilbert's two intended companions, and Gilbert in turn, to pacify his own kin, had decided to travel in England, where his uncle, another Noailles, was ambassador to the court of George III.

Much later La Fayette confessed how much fun the whole performance had been: "At nineteen, a youth is perhaps too fond of talking against the king he is about to combat, of waltzing in the ballroom of Lord Germain, royal minister to the American colonies, and encountering at the Opera that [General] Clinton whom he will meet again at [the Battle of] Monmouth."[8] Meanwhile a trusted agent was tending to serious business matters in Bordeaux: purchase of a vessel named the *Victoire* and equipment for 112,000 francs* from the shipbuilding firm of Reculès de Basmarins, Raimbaux & Co. Captain Le Boursier must have judged from the cargo that they were bound for the West Indies; La Fayette would direct him to alter the ship's course once they reached open water. He had orders to transport thirteen officers.

From Calais, then from London, Gilbert continued to lull his child bride with flowery letters: "I am leaving everyone I love; I leave you, dearest one, not knowing why indeed. But the die is cast and I must go . . . Farewell, dear one, in whatever country I sail to, I shall always love you tenderly" (February 20, 1777). He knew perfectly well what country he would land in six months later, and why, but he felt Adrienne was still under her parents' thumb and not to be trusted with his secret. "We have just dined at our ambassador's house and are leaving for the Opera; afterward we are invited to supper and a ball; we shall see a great many ladies tonight. I find Paris far superior to London, although we are very well received here. I am eager to see all these young ladies" (February 25). "The pleasures of London race by so fast, and I am amazed how lively they are . . . To get up from dinner at half past seven and eat supper between two and three [in the morning, of course] seems to me a very bad habit" (undated). "We dance, we sup, we stay out till all hours

*Today about 550,000 francs [$110,000]. Beyond the means of any individual, even the wealthy La Fayette; a quarter in cash, the balance payable in fifteen months.

a great deal, and our occupations have been social, for the most part . . . Tomorrow or the day after, we go to Portsmouth, armed with full instructions on what to see" (March 7)[9] . . . Mainly to see a lot of soldiers and weaponry taken aboard ship, one of which might be destined to end his life. He closed the last letter with an apology for having not yet written to his father-in-law, the Duc d'Ayen: "I shall delay writing him until I have a more interesting excursion to relate."

Deliberate irony? A week later he was back, in Chaillot, not Paris, at Kalb's house, just around the corner from his wife, also from his father-in-law, whom he had resolved not to see before leaving the country.

He works out a contract, predated December 7, 1776, with Silas Deane, who, "acting on behalf of the supreme Congress," appoints him to "the rank of major general."* Like a royal prince, he advances to the very heights of the military hierarchy without ever drawing his sword. Silas Deane had no authority to promote him thus, but there it is in writing, with lines added by La Fayette:

"I subscribe to the above terms and pledge to depart when and as Mr. Deane deems suitable, to serve the United States with all possible vigor, without remuneration or salary, reserving the right to return to Europe if family or my king should summon me."[10] A far cry from the commitment that regimental recruiters often demanded of enlistees at the garrison in Metz: twelve years' service, and death to deserters.

Then off he sails, without seeing Ségur again, but leaving his father-in-law a small bomb in the form of a letter:** "You will be stunned, father dear, at what I have to tell you; it has pained me more than you can guess not to consult you . . . I have found a unique opportunity to distinguish myself and to learn my profession: I am a general in the army of the United States of America. My zeal for their cause and my candor have won their confidence. For my part, I have done all I can to help them and shall always hold their interests dearer than my own. At this moment, father dear, I am in London, still awaiting word from my friends; I shall leave as soon as it arrives, without stopping in Paris; I shall sail on a vessel chartered by me and which I own . . . "[11]

A vein of resentment runs through the letter: the Duc d'Ayen had always treated his son-in-law condescendingly and is bound to be furious on discovering that Gilbert is indeed capable of acting decisively and that the family eventually will have to answer for it. As for the child bride, who is once again pregnant, Gilbert had misjudged her: he could have trusted her; she would not have betrayed him. She will bear the blow in silence and comment laconically in later years: "M. de La Fayette carried out the plan he had contemplated

---

*In fact this would make him deputy commander of an army, outranking all other company commanders.

**Predated, also, March 9, but not delivered until the 16th, when he was in Bordeaux.

for six months to go serve the cause of American independence. I was pregnant and loved him deeply."[12]

65

MARCH 1777

Whom Impulse Led Astray

Fabre d'Eglantine is sentenced to hang. Such a young, handsome fellow. What a shame. And all for love. Just what you might expect of a clown from Carcassonne. "Seek and ye shall find"; he wagered and lost. Someday someone will write an operetta about his romantic end, a buffoon dangling from a noose. Not the first one, either.

Catiche and he have had less than ten days of bliss, not enough time even to get bored. The girl's mother was not the type to let someone filch her pullet with the golden eggs. Upon discovering her daughter's flight, she badgered the authorities and got the mayor to station a watch at the gates of Namur— several hours too late to catch the fugitives. The mother also denounced poor Lieutenant Maye as an accomplice, and he has been clapped into prison. Then she offered a reward for information as to where, in what direction, they have fled. This province was Catholic, ruled by a prince-bishop, and the parish priest was the law unto himself. Money could buy safe conduct through Liège province, and they had none. Peered at, spied on, driven from shabby inns to a wagoners' lodging, Fabre and Catiche trudged the banks of the Meuse for some twenty-five miles on their way north to the sea, far away, remote, inaccessible as freedom itself. Their love had no chance to blossom, for hostile forces challenged their every step: wind and rain, vegetation too sparse to offer them shelter, fields too bare to cushion their love. Jambes, Andenne, Huy, Engis . . . Then the chief hurdle, Liège itself, whose citadel, atop the Carthusian hill, bars the Meuse. City of forts and cloisters, seat of the diocese. When they tried to turn into the plain and head for Maastricht, they were caught in Waremme.[1]

From then on things happen fast. Catiche is sent back to her mother to be married off. Fabre is returned to Namur to stand trial on charges of seducing and abducting a minor. In the courtroom, magistrate and defendant face each other. No witnesses, no lawyer. He is permitted to defend himself —or rather to counterattack in writing. He cannot deny the charge, having been caught in the act. On the other hand, the girl's own father eloped with his wife when she was fifteen and he thirty-five. Isn't he, too, exploiting "the charms of Madame Deresmond"? Didn't he have his eldest son sleep with the servant girl Catin in order to spy on his daughter . . . a daughter whose virginity was still intact when she met Fabre only because she had defended it successfully against her own father? Fabre swears this was his reason for abducting her, to remove her from such an atmosphere.

Keep talking, belated champion of innocence! Namur's judge is deaf. On March 20 he sentences Fabre d'Eglantine to be hanged "according to law and justice, and in conformity with the regulations."[2] Mitigating circumstances are brushed aside on March 22, 1777. Fabre has but a few hours to live.

Luckily for him, he was not the only one sentenced.

For an actor, whose life was worth precious little to begin with, justice was blind. But Namur's magistrate had also convicted two accomplices, both officers, one of whom was Lieutenant Maye. Light sentences: a short stint behind bars, stiff fines. Enough to make them scream for mercy. Their protests reached all the way to Brussels, where Prince Charles of Lorraine, governor general of the Austrian Lowlands under Maria Theresa, and viceroy of Belgium for twenty-five years, also commanded the army. Now, it was customary throughout Europe for generals to wink at the amorous escapades of their officers. No army could function effectively unless soldiers were allowed to chase girls. The same circumstances that brought death to an actor built prestige for a cavalry lieutenant.[3] And Charles of Lorraine needed to keep his men content, for rumors of an Austro-Prussian war over Bavaria were spreading through the garrisons.

Like loyal comrades, Fabre d'Eglantine's friends remember him when petitioning the governor on March 23, pleading to save their careers and his neck, urging clemency for a poor fellow "driven by youthful ardor, born in a climate where passions seethe; for a spirited lad whose lively, open nature works against him, who listened unwisely to his heart, whom impulse led astray."[4] Charles of Lorraine inclines to amnesty, for him, for them. He is unprepared for the shrill protests from Namur's magistrate, who, deprived of a hanging, drafts an opinion seeking to deny mercy to a wretch "practiced in all the refinements of vice, whose sole experience is of perverted and dissolute morals, whose sole resource is his undistinguished acting talent." What did the judge know about this? Had he gone to the theater? Had he studied Catiche casually but with sufficient intensity to produce his idyllic portrait of a "young girl of fifteen and a half, not only obedient, submissive, and devoted to her parents, but also well behaved, honest, and extremely shy, who was abducted, snatched, stolen from her home, from her family, from herself, and by whom? By a debaucher, corrupted by filthy, shameless vice" and so on. Pages and pages of slander, like talons squeezing the life out of Fabre. The judge's desperate appeal to the governor may be the very thing that saved Fabre's life.

What a lot of noise about a young rake! Charles of Lorraine is an aging connoisseur of good food and pretty women. Irritated, he waves off the vulture and sets Fabre d'Eglantine free on March 30. Poorer than ever, and amazed to be alive, he asks no questions and starts out at once for Paris, the seat of beggardom.

66

APRIL 1777

What Would You Do There?

La Fayette and Kalb leave Paris for Bordeaux on March 16, 1777. They hire a cabriolet, a light two-wheeled carriage "with room for travel bag and port-manteau," and doors with windows for privileged passengers, which they are. They pay three francs per post; the entire journey will cost nearly 250 livres* exclusive of food on the road, for they have decided not to stop for eating or sleeping. They reach Bordeaux on the 19th. They could choose among four routes: seventy-six posts via Vendôme, Tours, Poitiers, Niort, Saintes; seventy-six and a half via Orléans, Tours, Angoulême; seventy-five and a half via Chartres, Tours, Poitiers, Angoulême; seventy-six via Etampes, Orléans, Vierzon, Châteauroux, Limoges, Périgueux, Libourne. The average post was equivalent to one hour's travel with a pair of fresh horses. The postilions are forbidden to rein them in "except to catch their wind."[1] La Fayette himself barely had a chance to breathe—three days and nights on the road.

He arrives unheralded in this large city with a population of a hundred thousand, underrated in the eyes of the capital and the court, but presently changing character as it changes from viticulture and agriculture to maritime commerce on the Garonne.** Of all French cities, Bordeaux is shifting most rapidly from farming to overseas trade. Louis-Hyacinthe Dudevant, young son of a local sugar-refiner, recently published an *Apologie du commerce, essai philosophique et politique, avec des notes instructives* . . . [In Defense of trade, a philosophic and political essay with instructive notes], which has aroused considerable enthusiasm, especially for its epigraph heralding the new cult:

*About 1250 francs [$250] today.
**Bordeaux's merchant fleet numbered 79 vessels in 1730, 324 in 1777. During the same period the export trade grew from 110 to 750 dealers, including 25 slavers.

Puisse l'heureux lien des besoins mutuels
Du couchant à l'aurore unir tous les mortels.[2]

[May the happy bond of mutual needs
From sunset to sunrise unite all mortals.]

La Fayette is untouched by this mercantile spirit; on arrival, he goes straight to the house* of "the supreme military governor of Guyenne and Gascony," the king's military deputy. Another member of the Noailles clan, as it turns out, the Duc de Mouchy, recent successor to Maréchal de Richelieu, whose lavish, Borgialike style of living had stunned the Bordeaux region for sixteen years. From London to Bordeaux, then, Gilbert was a guest of one rich uncle after the other, the last being the father of his best friend, the Vicomte de Noailles, who had not been permitted to leave Paris.

All goes well. He is welcomed as a young aristocrat traveling for his education, and on March 20 he roams the bustling avenue parallel to the docks along the Garonne. The river is too wide to bridge; its harbor is as distant from the sea as those of Nantes, Rouen, or Hamburg. Large vessels avoid it because there are few solid berths and no upright piers. For several days the *Victoire* has been awaiting her passengers in the estuary at Pauillac; the longboat to ferry them there leaves from the Saint-Michel docks, "where calkers, shipwrights, and sailors toil, and the soldiers from Fort Louis come to 'tank up.' "[3] Vagabonds, starving beggars, and fortunetellers add an exotic touch to the backdrop of brand-new townhouses built by eighty shipowners doing a hundred millions' worth of business annually in the port.[4]

La Fayette never so much as glances at the seamy side of society. Everything has been arranged for him by another Dubois-Martin, brother of Broglie's secretary. He was the secret agent working in Bordeaux while La Fayette waltzed in London. One last formality: at the admiralty, he must sign the sailing permit issued to "Sieur Gilbert du Mottié [for Motier], Chevalier de Chavaillac [for Chavagnac], twenty years of age, tall, with blond [*sic*] hair."[5] The clerk is not observant: on the same permit Kalb is transformed into "Baron de Canne."

Like any veteran of the secret service, Kalb lived in mortal terror of countermanded orders and failed to share his companion's optimism. On March 20 he wrote to his wife: "We may yet be prevented from sailing. A thousand details delay us, and there is plenty of time for the ministry to be informed of the marquis's departure and to remand its orders before we get out to sea." And again on March 23: "We still do not know if there is opposition to our sailing; the ship will not be ready until tomorrow."[6]

In fact it was two days before they could board the longboat to Pauillac. Suddenly, on the Saint-Michel dock, a messenger appears frantically waving

*A relatively simple building on the corner of the Rue Porte-Dijeaux and the Rue Vital-Carles, formerly the mayor's mansion.

a letter from Versailles addressed to La Fayette at the governor's mansion. Sent by Coigny, a charter member of the Epée de Bois drinking set, it packed thunder: the Duc d'Ayen, enraged by his son-in-law's letter, had raised a storm with Vergennes and the king, who is prepared to issue a *lettre de cachet.*

La Fayette's confidence collapses like a house of cards. Kalb reads panic on the face of his neighbor in the longboat. If the Garonne had been a sluggish river, La Fayette never would have happened—one name fewer in the annals of French history. Kalb takes him in hand and gets him out to the ship to think things over: "If that letter had not been handed to him after we were already settled in the rowboat, I believe he would have chosen to turn back immediately."[7]

Panic affords a thick-skinned professional the chance to square accounts with this nineteen-year-old "general," this amateur they left on his hands. Kalb, like everyone else, assumes La Fayette to be a conceited ass. After dragging him aboard the *Victoire,* he persuades him (if only to protect their investment and the ship from seizure) to head for the nearest Spanish port and await further word. After all, no one has stopped them from sailing. On the morning of March 26 Kalb hands the pilot one last note to his wife: "In two hours we will be at sea. We raise anchor under marvelous skies. I will surely write to you before reaching America, for we will need to put into some European port or other and undoubtedly will wait over in San Sebastian for replies to the mail we sent to Paris."[8]

Kalb is determined to sail regardless of wind or weather, but La Fayette, whose nausea is not purely sea-induced, leans on him, seeking advice to justify retreat. When the *Victoire* veers southwest across the Gulf of Gascony in the soft light of early spring that casts a nacreous, wavelike glow on the ocean's face, Kalb is convinced that La Fayette will not leave: "If the marquis is foolish enough not to make some arrangement with the shipowner, he will have to pay dearly for it.

"I say foolish: the word is not too strong; besides, he has acted foolishly all along, from the day he decided to carry out his plan without heeding the warning signals . . . He asked my advice, and I felt duty-bound to urge him to obey the wishes of his father-in-law and the king's commands. I never would have counseled him to resist and to break with his family. If he had not kept insisting that he would win the Duc d'Ayen's support, I would have stopped him from going ahead; but he always said that his family approved of his plans, that his father-in-law himself intended to sail for America eventually with the Vicomte de Noailles, that Madame de La Fayette knew of and favored his designs. I always thought he was wrong not to confide to his wife that he was leaving. If he had told me in Paris what he has since admitted, I would have firmly opposed the whole thing. As planned, the affair will cost him dear."[9]

Kalb is forty-five, former lieutenant colonel in a German regiment, then brigade commander in the French army. For ten years he has roamed two continents, spying first for Choiseul, later for Broglie, and has done all right for himself.* In January 1768 he was shipwrecked off the coast of New York, where his clothes stiffened "like planks of ice." [10] He is ruthless and unfeeling. For a man like Kalb, it is easy to destroy a helpless, disoriented infant who suddenly awakens to the fact that he is naked and unarmed.

On March 28, off San Sebastian, the *Victoire* drops anchor in the tiny port of Los Pasajes in Guipuzcoa province, on the Bay of Biscay. French sailors called it "Le Passage" and made regular trips there. Opening out from a narrow inlet, its harbor is "good for large vessels," but shipmasters must be on the lookout for a pair of reefs barely covered by two low tidal basins, the Eastern and Western Basins on either side of the entrance. The tides "rush in and out of the harbor," [11] making matters worse for La Fayette, who is still seasick in his floating hotel and tortured by agonizing uncertainty. Nursing his resentment, Kalb measures the young man's mounting desire to turn back: "No point waiting here for replies to our mail to Paris; we already received one in Bordeaux, which arrived yesterday. By royal command, the marquis is ordered to return to Toulon and await the Duc d'Ayen and his sister, the Comtesse de Tessé, and to accompany them to Italy. There's the end of his expedition and his service to the cause of American independence. He is leaving for Bordeaux; from there, if possible, he will go to Paris, for he dreads the idea of Italy. So now I must wait for messages from La Fayette either from Bordeaux . . . or Paris . . . What a bore! I doubt that he will manage to rejoin me, and I have advised him to pay twenty thousand or twenty-five thousand francs for the privilege of canceling his contract with the shipowners . . ." [12] Selfish advice from Kalb, who stood to inherit the contract and to take command of the little expedition which was all ready to leave.

On March 31 La Fayette goes ashore to Los Pasajes and then on to Bordeaux via Saint-Jean-de-Luz and Bayonne. No one would have wagered a sou on his destiny that day. He wasn't proud of this retreat when dictating his *Memoirs*: "The letters from my family were dreadful . . . The consequences of defying the law and the power and wrath of the government needed no elaboration; the distress and pregnant condition of a loving wife, and the ideas of relatives and friends finally made up my mind." [13] Did he really have to come all the way to Los Pasajes to realize that his wife is with child? No, the truth is simple: they have scared him into submission. The visceral terror that grips a man unsure of himself, even though he may swagger, when he feels the ground slipping from under him: family, friends, and, to be sure, fortune. Coigny had sounded the first alarm on behalf of the queen and the elegant set; the Duc d'Ayen followed suit, plus the whole Noailles tribe (his London uncle, the ambassador, stormed: "I presented him at court! What is he trying

---

*From Kalb to Choiseul, August 28, 1767: "I doubt that the cost of carrying out your secret instructions will be less than two thousand écus, exclusive of travel and personal expenses."

to do to me?''). Only his wife said nothing, but her silence spoke louder than words.

Thirty-five posts from Bayonne to Bordeaux, with a frustrating delay on the way through Langon, whose postmaster charges "ten sous per wheel for ferrying carriages across the river."[14] On April 5 Gilbert appears not before Maréchal de Mouchy, who is apt to lock the door behind him, but M. de Fumel, military commander of Bordeaux, requesting permission to wait there pending instructions from Paris. As always, he is received with backbreaking deference. A La Fayette is a notable, unlike a Fabre d'Eglantine or even a Sade or a Mirabeau; he deserves special consideration. His ancestors have been ministers and governors. He is free to wait, and he waits. Champing at the bit, he roams Bordeaux, a city of inns with spacious stables and coachhouses, the caravansary that serves France, Spain, and the Atlantic trade.[15] He keeps open house at the Chapeau Rouge. He strolls down the tree-lined, recently land-scaped Allées de Tourny into the Place Dauphine, still new and fresh,* scaled down to human proportions by its encircling band of classic two-story façades. La Fayette is not in hiding. It would have been a simple matter to arrest him if anyone had cared to. The local aristocracy knew his address and assumed he was preparing for a trip to Italy. Perhaps the prospect of such a penitential pilgrimage, with his father-in-law holding one hand, his aunt the other, finally spurred him to get a grip on himself. They meant to treat him like a truant. The parental scorn he had wanted to escape is bobbing up again. How can he go back to being treated like a child by a father-in-law who had said to him only last winter: "That [America] will do for the Vicomte de Noailles, who is strong and eager and decisive about whatever he undertakes, but you, what would *you* do there?"[16] Gilbert realizes that Kalb is angry and that the other less important volunteers in Los Pasajes cannot know what to think: Dubois-Martin, who had made all the arrangements and then signed on as a major; a Valfort, a Fayols, a Bedaulx, a La Colombe, fourteen in all, including Kalb. How could La Fayette face them if one day they should meet after having sailed without him? It was not to be rid of them that he came to Bordeaux; he had meant well by acting thus and placing himself in limbo; he seeks to force destiny's hand and has written to the one man still powerful enough to smooth the way, the Comte de Broglie, who has been urging him to sail for the last six months.

But having drummed up the courage to sneak off as he did, La Fayette still lacks the nerve to defy the authorities, the establishment. It takes him a long time to do so, two weeks in Bordeaux, which is about the average wait for replies to messages to the capital.

A very long wait for the *Victoire*'s passengers, not to mention her crew, which finds itself reduced to swabbing the deck and chasing girls in Los Pasajes —but then, who cares about sailors in such straits? Any more than about post

*Completed in 1770.

horses. Kalb writes glumly to his wife on April 6: "I was flattered to receive word from the marquis in Bordeaux yesterday evening. If I hear nothing today or tomorrow, we may end up spending the rest of our lives here . . . It is absolutely certain that neither M. de Maurepas nor the Duc d'Ayen will allow him to rejoin us . . . [17] Our motives for coming to this port hold us here: we must have authorization either from the marquis or the shipowner to proceed on our way . . . He sent [from Bordeaux] a letter to Paris and awaits the reply. That proves how hard it is for him to abandon his plans and his ship* . . . I will not know what to expect before the 11th . . . This waiting is unbearable." [18]

Nothing on the 11th; but on the 12th "the post has just brought me a letter from the marquis dated the 5th, from Bordeaux. He tells me they have refused him permission to sail and he is afraid he may have to go to Toulon." Apparently he still had not ruled out the trip to Italy. On the 13th Marseilles, not Toulon, turns out to be his destination, "where he is commanded by the king to appear today [Kalb again to his wife, on April 15]. He says that this whole business has caused quite a stir at court, but he still hopes to win the Duc d'Ayen's sympathy and to rejoin me. He bids me not to sail before further word from him . . . If I have to wait till he reaches Marseilles, it means I am stuck here till the 26th."

But on April 17, instead of a letter, Gilbert de La Fayette turns up in person on the docks of Los Pasajes and boards the *Victoire* wearing postilion's clothes. Hoist anchor! We're off to America! What happened?

In Paris, skirmish among the princes: a weekly occurrence likely to flare up over a point of etiquette, a matter of policy, a lady. On one side, the Noailles clan, angrier in appearance than in fact, who seldom vociferate except to extricate themselves from some diplomatic blunder. On the other side, the Broglie tribe, defending the young corsair and his crew as nothing but a harmless adventure. Maurepas smiled and kept out of it. Louis XVI could not be bothered even to think about it. The queen and Coigny, partisans of the "English faction," had sounded the alarm earlier and then forgot about it. Silas Deane had been afraid of a reprimand from both Franklin and Vergennes; on April 2 he wrote to the latter: "To persuade a very brave and amiable young man to embrace our cause and to set an example to everyone with his native, hereditary [*sic*] valor certainly cannot be held against me." To Vergennes again on the 5th: "No country would be ashamed of him, and I am convinced that one day he will prove to the world that my present bias in his favor was warranted." [19] The tempest at court subsided—and instead of a *lettre de cachet*** settling the matter once and for all, La Fayette greets an old friend,

---

*Kalb's mentality is such that he cannot imagine any gap in La Fayette's thinking between the *plan* and the *ship*, between ideal and reality.

**Which exists only in La Fayette's fears or imagination to justify the endless suspense of his stay

the Vicomte de Mauroy, who arrives in Bordeaux on April 15 with a message from Broglie urging him to be on his way. Since the ministers have issued no formal injunction, it means the court is willing to overlook the affair. Silence implies consent. And just to prove it, Mauroy carries in his pocket a commission as major general in the rebel army signed by Silas Deane, who apparently was turning out generals by the dozen. Broglie's emissary delivers a message guaranteed to dispel any uncertainty on La Fayette's part: assurance that he will be the laughingstock of Paris if he goes back there. Fear of ridicule sweeps away all his other fears.[20]

Falling back into his old pattern, he informs Bordeaux's commandant that he is bound for Marseilles with Mauroy in a post chaise. Once past the city gates, he slips into his postilion's costume and off they gallop southwest, not east, with his companion lolling in the seat behind. No one pursues them, yet he plays cat-and-mouse. Kalb to his wife from Los Pasajes on April 7: "The marquis has just arrived and is resolved to come with us . . . We have decided to sail."[21]

And so they did on the morning of April 20, 1777.

67

APRIL 1777

The Fiat Lux *Has Not Arrived*

The court of Versailles has problems enough without worrying about a fugitive La Fayette. How can one pay much attention to a complaining Duc d'Ayen when the emperor is about to visit Versailles? Imagine, the emperor! Charles V's successor, Charlemagne's heir—to the title, if nothing else!

But on April 18, 1777, Joseph annoys everyone by stopping first in Paris, where he puts up at the Hôtel de Tréville* near the Luxembourg. A slender, agile, moderately tall young man of thirty-six, dressed in very ordinary "puce-colored" clothes and attended by three or four servants, climbs out of a spacious but otherwise unremarkable traveling coach. The "Count of Falken-

---

in Bordeaux. Never did he receive a royal order, which it would have been treasonable to disobey; only the admonitions of family and friends.

*Run by a German hotelkeeper named Schmelling, on the Rue de Tournon. It became the Hôtel Foyot and was demolished in 1950.

stein" has made his way inconspicuously through Germany and eastern France, thus avoiding the ceremony so distasteful to this innately modest personality. His mother complained of it in advance: "I hope he will not wish to dine in furnished rooms and will lodge at the Trianon when he goes to Versailles instead of in the town . . ." He had made his own arrangements, however, having instructed Ambassador Mercy-Argenteau "to avoid carefully the appearance of reception rooms . . . As to Versailles, I am quite determined not to stay in the palace or the Petit Trianon or any other royal holding or dependency. I wish to pay for my lodgings and would prefer to return nightly to Paris rather than destroy for a single night spent at court the whole edifice of my anonymity . . . Kindly find a couple of rooms for my use in the town of Versailles."[1]

It was his first escape—relative at that—from Maria Theresa's spies, and his first opportunity to live where and as he pleased. He was not about to let spy number one, Mercy-Argenteau, snatch away that freedom.

Joseph II has his faults, but stupidity is not one of them. He knows that Mercy-Argenteau's fortune hangs on Maria Theresa's favor and that she relies on him to inform her of everything. The fact that he performs so efficiently suggests a natural gift for snooping. Besides, he and the empress have worked out a system to keep her informed of her son's every movement in Paris. From Maria Theresa to Mercy: "For the duration of his trip you will send me your [usual] reports in a form that may be handed around* . . . but after the emperor's departure I expect a full report immediately on what has gone on in Paris during the emperor's visit. If by chance something interesting [that is, for her eyes and ears only] should come up of which I ought to be informed at once, you may entrust it to Starhemberg,** who is *au courant* and will see that it reaches me."[2] Maria Theresa was so conscious of having neglected to educate her ten surviving children that she mounted a veritable network of intelligence agents in high places (such as Mercy-Argenteau) to spy on them in all the courts of Europe into which she had married them. The resulting stacks of mail produced a torrent of self-renewing lamentations which became her life. No good could come of this visit, she predicted, exceptional as it was: two of her children putting their heads together spelled trouble: "In the end, I expect no positive results from his trip. Unless I am mistaken, one of two things will happen: either my daughter will win over the emperor with kind words and smiles, or else he will try her patience by preaching to her."[3]

But Vienna is two weeks from Paris and Joseph arrives determined to amuse himself as well as to accomplish what he came for. A conscientious ruler, he must reforge the alliance between France and Austria at a time when mounting

---

*That is, a normal diplomatic dispatch destined eventually for the state archives, which Joseph could read on his return.

**Military governor of Brussels.

Russo-Turkish pressure threatens war in the Balkans, when the Elector of Saxony's declining health may jeopardize the fragile balance of power among the German states. But the emperor is not going to reactivate the alliance merely by talking to Vergennes and Maurepas; he must somehow shift the marriage of Louis XVI and Marie Antoinette from fiction to fact. In 1776 their union left one point unsettled: they continue to sleep apart almost every night, a situation that dates back virtually to their wedding night and has not improved. Someone has to intervene, and it can only be Joseph, who, at fourteen, had carried his baby sister to the baptismal font. Neither Mercy-Argenteau nor Maria Theresa (the prudishness of whose correspondence borders on idiocy) nor anyone else really knows what goes on between the young couple. Joseph will do what he can to help them.

April 19, quarter past eight. The emperor, flanked by young Count Belgiojoso, leaves the Hôtel de Tréville, his assumed identity so effective that a crowd blocks the street. Behind a pair of fine horses, at half past nine he arrives at Versailles: the mystery of his person again being such that courtiers pack the antechambers. But the Abbé de Vermond "stands in the porte-cochère and privately conducts the emperor up side stairs and into the queen's apartments, having first made sure that no one saw the emperor. Their reunion was touching; they embraced and clung to each other in silence, then entered an inner room, where they spent nearly two hours alone together. Only then did they pour out their hearts, especially the queen, who was visibly agitated," Mercy reports in his pedantic fashion.[4] Yet he does not exaggerate Marie Antoinette's intense emotion, her joy at seeing this familiar face from her childhood, her eagerness to pour out her troubles to her older brother, her only bulwark against all the grief she has endured at the hands of the French, whom she can never quite understand. She is apprehensive, too, like any young girl who expects to be scolded. On December 16 she wrote to her mother: "Apart from satisfaction, my greatest joy would be if, after having seen how things really are, he [the emperor] could put to rest in the eyes of my dear mama the allegations people have brought against me. They distress me greatly . . . "[5] In fact, these frustrating "allegations" are more than she can handle; in leaning over backward to combat them, she slips into the very excesses of which she is perpetually accused. Horseracing, yes, and what of it? Her friends, the dozen or so young men and women in whose company she can escape the prison of court ceremony, what of them? Her childless marriage, yes, but whose fault is it? Yet she knows Joseph is bound to bring up Turgot's dismissal and blame her for it, for her jewels, her gambling, all the malicious gossip that Mercy has poured into his letters to Vienna. Just lately he reported to Maria Theresa: "It is plainer than ever that, despite her genuine joy at seeing her august brother again, the queen feels extremely uncomfortable about his impending visit and what he may think of this whole court, especially the style of life which the queen has adopted."[6]

Now sister and brother are face to face. Hapsburgs to the bone, their attractive features cannot erase the scars of degeneracy: an uncommonly high forehead, bulging eyes, and that protruding jaw which in turn makes the lower lip stick out like a pouting bud about to burst, a lip perpetually deprived of moisture, dry, chapped, cracked, painful, which, toward the end of Charles V's life, became infected.[7] Her jaw is the most striking badge of her heredity; his is the pair of "blue eyes exactly like his mother's, Hapsburg blue, pale, icy, and faintly clouded."[8] Yet he is well built and able to shift from a degree of arrogance to condescending charm.

For tactical reasons as well as through instinct, Marie Antoinette is the first to raise delicate questions, confronting them head on: the "circumstances attending marital intimacy . . . her habits, her frivolous pastimes, her craze for gambling, her companions, her favorites," Mercy recites jubilantly. Big brother is too embarrassed to deliver his prepared sermon and confines himself instead "to one or two comments on the importance of such topics, asking for time to reflect on them."[9]

Having weathered the opening assault, Marie Antoinette takes her brother's arm while the Bourbons pass in review privately in her chambers. Louis XVI first, of course: "The two monarchs embraced; the king made several comments indicating an honest desire to appear cordial and sincere; the emperor appreciated his intent."[10] His brother Leopold, Grand Duke of Tuscany, would soon learn his real opinion of the French sovereign: "The man is rather weak but not stupid. He has ideas, he has taste, but his apathy is mental as well as physical. He converses passably well; he has no desire to improve his mind and no curiosity; in short, the *fiat lux* has not arrived; the globe is still round." The rest of the Bourbons come off little better in his estimation: "Monsieur [the Comte de Provence] is an enigmatic creature; even more than [his brother] the king, he is icily unresponsive, and his paunch prevents him from walking properly. His wife is ugly, crude, and obviously Piedmontese; she does nothing but intrigue . . . The Comte d'Artois is a thoroughgoing fop. His wife, who alone produces children, is a hopeless imbecile."[11]

How they all love each other! Marie Antoinette, whose friendly relations with Artois provoked criticism, "confesses quite frankly that she takes no interest in her royal brother-in-law, and that if occasionally they go out together for sheer entertainment, all commerce between them ceases at the close of that entertainment." As to Provence, who recently had measles at the same time as Artois, "the queen made several remarks about him to the effect that whatever happened to Monsieur made little difference to her. The king, for his part, showed not the slightest affection at this time for his royal brothers."[12] And the royal aunts wage a cold war. Barricaded at Belleville, they plot against the queen as well as the king. More charitable still, Louise, a Carmelite, has quarreled openly with her nephew because, like a proper daughter of St. Theresa, she has asked him for an annual pension of two hundred thousand livres,* which he denied, reminding her that she had taken a vow of poverty.[13]

Joseph is then treated to a parade of ministers who get along no better: "Antipathy to M. de Saint-Germain is at its peak; everyone agrees that he is responsible for the general discontent among officers and their men . . . On the other hand, M. de Sartines has had sharp words with M. de Maurepas over the naval forces . . . " and "M. Taboureau, who no longer can endure the vexations of having to deal with M. Necker, has handed the king his resignation [April 11]."[14] At a glance, Joseph II sizes up the French government's major functional weakness: "Each minister is absolute master of his own department, but stands in constant fear of being replaced, not guided, by his sovereign. Thus, each man looks only to his own survival, and there is no cooperation without that in mind. The king is supreme when it comes to being handed from one slavemaster to another."[15] Anarchy and monarchy in the service of conservatism.

The same insightful analysis of his sister's private life: the club of "elders" all between thirty and forty years old in which Lauzun is losing credit because of political activity as well as mounting debts, while Coigny gains; in which Besenval and Breteuil are holding their own, while the Prince von Ligne is slipping—which is all right since he is Belgian and therefore an Austrian subject; the group of "youngsters," including a Hungarian whose rising popularity of late bears close watching, Count Esterhazy. As for the ladies, the story is simple: Lamballe retired upon receipt of a colossal stipend as superintendent of the queen's household, while Yolande de Polignac's star is rising. Her husband has just been named master of the horse, much to the chagrin of the Noailles tribe, who had been eyeing the office. That appointment alone has added eighty thousand francs** to the queen's household expenses.

But one day is not enough for Joseph to probe the bottomless pit of his sister's spending. He takes time out to explore Versailles, then Paris, and returns all excited about the dome of the Invalides, of whose very existence he informs Louis XVI:

> "You possess the most splendid building in all Europe."
> "What's that?"
> "The Invalides."
> "I've heard say."
> "What, you've never gone to see it?"
> "No, never."[16]

---

*A million francs [$200,000] today. That same pension had just been awarded by Louis XVI to his three other aunts, the Belleville set.   **400,000 francs [$80,000] today.

The King of France had never seen the Invalides, and Marie Antoinette's first thought was to take her brother on a tour of the English pleasure gardens which her husband is presently building for her near the Petit Trianon. A lot of digging is in process; they are turning under the gardens of Le Nôtre, who had "invented the art of surrounding oneself at great expense with a circle of tedium."* Oriental rock gardens, artificial brooks, trees of "many varieties" are going up near the foundations of the Temple of Love on the little island that has just been drained. There, on April 22, the emperor, the queen, and the king will "chat," as they say, informally, in a setting of scarlet-and-gold attendants, the mandatory "Trianon uniform" for courtiers, Compiègne's being green, Choisy's, blue. The ice is broken; they see each other for what they really are, and the court, already disappointed, begins to judge Joseph II with standard cruelty.

Strange fellow indeed, a preacher whose sermons hammer out admonitions and occasional paradoxes. "He is always the same," Marie Antoinette later writes to her older sister Maria Christina, to whom her relationship is like Leopold's to Joseph. "He makes very astute observations on what he sees and gives better advice than anyone else; at times, granted, he expresses it rather roughly, which robs his good ideas of their impact . . . The king is friendly to him and listens readily, being very timid and laconic, but when our brother flings one of his criticisms at him, he simply smiles and says nothing. The other day, however, he could not keep silent about certain charges leveled against the clergy by the emperor."[17] Monsieur, for his part, is too sensitive not to feel wounded to the quick, and Joseph's manner irritates him. He informs Sweden's Gustavus III, with whom he corresponds regularly: "The emperor is most cajoling and eager to protest his friendship; but under scrutiny, his protestations and openness conceal a desire to worm information, as they say, and to disguise his true feelings; he is maladroit, however, and with a bit of flattery, to which he is highly vulnerable, rather than being wounded by him, one wounds him easily. Then he becomes exceedingly indiscreet. His knowledge is quite superficial."[18]

Far too hasty an effort to comprehend one of the markedly incomprehensible figures of his day. Unstable as Joseph is, like all Maria Theresa's children, he alone among Europe's rulers can aspire to rival Frederick the Great, whom he feared and revered in his youth. An idealized foe. For years Joseph has dreamed of avenging Austria's suffering at the hands of Prussia by imitating that fascinating tyrant and reformer. Joseph yearns to take up the torch of Prussian despotism and sees himself as its latter-day Messiah informed by the fires of insurgent villages. But only after Maria Theresa is gone, this mother of his who detests war and consented to the partition of Poland under protest; who continues to persecute Protestants, yet would put down the barons and uplift the peasantry, whereas Joseph would let the barons pummel the masses

*Said the Vicomte d'Ermenonville.

into accepting what is best for them. He is tired of being a great statesman ignored by the world. The *philosophes* extol Frederick and Catherine of Russia. Who cares about Joseph? King of the Romans at twenty-three, emperor at twenty-four, he watched power and love trickle through his fingers, the power confiscated by his mother and Kaunitz, the love gone when Isabella of Parma, his adored first wife, died after two years of marriage, never having been able to put up with him. In revenge, he made life miserable for his second wife, Josepha of Bavaria, who also died. Now, having seduced Eleanor of Liechtenstein, he renounces love, save whatever he can coax from Vienna's prostitutes. He has no male heir. Leopold, his confidant, will inherit the empire, but not until Joseph has overhauled the present system and instituted the opposite of everything his mother does, including her attempts these past two years to stem the Bohemian uprisings by abolishing feudalism and transforming serfs into farmers. In January, Joseph complained of this to Leopold:

"Dearest brother, our domestic affairs are as entangled as ever, it is sad to see, especially when one knows that the reasons for it are mainly the personal attitudes and chicanery of subordinates. Her Majesty is more confused than I have ever seen her; she takes a dim and biased view of things, she pictures herself as defending a cause that everyone else opposes, though her adherents include only three or four advisers, whereas all the ministers and all honest men contest the upheaval she would bring about and which would ruin fortunes, cause untold disruption to the state, and eventually destroy it . . . her beliefs are so persistent, so pernicious, that one could not counter them with any remotely similar proposal; I do not attend her councils and so cannot tell you at present what they are cooking up, but it is practically impossible to approach Her Majesty calmly, for each time the wailing and the raving breaks out anew coupled with biting rebukes and suspicions, for she says that I forsake her, that I have joined the enemy, that I have been beguiled and won over by God knows whom—she imagines my friends, even my servants shape my opinions when they do not coincide with hers—in short, it's a mess . . . The empress seeks to annul the official schedule of *corvées* issued last year; she would abolish serfdom; she would regulate arbitrarily the terms of labor and leaseholds which landlords have established for centuries with their tenants; change the entire rural landholding system; reduce taxes and obligations of peasants without regard for the master, who thereby stands to lose half his income; depress prices, and create as many bankruptcies as there are landowners, many of whom have debts or commitments. This is the crisis we face . . ." [19]

A peculiar enlightened despot, unenlightened as to the only workable lever for reforming his empire: creation of a rural population loyal to the crown. His normal behavior ranging from irresistible charm to downright churlishness, his moods, his offensive generosity, his sarcastic civility reflect the contradictions operating in the Austrian eagle, whose two heads, mother and son, are locked in a fierce Oedipal contest that is paralyzing central Europe.

This explains Joseph's aggressive campaign to reform his sister's life. Far from being dazzled by the Trianon Palace with its obelisks, its pyramids, its temples, its Japanese footbridges, its gazebos and pagodas, he, like his friend the Prince von Ligne, is tempted to dismiss it as "the raving madness of a bad dream in a Graeco-English garden."[20] He estimates its cost quite accurately at two hundred thousand livres, payable from the royal treasury. Yet Joseph has learned, through Mercy,[21] that in January the queen was compelled to admit debts of 487,272 livres, mostly from gambling at lansquenet and faro,* two ruinous card games. In a single evening when the queen lost a hundred louis at faro (bankers from Paris were brought in to "deal out the cards"—that is, to advance funds), the Comte d'Artois also lost a hundred and Monsieur four hundred louis. Her jewelry bills are mounting also, and she pouts when her mother remarks on it. From Maria Theresa: "Reports from Paris say that you have paid 250,000 livres for bracelets." From Marie Antoinette: "I have nothing to say about the bracelets; I cannot imagine why anyone would annoy my dear mama about such bagatelles."[22]**

She cannot get off so easily with her brother, who starts to upbraid her. When she invites him to play faro, he answers: "No, I am not rich enough for those gentlemen." Her court at once judges him to be "a prince more eccentric than admirable."[23] Each entertainment causes a row between brother and sister.

This is not the same little Antoinette who stood staring in wide-eyed adoration at her cocky older brother in the park at Schönbrunn. Now she is a queen and reminds him all too frequently that he possesses only half a throne. She objects to his blunt remarks and his teasing. He discovers that she is "subject to those nervous complaints known as vapors," and has occasion to see her "weep copious tears whose effect was purely physical." He decides that her "tendency to become impatient and melancholy rules out any serious conversation."[24] Finally, on the night of April 22, having learned the causes behind his sister's hysteria, Joseph reveals to Leopold what was currently known as "the mystery of the French royal bedchamber": "This is the secret: in bed, he [Louis XVI] has good hard erections; he injects his organ, remains there motionless for two minutes or so, then withdraws, still stiff, without discharging, and drops off to sleep. It makes no sense, as from time to time he has nighttime ejaculations; he never completes the act itself, yet is content, saying merely that he did it out of duty and without the slightest enjoyment. If only I had been there once, I would have fixed things; he needs to be beaten

---

*Both similar to poker. The first had been introduced to France by German foot soldiers, or *lansquenets.* In the second game, a "banker" took on all other players. An aristocrat who played banker would have lost caste.   **The bagatelles cost 1,250,000 current francs [$250,000].

like an ass to make him discharge his spunk. With all this, my sister has little appetite for the whole business, and together they make a hopelessly clumsy pair."[25]

We know, therefore, that neither of the two had any sexual disability; Louis XVI was no victim of phimosis.* It was simply the marriage of two painfully inhibited young persons who were sadly misinformed, if not totally ignorant, about copulation, and whose fertility was an affair of state. Maria Theresa has sent her daughters to the altar without a hint of what to expect on their wedding night; shortly after her marriage, some nine years earlier, Maria Carolina of Naples, one of Marie Antoinette's sisters, had written thus: "The suffering is sheer martyrdom compounded by the fact that one is expected to look happy. I know what I am talking about, and I pity Antoinette, who has yet to face it . . . If faith had not whispered to me: Think of God! I would have killed myself rather than endure what I had to put up with for a week."[26]

As Joseph II aptly described Louis XVI's temperament in general, "the *fiat lux* has not arrived" to enlighten his marriage either. But the emperor intends to change that and, being neither shy nor prudish, advises his sister what to do . . . for on her more than on her husband must the light shine. Let her put aside her pride and show a little more tact—warmth, too, and perseverance. Joseph feels useful that night; not only did she listen to him, but she actually heeded what he said. Now if he would just stop harping on her spending habits . . .

DERUES

68

MAY 1777

God Give Me Strength!

Idle bystanders who flock to the Rue de Tournon for a glimpse of the emperor leaving his hotel on the morning of April 19, 1777, need only continue down the long street and on across the bridge arching both arms of the Seine to savor a very different spectacle: the Hôtel de Ville district is in an uproar over the discovery of a body in a cellar on the Rue de la Mortellerie. An autopsy was performed on the spot during the night, by candlelight. Crowds spill "halfway into the gutters" hoping to catch sight of the most celebrated criminal of the

*Abnormally constricted orifice of the prepuce.

day and his wife, the Derues couple. They arouse nearly as much attention as Joseph II.[1]

It was about time they found the corpse of Madame de Lamotte, who had been missing for close to three months. Two suspects had been arrested, he on March 15, she on April 10, as the investigation crawled along; the pair fiercely denied any involvement in the bodiless crime, and public opinion began to relent. Why persecute a poor grocer and his wife who protest their innocence, solely on the word of a country squire whose wife may have been stepping out behind his back? Of course Etienne Saint-Faust de Lamotte's fifteen-year-old son had also disappeared in Paris a few days after his mother. But why pounce on the Derues pair, why suspect them of locking up and killing the victims? The mother may simply have run off with her son. The Parisian petty bourgeoisie rallied behind the accused couple; the nobility sided with Lamotte. As the law courts generally were taken for servants of the rich, no contest between a grocer and a nobleman could turn out fairly. A man all in black save a white neckband and wearing a short sword, a combined civilian, soldier, and priest, rubs his hands jubilantly at the entrance to this sordid cellar —the picture of a well-pleased policeman. He is Inspector Hubert Mutel,* in charge of the case since March 3 on orders from the Paris chief of police:

> You are hereby requested, sir, in company with police officers Dutronchet and Le Houx, to go to the house of Madame Des Rues [*sic*] and question her as to events which M. de la Motte [*sic*] will describe to you and to act in this affair according to your duty.
>
> Lenoir[2]

What a case to sort out! A Burgundian squire brings suit over the disappearance of his wife and son, accusing a retired grocer named Derues of having been the last person to see Madame de Lamotte alive. The unraveling, on March 6, of a tangled tale *à la Beaumarchais* in the house of this former grocer, who is off "on business" somewhere in France, leaving his sullen wife to receive the inspectors. Just an ordinary grocer's wife? Heaven forbid! Marie-Louise, née de Nicolai, wife of Antoine-François de Cyrano Derues de Bury, lord of Buisson Soif and Valle Profonde. Furthermore, Nicolai is the name of the presiding judge of the court of accounts, one of the highest magistrates in the country. The investigation team had beaten a hasty retreat from the door of this tall, slightly horsy woman in her thirties, with dark hair and unremarkable features, who, though self-possessed, seemed too distinctly plebeian in manner to sustain her thoroughbred pedigree. Inspector Mutel had an excellent nose: he smelled a lie emanating from the four walls that housed his suspects on the Rue Beaubourg, in the maze of alleyways where the Rue de la Courroirie [strap-making] met the Rue des Vieilles-Etuves

---

*One of forty-eight inspectors attached to the law courts, comparable to present-day police investigators. Not to be confused with twenty-eight high inspectors, like Bruguières, who worked directly for the chief of police on "sensitive" (political) cases.

[leather-steaming] hard by the church of Saint-Julien-des-Ménétriers.* Like a sleuth, in the quiet of his study he had begun to compile a thick dossier: "Contradictions to and consequences of the replies of Madame Des Rues [*sic*] to interrogation on March 6."[3] More and more scraps of paper accumulated: "First consequence" . . . "Second consequence" . . . each showing the woman to have denied the facts. Going through them one by one, we can understand how Inspector Mutel unraveled the lie into which the Derues pair had burrowed.

To start with, she is no Nicolai, but the daughter of a coachmaker in Melun named Nicolais; it was her husband who, just after their wedding in 1772, had scratched out, then falsified the entry on the marriage contract to make it appear that he had wed an aristocrat.[4] On top of that, the name Cyrano de Bury is pure fiction, for he is the son of Michel Derues, ironmonger and grain dealer in Chartres; Bury is a dot on the map of Beauvaisis province where he has never set foot. Nor does he have any right to call himself "lord of Buisson Soif and Valle Profonde," not having yet paid the Lamottes for that estate near Villeneuve-le-Roi.** How could he afford to put down even a quarter of the 130,000 livres† he had contracted to pay them in 1775? The whole façade began to crumble, revealing a man drowning in debt, struggling for years to keep his creditors at bay, borrowing from Peter to pay Paul. A mythomaniac. A megalomaniac harassed by demands for payment from his tailor, his wood-splitter, his apothecary, his landlord, his baker—even his grocer! He wove a tissue of lies around one slim thread of truth: a legacy of some ten thousand livres—real this time—which his wife stood to inherit from a certain M. Despeignes-Duplessis, a rich Beauvaisis landowner who had died in 1770. But the estate's settlement dragged on for years, and even if she eventually were to get the money, it was already pledged to creditors.

In 1774 Derues had attempted the grand slam of all swindles, a scheme so ambitious as to eclipse, if not wipe out, all the others he had tried. He had heard that a provincial landholder was anxious to sell a desirable estate (1092 acres with château) which he could not afford to maintain: the property known as Buisson-Soif.‡ He came, he saw, he charmed the Lamottes, he concluded the deal. The fictitious Seigneur de Bury became a Burgundian landowner, theoretically at least, for the sellers continued to occupy the place pending receipt of something more substantial than the IOU's he handed out more freely than sweets from his former grocery. The point was that he believed it, and made others believe it. The Lamottes were even grateful that he allowed them to stay on. Several times a year the Derues pair went there for a visit and

*Patron saint of street musicians. [*Trans.*].
**Now Villeneuve-sur-Yonne.
†Today about 650,000 francs [$130,000].
‡*Le buisson de la soif* or "thirsting bush." The château no longer exists.

some good country air, though no one was quite sure who was host and who was guest. Waiting for that famous inheritance . . .

But three months, six months, a year, going on two years was stretching things a bit. On December 31, 1776, Madame de Lamotte, always more reticent and practical-minded than her husband, arrived in Paris on the water coach from Montereau to see what was what. Her only son had just become a boarder at the school run by Monsieur and Madame Donon on the Rue de l'Homme Armé not far from the Rue Beaubourg. Derues, of course, had picked out the school* and would not allow Madame Lamotte to stay anywhere but with them, though their rooms on the Rue Beaubourg were small and cramped. She had reserved lodgings on the Rue du Paon; he promptly canceled them. The money he owed her would be available shortly; meanwhile, why not allow M. Cyrano de Bury, who knew Paris like the back of his hand, to squire her around town? A whirlwind sightseeing tour ensued for her and her son, whenever he was free from classes, conducted by the indefatigable Derues. Music halls, theater, opera . . . At last she begged him for a respite; she was exhausted, her son also, peculiarly so; both of them felt feverish and dizzy. They complained of cramps, loss of appetite; the lad said his head reeled so that he was "afraid to walk in the street lest he fall down."

Paris is murder for people from Villeneuve-le-Roi.

Murder.

From January 25 to 30 Madame de Lamotte complained of intestinal disorders and indigestion. "She kept going to the bathroom." With unflagging good humor, Derues cheered her up and served her cup after cup of "herbal tea," the nutritive and medicinal values of which were well known to grocers and apothecaries. On the 30th she took to her bed and vomited incessantly. She slept most of the next day, her fecal discharges reeking so foully that only Derues dared to approach her bed. On the 1st of February she recovered miraculously, got out of bed, and dressed when Madame Derues happened to be out. She then went off to spend a few days in Versailles, having suddenly decided to purchase "an office for her son," the post of notary's clerk. After that, she vanished. She had lied, the little minx, invented stories to cover her traces, gone off on a fling, and used the hundred thousand livres Derues had paid her—yes indeed, on the very day she had been so ill . . .

So said Madame Derues to the inspector, displaying a document attesting

---

*Typical of the many small private schools where children of noble or upper-bourgeois families were "whipped into shape" before being shipped off to military or clerical institutions of higher learning. Six hundred livres (3000 francs) covered a year's tuition, board, and lodging in a "partitioned dormitory" with six other boys. He was free on Wednesday (not Sunday, since the school made them attend religious services) and could go out in the evening with his mother when she was in Paris.

to the payment duly executed before a notary in the Faubourg Saint-Honoré, Maître Cordier.

Yes, but . . . "Twelfth consequence" (and this particular finding convinced the inspector of foul play): as if by magic, the paper had been drawn up on instructions from Derues, no legal officer having testified to the presence of Madame de Lamotte. The honest but careless notary had been duped. And the date of the document, February 12, was well after the disappearance of the poor woman. No one except Derues had seen her since January 31, when she appeared to be in agony. Only Derues had witnessed her "recovery" and departure for Versailles.

And what about the Lamotte boy?

Six days after "his mother's departure" he had come to see Derues. Perfect timing: the grocer had just received a note—subsequently lost—from his mother asking to have her son come to Versailles. Derues even took the trouble to escort the lad to an appointed rendezvous "in the park," where Derues claimed to have seen Madame de Lamotte "with an elderly man who embraced the boy tenderly, too tenderly." Who knows, maybe it was the lad's real father! Derues stayed away from Ash Wednesday through the following Sunday, an unnecessarily long time just to take a schoolboy from Paris to Versailles. It gave him a chance to wind up some business, he explained . . .

So said Madame Derues, based on what her husband had told her. And would you like to know what really kept him away, Mr. Inspector, all during the month of March? The fact is that he went back to Versailles, and perhaps beyond, to chase that woman who had gone off romancing with our money and nary a word to that poor M. de Lamotte, who is taking it out on us now. The world is really a mean place.

The inspector had dashed over to the Donon school, where he found the schoolmaster and his wife in a rage. Their pupil had gone to Versailles for a few days "with his mother," according to advice from M. Derues, who subsequently informed them on the 20th that plans for the boy's schooling had been changed and he would not be returning at all. Some nerve!

Derues said, Derues sent word, Derues promised, always Derues. The civil authorities sent search parties to find him when it became apparent that he alone knew the whereabouts of the missing pair. Hubert Mutel had his searchers comb "cellars, cisterns, cesspools, and haylofts" in the neighborhood of the Rue Beaubourg.

Then on March 11 Derues had turned up at home to confirm all the things his wife had been saying. Where had he been looking—vainly—for the missing pair? Somewhere between Montargis and Nevers, he told them. Almost from their first meeting Inspector Mutel sensed that he was facing a murderer, that frail, pale, pinched little man with girlish features, yet articulate and sure of himself. A bundle of steel nerves. Just as he had gone along substituting one debt for another, Derues defended himself inch by inch with new lies to cover the old ones. For five days he held out glibly, while his tale began to crack and buckle, until M. de Lamotte received a fraudulent affidavit, supposedly from his wife, which would have proved she was still alive if the signature had not been forged. A Lyons notary had been hoodwinked by a strange woman, heavily veiled and falsetto-voiced, who walked into his office one day. Perhaps a man in disguise. Mutel established that Derues had returned from Lyons, not Montargis, on that same day. That did it. Arrest the man! Off to prison with him! But what the devil had he done with the bodies?*

The *Journal de Paris* reports on April 20: "The day before yesterday a female body was discovered in the cellar of a house on the Rue de la Mortellerie. It was removed after observance of the usual formalities." And on April 22 in the same paper: "The female body has been identified as that of the late lamented Madame de Lamotte, who disappeared the early part of last February." The long, narrow street parallel to the Seine stretched from the Place de Grève to the Quai des Celestins. About midway down the street,** under the sign of the Pewter Pot, a certain Madame Masson had hung out the notice "Cellar for rent" and on February 1, for an annual fee of fifty livres, had rented it to "a short, pale man with piercing eyes wearing a fine dress coat"; he was in urgent need of "storage space" for a number of *feuillettes*† of sherry wine sitting on the docks and threatening to spoil in the sun. A carter delivered a cask "the size of a *demi-queue d'Orléans*" and "a large bundle wrapped in gray canvas." The persistent excavations of stray dogs scratching at the cellar door eventually led to the digging up of the loose soil in which he had buried it. The bundle contained "the putrid, horrible remains of a woman with a bruised face and her nose half rotted away."

"All right, Derues, we've found your victim, we've found Madame de Lamotte's body!"

He fought on to the bitter end: "I don't recognize her."

Her husband did, alas, and the owner of the cellar identified Derues as the man in the fine dress coat. Caught dead to rights, he fell back on his last desperate defense.

"All right, so I lied in a way, for I was the one who hid the body. But I didn't kill Madame de Lamotte. She got very ill in my house and I took care of her. Those herbal teas? I tried to cure her. My own recipe. An ounce of manna,‡ two parts epsom salt, one part rhubarb, a pinch of saffron . . . [The rather superficial autopsy report also mentioned, without real conviction,

---

*It should be noted that during the inquest he was not forced to undergo a "preparatory interrogation" (torture inflicted to produce evidence in the case), whereas his final agony was preceded by a savagely cruel "preliminary torture."

**With rare exceptions, houses in Paris were not yet numbered.

†"*Feuillette*": storage butt containing about 132 liters. "*Demi-queue d'Orléans*": 230 liters.

‡Sugary exudation of certain plants.

traces of corrosive sublimate.*] Nothing helped. I found her dead on the last night in January. I was afraid people would say I killed her. I lost my head. I sent my wife away to relatives in the country and got rid of the body by renting a cellar under a false name."

"What about the child? THE CHILD?"

"He died in Versailles, awful coincidence! He was sick also. I took him there for a change of scenery and to keep him from worrying too much about his mother. They threw us out of the hotel because they thought he had smallpox. And maybe that's what he actually died of in my arms, on February 16, in rooms I rented from a cooper. I said I was the boy's uncle and had him buried under a false name for fear once again that someone would accuse me of poisoning him. I invented a story to make my wife feel better. She had nothing to do with it. She is innocent."

He refused to give up. The boy's body was exhumed on April 23. In Versailles and Paris the public talked of nothing but this affair, "which excites people far more than the war in America." Witnesses in Versailles, especially the cooper and the priest who buried the boy, condemn this "uncle" who refused up till the very end to call a doctor. The examining surgeons who perform a second autopsy conclude once again that the victim swallowed a massive dose of corrosive sublimate. To anyone who has followed the investigation step by step, it is obvious that Derues got rid of Madame de Lamotte and her son in order to avoid meeting a long-overdue bill and to create the impression that he held title to the estate of Buisson-Soif. He had gambled on crime like a madman—and lost. The only hazy question was to what degree his wife had been involved.

He swore, he continues to swear, he will swear to the end—as she does —that she knew nothing. Yet he also insists that he is no murderer.

"To the end," May 6, 1777, is no easy task, in the "inquisition chamber" of the Palace of Justice, where he is put to torture before being broken on the wheel in the public square. "Rough day," Robert Damiens** had murmured at daybreak twenty years earlier. The crowd milling about the gibbet has grown since early morning.

"I keep telling you that I didn't poison anyone." At that rate, his wife might just stand a chance. Her trial was cut short so that they could wind up his within twelve days, owing to popular pressure. How could she have been an accomplice in a crime he has never admitted, even to her? Yet Derues knows what lies ahead of him. Whatever benefit he stands to gain (the only concession life ever handed him) from his wife's fate will cost him more than all the worthless IOU's he has signed. When the "executioner of high justice,"

---

*A compound of mercury commonly used at the time for medicinal purposes. In small doses it was an effective antiseptic in treating pox; in large doses, highly poisonous.

**Drawn and quartered for attempting to assassinate Louis XV. [Trans.]

one of the Sanson tribe, sets down the stone bench called the "interrogation seat," clamps the victim's legs between two boards, and approaches with the sledgehammer and wooden wedges that will splinter his bones, "a foul odor pervades the interrogation chamber." Derues shits with fear.[5]

"God give me strength to endure: I am innocent! I did nothing wrong by hiding that poor dead woman. God give me strength!"*

"Ordinary" torture calls for four wedges driven into ankles and knees. When the second went in, "Derues cried out repeatedly: 'Oh, God, give me strength to uphold the truth.'"

At the fourth wedge: "Madame de Lamotte died of a natural upheaval, and her son refused to see a doctor . . ."

Four more wedges will be driven into those same gaping holes in his flesh: the "extraordinary" torture. Rather pointless, for the agony has made him unconscious. Now the only sounds are hammer blows, crunching bones, and the poor devil's moans. The clerk has an easy job: "At the first wedge of the extraordinary, he persisted in repeating the same thing . . . At the second wedge, was silent . . . At the third wedge, was silent."

It will take hours to bring him to, in front of a roaring fire. He was too weak to sign the court record. Around two o'clock, in the rain, they load him, in shirt sleeves, into a tumbril for the last act. An assistant headsman holds an umbrella over Maître Jean-Gilbert Segaud of the Sorbonne, curate of Saint-Martin, who will raise the crucifix before the condemned man, symbol of a living God who suffered as much as he. An umbrella, too, on the steps of Notre Dame for the court clerk who reads aloud the public confession, to which the dripping Derues screams: "I am innocent!"

The Place de Grève is packed. Hawkers do a brisk trade renting out ladders and stools from which to view the gibbet, which is no higher than a man's head. Meanwhile a competing spectacle goes on in the nearby Plaine des Sablons, where Louis XVI and Joseph II are reviewing the Swiss Guards. The emperor and the King of France side by side is an event rarer than a public hanging. But Derues draws bigger crowds than Joseph, if only among execution-goers, who wouldn't miss the show for anything in the world, the only public entertainment (besides religious processions) available to the crowd. For centuries, men in power have trained the poor to regard complaisance as a virtue, have provided them with stellar examples of refined cruelty unknown to wild beasts. Old Parisians recall city-wide celebrations that accompanied the hanging in 1763 of Geneviève Guérin and Antoinette Blanquet, two seventeen-year-olds falsely accused of a crime, and of Elizabeth Gommery in 1764, a serving maid convicted of stealing a tablecloth and a napkin; the burning alive of Charlotte Villemont in 1762, accused of having slandered the wife of her baker master;** Jacques-Philippe Crapet's death on the wheel that same

*Recorded verbatim by the clerk of the court.
**She had "falsely" charged her mistress with having tried to kill her.

year for having "conspired to murder the Comte de Donges" ten years before. To cool their impatience, old-timers review the spicy catalogue of "uxoricides," wife-killers, whose offending hand was cut off before they were burned alive; blasphemers whose tongues were ripped out; children from six to fourteen hanged by the arms until they fainted (from fifteen up, they were tortured and executed like adults); criminals branded with the iron or flayed alive; prostitutes condemned to ride naked through the streets on muleback; and that thieving Marie Croison, "rather pretty, solidly built, with an extraordinarily thick neck," who caused young Sanson the hangman, who was still new at his trade, to drag out her agony for an hour before finally strangling her on January 27, 1765.[6] Hardly worth cataloguing are Jean-Denis Desportes and Jean-Claude Lesguiller, hanged for stealing flour during the Grain War two years before. A toothsome spectacle that would have been, as the second fellow was only sixteen, had the civil guard not cleared the square for fear of riots. Disgraceful. Fortunately, the fans have had their consolation: thirty-two deaths by hanging, the wheel, or the stake in Paris since Good King Louis XVI came to the throne three years ago, for murder, acts of violence, rape, sodomy, "burglary or house-breaking with lock-picking," and "household thefts."* The magistrates tried to be fair: eleven times the gallows went up outside the Hôtel de Ville, but it traveled elsewhere, too—wherever space permitted: to the Place Maubert, the Croix-du-Trahoir, in the Halles, at the Foire Saint-Germain, facing the Opera, in the vicinity of the Saint-Martin and the Saint-Antoine gates, at the Gobelins tollhouse, even to some outlying districts when the courts decided to punish a local offender on the spot: Montfort-l'Amaury, Saint-Cloud, Fresne-les-Rungis, Montmartre, Viroflay, Vaugirard, and Bondy.[7]

But the best treat of all is the wheel, a matchless diversion imported from Germany two centuries before. The scaffold includes two instruments, corresponding to the two acts of torture: St. Andrew's Cross, to which the victim is strapped preparatory to being mashed to a pulp; and the wheel itself, off to one side, onto which the quivering human debris is removed and left lying, "staring at the sky for as long as it pleases God to grant him life."[8] When God felt generous to the Paris mob, sometimes it pleased Him to grant the wretched victim twenty-four hours of agony.

Across the Seine, Manon Phlipon has shut the tiny window in her "sanctuary" and plugs her ears to shut out the crowd's clamor. Each execution reminds her with a shiver of the one she saw on December 13, 1774, in the Place Dauphine right outside her window, when Antoine Chabert and Charles Cellier died on the wheel for murdering Chabert's father in her own neighborhood. First they

---

*Of a total of seventy-one arrests on criminal charges in the Paris region, handled chiefly by magistrates of La Tournelle, thirty-nine were sentenced to the galleys (ten for life), to prison, to banishment, to do public penance.

severed the parricide's hand and exposed it "on a pole above the main entrance to the city church of Notre Dame."[9] The young man howled in agony for twelve hours on the wheel while hundreds of youngsters, who would be twenty-five or thirty years old in 1792, were paraded past him. Though convinced, like any true daughter of the bourgeoisie, that justice was being done, Manon Phlipon had written thus to her friends the Canet sisters: "I was here when they came to drag me from my solitude to the window to show me not the horrid execution, but the sea of faces pressing forward to watch it. The size of the crowd is inconceivable. People are even standing on rooftops;* in fact, human nature is scarcely respectable when contemplated in the mass; it makes one think of a colony of ants overrunning an inch of ground. I can't imagine what motive whets the curiosity of thousands to watch two fellow creatures suffer . . . I was thinking of this all night before I saw anything. The poor parricide agonized for twelve hours on the wheel, screaming loud enough for Mama to hear in her bed."[10]

Derues is lucky: he is sentenced to burn immediately after his body is broken. The net effect is the same with or without the wheel. At any rate, he could not have lasted long; he is white as a sheet and looks all but dead when they take him to the Hôtel de Ville for the customary "final declarations," which are as solemnly accredited in the courts as the utterances of women in labor: "*Virgini parturienti creditur.*"** Besides, everyone knows that a man facing death fears the fires of hell. Would he dare to lie at such a time? He lies. With his last breath. "I am innocent. If they were poisoned, I am not guilty of it . . . " But is he still lying when he cries out for the hundredth time: "I want you to know that my wife is innocent, innocent of everything, I swear it! She had nothing to do with it. I used every trick I could think of to keep her in ignorance . . . She is guiltless. As for me, I am about to die." This time he signs the statement with a firm hand.[11]

The crowd grows impatient; it wants blood. But it must wait for Derues to embrace his wife, for whose sake, above and beyond the torture already suffered, he must yet endure the agony of damnation which he expects in return for lying. His torment is to be eternal. Could any of the priests and judges standing around him deceive themselves or deceive him about it? A rough day. A rough eternity.

"Raise our children† to fear God and love their duty. Above all, never let them forget how I died . . . "

He speaks to a creature also in torment, for she loves him. Her face is all bloody from dashing her head against the bars of her cell at the Petit

---

*Her own execution on November 8, 1793, will draw a smaller audience.

**"One must believe what is said by a woman in labor." The legal justification for torture rested on the conviction that a man in agony speaks the truth.

†A boy of three and a girl of two, left in the care of a faithful maidservant.

Châtelet. She sobs, she shrieks at the sight of that battered body that shared her life for five years. She falls to the ground, writhing. Back to her cell she goes, until they decide what to do with her.

"Let's get this over with," says Derues.

The gates of the Hôtel de Ville open at six. He mounts the gallows on the arms of the hangman's assistants and allows himself to be undressed by them "as if by valets,"[12] then stretches himself out, wearing only a shirt exposing his arms and legs,* on the two crossbars marked with "slots corresponding to the location of the hips, calves, upper and lower arms";[13] they tie him down tightly to keep him from struggling. His head, face upward, rests on a stone. Quivering, the crowd surges forward. No *Salve Regina,* which is reserved for hangings. Bastien, Charles-Henri Sanson's junior assistant, picks up a heavy iron bar an inch and a half thick and brings it down mercilessly some twenty times on the notches in the cross. Arms and legs broken. Derues still finds the strength "to cry out in anguish." No one pities him. No one supports him. His is the utter solitude "of the man who deserves what he got," citizen of the shadowy kingdom, exiled to the outer fringes of anti-humanity, scapegoat. His sentence says nothing of *retentum* or strangulation after two or three blows, an act of mercy which judges occasionally ordered. Derues is to be broken and burned alive. The crowd flinches at each stroke of the bludgeon. Women faint. Children wail. Jacques Dureau, fourteen-year-old apprentice engraver, suffers a nervous seizure and is taken to the hospital.

A few sound blows on the stomach still do not end it. They untie the battered, faintly pulsating mass of flesh and dump it on the pile of burning faggots to one side of the gibbet, at ground level. The shapeless heap twitches as they cover it with straw and kindling. Veteran execution-watchers are disappointed; once again it proves that the stake spoils the wheel. It's all over too quickly. Smoke billowing up through the moist air screens the final agony.

As the rainy spring night falls along the Seine embankment where the executioner has scattered the ashes, a crowd of beggars dashes for the stake, ready to fight over the spoils if civic guards were not there to keep order; they grab every shred of shirt, gather up the coals, and hunt for charred bones, which bring good luck. A single bone from a man burned at the stake is luckier than a splice of the hangman's noose and can be sold for more. By mid-May a bone chip, real or fake, from the body of Antoine Derues the poisoner will fetch as much as the knuckle bones of martyred saints brought back by the cartful after the Crusades and sold at the Buci crossroads: one louis per toe.[14]

---

*Women were not put to the wheel, "in deference to their need to maintain a respectable appearance."

69

MAY 1777

A New Revolution

On the evening of April 25, 1777, Joseph II and his sister planned to meet at the Paris Opera. "The monarch made his way to the queen's box. He chose to remain inconspicuous, but as the audience seemed eager to view him, the queen took her august brother's arm and led him to the front of the box. The whole theater burst into applause and cheers which interrupted the performance for several minutes."[1] Gluck's *Iphigenia in Aulis* was being presented, a reminder to Marie Antoinette of her great victory as dauphine. The best way to curry favor with her was through applause. There even was a rite observed by the whole cast when the queen was present; surely they would repeat it now. Act II, Scene 3: the singer taking the high priest's role (Le Gros, an overstuffed fellow, as the name suggests, "a terribly clumsy actor with a magnificent voice") alters the chorus: "Sing, let us praise our queen." He steps forward, bows to Marie Antoinette, who feigns surprise for the fourth or fifth time, and offers an aria instead:

> Chantons, chantons notre reine,   [Sing, let us praise our queen,
> Et que l'hymen qui l'enchaîne   And may her union
> Nous rende à jamais heureux!   Bring us eternal bliss!]

Thunderous, standing ovation. The chorus repeats the stanza, and everyone weeps. Even the emperor breaks into applause at the mention of the "union" he had so crudely discussed of late with his sister in the arbors of Trianon. Is there still time to make a happy marriage out of the coupling of two bumbling partners? And if his advice helps them to achieve coitus, will the resulting offspring mean "eternal bliss" to a nation of twenty-three millions? Whoever raises that question publicly may as well prepare himself for a brisk journey down the boulevard from the Opera to the Bastille.

But who thinks of such weighty matters when a new battle rages in the musical world, arousing the worst instincts in critics and audiences alike? As with opera buffa, or with Gluck's arrival on the Paris scene three years before, they will surely come to blows. "Music is ill-suited to France, since that art has never made the slightest headway there without provoking the wildest dissension, the most ridiculous furors . . . The great dispute just exploded between Gluckists and Piccinnists now afflicts all our literary efforts," asserts Meister, acting editor of the *Correspondance littéraire* while Grimm struts about Saint Petersburg.[2] Gluck's pre-eminence seemed to have gone unchallenged; the Opera rarely staged another composer after Marie Antoinette came to the throne. Triumph of *Orfeo* in August 1775. Failure of *Alceste* the next April, followed by a stunning comeback after Gossec had reworked the third act. French music was beating a dismal retreat. "However strongly the immortal cult of Rameau and Lully* may persist nowadays, their splintered adherents are falling off, or at least remaining silent." Still, with Piccinni's arrival in Paris last winter, Gluck's throne had begun to totter under the assault of Italian opera. Enthusiasts of opera buffa had united to entice him away from the gentle Neapolitan climate. France, as if hit by a summer storm, found herself torn apart by the riptide of German and Italian operatic styles. In January, Paris had acclaimed *La Buona Figliola.* ** "At that point the Gluck faction wavered, while the Piccinni-Sacchini-Traetta camp took courage." Marie Antoinette continued to support Gluck, though less consistently once she felt she had won the opening round. She had rejected Piccinni when Du Barry tried to pit him against Gluck, but now his visit is sponsored by the ambassador of Naples, where her sister Maria Carolina is queen. How could she not welcome him? She decided to be mildly hospitable. Excitement began to build for *Roland,* the new opera he was writing, with Marmontel providing the French libretto. "Another revolution is in store for us! What tyranny, these endless attempts to vary our pleasures! Can one change systems in music as in politics? . . . People who used to enjoy each other's company now shun it; even dinner parties, which so effectively reconciled diverse minds and temperaments, now reflect only constraint and defiance . . . No longer do people ask: is he a Jansenist, a Molinist,† a *philosophe,* or a strict Catholic? They ask: is he a Gluckist or a Piccinnist?"[3]

Joseph II is indifferent to all the fuss and agitation; he cares little for music and less for literature. He simply applauds whatever is shown him, and when comparing opera in Vienna and in Paris, the latter comes off second-best as he deplores "its informality, its chaos, its incredible license. Actors and actresses carry indecency to such a point that when they are off the stage the men wear only a white camisole over silver culottes, with a bandeau round their hair; the women, peignoirs." Devotees of the flesh loved it, for opera, like the

---

*Lully had died in 1687 and Rameau in 1764, only fifteen years before; yet in their predictable rush to enshrine new idols and inter old ones, Parisian audiences had tired of the two composers. They became "immortals."

**Staged by the Théâtre des Italiens. A theatrical version of Piccinni's *La Cecchina,* current hit of the Italian opera season.

†Luis Molina (1535–1600), Spanish Jesuit theologian. [*Trans.*]

theater, had its share of chartered libertines whose choice was simply made easier. As for the orchestra, it was like "an old coach drawn by scrawny horses whose driver was congenitally deaf."[4]

Inscrutable, the emperor compares the calm discipline of Viennese audiences—which is all he can appreciate—to the "wild shrieks and protracted bellows that fill the theater [in Paris] during a performance" . . . "to actresses on the brink of convulsions" who exhale "violent shrieks from their lungs, clutching their breasts, head thrown back, cheeks aflame, blood vessels bursting, stomach heaving . . . And most incredible of all is the fact that only these howls draw applause."[5] On that point—and probably that alone—Joseph and Jean-Jacques Rousseau agree.

In a box, a handsome man in his fifties, high forehead, bushy eyebrows, his regular features slightly marred by a pair of tightly sealed lips, registers the faintly smug self-confidence peculiar to academicians. Jean-François Marmontel is at the peak of his career. This Limousin farmer has swept to celebrity on the tide of poems and prose that pours from his restless pen. Early this year, his latest book, *Les Incas, ou la Destruction de l'Empire du Pérou,* two volumes in octavo, came out and was bought up by the publisher Panckouke for thirty-six thousand livres.* Famous author of *Bélisaire,* he is assured a niche in history alongside Voltaire or Diderot.** Nor did he lack the faint aroma of persecution that ennobled all great writers of the 1760's: a few weeks in the Bastille for insulting a duke. He labored over the last volumes of the *Encyclopédie,* black-penciling column after column of indigestible print. Elected to the Academy in 1763, he is on his way to becoming its perpetual secretary (in 1784). But he still is not properly subdued. *The Incas* betrays a distinct trace of contempt for the nobility—Spanish, of course—the conquistadors who had ground the Incas into dust two centuries before. "To depict the horrors of fanaticism, could one choose a broader or more striking stage than that half of the universe still reeking from its ravages? To the manners of a superstitious and savage race, can one find sharper contrast than the engaging, more civil manners of those unfortunate Peruvians, the most intelligent and perceptive people on the American continent?"[6] The trouble is, as Marmontel is the first to admit, "that his latest work is neither narrative nor verse." It straddles the two. Critics objected that by abandoning "the agreeable medium" for an experimental dip into lyrical morality, "M. Marmontel has undertaken a task beyond his powers."[7] Furthermore, he got himself into hot water by representing justice in the person of a Catholic rather than the Church, by making "virtuous Las Casas" the symbol of true faith in contrast to vice-ridden Valverde, "herald of intolerance and superstition." The *philosophes* resent this as

---

* 180,000 francs [$36,000].
**Bélisaire, an abstruse philosophic romance, all but unreadable today, earned him the wrath of the Sorbonne in 1767 because of one chapter pleading for tolerance.

much as the churchmen. He is trying to steer a middle course between two authorities. This explains the extreme touchiness of the man, who, after years of bachelorhood, now prepares to become "a good husband, good father, good family man," according to his "good friend" the Abbé Morellet.* The latter plainly admits "that it is not at all impossible for M. Marmontel's wife to have been made miserable by a number of her husband's shortcomings, in particular his exceeding irritability,"[8] the disappointed ambitions of the parvenu who never quite makes it, of the gifted person painfully aware that he has talent but not genius.

He resents genius. He ferrets it out and denounces it wherever it crops up, as at present in the musical world. Marmontel poses as patron and sponsor of Piccinni's genteel refinement versus the salutary storm unleashed on musical audiences by Gluck with the presentation of *Iphigenia.* He has originated a metaphor clever enough to discredit Gluck with the intelligentsia: Gluck is a Shakespeare of the lyric medium. But Shakespeare—who, in watered-down versions, is finally enjoying a limited revival in London under the actor Garrick's impetus—is the "drunken savage" rejected by Voltaire, a barbarian, a monster, still not published or staged in France, yet condemned all the same. Marmontel seizes upon his name like a bludgeon: "Is the ear or the mind of Frenchmen so insensitive that, in order to be moved, it requires this intense commotion?" [He has just asserted that "never has anyone made trumpets rumble, strings roar, and voices bellow" as Gluck does.] "Whoever seeks only to be shaken would do better to choose Shakespear [*sic*] over Racine," but if some regard Gluck as "the Shakespear [*sic*] of music, it does not follow that all Italian Racines ought to be banished from the stage."[9]

This is why Marmontel has trudged across the Rue Saint-Honoré every morning for four months to the furnished rooms he rented opposite his own house in order to lodge Piccinni, his wife, his eldest son "eighteen years of age, and a young English companion." Marmontel finds the composer "invariably abed, dedicated to the Italian practice of what they call *il sacrosanto far niente,*" and proceeds to torment the little man of forty-eight, "thin, pale, drawn, exceedingly polite, whose courteous manner bore a tinge of seriousness uncommon to most Neapolitans," but who spoke not a single word of French. It was a schoolroom for two: master and pupil. "Verse by verse, nearly word by word, I had to explain everything to him; and once he had grasped the sense of a section, I declaimed it aloud, stressing the accent, the prosody, the cadence of each verse, the pauses, the half-pauses, the phrasing."[10] Paradise for Marmontel; purgatory for Piccinni. Served him right for trading Naples for Paris and an annual stipend of six thousand livres** from Louis

*On October 11, 1777, Marmontel will wed a twenty-one-year-old niece of Morellet. The bridegroom is fifty-four.
**30,000 francs [$6000] today. He received nearly twice that amount from the court of Naples,

XVI. He had yet to recover from the shock of arriving in Paris on New Year's Eve in the coldest winter in ten years. "But, my dear sir, doesn't the sun ever shine in this place?"[11] He had Marmontel to contend with as well as the wintry blasts. Piccinni found it difficult to adjust.

As for Shakespeare, at least one person does not share the prevailing aversion to him: Diderot, on his hilltop in Sèvres. Now, just inside the entrance to Notre Dame in Paris stood one of those gigantic, crudely conceived statues of minor saints which invaded all churches in the fifteenth century. To touch them brought permanent relief from colic or gout, according to their manufacture; to lay eyes on them once a day ensured survival for twenty-four hours. Notre Dame had a St. Christopher, five or six times higher than a man, clad in a tunic so skimpy that female worshipers took to praying at his feet. "Ah, monsieur," Diderot recently wrote to Tronchin, as if in response to Marmontel, "this Shakespear [*sic*] was a dreadful mortal; he is neither the gladiator of ancient times nor the Apollo Belvedere; he is instead the crude, unshapely St. Christopher of Notre Dame, a Gothic colossus between whose legs all of us could pass without the tip of our heads so much as grazing his testicles."[12]

Gluck, however, seems totally detached from his own tourney. Swept to and fro between Vienna and Paris like a cork bobbing on the tide, he witnesses these events, never angry, never anxious. How different he is from the one-man exhibition he was three years ago. Something snapped inside him when his adopted daughter Marianne died in April 1776. His niece, some say, his beloved child, his life. He knew she was wasting away with consumption when he wrote Orpheus's lament, *"J'ai perdu mon Eurydice,"* never suspecting that death would snatch her so swiftly from him. Suddenly she was gone, his "ever so delicate, ethereal little muse, the sound of whose voice touched the soul."[13] When his wife told him the news, "he broke into agonized sobs; his friends feared the frenzy of his grief."[14] Suffering does not sit lightly on this solid man.

---

but was beginning to lose credit where once he had been idolized as a great innovator. Rome, too, had turned from him.

70

MAY 1777

I Am a Royalist by Profession

And since Joseph II wants to see everything of interest in and about Paris and Versailles, he might as well give the "Count of Falkenstein" an eyeful. His evening at the Opera began the whirl of social events. The "enlightened despot" inspects the France of Louis XVI on parade. His agenda paints a fresco of the new reign.

April 26: a horse race at Longchamps, compliments of the Comte d'Artois. Sunday the 27th, a day of combined prayer and entertainment at Versailles, where Joseph observes the spectacle of a "Sunday *in publico*: the king's levee, mass, a state dinner; all the while I was part of the crowd of onlookers.* I must admit it was amusing, and since I play roles so often, it teaches me something to watch others do the same."[1] Not everyone was taken in. "We have had the emperor here," writes the Comtesse de La Marck the next day; "he behaved with utmost simplicity . . . His trite remarks were repeated with a solemnity that would make you die laughing."[2] But there is nothing trite about the comment he makes one evening in Madame de Guéménée's drawing room, ill-tempered at having been dragged "to this gambling den" by his sister:

"Which side does Your Majesty espouse in the American business?"

"I am, madam, a royalist by profession."

The Vicomte de Noailles, who wanted to sail with La Fayette, is also there.

On April 28 Joseph goes to watch "the Swiss Guards regiment drilling." There, he is in his element; nothing pleases him so much as the military side of his "profession." On the 29th and 30th, Versailles, inch by inch. On the 1st of May he begins a tour of Paris that would make any visitor envious, prefaced by a chat with La Borde, former chamberlain (and millionaire farmer-general) to Louis XV, who furnishes him with "detailed figures on crown revenues and on the expenses and organization of the royal budget." The

*From a letter dated April 29, 1777, to his brother Leopold.

notion of espionage never enters the mind of an emperor or a financier of this caliber. Next Joseph is taken on a tour of the royal furniture storerooms at the corner of the Place Louis XV and the Rue Royale;* rather than a warehouse, it is a museum dedicated to the art of gracious living, behind whose sparkling white façade, barely twenty years old, stretch row after row of rooms displaying for privileged guests the choicest examples of furniture in the world, mirrors, bronze and silver ornaments, arms and armor, ready to be installed in châteaux, ministries, and the houses of royal favorites. The emperor also sees the famous set of tapestries, including those woven after designs by Dürer, which are taken out to decorate the weather-beaten walls of the Louvre for the Corpus Christi celebration. Later that day, shifting from aesthetic to technical contemplations, he visits "le Sieur de Trudaine to examine everything that has to do with public works." Philippe-Gilbert de Montigny is the son of the famous Daniel-Charles Trudaine, who died some thirty years ago and had built a splendid network of fine roads and bridges for Louis XV. Though he lacks his father's gluttony for work and his good health, the son does his best to combat waste and incompetence among provincial administrators; he heads a corps of engineers gathered here in their headquarters, the Hôtel des Ponts et Chaussées, armed "with models, machines, and blueprints." Joseph inspects them as on the parade ground, tossing out compliments right and left: he would like public works to function like the army. Turgot had fought vainly against such stubborn solidarity when the whole engineering establishment rose to defend the provincial *corvée* system as indispensable to the nation. This Trudaine, then, is one of Turgot's foes. How pale he looks, how scrawny, as if he had been inhaling the dust from his files.** The star attraction in the visitor's eye, however, is not Trudaine but an aging peacock, Jean-Rodolphe Perronet, taskmaster of the new Paris, who has just built the Pont de Neuilly, the world's first horizontal bridge—good riddance to centuries of arches and slopes! When they removed the arch from the bridge some five years earlier† and it looked so splendid, so neat and clean with its single uninterrupted span, King Louis XV and Madame du Barry were present, attended by the court and diplomatic corps. Joseph has already hastened to glimpse this bridge, which he would like to copy in Vienna over the Danube. Germany's emperor stands in awe of the architect, himself something of a sovereign by virtue of having directed construction of the main sewer system in Paris at the age of seventeen and, at thirty, the canals of Burgundy. The whole field of engineering has been transformed by his inventions, from his "saw for repairing piles under water" to his "non-tippable dump cart" and a device for "dredging

---

*Now the naval ministry.
**He will die in four months at the age of forty-five, leaving two sons who become involved in the André Chénier group and go to the guillotine on 8 Thermidor, Year II.
†In 1772. Removal of the arch entailed withdrawing the wood or iron carapace in which the stone construction was "molded." Perronet was born in 1708.

harbors and rivers." Perronet, who is slightly deaf, cocks his good ear in the direction of his interlocutor with that look of grave condescension which used to exasperate Condorcet. The architect is visibly content with Joseph, who will proceed to inform everyone that the two most beautiful sights in Paris are the Invalides and the Pont de Neuilly.

More fine buildings await his inspection at daybreak on the 2nd of May, when he visits La Salpêtrière, the municipal hospital and/or poorhouse built for Louis XIV by Le Vau to house the twenty thousand beggars turned out of Paris after the Fronde. This complex rivals the Invalides in its majestic proportions. The church, dedicated to St. Louis, manifests "a revival of the Cistercian tradition in the midst of the Splendid Century"[3]—accidental, since its design in the form of a Greek cross is a device for separating men, women, boys, and girls into four different naves "so that they may attend the same mass without intercommunicating." Communion without communication, a dream cherished by the Sun King, irresistible also, no doubt, to an emperor who will soon rule single-handed over an assortment of nations. Find some way to unite them, yet keep them compartmentalized . . . "At daybreak" Joseph leaves Paris, traveling up the Seine along the Left Bank; he passes vast stores of floating timber collected there to fuel the city; he rounds the horse market. The site* of this immense sponge intended to absorb the dregs of civil poverty was a field east of Paris which used to produce saltpeter for the royal regiments, like a pendant to the western sponge, the Invalides, which stanches the wounds of the military.

All this was refined, however, in Louis XV's time. The splayed nave no longer is necessary, as La Salpêtrière houses women only. Prison? Poorhouse? Insane asylum? The women themselves couldn't say which, for the words are synonymous. *"Lasciate ogni speranza."*** Seven thousand women live there, "governed by nuns of the Order of St. Claire."[4] "Prostitutes number twenty-four hundred." The uniform is simple, a burlap sack, as if the inmates were lepers. Joseph II glimpses only a few hundred on his rushed tour through "various rooms crowded with sewing maids, embroiderers, wool-weavers, and garment workers; mingled with the inmates are a number of voluntary boarders who come there seeking a dreary refuge from want." He lingers in kitchens "which are spotless; seven caldrons contain food for these seven thousand women; two caldrons can hold a whole ox; the daily ration for each person is one mug† of gruel, one ounce of meat, and three slices of bread." Such a diet guaranteed a rapid turnover, in vast cathedral-like halls "where the stench

*La Salpêtrière, still one of the main hospitals in Paris, is now located at 47 Boulevard de l'Hôpital near the Gare d'Austerlitz.
**"Abandon all hope." [*Trans.*]
†A mug or half-pint was the Parisian equivalent of slightly under half a liter. And in Paris the ounce weighed thirty-two grams.

spurs a visitor to leave as quickly as possible": "they sleep five women to a bed."[5] His hosts avoid showing the emperor a special wing reserved "for women deprived of their reason." Over a thousand of them, "in the most deplorable condition when their insanity is the sort that divests them of their instinctive cleanliness. Though the rooms are washed twice a day, these poor souls live in indescribable filth and are like the lowest animals. Madwomen subject to fits of rage are chained like dogs to the door of a kennel and separated from attendants or visitors by a long corridor shielded with grill-work. Food is passed to them through this grillwork, and straw for their bedding. Rakes are used to remove part of the waste that surrounds them."[6]

Joseph's curiosity is still not satisfied. The problem of eliminating poverty and insanity in large cities was equally acute in Vienna, London, Rome, Madrid, or Moscow. He heads south from Paris along the road to Burgundy, certain to find the air more tolerable on the slopes of Bicêtre, between the towns of Villejuif* and Gentilly, "a league outside Paris . . . That alone is enough to make the air less foul than in most city hospitals."[7] So one could say that the king has been charitable, at least to the male population, by keeping only women at La Salpêtrière and sending forty-five hundred poor devils to the healthier climate of Bicêtre, "the beggars' Bastille, " which would accommodate many more "if the Seine could be diverted to Bicêtre." They must make do, however, with "wells and a few canals that bring in water from Arcueil, which everyone drinks except the governors of the place, who have it delivered daily from the Seine." A precaution the governors do well to take, for the local water "flows through lead pipes and is known to be potentially toxic." One of Bicêtre's two wells is almost as famous as the Marly waterworks "for its depth, though mainly for its simple mechanical device for drawing up water in two buckets, one of which descends empty while the other rises full." The police chief has just found a way to save money, replacing the dozen horses which used to turn the giant wheel to hoist the buckets with some thirty "able-bodied prisoners; in this manner he removes them from the temptations of idleness, maintains their vigor, and procures for them something to add to their dinner."

But the smell gets progressively ranker as Joseph approaches the asylum, and, despite his iron constitution, he feels queasy at the entrance from the strong odor emitted by "this receptacle for the vilest, foulest dregs of society . . . vicious persons of every kind, swindlers, defaulters,** pickpockets, thieves, forgers, pederasts, etc. It is distressing to see them side by side with vagrants, epileptics, imbeciles, lunatics, the aged, and the infirm—known as

---

*Literally: Jew town. Built on the site of an ancient ghetto into which Louis IX ("Saint" Louis!) planned to herd the Jews of Paris.

**Persons paid to do errands they never did, including sixteen- and seventeen-year-olds. They are segregated "lest they be torn to pieces if someone recognized them."

'the good poor.' " Conditions in Bicêtre are more crowded than in La Salpêtrière: they sleep six to a bed in the vast St. Francis Hall, the stench of which caused Madame Necker to faint recently when she visited the good poor, and since then she has been actively promoting "the construction of beds that sleep no more than two persons."* Five or six hundred inmates are packed together there, a tenth of whom are dying. "You cannot enter even to bring them food except behind the tip of a bayonet." Joseph hurries past "the good poor," being more interested in the bad ones, occupants of Bicêtre's experimental cells. A difficult problem facing any ruler: how to get rid of the trash unclaimed by the gallows if you have no galleys. Here's an idea now, this cluster of narrow cells, more like cages, piled one atop the other like a beehive —from which no bee escapes. "They claim that the prisoners there are punished less than their crime merits and thus are being treated mercifully . . . They are given a few scraps of iron with which to make little things. The ones below [in the lowest tier of cages on the ground floor] are the best off; everyone envies them because they become tradesmen and provide work for the others, who never cease to bless and praise the place below." Prisoners communicate silently between floors by flashing bits of glass that act as mirrors to reflect light signals in some prearranged code. Joseph's arrival sets off some strange signals. "The cells take two things into account: providing the prisoner with a hole for his bodily needs, and an exit for getting to mass. The chapel is in the center; they go there on Sundays." They no longer attend vespers since the day in February 1756 when prisoners in the building known as the "Little Ditch" took advantage of their Sunday outing to attack the guards, seize weapons, and force their way out. Fourteen mutineers and two guards were killed. Several prisoners managed to escape, but local townspeople promptly turned them in: "Their coarse homespun garments gave them away." "When questioned as to the motive behind the revolt, the prisoners replied that their normal ration had been cut, though it consisted of nothing more than a bit of bread and a scrap of meat once a week . . . that they bore no one a grudge save the warden and the chief steward . . . and that, tired of living, they had heeded only their despair."

"The authorities took them at their word: several were hanged, others flogged by the headsman and locked up more securely."**

Joseph deserved an afternoon's relaxation at the Colisée, a kind of sprawling stucco barracks hastily thrown up the year before in the riotous gardens that reached from the Champs-Elysées to the Faubourg Saint-Honoré. The product of another gambling spree, speculation on Parisian holidays, it marks one more bourgeois attempt to mingle with the nobility. A handful of bankers have built

*Her campaign succeeds in 1780.
**In describing this episode, L. S. Mercier cannot resist quoting Vauvenargues: "If you cannot make people good, you have no right to make them suffer."

the Colisée as a ballroom for up to two thousand dancers. It can also host "nautical entertainments." The cost: three millions.*

An evening of opera.

Morning of May 3: craftsmen instead of prisoners. The emperor is about to visit the "royal manufactory of tapestries and furniture for the crown" founded by the Gobelin brothers in the Faubourg Saint-Marceau under François I, which Colbert took over for the throne when the heirs met financial hardship. Under Colbert, it blossomed into Europe's greatest enterprise, housed in its own mansion a hundred *toises*** long in the heroic days of the Sun King. Toward the end of his life, however, Louis XIV's campaigns undercut the factory's prosperity and kept the Gobelin works from making Paris a rival of Venice or Florence. It licensed its own jewelers, woodcarvers, painters, engravers, and sixty apprentices from all over the globe. The tapestry studios still operate; twenty years before, Jacques de Vaucanson made them world-renowned with his invention "of a loom for weaving figured stuffs." Vaucanson is there now, bent with age; in two years he will be seventy, but he would have come in a litter, if necessary, to greet the emperor who has seen in Vienna his mechanical figurine "that plays the flute, tambourine, and galoubet" and the famous mechanical duck that gobbles grain. Vaucanson shows his guest "the model of a new type of mill he has been designing for several years." As they converse, silent craftsmen carry on the work, some of whom "take twenty years to train." "Hunched over his loom, the weaver arranges his silks and colors . . . He cannot see what he is making; the right side faces away from him."[8] Certain completed tapestries, called "finished pieces," have taken ten years to make, and sell for forty thousand francs.† The daily wage of a master tapestry-weaver in the Gobelin factory, a top craftsman, is twenty-three sous for twelve hours of work. If he is sick more than a week, he loses his job.

Next Joseph heads for the royal gardens‡ not far from his hotel, where he pays a call on the dean of naturalists. Georges-Louis Leclerc de Buffon is ill and receives him in bed with the blissful self-assurance of a man for whom everything always turns out right—except matters of the heart. He had been eager to remarry, hoping to find happiness with some young submissive girl like Sophie de Monnier, whose parents had proposed the match seven years before. But Buffon is no romantic dreamer. Work dominates his life. He believes himself brighter than Diderot and more gifted than Voltaire, since he is about to complete the most coherent literary monument of all times. He had planned to write a fifteen-volume *Histoire naturelle générale et particulière* in

---

*Now fifteen millions [$3,000,000]. Eventually the money went down the drain, as the Colisée never caught on; Parisians felt it was out of the way and avoided it. It was demolished in 1784. Today its only surviving memento is the Rue du Colisée.

**The *toise* measured six feet or nearly two meters.

†Today 200,000 francs [$40,000].

‡Beginning even then to be known as the Jardin des Plantes, or botanical gardens.

1739, the year that Louis XV, by making him supervisor of the royal "natural-history collection" and the royal gardens, placed Buffon in the ideal position to have the botanical specimens of four continents at his fingertips. He is now working on volume thirty and cannot say how many more are to come.* Joseph has never laid eyes on a single page of it and dislikes books in general, yet feels it incumbent on him to hail the venerable naturalist—or perhaps philosopher, Joseph is uncertain which. At any rate, Buffon is what Diderot aspired to be for technology: the first to employ style as a tool for repairing and reducing the ever widening breach between science and literature.

"In what manner may I convey my gratitude and respect to Your Majesty?"

"Allow me to sit at your bedside. I wish to be instructed and have come to see my master."[9]

On hearing that, who could challenge the emperor's claim to be an enlightened despot? Still, Buffon is not prepared to present him with the fundamental issue, evolution, which he is "the first in modern times to have approached from a strictly scientific point of view."** It would be unseemly to inform a Hapsburg that his ancestor may have been an ape. They talk about the problems of plant adaptation in Vienna and Paris.

On May 4, another garden tour at the Palais Royal, ancestral mansion of the ducs d'Orléans, followed by a third performance of the Comédie Française, though now the emperor is visibly less interested in the acting than in the actresses. In the next few days he prowls "the pretty temple of Mlle Guimard and around the country house of Mlle Arnould, where they say he had dinner and good luck." His mother will never hear of this from Mercy-Argenteau, whose reports prudishly ignore the episode as well as the emperor's visit "to the house of M. de Monville, one of our most engaging voluptuaries,"[10] where the servants are dismissed once the supper table is set for the actresses and their noble guests. Joseph will also be received "in the superb mansion of M. de Beaujon, former banker to the crown," like La Borde. He ends up meeting as many bankers as peers of the realm, which merely indicates his knowledge of where the true poles of power lie, the fact that money and nobility are coming into balance on the social scales as demonstrated by the ascendance of Necker, to whom he speaks on three occasions. But the one official who really takes the emperor's fancy is the Comte de Saint-Germain, minister of war, a starchy fellow brimming with ideas on military reform, who by now is heartily detested at court and in the ranks. The emperor likes this unpatriotic Frenchman who complains to him "of the nation's frivolity and the difficulty of imposing discipline." Joseph urges him to press for military training "with the persistence of a philosopher and the courage of a soldier."[11]

---

*Buffon (1707–1788) never completed his *Natural History,* which ran to thirty-six volumes at his death.   **According to Darwin.

On May 5, in the theater at Versailles, he attends a performance of Rameau's *Castor et Pollux* at the queen's side. On the 6th he inspects troops on the Plaine des Sablons. The date on which Derues is mashed to a pulp. Also the date on which a request for extradition, signed by the Comte de Mirabeau and the Marquise de Monnier, is handed to the Dutch government by the French ambassador.

7 I

MAY 1777

Malicious and Underhanded Flight

A warrant had been out for them since break of day on August 25, 1776, and the descriptions issued to police were less than flattering. Mirabeau: "Medium height, florid features heavily pockmarked and freckled, wild-eyed when preoccupied, face perpetually smudged and sweaty, stocky neck, broad-shouldered, muscular build, wide stubby feet." Sophie de Monnier: "Rather tall with bad posture, head lists to one side, oversize feet for a woman, plump hands, stoop-shouldered, round-faced, bulbous slightly ruddy nose, square chin, small mouth with regular teeth, thick lips, chestnut hair, fair skin with good coloring. She has a habit of biting her lips. Her voice is low and strong, not very feminine. She mumbles a lot. Not bad-looking on the whole."[1]

At first they were taken for two young men when, in the middle of the night and soaked to the skin, they knocked at the door of Madame Bôle, an acquaintance of Mirabeau's in Verrières (Switzerland). They warmed themselves at her hearth and were offered wine and brandy while a room was prepared. Twin beds? Ah no, a double bed even if it has to be in the attic; just let them sleep till noon. To protect himself in the event of court action, Mirabeau had his hosts note that Sophie came to join him and that he had never left Switzerland. Flight, yes, but not abduction. Legally, the argument stands.

They were expected to be on their way the next morning, but stayed for three weeks, snug and safe with Madame Bôle. In hiding, if you will, two leagues from Sophie's husband, in sight of the border. If the French patrols ever caught them, it would not have caused much stir with the Swiss, who had other things on their mind. As yet, however, no one was trailing the lovers, for the Marquis de Monnier felt tired of playing jailer and in no rush to bring them to court. He was not anxious to look like a fool by having his wife marched back to him under guard. Sophie resolved to enjoy the interval before her parents inevitably took up the chase. The time it took to exchange letters between Pontarlier and Dijon gave the young pair a chance to raise cash from some of Sophie's jewelry and clothing which Mirabeau entrusted to Louise de Cabris in Lyons. They wanted to put by as much money as possible before leaving; Sophie had helped herself to part of the contents of her husband's strongbox,* but they needed more for the journey ahead.

The messenger dispatched to Louise finally returned—with barely half the amount they had anticipated. Obsessively bent on defying their father, Louise had kept some of the valuables and would claim later that she never received them.

They set out anyway on September 13, riding in open wagons across Switzerland to the Rhine, then on down to Basel by boat, and finally to Holland. The river meant freedom but not joy, not peace of mind. Anguish: Gabriel carried a heavy pistol and swore to blow his brains out rather than risk arrest. Sophie echoed him: "They shan't take me alive. I'll swallow the contents of this little packet."

Opium probably; she kept it with her day and night. On September 26 they arrived in Rotterdam confident that here was a seafaring paradise. "Holland is the Egypt of Europe . . . As it penetrates the country, each river bed grows statelier . . . In several places one sees the ocean [sic] rise twenty-two and a half feet above the continent. On one side of a narrow roadway runs a ditch; on the other, the sea."** Overhead, the fugitives watched great migrations of wild ducks and geese flying up the Rhine in the opposite direction, sweeping down in colonies to rest on canals and marshes, those aquatic highways that crisscross the Lowlands in a neat grid. "The country is flat, so are the towns. From a distance, because of the many canals with their tree-lined borders, they resemble clusters of hamlets all strung together; one has the impression of endless countryside, and the hamlets appear to have sprung up overnight as if by magic."[2] The Marquis de Sade, Gabriel's cousin, who made this journey in 1769, could not get used to "seeing such arrays of trees, houses, windmills, and boats":[3] a land that turns and moves with every breeze. There stood Rotterdam at the river's end, indissoluble union of Europe and the sea, its canals so deep that trading vessels unload their cargoes right on a merchant's front doorstep. City of sails, to be navigated only by dint of "a prodigious number of drawbridges."[4] They stayed a week, it was so beautiful; England's proximity may also have tempted them. But what about money? Gabriel was not about to turn stevedore. His skills reside in his pen or his sword. Amsterdam loomed—remotely—to all enlightened spirits as an assured haven of liberty. On to Amsterdam and its free press! In October they settle

*Endless arguments would follow as to how much she took: 30,000 livres [6000 new francs] the Ruffeys insisted; more likely it was only a tenth of that.

**According to Diderot, who has published (*Voyage en Hollande*) his discerning observations on his own recent journey to Holland.

down in the house of a tailor, M. Lequesne, descended from Protestants banished under Louis XIV, who "rented rooms, preferably to French nationals," in the Kalverstraat near the flower market.

Amsterdam is another Rotterdam that seems to be sinking into the sea. Same blur of houses and sails, but here ocean-bound vessels have difficulty navigating the inland waterways; Texel Island is gradually silting up. Ships must be raised by "camels": two enormous wooden chests attached to each side of a ship to produce a shallower draft. Thus laden, they flounder along by the hundreds into a harbor "half a league long" with its back to the North Sea, its face to the muddy bank of the Ij. Stretching from the outermost limits of the port, the semicircular ramparts look, on a map of the city, like a bow with a line of docks for its string. Within this arc lie ninety islands and three hundred bridges. A fog-bound Venice whose canals freeze in winter, whose 350,000 inhabitants are constantly on the move, "speak every known tongue, and sell every kind of goods; it is one of the strangest spectacles in the world."[5] Fine houses, freshly varnished and painted every color of the rainbow, their façades, their walkways, their enclosures immaculately scrubbed and swept by residents who never scrub themselves. "A Dutchman takes good care of his house because it is liable to mildew, and poor care of himself knowing there is no danger of mildew." Still, they are a healthy people: "You will find the men, women, and animals well fed. The women's faces are frequently ugly and stimulate very little desire to try to verify their reputation for broad bosoms or to explore their other charms."[*]

A handsome, unkempt city, like a slovenly girl caked with makeup. The muddy canals are strewn with garbage and rags. Badge of distinction: one travels along the city's narrow streets by sleigh, even in summer. Only magistrates and doctors may drive coaches, as wheel traffic undermines the stability of houses built on, or rather anchored to, piles.

Gabriel and Sophie have anchored there, too, with mixed feelings. But then uncertainty has dogged their steps ever since they left Dijon. They have not been happy in Holland, only pretended to be.

Because of money problems? Since when did debts thwart romance? The truth is that Sophie not only "detests them beyond belief" but cannot even understand how debts come to be. Until she ran away, she was used to having nothing but bare necessities and superfluities. She says she would rather "do without than owe money," but later on, toward the close of their affair, she admits "there were many things in Amsterdam which detracted from our perfect bliss." Not altogether cheerfully did she give up her plan to order for her Gabriel a dress suit trimmed with fur which they brought with them: "Then we will sell the marten pelt, too, since you won't let me put it on a rose-color suit. Let's not be afraid of poverty; lots of people live on far less than

---

[*]Both observations are Diderot's.

we."[6] But she has never really tried to get along without servants, nor has he. Her culinary efforts go down the sink; they must eat out or pay a servant to cook. They must buy fuel, wine instead of beer, entertain a bit, not only French acquaintances but also Dutch if they are to uphold their chosen alias, "Comte and Comtesse de Saint-Mathieu."* Yet work is something Mirabeau cannot stand; his motive for seeking an army commission was to avoid it.

Later they romanticize: "How many times did you tear yourself from my arms to go to work, to do unpleasant tasks! [Just how many times indeed!] But nothing was too unpleasant when you did it for Sophie, when you worked for Sophie. Sweetheart, you are the ideal suitor."[7]

Did she really think so? Sheer rhetoric! He is neither flirtatious nor persistent; he is innately lazy and polygamous. Able to turn out a pamphlet by working twenty hours at a stretch—so long as he could loll to his heart's content afterward. "How we loved our bed!" . . . Able to dash off page after page of honeyed nothings when they are apart, but incapable of wooing her for three days running when alone with this adorably exasperating, unbearably sweet woman, who turns out to be distinctly passive in bed when no longer frustrated. If only he could beat her now and then! But when do you beat honey? "Imagine that the girl resents my intelligence, my talents, etc. Imagine that she wouldn't care if I were extremely stupid or ignorant as long as I kept healthy and stayed with her . . . In fact, to tend the herd with me is the height of her ambition."[8] So they went on loving, and working, too, in fits and starts, he at translating or composing pamphlets, she at giving Italian lessons, her sole "professional competence," to pupils somewhat too old for her, said Gabriel, whose inferiority complex channeled itself into fits of jealousy. Ugliness gave him the right to cuckold her, but she had no such right. "Your Italian lessons were torment to me . . . My temperament is uneven, my sensitivity prodigious, my energy excessive."[9] "From six in the morning to nine at night I was working." Later he marvels at the memory of those thirty peaceful days after eight months of chaos. "An hour of music relaxed me . . . She kept my accounts, she worked, read, painted, checked my printer's proofs . . ."[10] But if it was all so blissful, why did he go off alone several times for a week or ten days, to Rotterdam, especially over Christmas and New Year's Day, which they had planned to spend together? On business? More likely to borrow money, the only "business" at which he was any good. He borrowed six or seven thousand livres during their stay in Holland; an average of twenty-five to thirty livres a day.** Unavoidable: chicken or rabbit cost a florin;† turkey, two florins; Levantine coffee (the best), fifteen sous; a pound of good tobacco, sixteen sous; pure Castile soap, one florin; three florins for a bottle of cham-

*The name of an estate in Limousin belonging to Mirabeau's maternal grandparents.
**Today 150 francs [$30].
†A Dutch florin was worth approximately two Louis XVI livres (also called francs); the ducat: a half-louis, or 500 modern francs [$100].

pagne, but for wine from the Cape and "old, very old Rhine wine, a ducat"; men's silk stockings, from seven florins to a ducat, and between three and four for women's; twelve florins for a tailor-made suit; ordinarily it cost two hundred florins to heat a house in winter with peat, wood, or coal,[11] but it costs them twice that amount, since the winter of 1776 turns out to be the coldest since 1709. Mirabeau found that "Holland is the costliest country in Europe." He spent weeks running from the "loan bank" (where they refused to underwrite a loan for the good and simple reason that they suspected his false identity) to the "chamber of petty affairs," which regulated all matters involving less than six hundred florins, and on to the chamber "of magistrates," something that resembled a civil court of appeals. The threat of "physical constraint" (that is, imprisonment for debt) hung over him from the beginning. The pair owned nothing seizable except themselves. Whatever time Gabriel did not waste in legal circuits was claimed by Dutch publishers. Diderot has denounced them lately as the sharpest swindlers in Europe: "Their shops are rats' nests, their printing houses the foulest hovels; they are loutish, lazy, grasping, and ignorant; they seek only their own interest—which they misunderstand." "Successful piracy is dooming the book trade."[12] How marvelous Holland seemed from Paris! How precarious it is to live by one's pen in a country where "the people are superstitious, hostile to philosophy or to religious tolerance,"* yet where "persecution does not exist. A materialist is viewed with horror but left alone" provided he is rich and an isolated case. "Anti-clerical publications are harder to come by than in France";[13] they are, of course, Holland's prize export item. Amsterdam turns out subversive literature (both political and pornographic) for European consumption, while booksellers use writers the way pimps do whores.

But moneylenders and booksellers don't take up all Mirabeau's time. He also went to the theater several times, leaving Sophie home. Just the theater? "It distressed me in Amsterdam when you visited the sluts, though I was sure you never laid a hand on them."[14] With actresses and "sluts" Sophie lumps "those horrid Freemasons," though she is not too sure who they are. She simply feels that all those people are keeping Gabriel from "minding the herd with her." Had they not been around, though, he would have found some other way to escape domestication. She wanted to possess him. He was determined to glow, to reshape the world—the image of his father. Sophie believed she had landed herself an ideal husband when in fact she simply had an affectionate mad dog on loan.

Masons of Amsterdam's Lodge of the Beloved, or of the Profound Silence Lodge in Rotterdam,** had given Mirabeau the hope that even in Holland

---

*The intolerance of Protestants there was as bad as that of Genevan Calvinists in private as well as diocesan matters.

**In all probability Mirabeau was initiated into the Lodge of the Perfect Union at La Rochelle in 1768 when a privileged prisoner on the Isle of Ré.

he could find equality if not fraternity. Inside the lodge no one treated him as a foreigner—they were too cosmopolitan for that—or a suspect. Some degree of unconventionality was the rule. Masonry enabled aristocrats as well as their hopeful imitators to attain invaluable social perspective, to escape the immobilizing constraints of their native habitat, always within the "cultivated" framework of the Enlightenment: a Freemason must express himself and behave like a gentleman, if only to conform to its esoteric rites. Not a mason was to be found among the Freemasons; Mirabeau would have been the first to complain if he had met one. There were just as many bourgeois as patricians.

In a single winter he designed a *Plan de réorganisation de la Franc-Maçonnerie* [Plan to reorganize Freemasonry]* and submitted it to his brothers;[15] an essay full of ideas on contemporary music bearing the curious heading: *Le Lecteur y mettra le titre* [The reader will supply the title]; a long satirical and irreverent narrative poem, *Parapilla* (perhaps two plagiarisms); and the pamphlet *Avis aux Hessois* [Advice to the Hessians]. Written with conviction, the latter is reminiscent of Mirabeau's earlier *Essai sur le despotisme*. It was also an attempt to reach out to America and escape choking to death in Europe.

The English crown eventually would crush the rebels, everyone agreed, but needed more troops to do the job. Not enough could be raised in Britain, so George III resorts to his favorite expedient: hiring soldiers from the petty German princes who have too many of their own to feed and keep busy. In February 1777 the Landgrave of Hesse-Cassel had bartered an "infantry corps," two or three thousand seasoned fighters, to the English "for the price of one hog per man" and was incensed when the first lot objected to being dispatched from Hanau in March. A full company mutinied on the Rhine en route through the Lowlands, where deserters were aided by Dutch peasants. More such mercenaries were assembled in the vicinity of Nijmegen despite protests from such "liberals" as Gabriel met in Rotterdam, most vocal among whom were the Van Haren brothers ("poet statesmen" unloved by the merchant class). After all, the beggars' revolt had freed the country from Spanish tyranny just two hundred years before. Partisans of the American cause needed a voice to express their discontent; Mirabeau was only too willing to shout. He dashed off the *Avis aux Hessois et autres peuples de l'Allemagne vendus par leurs princes à l'Angleterre* [Advice to the Hessians and other German peoples sold by their princes into bondage to England] and took it to Amsterdam's most prominent printer, Marc-Michel Rey (Rousseau's publisher):

"You will make money from it. I wrote the *Essai sur le despotisme,* which went to two editions in six weeks when Fauche handled it in Neuchâtel."

---

*In which the budding author, penniless as Job, yet extremely class-conscious, argues against taking "persons of small means" into the lodge: "Poverty makes men so desperate to escape it that we ought not to trust anyone in that condition."

Skeptical, Rey asked for further particulars from the "Comte de Saint-Mathieu," who disclosed his real name and obtained Fauche's written recommendation. As a result, a short anonymous pamphlet appeared in April attacking the principality of Hesse: "You are sold, and to what purpose, just gods! To combat people defending the most righteous cause . . . And why do you not emulate them instead of trying to destroy them? . . . When authority grows arbitrary and oppressive, when it scorns the rights it was designed to protect, when it breaks the contract that fixes and limits duties, then resistance is a duty and cannot be termed sedition . . . Whoever attempts to recover his liberty by fighting for it exercises a wholly legitimate right . . . Treason against the people is the worst crime, for a people is just as superior to its sovereign as the sovereign to the individual."[16] Mirabeau gained prestige among his fellow Freemasons and entree to all the publishers. He was on the way to join Linguet, Morande, and Beaumarchais as one of the popular pamphleteers of the day. Would this enable him to pay off his debts at last and enjoy some kind of stability? No, his doom was sealed.*

Fauche had informed on him by giving his address to the Marquis de Monnier: Neuchâtel is too close to Pontarlier for fellow notables not to "cooperate." A rich bookseller in Switzerland, even the "Prussian" sector, can look for advantage in doing a favor for a magistrate in Franche-Comté. Sophie's disappearance has left Pontarlier society in a permanent state of shock. An intolerable outrage to propriety! Nobles, magistrates, and prosperous bourgeois all urged the Marquis de Monnier to bring action for "abduction." But he was in no hurry: "I have no idea where my wife is. How can I prove she is living with that devil of a fellow?" Then along came Fauche to force his hand.

Sophie didn't care; Gabriel pretended not to. To her, France was a distant planet she had escaped forever. Stateless now, they were slowly gravitating either toward Amsterdam or Philadelphia. What harm could come to them in a free country?

Preliminary signal: Monnier dispatched a trusted manservant, Joseph Sage, to his wife with a magnanimous offer and money to pay her way home. Come back and all will be forgiven. She refused to see him. Mirabeau saw him, however, found out what plans were afoot in Pontarlier, and proposed some possible solutions. Sophie might return to France, for example, and enter a convent "which allowed her to go out during the day," providing she was assured an annual allowance of a thousand écus. Was this a trick of his or the first sign of waning interest? On his initial visit to Rotterdam, true to form,

---

*Later Mirabeau invents all kinds of stories about the *Avis aux Hessois*: he claims that the pamphlet triggered mutinies which actually occurred before its publication; that it was translated into five or six tongues, when only French and German editions are known; that the Landgrave of Hesse-Cassel immediately bought up every copy of the German edition in order to prevent their distribution. The landgrave ran no great risk as his soldiers were illiterate.

he had left several irons in the fire, one of which involved a friendly settlement of this uncomfortable situation. But can one "settle" a love affair? At that time she, in Amsterdam, wrote to him in Rotterdam: "Much as I want you to amuse yourself, sweetheart, I am flattered and content that you have not grown accustomed to the absence of your mistress . . . You do believe me, don't you? . . . Isn't it chilly sleeping alone? I think so . . . Good-by, dear one, I embrace you lovingly, I kiss your neck, your shoulders, your . . . * Good-by."[17]

After his messenger's return, and goaded by the Ruffey clan, Monnier brought suit in Pontarlier against the Comte de Mirabeau for abducting his wife. The whole thing was prearranged. The plaintiff's judicial colleagues conducted a closed hearing as snow began to melt on the rooftops. Jeanret the smuggler appeared for the prosecution. There was no defense; two ungovernable subjects were to be condemned *in absentia*. The court possessed one of several letters intercepted from Mirabeau the summer before which described his escape plan—an outright confession.

Sophie shut her ears to all this. Gabriel listened and grew anxious. Other reports reached him from France of family strife that had fueled gossip all winter long in the Paris salons. His father barricaded himself on the Rue de Seine or at Bignon with whichever children sided with him, generally the Du Saillant clan, which hoped to reap a fat inheritance; his mother, a boarder in the convent of La Trinité, was joined by Louise, who longed to bring the dispute to a head. Thirty years of marital wrangles suddenly burst into the open. The marquis had the talent, the friends, and the influence in high places; the marquise had the money, but he controlled it for the moment because she was a proven nymphomaniac who had handed out affidavits of virility to certain lovers, including valets, coachmen, etc. The marquis had got hold of a few of these letters and had them locked away in his arsenal of secret weapons together with "the letter of incest" which he planned to use against his son. Charming family! "The twenty years spent with my wife were twenty years of nephritic colic," the Friend of Man complained. On her side, Marie-Louise de Vassan-Mirabeau has just issued a statement accusing her husband of trying to force an abortion** on her, poisoning her, bringing prostitutes to the house, and giving her the pox on three occasions—in case the poison failed.

Since infancy Gabriel had been steering his way between two amicably separated monsters: she in Limousin, he in the Paris suburbs. This sordid background had not improved the boy's stability or moral development. Guided by the amount of money he hoped to extract from either parent, he sided with one or the other, depending on his needs and regardless of principle. In recent times he had fawned on his father because only his father could lift the son's proscription. Since his arrival in Holland, however, Gabriel

*The ellipsis is Sophie's.
**Despite the eleven children she bore him, five of whom survived.

turned to his mother, not only out of revenge but also because she had broken the truce by demanding legal division of property which could make her hugely rich and the marquis a pauper.

"I would give several years of my life to be near you in these moments of anguish and fear," Gabriel wrote to her, suggesting that he come and help her lawyer. "For no matter how clever he may be, he cannot know the domestic incidents as I do." At the same time, cynically, he parried Louise's attempts to stir their mother's wrath against the marquis. What about the "letter of incest" their father was now waving under the noses of government officials? "I thought I had formally denied all responsibility for those odious letters imputed to me."[18] As to Sophie, whom his mother urges him half-heartedly to send back to France: "The essential and incontrovertible fact is that they cannot prove I abducted Madame de Monnier because it isn't true and I can prove that I was not in France when she left." For the moment, they are living together, but "do you believe, dear Mama, that honor or duty commands me to send away a woman who has done so much for me?"[19] "Dear Mama" did not press the point; she needed her eldest son near. What better evidence could she produce than the testimony of a son—tarnished or not—against his father? She got her money's worth and more. Gabriel overdid it. He wrote and sent to his mother a statement to fling in the marquis's face. In return for which the marquis informed the court that "my son slept with my wife before sleeping with my daughter." This, it seems, was customary among the Le Vassan clan. Parisians were all agog. Stung to the quick, Gabriel responded with a pamphlet, published in March and entitled *Anecdote à ajouter aux nombreux recueils des hypocrisies philosophiques** [Supplementary anecdote to be added to the compendium of philosophic hypocrisies], which tore his father to shreds. Explosive opening: "The Friend of Man did nothing for his wife nor his children. He preached virtue, tolerance, order, and morality, yet was the worst husband and the most repressive, prodigal father."[20] "Prodigal" is a key word, indicating that his wife and son accuse the marquis not only of "mental cruelty" but also of squandering a fortune he merely managed and which was rightfully theirs. He underwrote costly physiocratic experiments, products of the sick mind of a presumptuous ignoramus "who had set himself up as law-giver to kings and farmers but could not tell a grain of rye from a grain of wheat."[21] The marquis could have swallowed, perhaps even forgiven, all save the last accusation, which ridiculed everything he had fought for all his life. Now the family feud narrowed to a bitter duel between father and son.

Prior to this, the elder Mirabeau had shared the Marquis de Monnier's attitude toward the fugitives: he was fed up and glad to be rid of them.

---

*Bearing the date December 15, 1776, supposedly printed in London, and signed "S.M." (Saint-Mathieu). A single copy of this small pamphlet in octavo is on file in the Bibliothèque nationale in Paris.

Inspector Bruguières,* one of the sleuths who had tracked Gabriel first from Dijon to Geneva the previous summer, then to Lyons and Lorgues, came to the marquis with his son's address and "an appeal for terms." He was sent away. "The wretch is in Holland and would be in peril if I meant to get him, but this is not the right moment."** He would not hear another word about him.

The marquis changed his tune after reading the "infamous pamphlet." If his son was spoiling for a fight, he would fight him tooth and nail. In the time it took a messenger to ride to the Ruffeys and back, Bruguières was put back on the job. Lenoir, chief of police, agreed to release him for a special assignment at no cost to the government, as Ruffey and Mirabeau senior each contributed one hundred louis† to pay his expenses.

Sophie is pregnant. They have decided to name the baby either Gabriel-Sophie or Gabrielle-Sophie. Will they ever reach that ultimate stage of passion, domesticity? Their first—and last—springtime together is harsh and unpleasant. In Holland "spring is simply the last throes of winter; northern winds begin to blow shortly before the vernal equinox and continue until just after the summer solstice; which is why trees rarely leaf out until the 12th of May."²² A depressing burden of debt hangs over them like the wind-driven clouds that choke the sky. Mirabeau is not sure exactly how much they owe, probably close to two thousand livres. If the "chamber of insolvents" should intervene, that would be the end. Give him time to turn out a few more pamphlets and everything will be different.

Bruguières arrives in Amsterdam on the 1st of May. Outside their house, he prowls the streets visibly enough to warn them that they are being watched. Strange fellow, more like a cavalry officer than a detective, with an air of distinction. Obviously a man of some breeding who, either from need or choice, went to work for Sartines and his successor, Lenoir. A good man to investigate matters in patrician circles which require a deft touch and the "capacity to communicate" with aristocratic suspects. This facility he now employs in establishing a cat-and-mouse relationship with Mirabeau. "As one gentleman to another, this is what I am supposed to do [but he doesn't spell it all out]. This is what you could do if I were to close my eyes . . . " After three or four days of bargaining, he impresses his victim as a rather likable soul. Did he take time to inquire into their financial situation? Possibly. On May 5 Mirabeau writes to his mother: "M. Bruguières is still here, but it doesn't worry me . . . [Maybe he has] decided that it might be useful to try to intimidate me. I don't know what else to think. It follows that I ought to

*Contemporary and later spellings vary (Brugnières, Brignières, etc.). An examination of the signature itself leaves no doubt, however, that de Bruguières is correct.
**Letter dated February 6, 1777, to his brother the Bailli de Mirabeau.
†Today 20,000 francs [$4000].

relax a bit, all the more since I owe over a hundred louis* and have less than six to my name. So I'm chained here. What can I do? Wait for a bomb and then do my best to muffle it."²³

The bomb is in Bruguières's pocket: an introduction from Vergennes to the Duc de La Vauguyon, French ambassador to The Hague, and a formal request to have the couple arrested. The official wording, in diplomatese, left no loophole unplugged: "M. de Monnier and his family, rightfully vexed by the malicious and underhanded flight of Madame de Monnier, which has been the object of lengthy investigation and oral testimony at the request of M. de Monnier in the state of Neufchâtel in (Swiss) Verrières, feel themselves bound by circumstance to address themselves to the court of France to solicit most strenuously the capture and extradition of M. le Comte de Mirabeau, author of the escape [*sic*], and of Madame de Monnier through the offices of the French ambassador to the High Powers** so that they may be removed and transferred to the city of Besançon, there to stand trial."²⁴ Gabriel and Sophie feel the trap about to be sprung on them when Bruguières suddenly vanishes. A vague, stifled threat hovers over Kalverstraat, where no neighbors greet them because they are two months behind in their rent. To the Marquis de Sade the Dutch had appeared to be "generally nice people, strongly attached to their own interests, totally absorbed by the idea of accumulating money and preoccupied with ways to do so; glad enough to be of service when it costs them nothing; apathetic, cold, and fundamentally rather blind to anything that does not produce money."²⁵ Sophie remains calm, but Gabriel begins to flounder about in this human wasteland. She believes they are safe because he "has become a naturalized Dutchman." All the Bruguièreses in the world cannot lay a finger on a free subject of the States-General of Holland . . . She is confused. What Mirabeau paid (dearly at that) is a type of tax levied on visitors in western Holland, specifically Amsterdam, one of the seven United Provinces, where he had acquired provisional, costly, and revocable citizenship. No man wallowing in debt could expect permanent civil status in Holland.

On May 6 in The Hague the Duc de La Vauguyon opens formal extradition proceedings.

*He actually owed more than 400.
**Official title of the governing body of the Low Countries.

72

She Is No Help to Him at All

On May 7 Joseph II does a good deed. He pays a visit to the "Institution for
the Deaf and Dumb" on the Right Bank, along the Rue Neuve-des-Petits-
Champs, "second carriage entrance on the left, over which the Abbé de l'Epée
has lodgings." A most impressive name for a private school like many others
in Paris. Pupils here, however, for whom the master is "at home on Tuesdays
and Fridays from seven till noon,"[1] are peculiar in that they can neither speak
nor hear.

It is the first school of its kind in the world. As a rule, deaf mutes from
both urban and rural families are left to drift toward idiocy. If abandoned, they
end up in the madhouse. Early in his career the Abbé de l'Epée, younger son
of a noble Versailles family and destined from birth for the priesthood, had
met two young deaf and dumb girls and their mother while visiting the poor.
The appealing look in their eyes, louder than words, had decided his life's
work. Hopeless idiots? Never. What about all the others whom no one would
talk to because they were mute? It struck him then and there "that one must
teach them through their eyes, through their minds, through the aid of drawing and sign language the things the rest of us learned by ear."[2] To his great
joy, he was able to rehabilitate the two girls, one of whom married and raised
a large family of normal children. The success of this experiment persuaded
him, like Bernard de Palissy, to burn all his household possessions and devote
his life to the deaf and dumb. When he tried to enlist the support of rich
patrons,* they spurned him. Throw money away on blighted children? Congenital infirmity was still looked upon as the wages of sin, meaning uncontrolled lust, though with less severity when the son of a magnate or a ruler
turned out to be permanently afflicted. With the poor, however, everyone
agreed: why invest money on marginal workers when there were not enough
schools to train those whose labor was becoming essential to industrial growth?
Unable to raise a sou, the Abbé de l'Epée sank his entire inheritance—not very
much, but it would have maintained him for life—into an "institution for the

*Madame de Pompadour for one. He applied to her no less than eight different times.

deaf and dumb." Cardinal de Fleury, the famous minister of Louis XV's minority, had noticed the energetic, idealistic young priest and decided to make him a bishop and put him in charge of a parish of perhaps a hundred thousand. The Abbé de l'Epée refused; he wished to serve the deaf and dumb. He did, and had been vegetating for the past thirty years in his four-room Paris diocese.

"His Majesty the Emperor presented gifts of an enameled box and a gold medallion to the Abbé de l'Epée." Far more than that, he brings him celebrity. Paris at last takes cognizance of this singular person. "The visit had an impact. Neither the abbé nor his school had aroused much interest heretofore; suddenly they became fashionable. Everyone insisted on seeing them."[3]

On May 8, with insatiable curiosity, Joseph sets out "after morning mass" to visit the royal printing house, "just past the third entrance gate, underneath the great gallery of the Louvre"—that old abandoned palace and erstwhile caravansary serving the whims of the court. A place to stable horses, rooms to house stage artists and bankrupt retainers. The royal printery "is the finest establishment of its kind in the world . . . The type cast on the premises is for [the crown's] exclusive use," superb eighteenth-century letters, each a marvel of elegant perfection. This is the artistic legacy of Garamond the engraver, who won the patronage of François I in undertaking "to purge lettering of all traces of Gothic influence." From then on, a *garamond* became the universal standard of excellence in typography. But what is the type used for? What do they print inside? Ordinances, public notices, administrative reports from the provinces—nothing.[4]

Farther down the Right Bank of the Seine, near the hill of Chaillot, the emperor discovers "an old building called the Savonnerie" because soap was made there in Henri IV's day. Since then it has housed "the royal manufacture of carpets, similar in style to Persian and Turkish designs," originally installed in the Louvre under Marie de Médicis. "The products made here surpass those of the Levant."[5] Farther along the river, at Passy, Joseph sees the favorite country abode of rich Parisians. "Its proximity to town, its mineral waters,* the open, animated perspective of most houses, make it much sought after by wealthy individuals seeking to relax from their occupations in wholesome air and to enjoy delightful outings in the Bois de Boulogne." Franklin took lodgings there, safe alike from the inquisitive public and from English spies. Not he, of all people, is the object of Joseph's visit, but rather "the royal physics laboratory," a spacious building at the foot of the Rue de la Paroisse, near the entrance to the Bois de Boulogne, where Louis XV had collected a clutter of optical and physical apparatus and left it in the care of the Abbé de Noël, a jovial priest known as "Père Noël" [Father Christmas]. Instruments

---

*"Passy has three kinds of waters: the old, the new, and the water containing acids and minerals that sells for seven sous a bottle."

that ranged from a microscope to a twenty-four-foot telescope which "Père Noël" had constructed in the hope of learning whether another planet existed beyond Saturn, as mathematicians had been asserting for some time against the arguments of astronomers; is it possible to discover through calculations a celestial body that no one has ever seen? Scholars will end up pinpointing the Virgin's heavenly throne with the help of algebraic equations! At present the Passy telescope magnifies Jupiter twice.

Amsterdam. Gabriel and Sophie begin to gather up their belongings in case they have to flee. But where to? They have no money even to cross the Channel to England.

May 9. The emperor and the king go hunting in Meudon, riding in the same carriage. They talk business. Joseph, a perpetual tourist, has personally visited every inch of his empire. He cannot understand this ruler who has not ventured from Versailles even as far as the Invalides and seems afflicted with locomotive paralysis:

"Go tour your provinces! It is the key to winning your people's affection. Start with Brest, for instance, since you intend to make it your chief military base, your balcony overlooking the Atlantic."

Louis XVI timidly objects that his two brothers are better suited to the role of traveling salesmen for the crown and have nothing else to do anyway. It so happens that Provence is going to leave—where else but for Provence?—and Artois for the west at the end of the month. The emperor is not satisfied. He takes up the question again that evening with the queen, "in a tone of voice that might seriously have offended" his sister, whom he had treated gently thus far. He informs her calmly that if the king decides to travel about, she should not accompany him "because she is no help to him at all." "This opinion was followed by several objections to the queen's undignified treatment of her husband, to the lack of respect in her speech, the haughtiness of her manner."[6] Marie Antoinette bristles. When will they get it through their heads that she is no longer a child? Not surprisingly, her brother has some trouble "persuading her to go to the king in his apartments." Would he also like to conduct her there with a candle? The marriage will not be consummated tonight either.

On May 10 the emperor visits the regimental armory of the French Guard, its entrance on the boulevard adjacent to the Chaussée d'Antin. There he is greeted by old Maréchal de Biron, uncle of Lauzun, their colonel, proud founder of this mini-military academy for a hundred-odd boys between the ages of eleven and sixteen, "sons of officers who show an aptitude for the art of warfare."[7] Theoretically, at sixteen they may choose another profession, but actually they are pre-cast as soldiers from boyhood because if they withdraw at the close of training, "their parents are obliged to repay the cost of their upkeep." "They are taught reading, writing, arithmetic, mathematics, geometry, civil and military engineering, vocal and instrumental music, dancing, German, and the full range of military exercises. His Majesty contributes ten sous daily for each pupil."*

A morning's pleasure, an afternoon's drudgery: attending a session of the Academy of Sciences, where Joseph stoically endures a lecture from M. Lavoisier "on alterations produced in the air under various conditions, and on the means of returning air fouled by human or animal respiration, or by any other cause, to a state of purity."[9]

Lavoisier positively beams. Not so much because of the honor paid to him today—actually, it is the attention of great scientists, not rulers, he seeks to attract—but because he is at the peak of his form, the most exciting period in the life of a successful research scientist. The year 1777 is his greatest. At last he has hit on a name for the "vital air" he discovered three years before and called successively "eminently breathable air," "dephlogisticated air," "oxygen principle," and finally just plain "oxygen." In his brand-new laboratory he has just performed the experiment which dethrones "atmospheric air." Mercury brought to the boil in a closed container consumed all the oxygen, which converted to a rust-colored oxide, leaving only four fifths of the original atmosphere, now turned to unrespirable "moffette" (shortly to be known as nitrogen). Lavoisier describes the experiment in great detail for the first time in the presence of an emperor who understands barely a word he says, little more than do the dozing academicians, for Lavoisier reads poorly and his style is ponderous. No one perceives the revolution underlying his blundering recitation: air ceases forever to be one of the four classic elements.

Lavoisier's research is not limited to oxygen experiments; he continues to pour out his energies in all directions. In one year alone he produced an article on "elastic aeriform fluids"; a "Report on the exceptionally cold winter of 1776 as compared to that of 1709";** an account of an investigation, carried out at the request of M. and Madame Necker, into prison conditions in those same institutions which Joseph had recently visited and which Lavoisier described as "crawling with filth, vermin, and corruption." He is running into surprising obstacles for so prominent a personality, a farmer-general and director of the state gunpowder commission: the penal administration is reluctant to cooperate with humanitarian muckrakers. "Wouldn't you think," Lavoisier soon writes to Madame Necker, "that, as prisons are more or less open to the

---

*Approximately 75 current francs [$15] per month. The complete training of one such French Guard cost the king about 6000 current francs over a period of six years. In comparison: at the end of May 1777, for the "month's outlay in connection with the imperial visit," Louis XVI hands over to his first chamberlain, Thierry, the sum of 6335 livres (31,000 current francs [$6200]) to cover household and kitchen expenses.[8]

**The two thermometers he put together for the occasion, more refined than the instruments used by Réaumur in 1732, may still be seen today in the "cellars" of the Paris Observatory.

public, we would have no difficulty visiting them?* Our task initially appeared to offend several magistrates. We were obliged to use guile and to take infinite precautions . . . "[10]

The subject he has been authorized to discuss today before the emperor is one of immediate concern, even if complicated in terms of its chemical ramifications. Joseph has been inhaling the problem ever since he came to Paris. The city stinks. People are virtually choking to death. In all the major European capitals, including Vienna and Paris, where sewers are still novelties, statistics tell the toll of "foul air."** Paris has the worst of any. Cemeteries that have mushroomed in every parish are becoming charnel houses. Even the churches reek of corpses putrefying in the crypts. On the Rue Saint-Denis "the flower vendors of Paris" gather to sell their wares alongside butchers who peddle their meat up and down the outside wall of the Cemetery of the Innocents, where towering mounds of petrified bones crowd the great vaulted structure built around a tiny twelfth-century chapel. Bodies are buried there, too, and Parisians who visit (with nostrils plugged) the cellar-to-attic mortuary conceive a strange vision of paradise from wall paintings that depict a *danse macabre* in which the pope and the emperor clasp hands with the insane.†† Proposals to burn the rapidly multiplying corpses before they asphyxiate the city invariably provoke outraged protests from churchmen: how then could God revive them? On the Day of Judgment, He would need the bones, not just ashes. So they walled up the vaults adjoining the charnel house, the stench from which drove neighboring tenants from their homes.

But there are worse dangers than the dead. The Seine has become the main catch-basin for the city's blood and excrement. Butchers slaughter their animals in the street outside their shops. "What could be more grisly and disgusting than to slit the throats of livestock and butcher the carcasses publicly? One walks in encrusted blood . . . Dismayed observers draw parallels between inhabitants of Bengal and those of the Rue des Boucheries‡ . . . In some streets near the butcher shops, which exhale a ghastly odor, vile prostitutes sit by the wayside at midday, publicly promoting their debauchery. It is not an attractive sight: these female creatures with their beauty patches and their makeup, monstrous and repulsive objects, hugely fat without exception, look more ferocious than bulls."[11]

As if blood were not enough of a problem, "each home has its private repository of corruption. Houses reek, leaving their tenants perpetually dis-

---

*Necker had appointed him "chairman" of a commission to study prisons, which also included Trudaine.   **Use of the word "pollution" was limited to a purely sexual connotation adopted by the Church—that is, "nocturnal pollution."

†Under pressure from Necker and Lenoir, the charnel house of the Innocents will be closed in 1780 and its bones strewn by the cartload in the Bois de Boulogne.

‡The analogy is L. S. Mercier's, as are the descriptions that follow; not to be confused with Lavoisier's style.

comfited. They are breathing air infected by the multitude of cesspools. Their 'nocturnal emissions' spread disease throughout whole neighborhoods . . . Because they are poorly constructed, these ditches often permit waste matter to seep into adjacent wells. This does not discourage the bakers from drawing water from those wells, and thus the most basic dietary staple inevitably is saturated with those mephitic, disease-ridden particles. To spare themselves the trouble of transporting fecal waste outside the city, 'these offenders' dump it at daybreak in ditches and gutters. This indescribable muck inches its way along city streets to the Seine and poisons the shores where water-carriers fill their buckets each morning with water that residents are compelled to drink."[12]

Such is the tasty diet of bread and water to which the Paris masses, some half-million strong, are condemned. After his hard afternoon, the emperor relaxes at an evening performance of the Comédie Française.

Still May 10. Pontarlier. The regional administrator for criminal affairs hands down his verdict in the case brought against Gabriel and Sophie by the Marquis de Monnier. They are sentenced *in absentia,* he, for "forcible abduction of a married woman," to lose his head and pay a fine of forty thousand livres* to the plaintiff, her husband; she, for adultery, to the annulment of her marriage contract and rights thereunder as well as forfeit of her dowry, and to life imprisonment and loss of her hair. Free love is costly in Louis XVI's reign if it tangles with the law. In the main square at Pontarlier, the public executioner of Besançon beheads Mirabeau in effigy; thus he endures the same fate as his cousin Sade in Aix-en-Provence. The lovers of Amsterdam have no idea of the cruelty and rapid performance of their sentence. To them, Pontarlier still seems the far end of nowhere. Their hopes revive; no one is harassing them. Miracle of miracles, Bruguières may have cleared out for good.

*Today 200,000 francs [$40,000].

73

Happy or Unhappy with Her

On May 12 Joseph II pays a visit to the new (twelve years old) veterinary school five miles outside Paris, between Alfort and Charenton. It is the principal repair and maintenance center for the nation's equine force and therefore its main source of agricultural and aggressive energies. What would become of a great power without its mounted units? The emperor dreams of cavalry charges across the plains of "Romany"—maybe even up the Danube to Bavaria. Tomorrow's hypothetical wars to the east and west are his consolation for all the bowing and scraping he must put up with from the French. To rival Frederick the Great! For that, Austria—or rather "the German Emperor," as Joseph is now called—will need an invincible striking force, a cavalry not at the mercy of sparse forage or epizootic disease. "The building is handsome and spacious. The natural-history collection includes a great many dissected specimens. One may observe very skillful operations being performed on horses; there is a fine chemistry laboratory and an apothecary who does nothing but prepare remedies for horses. They have a large forge and able blacksmiths to instruct apprentices. The school director is comfortably housed behind the courtyard."[1] He assures Joseph that once the school has trained one or two generations of army veterinarians, the French cavalry will be the finest in Europe. About 1806.

Same day, May 12. After lengthy deliberation, the Great Chamber of the Parliament of Paris ruled on the Marquise de Mirabeau's petition for "separation from bed and board" of her husband. She loses; the case is dismissed. The marquis has won the support of nearly every minister. The communal-property law will continue to apply to this elderly couple, but, by the same token, their separation agreement will become void; nothing prevents the marquise from insisting on cohabitation—the last thing in the world her husband wants. "There will be tales of their first night together"[2] in more than twenty years. And what's to become of "the black pussycat," Madame de Pailly, snugly ensconced now at Bignon? That same evening the marquise arrives at the family mansion on the Rue de Seine with two notaries, a woman companion, a magistrate friend, and two servants. Legal invasion. Forewarned, the housekeeping staff offers slight resistance. Escorted by a Swiss Guard, two valets, and her husband's own secretary, the marquise captures the field abandoned by her mate: the "nuptial" bedchamber, where she installs herself and orders supper served "promptly at ten thirty," then goes to bed, still attended by her inseparable companion, Madame de Neuville, from whom she refuses to part for even an hour. The Friend of Man has fled. Not far: he is staying with the Duc de Nivernais, a trusted friend on the nearby Rue de Tournon, and is kept informed of every move the marquise makes. He knows her like a book and is ready to pounce at the first opportunity. "She will always fall prey to her own violence."[3]

May 13. Claiming to be ill, she burrows into the bed she reconquered too easily for the victory to last. There she receives a battery of legal experts ushered in courteously—all except one. The marquis has barred the door to a certain Delacroix-Frainville, author of several insulting pamphlets published in Holland at Gabriel's instigation. And he is the lawyer she prefers. At six o'clock he arrives. The Swiss Guard stops him in the courtyard. She recognizes his voice, leaps out of bed, rushes downstairs into the court, into the street, hair disheveled, barefoot, a petticoat hastily slung over her nightdress—just what you'd expect of the Vassan tribe; like mother, like son. Gabriel must not be allowed to perpetuate that race. She shouts to passers-by; a crowd gathers around this poor, half-naked, half-hysterical woman who has never learned to control herself: Mirabeau's mother. She urges them to act as witnesses, and they are only too happy to help her subdue the porter, whom she pummels like a fishwife to get him to open the door to a house she claims is hers. The crowd groans menacingly when the Swiss Guard bundles her off. Scene from an opera buffa: she reappears, with breasts half exposed, in the window of the porter's lodge, where she delivers an incoherent diatribe studded with threatening references to "death" and "inheritance" before they can get her back to bed. She surrenders willingly once her nervous impulse has subsided. Like her son, she is not persistent.

She thinks the incident is over and done with. But she is lost; no woman of breeding makes a spectacle of herself or, even worse, appeals for aid to the common herd. God knows where *that* would lead!

Still May 13. The Hague, capital of the United Provinces. There, in the afternoon, Gabriel's and Sophie's fate is decided by a handful of important gentlemen who have never laid eyes on the pair. "The residence of government officials," Diderot observed, "has made The Hague an abode of espionage, and the idleness of its prosperous citizens an abode of busybodies. There are only foreign diplomats and representatives of the States,* all of whom scrutinize each other tirelessly and see each other rarely. It is perhaps the most beautiful town in the world. Its population is between thirty-eight and forty thousand."[4] Here is the summit of the strange economic-political pyramid of the United Provinces, a republic of traders and navigators from which the Americans take inspiration in drafting their Constitution. Bastard republic at that, forenoon of monarchy. It has its prince, not a king but a "hereditary stadtholder," so honored in deference to his glorious ancestor William of Orange. He is by birth "commander of armies on land and sea,"** but "the republic's ambition is to grow rich and not glorious. The average Dutchman aspires to be a merchant and to have an army no larger than is necessary to defend his borders, a navy sufficient to maintain and develop trade." The stadtholder, then, is something of a figurehead general, deluged with honor and mocked behind his back. "By restricting this office to one single family, it seems to me [Diderot] that they have discovered the secret of how to preserve a long succession of incompetents at the head of their fighting forces."[5] The "reigning" stadtholder, as they call him, of these past thirty years has the drooping look of an adjutant; he attends only to the leftovers: "He is fond of soldiering and whatever relates to it. He leads his troops in maneuvers and drills them in the Prussian manner."† He is married to a niece of Frederick the Great, "very pretty," Sade comments; "she dresses like a man, rides horseback, drives a carriage. They say she has inherited some of the militaristic traits of her forebears."[6] The House of Orange being thus relegated to a minor role, neither the stadtholder not his wife has heard a word about the Mirabeau affair. This has been the exclusive concern of the Duc de La Vauguyon, Louis XVI's ambassador, and Grand Pensioner Van Bleyswick, otherwise known as the prime minister, who holds the reins of power in a country whose leaders are honest enough to call themselves "pensioners" (one to each province and also one per large city), "a key post deriving its title from the pension paid as a salary to the incumbent."[7] In this democracy of money, an unconventional, unproductive couple is about to be crushed by the base of the pyramid, Amsterdam's magistrates, whose opinions the grand pensioner was obliged to solicit during the few days when Gabriel and Sophie thought no one was looking. Each province is sovereign; their deputies constitute the States-General, known to all the courts of Europe as "High and Mighty Lords."‡ "A deputy is invariably a rich landowner†† . . . He makes no

*That is, delegates from each of the seven provinces of the Lowlands.
**40,000 soldiers and twenty men-o'-war in 1777.
†The French will depose him following the "Batavian Revolution" and he will die in Germany in 1806. His son will mount the throne in 1815 as William I, the first king imposed on the Netherlands by the Holy Alliance.
‡Except the King of Spain, who still regards them as offshoots of rebellious beggars and addresses them simply as "Messieurs."
††And Diderot adds: "This seems only fair, since private interests always determine patriotic

decision without first referring it to his town and without the town submitting it to the local diet."[8] "Each town is a private republic governed according to its own laws, conventions, customs, by vote of the majority and without distinction as to civil status: that is the democratic side; the nobility looks after the safety of the region: that is the aristocratic side."[9] There is latent rivalry between these democratic tradesmen and military patricians, the latter forever bent on "puffing" the stadtholder to win his support. Mirabeau has alienated fellow aristocrats because of his ties to "republicans," as the partisans of liberty were known in Holland, whose good will he has also forfeited: the presence of an outlaw made them uncomfortable. From start to finish, every nut and bolt in the well-oiled Dutch machine betrayed him. The grand pensioner declares, on the afternoon of the 13th, before the assembled "High Powers," that there is cause to take into secret custody "in Rotterdam or Amsterdam" these two persons "charged with crimes in their native land . . . while acting with all due precaution." This, to make sure the pair does not go underground. First stage: they will have a hearing; they will be confined. In the second stage, after several days the grand pensioner will submit a report to the States-General "urging their release to the law officer charged to repatriate them." Immediate decision unprefaced by any debate: orders are issued to the bailiffs and magistrates of those two ports to seize the delinquents "if they can be found."[10] The wheels turn relentlessly, noiselessly.

The "delinquents" have yet to go into hiding. They have stayed right where Bruguières told the ambassador they were—who told the grand pensioner, who told the chief bailiff of Amsterdam . . . Still the same day as this decision, May 13, 1777, the French-language *Gazette d'Amsterdam* carries a piece of news that could set them dreaming. It is the first mention in any European publication of a young man who has had an astounding streak of good luck this spring: "The Marquis de La Fayette, who, for some time and without seeking royal approval, planned to sail to America and serve as a volunteer in the rebel army but was ordered at Saint-Sebastian to cancel his voyage and has since received royal sanction to travel for five months,* has taken the opportunity to ship out from Bordeaux, transfer to his own vessel moored at Saint-Sebastian, and continue on to America."[11]

In fact the *Victoire* has been at sea for three weeks, and once out, La Fayette had ordered the captain to head directly for the United States, not the Windward Islands.

---

feeling. A man who owns nothing and is able to carry all his possessions on his back has no homeland."

*This "dispatch" contains four erroneous details, the worst of which is the alleged "royal sanction." It illustrates the substitution of gossip for fact typical of the last quarter of the eighteenth century.

This man has defied the law and got away with it, escaped all that is about to come tumbling down on Mirabeau.

May 14, 1777. Yes, burgomaster, yes, chief magistrate, the Comte and Comtesse de Saint-Mathieu still reside on the street corner where the Kalverstraat intersects St. Lucy's Lane. But they seem a bit jumpy lately. In and out all the time. The count is trying to hire a carriage. Maybe the inquiry we made yesterday has alarmed them. Better not delay too long . . .

No time is wasted. The bailiff, flanked by magistrates Bicker and Ooster, appears at dusk at the front door. They find Sophie "making last-minute preparations to flee." Alone. Gabriel is in town with "friends"* and she is supposed to join him there so they won't be seen leaving together. He finally bestirred himself, but to what avail? "Out of senseless timidity, I waited too long to approach my friends, and they warned me to settle my debts at once; but it was too late. The very day I was arrested, people predicted on three different occasions that it would come to pass the next day. Fatal error! . . . That same night we had planned to escape." Without money? Just like that? Together, they might have tried it; alone, he lacks the courage born of desperation. "I knew she had been arrested. I never hesitated as to what course I must take. I felt compelled, both emotionally and morally, to be happy or unhappy with her. I gave myself up."[12] He appears, pale and puffy-eyed, like a ghost the investigators—and perhaps even Sophie—never expected to see.

An act that stands to his credit—for the moment. Sincere? Unquestionably. For the moment.

MIRABEAU FILS

74

MAY 1777

The Wretch Is in Irons

On May 13 a great reception took place at the Trianon Palace, a third (unconvincing) attempt to marry off Joseph II. A tiny bundle of nubile femininity, Madame Elizabeth, appeared before him smothered in satin and lace. If he had any taste at all for nymphets, she was no worse than many another and curtsied admirably. It would be a dream come true for Marie Antoinette and Maria Theresa to have a sister of Louis XVI wed the Emperor Joseph. A doubly

*Impossible to identify. Perhaps Freemasons.

cemented alliance. "This well-organized party became delightful, owing to the queen's gracious behavior. The king added a note of cheer and, to the extent his demeanor permits, appeared attentive to the emperor."[1] But nothing could ever come of this: Joseph is three times the girl's age and not inclined to remarry. His sexual preferences run to casual encounters with experienced, fleshy, and coarse prostitutes. As for the tiny princess, her all-girl world is an effort to redeem the loss of her sister Clothilde, who became the wife of the Prince of Piedmont two years before. Elizabeth had reacted with hysterical fits that frightened the court. To console her, her closest friend, Angélique de Mackau, a "little angel" of fifteen, is being married to a Bombelles in order for her to qualify as lady in waiting to the princess, who writes her after the wedding: "At last my wishes are granted and you are mine! How sweet it is to know that one more bond unites us! "

A waste of time. Sardinia's ambassador informs his foreign minister: "The emperor, who was not unacquainted with the many rumors alleging his projected marriage to Madame Elizabeth, has let it be known to Their Most Christian Majesties and to the whole royal family that he did not care to remarry."[2]

Despite this, he continues to act as "technical adviser" to his sister in matters of the bedchamber. Up to now the discussions have been with her alone, but tonight, at Trianon, Louis XVI shows signs of domesticity. It took him a month, his own sweet time. "The king confessed distress privately to His Imperial Majesty at having no children; he went into precise details about his physical condition and sought the emperor's advice."[3]

The next day "His Imperial Majesty" embarks on a cunningly disguised outing designed to approach a lady who attracts him far more than the little doll they wanted to stick him with for life: Europe's sovereigns were jealous of Louis XV's later years. Here is one sovereign "determined to see what their eyes have never seen and were so eager to see": that Du Barry woman. The pretext: traveling west from Versailles, what harm can it do to visit the great and small stables? And while at it, why not ride as far as the hillside overlooking the Seine to admire the famous Marly waterworks without which no fountains would play in the gardens of Versailles? The emperor's mind seems to wander as engineers explain the function of those giant wooden wheels, the pumps, the holding basins, the mains that crack and groan and gurgle for a quarter of a league to raise water five hundred feet from the river below. He cuts them short. They drive a short distance along a narrow path through the woods, to Luciennes (or Louveciennes, as it was also known), where Claude-Nicolas Ledoux, the architect now building a utopian community in the salt marshes of Franche-Comté, first proved himself five years earlier by designing a jewel: a pavilion for the king's mistress, slightly smaller but more cheerful than the Petit Trianon. It seems as if it would fit into the palm of your hand, yet sleeps twenty. The terrace overlooks a bend in the river and the countryside beyond. "The mantelpieces and doors were richly carved; the locks and metal fixtures were marvels of craftsmanship. The clocks, candelabra, and bronze ornaments were creations of the celebrated Gouthière."* A faint aura of sexuality hovers here. "All the paintings and sculptures represent sensual subjects; one might take it for the temple of lust . . . In every room Louis XV faces his mistress, sometimes as a medallion, sometimes as a bust or portrait . . . One drawing room depicts high points in the career of this royal mistress: her first appearance before the king, then in the arms of Louis the Beloved, and finally her presentation at court in robes of state."⁵ Like the lives of the saints unfolding on cathedral walls. Guardians of this temple, the countess's servants stand at the doors and windows; they feign dismay at the approach of "a distinguished-looking German traveler, Count von Falkenstein," then take him on a guided tour. But who is the solitary stroller seemingly caught by surprise on the pathway? It is the White Lady of the old monarchy who outreigned even Marie Leczinska. Du Barry. Her exile lasted but three short years, the time it took for Marie Antoinette to bury her resentment. Her progress from banishment to Louveciennes has been by leaps and bounds: a year in sumptuous quarters at the abbey of Pont-aux-Dames; a year in her newly acquired Château de Saint-Vrain near Montargis, where she entertained an average of twenty-five dinner guests. Then permission came for her to return here, an hour from Versailles. She is thirty-four, her beauty unmarked by grief. Her "widow-hood" is well cushioned by the "favors" she grants the Duc d'Aiguillon, the Prince von Ligne, and, more recently, lest she waste away, the Duc de Brissac. Dropping his alias, Joseph offers his arm for a tour of the park to this gay and blooming beauty, the kind of woman he appreciates. The antithesis of his mother. She simpers.

"Don't refuse me, madam. Beauty is always queen."

Gabriel and Sophie have been taken into custody in Amsterdam's Verbeeter-huis, but are separated by the full length of that immense, all but windowless building as glacial as the fortress of Joux. She is stunned and contemplates suicide. He grits his teeth, unwilling to accept any situation without a battle.

Initial interrogation, May 15. "The prisoners have declared that no abduction occurred; that the Comte de Mirabeau met Madame de Monnier not in France but in Switzerland, in her bedchamber; that they left the country for Holland, where they have resided for six or seven months** under the adopted name of Saint-Mathieu.

"Madame de Monnier has given no reason to oppose her removal to

---

*The then fashionable goldsmith. These bronze decorations had not been, and never would be, paid for: the king received credit. But as Louis XVI refused to honor Louis XV's debts on behalf of Madame du Barry, Gouthière went bankrupt and died in poverty.⁴
**Actually, ten days short of eight months.

France . . . but the Comte de Mirabeau has maintained that, having committed no crime, he should not be handed over to the official who has come here to take him back; and that he was prepared to return to France with assurance of safe conduct from the king."[6] In other words, he falls back on the same absurd logic that he resorted to in Provence when his debts first got him into trouble: appeal to the throne for a *lettre de cachet* to protect him from the law of the land. First, however, he wishes to protest to the States-General to gain time in the hope that his "friends" will intervene. This irritates the magistrates of Amsterdam, who insist on seeing a financial statement first. In twenty-four hours Gabriel dashes off a statement in which he is plainly banging his head against a wall: he argues "that his father's prestige alone determined the steps taken by the French government, and that his father is acting out of an unjustifiable hatred toward him."[7] Did they even bother to read it? The "High Powers" had no interest in the tangled relations between father and son; all they wanted to ascertain was the latter's financial solvency. The Duc de La Vauguyon shrewdly pledges to pay the prisoners' debts—and be reimbursed later by their families—if the extradition procedure is speeded along. It is, with rare rapidity: on May 17, 1777, the States-General sitting in The Hague "takes note of the declaration submitted by deputies of the City of Amsterdam, according to which they have consented to surrender the above-named persons, for particular reasons relevant to their circumstances, and without compromise now or ever to the rights and privileges of the City of Amsterdam." The government thus authorizes "the surrender of the afore-mentioned persons . . . to police officials of the City of Paris dispatched for that purpose."[8]

May 18, Amsterdam: the prisoners in the Verbeeterhuis are notified of the sentence of "surrender." They will be "transported" shortly. Let them chew their nails in the meantime. May 20, Paris: police officers appear at the Mirabeau house on the Rue de Seine, take the marquise into custody, and, over her protests, place her under house arrest with the nuns of the convent of Saint-Michel—by royal decree stemming from her recent scandalous behavior. It is one of the triumphant moments in the elder Mirabeau's life: "M. de Maurepas arranged things in the king's presence and before a commission composed of himself, the keeper of the seals M. Amelot,* and M. de Sartines. He [Maurepas] has known me for forty years; he is acquainted with the vexations and the nonsense I have had to put up with for fifteen of them; he has cut formalities to the bone, taken all necessary precautions, and since the other one's** madness and my distress have been all too evident, there was

---

*First chamberlain of the king's household (successor to Malesherbes) and empowered to issue *lettres de cachet.*

**The "other one" is his wife, who has just obtained from the royal magistrates a legal award rejected by the king only a week after their ruling.

no cause to delay."[9] Having just learned that his son is now in custody, he is bursting with excitement: "I was informed yesterday that the wretch is in irons . . . I wish it had been possible to turn the rascal over to the Dutch so that they could ship him off to the nutmeg colonies,* never to return, for no one does . . . So I locked him up, though everyone advised me against it and urged me to let him work out his own destiny, as the saying goes . . . My conscience warned me that apart from the crime he goes about sowing like weeds, this destiny inevitably would be to ruin our family name . . . For such a fellow, the worst fate would be to become an honest man; he would rather slit his own throat; but things have not gone that far yet."[10]

The marquis has even won a triple victory, having also obtained a *lettre de cachet* against his daughter. Louise de Cabris is commanded to leave Paris and return to the convent of La Déserte in Lyons. But this does not satisfy her father, who would like to see her in prison, too. "As long as I have not put her behind bars, I have done nothing. She is the moving force behind this band of thieves . . . She never gives up. Hers is the stuff of eternal damnation."[11]

The emperor accelerates his daily schedule. He wants to wind things up, fold his tents and be off by the month's end. A meeting of the Académie Française with D'Alembert holding forth, more shriveled than ever now that he has found out about the passionate love affair between Julie de Lespinasse and Guibert. "She died once for all the world and twice for me." But this grieving man, who seems to have lost everything there is to lose, bows and scrapes before the enlightened despot as if he might gain something thereby. "M. d'Alembert began with a number of new synonyms, including: Arrogance, Pride, Disdain, Simplicity, and Modesty; this gave him a chance to embroider on some of the merits of our august traveler." Joseph withstands the deluge of praise, knowing of Frederick the Great's admiration for D'Alembert, which is reason enough to listen to him now, but he fidgets under torrents of florid eloquence from the two ensuing speakers. "If one is to believe M. de La Harpe, our august visitor was somewhat distraught during M. Marmontel's address; and if one is to believe the latter, he was no less affected by that of M. de La Harpe."[12] In a single day the emperor reviews a parade of the greatest artists of the day: Pigalle, Pajou, Houdon, Coustou, Greuze, and Vernet. Without comment. Because he was advised to do so. "To save time and energy, I had to refuse all non-essential invitations. There is an abundance of acquaintances I felt compelled to forfeit."[13] When it comes to politics, however, he lacks neither intuition nor memory. Three or four names crop up in connection with his last discussions at court, key names for the present and perhaps the future. He sized up Maurepas as a bantam, sensing that everyone was waiting for that useless little bag of bones to disintegrate and

*Dutch colonies in the Pacific; Java was a major source of nutmeg.

give way to a truly effective prime minister who would resolve the savage rivalry between the Choiseul and Aiguillon factions, waning stars not yet convinced that their former brilliance is forever lost, and rising hopefuls such as the Noailles and Rohan clans. Madame de Guéménée, daughter of Maréchal de Soubise, is married to a Rohan. Her retainers back the Bishop-Coadjutor of Strasbourg, Louis-René de Rohan, a handsome, ostentatious, ambitious "prince of the church" who had served as ambassador to Vienna at the time of Marie Antoinette's marriage. The doddering Cardinal de La Roche-Aymon, Grand Almoner of France, is expected to die any day now and Rohan has been promised the office. But Maria Theresa and her son have taken a dislike to that scheming, womanizing grandee. Joseph sidesteps his request for an audience, thereby supporting the queen's instinctive aversion to that particular member of the Rohan tribe. He does it out of no concern for the country's welfare, however, for shortly thereafter, during his tour of southwestern France, he recommends the appointment of an even more worldly prelate, Loménie de Brienne, Archbishop of Toulouse, a seminary classmate of the Abbé de Mermond, who, with Austrian support, had become official reader to the French queen. For months now Vermond has been extolling Brienne as a financial wizard because he manages the fiscal affairs of his diocese in proper fashion. "His Majesty the Emperor writes that he has developed a very high opinion of the archbishop [of Toulouse]; that he considers him among the most able candidates for office and was urging his august sister to focus the king's attention on him. This advice impressed the queen and she showed the emperor's letter to the king."[14] So there's a stand-by in case the present fiscal administrator stumbles.

But Necker is making good progress for the moment; his Swiss bank effectively underwrites the royal treasury, and he continues to steer clear of internal political strife. But the services of a Protestant will not be appreciated forever.

Time for big brother to move on. The better he gets on with the king, the less his sister likes it. "On the 23rd there was another sharp exchange between the emperor and the queen . . . " On the 27th, in my [Mercy-Argenteau's] presence, a brief dispute arose in which the emperor stood firm." Before five or six other persons, he asserts that if he were Marie Antoinette's husband he would teach her to behave.[15] As a parting gift, he leaves her a long list of instructions spelling out "her two sets of duties: (1) as a wife to her husband; (2) as a queen." Page after pedantic page, in which he acts as her father, her confessor, her prosecutor, never her friend. She probably will not read the whole thing, which rolls on like a bill of indictment: "Do you make yourself necessary to the king? . . . Are you absolutely discreet as to his shortcomings and weaknesses? . . . Is your manner not somewhat too unceremonious? . . . Have you considered the effects of your relations and friend-

ships? . . . Have you weighed the disastrous consequences of gambling?"[16]
He means to be helpful and is simply repeating rumors which go to make up
the current patrician view of the queen. Rather than a gesture of friendship,
Joseph's memorandum is one of abysmal ignorance.

On May 30 the emperor leaves for a long, rambling tour of the provinces.
The good-bys take place at Versailles, close to midnight; brother and sister are
deeply affected. Despite the friction, they care for each other. Joseph finally
shows emotion: "It grieved me to leave Versailles, as I was truly fond of my
sister; there I enjoyed the kind of pleasant life I had long since given up
. . . It took every ounce of strength to drag myself away."[17] As for the queen,
"who tried too hard to keep a cheerful countenance, she suffered a violent
attack of hysterics the following evening"; relieved, saddened, frustrated at
having to choke back her impulses for a month, she will spend a day resting
at Trianon with Mesdames de Lamballe and de Polignac as companions.

Joseph sleeps a few hours and leaves Paris at daybreak, the normal thing
to do when making a journey in long stretches. The last Frenchman to see him
off as he enters his coach is the Abbé de Véri, who, even more than Mercy-
Argenteau, mans the secret communication lines between Hapsburgs and
Bourbons. The emperor is pleased with his "official performance" in Paris and
boasts of it to his brother Leopold: "You put up a better front than I, but I'm
a better charlatan, and in this country that is what you have to be. I can appear
reasonable and modest; I exaggerate a bit and give the impression of being
simple, natural, deliberate, overly so. The enthusiastic response to that really
embarrasses me." But Paris disappointed him. "There are very interesting
things to see, superbly equipped and designed institutions; they build with
astonishing care and luxury; there is great stress on appearance, but if one
looks for utility, the result is disappointing." What he really appreciated were
those servile courtiers who rushed to ingratiate themselves with the House of
Austria: "I found a readiness to speak of secret matters that was both useful
and surprising to me, though I shall take care not to reveal their names."[18]
A good list to lock away in the event of war between France and the Holy
Roman Empire.

75

The Sea Is So Sad

Franklin and Silas Deane were not overly optimistic about La Fayette's escapade. How will the Continental Congress receive this twenty-year-old greenhorn "general" their delegates are about to send them? What if the fool acts rashly just to show off and ends up with a bullet in his head? The Noailles family would love that! At present these two "envoys extraordinary" are still tolerated but ignored by the French court as it waits to see which way the war will go. With some trepidation, they write to the Congress on May 25, 1777, to announce that "the Marquis de La Fayette, a young gentleman of illustrious family and considerable fortune, has sailed for America aboard his own ship, accompanied by several distinguished officers, to serve in our army. He is extremely popular and everyone wishes him well. We can only hope that the reception he receives will make the country and his undertaking agreeable to him. Those who condemn his action as irresponsible still must applaud the spirit behind it, and we would like the courtesies and respect he is shown to facilitate our task here by pleasing not just his influential family and the court but the French nation as well. He has left behind him a pretty young wife, for whose sake chiefly we trust that his valor and his ardent desire to cover himself with glory will be tempered by his general's wisdom so that he risks no more than circumstances demand."[1]

In other words, receive him politely and bundle him up in cotton. But the letter will arrive after La Fayette, who is still "somewhere on the ocean," heavy-hearted, tossed about between two lives, and suddenly aware on May 30 that he has not written a single line to his wife. Perhaps there is time yet; America is not so far away now, and he ought to send word on arrival to poor Adrienne lest she think he has forgotten her.

"On board the *Victoire*, May 30, 1777. I write you from ever so far away, dear heart, and to this cruel separation there is added the dreadful uncertainty of when I shall have word from you. I hope it is soon; among my many reasons for being eager to reach port, none makes me more impatient than that. What fears and anxieties compound the aching sorrow of being separated from all that is dearest to me! How will you have taken my second departure? Will you love me less because of it? Will you have forgiven me? Will you have realized that whatever happened would have taken me from you, to wander idly, ingloriously through Italy with people opposed to my plans and to my way of thinking? These speculations did not spare me a rush of agony in those awful moments when my ship was leaving shore . . .

"Since my last letter, I have been gazing at the most tedious scenery; the sea is so sad, a sadness that we share, I think, it and I. I ought to have arrived by now, but the winds have delayed me cruelly; it will be another week or ten days, I suppose, before I can hope to reach Charleston. That is where I plan to land, and I look forward to it greatly . . .

Now let us speak of more important things: of you, of dear Henriette, and of her brother or sister. Henriette is so delightful that she gives me a fondness for girls. Whichever sex the new baby is, I shall greet it with open arms. Tell me and hasten my joy as soon as it is born. I do not know whether being a father twice over is the cause, but I feel more like a father than ever."[2]

Adrienne de La Fayette is eight months pregnant when he writes those lines. Henriette, their first-born, is fifteen months, and because her "more like a father than ever" had acquired that "fondness for girls" long before, her infrequent gurglings that he might have heard on rare visits home cannot have increased it much. He interrupts the letter and turns again to the small diction-ary he uses to practice his English during interminable spells of bad weather that keep him below deck. Neither the ocean nor his solitude inspires him. Gilbert is a product of the drawing room, and after a week or so his fellow officers' barracks tales bore him to tears. He is seasick from the intricate zigzagging movements of the *Victoire,* a great hulk of timber, tar, and canvas whose captain, for the past month, has used every trick known to the time-honored trade of sailing masters to capture the west winds which prevail at this time of year in the Atlantic and to run against them. They had sailed due south, between the Azores and Spain, in the direction of the Canary Islands, then veered westward into north equatorial waters, and on up past the northern tip of the Leeward Islands: the safest route, for if challenged by a British vessel, they could always claim to be on their way to the French Cape.*

Following the tide up through the Antilles would bring them close to Florida; they plan to hug the coast and try to slip past British warships to Charleston harbor, the nearest American port of entry—still far from the battlefront, but the captain could hardly be expected to risk delivering them to Philadelphia. The rest of the journey overland would teach them about the new country.

For the moment, there are six thousand miles to cover: two months on the open sea.

*Cap Haitien in Haiti. [*Trans.*]

76

I Certainly Have Made You Suffer

Sophie and Gabriel will have to wait eight days in the Verbeeterhuis prison before leaving Amsterdam. They are treated decently and denied nothing—except their freedom. The sentence pronounced in Pontarlier has reached Holland: the ax for him, prison for her. Not the crushing blow it would seem, as they hope for "something better." Such a verdict is applied only to commoners; for the nobility, the time-honored accommodation of royal authority protects—or else destroys. Now they hope for the very thing they were fleeing: privileged deportation. With their newly adopted prison mentality, they set about building a special relationship with their jailers. Soften the human wall around you if you cannot leap it.

And Sophie's meek, tear-swollen face would melt a rock. Ambassador de La Vauguyon visits her and seems genuinely distressed to learn what she faces. He offers to help; who can resist the gratitude of a victim? Bruguières joins in, with encouragement from Mirabeau: "Help her, comfort her, keep her from destroying herself." Her silence, like a death wish, is ominous; perhaps she really means to take her own life. Sincerity: Sophie's most appalling trait. Gabriel tells Bruguières that she wears a packet of opium about her neck. The detective lectures her: now that she is pregnant, how can she think of taking the life of their child, living witness to the year together they have managed to snatch from destiny? "Give me the poison and I will let you see the count again, right here." She yields. They are together again—in a cell. Gabriel elicits her promise not to contemplate suicide until the baby is born next winter. "But she also vowed that if by a certain time . . . she had no way and no hope of hearing from or co   nunicating with me, she would escape her bondage and her grief."[1]

Thus begins the indescribable friendship of Sophie and Gabriel with M. de Bruguières. Queer bird, this detective who needs to love and be loved. Self-interest cannot be his motive, even at long range, for only a seer or a fool could predict what Mirabeau's future holds. For the moment, a thankless job awaits him. Bruguières is obliged to escort the despairing couple across Holland, Belgium, and northern France to separate prisons. Out of preference as well as convenience, he would rather travel among friends. He is polite and considerate to Sophie; to Mirabeau, after ten days in prison, he becomes something of an accomplice. Bruguières urges him to pass the time with his pen: write letters to Sophie which he, Bruguières, will deliver personally, and pleas for justice to his mother and the French and Dutch officials. "Give those to me also; I'll see that they get there faster." Each evening Bruguières leaves the Amsterdam prison with Mirabeau's blessings and a packet of letters that he crumples in his fist. He knows it is unwise to tax official eyes and ears with protests that will only discredit the prisoner—not to mention the messenger. He writes instead, on behalf of the captives, to his superior Lenoir, chief of the Paris police, expressing himself with a freedom that indicates secure feelings about his job as well as a readiness to exceed his instructions. The secret agent turns attorney: "May 25, 1777. Sir, I have the honor to inform you that the extradition has been granted and therefore I shall leave with Madame de Monnier and young M. de Mirabeau, with a local police-officer escort, for my different destinations.

"Allow me, sir, to present an argument that strikes me as just and compelling.

"The Marquise de Monnier is the well-born daughter of a president of Parliament, the wife of the presiding magistrate of a sovereign court of law, the court of accounts in Dôle, and related therefore to persons of rank; and it is a stain to have been at Sainte-Pélagie.* The foolish act of running off with a young man is bad but not criminal until it becomes public and people laugh at a young woman of twenty-two deceiving a husband of seventy: her only crime is improper conduct.

"But, sir, old M. de Monnier is blind and half mad, and he loves his wife . . . M. de Monnier is apt to question the propriety of committing his wife to Sainte-Pélagie, a place for prostitutes, a place that dishonors her.

"Finally, sir, he is not the one who issued this order, yet the woman is his wife. Would it not be more fitting if she were placed in a respectable convent—Conflans, for instance, or any other—even if it required an order from the throne?

" . . . As a result, sir, I shall not conduct Madame de Monnier to Sainte-Pélagie without your confirmation. And since I will be traveling through Chauny in Picardy and plan to let her rest there for a day, kindly send your instructions to me care of M. de Matigny, chief of police in Chauny; if I receive

*That is, a stain on a woman's honor to have been imprisoned at Sainte-Pélagie, where Sophie is supposed to go, Bruguières has just discovered. It is in fact "an asylum for fallen women, married or unmarried, from substantial backgrounds, who have disgraced their family or caused a public scandal." Run by nuns and supported by society women, this prison in the Faubourg Saint-Germain ranked midway between Les Madelonettes "for women of high birth" and La Salpêtrière for common whores and the insane.²

none, or if their arrival is delayed beyond an extra day's wait, I will leave for Paris and come to you before conducting the lady to her destination."[3]

Bruguières's charity falls short of paying his share of the journey. Before they leave he has the couple turn over to him the flotsam of their shipwrecks: thirty-five louis,* over one third of which will go for travel expenses, two watches, a walking stick, a sword, pistols, a ring given to Sophie by Mirabeau, gold earrings, laces, and minor items. The whole lot will be deposited with the Paris police: all that remains of the Comte and Comtesse de Saint-Mathieu.

They journey by easy stages, first in clumsy, springless Dutch rattletraps that jolt along like wheelbarrows. Escorted to the border by Dirk Burger, Amsterdam's deputy bailiff, and by an "officer of the peace." Then the trio proceeds by stagecoach through the "Austrian Netherlands" and France, turning eastward into the Oise Valley to reach the ancient village of Chauny, still swarming with monks. The curious threesome passes unnoticed, except perhaps for Gabriel's outsize head; on the road and at each relay station they melt into the stream of ordinary travelers. No chains, no constraints. Bruguières is really not a bad sort; he promises to help them in Paris or wherever they are sent and even manages to cheer up Mirabeau, who christens him "Pylades."** Dry-eyed, Sophie bears her sorrow with dignity. They cannot hope to escape now; all avenues are blocked. They have gambled and lost. A faint tinge of emotional release colors their fatalism, as if they had set a nutshell adrift on the ocean. Knowing they will be separated, they vow that nothing worse can happen and act as if they believe it. At each stage of the journey they rent a room for three: Bruguières lets them take the double bed and retreats to the far alcove—but Gabriel's exhibitionism won't let him ignore the joys of the flesh.

It had been winter two weeks earlier when the trap snapped shut. Now as they enter France at the end of May, summer bursts, hot and choking. Dust from the roads clings to their skin. They had all but forgotten those fierce cloudbursts that fail now to water down the chalklike soil. It seems as if they have turned their backs forever on the sea. The continental climate is a foretaste of prison.

No news at Chauny from Lenoir. On to Paris, where they arrive on June 6, tense with uncertainty and spent from the heat. Skirting the northern fringe of the city along a short stretch of the Rue du Temple, they pass into the suburbs and along the Boulevard du Temple, where Bruguières lodges next door to a *guinguette* or country dancehall converted to a *café* when the word became fashionable: the Café Caussin. He leaves them in his flat and goes off to make inquiries. Evidence that he trusts them—also that they are exhausted. They have no energy to flee. Their spirit is broken.

---

*Today 3500 francs [$700].

**Faithful companion of Orestes in the tragic saga of the House of Atreus. Mirabeau was obsessed with that legend and had similarly baptized Briançon.

"Pylades" returns from the police chief's office beaming like a Cheshire cat. "Good news, friends, good news!" M. de La Vauguyon also has interceded in Sophie's behalf. Secretly, Jean-Charles Lenoir was delighted to relent. He abominates the Friend of Man and anyone remotely connected with Turgot: all those physiocrats and economists who made trouble in 1775 with their grain laws and then blamed Lenoir for doing nothing during the riots, which had cost him a year's disgrace. He tends to wink at morals charges when persons of rank are involved. Lenoir is no one's fool; this girl who deceived an old man arouses his sympathy, as Bruguières had guessed.[4] No, they will not send her to Sainte-Pélagie; instead, she can lodge with Mlle Douai on the Rue de Charonne and enjoy the good country air of Mesnil-Montant. A kind of "private prison" with all the comforts of home—which her parents must pay for. And Gabriel will keep that oversize head of his. Only in effigy is a nobleman beheaded for a crime of passion. He will go to the dungeons of Vincennes, like Diderot, like all the celebrated men of his time. He should consider it a favor. A promotion of sorts. A distinction. An honor. "Good news!"

"God save my friends from the king's mercy," sighed Sir Thomas More when informed that Henry VIII graciously had ordered him beheaded instead of hanged. Mirabeau says nothing; neither does Sophie, who is pale, speechless, deaf, and blind. For these lovers it is the moment of truth. Never before have they lived so intensely one through the other. Her silence is an effort to conserve her energy for survival. Gabriel has been in poor health for months, flare-ups of congenital ailments that never were properly treated in boyhood: kidney trouble, blurred vision, and, worse still, hemorrhages induced by fits of anger or grief. Bruguières hurries them along; he is anxious to get it over with. No public servant should be compelled to witness such suffering. The carriage to Vincennes is waiting, the coachman grows impatient. Mirabeau bleeds from the nose like a front-line casualty, which in fact he is. Turning to Sophie, he stammers, "I certainly have made you suffer."[5]

Her last glimpse of him is that blood-smeared face.

77

This Liberty That I Worship

" . . . The days pass; worse still, they resemble one another. More sky, more water, and the next day brings the same. Indeed, people who write volumes about ocean voyages must be heartlessly effusive, for I have known winds as unfavorable as any, I have endured gales . . . Well, I have seen nothing remarkable enough to write about."[1] No, La Fayette is definitely unreceptive to the romance of the sea.

On June 7, 1777, afraid that his "voyager's letter" to his wife will seem too short—less than a page per week—he resumes his narrative with a sigh. "I am still on this dreary plain, which is incomparably tedious. To console myself, I think of you and my friends. I think how pleasant it will be to see you again . . . " In self-defense, he repeats that he was appalled at the prospect of being dragged off to Italy as if to cure him of some undesirable girl. He argues with considerable persuasion; his cause is an endless source of inspiration to him. "As a defender of this liberty that I worship, and personally freer than anyone in coming as a friend to offer my services to this interesting republic, I bring nothing but genuine good will, no ambition, no selfish interest; in working for my glory I work for their happiness. I hope that on my account you will become a good American: it is natural for the pure in heart to feel thus. The fortune of America is bound up with the fortune of mankind."

Several days later he feels the relief that Christopher Columbus felt: "Today we see several kinds of birds, whose presence promises that we are nearing the coast . . . Good night; it is getting too dark to go on writing; for the past few days I have prohibited any light on board—see how prudent I am!"[2] Nighttime was in fact the time of greatest danger. The *Victoire* had only two guns, and strong winds from the Bahamas drove her close to the Florida coast, dangerously close to British vessels blockading the approach to southern ports. They would have to try to slip past the mobile barrier dividing the American mainland from the Leeward Islands, which they no longer could claim to have missed. Like the Roman general he was training to become, La Fayette had given an order to Captain Le Boursier which the latter was resolved not to carry out: blow the vessel up rather than surrender her. Better to steal past the enemy under cover of darkness.

"Land ho!" on the morning of June 13. But whose land? They navigate by compass with preposterous maps, and even though certain that Spanish-owned Florida is behind them, they have no idea what port they are entering. The flat shoreline is an interminable stretch of alluvion deposited over millions of years between the Allegheny Mountains and the Atlantic, one of the longest littoral plains on the entire continent. They are desperate to find some little covelike shelter from British guns. Charleston had been their target, but the winds have driven them past it. Finally, around midday, they sight a bay at the mouth of a river. An arm of land dotted with a dozen or so wooden fishermen's shanties is all that separates the *Victoire* from the the Atlantic. The big ship is not so conspicuous once her sails are furled. Kalb, always a reliable observer, reports two days later to his wife that they have landed at "North Island, at the entrance to the Bay of Georgetown, fifteen miles from that city, a port named South Inlet, in Carolina." Two-hundred-year-old towns in this country bear the names of English monarchs; quite by chance they have dropped anchor off George's rather than Charles's town. But Carolina (South Carolina in this instance, from which North Carolina has seceded under pressure from powerful Virginia) or, more accurately, the Carolinas were so named by French immigrants sent there by Admiral de Coligny shortly before the St. Bartholomew's Massacre. Two centuries before La Fayette, a Huguenot sailor from Dieppe, Jean Ribaut, had settled a fort, long since vanished, and named it Fort Caroline in honor of Charles IX, who was preparing to slaughter his fellow Huguenots. Charles of England then took over the region and the name of its principal port. Subsequently it was never quite clear whose economic or political influence prevailed. Which staple crop should grow there, and who should reap it? Indigo, rice,* tobacco, or cotton? For Britain, Spain, France, or the Indians? A region "up for grabs." The outcome, however, as everyone predicted, ultimately would depend on mass "importation" of African slaves, as it has been "observed that the warm, humid climate of South Carolina suited the Negro; he lived there and multiplied rapidly whereas white laborers died of fever; so the ambition of every emigrant from the day he arrived was to buy slaves, without whom no planter could grow anything. They tried Indians and Negroes, but soon found the former intractable and the latter amenable to servitude. They were as different, people said, as wild and domesticated animals."[3]

The first human beings La Fayette meets in America therefore are black. As the *Victoire* cannot enter shallow waters, Gibert, Kalb, and several other officers climb into a longboat manned by seven oarsmen and spend the afternoon rowing up the mysterious little inlet, at the end of which naked blacks gathering oysters signal that a town is near. They row on, straining against the

*From seeds accidentally imported from Madagascar in 1698.

incoming tide. Once it begins to ebb, they can go no farther. Suspicious at first, the blacks simply stand and watch the newcomers struggle. At length they condescend to explain as best they can that their master is a "pilot," a "lord," an English "officer" who lives at the far tip of the sandy island, well outside the "town," like some solitary godling guarding the river. They offer to conduct several of the strangers there in a flat-bottom boat. Darkness has fallen suddenly along with the wind. In the stifling night, mosquitoes devour them as they glide through the bullrushes. La Fayette and two companions surrender to the "noble savages," who deposit them on a beach from where they can see the lights of a house. They approach and knock at the door, which unleashes a chorus of fierce yelps. Shutters open just wide enough for gun muzzles to slide through: the tenants take them for British or Indian intruders.

Kalb the German speaks English; he shouts that they are French and want to become Americans. Cheers ring out.

They are welcomed with open arms "to the summer residence of Major Benjamin Huger, a highly respected South Carolinian who greets them warmly and with cordial hospitality."[4] A fairy-tale ending to the nightmare. La Fayette is pampered and indulged by a swarm of little boys and girls and servants. Never will he forget that first night of life in the New World, the cool room with a big bed enveloped in mosquito netting and, next morning, the lush greenery fairly exploding in the blistering sunshine outside the wooden house.* Of course he adapts readily to the supreme comfort he discovers in the land of liberty: slavery.

No purpose in traveling up to Georgetown anyway, a dull place whose shallows would be inaccessible to the *Victoire*. La Fayette, Kalb, and their companions go on to Charleston by land, with Major Huger leading the way. A pilot dispatched by the major will help the *Victoire*'s captain guide her back along the coast to Charleston in the estuary formed by the confluence of the Ashley and Cooper rivers, which enclose it like a jewel case.

The expedition becomes less cheerful crossing this virgin wilderness where hardly a mile at a stretch is bare. An eerie silence reigns over the strange world of riotous vegetation. The ocean is still too close for them to find lush forests. Trees rise from the mud and offer poor shade; "bald cypresses," whose limbs could be branches or eruptive roots, form impenetrable thickets, like giant porcupines to be circumvented. Their only respite is passage through an occasional forest of "swamp pines" that gives the four Frenchmen on foot a chance to catch their breath, as Major Huger has not been able to provide horses for everyone. During the long march they become acquainted, a novel experience for European aristocrats. Only La Fayette, Kalb, and Huger ride horses; even in miniature, the caste system applies. The others trudge along in the same clothes they wore on board ship, having nothing to change into.

*The same latitude as Bermuda, Madeira, and Marrakech.

Charles-François du Buysson, Kalb's friend, a young officer of petty nobility in search of fame and promotion, reflects on his shattered illusions: "After three days of marching, thus did we arrive at Charles-town [sic] looking like beggars and thieves. We were received accordingly"—they, the hikers, whom the three well-intentioned horsemen had sent on ahead into town to knock at doors and receive a hero's welcome—"having fingers pointed at us by the local populace after announcing that we were French officers come only for glory and to defend their liberty." Huger's welcome had created a false impression, for he was an exception to the traditional colonial distrust of the French who had been claiming the land for two centuries, often with Indian aid. "We were treated like highwaymen even by the French, who are numerous in Charles-town, most of them hopeless debtors or men dismissed from the ranks. Many come from French colonies.* The [French] governors get rid of as many undesirables as they can . . . by giving them letters of recommendation to Anglo-American [sic] generals. The first batch was well received, but as their conduct revealed them for what they were, no one trusts letters of recommendation anymore and today in America people avoid their bearers."[5]

False alarm. The damage is quickly repaired, even as to the weary hikers mistaken for buccaneers. After Major Huger introduces "a real Frenchman from France" in the person of La Fayette, the gentry of this pretty little town puts itself out to welcome him and his companions, who seem refreshingly different from the human dregs previously cast up on these shores. Charleston is a hundred years old—people are beginning to spell its name this way, in conformity with local pronunciation—at least the "new" Charleston is. Its colonists shifted it several miles toward the coast after discovering that the earlier settlement was standing chiefly on silt. It is the New York of the South, minus New York's accessibility to ships: the *Victoire* arrives the same day as La Fayette, but remains well outside the narrow mud-bound anchorage. Ten to twelve thousand Whites, twenty thousand Negroes. A blend of trade and leisure: settlers journey here from the interior in summer to enjoy the sea air and to cure the effects of miasmatic rice paddies. Tar and pitch from pine forests are piling up at the docks because of the British blockade. Welcome, Frenchmen! The traditional foe becomes number-one friend, whom they eagerly clasp to their bosoms. Du Buysson cannot understand it: insulted and rejected in the morning as Frenchmen from the islands; heroes in the evening, Frenchmen from France, compatriots of La Fayette, "whose reception would be worthy of a French general."[6] Thus, Gilbert's first letter from America to his "dear heart" overflows with optimism: "Simple manners, a desire to please, patriotism and love of liberty, a sense of equality reigns here universally"— the universe to which he is accustomed, of course, and which receives him as an honored guest: the one hundred or so prominent families who rule Charles-

*That is, the totality of French possessions in the New World, all relatively close together: Santo Domingo, the Antilles, and Guiana.

ton society, as is the case in every other southern city of America. La Fayette fails to mention the African slaves or the thousands of indentured Europeans brought here under contracts no better than slavery, the only difference being that they have sold themselves whereas the slaves were abducted. Why should he speak of it? He was brought up never to notice such persons. In describing a town to his wife, would he mention dungheaps outside the door? Having come to champion paradise, paradise is what he finds: "The richest and poorest of men are equal, and though there are some immense fortunes in this land, I challenge anyone to discover the slightest difference in their behavior to one another . . . The city of Charleston is among the handsomest, the most attractively laid out, and the most gracious that I have seen. American women are exceedingly pretty, simple, and charmingly well scrubbed . . . What delights me here is that all citizens are brothers.* In America there are no beggars and no persons of the class we call peasants. Every citizen owns his own property and all enjoy the same rights as the most powerful landowner. The inns are not like those in Europe: here the proprietor and his wife sit down with you and preside over an excellent table, and upon leaving, you pay without bargaining . . . " "To have come with me is the guarantee of a warm reception. I have just spent five hours at a dinner given in my honor by a resident of this city . . . We drank toasts and mumbled our English, which I am finally beginning to be able to speak a little. Tomorrow . . . I shall settle arrangements for our departure."

That was no small problem: a thousand miles to Philadelphia through the southern and central states. The route had to be mapped out, addresses and introductions obtained for the principal stopovers, horses purchased as well as traveling clothes and provisions for the journey. Not so very difficult, it would seem, but La Fayette, a man of great wealth in France, suddenly finds himself penniless due to inexperience. Until he left Paris his financial affairs had always been handled by stewards—his own, his aunts', or his father-in-law's. In Bordeaux he had had to work out a secret contract with the shipowners. And he was very proud of having thought up what seemed to him a good way to keep going in America: by selling off the *Victoire*'s cargo. But with aristocratic abandon he had signed (unread) a sort of promissory note for forty thousand livres** payable to Captain Le Boursier as warranty for the cargo, which the captain was free to sell if he so chose. Haunted by the British menace, Le Boursier cannot wait to leave for Santo Domingo, where he has other trading business. They quarrel and part ways. La Fayette wastes a week negotiating a

*Laws governing slavery in the Carolinas and Virginia sanctioned the on-the-spot killing of any Negro found "outside his plantation without a pass from his master." If charges were brought against a slave, even for stealing a chicken, a justice of the peace ordered the offender arrested and brought before a "jury of property-owners" who, by majority vote, could sentence him to death.

**Today 200,000 francs [$40,000].

loan of thirty-five thousand livres from these hospitable colonists at a horrendous interest rate of twenty percent. His only collateral is his signature. Fortunately, a good many French settlers in Charleston can vouch for the solvency of the Noailles family.

All is ready on the morning of June 25, when the little band sets out on the long journey to Philadelphia.

78

JUNE 1777

To Claim by Force of Arms One's Sacred Rights

Politics, science, or medicine? Poland, like Dupont de Nemours; England, on the brink of revolution; Holland, Prussia, or France? This month Jean-Paul Marat chooses medicine in France, as a bird chooses a branch or a single season's nesting place. He is a bachelor and determined never to tie himself to any woman or master. He is thirty-four.

The nest is comfortable and worth trying after a string of flea-ridden furnished rooms in Switzerland, France, and England: Marat is to become physician to the guardsmen of one of the king's brothers. A sinecure after the storm; many others would call it a haven. Such an opportunity doesn't knock twice. His benefactress was the Marquise de Laubespine, whom he had cured recently of a near-fatal lung disorder. They had tried in vain "essence of snails and frogs," followed by goat's milk, which compounded the patient's suffering by adding "intestinal diarrhea" to her "pulmonary consumption." At that point the young woman was told of a doctor, "an English subject [*sic*] who had recently restored several hopeless pulmonary cases to life"[1] and was currently trudging back and forth between Paris and Versailles in search of a stable practice. After thorough examination of the patient's sputum, Marat obtained rather dramatic results with a mixture of sweet almond extract and sodium nitrate, and an artificial mineral water of his own invention with properties similar to the "acidulated waters of Harrowgate." A foreign physician enjoyed special favor, being thought to possess mysterious cures. Promiscuous as all the other pretty young women who fluttered about the Comte d'Artois, this marquise welcomed the new doctor and his treatment; Marat, with his Sardinian looks, his deep, soulful eyes, his large, voracious mouth, pounced on the opportunity. His patient made astounding progress.

Which led to the royal appointment issued "this 24th day of June, 1777, by order of His Highness the Comte d'Artois in Versailles: upon reports of the good character, learning, and medical experience of M. Jean-Paul Marat, holder of degrees from several British medical faculties, as a mark of favor, His Highness has granted and does hereby grant him the office of Guards' Physician, desirous that said M. Marat shall enjoy all honors, privileges, and emoluments attached thereto and shall be so designated in all official and unofficial records."[2]

Each of Louis XVI's brothers had his own little "military household," of no use whatever except for display: a company each of Swiss Guards, of "guards at the door," of bodyguards, all noblemen: a paradise for parasites. Marat was number eleven of a string of physicians serving the Comte d'Artois: "court" physicians, "consulting physicians, and "duty" physicians (that is, serving in rotation). He would be required to look after two or three hundred robust fellows in the pink of health. Annual salary: two thousand livres.* A fine apartment is assigned to him on the Rue de Bourgogne in Paris, near the Bourbon Palace, where he may receive his patients in style. His problems are solved.

Has he even met the prince? Probably not, but will do so later at some official reception. While Marat's appointment is taking shape, Artois is off touring Normandy and Brittany, making so many blunders and looking so foolish that they will think twice before parading him through another province. Lately he has ordered "365 pairs of shoes and 365 pairs of buckles in order to wear different ones each day."[3] He particularly enjoyed Saint-Malo, where a mock naval battle was staged in his honor and, incidentally, to remind the British of French sea power now that rumors of war are spreading. "From atop the bastion of the powder magazine," a disheveled boy of nine peers down at "the young prince amid the crowd on the shore: in his glory and my obscurity, how unknown were the workings of fate!"[4] This is François-René de Chateaubriand, "abandoned to an idle childhood" after being consecrated to the Virgin two years earlier. Why fill a boy's head with learning when he is destined to command the king's navy? "I grew up at home without instruction . . . All the little ragamuffins in town had become my closest friends; I filled the courtyard and the staircases of the house with them. I resembled them perfectly; I spoke their language; I shared their manners and behavior; I was dressed like them, unbuttoned, and unkempt like them . . . My face was smudged, scratched, and bruised, my hands filthy. I looked so odd that my mother broke off scolding me to laugh and exclaim: 'How ugly he is!' "[5]

---

*Today 10,000 francs [$2000]; not a great deal, but there were generous "fringe benefits" including free housing.

Right now Marat is in the prime of his good looks and consciously exploiting them. He wears a sword. He makes vague efforts to discover titled ancestors. An urge for repose perhaps, the sudden fatigue of the *mezzo del cammin'* after two or three worn-out lives. "As long as I held the title of guards' physician to Artois, I retreated to the privacy of my consulting room."[6] This retreat brought increasing numbers of socially prominent "pulmonary cases" to his door. Business is booming; he could easily have specialized in lung disorders. Witness the four-page medical report he writes on a "chevalier"* with "severe chest pains, constant relatively high fevers and who has spat blood for over a year." Marat prescribes a diet before any medication: "Monsieur le Chevallier [*sic*] will carefully avoid any chill in the lower extremities: he will wear cork-soled shoes.

"He will eat no fried, salted, glutinous, or spicy dishes, no pastry, no vermicelli, lasagna, or fish. This also applies to coffee and brandies.

"His diet will consist of roast lamb, veal, beef, poultry, and game, of spinach, lettuce, sorrel, cardoon, salsify, asparagus, turnip, beets, as much or as little as desired, and plenty of boiled potatoes.

"His beverage at table will consist of tealike infusions of Florentine fennel or well-watered Burgundy.

"Monsieur le Chevallier will begin his cure by drinking, upon arising each morning, three glasses of mineral water mixed with a quart of warm milk. He will repeat this four hours after [midday] dinner."[7] The mineral water is Marat's own secret concoction. Then he goes on to prescribe certain pills and sodium-nitrate enemas. The chevalier was astounded at the speed of his recovery. Thinking that a miracle had occurred, he sought to express his gratitude at the foot of the prescription: "After drinking the mineral water** for twenty days, and my lungs having cleared up, he had me take drops of Mecca balsam† in a cup of warm milk. My cure was complete."[8]

"Since the age of sixteen I have been my own master. I lived two years in Bordeaux, ten in London, one in Dublin, one each in The Hague, Utrecht, Amsterdam."[9] Now Marat drops anchor in Paris. For how long? And why has he left England? From writer's disillusion, from political disenchantment. *The Chains of Slavery* had done poorly. He had made the mistake of bringing out

*Impossible to identify. The manuscript is in the Avignon archives and bears the chevalier's illegible signature.

**"M. Marat's artificial anti-pulmonary water" was to undergo chemical analysis in 1780 by the Abbé Teissier, "doctor-regent" of the Faculty of Medicine of the Sorbonne. It turned out to contain "limewater that has been precipitated by a tiny amount of alkaline base."[7]

†"Mecca balsam is a solid white resin much like a sulfate when aged. It is brought from Mecca by returning caravans of pilgrims and Mohammedan traders . . . It comes from the bark of a tree that grows in Arabia Felix . . . It is known to be excellent for healing sores and various other disorders" (*Encyclopédie*).

a second edition, and after turning salesman and touring the countryside from Carlisle to Berwick, from Newcastle to Edinburgh, lecturing to "patriotic societies of the kingdom," he found himself with an appalling overstock on his hands. He became tense: anyone who walked behind him in the street might be a Tory spy. They did indeed exist, for George III's agents kept an eye on political agitators and would have had no trouble tracing Marat, who lodged in furnished rooms or public inns. To assure himself of a sanctuary for the future, he had joined the Freemasons, who welcomed him to their ranks "in London on the 15th of July in the year of light 5774* and the year of Our Lord 1774" and made him "a third-degree Mason as it appears in the Registry of the Lodge of Free and Accepted Masons, duly constituted and assembled at Kings Head, Gerrard Street, Soho." [10]

Another "degree," this time in medicine, would give him social status. Initially, it was his desire for an auxiliary shelter that prompted him to wangle a medical degree from Edinburgh University, also during the summer of 1774, through the offices of two Scots physicians with "advanced" ideas, Dr. Buchan and Dr. James. As to holding degrees "from several British medical faculties" for which the Comte d'Artois's secretary pompously gave him credit, this is sheer invention. But then Marat invents a great deal at this stage of his career, not only because it is a normal tendency for those who become self-reliant too early in life but also out of the need to build a presentable image in the society where he had just begun to make his mark. [11]

His "medical image" linked to his "scholarly image" blossomed that summer in the wake of political setbacks in England. He gave up fiction forever, and pamphleteering temporarily. Toward the close of 1775 he published two medical treatises: *An Essay on Gleet* (blennorrhea, popularly known as "soldier's pox") and *An Inquiry into a Singular Eye Disease* (accidental presbyopia). [12] What connection, if any, is there between venereal disease and eye disease? Marat points to "the irritating effect of mercury" on the circular fibers surrounding the crystalline lens and to the fact that mercury was the accepted cure-all for the "shafts of Venus." In his earliest medical publications he was —occasionally—several hundred years ahead of his time. And he knew it. But they were mere trifles** in comparison to his philosophical/physiological *magnum opus*, a treatise on man that he has nursed along before, during, and after the tremors caused by his *Chains of Slavery* and while completing his doctoral requirements—in short, his major occupation from 1770 to 1775. It allows him to resolve (or think he has done so) all the contradictions and oddities of his intellectual training into one coherent system.

*God the Father was the first Mason; He had created the world exactly four thousand years before the birth of Christ.

**Not to be ignored, however, as they reveal what Professor H. Truc calls "genuine gifts of medical observation and therapeutic expertise, suggesting a thorough knowledge of pathology, physiology, and physics, especially the fields of optics and electricity." [13]

1772, in London, first edition of a 115-page *Essay on the Human Soul.** 1773, again in London, a second edition, substantially enlarged and with a new, less spiritual title more in keeping with the times: *A Philosophical Essay on Man*, subtitled "An inquiry into the principles and laws of the reciprocal influence of body and soul." An attempt to define approximately, in both scientific and philosophic terms, the mystery of human existence. The definitive title appears on the French version, expanded still further and bearing the author's name, J.-P. Marat, M.D.: *De l'Homme, ou des principes et des loix* [sic] *de l'influence de l'âme sur le corps et du corps sur l'âme* [Essay on Man, or principles and laws governing the influence of the soul on the body and of the body on the soul]; three volumes printed by Rey of Amsterdam in 1776, the same year that Rey brought out Mirabeau's *Avis aux Hessois* [Advice to the Hessians].[14] This explains Marat's frequent trips in 1775 and 1776 between England and Holland—where Masons in Mirabeau's Lodge of the Beloved gave him a fraternal welcome. It also explains why he suddenly left London for Paris on April 10, 1776: bundles containing the first edition of his book had been held up between Amsterdam and Rouen, owing to customs regulations rather than censorship. The French censors had no interest in the muddled pronouncements of some "English doctor" about "vital influx," yet Marat was convinced that they were out to ban the book and that British aristocrats in league with Parisian *philosophes* meant to muzzle him. He rushed over to France to promote the book, which he modestly claimed to be "far better than anything I have written thus far."[15] He was only partly successful, for sales were slow and the "publicity campaign" he tried to launch in the gazettes never really materialized. The book had no great impact.

Like many writers, Marat misjudged his own talents. His best work to date is *The Chains of Slavery*, which has vitality and cohesion. The *Essay on Man* is a hodgepodge; for all its bold and imaginative interpretation of numerous observations on "the mechanics of the human organism," it lacks order and restraint and winds up a somewhat pretentious effort at self-instruction. Instead of resolving his conflicts, he compares and contrasts them, thereby assuring himself a life of perpetual inner discord: the physician, the physiologist, and the philosopher wage a three-way struggle for self-expression. The *Essay on Man* reflects Marat's patchwork culture and the gnawing discontent he unconsciously harbored, for he was frustrated as much by his ignorance as by his learning. He attacks the atheism of Helvétius, protesting that "the *philosophes* invented systems instead of using experience as their guide," yet what experience allows him to assert that "man, like every animal, is composed of two distinct substances, soul and body,"[16] and to localize the spiritual seat in the meninges? The book is a jumble of ideas, a forum in which Marat professes a positivist philosophy—"the observation of facts is the sole basis of human knowledge"—only to contradict himself ten pages later with a spiritualist

*A single copy, with no author's name, exists in the British Museum.

doctrine—"the reason for intellectual differences is traceable to the disposition of organs. Impetuous Aeschylus, eloquent Fénelon, sublime Corneille, profound Montesquieu, insignificant Voltaire, indeed all human beings owe the individual twists and turns of their mind to their physical makeup." Fine, but apparently one man has managed to escape the norm and possesses a flawless constitution, the "sublime Rousseau," whom Marat invokes like a saint: "Lend me thy pen to celebrate all these wonders; lend me the enchanting gift to reveal nature in all her beauty . . . "[17] Dr. Marat races back and forth between materialism and idealism, between London and Paris, so to speak, occasionally intuitive, always abrasive. Totally lacking a sense of humor. Proud to discover that man possesses not only "the five senses universally recognized by fools as well as sages," but two more: hunger, which sits in his stomach, and thirst, "which sits simultaneously in the stomach and the esophagus." And the sense of touch is not limited to the skin: "it extends inside the body as well as over its surface. We perceive its sensation in love's gentle embraces and in the fierce pangs of indigestion."[18]

He looked for trouble and found it. "Insignificant Voltaire" lives, feebly, hardly more than a puff of air in snowbound Gex. But the puff, when so inspired, can still deliver an icy blast. Beware! In its issue of May 5, 1777, the *Journal de politique et de littérature* published Voltaire's scathing assessment of Dr. Marat, "a writer imbued with the noble desire to teach all men what they are and to reveal the mysteries they have long sought to explain . . . If a man has nothing better to say than that the soul resides in the meninges, he ought not to make such lavish display of self-contempt as to repel his readers whom he wishes to please . . . M. Marat believes he has discovered that neural fluid is the communication link between the two substances, body and soul. It is indeed a great discovery to have seen with one's own eyes the substance which links matter to spirit . . . " As to the soul's dwelling place, "leave that to the Lord, I beg you; he alone is in charge of accommodations and has not appointed you his quartermaster." "And when at last we have reached the end of this lengthy three-volume declamation, which heralds the absolute understanding of man, we are vexed to find only what has been repeated for three thousand years in as many different languages. It would have made more sense to stick to the description of man given in the second and third volumes of Buffon's *Natural History*,"[19] which had appeared twenty years earlier. That was Voltaire's way of politely perpetrating a slaughter.

The *Essay on Man* did not deserve such rough treatment from so high an authority, and charitable Diderot intervened to try to soften Voltaire's sentence. The book, after all, was an honest if clumsy effort to develop ideas that Buffon had merely stated. Though "Marat does not know what he is talking about" in regard to the action of the spirit on the body, Diderot found him "clear, firm, and precise" with respect to the action of the body on the spirit.[20] But as this roughneck had committed the unpardonable sin of invoking

Rousseau (who carefully avoided taking sides or defending his disciple—whose book he may never have seen), that was mandate enough for excommunication by the *philosophes.*

Marat's pride is hurt, though less than it appears; his scorn for Voltaire is strong enough, weathered enough, to withstand the assault. He composes a blazing rebuttal depicting himself as the victim "of an odious slander," but the reading public will never see it because La Harpe, editor of the *Journal de politique et de littérature,* refuses to print it. Voltaire, yes; Marat, no. When will he get it through his head that he is not in their league?

Marat wastes no time banging at those gates when other gates are yawning: salons close to the court open their doors to him. The Marat-Voltaire dispute was known to a few insiders. In fact, it added luster to Dr. Marat's growing reputation in the Comte d'Artois's circle, where no one dares take issue with the literary gazettes. But this year there are two Marats, just as there are two Beaumarchaises. The split personality is a device employed by certain fringe members of this select society which exploits and humiliates them. Marat grows quite cynical about it: "I like only those cases where there is little to be done and much to be gained."[21] Who would think, to watch this Marat playing the fop, strutting about like a peacock, affecting "studied elegance even as to his toilet,"[22] that another Marat, the same man, dips his pen in acid each evening in his handsome study on the Rue de Bourgogne "decorated with porcelains and well stocked with flowers," surrounded with pictures by Garnerey and Pfeiffer which he has personally chosen? (Marat was always interested in painting.) The vitriolic spark of his *Chains of Slavery* flares up again. The urgent tone noticeably absent from his medical treatises and the *Essay on Man,* the outraged cry of revolt rings out louder than ever in his largely unknown publication of the year 1777: *Plan de législation criminelle.*

Rousseau had written his *Discours sur l'inégalité* for a contest sponsored by the Academy of Dijon. In Marat's case it was an economics club, the Société Economique de Berne, that rekindled his combative fire by offering fifty louis for the best essay on desirable criminal legislation. An announcement of the competition in the *Gazette de Berne* had sparked his interest. The recent execution of Derues horrified him. He had visited the prisons of six nations and over and over had identified with the inmates. There, but for a stroke of luck or courage, go I . . . One of the books at his bedside was a treatise by Beccaria, an Italian reformer, on *Les Délits et les peines* [Legal offenses and their penalties], which took an extremely indulgent position toward criminals and condemned the cruelty of judges.*

Marat more or less repeats Beccaria's arguments and goes much further, progressing from the specific to the general, from an individual to the whole

---

*Published in Milan in 1764 and translated into French in 1770 by the Abbé Morellet. Beccaria, who was forty-two in 1777, had founded in Milan one of the most outspoken intellectual societies in all Italy, called *Il Caffè.*

rotten society. Destroy in order to rebuild. Level in order to equalize. Condemn those who condemn. Crime ultimately stems from one source: the rich oppressing the poor, who must "claim by force of arms the sacred rights of nature . . . For much too long now these hateful tyrants [the rich] have despoiled the earth: their rule will end. Therefore let us dare to approach the sacred precincts where arbitrary power lies entrenched, let us dare to tear aside the somber veil that masks its crimes, let us dare to snatch its deadly weapons ever fatal to innocence and virtue."[23]

This is somewhat different from the mood of political outrage in *The Chains of Slavery*. Here the critique of criminal justice serves to support economic indignation. Hunger, humiliation, and crime, the trinity of this regime, are exposed as indivisible.

THEY make him laugh with THEIR laws. But what a laugh! "Take a look at most of the nations on earth and what do you find? Only vile slaves and imperious masters. Are laws not the decrees of those who rule? As if they bothered to obey their own creations! They silence them at will; they violate them with impunity; then, to shield themselves from blame, they retreat behind sacred enclosures where no one dares follow . . .

"What is a crime? Violation of the law. But are any laws sacred to any government on earth? And can one regard rules as sacred unless each member of the state has had a voice in them? What are called thus are simply the commands of an arrogant master. Their authority therefore amounts to mute despotism imposed by the few upon the many . . .

"As soon as one part of a nation has no voice, [the laws] become partial, and society, in this respect, is merely a state of oppression in which man tyrannizes his fellow man."[24]

Projecting a vision that returns him to his central theme, Marat imagines a thief arraigned before his judges (and doomed to hang in most societies) who speaks thus:

"Am I guilty? I do not know; what I do know is that I have done nothing I ought not to have done. Survival is man's first duty; you yourselves know none more vital; he who steals to stay alive, if he cannot do otherwise, is simply exercising his rights.

"You accuse me of disrupting the social order. Why should I care about this so-called order which has always worked against me? Why should I care if you preach obedience to the law, you whom the law assures dominion over the suffering multitudes, a means to trap victims? Observe the law, therefore, since your prosperity depends on it; but what do I owe society, I who know only its horrors? . . .

"Wretched as we are, if only we could see an end to our suffering; but the poor man's lot is irrevocably fixed, and, barring some stroke of luck, misery is his forever. Who does not know the benefits reaped by those whom fortune favors? They need no talent, no merit, no virtue; the world bows to their will.

To the rich are allotted the great commercial ventures, the outfitting of merchant fleets, the provisioning of armies, the administration of public funds, the exclusive right to loot the state; to the rich are granted the lucrative enterprises, the manufacturing charters, the arming of vessels, the commercial investments. It takes gold to amass gold."[25]

79

LOUIS XVI

JULY 1777

MARIE ANTOINETTE

My Marriage Is Consummated

During this time Joseph II is touring France, something that Louis XVI chooses not to do. French rulers since Louis XIV had made a practice of letting their subjects come to them. The emperor himself is not overly fond of public contact; crowds bother him, rob him of his "affable composure" so admired in the salons, and have been known to make him downright rude. People pester him and waste his time. He has come to see France, not the French.

Two people, however, stir up considerable speculation in Paris and Versailles, not to mention foreign capitals, while Joseph hurtles along at a grueling pace, "grown much thinner" according to Viennese sources on his return home in August. Will he or will he not call on Voltaire and Choiseul? It is anyone's guess, for Joseph has not disclosed his plans.

To visit or not to visit Choiseul in semi-exile in Touraine? The emperor travels through Normandy and on into Brittany as far as Brest, where Sartines has begun building a maritime base against an eventual Atlantic war. He admires the harbor and the construction in progress, but frowns on "empty [powder] magazines and poorly armed vessels." He excites "a ripple of jealousy among ship captains by singling out one among them named Bougainville, a renowned sailor unloved by his colleagues."* He returns by way of Brittany's southern coast and the declining port of L'Orient, which Joseph finds "pretty

---

*Thus Mercy-Argenteau describes to Maria Theresa the man whose *Voyages autour du monde,* published in 1771, had made him Europe's best-known author—best-known to all save the empress and her ambassador. Foreign travel was not one of their passions. At the advanced age of thirty-six, Bougainville had shifted from the army to the navy, where, for this reason and because his new colleagues were jealous of him, he was not liked.

enough, but the East India Company's dissolution has dulled its luster."* Nantes, on the other hand, which pins its hopes on the "new" [West] Indies, "is a sizable city with able inhabitants. The mouth of the Loire, which traverses the country, is a unique position, although the constraints and taxes levied on navigation of French rivers and canals make land transport preferable in almost every respect."**

Is he going to visit Choiseul or not? Of course he will, since he has left the coast and "is working his way up the Loire to Tours along a sea wall," the great embankment built by Jeanne de Laval and the kings of Anjou to stem the river's tide from the north. "The scenery is splendid, much like the banks of the Po and the Reno near Ferrara."[1] Dusk falls slowly, gently, at this time of year on islands of golden sand and rows of houses made of native tufa stone bathed in the sun's glow. The banks of the Loire are at their loveliest in the month of June. Why not make the visit! Amboise is only fifteen miles from Tours, a single change of horses along this marvelous stretch of sunlight and water. Nestled in the forest of Amboise, the erstwhile "coachman of Europe" and architect of the Austrian alliance awaits an emperor's visit which will compensate for a king's neglect—and remind that king that Choiseul is still available for service. Marie Antoinette is counting on this and has asked her brother to call there. At the court of Versailles, Joseph had met two celebrated beauties of Choiseul's harem: the Comtesse de Brionne, his mistress, and the Duchesse de Grammont, his sister, who had aspired to succeed La Pompadour but found herself eclipsed by Jeanne Bécu (Du Barry). The Duchesse de Grammont had tried to harpoon Joseph:

"In your opinion, madam, what is the most fertile province in France?"

"It is Touraine, sire. My brother has a cottage there. He would be delighted to receive you."

The "cottage" of Chanteloup is a miniature Versailles whose feudal master, Choiseul, is also master of nearby Amboise and its forest. A stately palace with two wings, magnificent outbuildings, immense courtyards, great stretches of greenery designed by Le Camus, architect of the new grain market in Paris. A second Trianon emerges from the addition of a pink marble colonnade flanking the château. Inside are rooms filled with fine logwood and mahogany furnishings, exquisite paintings, trumeaux, ceiling decorations, Gobelin tapestries, draperies woven in Tours, velvets from Utrecht, toile de Jouy, damask, and chintz. "The second floor includes nine guest apartments,"[2] one of which is permanently reserved for the Comtesse de Brionne, one of the mistresses

---

*The latest dissolution, dated 1769, had been signed by Louis XV under pressure from liberal economists (including Necker), who argued correctly that to suppress monopolistic trade with the overseas markets France retained by the Treaty of Paris would revive commercial relations with the East Indies. Marion's *Dictionnaire des Institutions de la France au XVIIIᵉ siècle* asserts that "the saga of French overseas trading companies is an endless martyrdom."

**Vehicular traffic already had taken the lead over more rational means of transport!

whose occupancy his wife is obliged to tolerate, she whose dowry has purchased and embellished the estate. But when a Crozat du Chatel, clever and witty as she may be, marries a Choiseul-Stainville and brings him an immense fortune, she must hold her tongue. After all, one of her ancestors was a peasant.

The dairy farm adjoining the château boasts a herd of "sixty Swiss cows." The wine cellars are stocked "with Malmsey, Madeira, Cyprus, Malaga, Barsac, still and sparkling Champagne, Sherry, Vouvray, Sauterne, Volnay, etc. In a special bin they have stored away choice fruit brandies from Hendaye and Amboise, flagons of walnut, ratafia, kirsch, and orange liqueur, as well as Bourbonne water* for Madame de Grammont's exclusive use."[3]

The Duc de Choiseul's "cottage" is worth four million livres.** It merits an imperial visit if only to see a unique structure being built there: the Pagoda, set deep in "English-Chinese gardens," which, when completed, will make Choiseul the envy of his noble peers and even the king. A seven-tiered obelisk, actually six drawing rooms each smaller than the one below, all constructed of freestone. The inside stairway with its superb iron tracery climbs to a bell tower 120 feet high, offering a splendid view of the surrounding countryside. First you walk through the upstairs drawing room, which the duke is bent on transforming into a living memorial to himself: lately they have put up a marble plaque proclaiming that "Etienne-François, Duc de Choiseul, affected by tokens of friendship, kindness, and courtesy during his exile by the many persons who hastened to these precincts, has raised this monument to perpetuate his gratitude"—visitors' names in alphabetical order will be inscribed in gold on white marble tablets mounted on the wall alongside each of eight windows.† Choiseul intends to reserve one entire plaque for Joseph, Emperor of Germany, King of the Romans, King of Bohemia, King of Hungary, etc., whose titles surely will cover it completely. The estate's total force of 460 servants (including a liveried staff of fifty-four) has been "mustered and no expense spared to receive the queen's brother: a dazzling company has been assembled, a series of entertainments prepared, relay teams of splendid horses are strung out along the road"[4] (from Saumur to Amboise via Tours), and musicians stand ready to perform on the clarinet, horn, and bassoon aboard the illuminated "frigate" riding at anchor on the artificial lake.

To visit or not?

---

*Natural mineral water from piping-hot springs in Bourbonne (Champagne district).
**Today 20 million francs [$4 million].[5] The Pagoda is all that remains of Chanteloup, which, during the Restoration, falls into the hands of the Comte de Chaptal's son, a high official (and profiteer) of the Empire. Bankrupted in turn, as Choiseul will be, Chaptal junior sold the estate in 1823 to the famous "black gang" of real-estate speculators who destroyed more châteaux and monasteries than the Revolution. Chanteloup was destroyed stone by stone. Only the Pagoda and part of the gardens survive; they still make a historic excursion only three hours from Paris.
†The plaque bearing Choiseul's inscription still exists; the marble tablets are bare, however, and probably had their names removed during the Empire.

At Tours, an hour's distance from Chanteloup, Joseph orders the coachman to turn south and head for Poitiers. The devil take Choiseul. The devil take Marie Antoinette.

"I won't see him because I won't go there."

The subject is closed.

Now what about visiting Voltaire? If for no other reason than to thumb his nose at Frederick the Great over in Berlin, friend and foe by turns of King Voltaire, whose smile the "enlightened" rulers of Europe have been courting for thirty years. Joseph was crowned "King of the Romans"* in Frankfurt in 1764, beneath the faintly ironic gaze of young Goethe. A simple detour will gain him the prize all other sovereigns covet and none can claim: Ferney's blessings. Voltaire, for his part, had journeyed to Berlin and been a guest in Saint Petersburg, the darling of numerous princes. But a visit from the emperor—repository of the divine authority invented in Rome, revived by Charlemagne, and restored under Charles V—would have confirmed him as the pope of modern times, a bridge spanning the centuries. Joseph II at Ferney: a Canossa of the Enlightenment. A dream.

No hurry. First, the western tour. "La Rochelle is not a good harbor. They want to spend money to improve it; that would be a waste. Rochefort, a [naval] construction site on the Charente River, is nothing more than a shipyard . . . From there I went on to Bordeaux, a bustling city engaged mainly in the export of wines and brandies which it supplies to England and the North [of Europe]. The Garonne is a beautiful river and had two or three hundred sailing ships on it. It is also an active commercial waterway for goods from the islands of America and for trade with the American insurgents, a dozen or so of whose ships I saw there . . . On to Bayonne, across the moors, a desolate, barren region where, during a trip that lasted thirty-six hours, I counted no more than three villages." A side trip to Spain, in La Fayette's footsteps, as far as San Sebastian via Los Pasajes. Back to France and on to Toulouse, then "that splendid province of Languedoc with its delightful culture." Agde, Cette, Montpellier, Nîmes, Aix, Marseilles, Toulon, "the finest port I have seen . . . Despite this, I cannot tell why, the French fleet inspires no confidence. The crews are incompetent and poorly trained. I gathered this from the maneuvers I watched and from the constant disabling of their ships."[6] He intends to return home through the Rhône Valley and Switzerland to avoid the ceremony of Piedmont's court. This will bring him to Geneva, even nearer to Ferney than is Tours to Amboise. To visit or not to visit?

To visit! Frederick the Great predicts it reluctantly in a letter to Voltaire on June 17: "This self-styled 'count' will return home via Lyons and Switzer-

---

*Title of designated successors (hereditary or elected by a group of princes) to the throne of the "Holy Roman Empire of the German nation." French equivalent: the dauphin. Joseph was heir and also ruler.

land. I expect he will come to Ferney and will wish to see and hear the glory
of our century, the Virgil and Cicero of our times. If this visit takes place, I
flatter myself that your new acquaintances will not cause you to forsake old
ones and you will bear in mind that the throng of your admirers includes a
single soul at Sans Souci who is separate from the multitude."[7] Which of the
two regarded the other as supreme? Spare me his visit, Voltaire complains
feebly from the bed where he has lain dying for the past two months. "What
would bring a son of the Caesars to a little parish church, he whose true parish
ought to be St. Peter's in Rome?" The world's most enigmatic chapel, this one
at Ferney, rebuilt in 1761. Its triangular Masonic-style pediment bears three
Latin words, the pointed civility of which enrages the priesthood more than
heresy: DEO EREXIT VOLTAIRE. The first "Catholic" church dedicated to God
alone, not Christ or the saints.* "Who would want to visit a wretched watchmaker?" Voltaire gave himself away on that score, for nothing made him
prouder than his industrial successes, which some called exploitation, others
called charity. In his own way he was like Choiseul in Touraine, a petty
provincial lord of the Gex district, whose franchises he had defended (not
without personal gain) against French and Genevan neighbors. "As for my silk
manufacture, it has been flat on its back for a long time."[8]

In any event, he was the idol of Gex. The good folk of that village,
perched atop a slope midway between Voltaire's house and the road** on
which the emperor will have to pass, have cleared away stones where the coach
will turn left. In their Sunday best (on a Tuesday), they line the roadside,
watching, silent, dogged, rugged as "mobile timber." Will he visit?

He will not. But Joseph declines delicately, allowing his coachman to
come to a halt on the main road and start toward Ferney. Who ordered him
to stop? The emperor peers out the window in mock surprise:

"Where are you taking me?"

"To Monsieur de Voltaire's house, sire."

"No, straight ahead." Whereupon he turns to his equally astonished
chamberlain to announce, in a voice that all Europe will hear, "I am fond of
poets like Haller who are also God-fearing men."[9]

This traveler has a cruel streak; he enjoys playing cat-and-mouse. He stops
off in Berne to pay his respects to the aging Haller, more a scholar than a poet,
who has managed to combine religion (the Protestant variety, which did not
offend Joseph, who welcomed the chance to flout his mother's rabid Catholicism) with an astounding mastery of botany, surgery, and medicine. Whether
from sheer rapture or overexcitement, Haller dies two weeks after the em-

---

*Correct translation: "Dedicated to God by Voltaire." A freer version, to which the Sage reacted
with feigned shock, titillated the salons: "With God's help Voltaire gets a hard on." The chapel,
adorned by its pediment and inscription, still is there, the first building on the left to greet a visitor
standing at the gates of Ferney.

**National Highway 6, Paris to Geneva, that ends just a few kilometers away at the Swiss border.

peror's visit, whereas Voltaire, who has had to weather constant buffeting, responds with predictable wit: "Out of humility the emperor chose not to visit me. He was afraid I might not receive him."[10]

Maria Theresa always fidgets when her son is abroad. She knows how he is apt to behave. "I would much prefer that he had been to Chanteloup if only for an hour or so on his way through . . . Choiseul must be mortified . . . And he is not a man we ought to antagonize, for he may or may not return to power. I think he must resent the slight. I would be glad if the emperor had refrained from seeing that contemptible Du Barry woman." Still, he offered her one radiant consolation: "I am overjoyed that in passing through Geneva he avoided meeting that wretched Voltaire."[11] Having got this off her chest, she proceeds to pour out six pages of her woes as a woman and a ruler.

Good-by, Your Majesty. Your chief purpose in coming here was not to humiliate Choiseul or Voltaire but to help your sister make love halfway decently. The destiny of the world—your world, at least, and hers—hangs on Marie Antoinette's physiological responses. Being a man of the world, Joseph has grasped and faced up to the fact that in this case Austria must thrust forward though France hang back. A subject of intense speculation in all the courts of Europe, and for the rest of Joseph's trip the crude question of "Will they or won't they mate?" preys on the emperor's mind.

Chacun se demande tout bas:　　　　[All of us ask in whispers:
Le Roi peut-il? Ne peut-il pas?　　　Is the king able or not?
La triste Reine en désespère,　　　　The sad queen despairs,
　　Lère là.　　　　　　　　　　　　　　*Lère là.*

L'un dit: il ne peut l'ériger.　　　　Someone says: he can't get it up.
Un autre: il ne peut s'y nicher.　　　Another, he can't get it in.
L'autre: il est flûte traversière,　　　Still another: he's a transverse flute,
　　Lère là.　　　　　　　　　　　　　　*Lère là.*

Ce n'est pas là que le mal gît,　　　But that's not the real trouble
Dit le royal clitoris,　　　　　　　　Reports the royal clitoris:
Mais il ne vient que de l'eau claire,　All that comes out is rain water,
　　Lère là.[12]　　　　　　　　　　　　*Lère là.*]

First gleam of hope: Marie Antoinette consents to write about "it" calmly to her mother on June 16: "They say the Comtesse d'Artois is with child again. It is rather unpleasant for me to face after seven years of marriage. But it would not be fair to show resentment. I am not without hope; my brother can tell my dear mama how things stand. The king has spoken candidly and in confidence to him about this matter."[13] Maria Theresa is dying to hear more, but will have to wait for Joseph's return. What strange people they are, at once so outspoken and so prudish. "I look forward to hearing the promising results [of the trip] and also news of the state of your marriage, about which I have high hopes. But I must wait to hear this from his own lips when he returns. This puts me on edge, I confess, for in your life it is all or nothing* for you to produce heirs."[14] On July 15 Mercy-Argenteau reports good news: "The queen continues to behave more sensibly . . . Her Majesty visits the king more often, and nearly every day after lunch they spend an hour or two alone together in the privacy of their chamber."[15] The first and most elementary precept Joseph had preached: their nightly trysts had become torture to them both, a galling reminder of failure. Well, try it in the afternoon, when Louis XVI is not half asleep and she impatient to join her friends. One short month of willing, honest effort, the warmth of midsummer, perseverance, an older brother's advice . . . It can't have been a party, but on July 20, 1777, it ceases to be a disaster. Marie Antoinette fires off a victory dispatch to her mother on July 29: "Vergennes informs me that he is sending the mail with Breteuil.** This is a stroke of good fortune for me. The happiness I feel is vital to my whole life. My marriage was consummated over a week ago; the experiment [sic] has been repeated, and again yesterday more successfully than the first time . . . I do not think I am pregnant yet, but at least I can hope to be so one of these days."[16] Joseph's chest swells with pride. "The King of France has done the deed at last and now the queen may bear a child; they both have written to thank me, attributing it to my advice. I did indeed dwell on the subject in great detail in my conversations with him, and I came to the conclusion that laziness, clumsiness, and apathy were the only obstacles."[17] Was he not correct to estimate that Louis XVI is "ill-bred but well-intentioned," and that "if his intellectual faculties are feeble, he is not altogether an imbecile"?[18]

*Indeed, the choice was between remaining queen or being rejected. Throne or convent.
**Baron de Breteuil was the French ambassador to Vienna, successor to Cardinal de Rohan.

80

We Were Left Standing in the Street

The Marquis de La Fayette and his companions set out on their little caravan from Charleston to Philadelphia on June 25. Five hundred sixty miles as the crow flies, actually more than seven hundred since the one existing widened and tamped path (proudly known as a "highway") winds in and out, parallel to river beds wherever possible, plunging westward from time to time, leaping from valley to valley over straggling villages planted in the wilderness. My God, it's hot! Ninety-five in the shade, and not a breath of air once you leave the riverbank. It looks like a biblical expedition in search of the Promised Land, or, more to the point, a band of pioneers opening up new territories.

Three groups of pilgrims are strung out along the road. The officers have been assigned four lumbering wagons, which seem to roll on tree trunks, and in fact they do. Huge German work horses draw them, heavy, plodding animals transplanted to these shores by Hanoverian and Hessian colonists and adapted by now to the southern climate. "The marquis's aide de camp took it upon himself to act as our guide, though he had no idea what the country was like,"[1] and there was no map for the simple reason that no maps existed. At each stage of the journey they had to ask directions to the next town, and it was purely by accident that they ever reached Philadelphia, creeping along like snails. At the head of the march rides "one of the marquis's servants in a hussar's uniform"—who cares which regiment, for any uniform creates a favorable impression in this land. "The marquis's conveyance was like a traveling sofa supported by four springs and a forecarriage. A mounted servant acting as equerry* escorted it. The Baron de Kalb rode with the marquis. The two colonels who were La Fayette's advisers followed next in a two-wheeled vehicle. The third one carried the aides de camp,** the fourth, equipment,†

*Or squire (corruption of the French *écuyer*), the bottom rung of the ladder of nobility; above him was the knight (*chevalier*), a rank to which the squire aspired in feudal times.[2]
**Officers without official duties at the start, whom La Fayette thus classified on the spur of the moment, just as he calls "advisers" the two adventuresome colonels who had joined his expedition.　†In the broadest sense, embracing all the necessities of an army on the move: rations, ammunition, etc.

and bringing up the tail of the procession was a Negro slave on horseback."

The slave had cost less than the horse on the Charleston market. But the blessings and amenities of city life are forgotten after three hours on the road. The next day is sheer agony. The American South bares its true face, that of an untamed continent where nature stings, chokes, buries in sand, poisons, and demoralizes. "On the fourth day a number of vehicles were falling apart. Some of our horses, all old and winded, were either ready to drop or lame." They move on as best they can, like Cains in the forest fleeing the curse of torment-ing hordes of horseflies, mosquitoes, and gnats."* A far cry from "the delights conjured up by armchair novelists in European cities."[3] At the first oppor-tunity they buy more horses—as broken down as the first lot and just as costly. The Charleston loan sees them only as far as Petersburg, a twenty-two-day march, the road to depression for everyone save La Fayette, who celebrates their arrival in this relatively civilized place by dispatching a lively letter to the salons of Paris via "dear heart," his amanuensis: "You have the beginning of my travels. You know that I set out splendidly in a coach [sic]. You will discover that all of us are now on horseback, having smashed the carriages, an admirable habit of mine, and I expect to write you shortly that we have reached our destination on foot. It is somewhat tiring, but though several of my companions have suffered a good deal, it has affected me hardly at all."[4] This was the truth, both sides of it: he was equally oblivious to his own suffering and that of others. His optimism was insufferable; his cheerful dispo-sition became the eighth plague of the New World to his fellow officers, who didn't have such blissful ignorance or boundless hope, whichever you like. His endurance, too, a useful virtue acquired by growing up in Auvergne. "La Fayette's spirit would have fired the courage of anyone with far less than his," complained the Chevalier du Buysson, who "walked most of the way, often sleeping in the woods, dying of hunger, plagued by the heat, several of us suffering from fever and dysentery . . . I would venture to say that no Euro-pean military maneuver could be more rigorous than this journey. There [in Europe] the hardships are never constant; in fact, many pleasures compensate for them. But on this trip our misfortunes mounted from day to day, with no respite save the hope of arriving at last in Philadelphia." In Petersburg, thank God, things begin to look up. The infernal wilds of the Carolinas lie behind them; somewhere along the way they have crossed that imaginary line drawn by Charles I's surveyors into Virginia. America was so simple in those days: the northern colonies, outgrowth of the Plymouth settlement and called New England, and Virginia, matriarch of the South, mother of states that gradually cast off her influence, including not only Georgia and both the Carolinas but also Maryland. The South had begun life two or three hundred years earlier

*Thirty-six pests that plagued the travelers were named. Volney describes the gnat as a tiny black fly "worse than midges."

on Chesapeake Bay, whose coast lies about a hundred miles east of the expedition's present location. Once they have crossed the Potomac, which flows into the bay from the northwest, it will take them only a few days' march, through a more populous state with better roads, to reach the next major inlet along the coast, Delaware Bay, from where, like Crusaders glimpsing Jerusalem, they will move on to the City of Brotherly Love, the Mecca of modern times, Philadelphia. The only difference being that it will not have to be taken by force.

Or maybe it will, for after displaying all her worst physical features to La Fayette and his friends, America was about to show her worst face: incivility.

"After a thirty-two-day march we reached Philadelphia in an even sorrier state than when we arrived in Charleston." The last stretch of the journey had been relatively pleasant on "a wide, straight, well-kept road." Now and then they had the impression of traveling "along a garden path shaded by the oldest, handsomest trees that ever grew." Towns are closer together and more populated. Taverns are clean. Pennsylvania is not the South but the Center. They are travelers now, not trail-blazers. Farewell, Colonial America: the Nation is at hand. And these aristocratic disciples of Rousseau, accustomed to "the affectation of our elegant young dandies [among whom the Marquis de La Fayette had ranked conspicuously three months before] and to the contrast at home between the luxury of the upper classes and coarsely clad peasants or poor ragged masses," are pleasantly "surprised, on arriving in the United States, to find no such ostentation or misery anywhere."[5] In America there were only three classes: the very rich, the moderately rich, and the servant class, exclusive of slaves, who fell somewhere between the human and animal worlds.

The long pilgrimage is coming to a close: on the morning of July 27 La Fayette and his fellow officers reach Philadelphia, "scarcely five miles from the confluence of the Delaware and Schuylkill rivers." With a population of just over twenty thousand swollen by refugees from the North, it is indeed "a very large, very proud and beautiful city, for all its ninety years. The streets are wide, each crossing at right angles," and astonishing to the Frenchmen because they have sidewalks, unheard of at home. "Most houses are attractive, built of red or dark brick, with vestibules, colonnades, and here and there some superb exterior decorations; all of them have fairly high porches with rows of pillars underneath and seats enabling residents to sit on their front stoops in good weather to take the air."[6] It must have been the right weather: Philadelphia is a Turkish bath. But her merchant class is in no frame of mind to relax on the front stoop these grim summer mornings. The glorious excitement of declared independence is already in the past. The coming struggle is etched on people's faces. A British attack could come at any moment. Two months earlier they captured, then mysteriously evacuated, New Jersey. They could strike from the sea tomorrow.

Everything will change now that I am here, La Fayette decides hastily. But Philadelphians ignore this band of mud-spattered travelers up from the South. The effect is crueler than in Charleston, where at least people pointed at them. Philadelphia's streets are jammed with refugees from New York fleeing General Howe's advancing steamroller; "never had such a superb fighting force been seen" (half Hessian at that), seventeen thousand redcoats "mostly well-trained and well-equipped veterans."[7] Washington had barely eight thousand men to send against them once he managed to assemble his greenhorn army. His strategy has not changed for the past year: clever retreats, random thrusts or feints using militiamen whose units seem to slip away like sand through the fingers. The British withdrawal stunned him more than anyone, for they were in a position to demolish his Princeton defenses and sweep north to Philadelphia in three days. He may have bluffed them once again; Howe has sailed from New York, probably southward, and will disappear into the Delaware with those terrible floating fortresses of the royal navy. From the north or south, by land or sea, it is generally conceded that the cradle of independence will fall when the first British soldier enters the open city of Philadelphia. American forces—what they call an army—will have to retreat far inland in any number of directions. But is the struggle worth it? And where will they set up a new recruiting center? "The demoralizing effects of such news on the public caused great concern; it was feared that American volunteers would renounce the struggle if it appeared absolutely hopeless."[8]

The French travelers waste no time. After washing off the mud of their journey, they set out at once to call on the president of the Continental Congress. The city chokes with anguish in the early-morning light, its houses either abandoned by their owners or crammed with exiles from the north; in the streets, mingling with the citizenry, clusters of militiamen in nondescript uniforms, armed like weekend hunters, drift aimlessly in circles.

No sound of cannon fire. The invisible British may arrive tomorrow. This fear is worse than a siege. It is hard to find one's way through a maze of houses "without garden walks or public parks; the only outstanding buildings are the hospital, the town hall, the jail, the church of Christ, and the statehouse, which has spacious rooms."[9] Nearby lives Mr. Hancock, president of a vanishing Congress, most of whose delegates have gone to Baltimore rather than stay and be trapped in the capital. The Frenchmen rap at his door with its "gleaming brass knocker"[10] and present what they take to be unfailing credentials: letters of recommendation from American delegates in Paris . . .

They are shunted off to one Mr. Moose, a Congressman with barely five words of French at his command. La Fayette and Kalb explain themselves painfully. Moose listens politely, like a prison guard at the grating, and asks them to meet him the following day "outside the doors of Congress."

This is no figure of speech: the next morning they stand there in the dust, travelers from over the ocean, at the doors of the building where independence was first proclaimed. No one even asks them to come in and sit down. They must wait outdoors "a very long time." Reappearance "of Mr. Moose with another delegate. He informs us: 'This gentleman speaks fluent French. His job is to take care of everyone from your country, so you will have to deal with him from now on.'

"He went back inside, and the gentleman in question, Mr. Lovell, greeted us in the street and left us there after calling us, in perfectly good French, a band of adventurers."

Mr. Lovell doesn't mince words. Officers? High-ranking ones? And what would you have me do about it? We are inundated with officers, yours and ours! At the rate we're going, we'll have an army of French colonels and generals. Is there by any chance an engineer among you? Someone able to lay out trenches or design ramparts with proper gun emplacements?*

"We have charged Mr. Deane to send us four French engineers. Instead, he sends us M. du Coudray** with self-styled engineers who are not engineers and totally inexperienced artillerymen."

It is apparent that Silas Deane's popularity in the Congress is in eclipse. Franklin, on the other hand, has wasted no time: "He has sent us those four engineers." As to officers, "last year we were indeed short of them, but this year we have a great many, some very unskilled." Also, they prefer English-speaking ones. "British officers have come to serve us without our even asking." Having said this, Mr. Lovell wishes them a safe voyage home and shuts the door to America in their faces. This leaves Kalb, Mauroy, La Fayette, Du Buysson, and eight or ten others stranded on the streets of Philadelphia —worse than adrift in the Atlantic. "That was our initial reception. We were at a loss to know what to make of it: no one could have been more stunned than we"[11] on July 28, 1777.

*Just what Beaumarchais had been begging from Vergennes eighteen months earlier: "Gunpowder and engineers!"
**Whose ill-temper and pretentious airs had caused Beaumarchais such trouble when he was rigging out the *Amphitrite.*

81

JULY 1777

This Sick Society

Pierre-Victor Malouet, on the other hand, has been treated like visiting royalty this month by Dutch authorities in Surinam.* "Having arrived in Paramaribo on July 10 and been received with highest honor as royal commissioner in French Guiana, accredited with the Dutch government, I felt uncertain momentarily about my functions, which, unknown to me, had broadened."[1] Manifestly so. The Dutch colonists look to this notary's son from Auvergne to settle all their problems. At the age of thirty-seven, he finds himself in a position to reshape a tiny backward corner of the globe, a patch of land whose name is still somewhat undecided, on South America's shoulder between the Orinoco and the Amazon, just above the Equator.

This is happening nearly equidistant from Bordeaux, the port from which La Fayette sailed, and from Philadelphia, his destination. Malouet is two or three thousand miles from France and from America. But the spiritual distance is even greater, almost planetary, between the rough, bigoted settlers from France, Holland, and England, each group bound by the laws of its home country, and Americans who are setting a bad example for Europe by rising against their king. There is a world of difference between a Malouet and a La Fayette, even supposing the former had heard of the latter.

Malouet has been building a reputation over the past two years in naval and colonial administrative circles, and has consistently opposed French aid to the American rebels. Even more the antithesis of Beaumarchais than of La Fayette. In February 1775 Sartines, his patron, former minister of police and now naval minister, had given him a handwritten query from Louis XVI to answer: "Does it befit the government to furnish [them] with clandestine aid . . . to exchange ambassadors, to trade with them? Can this be done on sound moral grounds?" Malouet did not hesitate: "Sound political as well as moral policy dictates that we do just the opposite. All indications promise that the New England** will prove fiercer than the old one if she achieves independ-

---

*The Dutch called Dutch Guiana "the Regency of Surinam"; its capital was Paramaribo.
**That is, the thirteen colonies.

ence. Soon she will have surplus goods that she will want to sell to our colonies, and will first capture the market followed by the territory . . . North America, once it is free and powerful, will spread southward and become even richer . . . We must make every effort to halt this progress. Any other course will lead us astray and ruin us."[2] That was far closer to the thinking of Louis XVI and Vergennes than the quixotic musings of a La Fayette. It explains Malouet's favor at court and why a non-noble was awarded high posts overseas.

Yet we find him presiding over a "National Assembly" in May 1777, the pompous new designation of the Colonial Assembly of French Guiana, a body somewhat similar to provincial states which still met in certain parts of France. He had called the meeting on arrival in Cayenne in order to test the colonists' response to a program of reform. Any stimulus in that direction formerly had come from Martinique at the cost of interminable delay. He had been "shocked at his first glimpse of this colony" on landing there in November 1776. "The shabby appearance of the city [Cayenne] and the looks of its inhabitants gave me the worst impression of the nature and product of their labors. Trade restricted to articles of prime necessity, industry deprived of essential tools and manpower, competition stifled . . . the prejudices of ignorance and self-interest . . . Such is the spectacle of this sick society that greets the eyes of a healthy visitor." He had rolled up his sleeves and set to work to revive these failing markets, planted on the coast of "Amazonas" midway between rival Portuguese and Dutch colonies by the West Indies Company, that had proliferated uncontrolled for two centuries as if by some sort of rampant schizogenesis. "Without innovation, I was certain to fail, for I knew the institution was rotten and all its parts corrupt." Still, he was not about to fling the whole works to the winds; Malouet in action is the very image of "enlightened reform": "My aversion to untested programs and innovations left me no alternative but to combat each abuse at the source and as it came to my attention. I was compelled to root out all institutional and administrative vices, for they are what destroys the body politic. Similarly, I had to attack the colonists for their errors, their intolerance, and their practices or else make it possible to justify them . . . The more obstacles I foresaw, the more observers I needed to report the facts" as well as to keep a tight rein on Fiedmont, the military commander, an old bully ever eager for a scrap, who wanted to put up a fort wherever an Indian came out of the forest and would have spent every last louis of royal funding on gunpowder. To combat this attitude and the pervasive apathy among settlers, Malouet resorted to an experiment in pragmatic parliamentarism, a forum for some sixty to a hundred representatives on which the colony's future depended. "In this instance I had to proceed not by authority but by reason, by demonstration; my words and acts had to be public for I would have joined the ranks of blind overseers if I had written or proposed a plan without debate."[3] But "how do you win the good will of such people?" Guiana's settlers were victims of the tropical climate, rum, the prostitution of native black women, smallpox, and indifference. "One had to attack their most cherished habits . . . I hoped, by having them meet frequently at my house, to teach them more easily. Wasted effort; I had guests but no converts."[4]

His message, of course, was not noticeably evangelical. He was a missionary of profit. All his "wasted effort" had gone into persuading these people to enrich themselves systematically—in order to enrich the home treasury. They yawned and fell back into their hammocks; four years in Guiana took the vitality out of young and old alike, whose only interest was the day-long siesta. The colonists stared mutely at this dignified, faintly arrogant, gray-faced man who delivered long lectures and kept urging them to plow more land so as to replace the rapidly exhausted soil now under cultivation. He preached the blessings of new plants, including clove and nutmeg, which the administrator Poivre* recently had introduced to Cayenne from the Indian Ocean, unknown to the Dutch. Malouet planned a celebration around the blossoming of one of three clove shrubs that finally had taken root on Mount Gabrielle and which appeared, "from tip to toe, to have more cloves than leaves." The overseas trading company run by farmer-general Paulze, Lavoisier's father-in-law, had investments in the Guiana spice trade—and behind Paulze stood Monsieur, the king's brother, who is beginning to feel his life style cramped by his income.[5] Malouet had powerful backers at home, but it took four to six months for his letters to receive an answer, and meanwhile he was on slippery ground: the Amazon mud.

Do all natives of Riom retain its local color? Malouet and Gilbert Romme share the same basalt grayness worn by the churches and houses of this ancient circular town. The same boyhood memories of dusty law offices, a father, an uncle, a cousin, a grandfather in legal robes. Gilbert Romme is studying in Paris to become a doctor, or teacher, or scientist, but he is ten years younger than Pierre-Victor and lacks the latter's provincial springboard to success. His attorney father was not as rich as "Maître Pierre-André Malouet, Bailli d'Olliergues, notary and prosecutor for the crown in the district of Auvergne," and Gilbert was orphaned early in life. No penniless orphan can hope to compete with the eldest son of a well-to-do lawyer. Romme vegetates in Paris while Malouet governs French Guiana. Yet both must climb the same ladder of promotion and obtain the patronage of one or two noblemen, liberals in Gilbert's case, courtiers in Pierre-Victor's. Auvergne has left them a common legacy: they are industrious, they abhor wasting time, and they have no sense of humor.

Malouet is a good-looking man with graying hair, whose regular features

*This explains popular use of Cayenne pepper (*poivre*). Until then the Dutch had managed to retain a monopoly of the plant.

one forgets once his back is turned. He is complete, every peg in place as to both moral and physical makeup, inside and out, before the age of forty. He was a pupil of the Oratorians in Riom, like Gilbert Romme, then went on to their school in Juilly, the finest in the kingdom, where he "wore a monk's habit until the age of sixteen," though it involved no lasting commitment. There he received superb instruction in physics and geography. In his twenties, with Paris nearby, he sowed his share of oats, no more, no less than average. He flirted, wrote inflated verse, gambled, and ran up a few small debts, but returned promptly to the fold when, at eighteen, he was made diplomatic secretary to his father, the ambassador to Portugal. The young colt never kicked up his heels wildly; he took the bridle without a fuss. "The need to make a good appearance, to behave with dignity and circumspection in a superior [*sic*] society, curbed my flights of fancy." He became an elderly young man forever, the price of his security: "I learned to be silent, to listen attentively to whatever was worth remembering, to be bored at times without showing it, and to beware of first impressions . . . I received my first lessons in social formalities and acquired a taste for good company which always prompted me to shun whatever failed to resemble it."[6] He had no trouble adapting to the mold of naval administration and, while serving that ministry in Rochefort, had examined the entire correspondence of Colbert, his hero, for references to the design of that port. Disciple of Colbert and Choiseul: ideas and obedience. He will go far. His credit is high at court for being an outspoken defender of the civil bureaucracy whose interests he can be relied on to champion in the constant clashes between port officials and the professional sea dogs who make their own laws, the perpetual tug-of-war between commissioners and officers.* Malouet is a commissioner through and through.

Which is not to call him either foolish or spiteful. Whenever able to redress a wrong or uncover an injustice, he did so—unless it promised to involve him in some serious controversy. Denunciation without dispute is his method of operation. In Santo Domingo, where he worked for a year, he was vexed by the stupidity and cruelty of officials toward slaves as well as settlers. A revolt broke out led by a former army sergeant named Détrées. Détrées was hanged, much to the chagrin of Malouet, who never lifted a finger to save him. "A badly organized administrative system, in which I participated, unchecked and untempered authority, of which I was the instrument, could only offend my sensibilities. Still, I did not become discouraged"—and for good cause. He has just acquired "an additional vested interest in the prosperity of this colony: ten months after my arrival, I married,** became a property-owner, and was distressed to see property rights threatened by arbitrary regulations and by a system of military security as detrimental to trade as to farming."[7]

He is fighting not for the prosperity of mankind but for his own right to

*Malouet will rise to the rank of naval minister during the first Restoration.

**To a Mlle Béhotte, daughter of a prosperous planter in Cap Français.

prosper. Subtle difference. He disapproves of slavery. "I became a colonial slaveowner, though I did not support the system: its abuses and the dreadful acts of cruelty I knew about made my blood boil." But "theories and philosophic oratory have never led me astray." Slavery "is a necessary evil, but did it have to go to extremes? Since our colonies can only be farmed by blacks, who must be subservient to the landowners, why should this subservience not be defined so as to assure the slave as well as his master the protection of the law?"[8]

His answer was to standardize slavery, to give the slaves a share of the booty—short of freedom. The blacks who worked for Pierre-Victor Malouet probably were treated well.

For several years he had been planning to settle down in France and had bought in Santo Domingo, "independent of my wife's property, a coffee plantation which I expected to become highly productive. On this I anchored my plans for independence . . . I wanted to live in the country"[9] on the income from his colonial holdings. But the civil bureaucracy was not ready to release him. They wanted him to find out once and for all whether Guiana was a gold mine or a rotten apple. The court shifted its attitude regularly, depending on the emotional climate in the capital, which in turn hinged on the relative risks of speculation. In 1764, in an effort to recoup French losses under the Treaty of Paris, Choiseul had shipped some fifteen thousand inhabitants of Alsace and Lorraine to Guiana to found a tropical Canada or Louisiana.* Three birds with one stone: while purging Lorraine of German sympathizers who were grumbling about the brutalities of French occupation, he would be ridding the eastern provinces of extra mouths to feed and at the same time tapping the riches of a fabulous continent.

The deportees died of fever west of Cayenne in 1765. "The town and parish of Kourou has no remarkable sights save a giant cemetery where twelve thousand persons were buried in less than eighteen months."[10] The tropical climate could not solve the problem of what to do with the population of Lorraine. An error of judgment that was promptly forgotten. In 1768 Choiseul shifted the projected settlement to a better location on the River Approuague and called on adventurers from all over to ship there. Three thousand corpses, a million francs thrown to the winds. Choiseul pressed no further, but Louis XVI and Sartines began to feel the lure of Guiana. "In 1776, for the third time in twelve years, Cayenne became a new Peru. A Baron de Bessner, who aspired to govern the place, had everyone worked up about it . . . He returned from Cayenne, having sailed the rivers and tramped the jungles of that continent; he had seen the land covered with vanilla, sarsaparilla,** sassafras, native spices, fragments of precious stones . . . These tales, transformed into

*The Treaty of 1763 ceded Canada to England and Louisiana to Spain.
**Plant whose root has "medicinal and sudorific" properties.

positive facts in well-written memoirs, greatly impressed Monsieur's councillors, who convinced His Royal Highness that henceforth he must look to Guiana for the richest share of his appanage . . . I was charged by M. de Sartines to examine and report on all these plans."[11]

Malouet labored under no delusions. His pessimism conflicted with the wildest fancies of the third Guiana Company, which was already distributing layouts of coffee, tobacco, and cocoa plantations and planned to introduce viticulture and "large herds of steers; the last article in its prospectus dealt with the manufacture of *small cheeses,** which were expected to be highly profitable. I mention this extravagant notion only to demonstrate how far such fanciful cupidity can go."[12]

To repay him for being right, Maurepas, a firm believer in the politics of diversion, had sent him off to Guiana with a sneer. Wait and see who wins out, the expert or the charlatan. It would be even funnier if both perished. Malouet insisted on setting out before Bessner took over. Malouet has only a few months in which to avert another colonial disaster. This is why he is desperate to convert Cayenne's settlers to the blessings of a planned economy.

He had found consolation of sorts in his discoveries and in his work. Never will he forget landing in waters strewn with floating timbers that rolled in with the waves all along the shore, as if rivers were bringing the jungle oceanward; scarlet birds nesting in mangrove trees; flamingoes; monstrous sea creatures ranging from swordfish to giant rays; the baying of hundreds of wild dogs below the fortress of Cayenne, which stood out against the moonlit sky, the one sign of life, but otherwise a sign of death for ships entering "the vast deserted anchorage . . . " He had explored the interior along a network of interlocking rivers and canals "as complete as our royal highway system." He became acquainted with the monkeys of the Oyapock River region—"the monkey surely is at an infinite distance from man, but a few resemblances to our species would suffice to demand our sympathy; my hatred of despotism is such that I would not even impose it on animals"—this also applies to the apathetic but proud Indians,** whose independent spirit he admires. "We invited them to our villages to show them our prosperity and they were not tempted by it."[13] He struggled against the missionaries who "managed to assemble the Indians of the Bay of Vincent Pinson in the chapel . . . They taught them the catechism, baptized them, and made them attend mass by passing out a ration of *tafia*† each time. Once the casks ran dry, the Indians stayed in their huts," whereupon the missionaries dispatched a body of fusiliers to round them up. Malouet at once found himself with a minor revolt on his

---

*Malouet's emphasis.
**The two principal tribes in the Guianas were the Arawaks and the Caribs. How many? Not more than 20,000 between the Orinoco and the Amazon; less than 3000 in the French colony, according to Malouet.
†A rumlike distillate from sugar-cane juices. [*Trans.*]

hands, which he quelled peacefully because he understood that the Indians had greeted the head missionary's sermon with laughter. "The truth is that they spoke reverently of God as master of the universe, but mocked at heaven and hell. When the chief missionary informed them that they would roast in hell if they died unbaptized, they replied: 'Show us heaven and hell and whoever is there.' "[14]

Heaven and hell are really not so far away. One can find them both in Paramaribo, where Dutch neighbors seem to have a knack for colonialism, having pioneered settlements all over the globe with far better results than those French dilettantes. Their capital, where they receive Malouet with balls and fireworks, is the same distance along the coast from Cayenne as Poitiers from Paris. But the French port is a mere checkerboard of dingy shanties thrown together on sand, whereas the Dutch have built themselves a lively, immaculate community. Their wives drive about in gilt coaches dressed in colorful, bejeweled gowns. The humblest household boasts twenty in help, all Negro slaves of course, not those lazy Indians; no one can beat the Dutch for squeezing every last ounce of labor from a slave.

They break him in; if he resists, they punish, then kill him as an example to the others. After all, what would happen if slaves suddenly realized they outnumber their masters six to one? The slaveowners are imaginative and have made Paramaribo the capital of slow torture. They hang unruly blacks on tenterhooks; they flog them to death by degrees, day after day, to prolong the agony; they throw them into alligator-infested ponds kept for that purpose; they flay them alive; they cut off their hands, their arms, their legs, their testicles, and leave them to die in anguish on the steps of the church. Madame van Oggerdorp, wife of a respectable spice merchant, became offended by the expression of one of her servants and personally gouged his eyes out with the tip of her parasol, then had him thrown into the river from the six-oared pleasure craft with its damask-canopied deck that takes her boating. Judge van Stikker ordered a thirteen-year-old Negro girl disemboweled for having got herself pregnant without his permission. The dying mother and the fetus were exposed in the pillory of the slave market.[15] Paramaribo's social life is the envy of all other colonies. One reception follows another, interspersed with balls, musical gatherings, and theatrical performances put on by visiting players from Amsterdam in a tiny, charming theater lit by the same wax candles currently used in Europe. A carnival atop a volcano.

For even colonial Surinam has a problem, the same one that brought Malouet to these shores: "This proud colony was in seething ferment; the slave war preoccupied the Regency and had split the population into two camps."[16]

Slave war? Alas, even these wretched creatures had succumbed to original sin. They were disobedient and had fled Paramaribo like water through a sieve. First, one or two at a time, then in bands, they escaped to the jungle and formed small armies that preyed mercilessly on any settler who crossed their path. A name was given to these slaves who rejected the white man's law: runaways. By 1777 there are said to be thousands roaming the land—which gave Baron de Bessner a brilliant idea: to solve French Guiana's labor shortage since the Indians refuse to be recruited, why not entice the runaways to Cayenne? They could replace those weak-livered deportees from Lorraine who seem to die like flies the moment they set foot in the tropics. Put the slaves to work on French plantations. They must get the Dutch to agree so as not to antagonize them; it would never do to go to war over the issue. And as M. Malouet seemed to possess the gift of persuasion, he was selected for this diplomatic mission to Paramaribo.

Where he found himself in a hornets' nest. The business of the fugitive slaves had widened a rift in the Dutch colony between partisans of the stadt-holder and of the States-General that had not yet come to a head at home. There was general agreement that the runaways had to be brought under control but no agreement on how to do it. When the regimental colonel sent there by the Prince of Orange tried to impose his authority, the settlers refused to fund him. Here the "governor" is a civilian, whereas the French colonies are under the command of a military officer of noble birth. Paramaribo's governor, who must have been starved for congenial company, proceeds to pour out his worries to Malouet, a fellow civilian. He fears the commander of the army, who "announces publicly, encouraged by his supporters, that unless the colony's government is subservient to the stadtholder and under military control, there is bound to be trouble."[17] The colonel in question rushes over to Malouet the next morning to disclaim that view and to appeal to the Frenchman's sense of justice. Like some saintly legislator, Malouet is forced to decide the issue; he favors civilian rule, naturally, but seeks to avoid passing judgment. He listens in silence. Who knows how things will turn out among these Dutch? When they part at the end of July, with much bowing and scraping, Malouet is convinced that fear has grossly inflated the re-ported number of runaways. The poor creatures who have managed to slip off into the jungle are scattered and disorganized. Their only thought is to get as far away as possible. There are probably less than three thousand of them. And Bessner's idea is just another pipe dream, for the slaves have not fled the Dutch only to turn around and work for the King of France.

Malouet returns to Cayenne to attempt the possible, only the possible. He needs "fishermen and salters from Granville"* and about a hundred fishing boats with decks: the waters off Guiana teem with five-hundred-pound sea cows whose flesh tastes like pork. Fresh and preserved fish "would end our dependence on New England to provision the Antilles."[18] Send us good

*Fishing port on the English Channel. [*Trans.*]

breeding bulls and French Guiana alone soon could have a hundred thousand steers ready for market. Launch a chain of food-producing plantations, each worked by a hundred acclimatized slaves from Santo Domingo or Martinique, which in turn can feed another five hundred workers farming export crops. "At that rate, in twenty years the king would have a flourishing colony without having spent a sou more than it costs him today to support a flagging economy . . . But can programs of this magnitude be discussed fifteen hundred leagues from Versailles?"[19]

Versailles, where Maurepas has just promised Baron de Bessner the governorship of French Guiana.

82

JULY 1777

To Serve at My Own Expense

La Fayette wins the first victory of his career in the dusty streets of Philadelphia on July 28, 1777, just when everything seems to be coming apart. Through patience and dignity: a matter of perseverance. They have actually shown him and his companions the door. Keep calm; don't panic, don't give up. "We decided to wait and discover the reason for this insult before complaining about it."[1] They find out soon enough that no one is really angry at them; they are simply paying for the mistakes of invading hordes of adventurers from all over the map who had descended on American military headquarters. Mostly French, unfortunately, with a sprinkling of Germans, Poles,* Spaniards, and others. For six months Washington had been pleading with the Congress to do something about them. "We must either assign them a post or send them away. The first alternative is difficult; the second is disagreeable and perhaps impolitic if they are able men. But how are we to tell them from common adventurers? Meanwhile, I am plagued and wearied by the importunities of some, the discontent of others."[2] A decision had been made to reject these latest candidates without further ado, for times were grim and the threat of a British attack left no time to pick and choose.

First consolation: no one had a special grudge against the newcomers; the grievance was a general one. How could members of Congress tell the difference between a Du Coudray and a La Fayette? The distinction, a matter of

*Notably Pulaski and Kosciusko.

superior breeding on the latter's part, should become apparent on demonstration even to Moose and Lovell.

July 29: Gilbert composes an address to the Congress stating his position, the motives for his coming, and the terms of his understanding with Silas Deane. He knows exactly how to end it. If you gentlemen are indignant at people who try to take advantage of you, don't worry: "For the sacrifices I have made, it is my right to demand two favors: one is to serve at my own expense, the other, to begin my service as a volunteer."[3]

"The right to *demand* two *favors* . . ." The Congress perks up its ears at the unfamiliar style and the uncommon offer. A Frenchman who will cost us nothing? Suppose he has real ability?

July 30: Mr. Lovell, "the same person who received us so abominably," calls on the Frenchmen "accompanied by another member [of the Congress] at once more adroit and more tactful."[4] Maybe also better informed as to the peculiarities of the French nobility? Twenty-four hours of negotiations. A mutual decision is reached to do away with the arbitrary commissions handed out by Silas Deane to French volunteers. On July 31, on its own authority, Congress votes "to accept the services of the Marquis de La Fayette" as if he had just appeared out of the blue and to assign him "the rank and duties of major general* in the army of the United States . . . in consideration of his zeal, his illustrious family and connections . . . given the fact that he has left his home and country at his own expense . . . that he asks no salary or maintenance and simply desires to risk his life for our cause."[5] Signed: Pontius Pilate.

If Mirabeau, in his cell at Vincennes, had heard of this incident, it might have lessened his pain and bitterness: even if he had managed to make the tremendous leap from Amsterdam to America, they would have sent him packing as an unsavory character. Fame is to be had—for a price.

La Fayette's companions will have to recognize this. They are not related to the Noailles clan. They are not millionaires. La Fayette pressures his hosts to let Gimat and La Colombe stay on as his "aides de camp"; Captain de Chesnay is hired as a topographical engineer. As for the rest, out! Send them back where they came from and let them take it up with Silas Deane.

Kalb is beside himself with rage. Why should they take this young whippersnapper when here he stands, a veteran of years in America, an experienced soldier, right-hand man of the Comte de Broglie? An insult not just to him but also to the others whom he recruited. Mr. Hancock gets an earful: "I cannot tell you, sir, how deeply I resent this offense and how absurd it appears to have snatched these men from their homes, their families, their professions, to cross the ocean and brave untold perils only to be greeted with scorn by those from whom we expected only gratitude." In any event, this isn't the end of the matter: "Regretfully, I might be compelled to bring suit for damages against

*A rank then equivalent to colonel, or the commander of a division.

Mr. Deane or his heirs . . . ."[6] For the moment, let him scream his head off. No one bothers to answer. He and his fellow "misfits" can hang about Philadelphia as long as they wish. This is no land of savages; no one is chasing them away. But don't expect help if the British catch them. Lookouts spotted the enemy fleet rounding the Delaware coast on July 30. The little band that came together more or less accidentally at Los Pasajes disperses in a huff. Did La Fayette really exert himself to defend them? Or is he secretly relieved to see them go? After all, Kalb, not he, brought them here. Gilbert listens for the sound of gunfire. His one desire at the moment is to meet Washington, the commander-in-chief, on whom his military assignment depends.

Another man's hopes soon will be dashed. The Comte de Broglie, on his estate in Charente, had better forget his dreams of ruling the New World. Kalb writes to him: "The mere mention of it would be pointless. They would consider it a gross miscarriage of justice to Washington as well as an insult to their country."[7] Go buy yourself a new outfit, Monsieur le Comte; these Americans are odd enough to want fellow Americans to lead them. La Fayette has grasped this fact when he thanks John Hancock for his commission, and assures him of "the loyalty that every true American owes you."[8]

GEORGE WASHINGTON

83

JULY 1777

A Man Truly Made for This Revolution

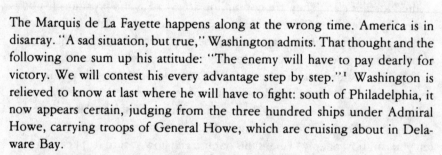

The Marquis de La Fayette happens along at the wrong time. America is in disarray. "A sad situation, but true," Washington admits. That thought and the following one sum up his attitude: "The enemy will have to pay dearly for victory. We will contest his every advantage step by step."[1] Washington is relieved to know at last where he will have to fight: south of Philadelphia, it now appears certain, judging from the three hundred ships under Admiral Howe, carrying troops of General Howe, which are cruising about in Delaware Bay.

Philadelphia takes on a different look in the first week of August as men and officers pour in, the last patriot units that are still more or less intact, a thousand strong, whom Washington had camped on the New Jersey border, near Princeton, since May, unsure whether the fighting would take them north or south. South it is. "Between you and me," Washington writes to his brother

John Augustine, "I fear the game is up . . . We will retreat, if necessary, beyond the Alleghenies."² This was his state of mind when he met La Fayette for the first time on the afternoon of July 31, 1777, at a languid and dreary luncheon in his honor given by Pennsylvania officials. For Gilbert, it was a memorable event. Like Joan of Arc singling out the dauphin at Chinon, he walks straight up to the commander-in-chief, "surrounded as he was by officers and citizens. His majestic face and bearing made it impossible not to recognize him. His gracious and noble welcome was no less distinctive."³

Washington is an imposing figure in his elegant blue-and-white uniform, trim and proper as everything else about him. At forty-five, he looks closer to fifty; some twenty years earlier he acquired a "lordly air, an imposing, awkward dignity"⁴ which, coupled with a certain mental and muscular dullness, suggests the gentleman farmer he is, more at ease on his plantation or in the army than in the drawing room. His smooth, sunburned features carry a scar from his first battle, against the French. He wears the inscrutable mask of a leader. No wrinkles. Remote gaze. An endless capacity for silence shields him from reproach. "This silence," he says, "which often can express feelings better than the most refined eloquence."⁵ Washington: a dense mass.

He is a feudal lord of the old America, which is now dying in order to stay alive, unaware that she will never be quite the same afterward. Washington, born on the banks of the Potomac not far from Chesapeake Bay, came of aristocratic English stock, opponents of Cromwell who had emigrated in 1657. Not rich to begin with: hard-working tobacco farmers. His father died early, leaving ten children from two marriages for George's mother, Mary Washington,* to care for. Mary still presides over the family estate like a queen mother, more feared than loved. "She was really a good person, but even in the midst of her goodness this majestic woman was awe-inspiring."⁶ "Majestic"; "awe-inspiring"; the same refrain is heard from Washington's associates. A good deal of his austerity must have come from his mother. She had armed her children for the peaceful conquest of ever widening vistas beyond the Potomac. One sure path was to marry them off to neighboring planters in order to consolidate the ancestral domain. Concentration of property. George's elder brothers had worked hard and died prematurely, leaving him head of the family. He started life as a surveyor, the only acceptable profession for a Virginian other than soldiering or farming: this involved measuring the land exactly so as to avert feuds between neighbors, though it took a day's journey on horseback to reach that neighbor.

Washington has fulfilled his family obligations. Twenty years of toil, planning, and social advancement have made him one of the richest landlords in Virginia. Mount Vernon,** his estate along the lower Potomac, covers two

*She dies in 1789, after her son becomes president.
**The "Mount of Vernon," named after the British admiral under whom his elder brother Lawrence Washington had served. Lawrence had bought the estate.

thousand five hundred acres. In 1777 he is master of 135 slaves.[7] As time passed, he took up arms on several occasions, like the warring barons of feudal times, against the French, or Indians, or both when they joined forces, and in support of westward expansion. It won him twofold notoriety: Europe execrated him, America revered him. Washington is the spark that set off the war of 1754 between English and French settlers, which, little by little, without the nations realizing it, led to the Seven Years' War that bled Europe white. There is a skeleton in Washington's past, the ghost of Captain de Jumonville, struck down somewhere "near the fork of the Ohio" at daybreak on May 28, 1754, by a surprise volley from Washington's musketmen. Thirty-two against forty. The opening battle of history's first world conflict. A hundred thousand deaths were to follow, but could not erase the memory of those first victims: because Jumonville had been betrayed, say the French: he came as a parliamentary observer. Not so, counter the English: he was leading a band of armed spies. The debate goes on for twenty-five years and fans the flames of ancient rivalries. The name of Washington became a refrain prior to the Declaration of Independence; he, along with Franklin, was probably the only American known in Europe—where he had never set foot. French literary gazettes had published the patriotic verses of a certain Thomas on "the murder of Jumonville, that monumental perfidy which cannot fail to outrage the centuries."[8] To which Virginians replied that their twenty-two-year-old colonel was merely doing his duty. Those were the seeds of his military glory, slow-growing at first because America did not have to go to war every year and also because Washington had fancied himself somewhat prematurely in command of an army, confirmed at the first hint of war, a liking for which he confessed to his brother: "I heard the whine of musket balls and, believe me, their song casts a spell."[9] He resigned his commission toward the close of 1754, slightly older than La Fayette now is, complaining that he was being treated unfairly. Two years later, under local pressure, they begged him to return and take command of the Virginia forces, a militia suffering from contagious and rampant desertion. The average militiaman enlisted for a year and saw no need to stay longer when there was no fighting. He returned to his tobacco farm. Washington had nothing but contempt for these overnight soldiers, "obstinate, conceited, cunning, of little or no use to the population and overcostly to the colony. The first rascal to appear sizes up the situation and wants to run things. If his opinions are ignored, he takes offense, turns on his heel in protest, and marches back home."[10] Exactly as Washington himself had done two years earlier, but he was a leader and had firm notions of how to discipline cocky recruits: "The most ruthless punishments, the most impressive examples." He ordered a gallows of record height, forty feet, raised in front of his regiment to hang three deserters (who normally would have gone before a firing squad) on July 27, 1757. There could be no doubt that Colonel Washington would be a tough and demanding wartime commander. He punished his men severely; thirty strokes of the lash were not enough: "That many strokes scarcely intimidate certain incorrigible fellows, some of whom have stated that they would gladly endure such punishment for a bottle of rum."[11] Flogging starts "with a thousand strokes of the lash."* When he turned in his commission for the second time late in 1758, again from injured vanity, he ran no risk of being flogged or hanged, for by then the thirteen colonies looked to him as the Hercules who would save them from all future crises. He counted on this. He did some local politicking meanwhile to bolster his status, for such was the custom among rich planters. Virginia's prominent citizens were invited to Mount Vernon. He advanced steadily through social connections, which he cultivated as systematically as his tobacco fields.

Silence enhanced his reputation more than public discourse. His mute opposition to British extortion had a greater impact on the South than Patrick Henry's** speeches. To his peers he offered an ideal well within their grasp: a conservative revolution. "My instinctive sense of liberty made me realize that the measures adopted several months before by the government [of George III] are contrary to all principles of natural justice."[12] And when George Washington says no, he means it. Unlike Franklin or Jefferson, he was not guided by philosophic principles. From childhood he learned to defend home and family against marauding Indians; if the British insisted on acting like savages, they would be treated so.

Enthusiasm? Not a trace. As a delegate to the Continental Congress of 1775, his mood seemed to reflect energetic fatalism. He went about in a cloud of profound sadness that eventually became a permanent fixture: sorrow rising to the surface of a successful life—successful except in love. Washington's one great passion (if he was capable of such a thing) had been the wife of his best friend, George William Fairfax, who owned the neighboring estate of Belvoir. Ten years of suppressed desire. He became engaged (purely in the interests of carrying on the family name) to Martha Dandridge, the Widow Custis, plump, pleasant, and well provided for. Four months before his wedding, Sally Fairfax confessed that she, too, had loved him secretly for ten years. Washington uttered a little groan as if struck by a bullet, married Martha Custis on January 6, 1759, and kept silent until the end of his days. The two couples saw a good deal of each other on the farm, at receptions, on hunting parties. Martha and Sally became close friends. They exchanged port wine and home-made sausage. Shortly before the Declaration of Independence, the Fairfaxes sailed back to England, where the bulk of their fortune lay. Washington was left with his farm, his political career, and a war. All that, only that. And a wife who bore him no children.

---

*This phrase recurs over and over again in Washington's correspondence.
**Patrick Henry (b. 1736), a self-made lawyer; his fierce condemnation of the crown roused Virginians in the early days of the Revolution.

In Philadelphia his silence had focused attention on him. The northern delegates elected him commander-in-chief in order to bind the South more firmly
to the cause. He thanked them in three sentences and went off to rejoin his
regiment near Boston. Letter to his wife on the day he left: "I am not the least
apprehensive about the toil and perils of the campaign ahead: my only regret
will be to think how lonely you will feel, I know, being left alone. I pray you
therefore to arm yourself with courage and spend your time as pleasantly as
possible . . . Since life is always uncertain, I enclose a will. I trust the benefits
it assures you in case I die will please you."[13]

He was positively convinced that Congress had made the right choice.
"No man who has ever served his country has worked more industriously and
zealously in the nation's interest to fulfill the duties entrusted to him than
have I."[14]

Now, after a year of this ugly war, no one had a word of blame for him.
The very shadow of his presence was comforting, and in December the Congress had granted him broad powers to "raise and assemble, promptly and in
the most efficient manner, sixteen infantry battalions in addition to those
already approved by Congress, to appoint officers . . . to raise, commission,
and equip three thousand light horse, three artillery regiments, and an engineers corps and to fix their pay . . . to deploy and appoint all officers below
the rank of brigadier general";[15] he also was given police powers and authorized to levy requisitions. Though a *de facto* military dictator, he continued to
conduct himself as an obedient servant of the Congress, to which he reported
punctually. Too punctually, it seemed, for the news he brought them was
generally dismal.

A single victory at the start: they had chased the enemy from Boston. But
then the British took New York and, after six months of bitter fighting, pried
Washington from the Hudson Valley. He had done his best to slow their
southward offensive with swift, brilliant thrusts like the now legendary one at
Trenton, just above the frozen Delaware River, on Christmas Day, 1776. The
British generals were dumfounded: who ever heard of attacking on Christmas?
Howe and Cornwallis, with a superiority of two or three to one, began their
tramp across New Jersey, expecting to fight European-type engagements
against the massed regiments of Louis XV or Maria Theresa. Washington, it
turned out, was carrying on hit-and-run warfare. Seven months of hide-and-
seek in and around Princeton and New Brunswick. Then came the British
withdrawal that was not a withdrawal but a falling back for support on her
incomparable lifeline, her proudest battle force, the fleet. Now they have been
sighted, those lions of the seas. Philadelphia's fate hangs in the balance, as if
anyone expected the city to hold out. The entire British force in America
numbered 32,575 men (including 11,618 in Canada).* Washington was never
quite sure of the size of his army; less than 15,000 in any event.[16]

At the luncheon on July 31 Washington also notices La Fayette, whose patrician manners contrast sharply with those of his Philadelphia merchant hosts. Not to mention those dimpled rosy cheeks among so many gaunt faces. Here is at least one person who hasn't given up the city for lost. "Tomorrow let me show you the defenses along the Delaware"—the magnetic current is flowing. No other American has responded to La Fayette with such unstinted cordiality; never has the heart of George Washington been conquered so speedily. Washington is burdened with guilt for France (or perhaps for himself?) over the death of Jumonville. And he needs officers of distinction to lead his democratic army. "In choosing officers, it is best to avoid having them come from the same background as their subordinates. The hierarchy of rank often is transferred from civil to military life . . . The first rule is to determine whether the candidate is truly a gentleman, whether he has a genuine sense of honor and a reputation to risk."[17] Since this relative of the Noailles clan is willing to pay his own way, unlike all the other Frenchmen who have come over in the past year, he passes the test.

La Fayette will proclaim to the world that at last he has found a father, the one he has been seeking ever since that ugly bullet (English, naturally) robbed him of his own parent at the Battle of Hastenbeck. A hint of complacency runs through his letter to the arrogant Duc d'Ayen: "Our general is a man truly made for this revolution, which, but for him, could never be achieved . . . I see how worthy he is of his countrymen's adulation . . . I admire, more and more with every passing day, the beauty of his mind and character . . . His name will be revered down through the centuries by all lovers of liberty and of mankind . . . I think the role he is performing gives me the right to tell the world how much I respect and admire him."[18] A clear message to his father-in-law, who had snubbed him mercilessly.

In the meantime, "dear heart," his wife, had given birth on July 1 to their second daughter, Adrienne, and the *Victoire* had foundered on a sand bar obstructing the entrance to Charleston harbor. Gilbert will have to deal with some heady insurance problems, but what does he care now that he has a chance to fight!

*Figures for June 1777.

84

A Mere Scratch, Dear Heart

La Fayette is on the brink of two battles: a real one at Brandywine Creek, and a psychological one by pressing his favor with Washington. He takes a grip on events, plunges ahead blindly, and triumphs—but not until September. Throughout the month of August, for the last time, his fate hangs in the balance.

Washington has returned to headquarters north of Philadelphia, not sure at first what to do. Where have the English gone? They were sighted at the mouth of the Delaware, but never entered it. The sea seems to have swallowed up their fleet. Now what? Will they head south, invade Charleston again, and overrun the Carolinas and Georgia? No, reports on August 4 say they are advancing due north toward the Hudson—which they left the month before. What an absurd war! Washington marches northward, tentatively, on August 8. Wait! Wait! A messenger gallops up two days later: British ships have reappeared at the mouth of the Delaware. The threat to Philadelphia from the river is more real than ever. Washington calls a halt and camps once again on the Pennsylvania–New Jersey border, about fifteen miles above Philadelphia. A hilly wilderness* where Neshaminy Creek lazily winds its way through ancient hunting grounds of the Bucks tribe and loops back on itself to form a convenient entrenchment. The army will wait there several days and prepare for a showdown. Will the British decide to land somewhere north of Philadelphia? In fact, after it merges with the Schuylkill, the Delaware narrows too rapidly to accommodate large vessels.

Meanwhile La Fayette cools his heels in town, waiting for his commission and trying to raise money: he is down to his last cent. By a stroke of fortune, the agent for "Rodrigo Hortalez & Co." is still in Philadelphia, an intelligent, capable, trustworthy young man named Théveneau de Francy, none other than the brother of pamphleteer Théveneau de Morande, whose scandalmongering *Gazetier cuirassé* had made him the king of extortionists in Du Barry's

*Today these hills form one of the principal green belts surrounding the sprawling Philadelphia metropolis on the east, about twenty miles from the city center.

day. Beaumarchais and Morande had kept in touch ever since their pact in 1774, and Morande introduced his younger brother to the playwright–shipowner–secret-agent, who was admirably positioned in Paris to launch a Burgundian novice "in the business world." Pleasant surprise: whereas the elder brother was a rotten plank from the start, the younger one matured into stout timber. Beaumarchais grew fond of the lad and lately has begun to treat him like a son. "You and I are one and the same."[1] Francy is authorized to deal freely as his agent in America and acts more or less as a secret commercial ambassador to the Congress, like Silas Deane to Vergennes. La Fayette, who had ignored Beaumarchais in France (upon the Comte de Broglie's advice), is delighted now to encounter that suspicious commoner's representative, who enjoys sufficient authority to lend the large sums required by an unsalaried major general to purchase horses, equipment, uniforms, servants, and all the paraphernalia of military life for himself and his aides.

On August 13 his commission comes through. On the 20th, outfitted from head to toe, he gallops off to join Washington, who now wonders what to do with this charming foreigner. An altogether captivating young man indeed, but does this qualify him for a military assignment? Now La Fayette had sent General Washington a series of glowing letters which helped to create certain false impressions about the writer. Washington warned the Congress on August 19: "I do not think you realize the breadth of his ambition . . . certain it is, if I understand *him,* that he does not conceive his commission is merely honorary, but given with a view to command a division of this army . . . he has said that he is young and inexperienced, but at the same time he has always accompanied it with a hint that so soon as *I* shall think him fit for the command of a division, he shall be ready to enter upon the duties of it, and in the meantime has offered his service for a smaller command."[2]

Gilbert is no fool. Having obtained this hard-won commission from Congress, he is not about to demand his pound of flesh from headquarters. If a misunderstanding, it is a stroke of tactical genius. He arrives at the Neshaminy Creek campsite on the afternoon of August 20 only to discover a state of confusion unlike anything he had ever seen at the officers' training academy in Metz. "About eleven thousand men, poorly armed and miserably clad, offered an amazing display; among the motley assortment of dress and occasional undress, the best garments were hunting blouses: loose-fitting gray sailcloth jackets common in the Carolinas."[3] At headquarters, however, Washington manages to come up with a touch of Virginian hospitality: plenty of food and drink at regular hours. He introduces La Fayette to his staff as if he, personally, had recruited him. What finer specimen of French court nobility could you ask for to boost officer morale? Of course no one knows what he went through to get here. La Fayette, with his aristocratic swagger, likes to hint that he is just the first swallow of this Franco-American spring. Even if Washington detects the Frenchman's excessive vanity, he refrains from pricking it in the hope that behind La Fayette stands a Broglie and Louis XVI, and that this lanky redhead heralds the arrival of warships, desperately needed artillery, and French troops by the thousands. Gilbert thus is authorized to sit in on the council of war of August 21 and is given the title of "major general in the service of the United States"—success! This assures him equal, if not superior, footing. And the privilege of witnessing a glorious blundering, for the pattern these past two months is repeating itself: the British have vanished again. But what did that messenger report back on August 7? Is theirs a ghost fleet? They are not attacking Philadelphia directly. Refrain: they must be heading for Charleston. So we head for Charleston? No, too little time. They travel by sea, but it would take us two months to cover the distance on land with all our arms and supplies. Let the Carolinians look out for themselves. We are marching north (another refrain) to recapture New York, which they left virtually defenseless.

Decision reached on August 20 and revoked two days later with great alarm. The president of the Congress informs Washington: "A message just arrived from Maryland signals the presence of about two hundred sails of Admiral Howe's fleet in Chesapeake Bay. The Congress consequently has ordered the immediate transfer of provisions and prisoners to safer ground."[4] If those gentlemen are moving out, things really must be serious. The ghost fleet has materialized again. Howe has elected to pursue a compromise operation instead of invading Philadelphia from the Delaware River, where it would be hazardous to land troops under fire, or sending his forces farther south. Chesapeake Bay is a gateway to Virginia, hub of the central and southern colonies; it offers countless opportunities for joint maneuvers between land and sea units. The British will come ashore as far north as possible (Chesapeake Bay, like the Delaware, stretches in a north-south direction, but is much wider); this will deliver them west of Philadelphia, which they will attempt to circle from the southwest, then attack from the east. They may even capture Washington's army if he persists in defending the beleaguered capital. There is no colonial fleet to evacuate his troops.

At last the situation becomes clear. The fearful uncertainty is ended. American marching orders are reversed: instead of heading north, they head south. Washington will try to block the road to Philadelphia. There is no time to assign duties to La Fayette; everyone is welcome to come along and be shot at. On August 24 La Fayette rides in Washington's parade through the city, a last brave show. Look at the closed shutters, the scowling faces on the street! Tory sympathizers are mixing their best punch for the redcoats. Washington has ignored this in planning the line of march: "The army will march single file through the city of Philadelphia," whose shape, from overhead, resembles a beef tongue stuck out from north to south, between the Schuylkill on the left, the Delaware on the right; the tip of the tongue marks their confluence. "The army will march down Front Street and up Chestnut to the Common.

About a mile outside the town the troops will halt to give the rear guard a chance to catch up and rejoin the column . . . Drummers and fifers will march in the middle of each brigade* and will play a tune for a quickstep, but with such moderation that the men may step to it with ease, and without either dancing along or totally disregarding the music, as too often happens."⁵ La Fayette rides starry-eyed in this funeral-like procession. His dream has come true. If tomorrow should mean the end of the world, he will die content. They pass the Schuylkill and at one point descend the right bank of the Delaware. They pitch camp in Chester just long enough to catch their breath. Where the royal army is hiding remains a mystery.

This time the redcoats are very close. You can see them, you can feel them. The fleet has sailed far up the Chesapeake and landed eighteen thousand men between Bel Air and Havre de Grâce—charming names contributed by the French. The upper Chesapeake is barely twenty miles from the lower Delaware. Philadelphia will hear cannon booming—rarely, for both sides lack artillery. The battle, actually a series of skirmishes, will start on September 11 on both sides of Brandywine Creek, where settlers once bought off the Indians with wine and spirits. A lazy, serpentine stream with east and west forks, fordable in autumn at some thirty-six different places. Washington throws up defenses wherever possible; they are boxed in by this foggy, thickly wooded region that offers no open space in which to deploy troops. They wait, they send out patrols, they guard against an attempt to turn their flank: Howe, by cutting them off from Philadelphia, could hurl them into the Delaware. Reinforcements have reached the Americans, as they always do in times of crisis; volunteers keep pouring in. A strange army this, unlike any other, where men actually come to fight, even against hopeless odds. Their ranks swell to nearly thirteen thousand. Another stroke of luck for La Fayette: he appears on the scene when there happens to be a shortage of officers to organize these plowmen turned soldiers.

On the eve of battle, September 10, he spends the night under Gideon Gilpin's roof, in a log cabin** that might have sheltered a missionary or trapper. Washington sleeps close by, within earshot, in the brick house of Benjamin Ring. Between the two, only trees, thick clumps of bushes, the constant movement of sentinels and dispatch runners. For two days they have hardly slept a wink. Early on September 11, 1777, La Fayette drinks in the sound he had been waiting since boyhood to hear: the dull roar of advancing armies. Twelve thousand infantry under Cornwallis and Knyphausen are marching up the two roads that converge at the Chadds Ford crossing. Washington masses his troops to bar their passage. La Fayette is at his side. He commands no unit, but acts as an aide to the commander-in-chief, sending and

*About a thousand men.
**Restored and preserved, the house, known (erroneously) as "General de La Fayette's headquarters," now stands in the sprawling suburbs southwest of Philadelphia.

receiving dispatches up and down the line. It is very hot and dusty. Five thousand redcoats—easy targets at long range for American gunners, whose own gray coats are far better camouflage—pour down steadily with the self-confidence of veterans from high ground above the stream, then halt at pre-scribed intervals to fling out a volley of musket balls. It is merely a diversion. Cornwallis has left Knyphausen and taken their main force upstream to at-tempt the flanking operation that Washington feared.

But Washington is cautious and distrusts his own instincts. He believes only what he can see or piece together from scraps of intelligence. He studies the approaching battle instead of actively shaping it. And he loses this one, the cost of hanging on to the defense of Chadds Ford until two in the afternoon, giving Cornwallis time to strike at his other flank. Now he is in a pincer grip: the worst peril lies upstream. La Fayette pleads to be sent there. Washington already has seen the plucky young Frenchman in action, herding panic-stricken runaways back to the lines. His indifference, or blindness, to danger is unwav-ering: bullets whistling past his ears have no more effect than mosquitoes. He wants to go? Let him go!

By half past four the battle has split in two: Washington, with the bulk of his army, faces Knyphausen's relentless advance foot by foot over Brandy-wine Creek at Chadds Ford. Three miles upstream, half the American columns have been sent to help General Sullivan stem Cornwallis's maneuver. This second skirmish takes place near the Birmingham Meeting House,* where colonists met for prayers and political debate. Hundreds of such meeting houses have spawned the citizens of the first free nation in modern times, which Hessian grenadiers under Cornwallis are doing their utmost to stamp out. The attackers make use of a tier of embankments to steady their long muskets and riddle the Americans with well-directed fire. Their volleys, faster and deadlier for being delivered by disciplined professionals, sow panic rein-forced by the sight of charging waves of redcoats. Two lines of defense crumble one after the other, and General Sullivan's retreat turns into a stam-pede. With shouts and gestures, La Fayette and his fellow officers urge terror-stricken defenders back into the ranks. No need to speak their tongue: pandemonium's language is universal. La Fayette leaps from his horse and plunges into the crowd of fleeing soldiers, cajoling and threatening. The bravest are rallied behind a knoll and regrouped around the Stirling Brigade, as the British pour in fresh troops and Cornwallis adds his reserves, outnum-bering the patriots ten to one. When this vast, outspread line of charging redcoats advances to within twenty paces, Sullivan's last unbroken regiment, which Stirling and La Fayette have helped to command, panics and takes to the woods, later to rejoin Washington, who has kept only a curtain of troops at Chadds Ford after realizing too late where the real battle lies. All he can do now is hold out long enough to turn a rout into an orderly retreat. One

*Still standing.

road bordering the Delaware lies open to Chester and Philadelphia. They must gain it somehow or risk total defeat.

When La Fayette goes to remount, he sees that he is wounded. How eagerly he had yearned for that musket ball in the left thigh! To bear a wound from one's first battle means good luck forever after, the old soldiers say. Gimat, his aide de camp, insists on applying a makeshift tourniquet. La Fayette ignores the injury until nightfall, having all he can do to help organize the flood of suvivors creeping toward Chester. "But how can you lean on a broken staff?" Washington observes wryly,[6] cognizant of the caliber of his undisciplined army. They come from all over to fight and then take to their heels. At Brandywine Creek, as at Kips Bay, General Washington threatened deserters with his sword, kicked their backsides, fired his pistol at runaways. A few of the day's casualties could be credited to him,[7] though he could have spared himself the trouble of helping the British. With this abject defeat, Philadelphia is lost.

The young Frenchman is borne by the retreating human wave to a small bridge just outside Chester.* "Amid the awful confusion, and with darkness fallen, it was impossible to recognize anyone."[8] He has withstood both panic and pain, retaining the calm composure needed to rally a handful of men and post sentinels at the bridge until Washington and his generals arrive. Only then does he put himself in the hands of Dr. William Magaw, a surgeon with the First Pennsylvania Regiment, who finds the whole leg so swollen that he has to slit open the riding boot in order to dress the wound. La Fayette has lost a great deal of blood and damaged several tendons. It is by no means the "scratch" he mentions in writing to his wife the next day from Philadelphia, which serves as a temporary shelter until Howe attacks the doomed city: "Just a few words, dear heart, which I send you through French officer friends who came here with me and failed to receive commissions, so are returning home.** Let me begin by telling you that I am well, because I must eventually tell you that yesterday we had a full-scale battle and did not emerge victorious. Our Americans, after holding firm for quite a spell, were finally routed; in trying to rally them, I was rewarded by milords the English with a musket ball in the leg, a mere scratch, dear heart; it has not damaged any bone or nerve, and I am beset with nothing worse than a few days on my back, which puts me in ill humor." The patriot cause suffered worse damage than he: "This incident, I fear, will bring far more troublesome times to America."[9]

*Now more or less a suburb of Philadelphia, about thirty miles southwest of the central city.
**Mauroy, probably. Kalb is stopped before he reaches the ship: the Brandywine disaster forces Congress to reconsider his application, and on September 15 they commission him a major general, like La Fayette. They will need him.

85

The Highway to Freedom

Depressed and running a low fever, La Fayette resolves to boost his dampened spirits. To crush America will take many more redcoats than are about to enter Philadelphia. Gilbert does not think of them or of his recent baptism by fire when he writes a second letter to Paris, conscious of the fact that his views will begin to mold public opinion. "Since you are now [October 1] the wife of an officer in the American army, I shall have to instruct you in certain matters. People will say to you: 'They have been beaten,' to which you must answer: 'That I cannot deny, but when two armies are equal . . . old soldiers always have the edge over raw recruits. Besides, they had had the pleasure of killing many, many more of the enemy than they have lost of their own men.' Then they will say: 'That is all very well, but Philadelphia has fallen, the capital of America, the highway to freedom . . . ' "[1]

That he could not deny. General Cornwallis had entered the city on September 26 with his army of British and German regulars, including several thousand Hessians—sold into foreign service by the Landgrave of Hesse-Cassel—who had mutinied in Holland the year before. Washington gathers the greater part of his militiamen at Germantown (originally a German settlement, as the name suggests), several miles outside Philadelphia. For the present, all he can hope to do is harass the enemy, keep him on the alert, and put off his occupation of the capital.

La Fayette is in Bethlehem, a good fifty miles farther north, between Emmaus and Nazareth.

When Quakers "shaken by the Holy Spirit," persecuted in Europe and America for refusing to persecute others, finally found refuge in the wilderness purchased by William Penn, they likened themselves to the Jews reaching the Promised Land. They gave biblical names to the towns they carved out of virgin forests. The Moravian Brothers, known as German Quakers, had fled central Europe and settled in Bethlehem after the third or fourth wave of religious repression following Jan Hus's martyrdom. Here, in one of their largest communities, they lived and worshiped peacefully, asking only that their pacifist ideals be respected. They were useless, therefore, to the Revolution but very useful in binding up its wounds, as were many Pennsylvania residents. Theirs was a charitable neutrality.

La Fayette was taken by boat with other casualties to Bristol, farther up the Delaware. There he was able to share the carriage of a member of Congress, Henry Laurens, who had also fled the capital and was seeking to rejoin his scattered colleagues. At last report, the Congress was camping out at York,* far west of Philadelphia and north of Baltimore, where its members dared not assemble so long as Howe's fleet held the Chesapeake. The doctors counseled La Fayette against making a long journey even by coach and to keep his leg elevated for at least a month. So Henry Laurens made a brief detour to drop him off with the Moravian Brothers.

"What a contrast between the peaceful religion of this community of brothers, their unity of interests, of education, of property ownership, the life of this great innocent family, and the scenes of carnage, the convulsions of civil war that I have just left behind."[2] A twinge of real bewilderment must have gripped him on reaching that Other World, where the taking of blood is forbidden. The register of the "House of the Moravian Brothers" in Bethlehem, transformed into a hospital for casualties of the Battle of Brandywine, records the entrance of many patients on Sunday evening, September 21, 1777: "The influx of strangers was too great for the inn to accommodate. Among them were many French officers, colonels, and even a general who is an illustrious nobleman." Wherever he went, Gilbert wasted no time announcing his pre-eminent ancestry.

He is cared for but not housed by the congregation, as he can well afford to pay room and board to Mrs. Barbara Beckel, "wife of Bethlehem's chief farmer." She lodges him on the second floor overlooking the main street. And what luck to have her daughter Liesel for his nurse, a fresh, charming young thing not yet twenty, who dresses all in white and is utterly fascinated by the "illustrious nobleman."

His eager eyes drink in this strange Quaker universe, whose "fundamental precept is to abuse no one in matters of religion and to treat as brothers all those who believe in a god** . . . It was a strange experience to see everyone addressing a sovereign [Pennsylvania's governor] familiarly and without removing his hat." Indeed, the Quakers had decided some time back not to bare their heads to anyone. They lived out their lives with broad-brimmed black hats glued to their stubborn skulls. Dark clothing all of a color; no wig, no war, no creed, no house of worship, no entertainments. "A govern-

---

*An inland town, not to be confused with the port of Yorktown farther south at the mouth of the Chesapeake.

**According to Voltaire, who was intrigued by the Pennsylvania experiment.

ment without priests, a people unarmed, citizens who are equal, almost before the law, and neighbors free of jealousy."* Franklin was always fond of them even if his sense of humor kept him from attending their meetings, which took place in any ordinary bare room, where the Holy Spirit never failed to invade someone and shake him like a sapling. Onto this society of purists the Moravian Brothers had grafted an element of asceticism reminiscent of Catharists and illuminati. Their "evangelical community" was very like primitive communism brightened with music, for each member learned to play an instrument, usually the flute, horn, or oboe. But the strict hierarchy of Ancients—who imposed an iron discipline on the congregation—Beginners, Progressives, and the Perfect, reintroduced a priestless priesthood and hidden political power in that Promised Land at the foot of the Alleghenies. "While the good Moravian Brothers were deploring my passion for soldiery,"[3] and despite the appetizing presence of Liesel Beckel, La Fayette was growing bored to death and complained bitterly of the slow healing process. "The wound is in the fleshy part of my leg and not near any bone or nerve . . . The surgeons [of the Moravian community] melt into ecstasies each time they change the bandage and insist it is one of the marvels of the age. I myself find it thoroughly tiresome and rather painful. A matter of taste. And that, dear heart, is the tale of what I pompously call my wound, just to give myself airs and attract attention."[4]

To pass the time he wrote stacks of letters, not just to dear heart; to Washington he offered advice on military strategy; he urged members of Congress whom he had met in Philadelphia to adopt certain political positions; to his cousin the Marquis de Bouillé, governor of the Leeward Islands, he suggested a plan of attack on the British Antilles. Bouillé politely reminds him that France is not at war with England. Objection overruled: La Fayette submits the plan to Maurepas after embellishing it with a diversionary tactic, a French assault "under the American banner." Maurepas throws up his hands at the nerve of this greenhorn strategist "who would strip Versailles bare to help the American cause; once he gets an idea into his head, there is no telling were he will stop."[5] But perhaps this rancorous old man long set in his ways is thinking back to another callow youth, who, catapulted into the naval ministry at fourteen, developed such interest in his work that by the time he reached La Fayette's present age he was devising schemes for invading the British Isles. In those days Maurepas had had a spark of life; now his main concern is to hang on, to "spare" himself. But his influence at court is still felt when he remarks on the impressive courage and verbal gifts of this survivor of the Battle of the Brandywine. It marks a turning point in official opinion: La Fayette ceases to be a target of ridicule.

In America he has won even more dramatic acclaim. Washington, whose authority grows with each defeat, wrote to the Congress immediately after the

*Voltaire again.

battle and commended La Fayette's conduct. He seems to have adopted him emotionally at some point between the Chadds Ford crossing and the bridge outside Chester where the young officer had stationed himself to await his commander-in-chief and father figure in the chaos of retreat and with a bleeding leg. Same disdain for the human fodder of war, ordinary soldiers who flee death. Same determination to resist the gloom of defeat. Same tenacity: functional in the older man, temperamental in the novice. After Brandywine, Washington and La Fayette begin to grasp their common historic destiny, even if Gilbert's initial boasting distorts their relationship somewhat: "All foreigners employed here are discontented, complaining, resentful, and resented. They cannot understand why I, a foreigner, am so well liked in America . . . For my part . . . as I am a good man, I am glad to be liked by everyone, foreigner or American . . . All the doctors here make a great fuss over me. A friend of mine has asked them to look after me; he is General Washington. This gentleman . . . has done me the honor to be my intimate friend.* His warm concern for my welfare has won my heart . . . We are as close as brothers, sharing each other's confidence and trust . . . Sending his personal surgeon to attend me, he urged him to treat me as if I were his son, for so he thinks of me."[6]

On October 4 Washington loses another battle, at Germantown. A trail of defeats too long to record. The Americans retreat again, but British forces concentrated in Philadelphia seem no better off for it. Like a pot-bound plant that cannot stretch its roots. They occupy a space, but the soil gives way. Even now the whirlwind is gathering; insurgents are slipping off down the Delaware to cut supply lines to the enemy fleet. Howe has repeated a classic British error: waging a leisurely war, failing to pursue, surprise, and destroy the foe. "They wasted precious time," La Fayette observes in later years, "and that was perhaps their greatest mistake in a war in which they made so many."[7]

He itches to be up and about in time to join in the reprisal. A month goes by before he is able to put on boots and ride again. He takes leave of his saintly hosts, who note in the register for October 16: "The French marquis, a charming and highly intelligent young man, came to say good-by; he asked permission to visit the Sister House, which we were only too pleased to grant. He went accompanied by an aide and expressed admiration for our institutions."[8]

Hypocrite! After those positive arguments he had written to his wife for her to promulgate at home: "Then they will say . . . 'Philadelphia has fallen' . . . 'the highway to freedom' . . . " So he had changed his tune, learned to sing out of both sides of his mouth. The hero of Brandywine must have cut a fine figure at receptions in the Hôtel de Noailles, when dear heart would read aloud his waggish portrait of the Quakers who were nursing him back to health:

*He has known him exactly two months.

"Then you counter politely thus: 'You are fools. Philadelphia is a dreary
town, open in all directions, its harbor already closed, rendered famous
(though I cannot imagine why) because it is the seat of Congress . . . It is full
of a scurvy kind of person, silly Quakers who do nothing but walk into a room
with broad hats on their heads and wait in silence for the Holy Spirit to
descend, until one of them, grown tired of waiting, gets up and spouts a great
many tears and a good deal of nonsense. So much for the people of Philadelphia. So much for this famous city, which, I can assure you, we shall get
back sooner or later.' "[9]

ROBESPIERRE FILS

86

NOVEMBER 1777

A Complete Change Came over Him

Munich in November, a forgotten Germany. Bavaria is buried under "warm
alpine snows" that drift in when the *Föhn* blows from the south and brings mild
winter weather from the Alps, whose white crests dot the horizon on clear
days. Is it the result of being squeezed between the Alps, the Danube, and the
Rhine, cut off from the mainstream of Europe's intellectual and martial life?
Bavaria, for the moment, is a relatively quiet spot on the continent and would
like to remain a loyal outpost of the Catholic Church, snugly sheltered by its
canons.

In Munich, too, forty thousand Germans go about their business peacefully, among the Nymphenburg Palace (local counterpart of Versailles), theaters, the museum, "which puts on marvelous balls and whose reading room
is rich in periodical sheets,"[1] "public walks that resemble English gardens,"
and many "academies of music." The season's two main events are the Carnival and the Christmas Fair; the interval is crowded with *dults,* minor holidays
that celebrate just about anything, such as the "Hit-the-Target Day" in August.
Between festivities a lot of work gets done—in the beer halls, which net
Bavaria over a million florins* annually, or in "a great number of shops that
make playing cards." There, on November 6, 1777, at some moment in the
endless chain of history, the father of Maximilien de Robespierre, "master of
languages," age forty-five, died of unknown cause and in unknown circumstances. The official certificate merely notes the death *"in München"* of
*About ten million francs [$2 million] today.

"Maximilianus de Robespierre de Aras [sic], *sprachmeister"* and his burial in the
Church of the Redeemer.* His children must have lost track of him and
assumed that he lived much longer than he did. He would have been sixty-
one in 1793. No one in Munich was in touch with Arras about this social misfit
cast up, while still a young man, onto the shores of a fading prince-elector.
That's another problem for the Bavarians: feuding Prussia and Austria are
bound to contest the elector's succession. Just when everything was so peaceful
. . . And why should anyone be interested in the whereabouts of this Frenchman, who may have had a falling out with the law in his homeland? His pupils
will have no trouble replacing him: Europe is full of such semi-vagabonds who
become schoolmasters because that or soldiering is the only profession open
to them.

But what was this Maximilien-Barthélemy-François Derobespierre** doing in
Munich? His true profession? Lawyer. His home soil? Artois. Family status?
Widower, father of four children. Legal encumbrances? None, save a few
debts. He was a runaway, pure and simple. An upper-middle-class citizen of
Arras who, like a sailor, packed up and went to sea. To pick up the trail of
this faceless individual, not a single portrait or description of whom has survived, we must work from whatever recorded clues exist between his birth and
death. An easy task, considering how few there are.

He was born in "the good town of Arras" on February 17, 1732. His
father, also named Maximilien Derobespierre, also a lawyer licensed by the
"superior provincial council of Artois," had married the daughter of a "bourgeois merchant" in accordance with the matrimonial tradition of social promotion practiced in this family since 1491, the husband providing "social status"
—nobility of the robe in this instance—and the wife, of "humbler origin,"
contributing "her dowry," as did Marie-Marguerite, "daughter of Bonaven-
ture Poiteau, bourgeois merchant, and Marie-Louise Graux," in 1731.[3] Again
traditionally, they named the first of their five children after the father, though
they called him Barthélemy.† Long before, Pierre Derobespierre or Jehan
Derobespierre had followed the same pattern to establish themselves "in
judicial circles" in Béthune, Carvin, or Arras, Austrian possessions at the time,
pleading in Latin and somehow surviving the intermittent strife peculiar to the
Fronde when French and Spanish armies under Turenne and Condé were
constantly warring in Flanders and Picardy. Having come under French sover-

*The discovery in February 1958[2] of this document, a copy of which subsequently was sent to
the town archives of Arras, finally resolved the long uncertainty as to the date and place of his
death. Conflicting tales had alleged the elder Robespierre to have died "in the Isles" (London)
or in America, but much later, as some sources maintain that he was alive during the Revolution
and followed his son's career from afar.
**Barthélemy was the name he usually used. The merger of his last name with the particle,
indicating his petty nobiliary extraction, was not uncommon at the time.
†Or sometimes François.

eignty only 120 years earlier, Artois province is "considered foreign" on the official tax rolls, along with Brittany, Franche-Comté, Provence, Languedoc, and others. A distinct advantage with respect to certain royal levies, but also a windfall for lawyers, since the strange statute generated hosts of lawsuits. The Derobespierres had plenty of work and promising careers—at least, the eldest sons did, who faithfully pursued the law from father to son with the blind devotion of reigning princes. The younger ones trained to become clerks, notaries, or tax collectors. One such example was Yves Robert-Spierre,* tax collector for the principality of Carvin-Epinoy, who managed, in 1696, to register his coat of arms blazoned thus: *Or a bend sable charged a demi-vol argent.*[4]

To return to Barthélemy: he was the first to break the pattern. As the eldest son, he was expected to take up his father's profession, yet at sixteen we find him a novice with the Premonstrants of Dommartin-en-Ponthieu. Mystical seizure or honest urge? Surely neither, for on June 17, 1749, several days or hours before making his vows, the young initiate confesses to his abbot that he "appeared desirous of taking holy orders only to content his father and mother."[5] He is permitted to leave at once; the church has enough unfrocked priests to contend with. Will he resume his law studies? Yes, but not in his hometown; he is sent to Douai to finish his degree.

There must have been friction between father and son. The elder Maximilien could not have been an accommodating sort, always bickering with relatives and his thirteen brothers and sisters. Late in life he had married a woman thirty years his junior. The children considered him a patriarch.

What caused the rift between father and son? This question invited all shades of local gossip, and much conjecture in later years. People said Barthélemy was chasing girls too much and was so "scatterbrained" that his father sent him off to the Premonstrants not to become a priest but to be kept under lock and key. A hopeless hothead, pure and simple, his father maintained. It was so easy in those days to rid the nest of ugly ducklings. But all this is muted, hinted at, nebulous. From Spanish occupation, Arras retained the faint aura of an ancient walled city, where bored young people wander aimlessly back and forth between two magnificent public squares, large and small, overlooked by gabled rooftops, each like its neighbor, and the gigantic abbey which the Benedictines of Saint-Vaast, the town's true aristocracy, are presently rebuilding on a lavish scale. A young lad "stuck on girls"—and his marriage will prove it—feels like:

---

*This whimsical spelling often finds its way into the newspapers in 1789 before Robespierre's fame is established. It will give rise to a tale picked up by the royalist gazette *Les Actes des Apôtres* [The Acts of the Apostles] claiming that *Robert-François* Damiens, the man who struck at Louis XV with a pocket knife, a native of Arras, was the great-uncle of Maximilien de *Robert-Pierre*. So Arras had cradled a regicide? The alleged relationship is pure myth.

Un malheureux, rélegué dans une île
Au sombre pays des patards

[A poor wretch stranded on an island
In the gloomy land of the *patard**]

asserted a French officer and amateur poet garrisoned in "the abode of yawns" which La Grande Mademoiselle [de Montpensier] had execrated a century before when, in the wake of Louis XIV, she was tiring of the first Lauzun.[6]

Though perhaps unstable, Barthélemy was never incompetent, as we know he became attorney for the Council of Artois on December 30, 1756, at the age of twenty-four, jointly with his father, whose good will he must have won—and kept through January 2, 1758, when he married Jacqueline-Marguerite Carraut, daughter of a brewer on the Rue Ronville.[7] So it's all patched up and tradition again takes the fore? The brewer will help his new son-in-law open his own office while old Maximilien's practice slowly dwindles. Life resumes its normal pattern after an adolescent fling . . .

But why did no relatives of the young couple sign the marriage certificate? A quiet ceremony, witnessed by strangers. A very unobtrusive wedding. Or a shotgun affair? Was Barthélemy the one who pressed for it, or was he dragged to the altar?

Four months and four days after the ceremony we find a birth certificate issued for another Maximilien, our own. Jacqueline Carraut, three years younger than her husband, was four and a half months pregnant at the time she married Barthélemy de Robespierre (the particle is now separate from the last name).

On the sixth of May 1758, I the undersigned baptized Maximilien-Marie-Isidore, born this day at two in the morning, offspring of the legitimate union of Maître Maximilien Barthélemy-François de Robespierre, attorney for the Council of Artois, and Jacqueline-Marguerite Carraut. The godfather was Maître Maximilien de Robespierre, paternal grandfather, attorney for the Council of Artois; the godmother was Marguerite-Marie Cornu, wife of Jacques-François Carraut, maternal grandmother, who affixed their signatures:

> De Robespierre/De Robespierre
> Mie-Marguerite Cornu
> G.-H.-P. Lenglart [curé][8]

Robespierre is born during the Seven Years' War. Europe becomes a bloody checkerboard through which the strategists wade: Frederick the Great, the Broglie clan for Louis XV, Daun and Laudon for Maria Theresa, along with Swedes, Russians, and Britons. Artesians** wait anxiously to see whether those accursed pawns will overrun their land. Washington has been named

*Popular name in Artois for a Flemish coin, from the Spanish *"pataca,"* meaning "piece of money." **Inhabitants of Artois province. [*Trans.*]

commander-in-chief but "retires" in a huff to Mount Vernon. Damiens, native of Arras, was dismembered six months earlier for slashing at the king with a knife; the censors pounce on this opportunity to halt publication of the *Encyclopédie,* which is only at volume seven, and D'Alembert breaks with Diderot out of sheer frustration. Madame de Pompadour favors Choiseul for a ministerial post, but her influence is fading. She governs Louis XV less than she governs France. Marat is fifteen and already traveling about. Voltaire has just written his *Essai sur les Moeurs* and secluded himself at Ferney, nevermore to roam.

Rousseau is writing *La Nouvelle Héloïse* and about to publish his *Lettre à d'Alembert sur les spectacles.* The year of Robespierre's birth marks the final break between the Encyclopedists and himself. Innovation's stronghold is developing cracks; the split between feeling and reason is building up. July will see publication of *De l'Esprit,* in which Helvétius sets out to "treat morality as a kind of experimental physics."

Barthélemy de Robespierre must have been an ardent fellow; his wife, though slight and possibly "pulmonic," went from one pregnancy to the next. Not the least exceptional: a Christian marriage in the Robespierre tradition.

February 8, 1760: birth of Marguerite-Marie-Charlotte.* December 28, 1761: Henriette-Eulalie-Françoise.

Maximilien senior died in 1762. His clients automatically shifted to his son, now one of the prominent lawyers in Arras and considered both eloquent and capable. A failure? "The number of cases he pleaded annually before the Council of Artois was considerable and never equaled later by his eldest son."[9]

January 21, 1763, birth of Augustin-Bon-Joseph, a fat little fellow forever known as "Bonbon." July 7, 1764, another oversize baby, so heavy that he strangles on the way out and dies. This last labor proved too much for the frail mother, who herself died on July 16, "aged twenty-nine or thereabouts."[10] Robespierre was six. He had never known his mother except pregnant and plaintive.

Custom decrees that one consoles the young widower and expects him to take a new wife within the year. Such a hot-blooded rover, and all that . . . Besides, he needs someone to care for the children.

But no, something else in Barthélemy goes awry. Is it triggered by grief, by frustration, or perhaps by long-dreamed-of independence? In later years Charlotte, his eldest daughter, mustering all her modesty and dignity, tries to explain it as simply as possible. This loss "came as a terrible blow to our poor father. He was inconsolable. He stopped going to court; he took no more cases; he gave himself up to the grief that consumed him. People urged him

*The only daughter still alive after Thermidor. She dies on August 1, 1834.

to go abroad for a change of scenery; he took that advice, but alas, we never saw him again . . . I have no idea where he died."[11] That is the only reference any of Barthélemy's children ever made to the parental abandonment that shattered their childhood.* Maximilien will never mention it or his father.

But the disappearance was gradual: Barthélemy did not run off impulsively like a stricken man. Rapid deterioration rather than sudden collapse. Intermittent flight. On October 16, 1764, his name still appears several times in the record of hearings before the Council of Artois.[12] Maybe he is beginning to "travel" a bit to refresh his spirit. By December 9, 1765, he is back and sending out a letter urging all lawyers in Arras to join in a collective message of sympathy to the royal family for the failing dauphin.** It is the only "personal" statement of his that we possess,[13] a mixture of royalist fervor and aggressiveness toward his colleagues. "All hearts soaring skyward in unison set the air resounding with their wails; they implore, they beseech, they clamor for the worthy object of their love to return . . . Ours are the only unheard voices! . . . I cannot imagine what has kept them still thus far . . . The one time we are called on to offer the king a pure, solemn, and indispensable gauge of attachment to the royal family, would we not dread the thought of someone saying that we never assembled? . . . Only by fulfilling today our primary duty as lawyers, in a noble and uncommon manner, shall we truly demonstrate the nobility of our profession."†

The slippage must have picked up and accelerated shortly thereafter. Clues are rare; we grope in the dark. On March 22, 1766: an IOU for seven hundred livres and ten sous made out to his sister Henriette. October 30, 1768, another such note made out to his mother. This is the first year his name does not appear on the roster of lawyers pleading before the Council of Artois. Disbarred? No, disappeared. His mother dies on May 17, 1770. He had already borrowed more than his share of his inheritance. Lawyers for the estate communicated with him at an address in Mannheim, in the Palatinate, where he may have begun teaching French for a living. He sends them the following waiver:

> I, the undersigned, licensed to practice law in the provincial Council of Artois, do hereby waive in behalf of my sisters all rights and claims both real and monetary to the estate of my late mother, acknowledging that I have already received from her more than the share to which I or my children would be entitled.
>
> Executed in Mannheim, June 8, 1770
> De Robespierre[14]

---

*Charlotte's *Memoirs* are not autograph but the efforts of a literary polygraph of the Restoration, Laponneraye, to whom she confided certain remembrances and documents. The sentence in question has the ring of authenticity.

**Louis XVI's father dies on December 20.

†He still signs his name as one word, "Derobespierre." The particle appears in official papers, but is not obligatory for everyday use.

He returned in the spring of 1772: last clue. Though not on the court roster, he pleaded two or three cases, as attested (for the last time) by the official record of hearings.[15] Then farewell to Arras forever—five years, until his death. This time, however, he leaves no forwarding address.

What became of his children? Rumors said they suffered shameless neglect. False rumors. Charlotte Robespierre later protests, with predictable dignity, the slanderous charges against her relatives:[16] "Those who have said that Maximilien was reduced to poverty in childhood are impostors."* No, never in dire need. Neither he nor his brother and sisters ever lacked food or shelter. But that was about it . . . All those proud children were forced to stomach at a tender age the acute humiliation of abandonment—Maximilien most of all, being the eldest and having been told so often that eventually he would carry on his father's fine practice and reputation. "A complete change came over him," his sister relates; "before that, like all children his age, he was scatterbrained, unruly, irresponsible. But the moment he found himself head of the family so to speak, being the eldest, he became composed, reasonable, industrious; he talked to us in a rather dignified manner and impressed us; when he joined in our games, it was to direct them."[17] He had adopted a more or less casual despair that stayed with him to the end.**

The brood scattered. Grandmother Carraut took the boys, and Robespierre's aunts the girls, though this was merely a prelude to the inevitable boarding schools for nuisance children. "Good" schools, for select pupils. Charlotte and Henriette were sent to the convent of Manarres in Tournai, a charitable institution that accepted twenty poor girls from approved families to be "lodged and instructed by an able schoolmistress in virtue and in the art of mending and sewing, or some other practical occupation."[18] The boys went straight into secondary schools. After a year in Arras, Maximilien received a scholarship from the Benedictines of Saint-Vaast to study in Paris at the high

---

*This time the citation is not from her *Memoirs* but from an autograph letter.
**Max Gallo notes the basic drives that motivate him from then on: "Maximilien thenceforth feels compelled to become a systematic person. Because his father lost his social position by shaping a life for himself without regard to custom or convention, Maximilien will try desperately to arrive in society, to become accepted. He makes every effort to hide his father's guilt, which he inherited simply for being his son, but also and chiefly because he feels guilty for sharing the public contempt for his father when he, the son, is still there. Isn't he responsible in some way for his father's death? Maximilien thus blames himself for both loving and hating his father, a feeling of guilt all the more acute since he idolized his mother, and is he not driven like everyone else to hold his father accountable for her death?

"This painful feeling also expresses a yearning, an awareness that 'something'—in this case a mother's warmth—has been lost forever.

"Guilt through the father and for the father, deep distress generated by that guilt and the loss of a mother who died prematurely from childbearing, will mark Maximilien Robespierre for life."

school which they founded in the fourteenth century and which subsequently had merged with Louis-le-Grand but kept a few openings for Benedictine protégés. Monseigneur de Conzié, Bishop of Arras, had put in a good word for the "deserving orphan." (After Barthélemy's final disappearance, people spoke of him in the past tense as if he were dead and buried; the teachers and pupils at Louis-le-Grand appear convinced of it.) Maximilien de Robespierre has been shut up in this famous school on the Rue Saint-Jacques since 1769, when he was eleven. Now, at nineteen, he is still not through. He is ever mindful (and ever reminded) of his "good fortune" in being the son of provincial gentry attending one of the finest royal institutions—and free! He has worked hard and wasted no time.* In return for such relentless industry, he can hope one day to become a lawyer in Artois—at the cost of a stunted childhood. "He was what you would call a good boy."[19] In 1771 his Latin composition won sixth prize** (*Maximilianus Maria Isidorus de Robespierre, Atrebas* [native of Arras], *e collegio Ludovici Magni*), and again in 1772. He did better in 1774 (fourth for Latin verse and composition), and still better in 1775, with two second prizes in Latin and a fourth in Greek. At the end of 1776 he took first place in rhetoric—French, at last!—the year his father died, unknown to the boy.

Several months later the Bishop of Arras visited Paris. Maximilien seeks an audience. He is thinking ahead. He would like to become acquainted with his benefactor, who until now has been a mere name on a list. Discuss his future. Obtain the promise of patronage he will need to establish himself in his native town. But appearing before a prince of the church, or any other prince for that matter, calls for making a good impression. And a good impression means that one is decked out in relatively lavish dress. It would never do to cast implicit blame on one's benefactor by turning up in a shabby old suit of clothes. Maximilien therefore pens the following petition to the bursar's deputy† of the Collège Louis-le-Grand:

> Sir, I am told that the Bishop of Arras is in Paris and I should like to see him. However, I have no proper suit of clothes nor other articles without which I cannot appear in public. I should be most grateful if you would take the trouble to explain my situation to him and help me to obtain what I need in order to appear in his presence. I remain, sir, respectfully, your very humble and obedient servant.
>
> De Robespierre ainé.[20]

---

*And drawn sufficient praise from his masters as to both character and academic achievement for them to deputize him to present, on his knees in the mud, the school's homage to Louis XVI on the latter's return from his coronation in June 1775.

**In a city-wide competition, funded by private donors, for schoolboys on set themes in various disciplines: Latin, rhetoric, etc. Other prize winners included the Abbé Delille, Lavoisier, La Harpe, Linguet, Calonne, Hérault de Séchelles, and Camille Desmoulins.

†School administrator in charge of funds for "needy" students.

87

DECEMBER 1777

In Matters of Faith, Reason Is Useless

"In Spain, three things on which the grandeur and opulence of a powerful monarchy reside are virtually ignored: the land, the people, and the wealth . . . Ten thousand [square] leagues of excellent soil, two or three million pairs of idle hands, and many millions of pesetas hidden away in private strongboxes: is there a richer mine in all the world?"[1] Thus complains the Irishman Bernard Ward, one of a host of high officials with whom Spain's ruler liked to surround himself and play the enlightened despot, though rarely to take their advice.

The Bourbons had been shifted about from throne to throne at the start of the century. Charles III, great-grandson of Louis XIV, with stronger claims to the French crown than the dukes of Orléans, has been reigning in Madrid for close to twenty years on top of twenty-five in Naples. He is king of many Spains rather than one. "Every city throughout the land is a miniature self-governing republic with its own code of laws," further observes Ward, who would like to serve as a latter-day John Law to the Spanish throne but feels helpless to cut away the overgrowth of local autonomy and privilege. Charles III's best advisers are attempting to do so, for the general welfare, they believe: you can sow more wheat on level ground. Also it will assure His Catholic Majesty greater authority over twelve million subjects.[2] But nothing can coax La Mancha or Castile, Catalonia, Galicia, Biscay, or Andalusia into thinking they are like everyone else. Many Aragonians still remember those pre-Bourbon days when all Europe compared their tiny kingdom to a paradise in the Golden Age, a community of citizens. Times have changed; all the Spains are merging into one. Not without a few shudders, however. Witness the tale of Don Pablo Olavide* at the close of this year, 1777.

He is nearly sixty. Who cares about his age? Did anyone ask Christ when he was born? Don Pablo Olavide is little more than a blurred profile, a symbolic victim kneeling in the choir of the Church of the Apostles adjoining

*Most of his French contemporaries, including Diderot, misspelled his name as "Olavidès." It should be pronounced "Olavidè."

Madrid's Square of the Holy Inquisition, awaiting sentence. In contrast to the shadowy dimness where his doom is about to be sealed, three bishops stand before the altar in gold chasubles that blaze in the glow of candlelight. Don Felipe Bertran, Bishop of Salamanca and grand inquisitor, intones in Latin a verdict that will silence forever the savior of the Sierra Morena, site of four-teen towns he had founded in ten years between Castile and Andalusia. One of Spain's impoverished communities owes its existence to him. Word of it crept over the border. Travelers ceased to bypass the Sierra; they journeyed there out of curiosity instead, via Madrid or Cordoba. The king had allowed him to turn a desert into a garden. But what of God? He was about to find out:

"You are an atheist. You claim to recognize no faith that is not explicit. You deny Providence. You maintain that heaven is not reserved for Catholics. You eat meat on Fridays. You cross your legs at mass. You advocate false doctrines, asserting that the earth revolves around the sun. You condemn the ringing of bells during storms to implore divine intervention. Your house contains indecent books and pictures. You exchange letters with the enemies of religion.* You have welcomed hundreds of heretics to your 'colony,' impious creatures who never pray to the Immaculate Virgin . . . "[3]

Olavide protests feebly. He has never ceased to protest from the moment his trial opened. He implores "the mercy never denied to those who seek it."

"I do not believe these settlers are without faith, therefore why must I be held personally responsible?"

Many did lack faith, unfortunately—the True Faith, the one Catholic answer to salvation. More than a third of the German and Flemish settlers imported ten years earlier to colonize the Sierra Morena were Protestants. On their tide drifted Friar Romuald, a Capuchin from Fribourg, self-appointed counselor to all those "Hessian plowmen" cast off by their local princes. After all, why assign them to the care of Spanish priests whose language they could not understand? Friar Romuald was a sour fellow who preached violently against Luther and Calvin. He had transferred to the banks of the Guadalquivir the obsessive theological issues currently tearing Germany apart. He had confused the "skepticism"—which was altogether relative and discreet—of the colony's "superintendent," Don Pablo Olavide, with Protestant doctrines he had been fighting all his life. Aided by spies and informers, the monk, like a termite, had bored away for ten years and eventually destroyed Don Pablo's career. Olavide had been fairly safe as long as Aranda, ardent foe of intoler-ance, remained prime minister. But the Catholic Church took its revenge on Aranda in 1774 when Charles III ordered him into gilded exile as ambassador to France. Deprived of official protection, Olavide was summoned to Madrid. He could guess why. No one goes unpunished for trying to change things in this country, even on the smallest scale. "In Spain it was a fundamental princi-

---

*Don Pablo had in fact corresponded with Voltaire and Rousseau, among others.

ple always to do what one had done the day before, in exactly the same way."[4] Two centuries before, Philip II had consulted his religious advisers to find out if it would be lawful to tamper with the Creator's handiwork by cutting a passage through the isthmus of Panama. No, the majority responded; those who dared to propose altering the face of the universe promptly found themselves in prison. The same struggle now dissolves into the same triumphant inertia; Romuald humbles Olavide:

"I do not believe I have ever said anything publicly that merits censure . . . Indeed, I have often discussed scholastic and theological questions with Friar Romuald. We have argued frequently on the subject . . . Is it reasonable to assume that I would express censurable opinions in front of a monk whom I knew to be my enemy, who wrote denouncing me to everyone, and who, down to the flood of letters I have provided this court, has threatened to drag me before the Inquisition?"

Last-ditch stand for honor's sake. Olavide knows that every Capuchin friar is a sworn vassal of intolerance and that his word outweighs the word of any layman, regardless of rank. Faith versus the True Faith is a hopeless battle.

"In fact the priest from Fribourg is, in my view, exceedingly superstitious. His conduct and his utterances bear this out. I was the true champion of a sane and sound religion which his doctrine degraded . . . Our disputes centered upon probable and acceptable matters of controversy . . . I am convinced that, in matters of faith, reason is useless because it cannot touch them . . . "

He does not discern the taint of heresy in his defense: one word alone, "reason," has acquired the blush of obscenity. A lifetime of courageous initiative in the service of his king trickles out along this dim, incense-laden trail of no return. As a young priest in Peru, he had used his own money to rebuild a church and theater after the Lima earthquake. The church was all right, but the theater damned him forever. He was banished from his South American birthplace, accused of unorthodoxy and, even at that stage, heresy. At the age of thirty, he had nearly succumbed to the fate awaiting him at sixty. But for the patronage of Aranda and a few enlightened grandees, his marriage to a rich widow, and the improved climate at the start of Charles III's rule when the king made an effort to end the bigotry of his late reigning brother . . . Olavide had made a remarkable comeback; from assistant magistrate of Seville, he went on to become intendant of Andalusia, then "superintendent of the Sierra Morena settlements," the development of which was sponsored by the country's "economic societies," comprising two or three thousand men of wealth and foresight who were hopeful of prodding Spain out of her lethargy, if only an inch at a time, and who corresponded among themselves with utmost caution.

Olavide did not even mention that matter to the inquisitors. They are still living in the Middle Ages. Why bother telling them about maize or grapes, mines or mills? The crucial question is whether or not he ridiculed publicly the traditional Catalan worship of the she ass, on which the man impersonating Christ rides in the Palm Sunday procession: "The people show special devotion to the sacred she ass, which is bedecked with ribbons and garlands and purses of silk; she used to wear a scapular until a priest banned it as seemingly irreverent."[5]

Never again will he ride through the Sierra Morena, an exhausting journey which he had made on arrival in Spain and which had dismayed other travelers, including Beaumarchais and Gorani,* during the 1760's. On the road south from Madrid to Cadiz, between El Viso and Bailen,** there was an eight-league stretch entirely desolate except for two windowless inns, whose proprietors, if the customer appeared well heeled, promptly alerted local bandits who shared the hills with wolves. Wheeled vehicles had to be abandoned at El Viso, as only mules could pick their way along a narrow, winding path flanking the rocky slopes. "For most of the journey" one failed to see a single "vineyard or tree or patch of healthy farmland, nothing but scattered meadows covered with thyme, melissa,† marjoram, wild thyme, and other aromatic sweet-smelling plants that yield only their fragrance to the traveler." Beyond Bailen, here and there, "wretched hovels where men and women, children, girls, boys, horses, mules, donkeys, sheep, dogs, cats, bedbugs, fleas, lice, a few snakes, spiders, and scorpions huddled one atop the other."[6] At first exposure, Olavide, like other foreign travelers, was outraged at the contrast between this miserable level of existence—the common denominator linking all the Spains—and the vain display of ecclesiastic splendor in every church. In Saragossa he could not kneel in good faith before four silver angels whose gilded wings were encrusted with sapphires: "The Virgin's crown is solid gold; her necklace, bracelets, and head ornaments are generally taken to be worth fifty million reals‡ . . . What madness! Would it not be better used to promote agriculture, trade, the arts? Should not most of it go toward constructing roads and waterways and making rivers navigable wherever possible?"[7]

The real "madness" was to have expressed his feelings aloud. Travelers went their way home; he remained. Besides, the initial support for the Sierra Morena farm communities had come not from the church but from the king: two million reals provided partly from property confiscated by the crown during the Jesuit expulsion. Spanish peasants were in no rush to be exiled to purgatory. And then Germany and Flanders had men for sale, literally—there were six thousand emigrants procured by a white-slaver named Gaspar Thur-

---

*Joseph Gorani (1740–1819) is a Milanese adventurer, a small-scale Casanova and fortune-hunter whose trail leads from Constantinople to Lisbon; his *Memoirs,* if not always reliable, are invariably colorful and lively.   **The site of General Dupont's defeat on July 23, 1808, at the hands of Spanish insurgents, marking the first serious setback to Napoleon's conquest.
†Lemon balm. [*Trans.*]
‡The real, or *royal* currency of Spain, was approximately equivalent to four French livres.

riegel for 586 reals a head. They landed one day at Malaga, itinerant craftsmen, landless farmers, driven from one province to the next and prostrate
from the heat. They asked for beer and were given heavy local wines that made
them sick. Olavide almost had a disaster on his hands when flimsily built
housing collapsed before it was even occupied. For these poor devils he had
founded an ideal community, worthy of the Friend of Man, in which entire
families died of dysentery. The rights of primogeniture were abolished; primary education became mandatory; municipal officers were elected and subject to recall; equal distribution of land, each farmer to have his own
herd . . . The survivors emerged: a nucleus had held fast. The hardiest human
vegetation had taken root. By 1770 the experiment was moving forward:
fourteen towns, two thousand families, five hundred artisans, thirteen thousand people all told, including day laborers and servants. Two thousand dwellings, fifteen inns, five bakeries, eleven flour mills, and four olive presses;
nearly a million saplings planted: mulberry, olive, poplar, and orange. Five
hundred thousand feet of grapevine.[8] On his last tour of inspection, when
already menaced by the Inquisition, Pablo Olavide found the eleven factories
opened in 1775 were turning out linen, silk, velvet, sailcloth, lace, soap, wax,
candles, nails, sewing needles, and crockery.

Olavide an atheist? He had built twenty-six churches. For a few short
months he had savored the pleasurable thought of having saved a host of souls
and set a precedent for Spain. Yet he did not think of himself as a saint. To
his judges he cried out:

"I stand accused of licentious acts in my youth,* sins for which I ask God's
forgiveness, yet I can see none against piety."

The settlers are saved, but he is doomed. Twenty-six churches, yes, but
not a single cloister. By failing to provide for monasteries in his community
plan, Olavide unwittingly had confessed to Encyclopedism. That is his crime:
"We are still too much the children and slaves of custom and prejudice to
realize that there are more useful and pious occupations than burning candles
in a house of worship."[9] At least a tenth of the country's male population
chooses celibacy as an alternative to poverty. Castration and security. The
solidarity of eunuchs. Like a giant lid, the priesthood sits heavily on all the
Spains, and the mere glimpse of another kind of existence—useful, prosperous, rational—looms like a revolutionary manifesto threatening to unfasten it.

Olavide's desperate struggle pits the useless against the useful.

They have taken away his hooded cape of knighthood in the Order of St.
James. He looks undressed in shabby beggar's garments such as he had never
worn. Ashen. Stunted.

*And not just then. "Though deeply obligated to his wife," Baron de Gleichen, Olavide's friend,
observes, "who made many sacrifices for his sake, he treated her shamelessly, forcing her to live
with a certain Doña Gracia, his mistress." But the Inquisition was not interested in that.

"We pronounce you a heretic and apostate.* You are a rotten limb of the faith. Never again shall you hold office. You are banished forever twenty leagues from the court, from the royal precincts, and from all large cities including those in Peru, your birthplace. You are forbidden to ride a horse or in a carriage. You will not wear a sword or embroidered garments. You will cover yourself only with roughspun the color of straw as a sign of repentance. For eight years you will remain cloistered under the constant guardianship of two monks who will never leave your side and will instruct you in your catechism for four years. They will require you to fast on bread and water every Friday and to recite a daily rosary plus seven *Ave Marias* and a *Credo.*"

Pablo Olavide has heard enough. He falls over in a faint. They carry him out.** The Sierra Morena settlements will manage without him;† they, unlike the man, are indispensable. Impossible to level towns and throw salt on their ruins. Traditions are fading.

A Spanish liberal, Nicolas de Azara, writes to his friend Roda: "How can things go on such as what Olavide has just been through? Humanity makes me weep tears of blood."[10] And Voltaire writing recently to Miranda:‡ "Monastic tyranny lives on. You may open your heart only to a very few, choice friends. You cannot whisper in the ear of a courtier that which an Englishman would declare before Parliament."[11] Under a regime midway between Spain's and England's, French men of letters begin to feel relatively secure. Diderot is compiling material for a short history of the affair. In January 1778 the *Correspondance littéraire* under Meister reports the Inquisition's sentence and is outraged that "the despotism of priests dares to revive right in our midst, before the eyes of all the world, such disgraceful, horrifying scenes."[12]

*As to the charge of apostasy (turning renegade), Olavide never forsook his vows or his faith.
**He escapes from the prisons of the Inquisition in 1781, slips into France, and meets Diderot. He lives there quietly throughout the Revolution. In 1797 he returns to Spain at the cost of a public confession and publication (probably under official pressure) of a "Gospel Triumphant" in which he declares his repentance, though not without certain reservations that can be read between the lines. He continues to be spied on and hounded by the Inquisition.
†La Carolina (named after Charles III), for example, between Madrid and Bailen, is a relatively important town today.
‡Father of the future *libertador*, a hero of the French victory at Valmy in 1792.

88

DECEMBER 1777

To Subdue a Blind and Ignorant Nation

Charles III in Madrid extended his protection all the way to Naples to an "enlightened minister," Tanucci, who had served him during his Neapolitan reign. The monarch had installed him there in 1759 as a kind of viceroy when switching thrones—in recognition less of Tanucci's intelligence than of his dependable vassalage. Like the Hapsburgs, the Bourbons regarded Italy as a colonial plum for the picking, and one of their major disputes with the pope was the latter's refusal to give up a part of it. Naples? Merely a sub-station in the western Mediterranean, a door to the gold mines of South America. The Italians hardly exist.

But enlightened Europe seems to be falling apart. A year before the Olavide affair, of which he washes his hands, Charles III had been vexed to learn that his nephew Ferdinand IV, King of the Two Sicilies, a feeble-minded boy who succeeded him on the throne of Naples, was flexing his muscles and had dismissed Tanucci.* Letter from the King of Spain to his old friend: "Believe me, no one laments your misfortune more than I. Let us help each other to endure the trials God wills upon us in our old age** . . . Rest assured that I will go on writing to you unless God inflicts some infirmity on me to prevent it, for I know you have served me well and I admire and love you."¹ Having said that, he turned right around and cashiered his own prime minister, Grimaldi of Genoa, whom he blamed for a disastrous military expedition against Morocco. He replaced him with Floridablanca, who had wangled the post of ambassador to Rome at the time of the papal conclave. One diplomat ousted another. In fact Charles III wanted to live out his days in peace, as Olavide has just discovered. The king had decided to shut out the light of reason the day he banished Aranda, Voltaire's friend, in 1773. On his arrival in Paris, Aranda had proved a great disappointment to the Encyclope-

---

*On October 27, 1776. The Kingdom of the Two Sicilies was the name adopted in 1130 for an amalgam that included Sicily proper and various "counties" of southern Italy: Apulia, Gaeta, Naples, and Amalfi.
**In 1776 Tanucci was seventy-nine; Charles III, sixty.

dists, who waited with open arms to greet "the Spanish Hercules," conqueror of the Jesuits—and saw instead a stout, toothless, jaundiced Spaniard come lumbering into their salons, where he rarely opened his mouth—for the good reason that he was stone deaf. Tanucci followed Aranda, and Dutillot in Parma, then Pombal on February 23, 1777; old men crumbling like a house of cards, exposing the shoddy caliber of European reformers whose names had become linked to the best and worst of the century: police-state methods in the service of limited ideals. The residue was frustration and resentment.

What of it? Ministers change, kings remain. Charles III devotes himself strenuously to hunting parties that occupy most of his day "every day of the year except Good Friday" and have tanned his skin the color of saddle leather. Visitors are startled by his "burnished" features, his habit of mending his own boots, and a faint resemblance to Henri IV of France as he goes racing by on the road to Aranjuez with forty guardsmen galloping behind. "Woe to him who was a poor rider: if he fell off, if he broke an arm or leg or his neck, it was his own misfortune. Men have been known to die from such falls, but accidents never stop the king." When a visitor came before him, "he rarely said a word and simply commented, 'Fine! Fine!' "[2] Bourbon constants whether they be French, Neapolitan, or Spanish: hunting and timidity. A rock of silence, behind which one can take shelter from stormy times.

The experiments of Sully, Richelieu, and Colbert had pointed the way, like radiant guideposts, to the fumbling, random efforts of Europe's great mid-century ministers. Single common denominator: the certainty that they personally incarnated a universal yearning for change. A generation of earth-bound eagles with clipped wings, able to hop but not fly. Louis XIV claimed, "I am the State"; these men claimed, "I am Reform." They all took the same path to power, by first winning the confidence of a king or regent, then displacing him and governing in his name, enhancing reality with a touch of the divine.

Nowhere had the poor risen, having been asked merely to go on obeying the same rules they never could understand. Nobles and clergy brooded and clung fast to their prerogatives. The middle classes had cooperated on the whole, but too sporadically to provide a solid base for the delicate balancing acts that went on between the central power and parliamentary or corporate bodies. Dictators of reform had known their heyday in the 1760's, about the time of the Jesuit expulsion; now they were about to fall, for European monarchs prepared to strike back.

These monarchs would have been foolish indeed not to exploit their advantage. Reactionary circles, including their own families and favorites, stood solidly opposed to any "enlightened" minister. Struensee's* disastrous

*Johann Friedrich Struensee (1737–1772), a physician born in Halle and a subject of Frederick the Great. He emigrated to Denmark, where he practiced medicine and letters somewhat in the style of Marat.

end in Denmark had sounded the alarm in 1772. Christian VII of Denmark had been subject to fits of insanity much like Charles VI of France. A brilliant, captivating madman. He took a fancy to the idealist German doctor, though not so strong a fancy as his wife, sister of England's George III. Struensee became her lover in 1768 and then went on to assume absolute power. Christian VII virtually abdicated in his favor by a transfer of authority such as Louis XIII would never have granted Richelieu: "The commands I give him verbally shall be set down by him in writing according to their proper interpretation . . . Such commands shall have the force of decrees issued from my own hand. They must be obeyed instantly."[3] The brief ensuing orgy of reform left Denmark reeling. More than a thousand fiats in three years. A confused profusion of just and arbitrary acts in the midst of which Struensee, drunk with his new power, and epicurean by temperament, reveled too often and too openly with his friends and spent most of his nights in the queen's bedchamber. "He had little use for public opinion and less for opinions different from his own . . . He failed to comprehend the full impact of habit and prejudice on the populace . . . He seemed to think that a minister hiding behind a curtain and pulling the strings of a puppet king had as much authority as an enlightened autocrat . . . His was an experiment in enlightened despotism that failed owing to neglect of the time factor."[*]

In return for which, in January 1772, they did to him what the Duc de Luynes had done to Concino Concini. A conspiracy of nobles invaded the king's bedchamber and extorted the same powers that Struensee had won. First, the order to arrest him and the queen. Struensee confessed to his liaison with her. They cut off one of his hands and put him to the wheel on April 28. The queen was sentenced to the block, then spared by intervention of George III, her brother. Her marriage was dissolved and she was banished forever to Hanover. A palace revolution thus overcame palace reform. The Danes could claim continuity as their excuse for installing Count Bernstorff, a moderate reformer by reputation, in Struensee's post, like Necker succeeding Turgot. His goal was to achieve in twenty years what Struensee tried to do in twenty months.

Three months later their neighbor Gustavus III had followed suit by clearing out the Swedish senate with artillery and a naval barrage. The term "royal revolution" came into use on that occasion. A defeat for old Senator Fersen and his Stockholm oligarchy, which had invented its own name for the half-century of power divided between throne and aristocracy: "the Era of Liberty." Vergennes, then ambassador to Stockholm, had shifted his support at the last minute to Gustavus III rather than the pro-French Hat party. That won him a ministry and maintained friendship between the two nations. As for

[*]According to Reverdil, a Swiss who had been Christian VII's tutor and was still active at court (quoted by François Bluche).

reform, Sweden gave it up. Frederick the Great was shriveling with age. Catherine II had Pugachev executed and shelved Diderot's plans for reform. In Vienna the intelligentsia pinned its frail hopes on Joseph II, but when would he really grasp the reins of power, and how? The reformation in northern and central Europe remained or was becoming a monarchic concern.

What of the south? Had "progressive" ministers taken refuge in the Latin countries? Some talked of a League of Reason under Bourbon leadership: Naples, Madrid, Parma—and Paris, once Louis XV was gone. It could have developed under Turgot's guidance . . . But Charles III sacked Aranda in 1773, introducing a new element into the stream of history: the accession to active political power of Maria Theresa's three daughters. Maria Amelia, Duchess of Parma, had dismissed Dutillot* in 1771, five years before Marie Antoinette sent Turgot packing in 1776, the same year that Maria Carolina of Naples cashiered Tanucci. They are sick of them.

Minister Dutillot wails: "I have tried [for Parma] many things; some are working. But I am faced with a degree of indolence and with limited resources. The situation calls for endless patience; in time there will be progress, slight, scarcely noticeable. We must never give up, though we die in our traces. What a life, monsieur!"[4] French by birth, he might have attached himself to the cause of reform in Spain or Naples instead of devoting his energies to far smaller game, the principalities of Parma, Piacenza, and Guastalla with their combined populations of three hundred thousand. From serving Philip V he had gone on to serve the future Charles III and later the Infante Philip, another son of Philip V,** who, by the Treaty of Aix-la-Chapelle, had been placed on the throne of Parma with his wife, Louise Elizabeth, the only daughter Louis XV had given in marriage. The French princess appreciated this industrious Frenchman. Dutillot had taken Parma to his heart and helped the duchy through a difficult period. He brought the Golden Age—in the French manner, to be sure. Casanova compared the court to Versailles: "The moment I entered its [Parma's] streets, I forgot that I was in Italy, for everything seemed ultramontane. I heard only French or Spanish from the lips of passersby, and those who spoke neither language seemed to be conversing in whispers."[5] This was the Dark Ages of the Italian language, when it became the idiom of beggars, as Alfieri so bitterly complains.

Dutillot had invested Parma with all the panoply of state: army, university, museums, hospitals, plantations, manufactories and mills. After carrying out rigorously the Jesuit expulsion, he had continued to oppose papal authority, which always claimed sovereignty over Parma. He persuaded the Infante Ferdinand to be inoculated against smallpox at fourteen (ten years

---

*Guillaume Dutillot, born in Bayonne in 1711, died in Paris on December 13, 1774.

**Philip V, father of Charles III, was originally the Duc d'Anjou, grandson of Louis XIV and destined by the latter to rule Spain.

before Louis XVI), in 1765, when he succeeded his father on the throne. But what good did it do to have saved the life of this dark-eyed, olive-skinned ingrate who resented Dutillot's association with his father? In 1769 Ferdinand wed Maria Theresa's second surviving daughter, Maria Amelia,* five years his senior, a frustrated, broken-hearted bride whose family had forbidden her to marry the Prince of Zweibrücken.** She would take out her grief on her young husband, whose hobbies included listening to carillons and roasting chestnuts. Sexually and emotionally deprived, she consoled herself, or at least kept busy, with the demands of government. Her mother ruled Vienna; why shouldn't she rule Parma? In 1775 "not a trace of her youth or beauty remains.† She, who always held herself so proudly, now has lost her graceful carriage and elegance. She is less cheerful, less lively. Her eldest daughter is the prettiest child imaginable, but has a streak of sadness that is distressing to see."[6] By now the phrasing of decrees has been altered to read thus: "We, my wife and I, hereby command . . . " To Dutillot, however, she wrote: "In my household I give the orders . . . I have sufficient authority to demand obedience here. I am German and know my rights. Do not forget that I can compel fear as well as love, so I would advise you to obey me."[7] In two years she managed to rid herself of Dutillot's annoying presence.

Maria Carolina of Naples took eight years to eject Tanucci; she needed that much time, having been led to the altar at fifteen by Ferdinand IV and as a substitute. The intended bride, her sister Maria Josepha, died three months before the wedding, but no one thought of postponing the ceremony for such a trivial reason. Maria Theresa had an endless fund of daughters to place. Maria Carolina found herself with a nonentity of a husband, typical of the last Bourbons, whose wits had been further dimmed by ignorant tutors provided by Tanucci. The minister had entrenched himself in Naples, like Dutillot in Parma, though he looked on it as merely a province of Spain and himself an agent of Charles III. He stopped at nothing to perpetuate forty years of power, twenty of which were virtually absolute. Joseph II was shocked: "If the king wishes to lunch in the garden, he must first ask Tanucci's permission."[8] The young Austrian bride set out to change the situation by filling the place her husband so readily ceded. "He is very ugly, but gradually one gets used to that.‡ As to his personality, it is better than I was led to expect. Still, I must confess that I shall never love him save out of duty."[9] In concert with Tanucci (though on this one point alone), she had urged Ferdinand to spend his time

---

*In homage to the Virgin, all the empress's daughters bore the first name Mary, followed by: Amelia, Carolina, Christina, and Antoinette.

**A Wittelsbach who later would rule Bavaria. The town of Zweibrücken (Two Bridges) in the Palatinate became the seat of a duchy and of a line of rulers, chiefly in Sweden.

†According to her elder sister, Maria Christina, future ruler of Belgium, who was appalled to find her so faded after six years of marriage.

‡Excerpt from her first letter after the wedding.

hunting—those Bourbon men apparently felt driven to wear themselves out!
—and fishing. He would disappear for days on a galiot* and row for hours on
end, swearing like a sailor, then appear at the Port Marina docks near the fish
market to sell his own catch to the highest bidder. She refused to let him roam
the countryside masquerading as an innkeeper to distribute wine to the peasants, with his noble escort similarly disguised.[10] Any monarch who mixed with
the public was courting disaster, even if it simply meant that he enjoyed
spending a few hours among his subjects. A queen who maintained her dignity
would gain esteem for it; no monarchy can afford to be without its Olympus.
At the age of twenty-three, Maria Carolina had only one more obstacle to
topple on the way to absolute rule over six million souls: the senescent minister
who drove out the Jesuits, also the Freemasons; who ignored the pope and
banned the *Encyclopédie*; who put up buildings for the grandees and muzzled
the poor. A reformer in the wrong country at the wrong time, who woke up
a doddering old man in eighteenth-century Naples and realized that he had
given his life to serving an Italian, not a Spanish, community. "I shall cause
Tanucci such trials and vexations that he will be forced to make room for me,"
Maria Carolina announced to her friends. "What do we care about Spain? I
shall never be queen as long as Tanucci remains at court . . . Listening to
Tanucci and Spain is like listening to the devil."[11]

She cast him out in October 1776. Marie Antoinette had cast out Turgot
in June.

Strategy on the part of the three daughters? A combined long-range operation
masterminded in Vienna by the imperial brood hen herself, Maria Theresa,
with an eye to ruling the Latin countries of Europe through her daughters?
There are whispers to this effect. If so, the Bourbons must look ridiculous on
those thrones that have fallen to the distaff. Skeptics are asking whether even
in bed they practice overturning alliances. Exaggerated gossip. The Hapsburgs
had outgrown their Machiavellian mood. On three occasions, as seen in connection with Marie Antoinette, Maria Theresa was shocked to discover that
her daughters were attempting to emulate her. Too young still, and too inept,
those good-for-nothing children . . . After which she resigned herself in
amazement to the triumphs of Carolina and Amelia. Diverting Naples and
Parma from the New Thinking and reorienting them toward Austria was a gift
from heaven. As for France, time would tell whether the birth of a dauphin
would provide Antoinette's springboard to power.

In all three cases, temperament is the crucial element: these German
princesses never forget that they are the daughters of an empress. Their dismal
experience with "nuptial bliss" makes them reach for the one sure source of
comfort: reflections of the mother image. Their revenge on life will be that

---

*A small boat propelled by sails or oars used exclusively for coastal traffic. The name derives from
"galley."

of pride. A reform-minded administrator, whatever shape he comes in, simply clutters their view. As politely as possible, they will try to compensate for the utter nullity of their husbands, whose annihilation must precede the ascent of queens. The queens have only to keep a steady head and use it. God in his immutable wisdom intended mankind to prosper by making Maria Theresa so fertile. All will be well as long as her daughters rule. Useful ministers shall be their servants. As added inducement, these ladies will have a chance to square accounts with another aspect of the monster men: they felt humiliated not just by their husbands and ministers but by their older brothers as well, Joseph and Leopold, who treated them as inferiors and whose wild notions of reforming the world are intolerable because they upset dear Mama.

Another queen, this time in Portugal, with none of the Hapsburg traits, has retired another tyrant. No sooner was the incompetent Joseph I laid to rest than his daughter Doña Maria, the first of that name, sent Pombal packing. Another fifty years of reform goes up in smoke. Pombal is a poor loser. His groans will echo far and wide, carried by the Duc du Châtelet, his instrument, who cannot resist paying a visit "in the town bearing his name," where Pombal has retired "to a tiny house with freshly plastered walls" behind which lodges Europe's most famous retiree excepting Choiseul:

"They blame me for being cruel, but I was forced to be. When I proclaimed the king's commands [his own in fact] and no one paid any attention, then I had to resort to force. Prisons and dungeons were the only means I could find to subdue this blind and ignorant nation."[12]

With prudent foresight, he had made sure that Joseph signed every edict —with or without reading it. That saved Pombal's life; relatives of his victims, rich and poor alike, shouted for his blood, and Queen Maria would have been happy to oblige. But when he produced reams of documents bearing her father's signature, she contented herself by banishing him to his country estate. Which is really not such a hardship. On his doorstep you may find "nearly two hundred persons to whom bread and soup are distributed . . . ." "The waters are excellent at Pombal . . ." " 'Come,' he invited, 'and share the frugal meal of a recluse' . . . Instead of the frugal meal he had promised, I sat at a laden table . . ." "M. de Pombal has brought a great many books with him; he reads or has someone read to him constantly: the books are all in French . . ." "Madame de Pombal is still quite attractive; she dresses with taste and elegance . . . At the height of the Marquis de Pombal's prosperity, both the mighty and the humble sat at her feet; her house was a miniature court. Visitors knelt to kiss her hand . . . German by birth, she shares the pride of her nation's great families . . . She tried to conceal her distress from me, but was not very successful. After ten minutes of conversation her eyes flooded with tears." Her husband does likewise: " 'This ordeal is beyond my power to withstand; and now the sun has lost its splendor and warmth . . . What is

Portugal today? What was it forty years ago?' . . . Tears welled up in his eyes."[13]

Weep, weep for yourselves, enlightened statesmen! Casualty list at the end of six years: Struensee, the elder Fersen, Dutillot, Aranda, Tanucci, Turgot, and Pombal. Kings, their mothers, their daughters, and their wives are recovering the reins of power. Relief is at hand.

VOLTAIRE DINING
WITH THE PHILOSOPHES

89

FEBRUARY 1778

The Brisk Jaunt to Eternity

Paris, February 10, 1778, four in the afternoon. The news rocks the city: Voltaire has come. He has not set foot in the capital for twenty-five years. He had already taken up residence outside Geneva when Louis XVI was born; Parisians of the king's generation know him only through his writing. "The sudden appearance of a ghost, a prophet, an apostle, could not have caused greater astonishment and admiration . . . This new prodigy momentarily suspended all other interests. He silenced rumors of war, legal intrigues, court scandals, and even the dispute raging between Gluckists and Piccinnists."[1] Where is he? When do we get to see him? Why did he come? Voltaire is in Paris: the great revenge. Can it be true?

He is a guest of his friend the Marquis de Villette, on the Rue de Beaune at the corner of the Quai des Théâtins,* "hemmed in by tremendous crowds. Carriages cannot pass. Standing throngs force back the oncoming tide.** The king of thought sits enthroned in the Hôtel de Villette opposite the deserted Tuileries Palace."[2] He is eighty-four years old.

Initial surprise of the select few privileged to meet him privately: Voltaire is handsome. He had managed to pursuade a whole continent that he was no more than a dried-up mummy. Pure flirtation, of which he was an accomplished master. Still, his own charm did not escape him. "It is impossible to describe the sparkle in his eyes or the grace of his features; what an enchanting smile! Not a single wrinkle fails to embellish it. How surprised I was," con-

*Now the Quai Voltaire. An inscription on the house recalls these times.
**The "crowd" in this case includes the middle class, the nobility, and small craftsmen.

fesses pretty Madame Suard, who caught his heart instantly, as did every attractive woman within reach, "when, instead of the decrepit head I expected to see, there appeared that lively and expressive face . . . In place of a bent old man, I beheld a person standing erect and tall, in a noble, though careless, attitude, and one whose step was still firm and brisk."[3]

Pigalle sculpted him seven years earlier in the nude, like a Greek god,* a commission which the sitter's admirers paid for by subscription. Voltaire complained about it bitterly: "I ought to have a face! You can hardly tell where it belongs! My eyes are sunk in three inches, my cheeks look like old parchment plastered over unanchored bones. The few teeth I had have vanished . . . No poor fellow has ever been sculpted in such a state!"

D'Alembert produced the right words to make him feel better: "Genius, as long as it breathes, always has a face . . . From those flashing eyes which nature has given you, M. Pigalle will coax the flame to vitalize his statue."[4]

Voltaire's eyes: two glowing coals. They can scorch a man.

No one believes him anymore, dating back to the time he announced that he was at death's door. "I am dying, literally . . . These spindle legs of mine have swollen into barrels."** But wait: "His ailment has settled into a violent attack of gout. As it is the first he has had in all of eighty years, people generally take it for the sign of a life that is not about to end."[5] He does, however, have great difficulty urinating—probably caused by retention of the bladder, a strangury, as it is called—and faces the constant threat of uremic poisoning. He has little appetite, and the slightest excitement brings up the few mouthfuls he had managed to get down. He is obliged to take a weekly enema in order "to go to the bathroom," but no one takes that seriously since, by his own admission long ago, he "was in the habit of taking a pill" when advised that a chronophage† was about to call. Convention, in those blessed times, upheld a man's right to swallow a laxative and shut his door to the world.

Dying or not, his resilience has everyone fooled: that inimitable way he has of leaping out of bed and wriggling into his trousers like a fish while dictating full speed to his secretary;‡ his prancing before the ladies, the trembling kisses impressed on white fingertips, the gnarled hands that never cease to grope; the nights he talks his dinner companions under their seats until two in the morning, then faints in a salon the next day. An iron rod. He makes everyone forget his real infirmity, which is that he has lived past eighty.

He must have forgotten it himself, else why would he be mad enough to

*This nude statue of Voltaire, one of the most powerful and original works of art to come out of the eighteenth century, is in the Museum of Fine Arts, Orléans.

**Letter to the Duc de Richelieu, February 12, 1773.

†"Devourer of time": a literary personality who drops by unannounced.

‡A scene sketched lately by the Swiss artist Huber, who caught it and many others with admirable wit and delicacy to provide a documentary film on Voltaire's last years at Ferney. Most of these canvases were acquired by Catherine II and now hang in Leningrad's Hermitage.

set out from Switzerland for Paris in early February, the worst season for travel, he who had not budged for twenty years? What has got into him? A would-be suicide. His excuse? A final display of his most controversial talent —a talent all but unchallenged in his day—that of playwright. His *Irène* is being staged even before he has finished writing it. Not a work he is proud of. In a letter dated July 25, 1778, he entreats the Duc de Richelieu* "to spare me the jibes that never fail to delight a social gathering, but which can prove fatal when one is exposed to that merciless audience. I am so ashamed of my abysmal ignorance, at my age, that I tremble as I speak to you."[6] It did not prevent him from investing every last ounce of energy in the undertaking, and cursing himself under his breath.

He leaves a warm nest in a chilly country, "this odd little kingdom in my alpine valley . . . Two [square] leagues of earth that yield very little but are their own master. Philosophers need two or three burrows to escape the dogs that chase them . . . When someone asks me: 'What do you do there, you rascal?' I reply, 'I rule, and I pity the slaves.'

"I have two parish priests [one in Ferney, one in Tournay] with whom I am rather pleased: I bankrupt one and beg from the other. My vassals bend low when I pass. In fact, I have a reputation for strewing their fields with twenty-four-sou gold pieces."[7] Inflated reputation: Lord Voltaire's tenants had to work hard for what they received, whether in the fields or in the watch factory, his pride and joy,** source of one-of-a-kind gifts that he sent all over Europe and of competition with his Genevan neighbors which ultimately alienated them as much as his declared atheism. This physiocratic and industrial paternalism brought into balance the many levels of his existence: country squire of Gex, nominal lord of two towns, yet answerable to the King of France, who left him alone as long as he stayed put; gentleman farmer who drained marshes and made fallow land fertile; Encyclopedist who had brought technology to a rural area; emperor of writers and philosophers, ruling for years by correspondence over the kings, the ministers, and the salons of Europe; chronicler of injustice, defender of lost causes championed by his pen: Calas, Sirven, de Lally-Tollendal, the Chevalier de La Barre . . . Happy? The word had little meaning for him. Smiling, yes, and generally serene, but subject also to fleeting fits of depression. "Where am I going? Is my past responsible for the future? Does anyone see the weeping man beneath the grinning mask?"[9] Who knows, perhaps now and then Ferney seemed too snug.

He designed the plans for his small château,† more the size of a manor

---

*Acting chamberlain for the year 1778, and in charge therefore of the Comédie Française for that year.

**Making 400,000 livres a year shortly before his death (about 200,000 francs [$40,000] today). It remained a modest-scale enterprise.[8]

†Still standing, at Ferney-Voltaire. Now privately owned, it may be visited at certain times, usually in groups. One should be prepared to meet Voltaire behind every door.

house; a far cry from Jean-Jacques Rousseau's two-room flat, but not quite as splendid as Choiseul's Chanteloup. A tree-lined road leads from the nearby village straight to the gate; on the left is Voltaire's church; on the right, a tiny gatekeeper's lodge. The château, a square building without wings, is not visible from the entrance, being hidden behind clumps of trees and meandering pathways. The approach is short; the "front garden" covers only a few acres. A vaguely classical façade; the vestibule dominated by a bulbous earthenware stove of German invention, a common fixture wherever homes need to be heated six months of the year with cord after cord of wood. On the right, a circular stone stairway leads to the sleeping quarters, which can accommodate only ten or a dozen persons. Opposite, the "main waiting room," where "unwelcome" visitors were parked; on the wall, grinning down at them, hung a lively portrait of Frederick the Great as a young man dressed in blue. On the left was the private drawing room for select callers, who waited breathlessly to be presented. From there they stepped directly into the small bedroom where Voltaire spent most of his "good" days and could listen with relish to unwanted visitors being shown out. Those he received found him in bed, "crowned with a nightcap fastened by a fresh ribbon and wearing a white satin bed jacket. Across from his bed hung the portrait of Madame du Châtelet* [by Nattier]. On one side of his bed he could always look up at figures of Calas and Sirven,** popular color prints that he treasured more than Raphael's Madonnas."[10] Those who went away unreceived still enjoyed his hospitality. "Every caller, every pilgrim, every devotee sat down, no matter what the hour, to a plump bird and a bottle of Moulin-à-Vent."[11]

His friends, the real ones, friends of his youth or even of the moment, might see him burst into the vestibule, grab them by the arm, and whisk them across the house. After passing through the library with its "six thousand volumes of every description: all the radiant mysteries of the human mind,"[12] they would come upon Ferney's splendid gardens: terraced beds of roses and jasmine, clumps of shrubbery set out in three's, trellised vines sloping down to the orchards, which extended to the wall at the edge of the woods. The Lake of Geneva, less than three miles away, added mildness and moisture to the air. But Voltaire turned his back on the lake, preferring to gaze over the horizon in the other direction at the Jura Mountains, snow-capped the year around, the peaks of La Faucille, and, beyond, France.[13]

Though the house was small, the grounds covered more than a thousand acres of farmland, vineyards, and woods. In 1778 several hundred mountain

---

*The woman he loved most and longest in his life. She died in 1749—after giving birth to a child by the poet Saint-Lambert, Voltaire's rival for her affections.
**The Calas family were Protestants in Toulouse convicted of murdering one of their members, who had actually committed suicide. The elder Calas died on the wheel. The Sirvens, a Protestant couple from Mazamet charged with killing their daughter to prevent her from becoming a Catholic convert, were forced to flee the country.

folk tenant the land and are wholly dependent on its master. Three years before, they had held a feast of thanksgiving to celebrate the recovery of his niece Madame Denis, who keeps house for the old man. "We have had regiments of infantry, cavalry,* cockades, kettledrums, fiddles, and an outdoor picnic for three hundred . . . The cavalcade included nearly a hundred riders in uniform, with all the equipment and precision of an army. When you realized that fifteen years before there were a scant twenty peasant families in this region, all starving, it was indeed odd to witness such a celebration, the splendor and cost of which not many towns in this kingdom could match." [14]

He leaves all that behind under snow as he sets out for Paris early on February 4, 1778. He felt exhausted already from the still journey familiar to men of letters, having sweated blood that winter not only to finish *Irène* but also to get *Agathocle* under way. What dreary themes for such a spirited soul! The Empress of Constantinople, a contemporary of Charlemagne, who defended idol worship against the iconoclasts, yet did not shrink from commanding that her son's eyes be put out.**The tyrant of Syracuse (Sicily) in the third century B.C., who was conquered by Hamilcar and then allied himself with the Carthaginians to crush his own rebellious subjects. The author of *Le Siècle de Louis XIV* used the staging of those warmed-over historical themes as an excuse to return to Paris. "Yet I am sorely afraid I am about to make the brisk jaunt to eternity, for I am worn out, and my limbs are in shreds for having been lately in Syracuse and Constantinople: I was so badly shaken up that I cannot budge"—letter dated February 2 to a friend, one of the last he wrote from Ferney. [15] French roads, after icy alpine passes, could be counted on to shake him up far worse.

If anything might have held him back, it was his tenant farmers. They were stunned. Among themselves, they swore they would never see him again, but to him they spoke of the rain or good weather, for they were not of his world. And his world pressed him to start on a journey.

A very small world, those three or four intimate friends who replaced the home he had never made. Wagnière, his secretary, ready to work at any hour, always on hand, yet bored at Ferney. Villette, urbane homosexual, son of a banker who made a fortune supplying the army and bought himself the title of marquis. Like Voltaire, Villette had too light a beard to shave but too much to let it grow; so they plucked each other. Villette had gained the great man's favor by presenting him with a fine pair of tweezers from Paris, better than any made in Geneva or Lyons. Voltaire had known Villette's mother as a young woman, and Villette was not averse to hinting that he might be his son. The young man had literary aspirations, dreams of the Academy . . . If he could bring Voltaire into his house, show him off as exclusive property, what a triumph that would be! At Ferney, in spite of his sexual proclivities, he has

*That is, parades on foot and on horseback.
**The Greek Church canonized her and made August 15 her feast day.

recently married the young Varicourt girl, one of those rosy, affectionate orphans that Voltaire loved to take under his wing. *"Belle et bonne,"* he called her. Penniless, charming figure, warm-hearted, and "philosophically inclined." The nocturnal ceremony took place by candlelight in Ferney's curious chapel: DEO EREXIT VOLTAIRE. Villette had changed his habits for a short spell, and Voltaire gloated in sad amusement: "The newlyweds are working night and day to make me a little philosopher . . . As for myself, I lie in bed alone and ramble on about it in poem and prose."[16] His love life was a sprinkling of vicarious pleasures. Belle et bonne urged him to visit her in Paris. One more reason to go.

The chief of this little band, however, its soul of decision, is Marie-Louise Denis, daughter of a Demoiselle Arouet, his niece therefore, formerly his mistress, and for the past twenty years mistress of his household. She is now sixty-six, ugly and ill-tempered. Indispensable. Under such circumstances, marriage is preferable to a wilted romance. The widow of a finance administrator for the army,* she had gone to live with her uncle about 1750, ostensibly to run his house. Eating was her great passion, and she ballooned into a dimpled barrel. A faint trace of Voltaire's wit had rubbed off on her from constant aping, but her product remained hopelessly vulgar. She drove him wild. There had been violent scenes, screaming ruptures between them. Several times he had tried to rid himself of this "mother-mistress *à la Molière*" (according to Frederick the Great), now toothless and irritable, whom he referred to as "the fat sow"[17] and who was not above filching a manuscript of his now and then. Money was her idol, and Voltaire's fortune, which no heir stood to inherit, was in the neighborhood of two million livres.** Though aware of her motives, he refused to give up his matron. Unsensual as he was, Voltaire clung to certain fond memories of her: "If my poor state of health permitted it, I would cast myself at your feet, I would embrace all your beauties. In the meantime, I press a thousand kisses to your round breasts, to your ravishing buttocks, to your whole body that so often stretched me taut as a bow and plunged me into floods of rapture."[18] With her, his pleasure had not been solely vicarious. The erstwhile passion had become habit. She was the only sexual content in Voltaire's life.

Madame Denis, like Wagnière, found Ferney tiresome. But it would be too simple to exaggerate their influence.

The fact is that Voltaire himself was bored at Ferney.

Linguet, who eyes events from exile in London, expects no good to come of the trip: "M. de Voltaire has suddenly forsaken the woods of Ferney that he seeded, the houses of Ferney that he built, the peace of Ferney that so con-

*In charge of the military expenditures of a military unit—and who never got poor from it. A client of Villette senior's banker associates.
**Ten million francs [$2 million] today.

tented him, for the mud, the strife, the incense of Paris. He alone will be able to tell very shortly whether the change has been beneficial."[19] He has nothing to fear but fatigue, for the danger of official retaliation is all but defunct now. No *lettre de cachet* was issued against Voltaire, who even retains the title of royal historiographer. "There never was any formal repudiation. I have always kept my office and the right to exercise it. If I were to ask permission, it would make them think I do not have it."[20] Intense psychological pressure had forced Voltaire into voluntary, not mandatory, exile. If he had gone back under Louis XV, they would have sucked him into some kind of wrangle. But what has he to fear from Louis XVI or Maurepas, as long as he avoids openly antagonizing them? He is returning to Paris, not Versailles.

February 3. Madame Denis and the Villette couple set out ahead, like heralds of the king. On the 5th, Voltaire, with Wagnière and a cook used to the master's diet, bundle into a coach crammed with cushions and foot-warmers. Much kissing of hands, much embarrassed sniffling on the part of simple folk unaccustomed to showing such emotion. He brags: "I left my manuscripts and papers in a terrible mess. I shall be back in six weeks to tidy them up."

They take the main road from Geneva to Paris. Rough-shod, the horses cover the first, and iciest, leg of the journey at a nearly steady trot over steep trails along the mountainside. Waterfalls streaming from the "Rhône's over-flows" bring down sheets of ice; Nantua has only one street, "which is the center of all activity."[21] They put up at the town's single inn, where "the trout compete with those of Geneva." February 6: the second, exhausting lap, from Nantua to Sennecey, brings them to Burgundy. In Bourg-de-l'Ain,* Voltaire is recognized while the horses are being changed. A large town with a popula-tion of five thousand, it provides a foretaste of the capital. People crowd around and jostle him; he has to lock himself in a room at the inn. Old Bon, in charge of the relay station, scolds one of his favorite postilions: "That's some horse you're bringing in. Better fetch another. Go ahead and kill all my horses, I don't give a damn. You're driving M. Voltaire."

For the first time in history, two writers have become familiar names to the illiterate: Voltaire and Rousseau.

February 7: Sennecey to Dijon via Chalon and Beaune. In Dijon, the Hôtel Croix d'Or, where city youngsters have bribed the waiters for the chance to take their places. Voltaire is serenaded beneath his window. If he had been willing to greet all the local gentry and academics who flocked to the entrance hall, he would have been up the whole night. He turns them away, including Sophie de Monnier's father, cantankerous old Ruffey, presi-dent of the court, with whom he recalls sharing two bottles of excellent Burgundy twenty-five years before in the very same inn.[22] But the dreary journey (with mud now replacing snow) added to the strain and excitement

*Now Bourg-en-Bresse.

has cut Voltaire's appetite; he scarcely touches his food or drink and sleeps hardly a wink. The choice was his own.

February 7: an early start. Rouvray, Vermenton, Auxerre, Joigny. They spend the night in Joigny, a town "beautified* with military barracks, entered by way of a bridge and several avenues of agreeable aspect." February 8: Villeneuve, sur l'Yonne, where Derues tried to become a landowner, much to the Lamottes' and his own misfortune; Sens, in whose cathedral the dauphin, Louis XVI's father, lies buried, having managed to instill in his son fear of all that Voltaire represents, panic in the face of reason; Le Pont-sur-l'Yonne, then on to Fontainebleau.

A coach axle breaks at Moret; such accidents are common on long, jolting rides. They stop along the banks of the Loing River with its damp, chilling mists and wait not quite two days for a wheelwright to make them a new axle. Alarmed at the delay, Villette gallops in from Paris and transfers them to his own coach. Voltaire, still badly shaken from the breakdown, asks his friend to have the coachmen slow up. "Tell them they are taking an unfortunate man to Paris to be cut into." Two possible interpretations of the word: taxes or surgery . . . February 10: dusk seems to have fallen at midday, or is the sun not yet up? Impenetrable gloom; then, on the heights near Villejuif, "the eye embraces Paris—that is to say, a giant grayish mound of towers and irregular buildings stretched out as far as you can see."[23] Voltaire is looking down on the slaughterhouse.

He was counting on Lekain, the greatest actor of the day, to perform his tragedy. First bad news on arrival: Lekain died the day before, February 8. Less than fifty years old. Worn out? Yes, but in love. Voltaire sleeps on the Rue de Beaune and shuts his door fast. Heavy-hearted? Perhaps, in his own way. He had deeply resented Lekain's refusal to act in some of his last plays and the need to cajole him into doing *Irène.* Still, that divine monster with his unruly shock of hair had so enhanced all the other works, the great and famous tragedies from *Mérope* to *Zaïre,* as to have inscribed his name permanently on each. Perversity; a bad omen. And all those people beating a path to his door! He retreats to his customary refuge: bed.

On the second floor of a brand-new, sparkling white, square town house with painted interiors by Van Loo and elegant furnishings. Lovingly, Villette had selected everything down to the doorknobs. The building fronts on an immaculate quay behind a low embankment. Louis XV's urban planners had worked in this vicinity to transform the sprawling clutter of ancient Paris. The Seine is murky these days, and foul; it flushes everything in its path. Here, at least, the river is contained, whereas a few miles upstream it washes over mud banks and disgraces the Hôtel de Ville. Paris is littered, like the Seine, with

---

*The verb is not ill-chosen. In those times, architects of public buildings tried for beauty as well as utility in designing churches, schools, town halls, hospitals, and even military facilities.

carriages and pedestrians edging into long lines, shepherded by Belle et bonne and Madame Denis. Hard to tell whether the ladies are weeding them out or packing them in. On February 11 and 12, in dressing gown and nightcap, Voltaire "receives half the city of Paris." "In a single day, a hundred blue sashes* have filed through the door." Academicians, dukes, and peers, the farmers-general, targets of his bitterest attacks . . . He waves his arms, wears himself out doing his inimitable act, unable to resist dazzling and seducing his audience. Overwhelmed, his visitors depart savoring each syllable the great man has uttered. Between bows, he dictates alexandrines to Wagnière in a last-minute attempt to rework his unworkable *Irène.*

Gluck appears on the 12th. "I postponed leaving for Vienna a day so that I might have the honor and pleasure of seeing you." Piccinni stops by on the 13th. So does Yolande de Polignac, who comes as the queen's ambassadress to assure him that he has nothing to fear even if Louis XVI seems to ignore him. Silence implies consent. The Comédie Française players arrive on the 14th. Madame Vestris will take the lead in *Irène*: "Madam, I worked for you last night like a young buck of twenty."[24] Villette is radiant in his impressario's role: "To see Voltaire, you must go through me. You want Voltaire? Here he is, but kneel first to Villette . . . "[25]

Ben Franklin brings his grandson "to receive a blessing." From what deity? Voltaire dresses for the occasion in a "suit of scarlet trimmed with ermine, a colossal Louis XIV wig, black and unpowdered, which all but buried his emaciated features, leaving visible only a pair of eyes that glittered like garnets."[26] Resting his hands on the head of the fifteen-year-old boy who kneels at his feet—or otherwise would tower over him by a foot—Voltaire murmurs: "God and Liberty." Twenty witnesses are weeping; he weeps, too.

Next come Madame Necker, Madame du Barry, Diderot, D'Alembert, Beaumarchais, Marmontel, blind old Madame du Deffand, and a captain of dragoons in female attire who stumbles over everyone's feet, the "Chevalière" d'Eon, now "in his fifties, with his foul oaths, his clay pipe, and his wig."[27] Few young persons. Most are elderly or at least middle-aged: men and women who called him master when he was twenty or thirty and whom he taught to combat absurdity with the only effective weapon: laughter. Voltaire's special laughter. He enabled them to survive the times. Because they were rich, of course, as well as cultivated, and could afford to buy and keep proscribed books. Because Madame de Pompadour, Choiseul, or Malesherbes protected them. Because right under the nose of church and state a radiant, unspoken, intellectual conspiracy came into being and bound them together. They all know each other. They support each other. Like one big family. In this last quarter of the century, history plainly is on the side of Voltairians. Too late perhaps. The populace gathered on the quay stares in mute incomprehension.

*Knights of the Order of the Holy Ghost.

Marat fulminates nearby, close to the Palais Bourbon. And if Louis XVI has not appeared, there is no chance that Rousseau will.

Rousseau drew his admirers not from the *"beau monde"* but from the middle classes, among whom he enjoyed certain islands of support. Manon Phlipon informs the Canet sisters scornfully that Voltaire's arrival "has created some stir . . . We are agreed as to our opinion* of this famous man. We admire him as a poet, as a man of learning and culture, but we set little store by his politics or philosophy. We also feel that he would have been wiser to stay home at Ferney and go on peacefully enjoying his fame, surrounded by his adoring subjects, instead of coming here and looking like an old fool hungering for flattery from a clever crowd."[28]

He falls ill on February 15.

VOLTAIRE

90

MARCH 1778

Unable to Betake Myself to Church

A silent spectator in bourgeois dress watches on the sidelines as the invasion of the Hôtel de Villette progresses: Jacob Tronchin, of Geneva's Tronchin dynasty, the councillors, physicians, and "manufacturers" who had courted Voltaire ten years before, then snubbed him when his industrial success threatened to rival theirs.

Voltaire grew anxious. Would his old friend Jacob come to the Rue de Beaune? He came, unsmiling. At Ferney or at Les Délices, Voltaire's Genevan property, the mood was relaxed and informal, but here in Paris it was like a state reception. And look what they are doing to the poor man! Jacob writes to his cousin François on February 14: "I saw Voltaire. I doubt that he will return to Ferney, as he intends, in May or June. They will have smothered him with embraces or vexations before that time. I found him weak and fatigued from the seventy-two relay posts he covered in four days, and from the first two nights after his arrival, most of which he spent finishing work on his *Irène*, as he is determined to see it staged while he is here . . . The throng of coaches in front of his door is worse than at the Opera."[1] Voltaire welcomes Jacob with open arms: there is always room for reconciliation when Rousseau is the

---

*Shared by her circle of "gentlemen" and bashful suitors, among whom Roland is nosing into the lead.

common foe. The Tronchins have done more than their share to deflate Jean-Jacques's influence among the Genevan populace, including persecution when necessary. After all, didn't *The Social Contract* invite workingmen to rise against the Calvinist bourgeoisie that governed them so wisely?

They embrace, but Jacob makes no attempt to conceal his annoyance and reappears the next morning with one of his many cousins, Théodore Tronchin, the celebrated and fashionable Paris physician. A crusader for inoculation. On this particular morning, Sunday, February 15, Voltaire suffers severe pain in the bladder. His legs are swollen. Dr. Tronchin urges him to rest and see fewer visitors. But he gets no cooperation from either Madame Denis or the Villette couple, who have not brought their prize to Paris just to let him drop out of sight. Independently, then, Tronchin decides to appeal to the public, and his plea appears in the *Journal de Paris* on February 20:

"I should like personally to have informed M. le Marquis de Villette [who managed to be out so as not to have to listen] that M. de Voltaire has been living, since his arrival in Paris, on capital resources, and that his true friends ought to wish that he spend only income. At the rate he is going, those resources will soon give out and we shall all be witnesses to, if not accomplices in, the death of M. de Voltaire."[2]

Aid to an endangered individual: old Tronchin minced no words. But what good is an appeal to the humane instincts of an inhuman society? The message precipitates even longer lines. If Voltaire is about to die, everyone wants to boast of having seen him alive. The patient himself is the worst offender. On the morning of February 20 when Tronchin's appeal is published, Voltaire gets out of bed and goes forth zestfully to do a day's battle with the Duc de Richelieu and the Comédie Française over the casting of *Irène*. "It is a curious sight to see these two old men and listen to them. They are about the same age. The duke is slightly younger,* yet, despite his elegant dress and decorations, he looked more worn out than M. de Voltaire in nightcap and dressing gown."[3]

Another species of visitor begins to circle Voltaire's house the moment Tronchin's appeal publicizes the fragile state of his health: the smell of death brings ravens. Late on February 20 he receives a letter signed, "Gauthier, priest": "Many persons admire you, sir; from the bottom of my heart I desire to be one of them; I should like that privilege if you are willing, and the choice is yours . . . I shall not forget you during the most holy sacrifice of the mass, and shall pray as fervently as I can to just and merciful God for the salvation of your immortal soul, which may be on the brink of judgment . . . My purpose is to render you the greatest service of all,"[4] which is to spare him from having his remains tossed into the public dump alongside dogs, actors, and suicides if he dies within the gates of Paris unanointed by the Church. This great broad mind had one tiny fear. At Ferney he could arrange whatever he

*Eighty-two in 1778.

wanted privately with the priests; once, as a matter of fact, when he was deathly ill, he had managed to become a Capuchin convert, which kept the salons howling with laughter. But in Paris, where thousands of eyes were on him, he had to choose between scandal or ridicule. The burial of an unrepentant sinner or the humiliation of acquiescence. Neither death nor damnation troubles him, only the gutter. A question of background, probably, or else the weight of his eighty-four years. Who knows? He muses. The priest's message is nicely put. Why not acquire an admiring confessor? Repeat the Capuchin "caper" on a broader level. This Gauthier is following orders, no doubt about it, but he sounds civilized enough. "Your letter, sir, seems to come from an honest man, and that alone persuades me to request the honor of your visit, on the day and hour of your choice . . . I shall soon appear before God, creator of all worlds. If you have something to tell me, I shall consider it my duty and honor to receive your visit." [5]

To understand Voltaire, one must accept the fact that he is not an atheist. The century's only atheist of comparable rank is Diderot.

Father Gauthier needs no second invitation: on February 21 he bursts like a bomb into Voltaire's drawing room, where the great man, lively as ever, is prancing about in front of twenty visitors. Out, everyone out! Voltaire suddenly goes limp at the sight of the cassock, hustles his admirers through the door, and closets himself with the priest. They feel each other out; they scrutinize each other. Who sent this messenger of the Infamous Thing? "M. de Voltaire listened to me attentively," relates Gauthier, a devout man and former Jesuit whose training had cultivated in him a respect for individuality that still guides his thinking and behavior. He is attached to the parish of Saint-Sulpice and says mass at the asylum for incurables. "M. de Voltaire told me that he loved God. I praised him for it and observed that he must demonstrate it." They lock swords. Voltaire had been expecting this fencing match for fifty years, never quite sure how he would come out of it. He had perfect confidence in his own inventive powers. "He listened to me intently, and the moment I stopped talking he inquired if I was acting on my own initiative. 'Yes,' I told him truthfully.

" 'What?' he retorted. 'You mean to tell me that the archbishop and the curé of Saint-Sulpice* have not advised you?'

" 'No, sir. If my coming here has been unpleasant, I ask your indulgence; and if it has given you pleasure, we have the Lord to thank.' " [6]

The priest was telling the truth. On his own, he was leading the race to convert Voltaire, but he also admits frankly that he will report the result of his endeavors to his superior that evening. "I left M. de Voltaire and asked if I could drop by to see him now and then; he consented readily." The breach is open. As to whether he consented readily or resignedly . . . He wanted an insurance policy guaranteeing him a decent burial, and this salesman was as

*Which served most parishioners on the Left Bank. Saint-Germain-des-Prés was still Church land.

good as another. Wagnière asks if he is content with M. Gauthier. "He told me he was a nice enough fool."[7] A useful commodity. Keep him on hand for emergencies, like a lucky charm. Meanwhile another, more frenzied church messenger bursts in, the Abbé Marthe, and shouts at Voltaire:

"This very moment, sir, you must make confession to me, and without fail! There's no escaping it. Hurry! I am here for the purpose."

Voltaire twits him. "On whose behalf have you come, Father?"

"Why, the Lord Himself has sent me."

"Then kindly show me your credentials."[8]

On Wednesday the 25th he has a hemorrhage.

Tuberculosis? No, more likely the fact that his whole body, including the blood vessels, was no sturdier than tissue paper. It was simply giving out. He lies in bed around midday, dictating to Wagnière, when suddenly he starts to "cough rather violently."

"Oh, I'm spitting blood."

The blood "spurted from his nose and mouth as when you turn on a fountain spout where the water is under pressure."[9] Madame Denis rushes in, followed by others. Will they understand? Voltaire believes he is dying and asks for the Abbé Gauthier. First they call Tronchin, who is furious. Didn't he warn them of this? He goes straight to work and removes two basins* of blood from that pallid body. It will keep him quiet at least. The hemorrhage activated by coughing fits continues for almost three weeks. No visitors are allowed. On the 26th, Voltaire writes to Gauthier: "You promised to come listen to me. Please do so as soon as you can," and his niece confirms the request the next day. She intends to bask in the reflected glory of a splendid funeral: "Madame Denis, M. de Voltaire's niece, would be pleased to have the Abbé Gauthier visit him; it would oblige her greatly." In the meanwhile Gauthier has cleared the matter with his superiors and made himself their temporary agent. He comes, but the patient is in no condition to talk. Come back on March 2. In the vestibule, the abbé crosses paths with the Duc de Richelieu, ardent defender of the faith, who had once declared that "we have nothing better to replace it with, and to attack it merely fosters civil unrest,"[10] while at the same time providing Louis XV with cast-off mistresses from his own bed. He is pleased to find the priest there, yes, but advises him "not to intimidate my schoolmate from Louis-le-Grand."[11]

Voltaire was beyond intimidation and quite self-possessed. Wagnière, a Protestant and the only person who maintains his dignity that day, casts searing looks at him. But what can a humble secretary say? In silent misery he witnesses the final skirmish, prelude to a life struggle gone down to defeat.

"I have asked you to come for the reason you know . . . [The word

*250–300 grams.

"confession" never passes the patient's lips.] If you like, we can get on with this little business right now . . . "

The priest informs him that he must first execute a formal written retraction.

"Let everyone leave; I wish to be alone with my friend the Abbé Gauthier."

Alone, if you will, with three sets of ears glued to the keyhole: Wagnière; the Abbé Mignot, Madame Denis's brother, a meddling cleric determined to elbow his way into the final act; and a M. de Villevieille. They overhear the priest imposing conditions. Wagnière shudders; the two others chide his foolishness. "I answered that I despaired not to know my master was confessing his sins but to think that he might be pressed into signing something that would dishonor him later. M. de Voltaire called me to bring him writing materials. He saw that I was upset and, with apparent surprise, asked me why. I was unable to tell him."[12] Like all good Calvinists, Wagnière lacks imagination and humor: he cannot translate winks. The poor man chokes with rage while Voltaire calmly writes out the required sanctimonious nonsense:

"I, the undersigned, hereby declare that, having vomited blood for the past four days, at the age of eighty-four, and unable to betake myself to church; and since the curé of Saint-Sulpice has been charitable enough to send me the Abbé Gauthier, a priest, I have made confession to him; and if God so wills it, I die in the holy Catholic religion in which I was born, trusting that in His divine mercy He will see fit to forgive my sins; and if ever I have disgraced the Church, I ask its pardon and God's.

"Signed: Voltaire, March 2, 1778, in the house of M. le Marquis de Villette."[13]

Villevieille and the Abbé Mignot are called in to witness the document. Wagnière refuses to join them. His anger is unwarranted; now *he* is the intolerant one. He cannot understand that, though this amounts to a profession of faith, a passport to the cemetery, it is not a retraction. Voltaire never put his signature to a single word disavowing a single work of his. Wagnière, the Protestant and skeptic, has the last word on March 2 even if he doesn't know it, for tucked into his wallet these past three days he carries Voltaire's true *credo,* written out in a firm, clear hand, the only parting message he cared to leave:

> I die worshiping God, loving my friends, not hating my enemies, and detesting superstition.
> February 28, 1778   Voltaire[14]

The Abbé Gauthier is not overly proud of his limited victory. He suggests that Voltaire take communion. But "I detest superstition." The patient politely refuses. "For the reason that I am spitting blood and might accidentally spit out something else."[15] The priest shows the so-called retraction to his superior and receives a scolding. It's not enough, not convincing, doesn't mean a thing. Does anyone expect the Church to make its peace with Voltaire on the strength of *that*? He's pulling our leg with all his ifs and buts.

Gauthier resumes his assault the next morning. New development: a Swiss Guard bars the door to the Hôtel de Villette. Is M. de Voltaire dying? No, he feels better today, but is receiving no callers. If he should need the services of a priest, he will get in touch directly with the curé of Saint-Sulpice. For the moment, it is best not to speak to him of death. He is recuperating.

"Besides, that priestly crowd bores me stiff."[16]

SANTERRE

91

MARCH 1778

An Expert Sense of Touch

On March 12, 1778, Antoine-Joseph Santerre is married in the old church of Arcueil.* Remarried, actually, at the age of twenty-six. Happiness at last? The young couple looks gloomy enough, not a promising sign. Yet Santerre had enjoyed so many advantages from the start.

In 1752, third of six children, he was born to Augustin and Marie-Marguerite Santerre, blood cousins in a family of brewers settled in northern France. For three or four generations the Santerres had been making beer, the poor man's drink and the most popular beverage when bad grape harvests drive the price of wine too high. Beer-making therefore is one of the few trades that flourish in hard times, when "beer consumption increases; by the same token, good times transformed beer drinkers into wine drinkers."** Antoine-Joseph came into the world at the threshold of an age that brought prosperity to brewers and hardships to others, the period of the Seven Years' War, when "towns acquainted only with wine" began to drink beer. A contemporary economist, Le Grand d'Aussy, mentions a few such instances "in Champagne, where in the space of a year four breweries opened in the same town."[1] Europe's misery having brought prosperity to the Santerre clan, the alliance between two family branches, one in Saint-Michel in Thiérache province (paternal), the other in Cambrai (maternal), provided the additional capital and experience needed to expand the business to Paris. Their first

---

*Suburb south of Paris. [*Trans.*]   **Noted by Fernand Braudel.

brewery opened in the Faubourg Saint-Marcel, the city's poorest quarter, where day laborers sprawled in the gutter. A second, larger one at 7 Rue Censier is where Antoine-Joseph was born. And on August 29, 1772, in his own name, he bought M. Acloque's brewery at No. 232 in the Faubourg Saint-Antoine for sixty-five thousand francs.

At the age of twenty? How could he do it? Besides that, he had come into his majority in 1770, the year his parents died, one after the other, his mother in childbed, his father of grief. The six orphans had responded with the courage bred into natives of Thiérache, where life is a struggle. Marguerite, the eldest girl, became mother to them all at fifteen. Baptiste, the eldest boy, stayed at home and helped her raise the four others. An improvised household. The two are fast becoming spinster and bachelor for life.* Armand-Théodore, who never liked the beer trade, has taken up glass-polishing near Corbeil. Young Claire** is at boarding school. Antoine and François, the youngest boy, are already independent brewers, the latter at Sèvres, the former for the past six years in the Faubourg Saint-Antoine, that new community of workers and craftsmen between the Bastille and the Place du Trône.[2]

Santerre married the first time on December 12, 1772, shortly after buying his brewery. Not without mishap. He had fallen in love long before with Marie François, the prettiest girl on the Rue Censier. They were childhood sweethearts; for them to marry would have been the most natural thing, as her father was also a brewer. Unfortunately, he had social aspirations and dreamed of finding a musketeer to wed his daughter. She, however, had eyes only for Antoine-Joseph, a lad as handsome as any musketeer, "who stood a comely five feet four inches, with attractive features, a shapely mouth, soft brown eyes (the left slightly smaller than the right), fine silky chestnut hair, carefully combed and powdered. His appearance was always extremely neat and trim."[3] All to his credit, but still he was not a nobleman. François the brewer stuck to his guns. The young lovers met secretly for months at mass or in the Royal Gardens. When Marie's father broached his plan to marry her to a musketeer, Santerre all but flung himself into the Seine: a passerby grabbed him off the railing on the Pont de La Tournelle. Marie suffered an epileptic seizure with fever and delirium. Dr. Petit, who looked after both these neighboring families, diagnosed her ailment and prescribed the one fitting remedy: "Let them marry! Do you want to kill your daughter?"

François was not a bad father at heart; he consented to the match. They made a nice young couple, at twenty and sixteen. Marie bloomed again.

On September 9, 1773, seven months pregnant, she slipped on the stairs of their house. The baby was stillborn. She bled internally and died. Santerre had known nine months of bliss.

---

*And continue to share the house on the Rue Censier until both die in their sixties.
**She marries the lawyer Panis, whom we meet later at the National Convention and on the Committee of Public Safety.

He never grieved. People of Thiérache suffer in silence. He submerged his sorrows in work: the brewery became his universe. He has put five years of his life into those cavernous buildings that constantly demand enlargement, for which reason it is better to make beer in the faubourg than in the center of town. A good deal of space is needed for the giant furnaces in the brewery tower that heat huge copper caldrons, like half-sections of a globe; for the malting beds high in the granaries where the grain reaches its peak of flavor; for the grinding mills turned by four sturdy horses. One of them is so large that all the neighbors call him Sans-pareil [Peerless]. Each year Santerre lends the animal "to a poor man with a large family who exhibits him at the Saint-Germain fair rigged up in a harness reminiscent of the trappings on war elephants."[4] Ever more room is required for the barreling process, when the huge vessels disgorge the "foamy malt" into casks that will distribute all over Paris the hazy delights of a brew that is basically barley, with additives which vary from year to year: poppyseed, dried mushroom, aromatic herbs, sweet bay leaf, and *espiotte des Flandres,* also called winter barley."[5] This small manufactory provides employment for a steadily growing work force: at least thirty pairs of hands are needed to begin operations, which is why the owner must have capital at the start. There are no poor brewers. In 1778 Santerre employs over fifty workmen, local folk who earn ten or twelve sous daily, thus "lower-class," unskilled laborers. They appreciate Santerre, who, unlike most other employers, "does not send them back to the poorhouse" if they get sick, but keeps their jobs open for them, sees that they are looked after at home, and visits them. He dresses like a gentleman, yet treats them with respect.

Also, he works alongside them for twelve hours a day, rotating mash by the cartful; the word for beer-making (*brasserie*) comes from this stirring motion (*brasser*), "for the most tiring operation involves the arm muscles." His reputation grows. No one can equal him, "whatever the season, whatever the quality of the barley," for knowing if the grain contains enough water when squeezed between the fingertips; if it yields to pressure and dissolves between the fingernails, it is ready to be removed from the dampening tun and allowed to germinate. At twenty-five, he is one of six or seven master brewers of Paris who can tell from experience "the right temperature for pouring off " the diluted malt into vats. "The solution must be neither too hot nor too cold . . . Too high a temperature prevents the beer from fermenting later on or the impurities from settling out . . . It is not easy to judge whether the solution is right. It involves an expert sense of touch in *feeling the water** by applying a fingertip to the surface. An immediate pricking sensation means it is right."[6] White or red "beer"? Santerre makes both. The red** takes longer to "cook." Three or four hours for the white; thirty to forty for the red.

*Diderot's emphasis in the *Encyclopédie* article.
**Later called "dark."

Santerre is unrivaled at "beating the foam" after the brew has been poured off for the last time into collecting vessels, where the fermentation continues and even increases "to a given strength or maturity, at which stage the beer can be filled into casks . . . The surface of the fermenting brew is entirely covered with a fluffy, expanding coat of foam. Then one must beat this foam with a long pole to stir it into the liquid."[7]

He has been beating the foam now for five years. At the end of each day he trudged wearily back to his lonely room and read literature on the brewing trade. He corresponded with M. Quinquet, an apothecary and chemist who proposes to make street lamps burn ten times brighter by injecting a current of air. He acts on Diderot's suggestion that a thermometer be substituted for plunging a finger into the brewing vats to test for proper heat. He has just decided to imitate the English by substituting a steam engine for horsepower at some of his grist mills. He welcomed information that his younger brother brought back from a visit to England, including a description of revolving millstones, which enables him to put British ale and porter on the market before any of his competitors in the Faubourg Saint-Antoine or Sèvres. In the salons of the capital, Santerre Beer is becoming a craze. But what about its maker? It's rough, at twenty-five, to keep one's nose forever to the grindstone. Friends worry about him, try to prod him out of his rut. They introduce him to widows older than he. Somewhere on the list is M. Deleinte, "former jeweler on the Rue Bourg-l'Abbé, now lord and master of the estates and châteaux of Arcueil and Cachant [sic]" south of Paris—the familiar route to respectability taken by Pierre-Augustin Caron to become "Seigneur de Beaumarchais." The Deleinte household seems to reel under a plague of daughters: twenty-six of them, and not a single son. Twenty of the girls died in infancy. In any event, the father resolves to marry off one of the survivors to Santerre. And does, in a country wedding barely two leagues from the steps of Notre Dame, though it seems like fifty. Peasant processions, fireworks, high mass. Mlle Deleinte is resigned; so is he. "Three or four days after the ceremony his wife made the belated and cruel confession to him that she did not love him and had wanted to marry someone else."[8]

Well, he still has the brewery.

MARCH 1778

The Sense of His Fame

Priests are not the only ones contesting Voltaire's bedside; doctors have come there, too. Wagnière, Voltaire's secretary, observes that "M. de Villette could not bear M. Tronchin and did not want him to continue attending M. de Voltaire. This situation became so inflamed that one day M. Tronchin grabbed his arm and dragged him out of the room. After that, they split into two camps." The gravediggers and the lifeguards. "I was witness to the most intolerable scenes in the patient's bedchamber when he was critically ill," about the first ten days of March. "From the row going on, you would have thought brawling peasants were at each other's throats."[1] The clamor becomes common gossip and filters into the gazettes. Voltaire's illness receives blow-by-blow press coverage. Tronchin started it all; Villette carries on, if only to protect himself. In the *Journal de Paris* of March 5 Voltaire's host addresses an open letter to Dr. Lorry, whose soothing bulletins conflict with Tronchin's pessimism: "To you I owe my peace of mind and that of my young wife. You have soothed his [Voltaire's] spirit. Friendship undoubtedly has generated the alarming apprehensions that M. Tronchin aroused in us. Any other physician might be suspected of creating monsters for the honor of combating them."[2]

Delightful spring: Parisians will be able to wager on Voltaire's condition, just as Londoners did on the Chevalier d'Eon's sex. Will he or won't he die? Meanwhile, still coughing up blood, he burrows under the bedcovers and scowls, mostly at himself for having made that ridiculous confession. He knows Tronchin is right; besides, Lorry is only carrying on Tronchin's treatment. For once, it is not the doctors who are killing Voltaire but the public, which he, its captive, is beginning to detest.

March 10. The Comédie Française company—Voltaire describes the members as "mediocre, with little intelligence and no guts, intractable, as if they had no need for my advice"[3]—comes to rehearse *Irène* in the drawing room. But Tronchin is there and insists on keeping his patient in bed with the curtains drawn. Loud groans. Can't he attend the opening? Just a short trip

across the Seine. Without him, the performance will fall flat. The audience
wants to see the author, not the play. Tronchin won't hear of it. Voltaire "is
still losing a lot of blood," or was up till Wednesday, when the doctor put him
on ass's milk, to which he consented, having at last seen the light of reason,
and now he flies at Madame Denis whenever she insists on "arranging the
dress rehearsal so that he may watch it": "What would that accomplish? Would
you have the company come here to sprinkle holy water on me?"[4]

No, positively, he will not go. He took his life in his hands—and may yet
lose it—to come to Paris from Ferney in the dead of winter and lie flat on his
back while the idol of his eye is being performed less than a mile away. Still,
he coughs less, the bleeding has stopped, while he lies there wan and listless
—above it all. On March 16 society and the court, including the queen, attend
the opening of *Irène* at the Comédie Française. Missing are Louis XVI, Rousseau, Marat—and Voltaire. People simply cannot understand this dreary
tragedy; they yawn and applaud. With nightcap pulled down over his ears,
Voltaire obviously is pleased to receive messengers from Pont-Royal bearing
tidings of the success of each of five acts. "Your news consoles but does not
cure me."

"Yet he was eager to know which parts, which speeches, which verses had
the greatest impact . . . It delighted him to hear that he was offsetting the
unfavorable public reaction to his confession."[5] Well, that's a relief. He gets
up and walks about for a short while on the 17th. By the 19th, visitors are
calling again in droves.

The audience at *Irène* had not fussed too loudly at the playwright's absence
because a rich little comedy in the loges provided diversion: two princes of
the blood had fought a duel that morning, a brother and a cousin of the king
who were sitting in the front row, obliged to behave themselves. Not a
common spectacle. What a court, what a ruling family! About to cut each
other's throats . . .

The affair harkens back to the Mardi Gras ball a week earlier, a splendid
social event held at the Opera. Warm, friendly atmosphere. The Comte d'Artois arrived drunk, a habit he was then developing, and staggered on the arm
of his current mistress, pretty Madame de Canillac from Auvergne.[6] The
couple crossed paths with the Duchesse de Bourbon, née Bathilde d'Orléans.* Twenty-eight, nymphomaniac, subject to nervous seizures. She had
been married sight unseen to the Prince de Condé's simple-minded son, six
years her junior. Shifty and depraved, this Duc de Bourbon was ever willing
to forgo a ball at the Opera for a night's entertainment at one of the luxurious
brothels that catered to his peculiar tastes.** Artois, Bourbon, Orléans: these

---

*Sister of the future Philippe Egalité.

**He was to become the last Prince de Condé and die during Louis-Philippe's regime in the
course of some mysterious masochistic rite.

intermarriages among cousins never kept the young blades from seeking greener pastures. How bored they were! Artois had slept with Bathilde de Bourbon, as had everyone else, and the Duc de Bourbon with Madame de Canillac, in line with a host of others. But drink had soured the king's brother that night, and his blood was up: he insulted the duchess in passing; she plucked off his mask and he, with engaging gallantry, soundly slapped her face, "which was black and blue the next day."

Being a thorough witch, she at once alerted her clansmen. Imagine anyone insulting the Houses of Orléans and Condé! Five days of secret negotiations behind locked doors in the royal apartments led, at daybreak on March 16, to a duel in the Bois de Boulogne "according to all the ancient canons of chivalry," which the Chevalier de Crussol, acting as the Bourbon second, halted at the first drop of blood: a nick on the Comte d'Artois's shoulder. The two cousins dined together and went off arm in arm to see *Irène*. But they, their wives, and their mistresses were part of the spectacle and made up for Voltaire's absence. Louis XIII would have sent them to the block. Louis XVI apparently intends to have them cloistered each for a week in one of their many châteaux. How will they take it?

Jacques-Pierre Brissot chronicles: "Never had Paris been livelier or more lustrous; never had life been so full of activity and excitement, the kind of excitement that stirs the soul of a cultivated, poetic, and philosophic population.* Among a dozen other interesting events, this was the time when Benjamin Franklin and Voltaire were visiting . . . I had attended the première of *Irène* . . . In two letters to the *Courrier de l'Europe* which marked my debut as a contributor to that paper [for four years he has oscillated between law and journalism], I wrote a review of the tragedy . . . In the same breath that I reported the tremendous ovation given to the play, I spoke of the equally tremendous ovation for Messrs Bourbon and Condé [the father had come with his son] when they appeared in the loge, and the silence that greeted Marie Antoinette and M. d'Artois on their arrival in the theater."[7] This is not to say they came together: Artois got there first, strutting like a peacock, his lower lip drooping as usual; next came the queen, each to an appointed seat. Before that there had been much "clapping of hands" for the Condés, whose ancestor, the first Duc de Bourbon, successor to the regent, had tried to castrate Louis XV—or at least turn him homosexual at the age of fifteen by slipping young pages into his bed—but presumably bit off more than he could chew. The Condés are still around, and Voltaire's admirers cheer them first and loudest. In defiance of Artois. "The ladies [of society] whose idol this prince once had been all turned against him, and Madame de Bourbon's cause appeared to have been adopted by her sex—that is to say, all across the nation."[8] A nation of two thousand well-feathered birds.

*And never had Brissot waxed so platitudinous. The culmination of four years of misguided and ill-advised literary endeavors.

In defiance of Marie Antoinette also. Besenval, the queen's escort, is struck
by the chilling silence at their entrance, prior to the mandatory round of polite
applause. "For some reason, the general public does not like the royal family,
or the queen, or the Comte d'Artois especially."[9] Everything seems to operate
in reverse, against the norm, this evening. An in-house dispute. Mindless
approval of an unstageable drama. Support for a rotten branch of the Bourbons
over a misbegotten prince and an oblivious queen. Excuse? *Irène.* It fared
better because Voltaire could not come. The two thousand gilded doves
assume they are watching a chess match that began with the Fronde and will
go on forever: a Condé advances here, an Artois there, a queen here, a
Pompadour there. What harm can it do? They all meet for dinner.

   Brissot is puzzled and applauds no one. He is one of the few persons in
the audience to really miss not seeing Voltaire. In a day or so he will be on
his way to England (France and England are not at war yet), where he hopes
to become a political orator and journalist like Beaumarchais or Linguet.
Anything to get rid of his clerk's robes. He will become associated with the
first liberal French-English gazette, the *Courrier de l'Europe,* something of a
"co-production" aimed at familiarizing European readers with the philosophy
and oratory of England's greatest Whigs, Fox and Burke, "whose speeches
everyone repeated, whose names everyone mispronounced . . . People admired the sublime and previously unacknowledged eloquence of those orators. And people wondered why George III calmly allowed himself to be
insulted by them instead of packing off some of the glib talkers to the Tower.
What, no *lettres de cachet?* No Bastille? The people must be sovereign, from
what we hear."[10] They favor the American insurgents, they protest over-
mechanization in the mines and factories of their own land. Brissot looks
forward to meeting such men, who are more his brothers than the French
snobs flocking around Voltaire fifty years too late. "In bidding adieu to
Paris,* in passing its gates, I felt released from a giant burden. How beautiful
the countryside looked! How fresh the air seemed! Just to breathe it was a
thrilling sensation!"[11]

At Versailles, however, a breath of fresh air makes its way in on March 20.
The King of France grants an audience to republicans. Who would have
predicted, much less imagined, it a year earlier? Perhaps only Beaumarchais.
He is lost in the crowd of courtiers applauding an event which certainly they
have done nothing to shape. But times do change. First Voltaire, then Franklin; no longer can they be fobbed off. Two old men have conquered the
younger generation at the close of this century, starting with the King of
France.

   Not just two old men. Beaumarchais is under fifty. His arm rests in a sling.

*On April 13, 1778.

In his rush to congratulate Franklin the previous December, he had so pressed his coachman to race to Passy from the Hôtel de Hollande the moment he heard of the great American victory at a place with an Indian name, Saratoga, that the coach tipped over. Beaumarchais ended up with a broken arm—final casualty of the Battle of Saratoga. He is jubilant.

On October 17, 1777, General Burgoyne's redcoat army of five thousand had surrendered to Generals Gates and Arnold. First decisive victory of the war for the militiamen, who had been taken for raiders rather than soldiers. In reality, neither Washington nor the Congress had done it deliberately. Incredible bungling on the part of Britain's high command had handed them this revenge for the loss of Philadelphia. Burgoyne led the units that were to march south from Canada and join Howe's advance northward from New York. Howe decided to capture Philadelphia instead. Was he wrong or right? On whose orders did he act?* England's success in the center colonies had settled nothing and, in the end, led to her defeat in the North. One thing is certain: George III's armies were uncoordinated. Two hundred leagues apart, they had to grope their way for lack of guidance from London.

In the eyes of Louis XVI and Vergennes, the Saratoga victory did not offset a long list of defeats. The insurgents still lacked credibility. But public opinion had shifted slightly, partly because of Beaumarchais and La Fayette, mostly because of the salons in Paris and Versailles where Franklin's tact and conciliation had had a tonic effect. Franklin a revolutionary? Barely a republican in those times. He had gone out of his way to court the good will of Maurepas, Vergennes, the queen, the Noailles clan, and the bankers. Inflammatory remarks of England's ambassador, Lord Stormont, who behaved like a petty tyrant, had worked to Franklin's advantage. Gradually he managed to persuade the French that their best interests lay in going to war not for America but against England. Anti-British feeling ran high: let's not forget dismantled Dunkerque, the loss of Africa, India, and Canada, the humiliations of 1763! Shall France go on kneeling fifteen years later to an empire that is falling apart? Necker was less reticent than Turgot about military spending. Saint-Germain, eccentric or not, had restored muscle to army discipline. And in between intrigues Sartines had concentrated on building up naval arsenals. Bored aristocrats longed for a fight, even Anglophiles like Lauzun, who thought of war with England as just another friendly sparring bout, slightly bloody and therefore more exciting than a horserace, after which they could all get together and talk about it.

Saratoga gave Vergennes the opportunity to take a risk without losing face. To recognize the United Colonies was not, after all, an act of war. If the British choose to see it as such, that's their business. Louis XVI and his minister

---

*Military historians are still arguing the point for lack of documentary evidence.

were tired of hanging back. Franklin was informed that he and his countrymen would be accredited by audience on March 20. Amen!

A wig or not? Once again people will say he did it on purpose. Never in human memory has a state official appeared bareheaded before the King of France. One had to wear curls or a wig. Franklin will have none of that. "Stoop down!" comes back like the refrain from his boyhood that helped him over so many hurdles. But he waited too long to call the wigmaker, who is on the verge of tears: "Alas, sir, this will never do! It is not my wig that is too small but your head that is too big!"[12] Cheerful omen.

Amen to him as well. He still has a fine head of long white hair. In his brown velvet suit, his wire-rimmed spectacles, his shoes with silver buckles, he looks neatly and properly attired for this momentous occasion. Vergennes precedes him, followed by Silas Deane, Arthur Lee, and two other compatriots up the grand stairway of Versailles between two rows of Swiss Guards presenting arms. Drums roll in the parade ground. The doors to the king's apartment open. A herald cries: "The ambassadors of the thirteen united colonies . . ."

Franklin weeps. He has reason to. The son of a tallow chandler from Milk Street, Boston, has come a long way. Today, Versailles is a symphony of blue and gold. Four years ago, in London, all was gray when George III stripped him of office. What he had been asking of England for thirty years France gave him in three months. A meaning to life. The promise of a homeland. A man can begin life afresh, or reshape it, at the age of seventy. But not alone, not just for himself. Men have died, are dying at this moment in Virginia, in Pennsylvania, in the Hudson Valley. Millions now and in the future will escape stagnation if they follow his example.

"He dresses like a Quaker. His pride seems to come from within."[13]

Lord Stormont gave formal notice the next day of his return to London.

March 26. Voltaire seems to have taken a new lease on life. For the second time he receives Madame Necker, who presents her daughter Anne-Louise-Germaine, an alert, bright-eyed child of twelve.* He has begun to go out a bit and toured the Place Louis XV, which he had never seen, in a carriage. It had been a vacant lot when he left Paris. On March 28 he calls on Turgot, attended by Condorcet. There he discovers a man wrecked by failure, immobilized by gout; which of the two will die first? Condorcet sees the older man rush up to this great victim of circumstance who could be his son. Turgot is the one Voltaire "holds up to those who complain to him about the decadence of our times."** He "waters his hands with tears, he kisses them, despite Turgot's attempts to pull them away, and cries out in a voice choked

*The future Madame de Staël.
**Condorcet *dixit.*

with sobs, 'Let me kiss the hand that has signed the people's welfare into law.' "[14] That was how highly he valued the freeing of the grain trade.

He seems to be composing each gesture, like the final act of the one truly successful drama he created: his life. March 30: an apotheosis is now in order. At four o'clock he steps into his coach, "azure blue, studded with stars," as if bound for his coronation. It *is* a coronation. He goes to the Academy, where two thousand persons cheer him in the courtyard of the Louvre. D'Alembert delivers a ponderous eulogy of Boileau, Racine, and Voltaire, giving precedence to the latter, who listens, lost in thought, in the costume of another age, buried under "a high wig of tight grizzled curls, which he combs every day and is very much like the one he wore forty years earlier; flowing lace cuffs, and the splendid sable furs sent to him several years before by the Empress of Russia."[15] The Academy is just an appetizer; crowds wait for him at the Comédie Française. "His approach to the Tuileries from the old Louvre Palace was the nearest thing to a public triumph. The whole Court of the Princes, which is immense, all the way to the edge of the Carrousel, was mobbed, with crowds overflowing onto the broad garden terrace, a throng that included all sexes, all ages, all levels of society. As soon as his coach rolled into view, there rose a great universal shout of joy; the cheers, the ovation, the excitement grew louder as he approached . . . Every post, every gate, every crossing was jammed with onlookers, and hardly had the coach arrived when people were climbing onto the dashboard and even up over the wheels to get a closer look at the divinity. Inside the theater, public acclaim, which seemed already to have reached its zenith, grew deafening as M. de Voltaire, seated in the box reserved for the gentlemen of the king's bedchamber, between Madame Denis and Madame de Villette, received from M. Brizard [an actor] a crown of laurel, which Madame de Villette set on the great man's head and he instantly snatched off, though the audience urged him to keep it on with thunderous applause and cheers rising from every corner of the hall and causing a sensational din . . .

"Before the curtain rose, the entire company came out on the stage. The hall was packed solid, right to the entrance to the pit, into which several women had descended after failing to find seats anywhere from which to glimpse the idol of such unrestrained fervor . . . The hall became clouded with dust thrown up by the ebb and flow of the excited crowd. This rapture, this wave of universal delirium lasted for twenty minutes and made it difficult for the actors to begin the play. It was the sixth performance of *Irène* . . .

"M. de Voltaire's exit from the theater was even more affecting than his entrance; he seemed bent under the weight of his years and of the laurel wreath crowning his head. He appeared deeply moved; his eyes, set in pale cheeks, glowed as brightly as ever, but one could not help feeling that his life now hung on the sense of his fame."[16] Just before that, a portrait bust of the great man had been unveiled on stage and garlanded with laurel before his very eyes, surrounded by actors in Greek costumes and spectators in contemporary dress, amid an incredible clamor of contrived and sincere emotion, shouting, cheering, laughter and tears, an outpouring of collective hysteria that will mark forever the lives of those present. A shining hour for the public more than himself. He is disappointed not to be received, like Franklin, at court. Louis XVI is resolved to ignore him. Yet this man, accused of shaking the throne and the altar, was born under Louis XIV, whose official historian he became; a word or two from his sovereign—no matter how insignificant a sovereign—would have meant more to him than the cheering throngs he has known for so long. That evening he weeps as much from exhaustion as from joy. They wanted not so much to acclaim him as to devour him, to grind him up. To have him.

"Good Lord, do you want to kill me?" They do. It was part of the contract with his public which François-Marie Arouet had accepted in taking the name Voltaire at the age of twenty-five, the year of Madame de Maintenon's death.

93

MAY 1778

The End Will Be Rough

Rousseauists continue to sulk. Manon Phlipon comments scornfully to Sophie Canet on April 25, 1778: "M. de Voltaire is expected to leave in a week, or so they say. He has joined the Freemasons. (This sort of club is much in fashion.) M. de la Dixmerie* improvised the following verses to commemorate the initiation of the Nestor of poets:

Au seul nom de l'illustre frère   [In the name of an illustrious brother
Tout Maçon triomphe aujourd'hui,   Every Mason triumphs today,
S'il reçut de nous la lumière,   If our light has shone on him,
Le monde la reçoit de lui.   He in turn sheds it on the world.]

You have to know something about the Freemason vocabulary to grasp the meaning of 'brother' and 'light.' There's nothing marvelous about it; it's sheer flattery, and that kind of thing approaches pure sham unless it is heartfelt, the

---

*Literary dilettante best known for his notes to the *Contes philosophiques*. He could well afford to flatter Voltaire, having borrowed extensively from him.

fruit of enthusiasm and sentiment."[1] The ceremony of admission had taken place on April 7. Voltaire went, dragging his feet, detesting such antics. It was just a formality: the Masonic high mass aimed at correcting abject universal surrender to Catholic dogma. Unthinkable that a man like Voltaire was not a Freemason by 1778. The ritual takes place at the Lodge of the Nine Sisters[2] (the Muses), which occupies its own special niche in European Masonry outside the Grand Orient.* It is a cosmopolitan forum for ideas and fads of the day, from illuminism to scientism. Young medical student Gilbert Romme has just been admitted, sponsored by Count Golovkin, a Russian-born transplant. Romme feels his Jansenist creed melt away like snow in the sun on contact with these people, whose belief in a supreme being is tempered with skepticism: Lalande, Condorcet, Bailly, Berthollet, Lacépède, Mercier, Fourcroy, and Jussieu.** Italians, English, Swedes, and Germans all come together here.

But even if these cultivated minds had declared their independence from the One True God, they still needed a liturgy to live by. That morning Voltaire played a little game with them, or, if you will, performed a rite of syncretism. Without even a smirk. Sober-faced as his hosts, the popes of the new era.

"The venerable Brother de Lalande has sought the opinion of the very respected Bacon de La Chevalerie, grand orator of the Grand Orient, and of all his lodge brothers . . . He has chosen the very respected Brother Count Stroganov to receive and prepare the applicant. The latter was introduced by Brother Chevalier de Villars, master of ceremonies of the lodge; and at the completion of his obligations, brothers of the pillars of Euterpe, of Terpsichore, and of Erato performed the first section of Guenin's third symphonia concertante. Brother Caperon conducted the orchestra; Brother Chic, first violinist serving the Elector of Mainz, led the second violins; Brothers Salantin, Caravoglio, Olivet, Balza, Lurschmidt, etc., hastened to express the joyful mood of the lodge by displaying talents well known to the public and even better known to the respected Lodge of the Nine Sisters.

"After receiving the signs, words, and tokens, Brother de Voltaire was seated facing East next to the Worshipful Master. A brother of the pillar of Melpomene placed a crown of laurel on his head, which he promptly removed. The Worshipful Master passed around him the apron of Brother Helvétius,† which the widow of that illustrious philosopher had presented to the Lodge of the Nine Sisters along with the Masonic jewelry he had worn as a

*The Grand Lodge of France. [*Trans.*]

**These others join later on: Brissot, Danton, Desmoulins, Cerutti, Petion, Rabaut-Saint-Etienne, and André Chénier.

Among the "brothers" who recite compliments to Voltaire that day is Philippe-Antoine Grouvelle, future secretary of the Executive Council, otherwise known as secretary-general of the government in January 1793. It is he who reads the death sentence to Louis XVI.

†Helvétius and Lalande had founded the lodge.

member, and Brother de Voltaire chose to kiss the apron before accepting it. In receiving the pair of women's gloves, he told Brother Marquis de Villette, 'Since they imply a sincere, tender, and deserving affection, I beg you to present them to Belle et bonne.' "[3]

"Belle et bonne": two words chosen not at random but as a final appeal for humanity. Beauty and goodness, qualities he has always sought, along with many others, in women and never found. None of them has been able to make his life "belle et bonne." Will Reine-Philiberte make dying any easier? He despises her husband. He is fed up with Madame Denis and has just raked her over the coals for allowing dozens of new verses, last-minute backstage fabrications, to be added without his approval to *Irène*. Wildly, in a fit of childish temper, he had shoved her into an armchair when she tried to wrap her arms around him like a giant, flabby vine; the chair she tumbled into was occupied by Captain Vivier, called Nicolas Toupet, a dragoon and former military commissioner in Santo Domingo, now unassigned and "available." He is thirty years younger than she and courts her with starched intensity. Unhurried, she lifts herself lazily off this well-placed cushion that did not plant itself there accidentally.* Does she think her uncle did not notice the byplay? Voltaire hesitates and stumbles in the circle of admiring or self-seeking assassins. Should he return to Ferney? He mentions it. The broom is in bloom there, and his gardeners are clipping the hawthorn hedges. But does he really want to go? Tronchin pleads with him: "I would give a hundred louis for you to be back at Ferney. You are too intelligent not to realize that no one transplants an eighty-four-year-old tree unless he wants to kill it. Leave within the week."

"But am I ready to leave?"

Sometimes he wishes Tronchin would answer no, sometimes yes. Leave Paris when he has just arrived? . . . What if the queen plans to grant him an audience? She might indeed, though not for the cause of literature, having never read a page of his, but because her retainers urge it. If only Mercy-Argenteau and the Abbé de Vermond were not watching at every keyhole and reporting back to Vienna. Maria Theresa would die if she heard about it.

Madame Denis will not hear any talk of returning to Gex. The triumphant reception of *Irène* had been her personal triumph. "Having been told of the conversation with Dr. Tronchin, she scolded him soundly and never forgave him."[4] Does Voltaire really want to go back? Is he really in a condition to make the choice? Since the 30th of March he has lived in a state of intense agitation, hopping from one impulse to the next. The Villettes and Madame Denis press him to buy a house in Paris. He does, on the Rue de Richelieu on April 27.

"It is a tomb I am buying, not a house."[5]

*Madame Denis will marry Nicolas Vivier, or du Vivier, in the coming months.

He was still looking too far ahead. But why complain if he insisted on taking a hand in his own destruction? "As he wished to work on Monday, May 11, he drank twenty-five cups of tea. He had been suffering from severe kidney pains for some time and from frequent attacks of urine stoppage. He was forbidden to drink stimulants." It is said that he was killed by overwork; but it was also a suicide by childishness. "He had a bad attack and was unable to sleep."[6]

May 12. In agony, he calls desperately for Tronchin. How could he guess that his niece and Villette refuse to let the doctor come? Instead, they call in the neighborhood apothecary, who hurries over with God knows what drug "that scalds the tongue" and makes him vomit. Fever sets in. His strength is gone.

"Will you try my remedy?" his old friend Richelieu proposes. "It does wonders for my gout . . . "

Opium diluted in water fermented with yeast. The beer of the dead. Richelieu had a recipe for every occasion, from cantharides for making love to opium for getting over it. Like a hopeless addict, he peddled his trash wherever he could. To Voltaire he sends a vial and instructions to take it in small doses. On May 13 or 14 Voltaire drank every drop of the laudanum. Enough to put an army to sleep.* This time Tronchin will have to be called. It's too late.

"The effect of poppy extract, taken intemperately, soon made itself felt: by morning his mind was gone and delirium set in for the next forty-eight hours. Tronchin tried to counteract the opium the only way he knew: with doses of acid, carefully measured so as not to aggravate his strangury. Gradually, Voltaire regained his senses; his speech returned, but remained slow and painful. Soon, however, he seemed to grow steadily weaker, and what decided his fate was paralysis of the stomach induced by the opium. He could no longer take food or drink."[7]

Where is *Belle et bonne?* She is there, dressed to the hilt, shadow of Madame Denis, who rushes about the house barking orders.

May 25. "Extreme prostration." He cannot take food. To D'Alembert he had confided: "I shall die laughing if I can."[8] How, among these vultures, when his only "friends" are Wagnière, loyal but languid, and Tronchin, a competent doctor but infuriated by his patient's resort to opium? Genevan resentment will stalk Voltaire to the grave. Tronchin writes to his brother: "Voltaire is very ill. He will give in to his moods, to cowardice, to the fear of relinquishing certainty for uncertainty . . . I believe he is deeply upset by his approaching death; I wager he does not joke about it. For Voltaire, the end

---

*There has been a great deal of argument as to whether he drank it himself or those caring for him administered it. One fact is plain: the vial had disappeared by the time Tronchin arrived. "Broken," he was informed.

will be rough. If he retains his wits, he won't find dying funny."⁹ Tronchin
was a God-fearing soul.

The idol of the salons, the hero of March 30, is guarded like a condemned
prisoner from May 25 onward by unloving guards. Cut off from his admiring
public, he begins to be ignored. He will not die laughing. There is nothing
to laugh at.

They intend to make him choke on his laughter. He will have to pay
dearly for the cheers and applause. His mind wanders. The priests resume their
assault. A few *"philosophes"* take turns standing watch to prevent extraction of
another confession that might turn into an explicit retraction. The great cen-
tury-long struggle of ideas is reduced to this small, white, reeking, speechless
heap: Voltaire on his deathbed. Yet he refuses to give up, this amazing bag
of bones. What lust to live! Nervous energy has always kept him going, and
the nerves are still there.

Madame Denis and Villette are annoyed that their golden hen is expiring
too rapidly. The niece fears that her uncle may change his will at the last
moment. She is his sole heir. Villette, so proud of himself for having caught
and caged the golden bird, dreads the thought of having to dispose of the old
man's body. What will he do with it? Finally, in belated disgust, Voltaire drives
them from his bedside. The sight of them makes him sick. Only Belle et bonne
may stay, and even she leaves something to be desired. He hoped for a woman
and got a statue.

They play for time by making the public think he is simply ailing. Parisians
are not prone to panic. Once before, in March, word went out that he was
failing; he won't fool them twice. Voltaire is immortal. Wait and see: soon his
doors will reopen to visitors.

Villette moves him out of his paneled, mirrored, tapestry-hung bedchamber. No one must see the condition he is in. Like an ailing bird fallen from
the nest, he is carried out to a small servant's lodge at the back of the garden.
Daylight blocked by the church of the Théatins, whose tall façade conceals the
arrival of spring. His last hours will be tolled from the belfry of this order of
black-robed monks founded in Italy and dedicated to the task of raising the
standards of all other orders.

May 29. Three priests attempt the final assault. Villette welcomes them.
If only they can arrange the question of burial . . . Gauthier again, flanked
by the Abbé de Fersac, vicar of Saint-Sulpice, with the Abbé Mignot trotting
behind. This makes it three against one, the three representing a hundred
thousand: for years he has been fighting those odds single-handed. He is down
to his last breath—they cannot steal *that* from him.

The Abbé de Fersac waves at him the text of a confession far more
elaborate than the previous one: to sign it would have meant signing away his
life's work. Three little men in black hovering over him, promising salvation.
But he recognizes only the Abbé Gauthier, presses his hand, murmurs some-

thing incoherent. Maybe he is delirious after all. Crafty as the devil, that one. Impossible to extract a single pen stroke from him. One word would do: the three witnesses could then publicly proclaim his repentance. Voltaire's surrender would be the greatest Catholic victory since Lepanto. The question they wish to ask him is the one question he has always evaded, the fundamental dispute between orthodox Christians and deists. A theological question. Metaphysics? Not really, for the whole structure of Catholic doctrine hangs on it:

"The curé drew closer to the bed and, after speaking to him of God, of death, and of his approaching end, he asked him in a rather loud voice, 'Monsieur, do you recognize the divinity of Christ?' "[10]

The divinity of Christ? Voltaire had written an essay on the subject for the *Dictionnaire philosophique,* that abominable heresy publicly condemned twelve years earlier in the wake of the Chevalier de La Barre's appalling execution. The vicar of Saint-Sulpice knows all about the book, having obtained permission to read it after it was banned. Anyone, even a nobleman, found to possess it goes to prison. Let's look up the article under the heading *"Divinité de Jésus"*; here is what it says: "The Socinians,* who are considered heretics, do not recognize the divinity of Christ. They dare to assert, in company with the philosophers of antiquity, Jews, Mohammedans, and many other sects, that the concept of a mortal God is monstrous, that the distance between God and man is infinite, and that it is impossible for the Infinite Being, immense and eternal, to have inhabited a perishable body . . .

"They also dare to argue that Christians spent three whole centuries formulating step by step the apotheosis of Christ and that they raised this astounding edifice merely for the edification of pagans who had deified mortals. At first, according to them, Christ was simply considered a man inspired by God; then as a creature more perfect than all others. Later on he was assigned a place above the angels, as St. Paul tells us. With every passing day his stature grew. He became an emanation of God produced by time. As if that were not enough, he was said to have been born before history began. Finally, he was made into God, consubstantial with God . . . Socinus sowed the seeds of his doctrine throughout Europe, and by the end of the sixteenth century he had all but created a new strain of Christianity: there had been three hundred other strains before his."[11]

Does he recall writing those lines? Does he understand why they are so desperate to extort a confession from him: to extirpate the blasphemous doubt his impudence had implanted in Christian thinking? His mind was wandering just then; the faces grew blurred. But the word "divinity" restores his reason and his courage. Voltaire, like a seasoned soldier, will die on his feet.

"Instantly [after the question was raised], M. de Voltaire appeared to gather his strength, tried to sit up, pulled himself away from the vicar whom

---

*Sect founded in northern Italy in the sixteenth century by Faustus and Laelius Socinus (Sozzini). Its followers rejected the Trinity, the divinity of Christ, and original sin.

he was practically embracing, and, with the arm he had had twined about the vicar's neck, made a gesture of anger and indignation apparently meant to reject this fanatical priest, and told him in a loud, clear voice: 'Let me die in peace,' then turned his back . . . The patient's hand grazed the vicar's calotte in motioning him away . . . The vicar must have felt defiled and his calotte disgraced by the touch of a *philosophe*; he brushed himself off and departed with the Abbé Gauthier."[12]

Voltaire's last conscious act. The defeated priests go off shaking their heads. Twenty-four hours of torment lie ahead of him, like Calas, whom he had pitied so for surviving that long on the wheel. Tronchin had done everything he could to help him and now is crazed with hate. This fanatical Calvinist feels compelled to subject a dying non-believer-in-the-divinity-of-Christ to the fires of hell. God be praised, Voltaire is in torment. All is well. "I wish that everyone who had been enchanted by his books could have witnessed his death. The spectacle is entirely overwhelming."[13] Next to the doctor-executioner stand two women named Bardy and Roger, paid to note every shocking detail of an unrepentant sinner's death. They refuse him water. They let him lie in his own excrement—a man who was obsessed with cleanliness. He is burning up. He pleads for "a pool of ice." See, he must be roasting in hell already. He dips his hand in his chamber pot, moistens his burning flesh with urine.* That was part of the plan.

Toward eleven o'clock on the night of May 30, 1778, Voltaire cries out and dies. It is hard to believe.

ROUSSEAU

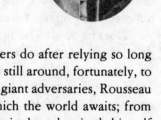

94

JULY 1778

Without Uttering a Single Word

Now that Voltaire is gone, what will the forecasters do after relying so long on Ferney for their political readings? Rousseau is still around, fortunately, to tell us at least how we ought to "feel." Of the two giant adversaries, Rousseau remains. He has yet to finish those *Confessions* which the world awaits; from time to time he turns out a *Rêverie*. Perhaps it was a mistake to barricade himself on the Rue Plâtrière and drive away those who wanted to arrange a truce with

---

*Giving rise a few weeks later to the myth of Voltaire "eating his own excrement," which the Catholic establishment duly propagated.

Voltaire. Feeling and reason could have met and clasped hands under the patronage of tolerance. As he grows older and looks back on the worst acts of his life—abandoning his own children, for example—he tends to become less critical of individuals and more charitable toward mankind. "Whoever is self-sufficient means no harm to anyone . . . Every morning, before daybreak, the bells of Saint-Eustache that I hear ringing for early mass* sound like a solemn admonition to judges and to all men to rely more confidently on their own intelligence; to oppress and despise weakness less; to trust more deeply in innocence and to show more concern for it; to care more about the lives and honor of fellow beings; to beware lest their eagerness to punish crime drive them to commit dreadful deeds."[1]

Is Voltaire included? No, too bitter a pill to swallow. Rancor that is social rather than literary or personal. All those people who acclaimed *Irène* and crowned its author have been admiring Jean-Jacques for thirty years, or so he claims. And their laughter strikes at the poor. Voltaire's laughter offends his ears. He did not visit the Sage in Paris, where his own public had forsaken him. The papers never mention him; no one knocks at his door. He has but two visitors: Corancez and Bernardin de Saint-Pierre. Still weak from his accident, he stays cozily ensconced on the Rue Plâtrière, where reeking sewers poison the air. Lack of exercise adds to the deterioration of his health.

On April 12, 1778, a Sunday in spring, Jean-Jacques Rousseau writes the last page of his life, the beginning of the *Dixième Rêverie,* which remains unfinished: "Today, Palm Sunday, my acquaintance with Madame de Warens dates back precisely fifty years." She was his "mama," the first woman to open his eyes to experience, the mysterious passion that had shaped his life. The memory of it billows up and sweeps him, like many men nearing the close of life, back to the womb, where it was snug and warm. He was luckier than most: his adopted mother slept with him. He idealizes that dreamlike reality now that the fire is damped: "She was twenty-eight then, born at the dawn of the century. I was going on seventeen and the sap rising in me, of which I as yet knew nothing, added heat to my natural sparkle. If it was not surprising for her to become fond of a lively, yet gentle and modest, rather good-looking youth, it was even less so for a charming, cultivated, gracious woman to inspire not merely my gratitude but more tender and unfamiliar feelings as well. The extraordinary thing is that this first experience shaped my life, set the course of my destiny forever after . . . Not a day passes without my recalling fondly and joyously that brief, unparalleled time of life when I was completely myself, undiluted, unrestrained, when I can truly say that I lived. Like the praetor disgraced by Vespasian who retired to his country estate, saying: 'I have spent seventy years on this earth and have lived for seven of them . . .' A preference for solitude and for contemplation took root in my heart alongside the warm

---

* *"La messe de la pie,"* an old popular expression based on the notion that the magpie comes to the window to steal food during the pre-dawn mass.

and exuberant feelings intended to nourish them. Noise and tumult shrink and stifle them; calm and tranquillity revive and inflame them. I need meditation in order to love. I obtained Mama's consent to move to the country."[2] The word "country" recurs twice in this soft, mellow *adagio,* the last music from his pen. No longer can he tolerate the city that is killing Voltaire. He refuses to die like a rat in a hole. To breathe deeply . . . The theme underlying everything he writes is an invitation to all men to return to nature. As if some invisible spring were compelling them to restore their balance, Rousseau sets out from Paris to Ermenonville in the same season that brings Voltaire to Paris from Ferney.

The Marquis de Girardin had clients who paid Jean-Jacques to copy music. Tactfully, to avoid offending him, the marquis suggested, through a doctor who was treating Rousseau's dizzy spells, that he bring Thérèse and stay "as long as he likes" at Ermenonville, north of Paris. The time is ripe: a yearning fills him to return to woods and meadows. On May 20, without telling anyone, he sets out. The marquis's carriage takes him through the forest of Ermenonville. He had forgotten the beauty of "fresh green trees free of fumes and dust." He regards the marquis and his wife and children as good people, like so many others for whom he had developed sudden attachments, often from necessity, only to change his mind and drop them a few months later. Now he won't have time to do that. On the other side of the forest he discovers what critics have insultingly called an English opera set—a set admirably suited to *La Nouvelle Héloïse.* After buying the Ermenonville property in 1763, Girardin, who is hopelessly addicted to British landscapes, loosed an army of gardeners on its barren soil, its dunes and marshes, transforming them gradually into a kind of Rousseauist attraction. Nature, freed from Le Nôtre's tyranny, though not allowed to roam at will, was forced to pattern itself after the reveries of Rousseau's lovers. Girardin recently published a treatise on landscape design, *De la composition des paysages, ou des moyens d'embellir la nature*; the estate merely illustrates his theories. A pond, poplar trees, not a single straight path, artificial ruins, artificial thatched cottages, artificial gravestones, bits of inscription etched on moss-covered rocks . . . "A mood of silence and serenity reigns over this peaceful sanctuary," he writes.[3] Rousseau feels that he is entering a world created by his own pen. It affects him deeply. Never again will he return to Paris. How could he, even for an hour? He sends word for Thérèse to pack their clothes and furnishings; she is used to it. While the marquis is having "a cottage in the orchard" built for them, they can live in a little summerhouse fairly secluded from the château. Jean-Jacques begins to unwind after years of tension. A deluge of fresh air and peaceful surroundings. The news of Voltaire's death upsets him, to Girardin's surprise. A foreboding.

"My existence was attached to his. He is dead; before long I shall follow him."[4]

He ceases to write, saying that he will wait until he has the urge. He enjoys walking free from the perils of coaches and open sewers. He collects plants to start "the herbarium of Ermenonville." Now and then he dines with his hosts at the château and sings "the ballad of the willow," accompanying himself on the spinet. Summer promises to be warm and stormy.

Rumors of war in the east and west. The Elector of Bavaria has died; Joseph II will try to snatch his territory. In Berlin, Frederick the Great frowns and alerts his army. Marie Antoinette, officially pregnant since April 19, intervenes repeatedly on her brother's behalf. Squalls at court, which must be laid at her door. Louis XVI and Vergennes play for time, having no desire to ruin themselves for Austria. Besides, by now it is plain that they are going to have to fight on the high seas. Imagine Louis XVI and Vergennes as buccaneers, sword in hand! The trick is to discover for what and against what France intends to send her armies of the poor to their slaughter, soldiers and sailors impressed from the ranks of those who are unwanted on the land or in the shops and who would otherwise end up in the poorhouse.

Under pressure from Franklin, La Fayette, Beaumarchais, and a host of others in the past, the present, the future (in respect to the latter, the reader is justified in taking the historian to task for flagrant intervention!), France will go to war, as she needs to wage one, in the Atlantic. On June 22 a messenger gallops from Brest to inform the court of Versailles that its worst fears have been realized. The start of a war invariably generates alarm and applause. "The frigate *La Belle Poule* captained by M. de La Clochetterie had spied an English squadron off the coast of Brittany . . . An English frigate approached him to ascertain his nationality and ordered him to come aboard and speak to the admiral. La Clochetterie replied that he was under no such orders from his government, was pressed to be on his way, and refused to comply. Whereupon the British ship opened fire on *La Belle Poule* and the battle was on, nearly at pistol range. It continued for five hours; at dusk the English ship turned tail and made off in the direction of her fleet without returning the cannon fire that *La Belle Poule* was still pouring into her poop. Half *La Belle Poule*'s crew was dead or wounded, and the ship itself so badly hit that it ran aground on the Brittany coast. The British vessel was out of commission."[5] By August, ladies of fashion in Versailles are wearing their hair *"à l'Indépendance ou le triomphe de la liberté,"* or simply a *"Belle Poule"* hairdo. Why complicate matters with the ancient issue of whether to support or attack the King of Prussia? From now on, the sun of heroes will rise in the west, unlike thousands of years of butchery in the heart of Europe. It will dissipate uncertainty only if France enters the lists. What about the victory at Saratoga? Disgraceful, when you come right down to it. Raw recruits defeating a regular army. What are things coming to? To set the situation right, we need a good solid victory from a standing army, preferably French, otherwise American, republicans, if it can't be helped—just let them be friendly to the monarchies. In this respect, it is all to the good that La Fayette and Washington have been beaten at Monmouth,* not far from New York. Colonial defeats and French victories alone will overcome the British. The war for America thus will assume its proper perspective: just another incident in the chronicle of monarchic rivalries. Headdresses *"à la liberté"* are unlikely to last through the winter. Such is the law of fashion. In any event, France can look forward jubilantly to the birth of a dauphin.

The spring of 1778 makes no promises. Will it bring desperate want, sufficiency, or shortages? Only time can tell.

On July 2, 1778, Jean-Jacques rises early.** He goes out for a walk, as he has always done when his health permitted, and is back by eight to breakfast with Thérèse and a serving woman. He asks Thérèse to go pay the locksmith's bill. Another mania of his: never run up debts. On her return, she hears groans: "He complained in turn of an unpleasant prickling sensation on the soles of his feet; of a chill up and down his spine, as if some icy fluid flowed there; of chest pains; and of a splitting headache that came and went, the agony of which he expressed by cradling his head between his hands and saying that he felt his skull was about to burst. Death came in the throes of one such seizure, when he fell out of his chair. We picked him up at once, but he was dead."[6] "Clutching my hands tightly in his, without uttering a single word," Thérèse asserts.[7]

Rumors of suicide are spread by the same tongues which reported that the dying Voltaire ate his own excrement. Have it your way, gentlemen; they died, each of them as best he could, as all of us hope to do.

Voltaire and Rousseau within two months. What shall we do? How shall we think and act? We may have to stand on our own two feet.

*June 28, 1778.
**Jean Guéhenno rightly demonstrates that here one must rely on the account left by Lebègue de Presles, a writer who was a house guest of the Girardins.

Notes

and

Index

Notes

1

1. *Correspondance littéraire* of Grimm, Diderot, Meister, etc., X, 341 (Paris, Garnier, 1879).

2

1. Paul Boiteau, *Etat de la France en 1789* (Paris, Perrotin, 1861). The estimation for 1774 appears on p. 4. Fifteen years later the population of France will reach at least 26 million. See Arthur Young, *Voyage en France*, Vol. III, *Population* (Paris, 1794).

2. Boiteau, *Etat de la France*, p. 12.

3. Paul Hazard, *La Crise de la conscience européenne*, 2 vols. in the collection *Idées* (Paris, Gallimard, 1969). See the first two chapters especially.

4. See the plates showing the *"Division générale"* [general division] of the world's four parts in the original edition of the *Encyclopédie*, or in the *Dictionnaire raisonné des sciences, des arts et des métiers* (supplement to Vol. I, *Afrique, Amérique et Asie*; supplement to Vol. II, *Europe*). In loaning me his complete collection of the 1788 edition of the *Encyclopédie*, Claude Tchou has provided me with a magnificent aid: he has enabled me to *live* for three years in the eighteenth century. As I write this book I constantly make use of the handsome plates in the *Encyclopédie*, which has been reprinted in full by Tchou (Paris, Cercle du Livre Precieux, 6 vols., 1967). To simplify these notes, I shall refer each time to the *Encyclopédie*.

5. Figures obtained from the *Bulletin of the United Nations*, December 1951.

4

1. Bernard Fay, *Benjamin Franklin, bourgeois d'Amérique* (Paris, Calmann-Lévy, 1929), I, 102.

2. *Ibid.*, II, 40.

5

1. *Correspondance et Journal intime du Comte Axel de Fersen, publiés par* Alma Soderjhelm (Paris, Kra, 1930), p. 16.

2. *Ibid.*, p. 35.

3. *Mémoires inédits* (presumed) of Mlle de Mirecourt (Paris, Albin-Michel, 1966).

4. L. S. Mercier, *Tableau de Paris*, original edition, published without the author's name in Amsterdam, 1784, III, 28.

5. Memoirs of the Prince de Ligne, cited in Gaston Maugras, *Le Duc de Lauzun et la Cour de Marie-Antoinette* (Paris, Plon, 1913), p. 97.

6

1. Louis de Loménie, *Beaumarchais et son temps* (Paris, Calmann-Lévy, 1879), I, 366.

2. *Correspondance littéraire*, X, 359.

3. Beaumarchais, *Oeuvres complètes* (Paris, Furne, 1835), p. 348.

4. *Ibid.*, p. 358.

5. *Ibid.*, p. 302.

6. Loménie, *Beaumarchais*, I, 357.

7. *Ibid.*, I, 348.

8. Beaumarchais, *Oeuvres complètes*, p. 309.

9. *Ibid.*, p. 310.

10. *Ibid.*, p. 326.

11. Gudin, cited in Loménie, *Beaumarchais*, I, 368.

12. Beaumarchais, *Oeuvres complètes*, p. 305.

7

1. Pouget de Saint-André, *Le Général Dumouriez, d'après des documents inédits* (Paris, Perrin, 1914), p. 317.

2. *Ibid.*, p. 36.

3. Bastille Archives, Dumouriez file, 1773 B.

4. Pouget, *Le général Dumouriez*, p. 316.

5. *Ibid.*, p. 28.

6. Arthur Chuquet, *Dumouriez* (Paris, Hachette, 1914).

8

1. Archives nationales, Minutier Central, XXIII, 724, and LVIII, 468.

2. André Maurois, *Adrienne, ou la vie de Madame de La Fayette* (Paris, Hachette, 1960), p. 19. What remains of the Hôtel de Noailles has become the Hôtel Saint-James on the Rue Saint-Honoré.

3. *Correspondance littéraire*, X, 408.

4. Maurois, *Adrienne*, p. 43.

5. Chavaniac is still standing and in fine condition, thanks to a Franco-American foundation. Its director, M. Durand, was most willing to show me the round room in which La Fayette was born and, among other fascinating

traces of the former inhabitants, a hole intentionally made in the thick wall of volcanic rock, by means of which La Fayette's grandmother, who had scant affection for callers, could observe undetected from her boudoir the visitors who entered the great courtyard, and possibly send word that she "wasn't at home."

6. A letter by La Fayette about his lineage, from the collection of Edmond de La Fayette, in Maurois, *Adrienne*, p. 44.

7. The most comprehensive biography of La Fayette is the monumental work by Etienne Charavay, *Le Général La Fayette* (Paris, Société de l'Histoire de la Révolution française, 1898), p. 653. It is a mine of information, unhappily marred by a hagiographic perspective and an antiquated style.

9

1. Maurice Tourneux, *Diderot et Catherine II* (Paris, Calmann-Lévy, 1899), pp. 470–84.

2. Denis Diderot, *Correspondance*, (Paris, Editions de Minuit, 1868), XIV, 14, 15. This colossal work by Georges Roth and Jean Varloot is a model of a modern critical edition.

3. André Billy, *Diderot* (Paris, Editions de France, 1932), p. 561.

4. Diderot, *Correspondance*, XIV, 12.

5. Billy, *Diderot*, p. 558.

6. *Correspondance littéraire*, XIV, 462.

7. A. Gaissinovitch, *La Révolte de Pougatchev* (Paris, Payot, 1938), p. 177.

8. *Ibid.*, p. 159.

9. Letter of the French ambassador to Russia, December 31, 1773. Affaires étrangères [Foreign Affairs], 1092 B A/R.

10. Denis Diderot, *Lettres à Sophie*

Volland, publiées par André Babelon (Paris, Gallimard), I, 129.

11. Diderot, *Correspondance,* XIV, 13.

12. Tourneux, *Diderot et Catherine II,* p. 61.

13. *Ibid.,* p. 482.

14. *Ibid.,* p. 457.

10

1. For my ability to understand Gluck and to write these pages, I am indebted to Jean and Brigitte Massin. They furnished me with notes extracted from Mannlich's memoirs (from which I quote here), and from G. Prodhomme's remarkable study *Gluck et la musique allemande.* In this section, unfootnoted passages in quotes come from these notes.

2. *Correspondance littéraire,* X, 417.

3. Gustave Desnoiresterres, *Gluck et Piccinni* (Paris, Didier, 1875).

4. Bachaumont, *Mémoires secrets sur la cour, la ville, etc.,* April 26, 1774, quoted by Desnoiresterres.

11

1. Gérard Walter, *Marat* (Paris, Albin-Michel, 1933), p. 23.

2. *Ibid.,* p. 14.

3. François de La Rochefoucauld, *Mélanges sur l'Angleterre au XVIIIᵉ siècle* (Paris, Guy le Prat, 1945), p. 123.

4. Paul Mantoux, *La Révolution industrielle au XVIIIᵉ siècle* (Paris, Genin, 1959), pp. 419–65.

5. Jean-Paul Marat, *Les Chaînes de l'esclavage,* 3rd edition, published by Havard in Paris in 1833. The other extracts from this work which follow are also taken from this edition.

6. Dr. Cabanès, *Marat inconnu* (Paris, Albin-Michel), p. 59.

12

1. Fersen, *Correspondance,* p. 45.

2. *Ibid.,* p. 46.

3. *Ibid.*

4. Reichard, *Guide des voyageurs en Europe* (Weimar, 1813), Vol. I, *La Grande Bretagne et l'Irlande.*

5. Gaston Maugras, *Le Duc de Lauzun et la Cour intime de Louis XV* (Paris, Plon, 1909), p. 385.

6. *Ibid.,* p. 386.

7. Extract from *Mémoire pour moi, par moi, Louis de Brancas, Comte de Lauraguais* (London, 1773), quoted in *Correspondance littéraire,* X, 224.

8. *Ibid.,* X, 225.

9. Bibliothèque Nationale Imprimerie, 8° LB/38–1270.

10. Paul Robiquet, *Théveneau de Morande* (Paris, Quanti, 1882), p. 28.

11. *Ibid.,* p. 30.

12. Gudin de La Brenellerie, *Histoire de Beaumarchais, mémoires inédits, publiés par* Maurice Tourneux (Paris, Plon, 1888), p. 109. The honest and provincial Gudin was to Beaumarchais rather what Dr. Watson was to Sherlock Holmes. A man of letters who was neither uninspired nor a genius, Gudin was fascinated by Pierre-Augustin and, despite their sketchiness, his remembrances are valuable for the light they shed on certain aspects of Beaumarchais's life. Thus the episode in question: biographers have presented Sartines's celebrated saying, "It is not enough to be censured, etc.," superficially, as if it were a drawing-room compliment. In fact it was a friendly but firm warning, a counter-move. Gudin accompanied Beaumarchais and Lauraguais to London in April 1774.

13. Pierre Pinsseau, *L'Etrange Destinée du Chevalier d'Eon* (Paris, Clavreuil, 1945), p. 137.

14. *Ibid.,* p. 139 and *passim,* for

the rest of this episode, set down in dialogue from D'Eon's text.

15. *Ibid.,* p. 141.

13

1. *Correspondance littéraire,* X, 188.
2. Museum of Versailles.
3. Duc de Choiseul, *Mémoires* (Paris, 1904), p. 220.
4. Emile Cantrel, *Nouvelles à la main sur la Comtesse du Barry* (Paris, Plon, 1861), p. 332.
5. *Ibid.,* p. 332.
6. Maugras, *Le Duc de Lauzun et . . . Louis XV,* p. 312.
7. Pierre de Nolhac, *Le Trianon de Marie-Antoinette* (Paris, Calmann-Lévy, 1924), p. 51.
8. *Ibid.,* p. 56.
9. Books consulted for the story of Louis XV's death and the return of La Du Barry: Cantrel, *Nouvelles à la main sur la Comtesse du Barry*; Edmond and Jules de Goncourt, *La Du Barry* (Paris, Charpentier, 1880); Ferdinand Dreyfus, *La Rochefoucauld-Liancourt* (Paris, Plon, 1903); *Journal de l'Abbé de Véri,* publié par Jehan de Witte (Paris, Tallandier, undated).
10. *Encyclopédie,* XVI, 120.
11. Dreyfus, *La Rochefoucauld-Liancourt,* p. 18.
12. *Correspondance secrète entre Marie-Thérèse et le Comte de Mercy-Argenteau,* publiée par D'Arneth and Geffroy (Paris, Firmin-Didot, 1875), II, 134 (cited hereafter as Mercy-Argenteau, *Correspondance*).
13. Fernand Braudel, *Civilisation matérielle et capitalisme* (Paris, Armand Colin, 1967), p. 59.
14. *Encyclopédie,* XVII, article "*Vérole.*"
15. Montyon, *Particularités sur quelques ministres des finances,* cited in Edgar Faure, *La Disgrâce de Turgot* (Pa-

ris, Gallimard, 1961), p. 11. Faure's book is a repository of exact information on the first twenty years of Louis XVI. It is from Faure that I have borrowed the physical description of the three ministers in question.

16. Maugras, *Le Duc de Lauzun et . . . Louis XV,* p. 428.
17. Soulavie, *Mémoires historiques et politiques du règne de Louis XVI* (Paris, Treuttel et Wurtz, Year X), I, 36.
18. E. and J. de Goncourt, *La Du Barry,* p. 186.
19. Dreyfus, *La Rochefoucauld-Liancourt,* p. 17.
20. *Journal* of the Abbé de Véri, I, 471.
21. *Ibid.,* p. 85.
22. *Lettres de Madame Roland,* publiées par Claude Perroud (Paris, Imprimerie nationale), new series, I, 36.
23. The episode is recounted in detail by the Abbé de Véri in his *Journal,* I, 87–9.
24. See the *Mémoires* of the Count d'Argenson, Vol. IV, cited by Gérard Walter in his preface to Faure, *La Disgrâce de Turgot,* p. 22.
25. Hilaire Belloc, *Marie-Antoinette* (Paris, Payot, 1932), p. 89.
26. *Mémoires* of the Abbé Morellet (Paris, Ladvocat, 1821), I, 223.

14

1. Cantrel, *Nouvelles à la main sur la Comtesse du Barry,* p. 338.
2. Letter from the Countess de Boufflers to Gustave III on July 20, 1774, in A. Geffroy, *Gustave III et la Cour de France* (Paris, Didier, 1867), I, 271.
3. Bernard Fay, *Louis XVI, ou la fin d'un monde* (Paris, Amiot-Dumont, 1955), p. 94.
4. *Correspondance inédite de Marie-Antoinette,* publiée par Count Paul Vogt

d'Hunolstein (Paris, Dentu, 1868), p. 69. The authenticity of this correspondence has been the subject of bitter dispute among historians, notably between the Count d'Hunolstein and Geffroy. Critical examination of the texts and comparison of them with incontestable records have proved their authenticity.

5. J. de Norvins, *Mémorial, publié par* Lanzac de Laborie (Paris, Plon, 1896), I, 5.

6. Dr. V. Galippe, *L'Hérédité des stigmates de dégénérescence et les Familles souveraines* (Paris, Masson, 1905), p. 370.

7. Fay, *Louis XVI,* p. 50.

8. Hunolstein, *Correspondance de Marie-Antoinette,* p. 70.

9. *Mémoires* of the Prince de Montbarey, II, 91, cited in Faure, *La Disgrâce de Turgot,* p. 9. Within these few lines is a condemnation of absolute monarchy, be it Charles Maurras's or Hitler's. Its proponents would convince us that the heir is best qualified to succeed to the throne and that this succession engenders the security of the system. There may not exist a son or grandson, an heir by blood or designation, who has truly been chosen by the ruler to succeed him. But once a man possesses absolute power, an inevitable megalomania leads him systematically to disregard all information on the real problems, which then must wait until his death for resolution.

10. Faure, *La Disgrâce de Turgot,* p. 17. In regard to this story of "the appeal to Maurepas," one that is apparently minor, but which captures the reign in all its superficiality and escapism, the author remarks: "It is one of those instances in which anecdotal history gets to the essential core of history and thus can show us its entire configuration."

15

1. J. P. Brissot, *Mémoires, publiés par* Claude Perroud (Paris, Picard, undated), I, 67.

2. *Ibid.,* p. 63.

3. *Ibid.,* p. 53. Brissot's ingenuous admission gives the lie to Maurice Jusselin's observation in the *Annales historiques de la Révolution française,* where Jusselin tries to exonerate him for this rather minor transgression.

4. *Ibid.,* p. 28.

5. *Ibid.,* p. 29.

6. *Ibid.,* p. 32.

7. Jean-François Primo, *La Jeunesse de Brissot* (Paris, Grasset, undated), p. 7.

8. Brissot, *Mémoires.*

9. *Ibid.,* p. 42.

10. *Ibid.,* p. 60.

11. *Ibid.,* p. 46.

12. *Ibid.,* pp. 64 and 65. This, the first known text by Brissot, dating from Chartres, 1774, was reprinted in Volume VI of his *Bibliothèque philosophique* in 1782.

13. *Ibid.,* p. 42.

14. *Ibid.,* p. 2.

15. *Ibid.,* p. 41.

16

1. Mirabeau, *Correspondance avec Sophie de Monnier* (Paris, undated), III, 450. His remark refers specifically to the episode mentioned.

2. The original is part of the Mirabeau papers in the Bibliothèque Paul Arbaud in Aix-en-Provence.

3. Georges Guibal, *Mirabeau et la Provence* (Paris, Fontemoing, 1901), I, 118.

4. See Antonina Vallentin, *Mira-*

beau avant la Révolution (Paris, Grasset, 1946). This is the most complete study of Mirabeau's youth.

5. Letter from the Marquis de Mirabeau to his brother, the bailiff, in August 1774, in Dauphin-Meunier, *La Comtesse de Mirabeau* (Paris, Perrin, 1908).

6. Louis de Loménie, *Les Mirabeau* (Paris, Dentu, 1879), I, 29.

7. Dauphin-Meunier, *La Comtesse de Mirabeau,* p. 75.

8. Dauphin-Meunier, *La Vie intime et amoureuse de Mirabeau* (Paris, Tallandier, undated), p. 146.

9. Letter from Mirabeau to Madame de Limaye, quoted in Dauphin-Meunier, *La Vie intime . . . de Mirabeau,* p. 136.

17

1. Letter dated June 2, 1774, in Gaston Maugras, *Le Duc de Lauzun et la Cour de Marie-Antoinette* (Paris, Plon, 1913), p. 3.

2. François Métra, *Correspondance secrète, etc.* (London, 1787), I, 4 (on June 4, 1774).

3. Duc de Lévis, *Souvenirs* (Paris, Ollendorf, 1910), p. 4.

4. *Journal* of the Abbé de Véri, I, 4.

5. Lévis, *Souvenirs,* p. 49.

6. Baron de Besenval, *Mémoires* (Paris, Year XIII), I, 39, 383.

7. Condorcet, *Eloge de M. le Comte de Maurepas,* an elegy delivered at the Royal Academy of Sciences, April 10, 1782, and included in *Correspondance littéraire,* XIII, 123.

8. The letter is quoted in full by the Goncourt brothers in *La Du Barry,* p. 196. This text concludes the debate about the exile of the favorite, which certain historians think was wrenched from a dying Louis XV by the priests,

an assertion they base on a transcription, predating her internment, in the records of the chief of police. It was not until May 12 and at Marie Antoinette's insistence that Louis XVI inaugurated his reign by issuing this order, which was not exactly an official document since it was addressed not to a governor of prisons but to a voluntary emergency council. As for the aunt, she was a lady Quantiny (sister to the mother Bécu), who was more a pensioner than a nun in the convent.

9. Extract from Hardy's *Journal,* cited by the Goncourts in *La Du Barry,* p. 196.

10. Métra, *Correspondance secrète,* I, 42.

11. Charles de Chambrun, *Vergennes* (Paris, Plon, 1944), p. 240.

12. *Journal* of the Abbé de Véri, p. 7.

13. *Ibid.,* p. 107.

14. Bachaumont, *Mémoires secrets,* p. 39.

15. Mercy-Argenteau, *Correspondance,* II, 161.

16. Gaston Maugras, *La Disgrâce du Duc et de la Duchesse de Choiseul* (Paris, Plon, 1903), p. 301.

17. *Ibid.,* p. 302.

18. Mercy-Argenteau, *Correspondance,* II, 162.

19. Lucien Perey, *La Fin du XVIIIe siècle: le Duc de Nivernais* (Paris, Calmann-Lévy, 1891), p. 226.

20. *Encyclopédie,* XX, article *"Inoculation."*

21. *Journal* of the Abbé de Véri, p. 476.

22. Mercy-Argenteau, *Correspondance,* II, 182.

23. Maugras, *Le Duc de Lauzun et . . . Marie-Antoinette,* p. 6.

18

1. Beaumarchais, *Oeuvres Complètes,* p. 709.

2. Loménie, *Beaumarchais,* I, 387.

3. The only known copy of this famous libel is the one that Kaunitz made in Vienna during the imprisonment of Beaumarchais (Vienna, *Haus-Hof und Staatsarchiv*). The original printed document, which Kaunitz sent to Louis XVI, has doubtless been destroyed.

4. Loménie, *Beaumarchais,* I, 389.

5. Paul Huot, *Beaumarchais en Allemagne* (Paris, Librairie internationale, 1869), p. 25.

6. Loménie, *Beaumarchais,* I, 392.

7. Gudin, *Histoire de Beaumarchais,* p. 125.

8. Vienna, *Haus-Hof und Staatsarchiv, Staatsabteilung Frankreich,* XXXVI, 110–13.

9. Loménie, *Beaumarchais,* I, 393.

10. Vienna, *Haus-Hof und Staatsarchiv, Staatsabteilung Frankreich,* XXXVI, 46–50.

11. Beaumarchais, *Oeuvres complètes,* p. 711. These two letters are in the same vein as the *Barbier* or the *Mémoires* on Goëzman. See also Huot, *Beaumarchais en Allemagne,* and Lomenie, *Beaumarchais,* I.

12. Letter from Beaumarchais to Gudin in Beaumarchais, *Oeuvres Complètes,* p. 715.

13. Huot, *Beaumarchais en Allemagne,* and Loménie, *Beaumarchais.*

14. Letter from Beaumarchais to Louis XVI, in Loménie, *Beaumarchais,* I, 396.

15. Vienna, *Haus-Hof und Staatsarchiv, Staatsabteilung Frankreich,* XXXVI, 11.

16. Constance-Lily Morris, *Marie-Thérèse, le dernier conservateur* (Paris, Plon, 1937), p. 273 (translated from the English by my mother, Marie Mavraud).

17. Mercy-Argenteau, *Correspondance,* II, 224.

18. *Ibid.,* II, 225.

19. Loménie, *Beaumarchais,* I, 399.

20. Huot, *Beaumarchais en Allemagne,* p. 108.

21. Loménie, *Beaumarchais,* I, 399.

22. Mercy-Argenteau, *Correspondance,* II, 225.

23. Loménie, *Beaumarchais,* I, 400.

24. Huot, *Beaumarchais en Allemagne,* p. 148.

19

1. *Journal* of the Abbé de Véri, p. 184.

2. *Journal historique,* cited in Maupeou, *Le Chancelier Maupeou* (Paris, Editions de Champrosay, 1942), p. 192.

3. Maupeou, *Le Chancelier Maupeou,* p. 19.

4. *Ibid.,* p. 131.

5. The best and most subtle defense of the Maupeou affair is that of Pierre Gaxotte in *Le Siècle de Louis XV* (Paris, Fayard).

6. *Journal* of the Abbé de Véri, I, 144.

7. According to Faure, *La Disgrâce de Turgot,* p. 31.

8. *Correspondance inédite de Condorcet et de Turgot* (Paris, Charavay, 1883), p. 185.

9. *Journal* of the Abbé de Véri, I, 158.

10. Fay, *Louis XVI,* p. 106.

11. *Ibid.*

12. Faure, *La Disgrâce de Turgot,* p. 54.

13. *Journal* of the Abbé de Véri, I, 112.

14. *Ibid.,* 160, 128.
15. *Ibid.,* 156.
16. *Ibid.,* 184.
17. Marcel Marion, *Dictionnaire des institutions de la France aux XVIIe and XVIIIe siècles* (Paris, Picard, 1969), p. 84.
18. Maupeou, *Le Chancelier Maupeou,* p. 228.
19. *Journal* of the Abbé de Véri, I, 160.
20. *Correspondance Condorcet-Turgot,* p. 160.
21. *Ibid.*
22. Maupeou, *Le Chancelier Maupeou,* p. 233.
23. *Correspondance littéraire,* X, 76.
24. Fay, *Louis XVI,* p. 108.

20

1. Loménie, *Beaumarchais,* I, 400.
2. Huot, *Beaumarchais en Allemagne,* p. 166.
3. Mercy-Argenteau, *Correspondance,* II, 226.
4. Letter to Mercy in Huot, *Beaumarchais en Allemagne,* p. 190.
5. Beaumarchais, *Oeuvres complètes,* p. 779.
6. Gudin, *Histoire de Beaumarchais,* p. 142.
7. Besenval, cited in Faure, *La Disgrâce de Turgot,* p. 46.
8. Turgot, *Oeuvres* (Paris, Schelle, undated), V, 504.
9. Mercy-Argenteau, *Correspondance,* II, 235.

21

1. Gaissinovitch, *La Révolte de Pougatchev,* p. 227.
2. *Ibid.,* p. 228.
3. *Ibid.,* p. 232.

4. *Ibid.,* p. 233.
5. *Ibid.,* pp. 97, 98.
6. François Bluche, *Le Despotisme éclairé* (Paris, Fayard, 1968), p. 200.
7. Gaissinovitch, *La Révolte de Pougatchev,* p. 234.
8. *Ibid.,* p. 28.

22

1. Pierre Jolly, *Du Pont de Nemours, soldat de la liberté* (Paris, Presses universitaires de France, 1956), p. 3.
2. *Ibid.,* p. 12.
3. *Ibid.,* p. 20.
4. *Ibid.,* p. 17.
5. Loménie, *Les Mirabeau,* II, 246.
6. Ambroise Jobert, *Magnats polonais et Physiocrates français* (Paris, Les Belles Lettres, 1941), p. 64.
7. *Ibid.,* p. 65.
8. *Ibid.,* p. 28.
9. *Ibid.,* p. 66.
10. Bluche, *Le Despotisme éclairé,* p. 308.
11. Jobert, *Magnats polonais,* p. 80.
12. Bluche, *Le Despotisme éclairé,* p. 306.
13. For a full account of this attempted program of national education, see Jobert, *Magnats polonais,* pp. 66–79.
14. Jolly, *Du Pont de Nemours,* p. 30.

23

1. Dauphin-Meunier, *Louise de Mirabeau, Marquise de Cabris* (Paris, Emile-Paul, 1914), p. 42.
2. Dauphin-Meunier, *La Vie intime . . . de Mirabeau,* p. 148.
3. According to the testimony of one of the plaintiffs in the trial that followed. *Ibid.,* p. 149.

4. Vallentin, *Mirabeau avant la Révolution,* p. 30.

5. Dauphin-Meunier, *La Comtesse de Mirabeau,* p. 114.

6. *Ibid.,* p. 126.

7. Letter from the Marquis de Mirabeau to Madame de Rochefort, September 25, 1774, in *ibid.,* p. 137.

8. Guibal, *Mirabeau et la Provence,* I, 137.

9. Vallentin, *Mirabeau avant la Révolution,* p. 124.

24

1. Janine Bouissounouse, *Condorcet, le philosophe dans la révolution* (Paris, Hachette, 1962), p. 63.

2. Faure, *La Disgrâce de Turgot,* p. 90.

3. *Correspondance Condorcet-Turgot,* p. 29.

4. *Ibid.,* p. 66.

5. *Ibid.,* p. 130.

6. *Ibid.,* p. 169.

7. *Ibid.,* p. 184.

8. *Ibid.,* p. 175.

9. Loménie, *Les Mirabeau,* II, 402.

10. *Ibid.,* II, 404.

11. Bibliothèque nationale, Fonds Joly de Fleury, 1159, p. 177, cited in Faure, *La Disgrâce de Turgot.*

12. *Journal historique,* cited in Faure, *La Disgrâce de Turgot,* p. 218.

13. René Girard, *L'Abbé Terray et la Liberté du commerce des grains* (Paris, Presses Universitaires de France, 1924), p. 63.

14. See in Presses Universitaires de France, Volume II of the giant *Histoire économique et sociale de la France (1660–1789)* (Paris, 1970), under the direction of Fernand Braudel and Ernest Labrousse. The work enables one to get a quick understanding of the grain problem, thanks to an enormous labor of assimilation.

15. *Correspondance Condorcet-Turgot* (June 21, 1772), p. 88.

16. Loménie, *Les Mirabeau,* II, 408. Also *Journal du Duc de Croy, publié par* Grouchy and Cottin (Paris, 1907), III, 153.

25

1. *La vie du pape Clément XIV (Ganganelli),* anonymous (Paris, 1775), private collection of the widow Desaints, Rue de Foin-Saint-Jacques, p. 92.

2. François Rousseau, *Règne de Charles III d'Espagne* (Paris, Plon, 1907), I, 405.

3. Daniel-Rops, *L'Ere des grands craquements* (Paris, Fayard, 1958), pp. 275–86, "A Major Offense: The Suppression of the Jesuits."

4. Fernand Hayward, *Le Dernier Siècle de la Rome pontificale* (Paris, Payot, 1927), I, 47.

5. Alexis de Saint-Priest, *Histoire de la chute des Jésuites au XVIIIᵉ siècle* (Paris, Amyot, 1844), p. 161.

6. Rousseau, *Charles III,* I, 407.

7. Saint-Priest, *La Chute des Jésuites,* p. 165.

8. Rousseau, *Charles III,* I, 406.

9. *La Vie du pape Clément XIV,* p. 285.

10. Hayward, *Le Dernier Siècle de la Rome pontificale,* pp. 25–8.

11. *Ibid.,* p. 52, and *La Vie du pape Clément XIV,* p. 245.

12. L. J. Rogier, *"Le siècle des lumières et la Révolution,"* in *Nouvelle Histoire de l'Eglise* (Paris, Le Seuil, 1966), IV, 46. This recent history, with a Catholic orientation, is the work most critical of the Ganganelli papacy. The expression "miserable property" is the President of Brosses's.

13. *Ibid.,* p. 75. This question, long debated, is no longer debatable:

the best Catholic historians acknowledge the bargain that was responsible
for the election of Clement XIV.

14. Saint-Priest, *La Chute des Jésuites*, p. 166.

15. Daniel-Rops, *L'Ere des grands
craquements*, p. 285.

16. Saint-Priest, *La Chute des Jésuites*, p. 166. All these details seem to
indicate that the infection from which
Clement XIV suffered had turned into
generalized gangrene.

17. *Journal* of the Abbé de Véri,
I, 203.

26

1. *Journal* of the Abbe de Véri,
I, 202.

2. *Correspondance Condorcet-Turgot*,
p. 251.

3. Faure, *La Disgrâce de Turgot*,
pp. 134, 136.

4. Fay, *Louis XVI*, p. 71.

5. *Journal* of the Abbé de Véri,
I, 64.

6. *Ibid.*, p. 205.

7. Marion, *Dictionnaire des institutions*, p. 336.

8. Geffroy, *Gustave III*, I, 304.

9. *Journal* of the Abbé de Véri, I,
214, 219.

10. *Correspondance littéraire*,
XI, 15.

11. *Ibid.*, XI, 16.

12. Beaumarchais, *Oeuvres complètes*, pp. 719, 720.

13. *Correspondance Condorcet-Turgot*,
p. 201. This was, on the part of Condorcet, a deeply rooted opinion.

14. Comte de Ségur, *Mémoires, ou
souvenirs et anecdotes* (Paris, Lecointe,
1842), I, 40.

15. Mercy-Argenteau, *Correspondance*, II, 248.

16. Bachaumont, *Mémoires secrets*,
p. 48.

17. *Journal* of the Abbé de Véri,
I, 79.

18. Bachaumont, *Mémoires secrets*,
p. 48.

27

1. Gilbert Lély, *Vie du Marquis de
Sade* (Paris, J. J. Pauvert, 1965). The
author specifies that Sade's Cadiz so-
journ in July 1773 was perhaps a
fiction designed to throw his pursuers
off the track. This biography is so
dense and detailed that one can follow
it only step by step.

2. *Ibid.*, p. 240.

3. A little girl, not yet six years
old, who will die at an early age.

4. *Ibid.*, p. 79.

5. *Encyclopédie*, II, 622.

6. Lély, *Vie du Marquis de Sade*, p.
247.

28

1. Hayward, *Le Dernier Siècle de la
Rome pontificale*, I, 57.

2. *Encyclopédie*, III, 819.

3. *Ibid.*

4. *La Vie du pape Clément XIV*,
p. 340.

5. Rogier, *Nouvelle Histoire de l'Eglise*, IV, 31.

6. Saint-Priest, *La chute des Jésuites*,
p. 189.

7. Jean Orieux, *Voltaire* (Paris,
Flammarion, 1966), p. 299.

8. Daniel-Rops, *L'Ere des grands
craquements*, pp. 287, 318, 323.

9. *Journal* of the Abbé de Véri,
I, 268.

10. Saint-Priest, *La chute des Jésuites*, p. 182.

29

1. Bibliothèque nationale, Dé-

partement des Imprimés, rés. p. Y. folio 317.

2. Bibliothèque nationale, Mus. rés. f. 1123 A. Below these lines one finds Baudron's music "engraved by Mlle Girard" of Roualt in Paris in 1775. But the composer's name will not be mentioned in later publications.

3. See the "Registre des feux" [Record of Special Effects] of the Comédie Française at the Library of the Comédie Française, ms. 587, February 1774.

4. Beaumarchais, *"Lettre modérée sur la chute et la critique du Barbier de Séville,"* in *Oeuvres complètes,* p. 87.

5. Jean Valmy-Basse, *Naissance et Vie de la Comédie-Française* (Paris, Floury, 1945), p. 160.

6. *Correspondance littéraire,* X, 511.

7. Beaumarchais, *"Lettre modérée,"* in *Oeuvres complètes,* p. 88.

8. *Ibid.,* p. 90.

9. René Pomeau, *Beaumarchais* (Paris, Hatier, 1967), p. 158.

10. Loménie, *Beaumarchais,* I, 467.

11. Pomeau, *Beaumarchais,* p. 166.

12. Beaumarchais, *"Lettre modérée,"* in *Oeuvres complètes,* p. 89.

13. *Correspondance littéraire,* X, 109.

14. Loménie, *Beaumarchais,* I, 462.

15. Beaumarchais, *"Lettre modérée,"* in *Oeuvres complètes,* p. 92.

16. Loménie, *Beaumarchais,* I, 478.

17. *Ibid.,* I, 479.

18. Beaumarchais, *"Lettre modérée,"* in *Oeuvres complètes,* p. 89.

19. Beaumarchais, *Compte rendu de l'affaire des auteurs dramatiques et des Comédiens Français* (Paris, Fournier, undated), p. 587.

30

1. Jean Cruppi, *Un avocat journaliste au XVIIIe siècle, Linguet* (Paris, Hachette, 1895), p. 390. This description of Linguet is taken from the journal of the bookseller Hardy.

2. Maupeou, *Le Chancelier Maupeou,* p. 214.

3. Cruppi, *Linguet,* p. 7.

4. Règlement du Collège d'Harcourt, Bibliothèque nationale 50 R. document 40, cited in Cruppi, *Linguet,* p. 8.

5. Cruppi, *Linguet,* p. 156.

6. *Ibid.,* p. 56.

7. *Ibid.,* p. 3.

8. *Ibid.,* p. 159 (phrase taken from *La Théorie des Loix*).

9. *Ibid.,* p. 359.

10. *Ibid.,* p. 337.

11. *Ibid.,* p. 364.

12. Registres du Conseil secret (Records of the Secret Council) of the Parliament of Paris, Vol. CCVIII.

13. Cruppi, *Linguet,* pp. 375, 376.

14. *Ibid.,* pp. 163, 166; all these extracts come from *La Théorie des Loix.*

15. *Ibid.,* p. 179.

16. "Linguet depicts the worker as the pariah of Europe; instead of turning to utopia or antiquity, his socialism manifests consciousness of the class struggle. In this sense, it is more a precursor of Marx than an ancestor of Fourier or of Cabet"—Jean Roux, *Précis historique et théorique de marxisme-léninisme* (Paris, Robert Laffont, 1969), p. 29.

17. *Correspondance littéraire,* XI, 29.

18. Encyclopédie, XXI (Vol. IV of the *Supplément*), 476. A lengthy article on the potato (forty columns!), signed "Engel," takes up part of Linguet's arguments again.

19. *Correspondance littéraire,* XI, 29.

20. Norvins, *Mémorial,* I, 74.

21. *Mémoires* of the Abbé Morellet, I, 226.

22. *Ibid.,* I, 229.

23. *Ibid.,* I, 95.

24. Norvins, *Mémorial,* I, 76.

25. *Encyclopédie,* XI, 749.

31

1. Alessandro Galante-Garrone, *Gilbert Romme, histoire d'un révolutionnaire* (Paris, Flammarion, 1971). This book is a repository of biographical information about one of the most admirable, significant, and misunderstood personages in the Revolution. It was published in 1959 by Einaudi in Milan. My wife and I took great pleasure in translating it. For Romme's letter of April 13, 1775, to Dubreuil, see p. 53.

2. M. de Vissac, *Romme le Montagnard* (Clermont-Ferrand, 1883), p. 25.

3. Galante-Garrone, *Gilbert Romme,* p. 47.

4. *Ibid.,* p. 44.

5. *Ibid.,* p. 49.

6. Daniel Mornet, *Les Sciences de la nature en France au XVIIIe siècle* (Paris, 1911), p. 21.

7. Galante-Garrone, *Gilbert Romme,* p. 46.

8. Vissac, *Romme le Montagnard,* p. 30.

9. Galante-Garrone, *Gilbert Romme,* p. 53.

10. Bachaumont, *Mémoires pour servir à l'histoire de la république des lettres* (Paris, n.p., n.d.), VIII, 291.

11. G. De Fournoux-La Chaze, "*L'Académie de Manège de Riom,*" in *Bulletin historique et scientifique de l'Auvergne,* 1943, p. 14.

12. Vissac, *Romme le Montagnard,* p. 35.

13. Galante-Garrone, *Gilbert Romme,* p. 67.

14. *Ibid.,* p. 67.

32

1. Fay, *Benjamin Franklin,* II, 137.

2. Reichard, *Guide des voyageurs en Europe,* Vol I, *Grande-Bretagne et l'Irlande,* p. 40.

3. Letter from Franklin to his friend Galloway, February 25, 1775, quoted in Cornélis de Witt, *Thomas Jefferson étude historique sur la democratie américaine* (Paris, Didier, 1861), p. 79.

4. *Considérations sur les mesures à prendre vis-à-vis de nos Colonies américaines* (London, 1774, undated and published anonymously, although the work of Matthew Robinson Morris, the second Baron Rokeby).

5. Lord Germaine, to the House of Lords, March 28, 1774.

6. Lord North, cited in Edouard Laboulaye, *Histoire des Etats-Unis* (Paris, Charpentier, 1866), Vol. II: *La Guerre de L'Indépendance,* p. 212.

7. *Ibid.,* II, 215.

8. Fay, *Benjamin Franklin,* II, 130.

9. *Ibid.,* II, 129: declaration by the Bishop of Saint Asaph.

10. Fay, *Benjamin Franklin,* I, 96.

11. *Ibid.,* II, 122.

12. Laboulaye, *Histoire des Etats-Unis,* II, 106.

13. *Ibid.,* p. 283.

14. *Ibid.,* p. 95.

15. D. Pasquet, *Histoire politique et sociale du peuple américaine* (Paris, Picard, 1924), I, 253.

33

1. Jolly, *Du Pont de Nemours,* p. 31.

2. Turgot, *Oeuvres complètes* (Paris, n.p., 1790), IV, 231.

3. *Mémoires* of the Abbé Morellet, I, 231.

4. Pierre Jolly, *Necker* (Paris, "Les Oeuvres françaises," 1947), p. 47.

5. Voltaire, *Oeuvres complètes* (Paris, Benchot), Vol. XL, letter #9392.

6. H. Grange, *"Necker jugé par Karl Marx,"* in *Annales historiques de la Révolution française,* XXVIII (1956), 61.

7. Faure, *La Disgrâce de Turgot,* p. 316.

8. *Ibid.,* p. 238. For the train of events of "the Grain War," see pp. 238-70.

9. Archives nationales, K 1022/25.

10. For facts relating to the Paris region following the Beaumont riot, I have made special use of Georges E. Rudé's article *"La Guerre des Farines,"* in *Annales historiques de la Révolution française,* XXVIII (1956), 139.

11. Archives nationales, Y 18682.

12. Bibliothèque nationale, Fonds Joly de Fleury, 1159/13.

13. Reichard, *Guides des voyageurs en Europe,* Vol. II, *France,* p. 135.

14. Archives nationales, Y 11441.

15. Bibliothèque nationale, Fonds Joly de Fleury, 1159/205.

16. Archives nationales, Y 18862.

17. Archives, Dept. of Seine-et-Oise, series B. Saint Germain-en-Laye.

18. *Ibid.,* Provostship of the Hôtel du Roy.

19. Archives nationales, Y 18862.

20. On the strength of a fanciful account in Métra's *Correspondance* (published in London ten years after the events), it was believed at one time that Louis XVI had been forced to harangue the eight thousand demonstrators surrounding the château personally! This is false. Moreover, it would have been highly unlikely. There was no contact between the king and the rioters during the Grain War.

21. Fernand Evrard, *Versailles, ville du Roi, étude d'économie urbaine* (Paris, 1935), p. 113.

22. Archives, Dept. of Seine-et-Oise, series B, Provostship of the Hôtel du Roy.

23. Fay, *Louis XVI,* p. 120.

24. Rudé, *"La Guerre des Farines,"* p. 149.

25. *Journal* of the Abbé de Véri, I, 290.

26. Fay, *Louis XVI,* p. 121.

27. *Correspondance Condorcet-Turgot,* pp. 212, 213.

28. *Ibid.,* p. 206.

29. Hardy, *Journal,* III, 58. This manuscript notebook is in the Archives nationales.

30. Métra, *Correspondance,* I, 343. Métra accurately reflects here the impression the Grain War made on the Paris bourgeoisie.

31. *Journal* of the Abbé de Véri, I, 291.

32. Léon Cahen, *"La Question du pain à Paris à la fin du XVIIIᵉ siècle,"* in *Cahiers de la Révolution française,* 1934.

33. Saltykov-Schedrin Library in Leningrad: "The condition of persons detained in the different prisons of Paris and elsewhere, relative to the bread, wheat, and grain that was pillaged," presented fully for the first time in the appendix of Faure, *La Disgrâce de Turgot.*

34. *Journal* of the Abbé de Véri, I, 290.

35. Faure, *La Disgrâce de Turgot,* p. 292.

36. *Ibid.,* p. 270. For Maréchal de Biron, see Maugras: *Le Duc de Lauzun et . . . Louis XV,* p. 360.

37. V. S. Lublinsky, *"Voltaire et la Guerre des Farines,"* in *Annales historiques*

de la Révolution française, XXXI (1959), 134.

38. Robert Christophe, *Les Sanson, bourreaux de père en fils* (Paris, Fayard, 1960).

39. Hardy, *Journal,* p. 225.

40. Archives nationales, Y 10525.

41. Robert Anchel, *Crimes et Châtiments au XVIIIᵉ siècle* (Paris, Perrin, 1933), p. 166.

34

1. Mercy-Argenteau, *Correspondance,* II, 329.

2. Victor-L. Tapie, *Monarchie et Peuples du Danube* (Paris, Fayard, 1969), p. 227.

3. François Fejtö, *Un Habsbourg révolutionnaire: Joseph II* (Paris, Plon, 1953), p. 136.

4. *Ibid.,* p. 136.

35

1. Chateaubriand, *Mémoires d'outre-tombe,* Edition des Classiques (Paris, Garnier, 1946), I, 37. The other unfootnoted quotations are taken from the first chapter of this same volume.

2. Chateaubriand has mixed up his childhood memories: the Dominicans have become the Benedictines here.

3. Charles Cunat: *Récherches sur plusieurs des circonstances relatives aux origines, à la naissance et à l'enfance de M. de Chateaubriand* (Paris, 1850), p. 10.

4. Abbé P. Nicoz, *Madeleine Morice, une mystique bretonne au XVIIIᵉ siècle* (Paris, Beauchesne, 1922).

36

1. *Encyclopédie,* XIV, 476.

2. *Correspondance Condorcet-Turgot,* p. 201.

3. *Ibid.,* p. 10.

4. *Journal de Papillon de la Ferté,* edited by Ernest Boysse (Paris, Ollendorf, 1887), p. 368.

5. *Ibid.,* p. 370.

6. *Ibid.,* p. 373.

7. *Ibid.,* p. 382.

8. *Ibid.,* p. 375.

9. Vicomte Fleury, *Le Prince de Lambesc, grand écuyer de France* (Paris, Plon, 1928), p. 143.

10. Belloc, *Marie-Antoinette,* p. 112.

11. Young, *Voyage en France,* I, 416.

12. H. Destainville, *"La Jeunesse de Danton,"* in *Annales historiques de la Révolution française,* V (1928), 424. This article, based largely on detailed analyses made by the departmental archives of l'Aube, is very convincing about the episode concerning Danton's escapade at the coronation, which has been much contested by some of his biographers.

13. *Ibid.,* p. 425.

14. Louis Madelin, *Danton* (Paris, Hachette, 1914), p. 6.

15. Bibliothèque of Troyes, *Catalogus Scholasticorum collegii,* ms. 357. The college of Oratorians occupied the actual site of the covered market at Troyes.

16. Reichard, *Guide des voyageurs en Europe,* Vol. II, *France,* p. 122.

17. Remembrances of Alexandre Rousselin, in Destainville, *"La Jeunesse de Danton,"* p. 428.

18. This is the opening phrase in Talleyrand's *Mémoires* (Paris, Jean de Bonnot, 1967), I, 3.

19. G. Lacour-Gayet, *Talleyrand* (Paris, Payot, 1933), I, 42.

20. Jean Orieux, *Talleyrand* (Paris, Flammarion, 1970), p. 116.

21. The account of Louis XVI's

coronation is reproduced almost in full in A. Chéruel, *Dictionnaire historique des institutions, moeurs et coutumes de la France* (Paris, Hachette, 1855), II, 1118.

22. Description taken from an article by Gustave Laurent, *"La Destruction de la Sainte-Ampoule,"* in *Annales historiques de la Révolution française,* III (1926), 148.

23. Mirecourt, *Mémoires.*

24. Talleyrand, *Mémoires,* I, 24.

25. Lacour-Gayet, *Talleyrand,* I, 37.

26. Talleyrand, *Mémoires,* I, 22.

27. *Ibid.,* I, 16–20.

37

1. Chéruel, *Dictionnaire des institutions,* II, 1121.

2. Mercy-Argenteau, *Correspondance,* II, 346.

3. *Ibid.,* p. 342.

4. Galippe, *L'Hérédité des stigmates de dégénérescence,* p. 213.

5. Mercy-Argenteau, *Correspondance,* II, 333.

6. *Ibid.,* II, 335.

7. *Ibid.,* II, 339.

8. *Ibid.,* II, 341.

9. Maugras, *La Disgrâce du Duc et de la Duchesse de Choiseul,* p. 322.

10. *Ibid.,* p. 323.

11. In his letter of July 17, 1775, Mercy gives Maria Theresa the substance of the conversation between Choiseul and the queen (*Correspondance* II, 356). But he could only repeat what Marie Antoinette had told him about it, and Maria Theresa began to distrust the old tale-bearer.

12. *Ibid.,* II, 358.

13. *Ibid.,* II, 361

14. *Ibid.,* II, 362.

15. *Ibid.,* II, 362.

16. *Encyclopédie,* V, 375.

17. *Ibid.,* V, 376.

18. *Journal de Papillon de la Ferté,* pp. 388, 304.

19. This episode, sometimes exaggerated and sometimes denied, has been the subject of a controversy. It is certain that it was Robespierre who delivered this speech. But nothing further is known, so I don't dwell on it. Paradoxically, the most probing account of this subject is found in the royalist pamphlet of the Abbé Proyart, who had been a professor at Louis-le-Grand: *La Vie et les Crimes de Robespierre* (Paris, 1795). Gérard Walter, in *Robespierre* (Paris, Gallimard, 1961), has sifted out its essential points.

38

1. Preceded by a brief, formal exchange at the fortress of Joux, when the governor had brought Sophie to visit the prison and had "shown" her his prisoner.

2. Paul Lacroix, *XVIIIe siècle: institutions, usages, contumes* (Paris, Didot, 1875), p. 396.

3. Vallentin, *Mirabeau avant la Révolution,* p. 137, and Dauphin-Meunier, *La Vie intime . . . de Mirabeau,* p. 174.

4. Paul Cottin, *Sophie de Monnier et Mirabeau* (Paris, Plon, 1903), p. x.

5. Claude Ferval, *La Jeunesse de Mirabeau* (Paris, Fayard, 1936), p. 90.

6. Loménie, *Les Mirabeau,* I, 411.

7. Cited in Vallentin, *Mirabeau avant la Révolution,* p. 126.

8. *Ibid.,* p. 129.

9. Marcel Chapron, *Mirabeau-Tonneau* (Paris, Editions Haussman), p. 27.

10. Vallentin, *Mirabeau avant la Révolution,* p. 135.

11. Dauphin-Meunier, *La Comtesse de Mirabeau,* pp. 146–71.

12. *Ibid.*, p. 172.

13. *Ibid.*, p. 176, but see also Dauphin-Meunier, *La Vie intime . . . de Mirabeau,* p. 161. On the spur of the moment Mouret claimed that Mirabeau was responsible for his wife's "theft" of four thousand livres and asserted it repeatedly. Mouret retracted this accusation in 1783 in a letter to Honoré. It was at the time of the Aix trial, when Mirabeau was feverishly collecting testimony for his own defense. It is very likely that he compensated the canteen-keeper for all or part of the sum in question, in order to clear himself of at least that charge.

14. Dauphin-Meunier, *La Vie intime . . . de Mirabeau,* p. 161.

15. *Ibid.*, p. 164.

16. Vallentin, *Mirabeau avant la Révolution,* p. 134.

17. Excerpts from the description of the fortress of Joux given by its governor, General Baille, at Savary in 1802 when Bonaparte confined Toussaint Louverture there. Today one may still visit Mirabeau's apartment and Toussaint's cell in the fortress of Joux.

18. Ferval, *La Jeunesse de Mirabeau,* p. 88.

19. Paul Claudel, *Partage de Midi,* Act I, Scene 4.

20. Vallentin, *Mirabeau avant la Révolution,* p. 142.

21. He will write this phrase to Sophie three years later from his prison in Vincennes.

39

1. José-Augusto França, *Une ville des lumières: la Lisbonne de Pombal* (Paris, S.E.V.P.E.N., 1965), p. 178.

2. José Pedro Machado, *Dicionario Etimologico da Lingua Portuguesa* (Lisbon, 1959).

3. França, *La Lisbonne de Pombal,* p. 14.

4. *Ibid.*, p. 23.

5. Nicolas-Roch Chamfort, *Oeuvres* (Paris, Club français du livre, 1960), p. 238.

6. França, *La Lisbonne de Pombal,* p. 175.

7. Galippe, *L'Hérédité des stigmates de dégénérescence,* p. 252.

8. The reflection of Luis da Cunha, an elderly diplomat influential at the court of the Braganzas. He had given young Carvalho a helping hand by recommending him in these very terms, in the 1750's, to the prince who would become Joseph I. França, *La Lisbonne de Pombal,* p. 178.

9. *Ibid.*, p. 176.

10. Bluche, *Le Despotisme éclairé,* p. 270. I have taken the basic picture of Portugal in 1775 from pages 260–72 of the same work.

11. *Ibid.*, p. 261.

12. França, *La Lisbonne de Pombal,* p. 108.

13. *Ibid.*, p. 109.

14. *Ibid.*, p. 114.

15. Saint-Priest, *La chute des Jésuites,* p. 22.

16. *Ibid.*, p. 14.

17. França, *La Lisbonne de Pombal,* p. 181.

40

1. A. Birembaut, *"La Correspondance de Lavoisier,"* in *Annales historiques de la Révolution française,* XXIX (1957), 346.

2. *Correspondance littéraire,* X, 349.

3. Edouard Grimaux, *Lavoisier* (Paris, Alcan, 1896), p. 104.

4. Bibliothèque de l'Arsenal, ms. 5806, p. 27.

5. Lucien Scheler, *Antoine-Laurent*

de Lavoisier et le principe chimique (Paris, Seghers), p. 45.

6. Hippolyte Gautier, *"Le Progrès des lumières,"* in *L'An 1789* (Paris, Delagrave), p. 337.

7. *Journal de Physique*, Vol. VI (1775).

8. Georges Bouchard, *Guyton-Morveau, chimiste et conventionnel* (Paris, Perrin), pp. 62, 167–9.

9. Scheler, *A.-L. de Lavoisier*, pp. 49–50.

10. *Ibid.*, p. 55.

11. *Ibid.*, p. 69.

12. Lavoisier, *Oeuvres*, V, 704, cited by Dujarric de La Rivière and Madeleine Chabrier in *La Vie et l'Oeuvre de Lavoisier d'après ses écrits* (Paris, Albin-Michel, 1959), p. 273.

13. *Ibid.*, p. 16.

14. *Ibid.*, p. 28 (extract from Lalande, *Notice sur la vie et les ouvrages de Lavoisier*).

15. *Ibid.*, p. 245 (Lavoisier, *Oeuvres*, IV, 225).

16. Count Mollien, *Mémoires d'un ministre du trésor public* (Paris, Guillaume, 1898), I, 65.

41

1. Boiteau, *Etat de la France en 1789*, p. 137.

2. *Journal* of the Abbé de Véri, I, 310.

3. Pierre Grosclaude, *Malesherbes, témoin et interprète de son temps* (Paris, Fischbacher, undated), p. 247.

4. *Ibid.*, p. 265.

5. *Ibid.*, p. 317.

6. Bibliothèque du Palais Bourbon, Z 492, document 19, folios 29 and 30.

7. Bibliothèque nationale, new acquisitions, 3531, folio 29.

8. Grosclaude, *Malesherbes*, p. 203.

9. Boissy d'Anglas, *Essai sur le vie*

de M. de Malesherbes, quoted in Faure, *La Disgrâce de Turgot*, p. 343.

10. *Journal* of the Abbé de Véri, I, 311.

11. Pages discovered by Grosclaude, *Malesherbes*, p. 320, in the Rosanbo family archives, carton II, dossier I.

12. *Isographie des hommes célèbres* (Paris, Alexandre Mesnier, 1828), Vol. II.

13. Grosclaude, *Malesherbes*, p. 322.

14. *Journal* of the Abbé de Véri, I, 317.

15. Grosclaude, *Malesherbes*, p. 325.

16. An observation by Besenval in his *Mémoires*, reported in Faure, *La Disgrâce de Turgot*, p. 345.

42

1. Assessment of the Duchesse d'Ayen by her daughter Madame de La Fayette, cited in Maurois, *Adrienne*, p. 22.

2. Lettre inédite of La Fayette, Chambrun family archives, cited in Maurois, *Adrienne*, p. 49. The extracts from the letters which follow have the same source (pp. 49–60).

3. According to the Comte de La Marck (*ibid.*, p. 55).

4. A. Bardoux, *La Jeunesse de La Fayette* (Paris, Calmann-Lévy, 1892), p. 16.

5. Ségur, *Mémoires*, I, 110.

6. Bibliothèque municipale of Metz, L S/G 112/3.

7. *Histoire universelle des armées* (Paris, Robert Laffont, 1966), III, 32.

8. Ghislain de Diesbach, *George III* (Paris, Berger-Levrault, 1966), pp. 115–21. The author confuses the little daughter whose birth had caused a public "scandal" and a sister who was

born to Gloucester a year later. The latter died at nine months and King George denied her burial in Westminster Abbey. This ultimate affront outraged the Gloucester family and decided them on leaving. Their first daughter, Sophie Mathilde, will live until 1844.

9. Charlemagne Tower, *Le Marquis de La Fayette et la révolution d'Amérique* (Paris, Plon, 1902), I, 15.

10. *Ibid.*, I, 16.

43

1. Moncure Daniel Conway, *Thomas Paine et la révolution dans les deux mondes* (Paris, Plon, 1900), p. 41.

2. *Ibid.*, p. 23.

3. Letter to Franklin, *ibid.*, p. 33.

4. *Ibid.*, p. 4.

5. *Ibid.*, p. 5.

6. Concerning Chalmers, *ibid.*, p. 16.

7. *Ibid.*, p. 17.

8. *Ibid.*, p. 18.

9. *Ibid.*, p. 26.

10. Bernard Fay, *George Washington, gentilhomme* (Paris, Grasset, 1932), p. 189.

11. D. Pasquet, *Histoire politique et sociale*, I, 256.

12. Conway, *Thomas Paine*, p. 24.

13. *Ibid.*, p. 27.

14. Pasquet, *Histoire politique et sociale*, I, 258.

15. De Witt, *Thomas Jefferson*, p. 86.

44

1. *Correspondance littéraire*, X, 415.

2. Maugras, *Le Duc de Lauzun et . . . Marie-Antoinette*, p. 72. Information which will follow about his youth and the Lauzun family is, with certain exceptions, taken from the preceding work by the same author, *Le Duc de Lauzun et . . . Louis XV*.

3. A. Franklin, *"La Vie de Paris sous Louis XVI (début du règne),"* in the collection *La Vie privée d'autrefois* (Paris, Plon, 1902), p. 172.

4. *Ibid.*, p. 169.

5. Mercier, *Tableau de Paris*, V, 221.

6. Letter of August 23, 1775, cited in Mercy-Argenteau, *Correspondance*, II, 369.

7. Duc de Castries, *Henri IV, roi de coeur, roi de France* (Paris, Larousse, 1970), pp. 211–21. This rigorously honest book sheds light on the "squaring of accounts" which was the policy for sixteen years of the *soi-disant* Good King Henri's reign, giving it the reputation of genteel gangsterism between the Bourbons of Navarre and rival families. Not surprisingly, Ravaillac's dagger marked the climax of this.

8. Duc de Lauzun, *Memoires* (Paris, Fayard, undated), p. 31. His appreciation of Madame Czartoryska, above, is from the same text, p. 53.

9. *Ibid.*, p. 11.

10. *Ibid.*, p. 27. The authenticity of these memoirs has sometimes been questioned just because of the seriousness of accusations like this one. G. Maugras, in comparing the text and diplomatic correspondence, has shown that they are indeed the work of Lauzun.

11. Maugras, *Le Duc de Lauzun et . . . Louis XV*, p. 440.

12. Lauzun, *Mémoires*, p. 8.

13. According to the Duc de Lévis, cited in Faure, *La Disgrâce de Turgot*, p. 335.

14. Ségur, *Mémoires*, I, 50.

15. Lauzun, *Mémoires*, p. 26.

16. Mercier, *Tableau de Paris*,

VIII, 40. The underlined words follow the original text.

17. Roger Baschet, *Mlle Dervieux, fille d'Opéra* (Paris, Flammarion, 1943), p. 82.

45

1. J. Rives Childs, *Restif de La Bretonne, témoignages et jugements; Bibliographie* (Paris, Briffaut, 1950), p. 226.

2. Restif de La Bretonne, *M. Nicolas* (Paris, undated), 2nd edition, X, 134.

3. Restif de La Bretonne, *La Vie de mon père,* note on page 3 of the 6th edition, that of 1788—which does not prevent the author from constantly spelling his father's name Edme *Rétif.*

4. *Correspondance littéraire,* IX, 160.

5. Mlle de Lespinasse, *Lettres* (Paris, Eugène Asse, 1882), p. 290.

6. Marc Chadourne, *Restif de La Bretonne, ou le siècle prophétique* (Paris, Hachette, 1958), p. 183.

7. According to Charles Montselet, in 1854 (*Rétif de La Bretonne, sa vie et ses amours*), cited by Rives Childs, *Restif,* p. 67. And Montselet added: "*Le Paysan perverti* is a novel without precedent in literature, a vigorous work which has its roots in the heart of humanity, a cynical work one could never make into a bad book, written by a peasant caught up in the middle of a society of marquises and duchesses, each of whom bore around her neck an imperceptible red cord."

8. François Prigault, *"Restif de La Bretonne communiste,"* article in *Mercure de France,* December 12, 1913.

9. Rives Childs, *Restif,* p. 85.

10. *Correspondance littéraire,* XI, 171, 161.

11. Chadourne, *Restif,* p. 163.

12. *Ibid.,* p. 173.

13. *Ibid.*

14. *Ibid.,* pp. 175–8. See also the episode recounted at great length in *M. Nicolas.*

15. According to the description of his friend Cubières, quoted in Chadourne, *Restif,* p. 196.

46

1. The text, which is located at the Archives des Affaires étrangères [Foreign Affairs] and at the Bibliothèque municipale in Tonnerre (R. 17), is published in full in Pinsseau, *L'Etrange Destinée du Chevalier d'Eon,* p. 184. This "transaction" is pre-dated October 5, D'Eon's birthday, in 1728, through a kind of courtesy on Beaumarchais's part. According to D'Eon, Beaumarchais wished to bestow on the "lady-knight" a new "baptism." In any case, two of D'Eon's Christian names were arbitrarily feminized in this text. He had been baptized on October 7, 1728, at Tonnerre: Charles-Geneviève-Louis-Auguste-André-Timothée. The second of these names did not in any way indicate that the child's gender was feminine. This was, as happened frequently, the first name of D'Eon's godmother.

2. Loménie, *Beaumarchais,* I, 433.

3. Marquise de la Rochejaquelein, *Mémoires* (Paris, Beaudoin, 1823), p. 21.

4. Frédéric Gaillardet, *Mémoires sur la Chevalière d'Eon* (Paris, Dentu, 1866), p. 99. Gaillardet's book should be used with caution and only for the documents quoted in it. The book is closer to fiction than to history.

5. Bachaumont, *Mémoires secrets,* X, 325.

6. Pinsseau, *Le Chevalier d'Eon,* p. 132.

7. *Ibid.,* p. 146.

8. *Ibid.*, p. 119. Pinsseau cites in full the text of this curious judicial document.

9. Gaillardet, *La Chevalière d'Eon*, p. 186.

10. Archives nationales, K 157: secret correspondence from Louis XV to the Comte de Broglie, November 12, 1767.

11. Duc de Broglie, *Le Secret du Roi* (Paris, Calmann-Lévy, 1878), II, 468.

12. E. Boutaric, *Correspondance secrète inédite de Louis XV sur la politique étrangère* (Paris, Plon, 1866), II, 440.

13. Bibliothèque municipale of Tonnerre, Fonds d'Eon, "*Campagnes du Sr. de Beaumarchais,*" R. 22 and 24.

14. Pinsseau, *Le Chevalier d'Eon*, p. 254.

15. Bibliothèque municipale of Tonnerre, d'Eon, R. 10.

16. Gudin, *Histoire de Beaumarchais*, p. 173.

17. *Ibid.*, p. 176.

18. Loménie, *Beaumarchais*, II, 92.

19. Gudin, *Histoire de Beaumarchais*, p. 178.

47

1. *Lettres de Madame Roland, publiées par* Claude Perroud (Paris, Imprimerie nationale, 1913), new series, I, letter to Sophie Cannet of January 5, 1776, p. 356. I owe a great debt to Monsieur Jean Guillermet, nephew of Claude Perroud, for the loan of this inestimably valuable collection, one of the most significant correspondences in the history of the Revolution. To simplify the references, when it is possible I will limit myself to indicating: Roland, *Lettres* (C.P.), volume number, and page.

2. Georges Huisman, *La Vie privée de Madame Roland* (Paris, Hachette, 1955), p. 9.

3. Madame Roland, *Mémoires* (Paris, Ollendorf, undated), p. 72.

4. Huisman, *Mme Roland*, p. 14.

5. Roland, *Lettres* (C.P.), new series I, 541.

6. Madeleine Clemenceau-Jacquemaire, *Vie de Madame Roland* (Paris, Tallandier, 1929), I, 17.

7. C. A. Dauban, *Etude sur Madame Roland et son temps*, with a facsimile of Madame Roland's letters to Buzot (Paris, Plon, 1864), p. lii. Jean Guillermet has loaned me the precious copy that belonged to Claude Perroud and enriched the annotations of this volume.

8. Roland, *Mémoires*, p. 125.

9. Published in Paris by the Debure brothers and in Orléans, where he took a degree in law, by the widow Rouzeau-Montaut, in 1775.

10. Roland, *Lettres* (C.P.), new series, I, 355.

11. Roland, *Mémoires*, p. 72.

12. Roland, *Lettres* (C.P.), new series, I, 356.

13. *Ibid.*, I, 362.

14. *Ibid.*, I, 370.

15. *Ibid.*, I, 378.

16. *Ibid.*, I, 358 (passage from a historic letter dated January 11; it also recounts Roland's visit).

17. *Ibid.*, I, 379.

18. *Ibid.*, I, 381.

48

1. *Journal* of the Abbé de Véri, I, 370.

2. Montbarey, *Mémoires*, II, 640.

3. *Journal* of the Abbé de Véri, I, 373.

4. Faure, *La Disgrâce de Turgot*, pp. 386, 387.

5. *Journal* of the Abbé de Véri, I, 425.

6. *Dépenses de la Maison du Comte de Provence en 1774, publiées par* J. A. Blanchet (Paris, Lechevalier-Cheronnet, 1897).

7. Grosclaude, *Malesherbes,* p. 330.

8. *Ibid.,* p. 332.

9. *Journal* of the Abbé de Véri, I, 373.

10. Expilly, *Dictionnaire de la France* (Paris, 1768), V, 401. It is advisable to correct Expilly's population estimates—they are always pessimistic. Try adding a good ten percent to his total for 1768 (600,000) and adding the 30,000 births in excess of the deaths, as figured according to "the general statement of births, marriages, and deaths in the parishes of the city and suburbs of Paris," begun on Colbert's initiative in 1670.

11. Grosclaude, *Malesherbes,* p. 346.

12. *Ibid.,* p. 349.

13. *Ibid.,* p. 348.

14. Mercy-Argenteau, *Correspondance,* II, 415.

15. *Ibid.,* II, 426.

16. *Correspondance Condorcet-Turgot,* p. 237.

17. Mercy-Argenteau, *Correspondance,* II, 366.

18. Dupont, cited in Faure, *La Disgrâce de Turgot,* p. 360.

19. Jolly, *Du Pont de Nemours,* p. 33.

20. *Ibid.,* p. 33.

21. *Correspondance Condorcet-Turgot,* p. 252.

22. *Ibid.,* p. 263.

23. Faure, *La Disgrâce de Turgot,* p. 424.

24. *Journal* of the Abbé de Véri, I, 391.

25. *Ibid.,* p. 393.

26. François Hincker, *Les Français devant l'impôt sous l'ancien régime* (Paris, Flammarion, 1971), p. 95.

27. Faure, *La Disgrâce de Turgot,* p. 451.

28. *Ibid.,* pp. 452–5.

29. *Ibid.,* p. 455.

49

1. The expression is Soulavie's, who will publish under the Consulate the first known history of the reign of Louis XVI. This history is full of approximations but also full of useful information.

2. *Journal* of the Abbé de Véri, I, 488.

3. Mercy-Argenteau, *Correspondance,* II, 393 (letter from Marie Antoinette to Maria Theresa on November 12, 1775).

4. *Journal* of the Abbé de Véri, I, 400.

5. Mercy-Argenteau, *Correspondance,* II, 403.

6. *Ibid.,* II, 406.

7. Maugras, *Le Duc de Lauzun et . . . Marie-Antoinette,* p. 43.

8. *Ibid.*

9. Mercy-Argenteau, *Correspondance,* II, 388.

10. *Ibid.,* II, 392.

11. *Ibid.,* II, 445.

12. Maugras, *Le Duc de Lauzun et . . . Marie-Antoinette,* p. 81.

13. *Ibid.,* p. 83.

14. Mercy-Argenteau, *Correspondance,* II, 390.

15. Maugras, *Le Duc de Lauzun et . . . Marie-Antoinette,* p. 105.

16. Comte R. de Gontaut-Biron, *Le Duc de Lauzun* (Paris, Plon, 1937), p. 44.

17. Lauzun, *Mémoires,* p. 95.

18. Lévis, *Souvenirs,* p. 159.

19. Lauzun, *Mémoires*, p. 101.

20. *Ibid.*, p. 110.

21. *Journal* of the Abbé de Véri, I, 407.

22. *Encyclopédie*, VII, 777.

23. Faure, *La Disgrâce de Turgot*, p. 401.

24. Grosclaude, *Malesherbes*, p. 393.

25. *Ibid.*

26. *Journal* of the Abbé de Veri, I, 449.

27. *Ibid.*, p. 488 (letter to Horace Walpole, March 6, 1776).

28. According to the memoirs of Dupont, cited in Faure, *La Disgrâce de Turgot*, p. 492.

29. It was bound to be interminable, a river of twelve pages whose very length was of a nature to indispose Louis XVI. The most complete text is obtainable in the *Journal* of the Abbé de Véri, I, 450–7, and even then the abbé says that he only "transcribed a few phrases" from it.

30. Faure, *La Disgrâce de Turgot*, p. 508.

31. *Ibid.*, p. 509.

32. *Correspondance Condorcet-Turgot*, p. 273.

33. *Ibid.*, p. 227.

34. Braudel et Larousse, *Histoire économique et sociale*, II, 680. The observation which follows on the banning of labor associations is borrowed from him as well.

35. *Sur la législation et le commerce des grains*, cited by H. Grange in *Annales historiques de la Révolution française*, XXIX (1957), 33. The author of the article observes in this connection: "Turgot had a passion for logic, a taste for systemizing that went so far as to stifle human feelings. He would have made an admirable English Puritan, naturally identifying investments with

asceticism, the accumulation of capital with saintliness" (p. 32).

36. *Journal* of the Abbé de Véri, I, 431.

37. *Ibid.*, I, 430 (letter to Véri on May 10).

38. Maugras, *Le Duc de Lauzun et . . . Marie-Antoinette*, p. 112.

39. *Ibid.*, p. 115.

50

1. Marquis de Ségur, *Julie de Lespinasse* (Paris, Calmann-Lévy, 1905), p. 155. All the other quotations in this sequence without a numbered reference will be taken from the same work.

2. *Ibid.*, p. 109. The text is from La Harpe.

3. André Beaunier, *La Vie amoureuse de Julie de Lespinasse* (Paris, Flammarion, 1925), p. 35.

4. "They all believe it is Monsieur de Mora's death that kills me. My friend, if they knew that it is you, that it is your marriage that deals the mortal blow! How they would hate me! How despicable I would seem to them! Ah! They would not accuse me more loudly or more vigorously than my conscience does already!" Letter to Guibert on August 7, 1775, in Ségur, *Julie de Lespinasse*, p. 504.

5. Joseph Bertrand, *D'Alembert* (Paris, Hachette, 1889), p. 6.

6. Letter from the Marquis Abel de Vichy dated May 28, 1776. *Ibid.*, pp. 521.

51

1. *Lettres originales de Mirabeau écrites du Donjon de Vincennes pendant les années 1777, 78, 79 et 80, contenant tous les détails sur sa vie privée, ses malheurs, et ses amours avec Sophie Ruffei [sic], Marquise de Monnier, recueillies par P. Man-*

nier, *Louise de Mirabeau,*
ery significant for what it
ut Louise's manifest
plex and tells about the
she would soon be play-
brother and Sophie. It is,
letter of a young girl at
, flayed alive, being
her father, her brother, her
r lover.
tres de Mirabeau, I, 312.
ciété des études robespier-
Mirabeau et leur temps, re-
Colloque
ovence (Paris, 1968), p.

ottin, *Sophie de Monnier et*
p. 46.
ettres de Mirabeau, to his fa-
Vincennes, I, 289.
Vallentin, *Mirabeau avant la*
p. 152. Extract from an un-
r from Sophie to Mirabeau.
olloquy on *Les Mirabeau et*
p. 197.
Archives nationales, K 164, 2,
pallingly misspelled text is in
uise's hand).
Archives nationales, K 164,

Vallentin, *Mirabeau avant la*
, p. 148.
Dauphin-Meunier, *Louise de*
, p. 110.
From the "journal of Mira-
ways the same source (see

52

Letter from Goethe to Herder
ch 25, 1775, in Charles Du
ethe (Paris, Corrêa, 1949), p.
he main part of this book is dean exhaustive study of "the
six-year-old Goethe."
Ibid., letter from Goethe to

Herder, May 12, 1775, p. 280. The translation of the passages from Goethe has been dusted off.

3. *Ibid.*, p. 301. Letter to Jeanne Fahlmer, November 22, 1775.

4. Goethe, *Souffrances du jeune Werther* (Paris, Livre de Poche, 1959), edition brought out by Antoine Blondin.

5. Du Bos, *Goethe*, p. 265.

6. *Ibid.*, p. 258. The ode from which these verses were taken was written in 1777.

7. Richard Friedenthal, *Goethe, sa vie et son temps* (Paris, Fayard, 1963), p. 201.

8. Goethe, *Werther*, p. 15.

9. Du Bos, *Goethe*, p. 270.

10. *Ibid.*, p. 298.

11. *Ibid.*, p. 259.

12. Jean-Marie Carré, *La Vie de Goethe* (Paris, Gallimard, 1927), pp. 22, 24.

13. Friedenthal, *Goethe*, p. 36.

14. Goethe, *Werther*, p. 24.

15. *Ibid.*, p. 26.

16. *Ibid.*, p. 71.

17. *Ibid.*, p. 141.

18. Adrien Fauchier-Magnan, *Les Petites Cours d'Allemagne au XVIIIᵉ siècle* (Paris, Flammarion, 1947), p. 41.

19. Goethe, *Werther*, p. 88.

20. *Ibid.*, p. 18.

21. Du Bos, *Goethe*, p. 257.

22. Friedenthal, *Goethe*, p. 163.

23. *Ibid.*, p. 167.

24. *Ibid.*, p. 105.

25. *Ibid.*, p. 190. Same reference for the letter above by Madame von Stein.

26. Du Bos, *Goethe*, p. 317.

27. Friedenthal, *Goethe*, p. 112.

28. Goethe, *Werther*, p. 42.

29. *Ibid.*, p. 79.

30. Du Bos, *Goethe*, p. 287.

uel, *citoyen français* (Paris, Garnery Librairie, Rue Serpente, no. 17, 1792, Year IV). It concerns Manuel, the public prosecutor for the Commune, who will be guillotined under the Terror. What has been exaggeratedly called "the journal" of Mirabeau is found on p. 394 of Vol. IV and consists of just three pages. It is nothing more than a memento, but useful to the researcher.

2. *Ibid.*, I, 300. Letter to his father, written from Vincennes in December of 1777.

3. Dauphin-Meunier, *La Comtesse de Mirabeau*, p. 193.

4. See the brochure published in September 1970 by the Fondation Claude-Nicolas Ledoux for the benefit of "L'Association pour la Renaissance des Salines Royales, Arc-et-Senans, 25," under the title: *Actualité de Claude-Nicolas Ledoux*. A visit to this building, which still stands, produces an intensely emotional reaction. Since 1970 these buildings have housed the Centre International de Réflexion sur le Futur.

5. Dauphin-Meunier, *La Comtesse de Mirabeau*, p. 196.

6. Anne and Claude Manceron, *Mirabeau, l'homme à la vie brûlée* (Paris, Dargaud, 1969), p. 64.

7. Dauphin-Meunier, *La Vie intime . . . de Mirabeau*, p. 183.

8. *Lettres de Mirabeau*, I, 24.

9. Vallentin, *Mirabeau avant la Révolution*, p. 143.

10. *Ibid.*

11. *Ibid.*, p. 144.

12. Duc de Castries, *Mirabeau ou l'échec du destin* (Paris, Fayard, 1960), p. 104.

13. *Ibid.*, p. 105.

14. Dauphin-Meunier, *La Vie intime . . . de Mirabeau*, pp. 215–20.

15. *Ibid.*, p. 221.

16. This notable letter is found in Dauphin-Meunier, *Louise de Mirabeau*, p. 95. It is very significant for what it shows us about Louise's manifest Oedipus complex and tells about the double game she would soon be playing with her brother and Sophie. It is, as well, the letter of a young girl at her wits' end, flayed alive, being crushed by her father, her brother, her husband, her lover.

17. *Lettres de Mirabeau*, I, 312.

18. Société des études robespierristes, *Les Mirabeau et leur temps*, records of the Colloque d'Aix-en-Provence (Paris, 1968), p. 186.

19. Cottin, *Sophie de Monnier et Mirabeau*, p. 46.

20. *Lettres de Mirabeau*, to his father from Vincennes, I, 289.

21. Vallentin, *Mirabeau avant la Révolution*, p. 152. Extract from an undated letter from Sophie to Mirabeau.

22. Colloquy on *Les Mirabeau et leur temps*, p. 197.

23. Archives nationales, K 164, 2, 27 (the appallingly misspelled text is in the marquise's hand).

24. Archives nationales, K 164, 2, 92.

25. Vallentin, *Mirabeau avant la Révolution*, p. 148.

26. Dauphin-Meunier, *Louise de Mirabeau*, p. 110.

27. From the "journal of Mirabeau," always the same source (see note 1).

52

1. Letter from Goethe to Herder on March 25, 1775, in Charles Du Bos, *Goethe* (Paris, Corrêa, 1949), p. 275. The main part of this book is devoted to an exhaustive study of "the twenty-six-year-old Goethe."

2. *Ibid.*, letter from Goethe to

Herder, May 12, 1775, p. 280. The translation of the passages from Goethe has been dusted off.

3. *Ibid.*, p. 301. Letter to Jeanne Fahlmer, November 22, 1775.

4. Goethe, *Souffrances du jeune Werther* (Paris, Livre de Poche, 1959), edition brought out by Antoine Blondin.

5. Du Bos, *Goethe*, p. 265.

6. *Ibid.*, p. 258. The ode from which these verses were taken was written in 1777.

7. Richard Friedenthal, *Goethe, sa vie et son temps* (Paris, Fayard, 1963), p. 201.

8. Goethe, *Werther*, p. 15.

9. Du Bos, *Goethe*, p. 270.

10. *Ibid.*, p. 298.

11. *Ibid.*, p. 259.

12. Jean-Marie Carré, *La Vie de Goethe* (Paris, Gallimard, 1927), pp. 22, 24.

13. Friedenthal, *Goethe*, p. 36.

14. Goethe, *Werther*, p. 24.

15. *Ibid.*, p. 26.

16. *Ibid.*, p. 71.

17. *Ibid.*, p. 141.

18. Adrien Fauchier-Magnan, *Les Petites Cours d'Allemagne au XVIIIᵉ siècle* (Paris, Flammarion, 1947), p. 41.

19. Goethe, *Werther*, p. 88.

20. *Ibid.*, p. 18.

21. Du Bos, *Goethe*, p. 257.

22. Friedenthal, *Goethe*, p. 163.

23. *Ibid.*, p. 167.

24. *Ibid.*, p. 105.

25. *Ibid.*, p. 190. Same reference for the letter above by Madame von Stein.

26. Du Bos, *Goethe*, p. 317.

27. Friedenthal, *Goethe*, p. 112.

28. Goethe, *Werther*, p. 42.

29. *Ibid.*, p. 79.

30. Du Bos, *Goethe*, p. 287.

53

1. Victor Alfieri, *Mémoires* (Paris, Didot, 1862), titles and subtitles of these four first periods. All the other unfootnoted quotations in this sequence are taken from the same work, pp. 19–186.

2. Giuliano Procacci, *Histoire des Italiens* (Paris, Fayard, 1970), p. 220. And the author adds: "It is certainly not an accident that two of the fathers of Italian literature in the eighteenth century, Alfieri and Goldoni, were essentially playwrights, which is to say they chose an eminently public genre."

3. Marquis de Sade, *Voyage d'Italie ou dissertations critiques, historiques, politiques et philosophiques sur les villes de Florence, Rome, et Naples, 1775–1776, texte inédit* published in *Oeuvres complètes du Marquis de Sade* (Paris, Cercle du livre précieux, 1967), XVI, 126.

4. *Ibid.*, p. 126.

54

1. *Ibid.*, p. 164.

2. *Ibid.*, p. 183.

3. Lély, *Vie du Marquis de Sade*, p. 257.

4. Sade, *Voyage d'Italie*, p. 188.

5. *Ibid.*, p. 359.

6. Hayward, *Le Dernier Siècle de la Rome pontificale*, p. 66.

7. *Ibid.*, p. 61.

8. Daniel-Rops, *L'Ere des grands craquements*, p. 394. The quotation of St. Leonard which follows is from the same source.

9. *Ibid.*, p. 400.

10. Hayward, *Le Dernier Siècle de la Rome pontificale*, p. 66.

11. Sade, *Voyage d'Italie*, p. 125.

12. "In his preface to *Itinéraire de Paris à Jerusalem,* Chateaubriand warns us that he made his journey not in or-

der to write this book but to research settings for his poetic novel *Martyrs,* and that the *Itineraire,* which contained those descriptions, was never intended to see the light of day. Certainly the Marquis de Sade in composing his *Voyage d'Italie* didn't know that twenty years later he would use it to illustrate certain episodes in a novel of his own. But if the purposes were different, the results are analogous and this similarity was worth pointing out"—Gilbert Lély in his foreword to *Voyage d'Italie,* p. xi. When Lély writes "twenty years later," he bases it on the date of publication (1797) and not the composition of *L'Histoire de Juliette.*

13. Sade, *Voyage d'Italie,* p. 136.

14. Sade, *Histoire de Juliette ou les prospérités du vice* (giving rise immediately to *La Nouvelle Justine ou les malheurs de la vertu*) (Paris, Cercle du livre précieux, 1967), IX, 25, 31.

15. Sade, *Voyage d'Italie,* p. 137.

16. *Ibid.,* p. 147.

17. *Ibid.,* p. 160.

18. *Ibid.,* p. 166.

19. Sade, *Histoire de Juliette,* p. 33.

20. Sade, *Voyage d'Italie,* p. 298.

21. *Ibid.,* p. 222.

22. *Ibid.,* p. 319.

23. *Ibid.,* p. 283.

24. *Ibid.,* pp. 365, 366.

25. Sade, *Histoire de Juliette,* p. 59.

55

1. *Mémoires de Barras, présentés par* Paul Vergnet (Paris, Editions littéraires et artistiques, 1946), p. 74. These posthumous memoirs compiled by Rousselin de Saint-Albin, then published by Georges Duruy in 1895, should be used with caution. They have followed Barras's own texts closely enough, but because of the author's mixture of cynicism and caution, the most flagrant

falsehoods alternate with flashes of truth. One obtains the latter only by cross-checking.

2. *Ibid.,* p. 73.

3. Young, *Voyage en France,* II, 72. *Ibid.,* for the two descriptions that follow in quotes.

4. Reichard, *Guide des voyageurs en Europe,* Vol. II, *France,* p. 159.

5. 985,601 inhabitants, taken in a census by Arthur Young in 1789 for the four departments of the High and Low Alps, the Var, and Bouches-du-Rhône. He should add the Vaucluse, still Comtat-Venaissin in 1789, where the way of life and the distribution of the classes were identical or very nearly so (*Voyage en France,* III, 207). The population was 5 percent smaller in 1776 than in 1789.

6. Jacques Vivent, *Barras, le "roi" de la république, 1755–1829* (Paris, Hachette, 1938), p. 17.

7. *Ibid.,* p. 14.

8. Note of Paul Vergnet in the margin of *Mémoires de Barras,* p. 73.

9. Jean-Paul Garnier, *Barras, le roi du Directoire* (Paris, Perrin, 1970), p. 21.

10. *Mémoires de Barras,* pp. 72, 73.

11. *Ibid.,* p. 73.

12. *Ibid.,* p. 74.

13. Young, *Voyage en France,* II, 73.

14. Reichard, *Guide des voyageurs en Europe,* Vol. II, p. 57.

15. Cuvillier junior and Bouin, *Essai d'un dictionnaire des principaux ports et mouillages du monde connu* (Paris, Librairie du commerce, 1845), I, 142.

16. Chevalier de Mautort, *Mémoires* (Paris, Plon, 1895), p. 116.

17. *Ibid.,* p. 115.

56

1. Laboulaye, *Histoire des Etats-Unis,* II, 327.

2. *Ibid.* The full text of the Declaration is found in II, 321.

3. D. Pasquet, *Histoire politique et sociale,* I, 216.

4. Fay, *Benjamin Franklin,* I, 82, and *passim.*

5. Observation of Dr. Kush, quoted in Volney, *Tableau du climat et du sol des Etats-Unis,* in the *Oeuvres* of Volney (Paris, F. Didot, 1838), p. 659.

6. *Ibid.* (but the text is that of Volney himself), p. 658.

7. The expression is John Adams's, quoted in Hannah Arendt, *Essai sur la révolution,* translated from the English (Paris, Gallimard, 1967), p. 206.

8. De Witt, *Thomas Jefferson,* p. 76.

9. Pasquet, *Histoire politique et sociale,* p. 201.

10. Letter from Jefferson to Samuel Kerchival, July 12, 1816, forty years to the day after the celebration in Philadelphia (in De Witt, *Thomas Jefferson,* p. 20).

11. André Maurois, *Histoire des Etats-Unis* (Paris, Albin Michel, 1943), p. 141.

12. To Thomas Pickering, forty-six years later. John Adams was then eighty-six years old, and Jefferson, who was only eighty, accused Adams of being senile and questioned his account. However, Adams based it on notes he had taken in 1776 and his story appears to be authentic.

13. *Autobiography,* in *Works of Jefferson,* I, 19, quoted in De Witt, *Thomas Jefferson,* p. 110.

14. See facsimile in Claude Manceron, *Histoire des révolutions en mille im-*

ages (Paris, Laffont-Pont-Royal, 1963), plate 213.

15. Reported by John Adams in De Witt, *Thomas Jefferson,* p. 107.

16. Conway, *Thomas Paine,* pp. 39–52. See also Maurois, *Histoire des Etats-Unis,* p. 140.

17. To General Gates, March 23, 1776, in De Witt, *Thomas Jefferson,* p. 98.

18. To François Dana, June 12, 1776, in *ibid.,* p. 106.

19. Arendt, *Essai sur la révolution,* p. 189. Excerpt from a letter from Jefferson to Henry Lee, May 8, 1825.

20. De Witt, *Thomas Jefferson,* p. 18.

21. *Ibid.,* p. 4.

22. *Ibid.,* p. 35. Excerpt from his *Autobiography.*

23. Conway, *Thomas Paine,* p. 52.

24. Letter to Joseph C. Cabell of February 2, 1816, in Arendt, *Essai sur la révolution,* p. 184.

25. *Ibid.,* p. 172.

26. De Witt, *Thomas Jefferson,* p. 9.

27. Laboulaye, *Histoire des Etats-Unis,* II, 327.

57

1. For this sequence I have followed Sophie and Mirabeau step by step with the aid of Dauphin-Meunier, whose considerable work in the two books already cited (*La Vie intime et amoureuse de Mirabeau,* pp. 234–59, and *Louise de Mirabeau,* pp. 110–40) enables one to give a truthful account of the elopement. All the quotations and unfootnoted information derive from these two books.

2. "Journal of Mirabeau," in the *Lettres de Mirabeau,* published by Manuel in 1792. See note 1 to Chapter 51.

3. H. O. Reichard, *Guide de la Suisse, 1793* (Geneva and vicinity), (Paris, re-edited by the Editions de la Courtille).

4. Cottin, *Sophie de Monnier et Mirabeau*, p. 1.

5. Dauphin-Meunier, *La Comtesse de Mirabeau*, p. 210.

6. L. G. Pelissier, *Mirabeau en Savoie et le gouvernement sarde* (Toulouse, Privat, 1892), p. 19.

7. Ferval, *La Jeunesse de Mirabeau*, p. 136, and Alfred Stern, *La Vie de Mirabeau* (Paris, Emile Bouillon, 1895), I, 129.

8. Cottin, *Sophie de Monnier et Mirabeau*, p. 4.

9. Notably August 3, 1776. I have drawn these names from Paul Cottin's work, cited above; it is particularly valuable for the months of July and August of 1776, when these letters permit one to follow Sophie day by day. The five quotations from Sophie which follow come from the same source, pp. 17, 19, 27, 47, and 54.

10. *Ibid.*, p. 113.

11. Letter to Sophie on July 12, 1870, in *Lettres de Mirabeau*.

12. Colloquy on *Les Mirabeau et leur temps*: R. Barny, "L'amour dans les oeuvres de Mirabeau et de Rousseau," pp. 194, 196.

13. Cottin, *Sophie de Monnier et Mirabeau*, p. 6.

14. This letter will be forwarded by the Ruffeys to the Marquis de Mirabeau, who will send a copy of it to Emilie, thus to the Marignane family. Mirabeau fils will regret it bitterly at the time of the Aix trial. It will be too late: the judges and Louise herself, who will never forgive her brother, will know about it then.

15. Cottin, *Sophie de Monnier et Mirabeau*, p. 48.

16. *Ibid.*, p. 43.

17. *Ibid.*, p. 31.

18. *Ibid.*, p. 37.

19. *Ibid.*, p. 19.

20. *Ibid.*

21. *Ibid.*, p. 30.

22. *Ibid.*, p. 44.

23. *Ibid.*, p. 52.

58

1. Manon's own expression in a letter of February 29, 1776, recounting her escapade to Sophie Canet (Roland, *Lettres* [C.P.], new series, I, 382). The rest of Manon's story is taken from the same text. Claude Perroud provides this detailed information on Moré's character in the preface of this edition.

2. Jean Guéhenno, *Jean-Jacques, en marge des confessions* (Paris, Grasset, 1948), pp. 218, 220. This book forms the first third of the estimable biographical trilogy that contributes more to our knowledge of Rousseau than all other works.

3. Vol. VII of *Confessions*, quoted by R. G. Schwartzenberg on p. 11 of his introduction to *Le Contrat Social*, published in the collection *Pour la politique aujourd'hui* by Pierre Seghers (Paris, 1971).

4. According to a description by Bernardin de Saint-Pierre, cited in Jean Guéhenno, *Jean-Jacques, grandeurs et misère d'un esprit* (Paris, Gallimard, 1952), p. 285. This is the last third of the trilogy mentioned above.

5. Guéhenno, *Jean-Jacques, grandeurs*, p. 316.

6. *Ibid*, p. 291.

7. All this follows a description by Bernardin de Saint-Pierre. See also Pierre Gaxotte, *Paris au XVIIIᵉ siècle* (Paris, Arthaud, 1968), p. 335.

8. *Correspondance littéraire*, XI, 287.

9. Cited in Guéhenno, *Jean-Jacques, grandeurs,* p. 264.

10. *Encyclopédie,* V, 347. This premonition has been noted by Henri Guillemin in *Pas a Pas* (Paris, Gallimard, 1969), p. 33.

11. Mercier, *Tableau de Paris,* V, 26.

12. *Guide des amateurs et des étrangers voyageurs à Paris* (Paris, Hardouin et Gattey, "booksellers to Her Serene Highness the Duchesse d'Orléans, at the Palais Royal, under the left arcades, nos. 13 and 14," 1787), I, 616.

13. Rousseau, *Les Rêveries du promeneur solitaire* (Paris, Garnier-Flammarion, 1964), p. 46. It concerns the second walk. Rousseau's story of the accident, which follows, is drawn from the same text.

14. *Guide des amateurs,* I, 618.

59

1. Roger Lafon, *Beaumarchais, le brillant armateur* (Paris, Société d'éditions géographiques, maritimes et coloniales, 1928), p. 85.

2. Loménie, *Beaumarchais,* II, 92.

3. *Ibid.,* II, 115.

4. *Ibid.,* pp. 99–105.

5. Archives des Affaires étrangères, correspondance politique, Angleterre [Archives of Foreign Affairs, political correspondence, England], 516, pp. 11, 12.

6. Loménie, *Beaumarchais,* II, 107.

7. Maurois, *Histoire des Etats-Unis,* p. 152.

8. Lafon, *Beaumarchais* p. 41.

9. I copied out, from Beaumarchais's minuscule handwriting, his coding of this note and decoding of Lee's answer, at the Beaumarchais exposition of the Bibliothèque nationale in 1966, catalogue numbers 323 and 324.

10. Loménie, *Beaumarchais,* II, 120.

11. *Ibid.,* II, p. 123.

12. *Ibid.,* II, p. 129.

13. Copied from Beaumarchais's minutely handwritten letter of August 18, 1776, at the 1966 exposition of the Bibliothèque nationale, catalogue no. 327.

60

1. Fay, *Benjamin Franklin,* II, 156.

2. Maurois, *Histoire des Etats-Unis,* p. 147.

3. Gaston Martin, *Nantes au XVIIIᵉ siècle, l'ère des négriers* (Paris, Felix Alcan, 1931), p. 289. The coincidence of the decline of the Nantes slave trade and the death of Louis XV is not my discovery. See Leon Vignois's article *"Pourquoi la date de 1774?"* in *Revue d'Histoire coloniale et économique* (Paris, 1928.)

4. See Franklin's portrait by Josèphe-Sifrède Duplessis, in 1783, in Jacques Ahrweiller, *Benjamin Franklin, premier savant américain* (Paris, Seghers, *Savants du monde entier,* 1965), p. 32.

5. Young, *Voyage en France,* I, 245.

6. *Ibid.,* I, 247.

7. *Ibid.,* I, 250.

8. Lafon, *Beaumarchais,* p. 96.

9. *Encyclopédie,* VIII, 742.

10. Lafon, *Beaumarchais,* p. 86.

11. *Ibid.,* p. 89.

12. *Ibid.,* p. 90.

13. *Ibid.,* p. 91.

61

1. Diderot, *Correspondance,* XIV, 208.

2. *Ibid.,* letter at the beginning of June 1776, XIV, 198.

3. *Ibid.*, XIV, 198. In the same letter to Wilkes, Diderot submitted to him the very dense "Declaration against the English oppressors." Only a few lines long, it ends with: "Tell me how long you have resolved to make your enemies laugh."

4. *Ibid.*, XV, 16. Clugny died on October 18.

5. Lady Blennerhassett, *Madame de Staël et son temps* (Paris, Westhausser, 1890), I, 100.

6. *Ibid.*, I, 125. The word is that of the comptroller general of Invau, predecessor of the Abbé Terray.

7. Jolly, *Necker*, pp. 98, 107.

8. *Ibid.*, p. 122.

9. *Ibid.*, p. 79.

10. According to the Baroness d'Oberkich. *Ibid.*, p. 73.

11. Diderot, *Correspondance*, XIV, 51.

12. *Ibid.*, XIV, 150. He discusses it in a letter to Sartines.

13. *Ibid.*, to Grimm on October 14, 1776.

14. *Ibid.*, in his last known letter to Sophie Volland, September 3, 1774.

15. *Ibid.*, XV, 30; to Grimm in mid-December 1776.

16. *Ibid.*, XV, 33.

17. *Ibid.*, XIV, 227.

18. *Ibid.*, XV, 24.

62

1. *Ibid.*, XIV, 71. This is an excerpt from *Voyage en Hollande*, compiled in 1774.

2. Roussel d'Epinal, *Correspondance amoureuse de Fabre d'Eglantine*, 3 vols. (Paris, 1796) (Bibliothèque nationale Z 48 660), cited in Louis Jacob, *Fabre d'Eglantine, chef des fripons* (Paris, Hachette, 1946), p. 27.

3. Marcel Rufas, *"Les Origines sociales de Fabre d'Eglantine,"* in *Annales*

historiques de la Révolution française, 1960, p. 294.

4. Jacob, *Fabre d'Eglantine*, p. 15.

5. *Ibid.*, p. 16.

6. Rufas, *"Les Origines sociales,"* pp. 295, 296.

7. Jacob, *Fabre d'Eglantine*, p. 18.

8. *Ibid.*, p. 22.

9. Georges de Froidcourt, *Le Procès de Fabre d'Eglantine devant le magistrat de Namur en 1777* (Liège, Protin and Vindor, 1941). The quotations and detailed information which follow will be taken from this book or from Roussel d'Epinal, *Correspondance amoureuse de Fabre d'Eglantine*.

63

1. Lély, *Vie du Marquis de Sade*, p. 153.

2. *Ibid.*, p. 265.

3. *Ibid.*, pp. 258–67. The tangled maze of these few months has been unraveled remarkably by G. Lély.

4. *Ibid.*, p. 267.

5. *Ibid.*, p. 269.

64

1. *Correspondance littéraire*, XI, 363. The letter is dated May 18, 1776.

2. Ségur, *Mémoires*, I, 110.

3. Tower, *La Fayette*, I, 26.

4. La Fayette, *Mémoires*, cited in Maurois, *Adrienne*, p. 63.

5. Archives des Affaires étrangères, correspondance politique, Etats-Unis, I, 304–7. Presented at the La Fayette exhibition at the Archives nationales in 1957.

6. Tower, *La Fayette*, I, 23.

7. *Ibid.*, I, 25.

8. *Mémoires de ma main*, written at La Fayette's dictation; cited in Tower, *La Fayette*, p. 31.

9. Until the publication of these

lettres inédites in Maurois, *Adrienne,* it was firmly believed, on the basis of La Fayette's *Mémoires,* that he had virtuously refused to visit Portsmouth to avoid being suspected of spying before his departure. He certainly seems to have been there, however.

10. Tower, *La Fayette,* I, 33.
11. Maurois, *Adrienne,* p. 69.
12. *Ibid.,* p. 76.

65

1. Froidcourt, *Le Procès de Fabre d'Eglantine,* pp. 30–72.
2. Jacob, *Fabre d'Eglantine,* p. 33.
3. Georges Lefebvre's note on Froidcourt's book, in *Annales historiques de la Révolution française,* 1951, p. 309.
4. Jacob, *Fabre d'Eglantine,* pp. 33, 34. *Ibid.* for the judge's texts which follow.

66

1. Reichard, *Guide des voyageurs en Europe,* Vol. II, *France,* p. 113.
2. Alfred Leroux, *Etude critique sur le XVIII siècle à Bordeaux* (Bordeaux, Féret et fils, 1921), p. 169. The particulars about both Bordeaux's economic development and its shipowners are taken from this book.
3. *Ibid.,* p. 5.
4. *Ibid.,* p. 174.
5. Kept at the Bordeaux court of commerce. List of passengers from January 19, 1777, to May 19, 1780, folio 9.
6. Tower, *La Fayette,* I, 43.
7. *Ibid.,* I, 47.
8. *Ibid.,* I, 43.
9. *Ibid.,* I, 47.
10. Vicomte de Noailles, *Marins et Soldats français en Amérique* (Paris, Perrin, 1903), p. 6. The excerpt from the letter from Kalb to Choiseul, given

here as a note, is taken from the same book, p. 5.
11. *Dictionnaire des ports et mouillages* (Paris, Librairie du Commerce, 1845), I, 147.
12. Tower, *La Fayette,* I, 45.
13. *Ibid.,* I, 46.
14. Reichard, *Guide des voyageurs en Europe,* Vol. II, *France,* p. 125.
15. Leroux, *Le XVIIIe siècle à Bordeaux,* pp. 9, 182.
16. Maurois, *Adrienne,* p. 65.
17. Tower, *La Fayette,* I, 47.
18. *Ibid.,* I, 48. Same source for Kalb's two texts which follow.
19. *Ibid.,* I, 38.
20. Bardoux, *La Jeunesse de La Fayette,* p. 37.
21. Tower, *La Fayette,* I, 49.

67

1. Mercy-Argenteau, *Correspondance,* III, 2, and II, 541.
2. *Ibid.,* III, 3.
3. *Ibid.,* III, 2.
4. *Ibid.,* III, 50.
5. *Ibid.,* II, 534.
6. *Ibid.,* II, 542.
7. Galippe, *L'Hérédité des stigmates de dégénérescence,* p. 97.
8. Fejtö, *Joseph II.* The following moral and physical profile of Joseph II will be taken from this book.
9. Mercy-Argenteau, *Correspondance,* III, 50.
10. *Ibid.,* III, 51.
11. *Lettres de Joseph II à son frère Léopold,* published in Vienna by Von Arneth; cited in Maugras, *Le Duc de Lauzun et . . . Marie-Antoinette,* p. 129.
12. Mercy-Argenteau, *Correspondance,* II, 467.
13. *Ibid.,* III, 33.
14. François de Lescure, *Correspondance secrète inédite sur Louis XVI, Marie-Antoinette, la Cour et la ville, de*

1777 à 1792 (Paris, Plon, 1866), I, 43–5. This work will henceforth be cited as *Correspondance secrète.*

15. Letter to Leopold on May 11, 1777. Mercy-Argenteau, *Correspondance.* III, 62.

16. *Correspondance secrète.* I, 52.

17. Hunolstein, *Correspondance inédite de Marie-Antoinette,* p. 92.

18. Geffroy, *Gustave III,* II, 390.

19. Fejtö, *Joseph II,* p. 140.

20. Nolhac, *Le Trianon de Marie-Antoinette,* p. 100. The other descriptions of the Trianon in 1777 are taken from the same work.

21. Mercy-Argenteau, *Correspondance.* III, 7.

22. *Ibid.,* II, 485, 487.

23. Madame Campan's expression. Fejtö, *Joseph II,* p. 161.

24. Mercy-Argenteau, *Correspondance,* II, 489.

25. Fejtö, *Joseph II,* p. 167. This key letter from Joseph II to Leopold on June 9, 1777, solves the famous puzzle of Louis XVI's impotence.

26. Morris, *Marie-Thérèse,* p. 262.

68

1. Georges Claretie, *Derues l'empoisonneur, une cause célèbre au XVIIIe siècle* (Paris, Charpentier, 1907), p. 217. For this entire sequence I have followed the detailed reconstruction of the double crime and of the trial that this book contains, comparing it with the documents preserved in the Archives nationales.

2. Archives nationales, Y 13 299.

3. Inspector Mutel's notes make fascinating reading for fanciers of old news columns; they are preserved in the same dossier at the Archives, in the appendix to the Derues trial: Y 13 299.

4. Archives nationales, X 2b 1 364.

5. According to the journal of Hardy the bookseller.

6. All these facts are cited in Anchel, *Crimes et Châtiments,* Chapters II ("Various Categories of Criminals"), p. 31, and VII ("The Gallows"), p. 165. Some detailed information about the torture of Derues will be taken from the same work, Chapter VIII ("The Wheel"), p. 181.

7. H. Monin, *L'Etat de Paris en 1789,* studies and documents on the Ancien Régime in Paris (Paris, Jouaust et Noblet, 1889), p. 91.

8. *Ibid.,* p. 92.

9. *Ibid.,* p. 93.

10. Roland, *Lettres* (C.P.), new series, I, 240, letters of December 13 and 14, 1774.

11. Archives nationales, X 2b I 364.

12. Hardy, *Journal,* in Claretie, *Derues l'empoisonneur,* p. 285.

13. Anchel, *Crimes et châtiments,* p. 184.

14. *"Le trafic des reliques au XVIIIe siècle,"* in *Annales du XVIIIe siècle,* XXXVI, 21.

69

1. Mercy-Argenteau, *Correspondance,* III, 54.

2. *Correspondance littéraire,* XI, 456.

3. *Ibid.,* as well as the two preceding quotations, XI, 457, 461.

4. Desnoiresterres, *Gluck et Piccinni,* p. 91. The expression about "the old coach drawn from afar" is from Mercier, *Tableau de Paris,* adapted here by the author.

5. J.-J. Rousseau, *Oeuvres complètes* (Paris, Pourrat, 1831), VIII, 483. Let-

ter from Saint-Preux to Madame
d'Orbe in *La Nouvelle Héloïse*.

6. *Correspondance littéraire*, I, 239.

7. *Ibid.*, p. 454.

8. *Mémoires* of the Abbé Morellet,
I, 239.

9. Desnoiresterres, *Gluck et Piccinni*, p. 159.

10. *Ibid.*, pp. 183, 191.

11. *Ibid.*, pp. 182, 183.

12. Diderot, *Correspondance*, XV,
38, letter of December 18, 1776. Editors point out that the statue in question will be smuggled away in 1786 by
the "clergy of the Enlightenment" and
that Victor Hugo will defend it forty
years later in his inaugural speech
before the Académie Française.

13. *Essais de Mémoires sur M. Suard*
(Paris, Didot, 1820), p. 98.

14. Desnoiresterres, *Gluck et Piccinni*, p. 142.

70

1. Mercy-Argenteau, *Correspondance*, III, 55. The details which follow
on Joseph II's voyage will be drawn
from the same volume, pp. 55–87.
Mercy-Argenteau had put together for
Maria Theresa what was really a little
journal of her son's long trip; one must
balance and supplement it with passages from Joseph's letters to Leopold
and with the memoirs of several contemporaries.

2. *Ibid.*, III, 91.

3. *Dictionnaire de Paris* (Larousse,
Paris, 1964), p. 520.

4. The details which follow about
La Salpêtrière are drawn from a lively
account of a journey to Paris by two
young natives of Nancy: *La Vie parisienne sous Louis XVI* (Paris, Calmann-Lévy, 1882). For this citation, p. 49.

5. *Ibid.*, p. 50.

6. *Ibid.*, p. 52.

7. Mercier, *Tableau de Paris*,
VIII, 5. The unfootnoted quotations
about Bicêtre which follow will be
taken from the same description: the
first chapter of Vol. VIII of the Amsterdam edition.

8. *La Vie parisienne sous Louis XVI*,
p. 47.

9. *Correspondance littéraire*,
XI, 471.

10. *Ibid.*, XI, 472.

11. Mercy-Argenteau, *Correspondance*, III, 61.

71

1. Pelissier, *Mirabeau en Savoie*,
pp. 2–4.

2. Diderot, *Voyage en Hollande*, in
Oeuvres Complètes, XI, 336–43. Other
unfootnoted passages in this sequence
will be drawn from the same text,
which gives a picture of the Low
Countries at the time of Mirabeau's
stay.

3. Sade, *Voyage de Hollande en
forme de lettres*, in *Oeuvres inédites, publiées
par* Gilbert Lély (Paris, Jean-Jacques
Pauvert, n. d.), XV–XVI, 93.

4. *Ibid.*, p. 94.

5. Reichard, *Guide des voyageurs en
Europe*, Vol. I, *Hollande*, p. 122.

6. Cottin, *Sophie de Monnier et
Mirabeau*, p. 30.

7. *Ibid.*, p. 31.

8. Vallentin, *Mirabeau avant la
Révolution*, p. 167.

9. *Ibid.*, p. 166.

10. Dauphin-Meunier, *La Vie
intime . . . de Mirabeau*, p. 270.

11. Diderot, *Voyage en Hollande*,
pp. 396, 397.

12. Diderot, letter to Caroillon de
Vandeul dated September 3, 1774, in
Oeuvres complètes, XI, 1038, and *Voyage
en Hollande*, p. 384.

13. *Ibid.*, p. 403.

14. Cottin, *Sophie de Monnier et Mirabeau,* p. xxxi.

15. Vallentin, *Mirabeau avant la Révolution,* pp. 167–70.

16. *Ibid.,* p. 163. The last two phrases of this quotation are taken from "Response to a Response" in *Avis aux Hessois;* Mirabeau presented it in somewhat the same manner as Molière had conceived *La Critique de l'Ecole des Femmes* after the publication in France of a mild pamphlet against his first work. But he later published the two texts together.

17. Cottin, *Sophie de Monnier et Mirabeau,* p. 57.

18. Dauphin-Meunier, *La Vie intime . . . de Mirabeau,* p. 276.

19. *Ibid.,* p. 279.

20. Vallentin, *Mirabeau avant la Révolution,* p. 173.

21. Stern, *La Vie de Mirabeau,* I, 139.

22. Diderot, *Voyage en Hollande,* p. 336.

23. Dauphin-Meunier, *La Vie intime . . . de Mirabeau,* p. 289.

24. *Ibid.,* p. 289.

25. Sade, *Voyage de Hollande,* p. 103.

72

1. *Guides des amateurs,* I, 172.

2. M. N. Bouillet, *Dictionnaire universel d'Histoire et de Géographie* (Paris, Hachette), p. 1078.

3. Mercy-Argenteau, *Correspondance,* III, 63.

4. *Guide des amateurs,* p. 376.

5. *Ibid.,* pp. 1, 12.

6. Mercy-Argenteau, *Correspondance,* III, 79.

7. *Guide des amateurs,* p. 112.

8. "Manuscrit autographe des comptes de Louis XVI," preserved in the Archives nationales: expenditures for 1777.

9. *Correspondance littéraire,* XI, 472.

10. Grimaux, *Lavoisier,* p. 130.

11. Mercier, *Tableau de Paris,* I, 109.

12. *Ibid.,* I, 111.

73

1. *La Vie parisienne sous Louis XVI,* p. 95.

2. Loménie, *Les Mirabeau,* II, 597.

3. *Ibid.,* II, 604. This opinion of the Marquise de Mirabeau refers to her son Gabriel, not her husband.

4. Diderot, *Voyage en Hollande,* p. 419.

5. *Ibid.,* p. 359.

6. Sade, *Voyage de Hollande,* p. 98.

7. Bouillet, *Dictionnaire universel,* p. 1466.

8. Diderot, *Voyage en Hollande,* p. 355.

9. *Ibid.,* p. 350.

10. Cottin, *Sophie de Monnier et Mirabeau,* p. xxxvi.

11. Charavay, *Le Général La Fayette,* p. 15.

12. Dauphin-Meunier, *La Vie intime . . . de Mirabeau,* p. 291.

74

1. Mercy-Argenteau, *Correspondance,* III, 65.

2. E. M. du L. (signature of a Carmelite nun), *Madame Elisabeth de France* (Paris, Perrin, 1931), pp. 39–46.

3. Mercy-Argenteau, *Correspondance,* III, 80.

4. Perey, *Nivernais,* p. 220.

5. *La Vie parisienne sous Louis XVI,* p. 99.

6. Cottin, *Sophie de Monnier et Mirabeau,* p. xxxvii.

7. *Ibid.,* p. xxxviii.

8. *Ibid.,* p. xxxix.

9. Loménie, *Les Mirabeau*, II, 607.

10. Vallentin, *Mirabeau avant la Révolution*, p. 176.

11. Loménie, *Les Mirabeau*, II, 608.

12. *Correspondance littéraire*, XI, 473.

13. *Ibid.*, XI, 474.

14. Mercy-Argenteau, *Correspondance*, I, 328, and III, 95.

15. *Ibid.*, III, 81.

16. *Ibid.*, III, 82.

17. *Ibid.*, III, 86.

18. *Ibid.*, III, 77, 96. Letters from Joseph to Leopold.

75

1. Charavay, *Le Général La Fayette*, p. 16.

2. *Mémoires, Correspondance et Manuscrits* of General La Fayette, published by the family (Paris, Fournier, 1838), I, 84.

76

1. Dauphin-Meunier, *La Vie intime . . . de Mirabeau*, p. 294.

2. Jacques Hillairet, *Gibets, Piloris, et Cachots du vieux Paris* (Paris, Editions de Minuit, 1956), p. 308.

3. *Lettres de Mirabeau*, edited by Manuel, appendix to Vol. IV, p. 389.

4. *Mémoires tirés des archives de la police de Paris* (Paris, Dentu, 1838), II, 367.

5. Dauphin-Meunier, *La Vie intime . . . de Mirabeau*, p. 298.

77

1. Tower, *Le Marquis de La Fayette*, I, 53.

2. *Ibid.*, I, 54.

3. Laboulaye, *Histoire des Etats-Unis*, I, 371.

4. Tower, *Le Marquis de La Fayette*, p. 163.

5. The handwritten manuscript of Du Buysson is reproduced in B. F. Stevens, *Facsimiles of Manuscripts in European Archives Relating to America, 1773–1783* (Washington), Vol. VI, no. 608.

6. *Ibid.*, Vol. IV, no. 652.

78

1. Cabanès, *Marat inconnu*, p. 108.

2. Archives nationales, R/I-519 (Ancien Régime).

3. *Correspondance secrète*, I, 56.

4. Chateaubriand, *Mémoires d'outre-tomb*, I, 58.

5. *Ibid.*, I, 48.

6. Cabanès, *Marat inconnu*, p. 99.

7. *Ibid.*, p. 110.

8. *Annales historiques de la Révolution française*, 1933, p. 534, a document identified at the library at Avignon, No. 6303 of the Requien collection of autographs.

9. Autobiographical article by Marat in *Le Publiciste parisien*, No. 147, dated June 28, 1790.

10. Georges de Froidcourt, *"Le Diplôme maçonnique de Marat,"* in *Annales historiques de la Révolution française*, 1935, p. 545.

11. Walter, *Marat*, p. 39.

12. Jean Massin, *Marat* (Paris, Club Français du Livre, 1960), p. 42. On the following page the author rightly supports the reservations held by Gottschalk, Marat's American biographer, concerning the other vagaries of Marat's life in England, which have not been substantiated: his request to marry the sister of a Dr. Aikin, his imprisonment at Woolwich for stealing medals from the Oxford Museum in 1776, and his activity as a veterinarian.

This period of Marat's life is already sufficiently muddy, in the sense of water roiled by the wind, so that one should not fish here for daring hypotheses.

13. Cabanès, *Marat inconnu,* p. 83.

14. *Ibid.,* p. 57.

15. *Ibid.,* p. 139.

16. *Ibid.,* p. 141.

17. Massin, *Marat,* pp. 44–45.

18. Cabanès, *Marat inconnu,* p. 147. See also Albert Riquez, *Le Docteur Marat, son système physiologique* (Paris, Maloine, 1908).

19. Cabanès, *Marat inconnu,* pp. 151–5.

20. Diderot, *Eléments de physiologie, l'Ame,* cited in Walter, *Marat,* p. 49.

21. Walter, *Marat,* p. 50.

22. According to his own confessions during the Revolution to Harmand de la Meuse, in Massin, *Marat,* p. 47.

23. Cited in Walter, *Marat,* p. 60.

24. Cited in Massin, *Marat,* p. 50.

25. *Ibid.,* p. 51.

79

1. Mercy-Argenteau, *Correspondance,* III, 104. The rest of the unfootnoted information on Joseph II's tour of France will be taken from the same letter.

2. Maugras, *La Disgrâce du Duc et de la Duchesse de Choiseul,* p. 115.

3. *Ibid.,* p. 118.

4. Maugras, *La Disgrâce . . . de Choiseul,* p. 355.

5. 4,060,000 livres exactly. This detail is interesting, for it allows one to know the value of a huge princely estate of the time. These four million livres represent the assessment of Chanteloup by the accountants of the royal treasury, as guaranty for the same

sum Choiseul borrowed from Louis XVI in 1784, at the height of his ruin. See Edouard André's and Roland Engerand's interesting pamphlet *Le Domaine de Chanteloup* (Chanteloup, 1958). It is available for sale at the estate.

6. Joseph II's letters to Leopold, June 9 and July 3, 1777: Mercy-Argenteau, *Correspondance,* III, 104.

7. Orieux, *Voltaire,* p. 734.

8. *Ibid.,* p. 735.

9. Fejtö, *Joseph II,* p. 165.

10. *Ibid.,* p. 166.

11. Mercy-Argenteau, *Correspondance,* III, 98 (letter from the empress to Mercy on July 31).

12. Song quoted in Fay, *Louis XVI,* p. 140. The song circulated in several salons very close to the court and most certainly among the people in 1777.

13. Mercy-Argenteau, *Correspondance,* III, 85.

14. *Ibid.,* III, 87.

15. *Ibid.,* III, 92.

16. Fay, *Louis XVI,* p. 160. See also in the same work the long note on p. 388, where the author proves irrefutably that no surgery was performed on Louis XVI in the interim between Joseph II's departure and the consummation of the king's marriage. The diary and records of the king, which were meticulously kept each day in his own hand, show that he was not immobilized for fifteen days, the minimum amount of time necessary for healing. He hunted almost every day of the summer. Contrary to what authors like Cabanès impulsively affirm, no record of this operation exists, and for good reason. Besides, the crudeness and detail of Joseph II's letters to Leopold are an unwitting record, far

more convincing, of a couple's victory over inhibition, accomplished by simple psychological methods. The story of phimosis and an operation was born out of the boasting of certain court doctors—Lassone, for one—who took on enigmatic, smug airs when Marie Antoinette revealed her pregnancy so that they would get part of the credit for the success. The texts of *Nouvelles à la main* by Bachaumont, quoted by Fay, *op. cit.,* concerning this alleged operation, do not support these suppositions.

17. Fejtö, *Joseph II,* p. 168.
18. *Ibid.,* p. 167.

80

1. Handwritten manuscript of Du Buysson, already cited in note 5 of Chapter 77, in Tower, *Le Marquis de la Fayette,* I, 167. The rest of the unfootnoted information in this sequence on La Fayette's voyage comes from the same source.

2. Marion, *Dictionnaire des Institutions, "Ecuyer."*

3. Volney, *Tableau des Etats-Unis, (Oeuvres,* Paris, Firmin Didot, 1838), *op. cit.*, p. 634.

4. Tower, *Le Marquis de La Fayette,* I, 168.

5. Ségur, *Mémoires,* I, 340. It is certain that Ségur did not accompany La Fayette on this first voyage. But he will catch up with him in 1782; his description of the Philadelphia vicinity and the town itself echoes the impressions of the Chevalier du Buysson.

6. *Voyages au continent américain par un François [sic] en 1777 et réflexions philosophiques sur ces nouveaux Républicains,* Bibliothèque nationale, manuscripts, Ms. fr. 14 695, folio 16.

7. Tower, *Le Marquis de la Fayette,* I, 200.

8. Marshall, *Life of Washington,* II, 350, cited in Tower, *Le Marquis de La Fayette,* I, 193.

9. Ségur, *Mémoires,* I, 350.

10. *Ibid.,* I, 339.

11. Here I followed Du Buysson's account step by step; its unintentional humor is worthy of a novel. In Tower, *Le Marquis de La Fayette,* I, 169.

81

1. Malouet, *Mémoires* (Paris, Plon, 1874), I, 148.

2. *Ibid.,* I, 442.

3. *Ibid.,* I, 403.

4. *Ibid.,* I, 405.

5. *Ibid.,* I, 389. A remark by Louis XVIII in 1814 to an administrator of Guadeloupe: "I have always been told that they make a fortune in America," same source.

6. *Ibid.,* I, 3–7.

7. *Ibid.,* I, 33.

8. *Ibid.,* I, 41.

9. *Ibid.,* I, 44.

10. *Ibid.,* I, 115.

11. *Ibid.,* I, 77.

12. *Ibid.,* I, 129.

13. *Ibid.,* I, 134.

14. *Ibid.,* I, 141.

15. Captain Van Moeren, *Récit d'une expédition à Surinam contre les nègres marrons* (Paris, Club du livre de voyages, 1958), pp. 70–82.

16. Malouet, *Mémoires,* I, 148.

17. *Ibid.,* I, 152.

18. *Ibid.,* I, 441.

19. *Ibid.,* I, 447.

82

1. According to Du Buysson, in Tower, *Le Marquis de La Fayette,* I, 170.

2. Letters from Washington to Hancock and to Richard Henry Lee,

February 20 and May 17, 1777, in *ibid.*, I, 171.

3. *Ibid.*, I, 172.

4. *Ibid.*, I, 173, according to Du Buysson.

5. *Journals of Congress*, III, 303, in *ibid.*, I, 173.

6. Tower, *Le Marquis de La Fayette*, I, 176.

7. *Ibid.*, I, 179.

8. *Ibid.*, I, 175.

83

1. *Ibid.*, I, 183. (Tower takes Washington's writings from Marshall's seven-volume biography, written in 1837.)

2. Cornélis de Witt, *Histoire de Washington et de la fondation de la république des Etats-Unis* (Paris, Didier, 1859), p. 99.

3. *Mémoires* of La Fayette, in Tower, *Le Marquis de La Fayette*, I, 202.

4. Fay, *George Washington*, p. 122.

5. *Ibid.*, p. 158.

6. De Witt, *Washington*, p. 12.

7. Fay, *George Washington*, p. 168.

8. *Ibid.*, p. 115.

9. *Ibid.*, p. 92.

10. *Ibid.*, p. 125.

11. De Witt, *Washington*, p. 105.

12. Fay, *George Washington*, p. 187.

13. De Witt, *Washington*, p. 44.

14. Fay, *George Washington*, p. 138. This is an excerpt from a letter from young Washington to the Governor of Virginia, William Dinwiddie, at the time of his first campaign. Since that time his self-satisfaction had only increased.

15. De Witt, *Washington*, p. 107.

16. *Ibid.*, p. 113.

17. *Ibid.*, p. 109.

18. Tower, *Le Marquis de La Fayette*, I, 229.

84

1. Lafon, *Beaumarchais*, p. 71.

2. Tower, *Le Marquis de La Fayette*, I, 207: letter from Washington to Benjamin Harrison.

3. *Mémoires* of La Fayette, in *ibid.*, I, p. 205.

4. Tower, *Le Marquis de La Fayette*, I, 208.

5. *Ibid.*, I, 209.

6. De Witt, *Washington*, p. 96.

7. *Ibid.*, p. 97.

8. *Mémoires* of La Fayette, in Tower, *Le Marquis de la Fayette*, I, 219.

9. Letter to his wife on September 12, in Tower, *Le Marquis de La Fayette*, I 223.

85

1. Maurois, *Adrienne*, p. 84.

2. Tower, *Le Marquis de La Fayette*, I, 223. This is an excerpt from La Fayette's *Mémoires*. We will find that he sang quite a different tune in his correspondence at the time.

3. *Mémoires* of La Fayette, in Tower, *Le Marquis de La Fayette*, I, 224.

4. In his letter of October 1, cited above.

5. Tower, *Le Marquis de La Fayette*, I, 225.

6. Again in his letter of October 1.

7. *Mémoires* of La Fayette, in Tower, *Le Marquis de La Fayette*, I, 222.

8. Tower, *Le Marquis de La Fayette*, I, 224.

9. Maurois, *Adrienne*, p. 85.

86

1. Reichard, *Guide des voyageurs en Europe*, Vol. III, *Germany*, p. 117. Other details on Munich come from this description.

2. *Annales historiques de la Révolu-*

tion française, letter of R. Garmy, XXX (1958), 96.

3. H. Buffenoir, *"Fausse légende sur la famille de Robespierre,"* in *Annales historiques de la Révolution française,* III (1910), 104.

4. Bernard Nabonne, *La Vie privée de Robespierre* (Paris, Hachette, 1938), p. 9.

5. *Ibid.,* p. 10.

6. *Ibid.,* p. 11.

7. Max Gallo, *Maximilien Robespierre, histoire d'une solitude* (Paris, Perrin, 1968), p. 28.

8. Buffenoir, *"Fausse légende."*

9. Nabonne, *Maximilien Robespierre,* p. 14.

10. Hector Fleischmann, *Robespierre et les femmes* (Paris, Albin-Michel), p. 21.

11. Excerpt from *Mémoires* of Charlotte Robespierre, cited in Nabonne, *Maximilien Robespierre,* p. 15.

12. Buffenoir, *"Fausse légende."*

13. Louis Jacob, *"Une Lettre du père de Robespierre,"* in *Annales historiques de la Révolution française,* XVI (1939), 169.

14. Nabonne, *Maximilien Robespierre,* p. 17.

15. *Ibid.,* p. 18.

16. Letter from Charlotte de Robespierre to a staff member of the *Universel,* May 24, 1830, in *Revue rétrospective,* I (1883), 406.

17. Cited in Gallo, *Maximilien Robespierre,* p. 30.

18. Nabonne, *Maximilien Robespierre,* p. 26.

19. Letter by Langlet junior, formerly canon of the Arras cathedral, who was himself a bursar at Louis-le-Grand, dated the 16th of Thermidor, Year II, in Fleischmann, *Robespierre et les femmes,* p. 26.

20. Nabonne, *Maximilien Robespierre,* p. 38.

87

1. Bernard Ward, *Proyecto economico, etc.,* published in Madrid in 1782. Cited in Jean Sarrailh, *L'Espagne éclairée de la seconde moitié du XVIIIe siècle* (Paris, Klincksiek, 1964), p. 178.

2. Gorani, *Mémoires* (Paris, Gallimard, 1944), I, 310. Gorani ends with an estimate of the Spanish population, based on figures of the economist Ustariz.

3. Rousseau, *Règne de Charles III,* II, 51. The unfootnoted information on the Olavide affair in this sequence comes from the same source.

4. According to observations of the Duc des Cars, reported in Sarrailh, *L'Espagne éclairée,* p. 25.

5. Sarrailh, *L'Espagne éclairée,* p. 653.

6. Gorani, *Mémoires,* p. 292.

7. *Ibid.,* p. 293.

8. Rounded-off totals; the exact figures are cited in Rousseau, *Règne de Charles III,* II, 50.

9. *Encyclopédie,* article *"Pain Bénit,"* XI, 751, cited in Sarrailh, *L'Espagne éclairée.*

10. Sarrailh, *L'Espagne éclairée,* p. 623.

11. *Ibid.,* p. 313.

12. *Correspondance littéraire,* XII, 44.

88

1. Rousseau, *Règne de Charles III,* II, 99.

2. Gorani, *Mémoires,* p. 301.

3. Cited in Bluche, *Le Despotisme éclairé,* p. 283.

4. *Ibid.,* p. 233. Excerpt of a let-

ter from Dutillot to Algarotti in 1762.

5. *Ibid.*, p. 224.

6. Morris, *Marie-Thérèse*, p. 265.

7. *Ibid.*, p. 263.

8. Bluche, *Le Despotisme éclairé*, p. 216.

9. Morris, *Marie-Thérèse*, p. 262.

10. André Bonnefons, *Marie-Caroline, reine des Deux-Siciles* (Paris, Perrin, 1905), p. 3.

11. Ferrer del Rio, *Historia de Carlos III* (Madrid, 1847), untranslated, III, 167.

12. *Voyage du ci-devant Duc du Châtelet en Portugal, publié par* J. F. Bourgoing (Paris, Buisson, Year VI), p. 116.

13. *Ibid.*, p. 117–23.

89

1. *Correspondance littéraire*, XII, 53.

2. Arsène Houssaye, *Le Roi Voltaire* (Paris, Michel Lévy, 1858), p. 290.

3. Jean-Baptiste Suard, *Mélanges de littérature* (Paris, Dentu, 1803), II, 5.

4. Cited in Orieux, *Voltaire*, p. 690.

5. Letter from the Prince d'Hennin to the Duc d'Aiguillon on February 22, 1773; Archives des Affaires étrangères, 80, Geneva, 1773, no. 7.

6. Paul d'Estrée, *La Vieillesse de Richelieu* (Paris, Emile-Paul, 1921), p. 196.

7. Houssaye, *Le Roi Voltaire*, p. 246.

8. *Ibid.*, p. 249.

9. *Ibid.*, p. 251.

10. *Ibid.*, p. 271.

11. *Ibid.*, p. 272.

12. *Ibid.*, p. 248.

13. I am extremely grateful to Madame Gauthier, proprietress of the Château de Ferney in 1966, for not withholding from my wife and myself the welcome that Voltaire was quite right to withhold from those who rang unexpectedly at the iron entrance gate of the estate. Thanks to Madame Gauthier, we were able to get acquainted with the secrets of Ferney.

14. Letter from the Prince d'Hennin of May 23, 1775 (see note 5 above, 81, Geneva).

15. Gustave Desnoiresterres, *Retour et Mort de Voltaire* (Paris, Didier, 1876), p. 187. This book is the last in a series of eight volumes: *Voltaire et la société du XVIIIe siècle.* I will draw from it for the rest of this sequence, and for that which deals with Voltaire's death.

16. Orieux, *Voltaire*, p. 727.

17. *Ibid.*, p. 662.

18. *Ibid.*, p. 483. This excerpt dates from 1748. I drew it from Theodore Bestermann's huge edition (in 102 volumes!) of Voltaire's *Correspondance* (Geneva, Institut Voltaire, 1955). By 1778 Voltaire had had no sex life for a long time, but erotic memories played a big role in his life.

19. Linguet, *Annales politiques* (London, 1778), III, 387.

20. Letter to Chabanon on August 3, 1775, in Desnoiresterres, *Mort de Voltaire*, p. 186.

21. Reichard, *Guide des voyageurs en Europe*, Vol. II, *France*, pp. 140–4, route from Paris to Geneva.

22. Mignard, *Voltaire et ses contemporains bourguignons* (Dijon, 1874), p. 137.

23. *Guide Reichard*, II, 138.

24. Desnoiresterres, *Mort de Voltaire*, p. 201.

25. Orieux, *Voltaire*, p. 745.

26. Houssaye, *Le Roi Voltaire*, p. 379.

27. *Correspondance littéraire*, XII, 162.

28. Roland, *Lettres* (C.P.), new series, II, 211, March 6, 1778.

90

1. Henry Tronchin, *Le Conseiller François Tronchin et ses amis* (Paris, Plon, 1895), p. 375.

2. *Journal de Paris*, 1778, p. 204.

3. *Mémoires secrets pour servir à l'histoire de la république des lettres* (First edition, Paris, n.p., n.d.) XI, 113.

4. Voltaire, *Oeuvres complètes* (Paris, Benchot), LXX, 449.

5. *Ibid.*, LXX, 451.

6. Elie Harel, *Voltaire: particularités curieuses de sa vie et de sa mort* (Paris, 1817), p. 109. One finds here *in extenso* the Abbé Gauthier's memoir concerning the circumstances of Voltaire's death; it was addressed to the Archbishop of Paris.

7. Desnoiresterres, *Mort de Voltaire*, p. 222.

8. *Correspondance littéraire*, IX (Furne edition), 497, February 1778.

9. Desnoiresterres, *Mort de Voltaire*, p. 228.

10. D'Estrée, *La Vieillesse de Richelieu*, p. 203.

11. Orieux, *Voltaire*, p. 749.

12. Longchamp and Wagnière, *Mémoires sur Voltaire* (Paris, André, 1826), I, 131.

13. *Correspondance littéraire*, XII, 87.

14. Original deposited in 1809 at the Bibliothèque nationale, manuscript department, F.R. 11 460.

15. Letter from D'Alembert to Frederick II on July 3, 1778, in D'Alembert, *Oeuvres* (Paris, Belin, 1822).

16. Desnoiresterres, *Mort de Voltaire*, p. 246. Voltaire said this to his second doctor, Lorry.

91

1. Cited in Braudel, *Civilisation matérielle et capitalisme*, p. 179. Le Grand d'Aussy's work appeared in 1782.

2. A. Carro, *Santerre, général de la République française; sa vie politique et privée d'après les documents originaux laissés par lui et les notes d'Augustin Santerre, son fils aîné* (Meaux, imprimerie Jules Carro), pp. 1–12. Most of the biographical details in this sequence come from this source.

3. *Ibid.*, p. 17.

4. *Ibid.*, p. 16.

5. *Encyclopédie*, article "Brasserie," II, 400.

6. *Ibid.*, II 403.

7. *Ibid.*, II, 404.

8. Carro, *Santerre*, p. 14.

92

1. Longchamp and Wagnière, *Mémoires sur Voltaire*, I, 129.

2. Number 64 of 1778, p. 225.

3. Desnoiresterres, *Mort de Voltaire*, p. 261.

4. *Ibid.*, p. 261.

5. *Mémoires secrets* (First edition, Paris, n.p., n.d.), XI, 165.

6. Fay, *Louis XVI*, p. 167.

7. Brissot, *Mémoires*, p. 141.

8. *Correspondance littéraire*, XII, 67.

9. *Ibid.*, XII, 53, quotation in a footnote from the *Mémoires* of Besenval.

10. Brissot, *Mémoires*, p. 160.

11. *Ibid.*, p. 140.

12. Fay, *Benjamin Franklin*, II, 199.

13. *Ibid.*, II, 201.

14. Desnoiresterres, *Mort de Voltaire*, p. 278.

15. *Correspondance littéraire*, XII, 69, note. The story of Voltaire's coro-

nation is taken from these same pages. This time Meister was a good reporter.

16. *Ibid.*, XII, 68–73.

93

1. Roland, *Lettres* (C.P.) p. 261.

2. The Masonic Archives of Paris were burned by the Gestapo during the occupation. But there is a fairly serious work on the Lodge of the Neuf Soeurs (Nine Sisters) which is quoted by Galante-Garrone in *Gilbert Romme*: L. Amiable, *Une loge maçonnique d'avant 1789: Les Neuf Soeurs* (Paris, 1798).

3. Archives générales des sociétés secrètes non politiques [general archives of non-political secret societies], in *Le Globe* (Paris, 1839), I, 381.

4. Longchamp and Wagnière, *Mémoires sur Voltaire*, I, 144.

5. *Ibid.*, I, 152.

6. *Ibid.*, I, 154.

7. According to the testimony of La Harpe in *Correspondance littéraire*, XII, 83.

8. In a letter of June 27, 1766.

9. Gaberec, *Voltaire et les Genevois* (Paris, Cherbulliez, 1857), p. 166.

10. The scrupulously reconstructed scene is in the *Journal des Débats* of January 30, 1869; it follows a synthesis of accounts by priests, by Madame de Villette, and a long letter from D'Alembert to Catherine II. See Desnoiresterres, *Mort de Voltaire*, p. 361.

11. Voltaire, *Dictionnaire philosophique* (Paris, 1964), pocket edition Garnier-Flammarion, with an introduction by René Pomeau, p. 167.

12. Desnoiresterres, *Mort de Voltaire*, p. 362.

13. Orieux, *Voltaire*, p. 772.

94

1. Excerpt from *Dialogues* by Rousseau, which were published for the first time in London in 1780. Cited in Guéhenno, *Jean-Jacques, grandeurs et misère d'un esprit*, p. 306. I follow Guéhenno in his detailed and inspired reconstruction of Rousseau's final hours.

2. Rousseau, *Rêveries d'un promeneur solitaire*, p. 171.

3. Guéhenno, *Jean-Jacques, grandeurs*, p. 329.

4. *Ibid.*, p. 328.

5. Fay, *Louis XVI*, p. 174. This is the best summary of this "skirmish" that the whole world awaited in order to begin the war.

6. Guéhenno (quoting Lebègue de Presles), *Jean-Jacques, grandeurs*, p. 330. Rousseau succumbed to a cerebral hemorrhage.

7. *Ibid.*, p. 331.

Index

A NOTE ABOUT THE AUTHOR

Claude Manceron was born in 1923, the son of a French naval officer and a Greek princess. His formal schooling ended after he was crippled by polio at age eleven, but he continued to read and became a teacher and a writer—at first of historical novels. His research, undertaken to make the characters' backgrounds authentic, led him to give up fiction and become a historian. He has been working on the Age of the French Revolution series since 1967. M. Manceron has given up teaching to devote himself full time to this work. He and his wife, Anne, live in a small village in the south of France, where they do research and write.

A NOTE ABOUT THE TRANSLATOR

Patricia Wolf is a native New Yorker who worked for many years for the internationally known firm of Wildenstein and Company. Her interest in pre-Revolutionary France was sparked by the visual splendors of Wildenstein's rich collections housed in their New York gallery and in the family's *hôtel particulier* on the Rue La Boëtie in Paris. Books she has translated from the French include: Jean Lacouture's *The Demigods,* Jacques Ellul's *Autopsy of Revolution,* Patrick Modiano's *Night Rounds,* Jean Orieux's *Talleyrand,* and Maurice Pons's *Mademoiselle B.* Mrs. Wolf now makes her home in the San Francisco Bay area with her husband, an urban planner and attorney.

A NOTE ON THE TYPE

The text of this book was set, via computer-driven cathode-ray tube, in Garamond, a modern rendering of the type first cut by Claude Garamond (1510–1561). Garamond was a pupil of Geoffroy Tory and is believed to have based his letters on the Venetian models; it is to him we owe the letter we know as old-style.